Stress, Anxiety and Depression

Stress, Anxiety and Depression

Editor: Jerry Colwell

AMERICAN
MEDICAL PUBLISHERS
www.americanmedicalpublishers.com

AMERICAN
MEDICAL PUBLISHERS
www.americanmedicalpublishers.com

Cataloging-in-Publication Data

Stress, anxiety and depression / edited by Jerry Colwell.
p. cm.
Includes bibliographical references and index.
ISBN 979-8-88740-478-3
1. Stress (Psychology). 2. Anxiety. 3. Depression, Mental. 4. Mental health.
5. Psychology. 6. Psychiatry. I. Colwell, Jerry.
BF575.S75 S77 2023
155.904 2--dc23

American Medical Publishers,
41 Flatbush Avenue,
1st Floor, New York,
NY 11217, USA

ISBN 979-8-88740-478-3 (Hardback)

Contents

Preface

In my initial years as a student, I used to run to the library at every possible instance to grab a book and learn something new. Books were my primary source of knowledge and I would not have come such a long way without all that I learnt from them. Thus, when I was approached to edit this book; I became understandably nostalgic. It was an absolute honor to be considered worthy of guiding the current generation as well as those to come. I put all my knowledge and hard work into making this book most beneficial for its readers.

Anxiety refers to an emotion characterized by an unpleasant state of inner conflict and subjectively unpleasant emotions of dread over anticipated events. Nervous behavior, such as pacing back and forth, somatic complaints, and rumination accompanies anxiety. It is a feeling of uneasiness and worry, generally unfocused and generalized as an overreaction to a circumstance that is subjectively alarming. A mental state characterized by a poor mood and aversion to activity is referred to as depression. Anhedonia is the key symptom of depression. It refers to a loss of interest or decreased feeling of pleasure in certain activities that normally bring happiness to the individuals. Stress is an organism's reaction to a stressor, such as an environmental situation, which can be physiological, biological, or psychological. It is the body's response to a situation that includes a threat, a challenge, or a physical or psychological barrier. This book explores all the important aspects of stress, anxiety and depression in the present day scenario. It will serve as a valuable source of reference for graduate and post graduate students.

I wish to thank my publisher for supporting me at every step. I would also like to thank all the authors who have contributed their researches in this book. I hope this book will be a valuable contribution to the progress of the field.

Editor

1

Dynamic Effects of Early Adolescent Stress on Depressive-Like Behaviors and Expression of Cytokines and JMJD3 in the Prefrontal Cortex and Hippocampus of Rats

*Rui Wang, Wei Wang, Jingjing Xu, Dexiang Liu, Hong Jiang and Fang Pan**

Department of Medical Psychology and Medical Ethics, Cheeloo College of Medicine, Shandong University, Jinan, China

Correspondence:
Fang Pan
panfang@sdu.edu.cn

Aims: Expression of inflammatory cytokines in the brain has been reported to be involved in the pathogenesis of and susceptibility to depression. Jumonji domain-containing 3 (Jmjd3), which is a histone H3 lysine 27 (H3K27) demethylase and can regulate microglial activation, has been regarded as a crucial element in the expression of inflammatory cytokines. Furthermore, recent studies highlighted the fact that lipopolysaccharides induce depressive-like behaviors and higher Jmjd3 expression and lower H3K27me3 expression in the brain. However, whether the process of Jmjd3 mediating inflammatory cytokines was involved in the susceptibility to depression due to early-life stress remained elusive.

Methods: Rats exposed to chronic unpredictable mild stress (CUMS) in adolescence were used in order to detect dynamic alterations in depressive-like behaviors and expression of cytokines, Jmjd3, and H3K27me3 in the prefrontal cortex and hippocampus. Moreover, minocycline, an inhibitor of microglial activation, was employed to observe the protective effects.

Results: Our results showed that CUMS during the adolescent period induced depressive-like behaviors, over-expression of cytokines, and increased Jmjd3 and decreased H3K27me3 expression in the prefrontal cortex and hippocampus of both adolescent and adult rats. However, minocycline relieved all the alterations.

Conclusion: The study revealed that Jmjd3 might be involved in the susceptibility to depressive-like behaviors by modulating H3K27me3 and pro-inflammatory cytokine expression in the prefrontal cortex and hippocampus of rats that had been stressed during early adolescence.

Keywords: Jumonji domain-containing 3, depression, early-life stress, H3K27me3, cytokine, adolescent, epigenetic

INTRODUCTION

Depression, a major psychiatric disorder that affects approximately 16% of the entire population, has the cardinal symptoms of low mood, anhedonia, and cognitive impairment (1). A large number of studies revealed that neuroinflammation is closely related with the pathogenesis of depression (2, 3). Elevated levels of pro-inflammatory cytokines such as interleukin-1β (IL-1β) and IL-6 were observed in the periphery and cerebrum of depressed patients (4–6), and this increase could be reversed after antidepressant therapy (7). Also, some patients suffering from chronic inflammatory diseases (e.g., cardiovascular diseases) had a higher incidence rate of depression (8). In addition, 50% of the hepatitis C patients receiving interferon-α (IFN-α, a pro-inflammatory cytokine) treatment had depressive symptoms (9, 10). Our previous studies also suggested that both chronic mild stress in rats and the administration of lipopolysaccharides (LPS) in mice induced an increase in pro-inflammatory cytokines in the prefrontal cortex and hippocampus as well as depressive-like behaviors (11, 12). Those studies suggested that neuroinflammation, particularly overproduction of cytokines, plays a critical role in the etiopathogenesis of depression.

Microglial activation is one vital factor that contributes to neuroinflammation. Microglia, the primary immune cells of the brain, are regarded as the main source of inflammatory cytokines when they are activated by diverse stress (13–15). Studies have confirmed that primed microglia generally have two functional subtypes, the "classical activation" type and the "alternative activation" type (16, 17). Classical activation of microglia is closely associated with the neuroinflammatory response caused by the upregulation of pro-inflammatory cytokines [e.g., IL-1β, IL-6, tumor necrosis factor-α (TNF- α)] and free radicals such as nitric oxide, further inducing dysfunction of neural networks in the central nervous system (CNS) (18). In contrast, alternative activation of microglia releases anti-inflammatory cytokines. There exist three pathological conditions after microglial activation: (1) tissue damage, (2) inflammatory responses, and (3) hormonal disorder or stress (19). When the periphery was in an inflammatory state, pro-inflammatory cytokines (e.g., IL-1β) crossed the blood brain barrier by saturated transportation and activated microglia and later further triggered the inflammatory cascade (19). Among other factors, studies indicated that stress was a crucial contributor in the activation of microglia (13). It was reported that chronic stress induced an increase in the microglial number and caused morphological changes (20). More importantly, recent studies showed that microglia could memorize early-life stress. The memory-primed microglia had a stronger activation when reacting to stress, even to the slightest stimuli, again in later life (21). However, in the case of classical activation, the relationship between neuroinflammatory response and susceptibility to depression was unclear in the case of individuals who had been exposed to stress early in life.

Environmental stressors can modify the expression of susceptible genes, thereby, leading to the susceptibility mechanisms of depression in which histone methylation plays an important role (22). The Jumonji domain-containing 3 (Jmjd3, KDM6B), which is deemed as a histone H3 lysine 27 (H3K27) demethylase that specifically demethylates trimethylated H3K27 (H3K27me3), is associated with transcription repression. Previous studies reported that Jmjd3 could be induced by nuclear factor-kappa B (NF-κB) in response to inflammatory stimuli such as LPS (23, 24). Increased Jmjd3 could demethylate repressive H3K27me3 epigenetic marks in promoters and gene bodies. Therefore, the expression of pro-inflammatory genes was potentiated, thereby, causing an inflammatory status in the CNS (23–26). Meanwhile, GSK-J4, as a selective Jmjd3 inhibitor, could limit the inflammation accompanied by a reduction in the levels of pro-inflammatory cytokines (27, 28).

Based on all the above studies, the present study first hypothesized that early-life stress induced susceptibility to depressive-like behaviors and expression of pro-inflammatory cytokines by the activation of microglia in the brain. Second, our study hypothesized that Jmjd3 was involved in the susceptibility to those alterations by modulating pro-inflammatory cytokines. In this study, chronic unpredictable mild stress (CUMS) was used to establish an animal model of depression in adolescence. Depressive-like behaviors, pro-inflammatory cytokine expression, microglial activation, as well as Jmjd3 and H3K27me3 expression in the prefrontal cortex and hippocampus were determined by a sucrose preference test (SPT), open field test (OFT), elevated plus maze (EPM), and Morris water maze (MWM), as well as by immunohistochemistry and immunoblotting. The purpose of this study was to evaluate the dynamic effects of CUMS in early-life on behavioral changes, cytokine expression, and Jmjd3 and H3K27me3 expression. As a second generation semi-synthetic tetracycline antibiotic, minocycline plays a neuroprotective role in many neuroinflammatory diseases of the CNS (29). It has been reported that minocycline is a microglial activation inhibitor and can suppress the secretion of pro-inflammatory cytokines such as IL-1β (30) and relieve stress-induced depressive- and anxiety-like behaviors in adult rats (31). Our goal was to investigate the effects of minocycline on relieving behavioral dysfunction, cytokine expression, and Jmjd3 and H3K27me3 expression in stressed adolescent and adult rats.

MATERIALS AND METHODS

Animals

Sixty male 21-day-old Wistar rats were obtained from the Experimental Animal Center of Shandong University and were housed in groups of five, with each cage maintained under standard laboratory conditions (12 h light/dark cycle, 25°C), with food and water provided *ad libitum* during the study. All procedures of this study were carried out with the approval of the Animal Ethics Committee of Shandong University.

Experimental Design

After a 7-day acclimatization, the rats were randomly divided into three groups ($n = 20$ in each group): control group (C), CUMS group (S), CUMS and minocycline group (S+M). The C group was the normal control, whereas the S group was exposed to CUMS for 3 weeks. The S+M group received both the CUMS procedure and the minocycline treatment. After 3 weeks of drug

TABLE 1 | Schedule of unpredictable chronic mild stress.

Time	Type of stress
Day 1	Heat stress (45°C, 5 min)
Day 2	Light/dark cycle reversal
Day 3	Radio noise in the room (8 h)
Day 4	Water deprivation (24 h)
Day 5	Pinching tail (1 min)
Day 6	Food deprivation (24 h)
Day 7	Foot shock (30 mV, 10 s duration for a total of 10 min)
Day 8	Radio noise in the room (8 h)
Day 9	Heat stress (45°C, 5 min)
Day 10	Food deprivation (24 h)
Day 11	Pinching tail (1 min)
Day 12	Water deprivation (24 h)
Day 13	Foot shock (30 mV, 10 s duration for a total of 10 min)
Day 14	Light/dark cycle reversal
Day 15	Food deprivation (24 h)
Day 16	Pinching tail (1 min)
Day 17	Radio noise in the room (8 h)
Day 18	Light/dark cycle reversal
Day 19	Heat stress (45°C, 5 min)
Day 20	Foot shock (30 mV, 10 s duration for a total of 10 min)
Day 21	Water deprivation (24 h)

administration and animal modeling, 10 rats from each group were randomly selected to undergo behavioral tests. The order of the behavioral tests was as follows: the SPT, then the OFT, the EPM test, and finally the MWM test. Later, at the age of 55 days, the 30 selected rats were sacrificed. The remaining 30 rats were raised to adulthood, and then they underwent the behavioral tests. Afterwards, these rats were sacrificed at the age of 90 days (see **Supplementary Material**). Therefore, our study had six groups altogether: the adolescent control group (AdoC); the adolescent CUMS group (AdoS); the adolescent CUMS and minocycline group (AdoS+M); the adult control group (AduC); the adult CUMS group (AduS); and the adult CUMS and minocycline group (AduS+M).

CUMS Procedure and Drug Administration

The CUMS was applied to all groups except for the control group, using a previously described method (32, 33). Rats were exposed to one of the following seven stressors randomly every day: food deprivation (24 h), water deprivation (24 h), radio noise in the room (8 h), heat stress (45°C, 5 min), foot shock (30 mV, 10 s duration for a total of 10 min), light/dark cycle reversal, and pinching tail (1 min) (see **Table 1**). Rats in the S+M group were treated with minocycline (intragastric, 40 mg/kg, diluted in saline) 30 min before CUMS for 3 weeks (17).

Behavioral Tests

Sucrose Preference Test (SPT)

The SPT was used to evaluate the level of anhedonia (34). Rats were trained to adapt to the 1% sucrose solution in a quiet environment before the test. In the first 24 h, each cage was provided with two identical bottles of the sucrose solution. Subsequently, in the second 24 h, each cage was provided with one bottle containing water and another bottle with the sucrose solution. After 48 h of adaptation, the rats were housed alone and deprived of water and food for 24 h. Later, two pre-weighed bottles with water and sucrose solution, respectively, were simultaneously placed in each cage. After 1 h, the two bottles were weighed again and the consumption was calculated. The sucrose preference was expressed as the sucrose preference (%), which was calculated as [sucrose consumption/(sucrose consumption + water consumption)].

Open Field Test (OFT)

The OFT was used to determine the autonomous and exploratory behaviors of rats in a novel environment (35). The apparatus for the OFT was a white wooden box without a top structure (100 cm diameter and 50 cm wall height). The bottom of the apparatus was divided into 25 squares. The rats were placed one at a time into the central square and were allowed to freely explore the field for 5 min. The locomotion activity (the number of crossings), rearing, and grooming behaviors of the rats were recorded by a SMART video tracking system (SMART v3.0, Panlab, Spain). After each test, we cleaned the device with alcohol before inserting the next rat.

Elevated Plus Maze (EPM)

The EPM was used to test the anxiety level of the rats (36). The apparatus was elevated 50 cm from the ground. Two opposing open arms (30 cm long × 15 cm high) and two closed arms formed a cross around the central platform (5 cm × 5 cm). Each rat was individually placed onto the central platform facing an open arm and was allowed to freely explore the maze for 5 min. The number of entries into each arm was reported by the video tracking system (SMART v3.0, Panlab, Spain). A lower ratio of open arm entries to total entries signified a higher level of anxiety in the rat. We cleaned the apparatus after each test before inserting the next rat.

Morris Water Maze (MWM)

The MWM was used to determine the spatial memory and the learning ability of rats (37). The apparatus was a circular black tank (120 cm diameter and 50 cm height) and was filled with warm water (22°C). The software assigned four quadrants to the surface of the water. The platform (13 cm diameter and 29 cm height) was placed at the center of the target quadrant (quadrant II) and was 1–2 cm below the surface of the water. The movement of each rat was tracked and recorded using the SMART video tracking system (SMART v3.0, Panlab, Spain). A training period was carried out for 5 consecutive days, four times a day. The rats were gently placed into a random quadrant facing the wall and were allowed to swim freely to find the platform within 60 s, followed by a 20-s reprieve on the platform. Rats that failed to find the platform were manually placed on the platform for a 20-s break. The sixth day was the testing period; the rats were placed into quadrant IV and allowed to swim freely for 60 s in the maze without the platform. The number of across the target quadrant and the platform were recorded.

Pro-inflammatory Cytokine Expression Analysis

Sample Collection

Five rats from each group were randomly selected after completing the behavioral tests and then were decapitated immediately after being anesthetized. The whole brain was taken out of the skull carefully after opening the skull along the sagittal suture. Both sides of the prefrontal cortex and the hippocampus were isolated, and the samples were stored at −80°C. All the processes were performed on ice.

Protein Extraction

Lysis buffer and 1% protease inhibitor (phenylmethanesulfonyl fluoride) were added according to the weight of the sample. The tissue homogenate was centrifuged at 12,000 rpm for 25 min at 4°C, and then, the supernatant was extracted. The protein concentrations were determined by a Micro Bicinchoninic Acid Protein Assay Kit (Beyotime Institute of Biotechnology, China).

Enzyme-Linked Immunosorbent Assay (ELISA)

According to the ELISA kit instruction book (Tianjin Anoric Bio-technology Co., Ltd, China), different concentrations of standards and samples were added in a particular order to the 96-coated well plates. Subsequently, a biotin-antibody diluent was added to the samples, followed by 100 μL of an enzyme conjugation liquid. After incubation at 37°C for 60 min, the coated microwell plates were washed five times with a prepared washing liquid. The solutions of TMB I, TMB II, and stopping liquid were added to the plates in turn. The iMark Microplate Absorbance Reader (Bio-Rad Labs, Hercules, CA, USA) was used to detect the optical density at 450 nm. According to the standard curve drawn from the optical density of the standard, the concentration of each sample was calculated.

Histological Measurements

In order to observe the changes in microglial number and morphology, ionized calcium-binding adapter molecule 1 (Iba-1), a microglial marker, was detected by immunofluorescence as in a previous study (31). Five rats in each group were randomly chosen to receive a heart perfusion with 50 mL saline and 100 mL 4% paraformaldehyde (PFA) in phosphate buffer (0.1 M, pH 7.4) after being deeply anesthetized with pentobarbital. After that, the brains were removed and fixed in 4% PFA for 24 h at 4°C. After paraffin embedding, the brain samples were cut into 4 μm sections. The sections were incubated in citrate buffer (pH 6.0) to facilitate antigen retrieval at high temperature. The tissues were uniformly covered with 3% bovine serum albumin (BSA) and were blocked for 30 min at room temperature. Afterwards, the sections were incubated with rabbit anti-Iba1 antibody (1:200, Abcam, USA) at 4°C overnight. After washing thrice with phosphate-buffered saline (PBS), the sections were incubated with a secondary antibody (goat anti-rabbit, Alexa 594 conjugated, 1:1000, Invitrogen, USA) for 50 min in the dark. After three washes in PBS, the nuclei were stained with 4′,6-diamidino-2-phenylindole (DAPI) for 10 min in the dark. Later, the sections were sealed with an anti-fluorescence quenching sealant and observed under a Nikon Eclipse TI-SR microscope. The images were captured with a color camera (Nikon DS-U3).

The expression of inducible nitric oxide synthase (iNOS) was determined using immunohistochemical analysis. The paraffin sections were placed in citrate buffer (pH 6.0) in a microwave oven for antigen retrieval. After natural cooling, the sections were removed and washed with water and PBS. Subsequently, the sections were incubated with 3% H_2O_2 for 10 min and were blocked with 3% BSA for 30 min. Next, the sections were incubated with rabbit anti-iNOS antibody (1:200, Abcam, USA) at 4°C overnight. After washing thrice with PBS, the sections were incubated with a biotinylated secondary antibody at 37°C for 30 min. After washing with PBS, the sections were incubated with a streptavidin-biotin complex. Later, the sections were dyed with diaminobenzene and observed microscopically. The images were captured with the above mentioned microscope camera.

Epigenetic Markers and iNOS in the Western Blot Analysis

Sample collection and protein extraction were performed in a manner similar to ELISA. Protein concentrations were mixed with a 5× Laemmli loading buffer and then were heated at 100°C for 5 min. Subsequently, 20 μg of the protein sample was loaded in a prepared sodium dodecyl sulfate-polyacrylamide gel (5% stacking gel and 8 or 10% resolving gel, according to the molecular weight of the protein) and was separated by electrophoresis. The protein was electro-transferred to polyvinylidene difluoride (PVDF) membranes (Bio-Rad, CA, USA). The PVDF membranes were blocked with 5% defatted milk in a Tris buffered saline with 0.1% Tween-20 (TBST) for 90 min at room temperature and were incubated with primary antibodies against iNOS (1:500, Abcam, USA), Jmjd3 (1:800, Abcam, USA), H3K27me3 (1:1000, Biogot Technology, Co., Ltd), and β-actin (1:5000, Biogot Technology, Co., Ltd) at 4°C overnight. The secondary antibodies (1:10000, ZSGB-BIO, China) were incubated for 60 min at room temperature. After washing thrice with TBST, the PVDF membranes were incubated with a prepared enhanced chemiluminescence mixture (Millipore Corp, Billerica, MA, USA) for 1 min and were visualized on film in the dark. The gray value of the bands was quantified with the Image J 14.0 software.

Statistical Analysis

All experimental data were presented as the mean ± SEM. The SPSS 17.0 software was utilized to analyze the data. The adolescent groups and adult groups were analyzed separately.

Data were analyzed using a one-way analysis of variance followed by Tukey's *post hoc* test. Significance levels were set at $p < 0.05$.

RESULTS

Behavioral Test

Comparison of Depressive-Like Behavior and Anxiety-Like Behavior Alterations Between Groups

Figure 1A illustrates the results of the SPT. In the adolescent groups, the percentage of sucrose consumption [$F_{(2, 27)} = 16.08$, $p < 0.001$] in the AdoS group was lower than the AdoC group ($p < 0.001$) and the AdoS+M group ($p < 0.001$). The same results could be seen in the adult groups; the percentage of sucrose consumption in the AduS group [$F_{(2, 27)} = 8.21, p = 0.002$] was lesser than the AduC group ($p = 0.041$) and the AduS+M group ($p = 0.001$). The results indicated that stress in early adolescence decreased sucrose preference in both adolescent and adult rats, but treatment with minocycline could reverse the decrease in sucrose consumption.

Figures 1B–D illustrate the results of the OFT. **Figure 1B** shows the number of crossings in the OFT for the adolescent groups [$F_{(2, 27)} = 9.47$, $p = 0.001$] and adult groups [$F_{(2, 27)} = 7.40, p = 0.003$], respectively. The number of crossing in the AdoS group was lesser than the AdoC group ($p = 0.001$) and the AdoS+M group ($p = 0.017$). Similarly, the AduS group had a lesser number of crossing than the AduC group ($p = 0.003$). Treatment with minocycline resulted in an increased number of crossing in the AduS+M group ($p = 0.027$) when compared with the AduS group. **Figure 1C** shows the number of rearings in the OFT for the adolescent groups [$F_{(2, 27)} = 7.05$, $p = 0.003$] and

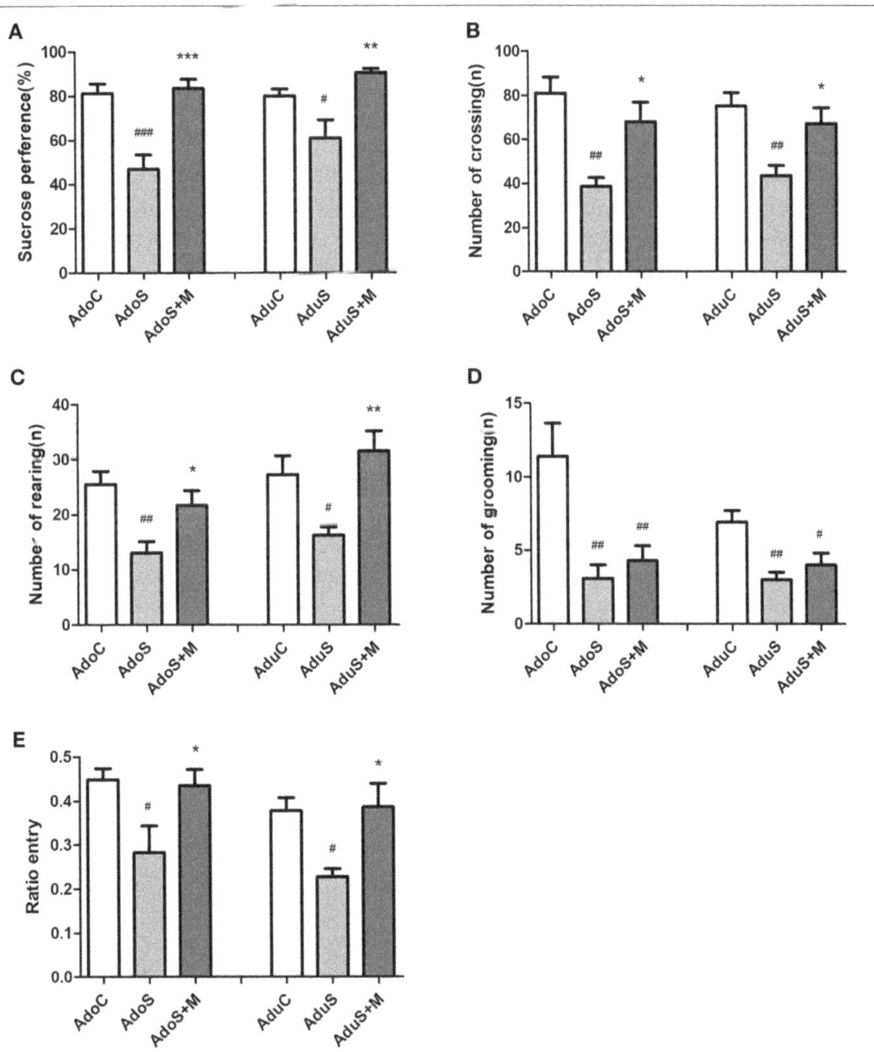

FIGURE 1 | CUMS induced depressive-like behaviors, while minocycline treatment reversed the alteration in both adolescent and adult rats. **(A)** Sucrose preference percentage in the SPT; **(B)** Number of crossing in the OFT; **(C)** Number of rearing in the OFT; **(D)** Number of grooming in the OFT; **(E)** Open arm entries ratio in the EPM test; Results were expressed as the mean ± SEM ($n = 9$ or 10 in each group). #, ##, and ### indicate $p < 0.05$, $p < 0.01$, and $p < 0.001$ vs. C group, respectively; *, **, and *** indicate $p < 0.05$, $p < 0.01$, and $p < 0.001$ vs. S group, respectively. AdoC, adolescent control group; AdoS, adolescent CUMS group; AdoS+M, adolescent CUMS and minocycline group; AduC, adult control group; AduS, adult CUMS group; AduS+M, adult CUMS and minocycline group.

adult groups [$F_{(2, 27)} = 6.91, p = 0.004$]. In the adolescent groups, the AdoS group showed lower numbers of rearing than the AdoC group ($p = 0.003$). Moreover, treatment with minocycline normalized the behavioral deficit when compared with the AdoS group ($p = 0.044$). In the adult groups, the number of rearing in the AduS group was lower than the AduC group ($p = 0.038$) and the AduS+M group ($p = 0.004$). **Figure 1D** shows the amount of grooming in the adolescent groups [$F_{(2, 27)} = 8.72, p = 0.001$] and adult groups [$F_{(2, 27)} = 7.65, p = 0.002$]. Both the AdoS group and the AduS group had lesser number of grooming than the AdoC group ($p = 0.002$) and the AduC group ($p = 0.002$), respectively. However, minocycline treatment had no effect on the amount of grooming either in adolescent or in adult rats. These results indicate that stress reduced automatic and exploratory behaviors in both adolescent and adult rats. Moreover, as an inhibitor of microglial activation, minocycline normalized most of the behavioral changes in both adolescent and adult rats.

Figure 1E shows the ratio of entry into the open arm in the EPM test in the adolescent and adult groups. The AdoS group [$F_{(2, 26)} = 4.63, p = 0.019$] had a significantly lower ratio of entry than the AdoC group ($p = 0.027$) and the AdoS+M group ($p = 0.045$). Similarly, there was a significant reduction of open arm entries ratio in the AduS group [$F_{(2, 27)} = 5.87$, $p = 0.008$] when compared with the AduC group ($p = 0.02$) and the AduS+M group ($p = 0.014$). These results indicate that stress in early adolescence induces anxiety-like behaviors in both adolescent rats and adult rats and that minocycline treatment improves abnormal behaviors.

Comparison of Cognitive Impairment in the MWM Test Between Groups

Figure 2 presents the results of the MWM test. **Figure 2A** presents the number of times through the platform during the probe test in the adolescent groups [$F_{(2, 27)} = 6.66, p = 0.004$] and adult groups [$F_{(2, 27)} = 8.25, p = 0.002$]. Compared with the AdoC group ($p = 0.019$) and the AdoS+M group ($p = 0.006$), the number of times through the platform decreased significantly in the AdoS group. The AduS group also had lower number of times through the platform than the AduC group ($p = 0.008$) and the AduS+M group ($p = 0.003$). **Figure 2B** shows the percentage of entries into the target quadrant in the adolescent groups [$F_{(2, 27)} = 5.47, p = 0.01$] and adult groups [$F_{(2, 27)} = 3.11, p = 0.061$]. The AdoS group had reduced percentage of entries when compared with the AdoC group ($p = 0.024$) and the AdoS+M group ($p = 0.018$). However, there were no significant differences in the three adult groups. These results suggest that stress in early adolescence induced learning and memory impairment, and the inhibitor of microglial activation could reverse the damages.

Comparison of Pro-inflammatory Cytokine Expression in the Prefrontal Cortex and Hippocampus Between Groups

Figures 3A,B show cytokine expression in the prefrontal cortex. As **Figure 3A** shows, the levels of IL-1β increased in both the AdoS group [$F_{(2, 12)} = 60.57, p < 0.001$] ($p < 0.001$) and the AduS group [$F_{(2, 12)} = 5.63, p = 0.019$] ($p = 0.04$), when compared with the AdoC group and the AduC group, respectively. However, these increases were attenuated by minocycline treatment in both adolescent and adult rats ($p < 0.001$; $p = 0.027$). **Figure 3B** shows the levels of IL-6 in the prefrontal cortex. The AdoS group had increased levels of IL-6 when compared with the AdoC group [$F_{(2, 12)} = 5.60, p = 0.019$] ($p = 0.045$) and the AdoS+M group ($p = 0.026$). The same change tendency was observed in the adult groups. There was an increased level of IL-6 in the AduS group when compared with the AduC group [$F_{(2, 12)} = 5.58, p = 0.019$] ($p = 0.032$) and the AduS+M group ($p = 0.035$).

Figures 3C,D show cytokine expression in the hippocampus. **Figure 3C** shows the levels of IL-1β in both the adolescent groups [$F_{(2, 12)} = 6.64, p = 0.011$] and the adult groups [$F_{(2, 12)} = 7.74$, $p = 0.007$]. The same change tendency that was observed in the prefrontal cortex was seen in the hippocampus; the AdoS group and the AduS group had higher levels of IL-1β than the AdoC group ($p = 0.013$) and the AduC group ($p = 0.02$), respectively.

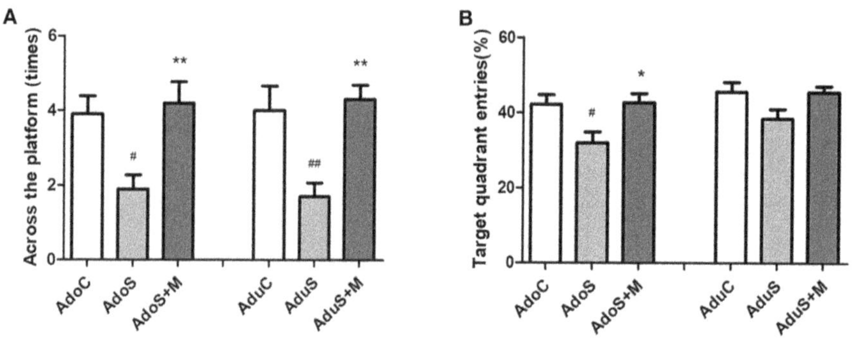

FIGURE 2 | CUMS induced spatial learning and memory impairment, while minocycline treatment reversed the alteration in both adolescent and adult rats. **(A)** Number of crossings of the platform in the MWM test; **(B)** Target quadrant entries percentage in the MWM test. Results are expressed as the mean ± SEM ($n = 10$ in each group). # and ## indicate $p < 0.05$ and $p < 0.01$ vs. C group, respectively; * and ** indicate $p < 0.05$ and $p < 0.01$ vs. S group, respectively. AdoC, adolescent control group; AdoS, adolescent CUMS group; AdoS+M, adolescent CUMS and minocycline group; AduC, adult control group; AduS, adult CUMS group; AduS+M, adult CUMS and minocycline group.

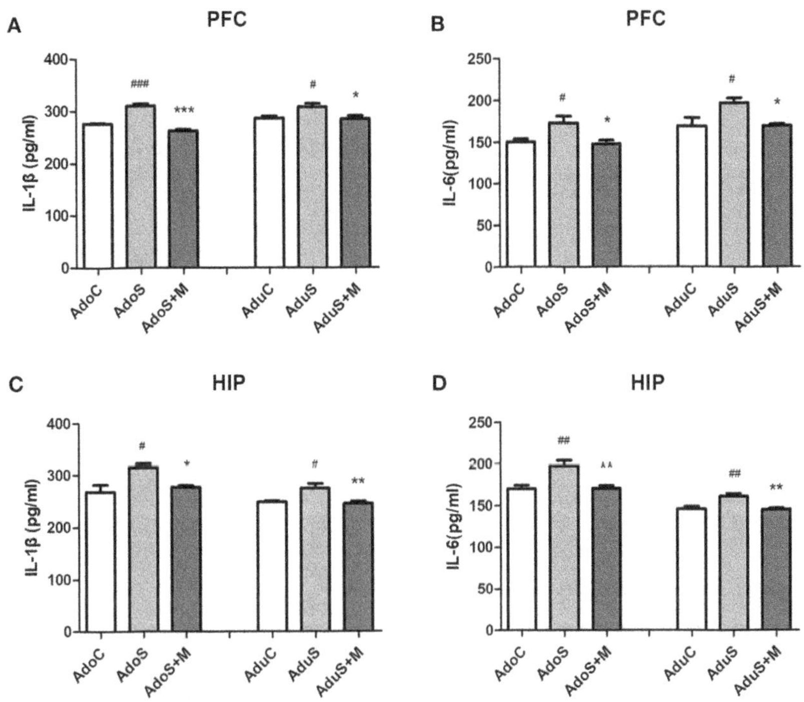

FIGURE 3 | The levels of cytokines in the prefrontal cortex and hippocampus of both the adolescent and adult groups. **(A)** IL-1β expression in the prefrontal cortex; **(B)** IL-6 expression in the prefrontal cortex; **(C)** IL-1β expression in the hippocampus; **(D)** IL-6 expression in the hippocampus. Results are expressed as the mean ± SEM ($n = 5$ in each group). #, ##, and ### indicate $p < 0.05$, $p < 0.01$, and $p < 0.001$ vs. C group, respectively; *, **, and *** indicate $p < 0.05$, $p < 0.01$, and $p < 0.001$ vs. S group, respectively. AdoC, adolescent control group; AdoS, adolescent CUMS group; AdoS+M, adolescent CUMS and minocycline group; AduC, adult control group; AduS, adult CUMS group; AduS+M, adult CUMS and minocycline group.

Minocycline decreased the levels of IL-1β in both adolescent ($p = 0.042$) and adult ($p = 0.009$) rats. **Figure 3D** shows that the levels of IL-6 increased in both the AdoS group [$F_{(2, 12)} = 9.91$, $p = 0.003$] ($p = 0.005$) and the AduS group [$F_{(2, 12)} = 11.03$, $p = 0.002$] ($p = 0.004$), when compared with the AdoC group and the AduC group, respectively. Minocycline decreased the levels of IL-6 in both adolescent ($p = 0.007$) and adult ($p = 0.004$) rats.

Comparison of Microglial Activation in the Prefrontal Cortex and Hippocampus Between Groups

Figure 4A shows the Iba-1 (as the microglia marker) expression in the prefrontal cortex in adolescent groups. **Figure 4C** shows the Iba-1 expression in the prefrontal cortex in adult groups. Fewer branches and larger cell bodies of the microglia in the prefrontal cortex were observed in the stressed group when compared with the C group and the S+M group in both adolescence and adulthood. **Figure 4E** shows the count of cells that positively express Iba-1 in the prefrontal cortex. We observed that the Iba-1-labeled microglial cells had a larger soma size and were more abundant in the AdoS group [$F_{(2, 12)} = 31.58$, $p < 0.001$] ($p < 0.001$) and the AduS group [$F_{(2, 12)} = 9.64$, $p = 0.003$] ($p = 0.037$), when compared with the AdoC group and the AduC group, respectively. Meanwhile minocycline treatment reversed the changes in the rats of the AdoS+M group ($p < 0.001$) and the AduS+M group ($p = 0.003$).

Figure 4B shows the Iba-1 expression in the hippocampus in the adolescent groups. **Figure 4D** shows the Iba-1 expression in the hippocampus in the adult groups. Fewer branches and larger cell bodies of the microglia in the hippocampus were observed in the stressed group when compared with the C group and the S+M group in both adolescence and adulthood. **Figure 4F** shows the count of cells that positively express Iba-1 in the hippocampus. In adolescence, the AdoS group [$F_{(2, 12)} = 61.32$, $p < 0.001$] had a significantly increased number of microglia when compared with the AdoC group ($p < 0.001$) and the AdoS+M ($p < 0.001$) group. The adult groups had the same change tendencies in that stress increased the number of microglia in the AduS group [$F_{(2, 12)} = 10.02$, $p = 0.003$] when compared with the AduC group ($p = 0.035$), and minocycline suppressed the activation in the AduS+M group ($p = 0.002$).

Comparison of iNOS Expression in the Prefrontal Cortex and Hippocampus Between Groups

Figure 5A shows the iNOS (M1 activation marker) expression in the prefrontal cortex and hippocampus in immunohistochemistry. **Figure 5B** shows the count of cells that

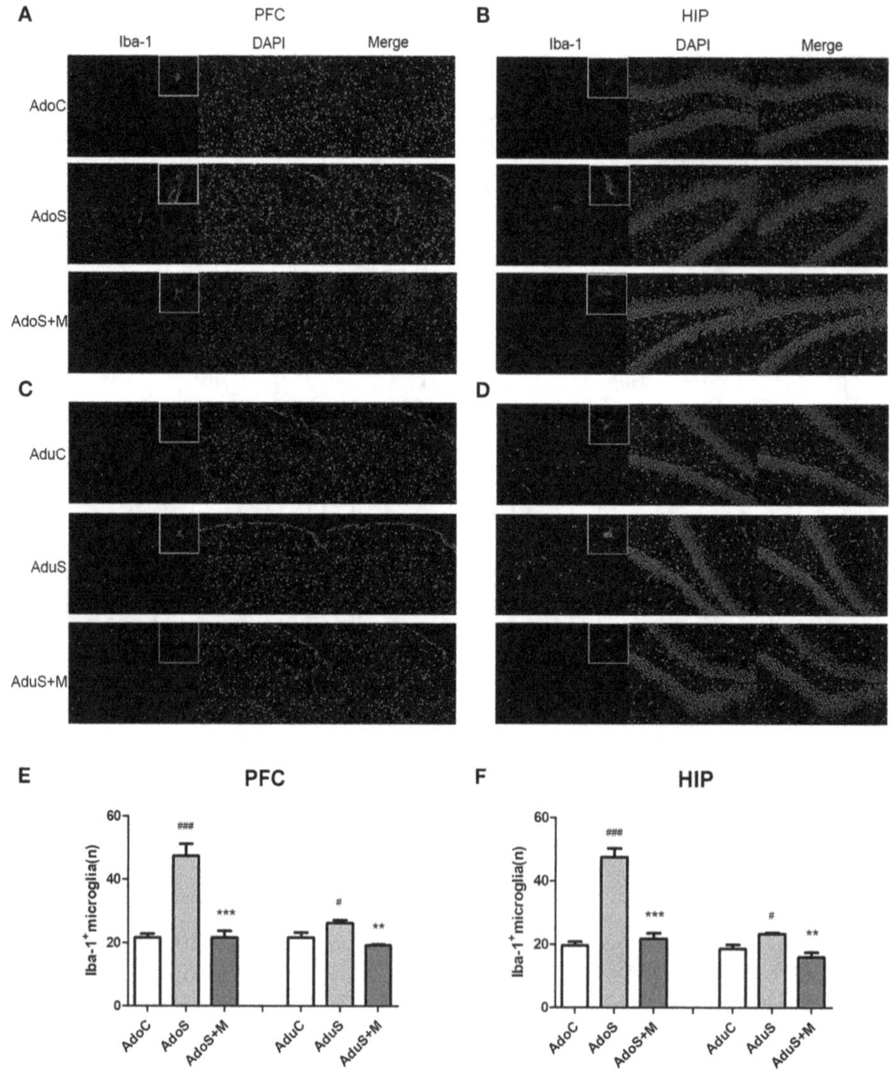

FIGURE 4 | CUMS induced microglial activation in the prefrontal cortex and hippocampus of both the adolescent and adult rats, while minocycline reduced the alteration. **(A)** Iba-1/DAPI (red/blue) staining (×200) in the prefrontal cortex of adolescent rats; **(B)** Iba-1/DAPI (red/blue) staining (×200) in the hippocampus of adolescent rats; **(C)** Iba-1/DAPI (red/blue) staining (×200) in the prefrontal cortex of adult rats; **(D)** Iba-1/DAPI (red/blue) staining (×200) in the hippocampus of adult rats; **(E)** Iba-1$^+$ cell counts in the prefrontal cortex; **(F)** Iba-1$^+$ cell counts in the hippocampus. The results are expressed as the mean ± SEM (n = 5 each group). # and ### indicate $p < 0.05$ and $p < 0.001$ vs. C group, respectively; ** and *** indicate $p < 0.01$ and $p < 0.001$ vs. S group, respectively. AdoC, adolescent control group; AdoS, adolescent CUMS group; AdoS+M, adolescent CUMS and minocycline group; AduC, adult control group; AduS, adult CUMS group; AduS+M, adult CUMS and minocycline group.

positively expressed iNOS in the prefrontal cortex. In adolescent rats, CUMS could induce iNOS expression [$F_{(2, 9)} = 15.76$, $p = 0.001$] ($p = 0.001$), while minocycline treatment reversed the alteration ($p = 0.049$). In adult rats, the stress-exposed rats also had higher iNOS expression than the AduC group [$F_{(2, 9)} = 13.12$, $p = 0.002$] ($p = 0.003$). Minocycline treatment also reversed the alteration ($p = 0.005$). **Figure 5C** shows the count of cells that positively express iNOS in the hippocampus. In the adolescent groups, the AdoS group had higher iNOS expression than the AdoC group [$F_{(2, 9)} = 10.03$, $p = 0.005$] ($p = 0.025$) and the AdoS+M group ($p = 0.005$). In the adult groups, the expression of iNOS also increased in the AduS group [$F_{(2, 9)} = 27.07$, $p < 0.001$] ($p < 0.001$) when compared with the AduC group and the AduS+M group ($p = 0.001$).

Figure 5D shows the expression of iNOS in the prefrontal cortex in Western blot. In the adolescent groups, the AdoS group [$F_{(2, 12)} = 24.15$, $p < 0.001$] had higher levels of iNOS expression than the AdoC group ($p < 0.001$) and the AdoS+M group ($p < 0.001$). In the adult groups, the expression of iNOS increased in the AduS group [$F_{(2, 12)} = 8.84$, $p = 0.004$)] when compared with that in the AduC group ($p = 0.01$) and the AduS+M group ($p = 0.008$).

Figure 5E shows the iNOS expression in the hippocampus in Western blot. Increased iNOS expression was seen in the AdoS group [$F_{(2, 12)} = 14.42$, $p = 0.001$] when compared with the AdoC

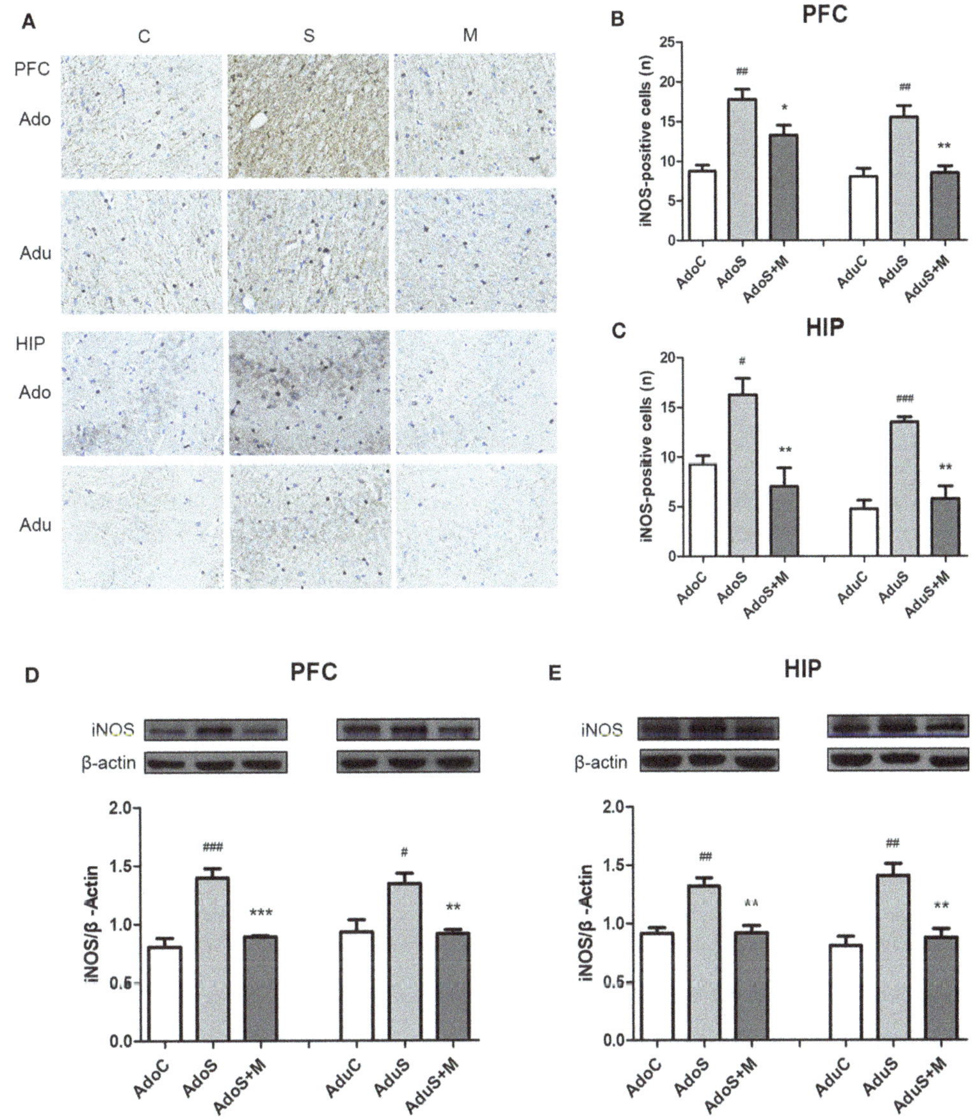

FIGURE 5 | CUMS induced M1 marker iNOS expression in the prefrontal cortex and hippocampus of both adolescent and adult rats, while minocycline treatment reduced the expression. **(A)** iNOS expression in the prefrontal cortex and hippocampus in immunohistochemistry (×400); **(B)** iNOS-positive cell counts in the prefrontal cortex; **(C)** iNOS-positive cell counts in the hippocampus; **(D)** Western blot analysis of iNOS in the prefrontal cortex; **(E)** Western blot analysis of iNOS in the hippocampus. Results are expressed as the mean ± SEM ($n = 4$ each group; $n = 5$ each group). #, ##, and ### indicate $p < 0.05$, $p < 0.01$, and $p < 0.001$ vs. C group, respectively; *, **, and *** indicate $p < 0.05$, $p < 0.01$, and $p < 0.001$ vs. S group, respectively. AdoC, adolescent control group; AdoS, adolescent CUMS group; AdoS+M, adolescent CUMS and minocycline group; AduC, adult control group; AduS, adult CUMS group; AduS+M, adult CUMS and minocycline group.

group ($p = 0.001$), but minocycline treatment normalized the alteration in the AdoS+M group ($p = 0.002$). The AduS group [$F_{(2, 12)} = 13.99, p = 0.001$] had higher levels of iNOS expression than the AduC group ($p = 0.001$). Similarly, minocycline reduced the expression of iNOS in the AduS+M group ($p = 0.003$) when compared with the AduS group.

Comparison of Expression of Jmjd3 and H3K27me3 Between Groups

Figure 6A shows Jmjd3 expression in the prefrontal cortex in every group in adolescence and adulthood using Western blot. In the adolescent group, Jmjd3 levels showed significant group effects [$F_{(2, 12)} = 21.23$, $p < 0.001$]. Stress induced the expression of Jmjd3 in rats of the AdoS group ($p = 0.001$) more strongly than in the AdoC group. Nevertheless, minocycline decreased the level of Jmjd3 expression in the AdoS+M group when compared with the AdoS group ($p < 0.001$). In adult groups, increased Jmjd3 expression was seen in the AduS group [$F_{(2, 12)} = 54.72$, $p < 0.001$] ($p < 0.001$) when compared with the AduC group. Minocycline reversed the alteration ($p = 0.037$ AduS group vs. AduS+M group).

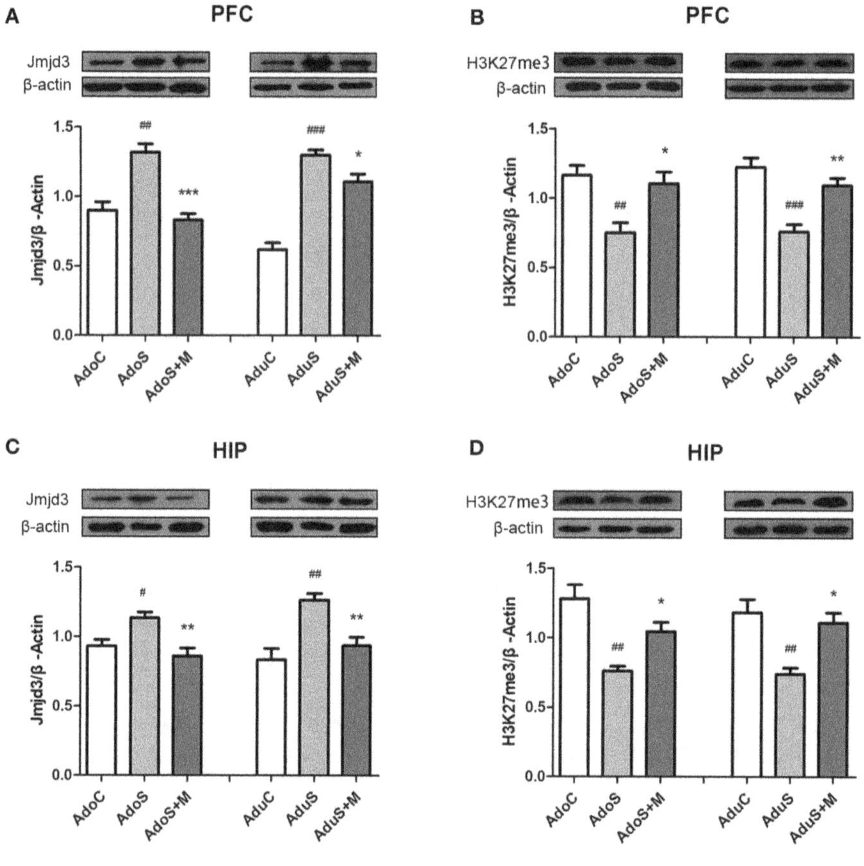

FIGURE 6 | The expression of Jmjd3 and H3K27me3 in the prefrontal cortex and hippocampus detected by Western blotting. **(A)** Western blot analysis of Jmjd3 in the prefrontal cortex; **(B)** Western blot analysis of H3K27me3 in the prefrontal cortex; **(C)** Western blot analysis of Jmjd3 in the hippocampus; **(D)** Western blot analysis of H3K27me3 in the hippocampus. Results are expressed as the mean ± SEM (n = 5 each group). #, ##, and ### indicate $p < 0.05$, $p < 0.01$, and $p < 0.001$ vs. C group, respectively; *, **, and *** indicate $p < 0.05$, $p < 0.01$, and $p < 0.001$ vs. S group, respectively. AdoC, adolescent control group; AdoS, adolescent CUMS group; AdoS+M, adolescent CUMS and minocycline group; AduC, adult control group; AduS, adult CUMS group; AduS+M, adult CUMS and minocycline group.

Figure 6B shows H3K27me3 expression in the prefrontal cortex in both adolescent and adult groups. The AdoS group had a markedly decreased H3K27me3 level when compared with the AdoC group [$F_{(2, 12)} = 8.56$, $p = 0.005$] ($p = 0.006$). Whereas, animals in the AdoS+M group showed a significantly higher H3K27me3 level when compared with the AdoS group ($p = 0.017$). In adult groups, stress induced the reduced expression of H3K27me3 in the AduS group [$F_{(2, 12)} = 16.38$, $p < 0.001$] ($p < 0.001$) when compared with the AduC group, while minocycline treatment could reverse the decreased expression in the AduS+M group ($p = 0.005$).

Figure 6C shows Jmjd3 expression in the hippocampus of adolescent and adult groups using Western blot. The same change tendencies in Jmjd3 expression in the hippocampus were observed as in the prefrontal cortex. Stress induced the over-expression of Jmjd3 in rats from the AdoS group [$F_{(2, 12)} = 8.24$, $p = 0.006$] ($p = 0.033$) when compared with the AdoC group. However, minocycline treatment decreased the level of Jmjd3 expression in the AdoS+M group when compared with the AdoS group ($p = 0.005$). In the adult groups, the AduS group [$F_{(2, 12)} = 12.24$, $p = 0.001$] ($p = 0.001$) had an increased Jmjd3 expression when compared with the AduC group; however, minocycline reversed the alteration ($p = 0.009$).

Figure 6D shows H3K27me3 expression in the hippocampus in both adolescent and adult groups, which had the same change tendency as the prefrontal cortex. The AdoS group had a markedly decreased H3K27me3 level when compared with the AdoC group [$F_{(2, 12)} = 12.70$, $p = 0.001$] ($p = 0.001$). Nevertheless, animals in the AdoS+M group showed a significant increase in H3K27me3 levels when compared with the AdoS group ($p = 0.044$). Similarly, the AduS group had lower H3K27me3 levels than the AduC group [$F_{(2, 12)} = 10.35$, $p = 0.002$] ($p = 0.003$). Meanwhile, minocycline treatment reversed the decrease in the AduS+M group when compared with the AduS group ($p = 0.01$).

DISCUSSION

The present study revealed that CUMS in the adolescent period induced short-term and persistent depressive-like behaviors, high levels of pro-inflammatory cytokines, microglial activation, and increased Jmjd3 and decreased H3K27me3 expression in the prefrontal cortex and hippocampus. The results indicate that the alteration of Jmjd3 and H3K27me3 expression plays a critical role in susceptibility to depressive-like behaviors in rats that had early-life stress experiences.

Previous studies suggested that social-psychological stress exposure in early-life increases the risk of mood disorders (38). Our previous study revealed that CUMS and acute stress in early life induce long-term dysfunctional behaviors, which supports the conclusion that early-life stress has long-lasting effects on individual behaviors (33, 39). Consistent with the above study, CUMS in the adolescent period induced depressive-like behaviors and memory damage in both adolescent and adult animals in our present study. Moreover, minocycline, the microglial activation inhibitor, attenuated the abnormalities of behaviors in adolescent and adult groups, which indicates that inhibition of microglial activation could relieve the depressive-like behaviors. These results suggest that early-life stress gives rise to long-lasting behavioral disorders (40, 41) and also that microglial activation is involved in behavioral abnormalities (42).

An increasing number of studies suggest that some pro-inflammatory cytokines are closely linked to the pathogenesis of depression under stress by a mechanism in which cytokines decrease the levels of serotonin, noradrenaline, and dopamine in the limbic system and stimulate the hypothalamic-pituitary-adrenal (HPA) axis to release glucocorticoids (2). In addition, pro-inflammatory cytokines could induce sickness-like behaviors independently; for example, IL-1β decreased locomotor activity (35). Cytokines also initiate the cycle of pro-inflammatory responses by giving rise to a cascade of inflammatory cytokine responses when the patient is suffering from psychological stress (43). The present study showed that CUMS induced significantly increased levels of IL-6 and IL-1β in both the hippocampus and prefrontal cortex. However, minocycline treatment attenuated these alterations. More importantly, adult rats in the CUMS group showed higher levels of IL-6 and IL-1β in both the hippocampus and prefrontal cortex along with depressive-like behaviors. Hence, our results demonstrate that higher levels of pro-inflammatory cytokines in the brain induced by CUMS during the adolescent period are associated with vulnerability to depression in adulthood.

Previous studies pointed out that classical microglial activation facilitates the occurrence of depression by pro-inflammatory cytokines during which stress plays an important role. First, stress induces HPA axis activation, and massive amounts of glucocorticoids are released into the prefrontal cortex and hippocampus, where they are susceptive to the corticosterone surge. Microglia express a large number of glucocorticoid receptors, whereupon stress induces microglial activation. Secondly, stress induces pro-inflammatory cytokine (IL-1β) over-expression in the CNS leading to the activation of microglia (44, 45). In order to clarify the role of microglial activation in neuroinflammation from adolescence to adulthood caused by CUMS in adolescence, the present study examined the Iba-1 and iNOS expression in the prefrontal cortex and hippocampus in both adolescent and adult rats. The results show that Iba-1 and iNOS are over-expressed in the prefrontal cortex and hippocampus of stressed rats when compared with their expression in unstressed rats. Furthermore, the morphology of microglia underwent a noticeable change from a ramified morphology to an amoeboid shape in stressed rats. These results are consistent with previous studies that showed that microglia increased in number, and hyper-ramified properties arose in response to chronic stress (46). Moreover, similar results were detected in adult rats, which support the argument that early-life stress could lead to long-term pro-inflammatory effects and classical microglial activation (47). Our results support the "two-hit" theory of the involvement of neuroinflammation in the etiology of mental disorders, which proposes that early-life stress primes or sensitizes microglia. Stress in later life can provoke the sensitized microglia, which can generate an exaggerated response and increase the risk of development of a mental disorder (44). Therefore, our results expanded the conclusion that stress-induced microglial activation in early-life is closely linked to the susceptibility to depression. Moreover, the present study illustrates the role of minocycline in microglial activation in early-life stress-induced depression. Consistent with previous studies (31, 48), minocycline administration reduced depressive-like behaviors and inhibited the expression of pro-inflammatory cytokines. These results imply that minocycline has the potential to be used as a treatment for depression by targeting microglial activation.

Recent research has demonstrated that Jmjd3 can remove the tri-methylation and di-methylation marks of H3K27 and then lead to gene expression. Most importantly, Jmjd3 was induced both by inflammation and by stress (23, 49). Jmjd3 decreased the level of repressive H3K27me3 marks at the promoters of NF-κB-driven inflammatory genes such as IL-1β (50). Thus, the higher expression of Jmjd3 participated in inflammation by enhancing the transcription of inflammatory genes via the NF-κB signaling pathway (49). In addition, NF-κB transcription factors were the driving forces for microglial activation (50). Hence, Jmjd3 was a key factor in a cascade of inflammatory cytokine response (23, 28, 49, 50). In this study, we investigated the alterations of Jmjd3 and H3K27me3 expression under stress and found that CUMS induced increased Jmjd3 expression and decreased H3K27me3 expression in the prefrontal cortex and hippocampus. These results imply that the downregulation of H3K27me3 by Jmjd3 mediated the expression of cytokines. It is important to note that minocycline, as an inhibitor to microglial activation, could reverse all the alterations in both adolescent and adult animals. Our results, for the first time, highlighted that Jmjd3 plays a key role in the inflammatory response to CUMS and mediates the susceptibility to depression by regulating microglial activation and pro-inflammatory cytokine expression in the prefrontal cortex and hippocampus.

CONCLUSIONS

Exposure to CUMS in the adolescent period induced long-term depressive-like behaviors, increased pro-inflammatory cytokine expression and microglial activation, increased Jmjd3 expression, and decreased H3K27me3 expression in the prefrontal cortex and hippocampus of adolescent and adult rats. Meanwhile, minocycline, a microglial activation inhibitor, mitigated all the alterations. Our study suggests that Jmjd3 might be involved in the susceptibility to depression by modulating the microglial activation and pro-inflammatory cytokine expression.

LIMITATION

This study has limitations. First, primed microglia have two functional subtypes, "classical activation" and "alternative activation." The present study only discussed the "classical activation," and no indicators of the "alternative activation" were included. Second, Jmjd3 is an important epigenetic element in microglial activation. Lack of a Jmjd3 inhibitor limits the understanding about the role of Jmjd3 in susceptibility to depression induced by early-life stress.

ETHICS STATEMENT

In the handling and care of all animals, the international guiding principles for animal research, as stipulated by the World Health Organization (WHO) Chronicle (World Health Organization, 1985) and as adopted by the Laboratory Animal Center, Shandong University, were followed.

AUTHOR CONTRIBUTIONS

FP conceived and designed the experiments. RW performed most of the experiment and analyzed the data. FP and RW wrote and refined the article. WW participated in the animal modeling and behavioral experiments. JX assisted in laboratory work and figure preparation. DL and HJ supervised the acquisition of results.

FUNDING

This work was supported by funding from National Natural Science Foundation of China (no. 31371036; 31771220).

REFERENCES

1. Jo WK, Zhang Y, Emrich HM, Dietrich DE. Glia in the cytokine-mediated onset of depression: fine tuning the immune response. *Front Cell Neurosci.* (2015) 9:268. doi: 10.3389/fncel.2015.00268
2. Jeon SW, Kim YK. Neuroinflammation and cytokine abnormality in major depression: cause or consequence in that illness? *World J Psychiatry* (2016) 6:283–93. doi: 10.5498/wjp.v6.i3.283
3. Slavich GM, Irwin MR. From stress to inflammation and major depressive disorder: a social signal transduction theory of depression. *Psychol Bull.* (2014) 140:774–815. doi: 10.1037/a0035302
4. Kohler CA, Freitas TH, Maes M, de Andrade NQ, Liu CS, Fernandes BS, et al. Peripheral cytokine and chemokine alterations in depression: a meta-analysis of 82 studies. *Acta Psychiatr Scand.* (2017) 135:373–87. doi: 10.1111/acps.12698
5. Torres-Platas SG, Cruceanu C, Chen GG, Turecki G, Mechawar N. Evidence for increased microglial priming and macrophage recruitment in the dorsal anterior cingulate white matter of depressed suicides. *Brain Behav Immun.* (2014) 42:50–9. doi: 10.1016/j.bbi.2014.05.007
6. Zhang HX, Xu YQ, Li YY, Lu MF, Shi SX, Ji JL, et al. Difference in proinflammatory cytokines produced by monocytes between patients with major depressive disorder and healthy controls. *J Affect Disord.* (2018) 234:305–10. doi: 10.1016/j.jad.2017.12.099
7. Dahl J, Ormstad H, Aass HC, Malt UF, Bendz LT, Sandvik L, et al. The plasma levels of various cytokines are increased during ongoing depression and are reduced to normal levels after recovery. *Psychoneuroendocrinology* (2014) 45:77–86. doi: 10.1016/j.psyneuen.2014.03.019
8. Goodwin RD, Davidson KW, Keyes K. Mental disorders and cardiovascular disease among adults in the United States. *J Psychiatr Res.* (2009) 43:239–46. doi: 10.1016/j.jpsychires.2008.05.006
9. Choi JS, Kim W, Sohn BK, Lee JY, Jung HY, Oh S, et al. Association of changes in mood status and psychosocial well-being with depression during interferon-based treatment for hepatitis C. *Psychiatry Investig.* (2017) 14:314–24. doi: 10.4306/pi.2017.14.3.314
10. Cooper CM, Godlewska B, Sharpley AL, Barnes E, Cowen PJ, Harmer CJ. Interferon-alpha induces negative biases in emotional processing in patients with hepatitis C virus infection: a preliminary study. *Psychol Med.* (2018) 48:998–1007. doi: 10.1017/S0033291717002379
11. Jiang H, Wang Z, Wang Y, Xie K, Zhang Q, Luan Q, et al. Antidepressant-like effects of curcumin in chronic mild stress of rats: involvement of its anti-inflammatory action. *Prog Neuropsychopharmacol Biol Psychiatry* (2013) 47:33–9. doi: 10.1016/j.pnpbp.2013.07.009
12. Zhao Y, Zhang Y, Pan F. The effects of EGb761 on lipopolysaccharide-induced depressive-like behaviour in C57BL/6J mice. *Cent Eur J Immunol.* (2015) 40:11–7. doi: 10.5114/ceji.2015.49427
13. Frank MG, Baratta MV, Sprunger DB, Watkins LR, Maier SF. Microglia serve as a neuroimmune substrate for stress-induced potentiation of CNS pro-inflammatory cytokine responses. *Brain Behav Immun.* (2007) 21:47–59. doi: 10.1016/j.bbi.2006.03.005
14. Hinwood M, Morandini J, Day TA, Walker FR. Evidence that microglia mediate the neurobiological effects of chronic psychological stress on the medial prefrontal cortex. *Cereb Cortex* (2012) 22:1442–54. doi: 10.1093/cercor/bhr229
15. Kreisel T, Frank MG, Licht T, Reshef R, Ben-Menachem-Zidon O, Baratta MV, et al. Dynamic microglial alterations underlie stress-induced depressive-like behavior and suppressed neurogenesis. *Mol Psychiatry* (2014) 19:699–709. doi: 10.1038/mp.2013.155
16. Colton CA. Heterogeneity of microglial activation in the innate immune response in the brain. *J Neuroimmune Pharmacol.* (2009) 4:399–418. doi: 10.1007/s11481-009-9164-4
17. Xu N, Tang XH, Pan W, Xie ZM, Zhang GF, Ji MH, et al. Spared nerve injury increases the expression of microglia M1 markers in the prefrontal cortex of rats and provokes depression-like behaviors. *Front Neurosci.* (2017) 11:209. doi: 10.3389/fnins.2017.00209
18. Nakagawa Y, Chiba K. Role of microglial m1/m2 polarization in relapse and remission of psychiatric disorders and diseases. *Pharmaceuticals* (2014) 7:1028–48. doi: 10.3390/ph7121028
19. Song C. The effect of thymectomy and IL-1 on memory: implications for the relationship between immunity and depression. *Brain Behav Immunity* (2002) 16:557–68. doi: 10.1016/S0889-1591(02)00012-0
20. Walker FR, Nilsson M, Jones K. Acute and chronic stress-induced disturbances of microglial plasticity, phenotype and function. *Curr Drug Targets* (2013) 14:1262–76. doi: 10.2174/13894501113149990208
21. Kato TA, Kanba S. Are microglia minding us? Digging up the unconscious mind-brain relationship from a neuropsychoanalytic approach. *Front Hum Neurosci.* (2013) 7:13. doi: 10.3389/fnhum.2013.00013

22. Tsankova NM, Berton O, Renthal W, Kumar A, Neve RL, Nestler EJ. Sustained hippocampal chromatin regulation in a mouse model of depression and antidepressant action. *Nat Neurosci.* (2006) 9:519–25. doi: 10.1038/nn1659
23. De Santa F, Narang V, Yap ZH, Tusi BK, Burgold T, Austenaa L, et al. Jmjd3 contributes to the control of gene expression in LPS-activated macrophages. *EMBO J.* (2009) 28:3341–52. doi: 10.1038/emboj.2009.271
24. Yu S, Chen X, Xiu M, He F, Xing J, Min D, et al. The regulation of Jmjd3 upon the expression of NF-kappaB downstream inflammatory genes in LPS activated vascular endothelial cells. *Biochem Biophys Res Commun.* (2017) 485:62–8. doi: 10.1016/j.bbrc.2017.02.020
25. Das ND, Jung KH, Choi MR. Gene networking and inflammatory pathway analysis in a JMJD3 knockdown human monocytic cell line. *Cell Biochem. Function* (2012) 30:224–32. doi: 10.1002/cbf.1839
26. Przanowski P, Dabrowski M, Ellert-Miklaszewska A, Kloss M. The signal transducers Stat1 and Stat3 and their novel target Jmjd3 drive the expression of inflammatory genes in microglia. *J Mol Med.* (2014) 92:239–54. doi: 10.1007/s00109-013-1090-5)
27. Donas C, Carrasco M, Fritz M, Prado C, Tejon G, Osorio-Barrios F, et al. The histone demethylase inhibitor GSK-J4 limits inflammation through the induction of a tolerogenic phenotype on DCs. *J Autoimmun.* (2016) 75:105–17. doi: 10.1016/j.jaut.2016.07.011
28. Kruidenier L, Chung CW, Cheng Z, Liddle J, Che K, Joberty G, et al. A selective jumonji H3K27 demethylase inhibitor modulates the proinflammatory macrophage response. *Nature* (2012) 488:404–8. doi: 10.1038/nature11262
29. Bahrami Z, Firouzi M, Hashemi-Monfared A, Zahednasab H, Harirchian MH. The effect of minocycline on indolamine 2, 3 dioxygenase expression and the levels of kynurenic acid and quinolinic acid in LPS-activated primary rat microglia. *Cytokine* (2018) 107:125–9. doi: 10.1016/j.cyto.2017.12.013
30. Kobayashi K, Imagama S, Ohgomori T, Hirano K, Uchimura K, Sakamoto K, et al. Minocycline selectively inhibits M1 polarization of microglia. *Cell Death Dis.* (2013) 4:e525. doi: 10.1038/cddis.2013.54
31. Wang YL, Han QQ, Gong WQ, Pan DH, Wang LZ, Hu W, et al. Microglial activation mediates chronic mild stress-induced depressive- and anxiety-like behavior in adult rats. *J Neuroinflammation* (2018) 15:21. doi: 10.1186/s12974-018-1054-3
32. Pan Y, Chen XY, Zhang QY, Kong LD. Microglial NLRP3 inflammasome activation mediates IL-1beta-related inflammation in prefrontal cortex of depressive rats. *Brain Behav Immun.* (2014) 41:90–100 doi: 10.1016/j.bbi.2014.04.007
33. Xu J, Wang R, Liu Y, Liu D, Jiang H, Pan F. FKBP5 and specific microRNAs via glucocorticoid receptor in the basolateral amygdala involved in the susceptibility to depressive disorder in early adolescent stressed rats. *J Psychiatr Res.* (2017) 95:102–13. doi: 10.1016/j.jpsychires.2017.08.010
34. Willner P, Sampson D, Sophokleous S, Muscat R. Reduction of sucrose preference by chronic unpredictable mild stress, and its restoration by a tricyclic antidepressant. *Psychopharmacology* (1987) 93:358–64.
35. Swiergiel AH, Dunn AJ. Effects of interleukin-1β and lipopolysaccharide on behavior of mice in the Elevated Plus-maze and open field tests. *Pharmacol Biochem Behav.* (2007) 86:651–9. doi: 10.1016/j.pbb.2007.02.010
36. Adamec R, Hebert M, Blundell J, Mervis RF. Dendritic morphology of amygdala and hippocampal neurons in more and less predator stress responsive rats and more and less spontaneously anxious handled controls. *Behav Brain Res.* (2012) 226:133–46. doi: 10.1016/j.bbr.2011.09.009
37. D'Hooge R, Deyn PPD. Applications of the Morris water maze in the study of learning and memory. *Brain Res Rev.* (2001) 36:60–90. doi: 10.1016/S0165-0173(01)00067-4
38. Heim C, Nemeroff CB. The role of childhood trauma in the neurobiology of mood and anxiety disorders preclinical and clinical studies. *Biol. Psychiatry* (2001) 49:1023–39. doi: 10.1016/S0006-3223(01)01157-X
39. Li CT, Liu Y, Yin SP, Lu CY, Liu DX, Jiang H, et al. Long-term effects of early adolescent stress: dysregulation of hypothalamic–pituitary–adrenal axis and central corticotropin releasing factor receptor 1 expression in adult male rats. *Behav Brain Res.* (2015) 288:39–49. doi: 10.1016/j.bbr.2015.04.007
40. Murgatroyd CA, Pena CJ, Podda G, Nestler EJ, Nephew BC. Early life social stress induced changes in depression and anxiety associated neural pathways which are correlated with impaired maternal care. *Neuropeptides* (2015) 52:103–11. doi: 10.1016/j.npep.2015.05.002
41. van Bodegom M, Homberg JR, Henckens M. Modulation of the Hypothalamic-Pituitary-Adrenal axis by early life stress exposure. *Front Cell Neurosci.* (2017) 11:87. doi: 10.3389/fncel.2017.00087
42. Wang HT, Huang FL, Hu ZL, Zhang WJ, Qiao XQ, Huang YQ, et al. Early-Life social isolation-induced depressive-like behavior in rats results in microglial activation and neuronal histone methylation that are mitigated by minocycline. *Neurotox Res.* (2017) 31:505–20. doi: 10.1007/s12640-016-9696-3
43. Iwata M, Ota KT, Duman RS. The inflammasome: pathways linking psychological stress, depression, and systemic illnesses. *Brain Behav Immun.* (2013) 31:105–14. doi: 10.1016/j.bbi.2012.12.008
44. Calcia MA, Bonsall DR, Bloomfield PS, Selvaraj S, Barichello T, Howes OD. Stress and neuroinflammation: a systematic review of the effects of stress on microglia and the implications for mental illness. *Psychopharmacology* (2016) 233:1637–50. doi: 10.1007/s00213-016-4218-9
45. McNamee EN, Griffin EW, Ryan KM, Ryan KJ, Heffernan S, Harkin A, et al. Noradrenaline acting at beta-adrenoceptors induces expression of IL-1beta and its negative regulators IL-1ra and IL-1RII, and drives an overall anti-inflammatory phenotype in rat cortex. *Neuropharmacology* (2010) 59:37–48. doi: 10.1016/j.neuropharm.2010.03.014
46. Tynan RJ, Naicker S, Hinwood M, Nalivaiko E, Buller KM, Pow DV, et al. Chronic stress alters the density and morphology of microglia in a subset of stress-responsive brain regions. *Brain Behav Immun.* (2010) 24:1058–68. doi: 10.1016/j.bbi.2010.02.001
47. Gong Y, Tong L, Yang R, Hu W, Xu X, Wang W, et al. Dynamic changes in hippocampal microglia contribute to depressive-like behavior induced by early social isolation. *Neuropharmacology* (2018) 135:223–33. doi: 10.1016/j.neuropharm.2018.03.023
48. Singhal G, Baune BT. Microglia: an Interface between the loss of neuroplasticity and depression. *Front Cell Neurosci.* (2017) 11:270. doi: 10.3389/fncel.2017.00270
49. Na J, Lee K, Na W, Shin JY, Lee MJ, Yune TY, et al. Histone H3K27 demethylase JMJD3 in cooperation with NF-kappaB regulates keratinocyte wound healing. *J Invest Dermatol.* (2016) 136:847–58. doi: 10.1016/j.jid.2015.11.029
50. Salminen A, Kaarniranta K, Hiltunen M, Kauppinen A. Histone demethylase Jumonji D3 (JMJD3/KDM6B) at the nexus of epigenetic regulation of inflammation and the aging process. *J Mol Med.* (2014) 92:1035–43. doi: 10.1007/s00109-014-1182-x

2

Inhibition of GALR1 in PFC Alleviates Depressive-Like Behaviors in Postpartum Depression Rat Model by Upregulating CREB-BNDF and 5-HT Levels

Hui Li[1], Tong Wang[2], Cuige Shi[3], Yutao Yang[2], Xiaoxiao Li[2], Yan Wu[1] and Zhi-Qing David Xu[2*]*

[1] *Department of Anatomy, Capital Medical University, Beijing, China,* [2] *Beijing Key Laboratory of Neural Regeneration and Repair, Beijing Laboratory of Brain Disorders (Ministry of Science and Technology), Department of Neurobiology, Beijing Institute of Brain Disorders, Capital Medical University, Beijing, China,* [3] *Department of Cell Biology, National Research Institute of Family Planning, Beijing, China*

***Correspondence:**
Hui Li
lihui5945@163.com
Zhi-Qing David Xu
zhiqingx@ccmu.edu.cn

Estrogen (E2) withdrawal is a core pathology mechanism for postpartum depression (PPD). Galanin (GAL), an estrogen-inducible neuropeptide has also been reported to be associated with depression. However, it still remains unclear which GAL receptors (GALRs) are involved in PPD pathologic process. In the present study, we discovered that the expression of GALR1, rather than GALR2/3, was upregulated with a region-specific pattern in the prefrontal cortex (PFC) of E2 withdrawal induced PPD model rats. Meanwhile, c-fos was also upregulated only in PFC in the same animal model. Injection of GALR1-siRNA into the bilateral PFC ameliorated depressive-like behavior of PPD rats, suggesting that the upregulation of GALR1 in PFC is involved in PPD. Moreover, Western Blot and HPLC assays demonstrated that the downregulation of CREB-BDNF signaling and 5-HT levels in the PFC of PPD rats were reversed after GALR1-siRNA injection. These comprehensive results suggest that the knock down of GALR1 in PFC alleviates depressive-like behaviors and reverse downregulation of CREB-BDNF and 5-HT levels in PPD rat model.

HIGHLIGHTS

Expression level of GALR1 mRNA was significantly increased in PFC of estrogen withdraw-induced PPD rats.
Injecting GALR1-siRNA into PFC alleviated depressive-like behavior and reversed the decrease of 5-HT level and CREB/BDNF signaling in PFC of PPD rats.

Keywords: PPD, PFC, GALR1, CREB, BDNF, 5-HT

INTRODUCTION

Postpartum depression (PPD) is a severe mental disorder that affects both mother and their babies, with an estimated prevalence of 10–15% worldwide (1). The DSM-5 defines postpartum depression as the depressive episode that begins 4 weeks after delivery (2) and may last for 12 months, clinically (3). In some serious scenarios, patients may tend to commit infanticide and are more likely to abuse their babies (4).The widely accepted hypothesis of PPD is that the withdrawal of estrogen (E2) plays a cortical role in the onset of PPD (5). Clinical studies have shown that women tend to exhibit more symptoms of depression during times of large hormonal changes. Thus, the onset of PPD is thought to arise, at least in part, from the dramatic fluctuations in the levels of the gonadal hormones during the postpartum period, and patients showed strong correlation between lower estradiol level in umbilical cord blood and depressive mood during the postpartum period (4, 6). Moreover, the E2 therapy has a greater improvement in depression scores compare with placebo among patients with severe PPD. However, interfering with breastfeeding, is a major concern for E2 therapy in PPD (6, 7) and searching for a new therapeutic target is emergency for PPD treatment. Galanin (GAL) is an estrogen-inducible neuropeptide, which is widely distributed in central and peripheral nervous system, as well as endocrine system (8). It has been demonstrated that GAL system plays an important role in depression, and drugs that target galanin receptors can modulate stress-related behaviors (9–11). GAL exerts its function via its receptors: galanin receptor 1 (GALR1), galanin receptor 2 (GALR2), and galanin receptor 3 (GALR3). It's signaling via multiple transduction pathways, including inhibition of cyclic AMP/protein kinase A (GALR1, GALR3) and stimulation of phospholipase C (GALR2) (8). Our recent study revealed that the knockdown of GALR1 in the ventral periaqueductal gray reverses depressive-like behavior of chronic mild stress (CMS) rats (12). Meanwhile, it has been reported that GAL neurons in the medial preoptic area govern the parental behavior in female rats (13). Moreover, the expression of GALR1 mRNA varies across the estrous cycle in the preoptic area and is elevated in females more than males (14). However, it still remains unclear which GAL receptors (GALRs) are involved in PPD pathologic process.

In the present study, utilizing an ovarian-steroid withdrawal-induced PPD rat model, we examined the change of GALRs expression in several brain regions associated with mental disorders, including prefrontal cortex (PFC), central amygdala (CeA), and ventral hippocampus (VH). In addition, we explored whether or not there was a causal link between change of GALR1 expression and depression-like behaviors in PPD model rats and possible signaling mechanisms involved.

METHODS

Animals and Housing

Female Sprague Dawley rats (160–180 g) were used in the present study (Capital Medical University, China). To minimize the stress, the female rats were acclimatized for 1 week before ovariectomy. The rats were group housed in a room with controlled temperature (22–24°C) and light (12-h light/dark cycle). All rats had free access to food and water. The study was approved by the Animal Care Committee at Capital Medical University. It was the minimal animal number for meeting statistical analysis requirements.

Ovariectomy

All surgeries were performed using an aseptic tip technique. Rats were anesthetized with 6% chloral hydrate (6 ml/kg) administrated i.p., and fixed at the prone position. A 1.5 cm longitudinal dorsal incision was made using an aseptic technique (15). The incision was then pulled laterally to open the muscular layer and peritoneum. The ovaries and fallopian tubes were identified and the ovaries were removed. The skin was sutured and penicillin was administered to prevent infection. The control rats were sham-operated. The rats were housed separately following surgery and allowed 1-week recovery to eliminate estrogen and progesterone.

Procedure

Hormones Administration

The rats were divided into five groups: control group ($n = 8$), PPD group ($n = 8$), PPD + siRNA group ($n = 8$), PPD+ scramble group ($n = 8$), and PPD_E group ($n = 8$). Rats in PPD group, PPD + siRNA group, PPD+ scramble group, and PPD_E group were ovariectomized bilaterally. Rats were administrated vehicle or hormones subcutaneously at 9:00 am for 23 days from 1 week after ovariectomy. The control group was injected with 0.3 ml polyethylene for 23 days. The PPD group, PPD + siRNA group, PPD + scramble group, and PPD_E group were injected with 2.5 μg estradiol dissolved in 0.2 ml polyethylene and 4 mg progesterone (0.1 ml) for the first 16 days and 50 μg estradiol dissolved in 0.3 ml polyethylene from day17 to day23. From day 24 till to the behavioral tests were completed, rats in PPD_E group continued receiving a high dose of estradiol (50 mg), while the PPD group, PPD + siRNA group, and PPD+ scramble group were injected with 0.3 ml polyethylene during the same time. The first 23 days were considered the "pregnant" period, after which were considered the "postpartum" period (16) (**Figure 1**).

siRNA Interference

The green fluorescent protein (GFP) reporting lentivirus encoding the siRNA to Galr1 and scramble (12) were injected into the bilateral PFC of rats in PPD + siRNA group or PPD + scramble group, respectively. The surgery was carried out 4 weeks before the behavioral tests. Rats were anesthetized with 6% chloral hydrate and placed on a stereotaxic apparatus (Benchmark). A hole was drilled on the skull based on the coordinate: AP+3.2 mm; ML±/−0.6 mm; DV −4.0 mm (below surface of the skull) from Bregma, according to the atlas of Paxinos and Watson (17). Three micro liters of siRNA or scramble was injected with a 10 μl microsyringe (Hamilton) for 15 min. The needle remained in place for another 15 min. The injection site was verified from 30 μm coronal sections under a fluorescence microscope. Rats were allowed one-week recovery.

Behavior Tests

Forced Swimming Test

Forced swimming test (FST) was conducted 3 days after the termination of estrogen administration in PPD group. Rats in PPD_E group were tested 2 h after the injection. The FST was carried out on rats as described in our earlier study (18), with slight modifications. Briefly, rats were individually placed in a transparent glass cylinder (64 cm height and 22 cm diameter) filled with tap water with depth of 30 cm at 25 ± 2°C. Each test session lasted for 5 min and was recorded by a camera connected to ANY- maze video tracking software (Stoelting Co.,

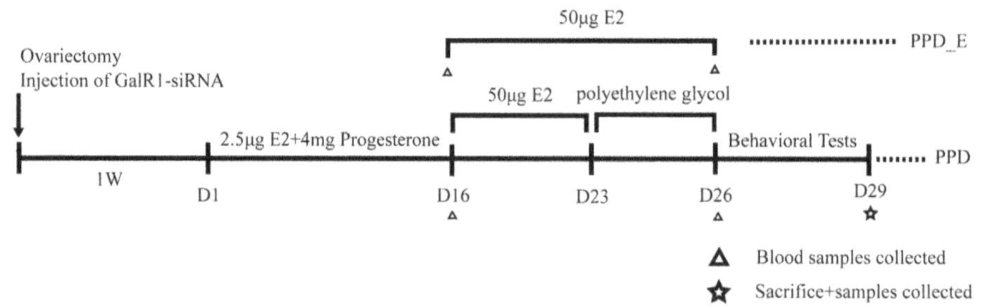

FIGURE 1 | Time schedule for the experiment. Behavioral tests included forced swimming test and sucrose preference test.

IL, USA) which automatically calculated the climbing time and immobile time. The water was changed and containers were cleaned thoroughly between rats in order to minimize any effects of other subjects. Rats were dried and returned to their cages after the test.

Sucrose Preference Test

The sucrose preference test was carried out on rats as described in our earlier study (12), All rats were trained to consume 1% sucrose solution 1 week before the test to habituate to the new solution. Animals were water-deprived 24 h before the test. The test was conducted at 11:00 a.m. 2 h following the estrogen injection in PPD_E group. Rats were placed in separated cages with no access to food. Two pre-weighed bottles were placed on each cage, one filled with tap water, the other one filled with 1% sucrose solution. The placement of two bottles (left/right) was counterbalanced and interchanged 30 min after the test started. After 1 h, bottles were re-weighted to determine the volume of the sucrose solution consumed and the sucrose preference presented by the percentage of the sucrose solution consumed.

Radioimmunoassay for Estradiol

Before the surgery and sacrifice, the rats were anesthetized with 6% chloral hydrate (6 ml/kg) administrated i.p., (at 9:00–10:00 a.m). Blood samples were collected from the retroorbital sinus using a heparan capillary tube then put into the anticoagulation tube. 20 min later, the blood was collected in Eppendorf tubes. The samples were centrifuged at 3,000 rpm (rounds per min) for 10 min. Plasma concentration of estradiol was determined by radioimmunoassay kit (Laerwen Co., LTD., Shenzhen, China) following the standard procedures.

Microdissection of PFC, CeA, and VH Sample Preparation

At the end of the behavioral tests, animals were sacrificed under anesthesia. Brains were rapidly separated from the skull and sliced using a 1-mm brain matrix. PFC, CeA, and VH were dissected on ice using stereotaxic coordinates. Each brain tissue was put into an Eppendorf tube and then rapidly shock-frozen on dry ice and stored at −80°C for later RNA extraction. The positions of the cannula were verified by crystal violet staining and only the rats with an exact localization were included in the statistical analysis.

Quantitative Real-Time PCR (Q-PCR)

Total RNA of brain tissues or PFC neurons was extracted using RNeasy Lipid Tissue Mini Kit (Qiagen, Germany) or RNeasy Micro Kit (Qiagen, Germany) following the manufacturer's instructions, respectively. Total RNA was dissolved in 30 μl RNase-free water provided in the kit. RNA concentrations were assessed using NanoDrop (Thermo Scientific, DE, USA) with 260 /280 nm ratios between 1.9 and 2.1. Transcriptor First Strand cDNA Synthesis Kit (Roche, IN, USA) was used to reverse-transcribe RNA (1 μg) into cDNA according to the manufacturer's instruction.

Quantitative PCR (Q-PCR) was performed following the reverse transcription. The total volume of Q-PCR reactions was 20 μl containing 8 μl distilled water, 10 μl SYBR Green Mix (Applied Biosystems, UK), 1 μl cDNA, and 1 μl primers (forward + reverse). The sequences of the primers used in this study were as followed: GAPDH-specific primers were forward: GACCACCCAGCCCAGCAAGG, reverse: TCCCCAGGCCCCTCCTGTTG. GALR1-specific primers were forward: TCGGGACAGCAACCAAAC, reverse: TGCAGATGATTGAGAACCTTGG. GALR2-specific primers were forward: GCCGCCATCGGGCTCATCTG, reverse: GTCGAGGTGCGCTCCATGCT. Amplification reaction protocol included 2 min at 60°C, 10 min at 95°C, followed by 40 cycles reaction as: 15 s of denaturing at 95°C and 1 min of annealing at 60°C. Samples were held at 10°C at the end of each amplification reaction. GAPDH was used as the internal reference for each sample.

Western Blot

Total proteins were extracted using Buffer C lysis buffer. The protein concentrations were measured by bicinchoninic acid (BCA) assay. Forty micrograms of proteins were concentrated at 80 mV and separated at 100 mV using 10% sodium dodecyl sulfate-polyacrylamide gel (SDS-PAGE). Proteins were then transferred to a polyvinylidene difluoride (PVDF) membrane (Millipore, MA, USA) for 2 h at 300 mA following the electrophoresis. Membranes were blocked with 10% milk at room temperature for 1 h and incubated with the following primary antibodies: c-fos (sc-413, mouse monoclonal, Santa Cruz CA), BDNF (ab226843, rabbit polyclonal antibody; abcome echnology), CREB and phospho-CREB (sc-377154, sc-81486, mouse monoclonal, Santa Cruz, CA) at 4°C overnight.

Membranes were washed 3 times (10 min × 3) with Tris-buffered saline-Tween (TBST) and incubated with horseradish peroxidase (HRP)-conjugated secondary antibody (1:5,000, Applygen, Beijing, China) for 1 h at room temperature followed by washing 3 times (10 min × 3) with Tris-buffered saline-Tween (TBST). Proteins were developed using an enhanced chemiluminescence (ECL) reagent kit (Applygen, Beijing, China) and radiographic films (Carestream, Xiamen, China). α-tubulin (ABT170, rabbit polyclonal, 1:10,000, Millipore, Temecula, USA) was used as the internal reference.

Determination of 5-HT and 5-HIAA Levels

The levels of 5-HT and its metabolite 5-HIAA in PFC and VH was measured using high-performance liquid chromatography with anelectrochemical detector (HPLC-ECD). Model 5600A CoulArray Detector System and CoulArray for Wingdows® 32 application software (ESA, USA) was used for detection and data analysis. PFC and VH tissues were dissected and stored at −80°C. Pre-weighted tissues were placed into Eppendorf tubes and homogenized in 200 μl of fluid A (0.4 M perchloric acid) for 10 s on ice. Samples were centrifuged at 12,000 rpm for 20 min at 4°C after placing on ice for 1 h, away from light. 80 μl of fluid B (mobile phase) was added into 160 μl of supernatant and vortex mixed. Samples were centrifuged at 12,000 rpm for 20 min at 4°C after placing on ice for 1 h, 200 μl of supernatant was extracted and kept at −80°C away from light. 200 μ of each sample was used for analysis. The flow rate was 1.0ml/min. The voltages of the four CoulArray channels were −150, 100, 220, and 400 mV, respectively.

Data Analyses

Data were presented as mean ± SEM (standard error of measurements).Statistical analysis was carried out using SPSS16.0. Animals with incorrect injection positions were excluded from statistical analysis. Data were analyzed with one-way ANOVA and the follow-up *post hoc* Tukey HSD multiple comparison tests were selected to compare mean values in each group. $P < 0.05$ was considered to be statistically significant.

RESULTS

E_2 Withdrawal- Induced Depressive-Like Behaviors in PPD Rats

E_2 levels were assessed after the 16-day 2.5 μg E_2+4 mg progesterone treatment and after the 7-day 50 μg E_2 treatment, respectively (**Figure 1**). There was no significant difference in plasma E_2 level among three groups on the 16th day ($p > 0.05$) (**Figure 2A**), while the E_2 level was significantly elevated in PPD_E group after 23-day injection ($p < 0.05$) (**Figure 2B**).

Behavioral tests were conducted 1 week after the termination of estrogen administration in PPD group, while rats in PPD_E group kept receiving a high dose of estrogen. In forced swimming test, the climbing time was decreased in PPD group compared with the other two groups ($p < 0.01$, $p < 0.05$) (**Figure 2C**). However, rats in PPD group showed significantly increased immobility time ($p < 0.05$, $p < 0.01$). Sucrose consumption test showed that the PPD rats consumed less sucrose than the Ctrl rats, indicating that PPD rats performed anhedonia symptom. Meanwhile, the estrogen treatment reversed sucrose consumption to normal level in PPD_E group ($p < 0.01$, $p < 0.05$) (**Figure 2E**). There was no significant difference between Ctrl group and PPD_E group in forced swimming test and sucrose consumption test (**Figure 2D**), which is consistent with previous reports (16, 19). Maybe the dose used is not sufficient enough to influence the behavior results, though it is already higher than Ctrl.

E_2 Withdrawal Elevated GALR1 Expression in PFC in PPD Group

The protein level of c-fos in PFC was significantly increased in PPD rats compared with Ctrl and PPD_E group ($p < 0.05$) (**Figure 3A**), but not in the VH and CeA (data not shown). The expression of GALR1 and GALR2 was analyzed in PFC, CeA, and VH brain regions. The mRNA level of GALR1 in PFC was significantly increased in PPD group compared with Ctrl and PPD_E group ($p < 0.05$) (**Figure 3B**), while in VH or CeA, the difference among the groups was not significant (**Figures 3C,D**) ($p > 0.05$). There was no difference in the expression of GALR2 in any brain regions tested ($p > 0.05$) (**Figures 3B–D**). It needs to be mentioned that the expression of GALR3 in rat brain is low abundance exclude hypothalamus and pituitary (20), and our data show the CT value of GALR3 in the PFC is near 37 (data not shown). Therefore, GALR3 was not analysis here.

Injection of GALR1-siRNA Into PFC Reversed Depressive-Like Behaviors in PPD Rats

GALR1-siRNA was injected into the bilateral PFC of ovariectomized rats, following estradiol withdrawal procedure (**Figure 1**). The coordinates for the PFC were AP +3.2, ML ±/−0.6, H −4.0 mm from Bregma (17) and the injection sites were confirmed by GFP fluorescence (**Figure 4A**). The efficiency of GALR1 interference was verified by Q-PCR. The expression of GALR1 was significantly decreased in PPD + siRNA group compared with PPD and PPD + scramble groups in the PFC ($p < 0.05$), while no significant difference between PPD and PPD + scramble group was observed ($p > 0.05$) (**Figure 4B**).

Behavioral tests were carried out 4 weeks after GALR1-siRNA injection. In forced swimming test, PPD. and PPD + scramble rats showed less climbing time ($p < 0.05$) and more immobility time than Ctrl rats ($p < 0.01$) (**Figures 4C,D**), while no significant difference was seen between PPD + siRNA and Ctrl rats ($p > 0.05$) (**Figures 4C,D**). In sucrose preference test, PPD and PPD + scramble rats consumed less sucrose than Ctrl rats ($p < 0.05$) while GALR1-siRNA injection reversed sucrose consumption to normal level compared with Ctrl group ($P > 0.05$) (**Figure 4E**).

CREB-BDNF Signaling Involved in the Antidepressant Effect of GALR1-siRNA in the PFC of PPD Rats

CREB and phospho-CREB protein levels were assessed with WB. The expression of CREB was significantly decreased in PPD and PPD + scramble group, while GALR1-siRNA injection

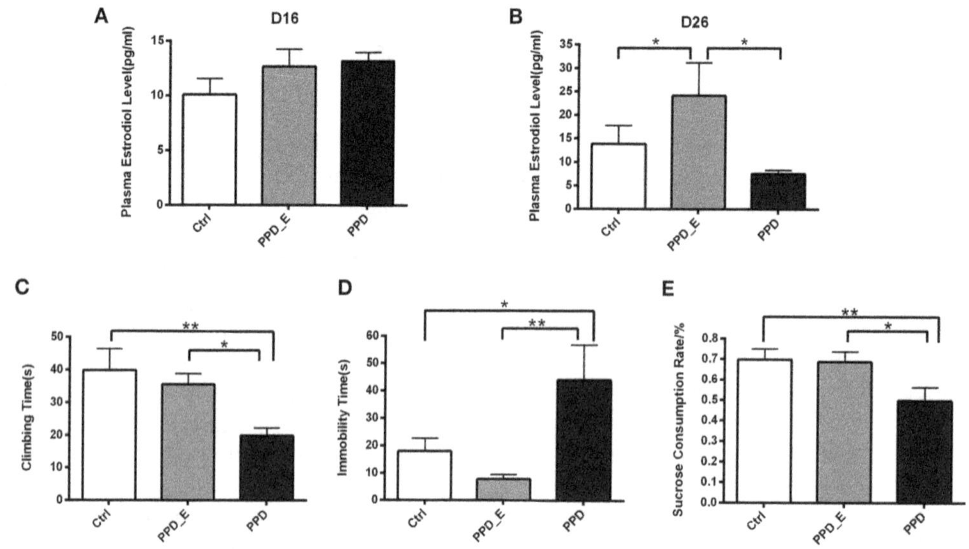

FIGURE 2 | Estradiol withdrawal-induced depressive-like behaviors in PPD rats. **(A)** After the 16-day 2.5 μg E2+4 mg progesterone treatment schedule, all groups had no significant difference in plasma estradiol levels. **(B)** After the 7-day 50 μg E2 treatment schedule, PPD_E group showed a significant increase of plasma estradiol levels. **(C)** PPD group showed reduced climbing time than Ctrl and PPD_E group in forced swimming test. **(D)** PPD group showed increased immobility time than Ctrl and PPD_E group in forced swimming test. **(E)** PPD group showed a significant decrease of sucrose consumption than Ctrl and PPD_E group in sucrose preference test. Data were represented as mean ± SEM ($n = 6$–8 in each group)$^*p < 0.05$ compared to PPD_E group **(A, B)**; $^*p < 0.05$, $^{**}p < 0.01$ compared to PPD group **(C–E)**. Data were analyzed by one-way ANOVA followed by *post-hoc* Tukey HSD multiple comparison tests.

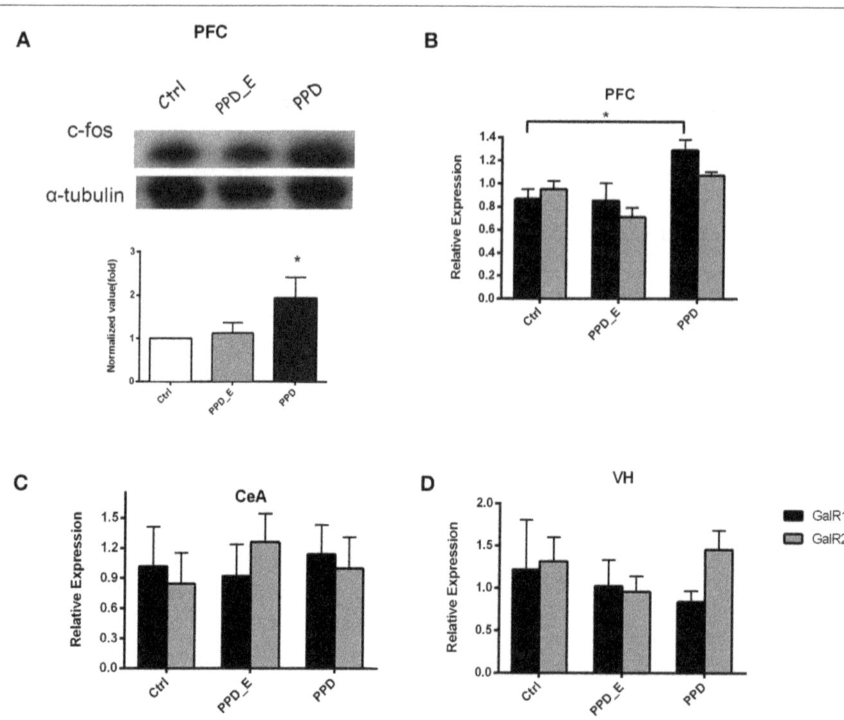

FIGURE 3 | The expression of c-fos and GALR1 was significantly increased in the PFC in PPD group. **(A)** In PFC, c-fos protein level was significantly increased in PPD group compared to Ctrl and PPD_E groups. **(B)** PPD group showed an increase of GALR1 mRNA level compared to Ctrl and PPD_E group in PFC, while there was no difference in GALR2 expression between groups. **(C)** There was no difference in GALR1 or GALR2 expression between groups in CEA. **(D)** There was no difference in GALR1 or GALR2 expression between groups in VH. Data were represented as mean ± SEM ($n = 6$–8 in each group). $^*p < 0.05$ compared to Ctrl group. Data were analyzed by one-way ANOVA followed by *post-hoc* Tukey HSD multiple comparison tests.

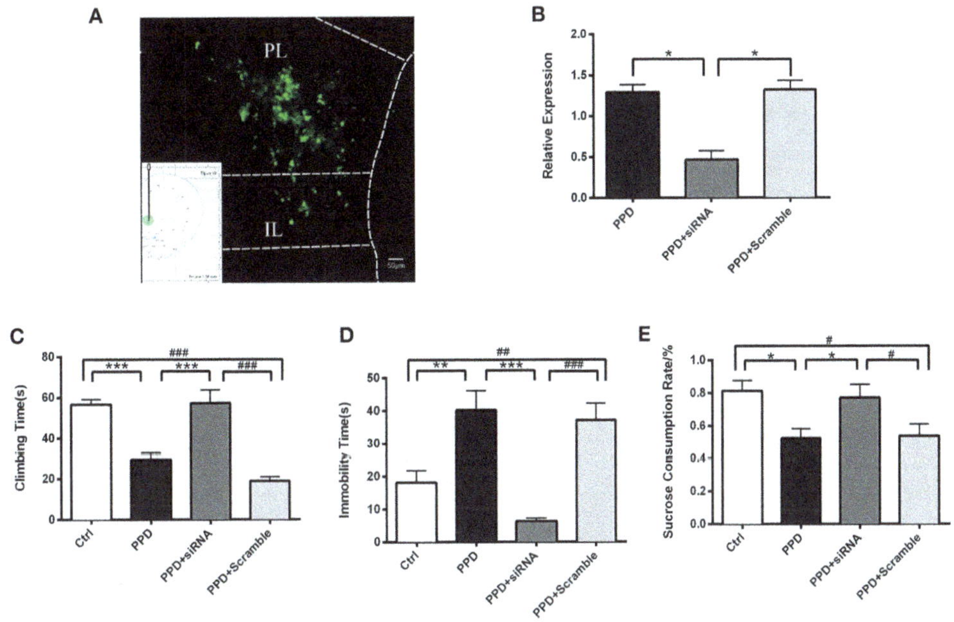

FIGURE 4 | Injection of GALR1-siRNA into PFC reversed depressive-like behaviors. **(A)** A low magnification (10 ×) representative image of coronal brain sections showing the injection sites. The success of AAV vector injection into the PFC was confirmed by GFP fluorescence. **(B)** GALR1 mRNA level significantly decreased in the PFC after GALR1-siRNA treatment compared to PPD group and PPD + Scramble group. **(C)** Climbing time elevated to normal level after GALR1-siRNA treatment. **(D)** Immobility time significantly decreased in PPD + siRNA group compared to PPD groups. **(E)** Decreased sucrose consumption was reversed after GALR1-siRNA treatment. Data were represented as mean ± SEM (n = 6–8 in each group). *$p < 0.05$, **$p < 0.01$, ***$p < 0.001$ compared to PPD group; #$p < 0.05$, ##$p < 0.01$, ###$p < 0.001$ compared to PPD + Scramble group **(A–C)**. ***$p < 0.001$ compared to Ctrl group. Data were analyzed by one-way ANOVA followed by *post-hoc* Tukey HSD multiple comparison tests. Scale bar = 50 0m.

increased CREB expression to normal level compared to PPD group ($p < 0.001$), PPD + Scramble group, ($p < 0.05$), and Ctrl group ($p > 0.05$); The expression of P-CREB was significantly decreased in PPD and PPD + scramble group, while GALR1-siRNA injection increased phospho-CREB expression to normal level compared to PPD group ($p < 0.001$), PPD + Scramble group ($p < 0.01$) and Ctrl group ($p > 0.05$),(**Figure 5A**). The expression of BDNF was significantly decreased in PPD and PPD + scramble, while GALR1-siRNA injection reveres E2 withdrawal induced decreased BDNF levels compared to PPD group ($p < 0.01$), PPD + Scramble groups ($p < 0.01$), and Ctrl group ($p > 0.05$) (**Figure 5B**). All those data suggest that 4. CREB-BDNF signaling involved in the antidepressant effect of GALR1-siRNA in the PFC of PPD rats.

Injection of GALR1-siRNA Into PFC Reversed the Decreased Levels of 5-HT and 5-HIAA in the PFC

HPLC was carried out to test the 5-HT and its metabolite 5-HIAA levels in PFC and VH. The levels of 5-HT and 5-HIAA in PFC were decreased in PPD and PPD +Scramble rats compared to Ctrl rats (**Figures 6A,B**). However, they were significantly increased in PPD+ siRNA rats compared to PPD and PPD +Scramble rats ($p < 0.05$). there is no significant difference between PPD+ siRNA and Ctrl group ($p > 0.05$) (**Figures 6A,B**). There was no significant difference of the 5-HT and 5-HIAA levels in the VH between all groups (**Figures 6C,D**).These results suggested that GALR1 interference may exert anti-depressant effect associated with up-regulation of 5-HT and 5-HIAA levels in the PFC.

DISCUSSION

In the present study, E2 withdrawal paradigm induced depressive-like behavior and upregulation of GALR1 and c-fos expression with a region specific pattern in the PFC of PPD rats. Treatment of GALR1-siRNA in PCF reversed depression-like behavior accompanied with the reversion of down-regulated CREB-BDNF and 5-HT levels.

The pathophysiology of PPD is considered to be triggered by the rapid decline in reproductive hormones following pregnancy. Besides post-partum period, lower E2 levels also associated with depression symptoms, it has been shown that CUMS-OVX rats demonstrated longer immobility time in FST test and lower sucrose preference than CUMS-intact female rats (21). However, so far most studies of depression model focus in male rats, the data about estrogen is very limited.

Consistent with other studies (16, 19), our data demonstrated that E2 withdrawal paradigm-induced depression-like behavior including decreased sugar preference, which implied this paradigm was sufficient to produce "anhedonia" in rats, suggesting that the establishment of E2 withdrawal rat model

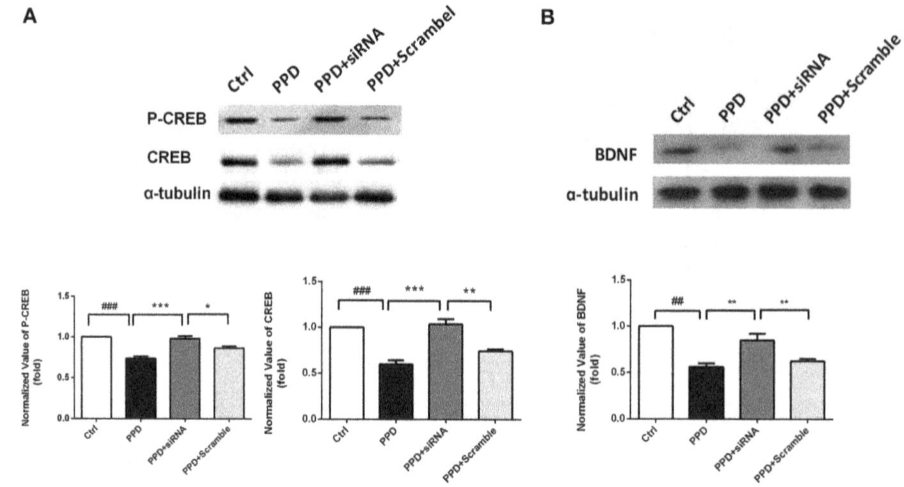

FIGURE 5 | siRNA-GALR1 interference reversed the decreased protein levels of CREB, P-CREB and BDNF in the PFC. All data are expressed relative to Ctrl group.**(A)** CREB and P-CREB protein levels were significantly decreased in PPD groups, while GALR1-siRNA treatment up-regulated CREB and P-CREB levels to normal.**(B)** BDNF protein levels were significantly decreased in PPD groups, while GALR1-siRNA treatment upregulated BDNF protein levels. Values are expressed as mean ± SEM. ($n = 3$ in each group)* $p < 0.05$, ** $p < 0.01$, *** $p < 0.001$ compared to PPD + siRNA group. ## $p < 0.01$, ### $p < 0.001$ compared to Ctrl group.

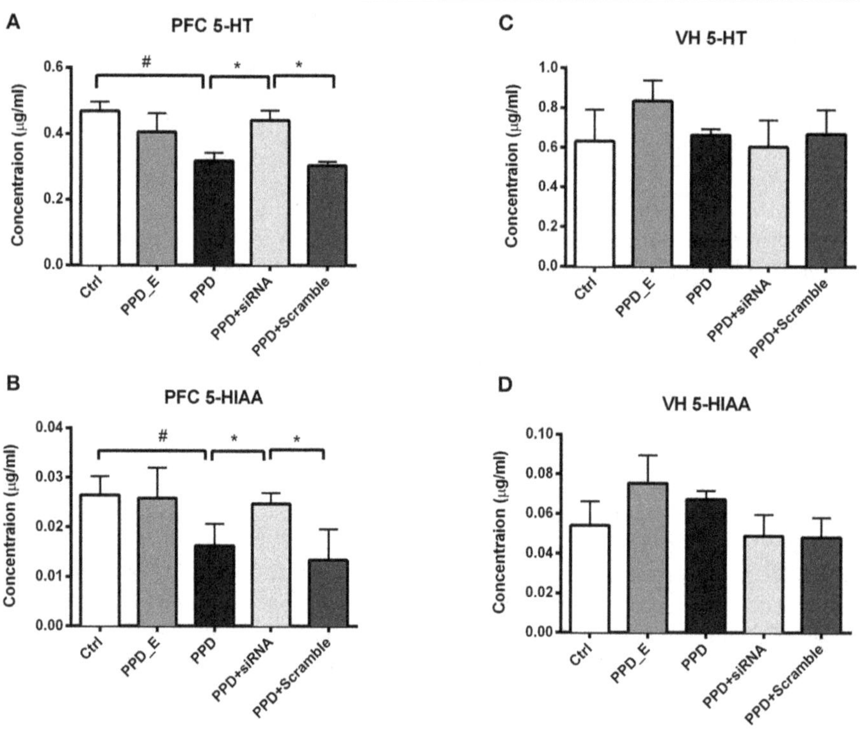

FIGURE 6 | siRNA-GALR1 interference reversed down-regulation of 5-HT and 5-HIAA levels i in the PFC. **(A)** PPD + siRNA group showed significantly increased 5-HT levels in the PFC compared to Ctrl and PPD + Scramble group. **(B)** PPD + siRNA group showed significantly increased 5-HIAAlevels in the PFC compared to Ctrl and PPD + Scramble group. **(C)** There was no difference in 5-HT levels in VH between groups. **(D)** There was no difference in 5-HIAAlevels in VH between groups. Data were represented as mean ± SEM ($n = 6$–8 in each group). * $p < 0.05$ compared to PPD + siRNA group. # $p < 0.05$ compared to Ctrl group. Data were analyzed by one-way ANOVA followed by *post-hoc* Tukey HSD multiple comparison tests. VH: ventral hippocampus.

is an effective approach to investigate the mechanism of PPD. Moreover, the depressed symptoms in rodents is prevented by prolonging exposure to high levels of E2 through the "post-partum period," suggesting that E2 plays antidepressant roles at least partially in this paradigm and further confirmed that the PPD is associated with E2 withdrawal (16). It has been shown that E2 complementary treatment plays antidepressant roles in OVX mice. However, it interferes with breastfeeding, which is a major concern in the treatment of PPD (22–24). Therefore, searching for a new therapeutic target is emergency for PPD treatment.

The monoamine-deficiency is one of the hypothesis of major depression (25). Menopausal depressive rats also showed decreased 5-HT levels in cerebral spinal fluid (26). Various studies showed that neuropeptide GAL has direct and indirect inhibitory effect on both NA and 5-HT neurons (27). It has been demonstrated that GAL system is associated with major depression in a postmortem brain study (9). Our recent study has also shown that the increased expression of GalR1 in the ventral periaqueductal gray of chronic mild stress rats is related to depression-like behavior (12). In the present study, we found that in PPD rats, GALR1 was significantly and selectively upregulated in PFC, but not in other brain regions. Meanwhile, c-fos, which is widely used as a marker for the activation of neurons in the brain (28), was also up-regulated only in the PFC in PPD rats. PFC is one of the regions involved in cortico-limbic circuits and is important in the development and treatment of depression (29). A recent proton magnetic resonance spectroscopy study showed glutamatergic dysfunction and neuronal damage occurred in dorsolateral prefrontal cortex in PPD patients (30). It has been shown that GALR1 is high expression in the mPFC (31), Taken together, all those data suggest that upregulation of GALR1 in PFC may be involved in PPD. To further demonstrate the causal link between change of GALR1 expression and depression-like behaviors in the PPD rats model, knocking down GALR1 in the bilateral-PFC with a siRNA technique was carried out and depressive-like behavior was ameliorated in PPD rats after GALR1-siRNA treatment. More interestingly, we found that higher expression of GALR1 was accompanied with lower expression of cAMP response element binding protein (CREB) and BDNF in the PFC of PPD rats. GALR1-siRNA injection reversed the decreased levels of p-CREB, CREB, and BDNF. It has been known that acitivation of GALR1, a Gi protein-coupled receptor, inhibits cyclic adenosine monophosphate synthesis and its downstream molecule CREB (31–33). Meanwhile, chronic administration of antidepressants increases the expression, phosphorylation, and function of CREB, and its downstream target gene BDNF in the limbic brain regions related to depression (29, 34, 35). All those implied that GALR1-siRNA-induced reversion of CREB-BDNF signaling might be involved in the antidepressant role of GALR1-siRNA.

Our HPLC results showed that the 5-HT and 5-HTAA levels were decreased in PFC of PPD rats. Moreover, this downregulation of 5-HT and 5-HTAA was ameliorated after GALR1-siRNA injection in the PFC. Decreased 5-HT level in the PFC associated with depression (36, 37). The concentration of 5-HT in PFC is depended on release and reuptake of 5-HT. Though it is well-known that GALR1 mRNA expresses in DR neurons (6) and very likely GALR1 protein also expresses in the terminal of DR neurons. Therefore, GALR1 might be involved in modulating release or/and reuptake of 5-HT. But local injection of GALR1-siRNA in PFC is not able to knockdown GALR1 expressed in the terminal of DR neurons as receptor protein is synthesized in the cell body. On the other hand, PFC neurons project to dorsal raphe and modulate serotonergic neurons activity as well as 5-HT releasing in target regions including PFC (38). GALR1 is highly expressed in PFC, and GALR1 mRNA level was significant increase in PFC of major depression patients (9). Thus, if the PFC-DR neurons expressing GALR1, blocking GALR1 might cause de-inhibition of PFC-DR neurons and in turn, enhance 5-HT release in PFC. However, because of lacking selective antibody against GALR1, it is still unknown whether PFC-DR neurons expressing GALR1. Meanwhile, it has been reported that astrocytes in PFC expresses 5-HT and transpoters and might be also involved in modulation of 5-HT concentration in PFC (39). It is also been reported that GALR1 expresses in astrocytes in the brain (40). Thus, local injection of GALR1-siRNA might knockdown astrocytes-expressing GALR1 and enhance release or inhibit reuptake of 5-HT. But the expression of GALR1 on astrocytes is also needed to be determined with selective antibody. In the present study, lower level of 5-HT in PPD model rats and ameliorated depression-like behavior together with reversed 5-HT level after GALR1-siRNA treatment suggesting that antidepressant effect of GALR1-siRNA might be mediated by reversing downregulation of 5-HT in PFC. Thus, GAL regulates 5-HT levels by modulating not only activity of 5-HT neurons (via GALR1/R3) in DR, the main source of 5-HT ascending system (41, 42), but also releasing or/and reuptaking of 5-HT (via GALR1) in PFC, the projection region of 5-HT ascending system.

It has been demonstrated that interaction between BDNF and 5-HT is involved in depression by influencing neuronal plasticity and depression susceptibility(43–45). Our data showed that GALR1-siRNA reversed PPD-induced downregulation of BDNF and 5-HT in PFC, suggesting that the interaction of BDNF and 5 HT might be involved in antidepressant effect of GALR1-siRNA. However, it is needed to be determined in future study.

Meanwhile, the etiology of PPD is a complex interaction of psychological, social and biological factors. It has been reported that, in addition to estrogen system, hypothalamic-pituitary-adrenal (HPA) axis disorder, gestation stress are involved in PPD (18, 46). In future study, we will continue study the effects of GAL signaling in other pathways of PPD.

CONCLUSION

The present results, based on the rat PPD depression model, provide evidence for involvement of GALR1 in the PFC in depression-like behavior. Thus, a GALR1 antagonist acting in the PFC may have antidepressant actions in PPD.

AUTHOR CONTRIBUTIONS

HL and Z-QX designed experiments. TW and CS carried out behavior and qPCR test. YY carried out WB test. XL carried out HPLC test. YW analyzed experimental results. HL and Z-QX wrote the manuscript.

ACKNOWLEDGMENTS

This research was supported by grants from the National Natural Science Foundation of China (81401119, 81671345, 31271154), the Beijing Natural Science Foundation (KM/KZ201610025026, 7172018, 7162016), the Beijing Brain Project (Grant Z1611000002 16142).

REFERENCES

1. Halbreich U. Postpartum disorders: multiple interacting underlying mechanisms and risk factors. *J Affect Disord.* (2005) 88:1–7. doi: 10.1016/j.jad.2005.05.002
2. Association AP. *Diagnostic and Statistical Manual of Mental Disorders.* 5th ed. Arlington, VA: American Psychiatric Publishing (2013).
3. Grigoriadis S, VonderPorten EH, Mamisashvili L, Tomlinson G, Dennis CL, Koren G, et al. The impact of maternal depression during pregnancy on perinatal outcomes: a systematic review and meta-analysis. *J Clin Psychiatry* (2013) 74:e321–41. doi: 10.4088/JCP.12r07968
4. Brummelte S, Galea LA. Depression during pregnancy and postpartum: contribution of stress and ovarian hormones. *Prog Neuropsychopharmacol Biol Psychiatry* (2010) 34:766–76. doi: 10.1016/j.pnpbp.2009.09.006
5. Hendrick V, Altshuler LL, Suri R. Hormonal changes in the postpartum and implications for postpartum depression. *Psychosomatics* (1998) 39:93–101. doi: 10.1016/S0033-3182(98)71355-6
6. DelRosario GA, Chang AC, Lee ED. Postpartum depression: symptoms, diagnosis, and treatment approaches. *Jaapa* (2013) 26:50–4. doi: 10.1097/01720610-201302000-00009
7. Stewart DE, Vigod S. Postpartum depression. *N Engl J Med.* (2016) 375:2177–86. doi: 10.1056/NEJMcp1607649
8. Lang R, Gundlach AL, Holmes FE, Hobson SA, Wynick D, Hökfelt T, et al. Physiology, signaling, and pharmacology of galanin peptides and receptors: three decades of emerging diversity. *Pharmacol Rev.* (2015) 67:118–75. doi: 10.1124/pr.112.006536
9. Barde S, Rüegg J, Prud'homme J, Ekström TJ, Palkovits M, Turecki G, et al. Alterations in the neuropeptide galanin system in major depressive disorder involve levels of transcripts, methylation, and peptide. *Proc Natl Acad Sci USA.* (2016) 113:E8472–81. doi: 10.1073/pnas.1617824113
10. Kormos V, Gaszner B. Role of neuropeptides in anxiety, stress, and depression: from animals to humans. *Neuropeptides* (2013) 47:401–19. doi: 10.1016/j.npep.2013.10.014
11. Picciotto MR, Brabant C, Einstein EB, Kamens HM, Neugebauer NM. Effects of galanin on monoaminergic systems and HPA axis: potential mechanisms underlying the effects of galanin on addiction- and stress-related behaviors. *Brain Res.* (2010) 1314:206–18. doi: 10.1016/j.brainres.2009.08.033
12. Wang P, Li H, Barde S, Zhang MD, Sun J, Wang T, et al. Depression-like behavior in rat: involvement of galanin receptor subtype 1 in the ventral periaqueductal gray. *Proc Natl Acad Sci USA.* (2016) 113:E4726–35. doi: 10.1073/pnas.1609198113
13. Wu Z, Autry AE, Bergan JF, Watabe-Uchida M, Dulac CG. Galanin neurons in the medial preoptic area govern parental behaviour. *Nature* (2014) 509:325–30. doi: 10.1038/nature13307
14. Faure-Virelizier C, Croix D, Bouret S, Prévot V, Reig S, Beauvillain JC, et al., Effects of estrous cyclicity on the expression of the galanin receptor Gal-R1 in the rat preoptic area: a comparison with the male. *Endocrinology* (1998) 139:4127–39.
15. Kim EU, Spear LP. Sex-dependent consequences of pre-pubertal gonadectomy: Social behavior, stress and ethanol responsivity. *Behav Brain Res.* (2016) 296:260–9. doi: 10.1016/j.bbr.2015.09.022
16. Galea LA, Wide JK, Barr AM. Estradiol alleviates depressive-like symptoms in a novel animal model of post-partum depression. *Behav Brain Res.* (2001) 122:1–9. doi: 10.1016/S0166-4328(01)00170-X
17. Paxinos G, Watson C. *The Rat Brain in Stereotactic Coordinates.* San Diego, CA: Academic Press (1998).
18. Wang T, Shi C, Li X, Zhang P, Liu B, Wang H, et al. Injection of oxytocin into paraventricular nucleus reverses depressive-like behaviors in the postpartum depression rat model. *Behav Brain Res.* (2018) 336:236–43. doi: 10.1016/j.bbr.2017.09.012
19. Stoffel EC, Craft RM. Ovarian hormone withdrawal-induced "depression" in female rats. *Physiol Behav.* (2004) 83:505–13. doi: 10.1016/j.physbeh.2004.08.033
20. Smith KE, Walker MW, Artymyshyn R, Bard J, Borowsky B, Tamm JA, et al. Cloned human and rat galanin GALR3 receptors. pharmacology and activation of G-protein inwardly rectifying K+ channels. *J Biol Chem.* (1998) 273:23321–6. doi: 10.1074/jbc.273.36.23321
21. Mahmoud R, Wainwright SR, Chaiton JA, Lieblich SE, Galea LAM. Ovarian hormones, but not fluoxetine, impart resilience within a chronic unpredictable stress model in middle-aged female rats. *Neuropharmacology* (2016) 107:278–93. doi: 10.1016/j.neuropharm.2016.01.033
22. Heydarpour P, Salehi-Sadaghiani M, Javadi-Paydar M, Rahimian R, Fakhfouri G, Khosravi M, et al. Estradiol reduces depressive-like behavior through inhibiting nitric oxide/cyclic GMP pathway in ovariectomized mice. *Horm Behav.* (2013) 63:361–9. doi: 10.1016/j.yhbeh.2012.12.005
23. Kandi P, Hayslett RL. Nicotine and 17beta-estradiol produce an antidepressant-like effect in female ovariectomized rats. *Brain Res Bull.* (2011) 84:224–8. doi: 10.1016/j.brainresbull.2010.12.012
24. Fitelson E, Kim S, Baker AS, Leight K. Treatment of postpartum depression: clinical, psychological and pharmacological options. *Int J Womens Health* (2010) 3:1–14. doi: 10.2147/IJWH.S6938
25. Belmaker RH, Agam G. Major depressive disorder. *N Engl J Med.* (2008) 358:55–68. doi: 10.1056/NEJMra073096
26. Gu S, Jing L, Li Y, Huang JH, Wang F. Stress induced hormone and neuromodulator changes in menopausal depressive rats. *Front Psychiatry* (2018) 9:253. doi: 10.3389/fpsyt.2018.00253
27. Xu ZQ, Zheng K, Hokfelt T. Electrophysiological studies on galanin effects in brain–progress during the last six years. *Neuropeptides* (2005) 39:269–75. doi: 10.1016/j.npep.2005.02.003
28. Kovacs KJ. Measurement of immediate-early gene activation-c-fos and beyond. *J Neuroendocrinol* (2008) 20:665–72. doi: 10.1111/j.1365-2826.2008.01734.x
29. Koenigs, M. Grafman J. The functional neuroanatomy of depression: distinct roles for ventromedial and dorsolateral prefrontal cortex. *Behav Brain Res.* (2009) 201:239–43. doi: 10.1016/j.bbr.2009.03.004
30. Rosa CE, Soares JC, Figueiredo FP, Cavalli RC, Barbieri MA, Schaufelberger MS, et al. Glutamatergic and neural dysfunction in postpartum depression using magnetic resonance spectroscopy. *Psychiatry Res Neuroimag.* (2017) 265:18–25. doi: 10.1016/j.pscychresns.2017.04.008
31. Mitsukawa K, Lu X, Bartfai T. Galanin, galanin receptors, and drug targets. *Exs* (2010) 102:7–23. doi: 10.1007/978-3-0346-0228-0_2
32. O'Donnell D, Ahmad S, Wahlestedt C, Walker P. Expression of the novel galanin receptor subtype GALR2 in the adult rat CNS: distinct distribution from GALR1. *J Comp Neurol.* (1999) 409:469–81. doi: 10.1002/(SICI)1096-9861(19990705)409:3<469::AID-CNE10>3.0.CO;2-Q
33. Hokfelt T, Tatemoto K. Galanin—25 years with a multitalented neuropeptide. *Cell Mol Life Sci.* (2008) 65:1793–5. doi: 10.1007/s00018-008-8152-9
34. Thome J, Sakai N, Shin K, Steffen C, Zhang YJ, Impey S, et al. cAMP response element-mediated gene transcription is upregulated by chronic antidepressant treatment. *J Neurosci.* (2000) 20:4030–6. doi: 10.1523/JNEUROSCI.20-11-04030.2000
35. Suda S, Segi-Nishida E, Newton SS, Duman RS. A postpartum model in rat: behavioral and gene expression changes induced by ovarian steroid deprivation. *Biol Psychiatry* (2008) 64:311–9. doi: 10.1016/j.biopsych.2008.03.029
36. Aboul-Fotouh S. Behavioral effects of nicotinic antagonist mecamylamine in a rat model of depression: prefrontal cortex level of BDNF protein and monoaminergic neurotransmitters. *Psychopharmacology* (2015) 232:1095–105. doi: 10.1007/s00213-014-3745-5

37. Erburu M, Muñoz-Cobo I, Diaz-Perdigon T, Mellini P, Suzuki T, Puerta E, et al. SIRT2 inhibition modulate glutamate and serotonin systems in the prefrontal cortex and induces antidepressant-like action. *Neuropharmacology* (2017) 117:195–208.
38. Warden MR, Selimbeyoglu A, Mirzabekov JJ, Lo M, Thompson KR, Kim SY, et al. A prefrontal cortex-brainstem neuronal projection that controls response to behavioural challenge. *Nature* (2012) 492:428–32. doi: 10.1038/nature 11617
39. Malynn S, Campos-Torres A, Moynagh P, Haase J. The pro-inflammatory cytokine TNF-alpha regulates the activity and expression of the serotonin transporter (SERT) in astrocytes. *Neurochem Res.* (2013) 38:694–704. doi: 10.1007/s11064-01 2-0967-y
40. Hosli E, Ledergerber M, Kofler A, Hösli L. Evidence for the existence of galanin receptors on cultured astrocytes of rat CNS: colocalization with cholinergic receptors. *J Chem Neuroanat.* (1997) 13:95–103.
41. Swanson CJ, Blackburn TP, Zhang X, Zheng K, Xu ZQ, Hökfelt T. Anxiolytic- and antidepressant-like profiles of the galanin-3 receptor (Gal3) antagonists SNAP (3788)9 and SNAP (3982)99. *Proc Natl Acad Sci USA.* (2005) 102:17489–94. doi: 10.1073/pnas.05089 70102
42. Xu ZQ, Zhang X, Pieribone VA, Grillner S, Hökfelt T. Galanin-5-hydroxytryptamine interactions: electrophysiological, immunohistochemical and *in situ* hybridization studies on rat dorsal raphe neurons with a note on galanin R1 and R2 receptors. *Neuroscience* (1998) 87:79–94.
43. Martinowich K, Lu B. Interaction between BDNF and serotonin: role in mood disorders. *Neuropsychopharmacology* (2008) 33:73–83. doi: 10.1038/sj.npp.1301571
44. Gotlib IH, Kasch KL, Traill S, Joormann J, Arnow BA, Johnson SL. Coherence and specificity of information-processing biases in depression and social phobia. *J Abnorm Psychol.* (2004) 113:386–98. doi: 10.1037/0021-843X.113.3.386
45. Murphy FC, Sahakian BJ, Rubinsztein JS, Michael A, Rogers RD, Robbins TW, et al. Emotional bias and inhibitory control processes in mania and depression. *Psychol Med.* (1999) 29:1307–21. doi: 10.1017/S0033291799001233
46. Dickens MJ, Pawluski JL. The HPA axis during the perinatal period: implications for perinatal depression. *Endocrinology* (2018) 159:3737–46. doi: 10.1210/en.2018-00677

3

Hydrogen Sulfide Antagonizes Chronic Restraint Stress-Induced Depressive-Like Behaviors via Upregulation of Adiponectin

Qing Tian [1†], *Lei Chen* [1,2†], *Bang Luo* [1,3†], *Ai-Ping Wang* [2*], *Wei Zou* [1,2], *Yong You* [1,3], *Ping Zhang* [1,2] and *Xiao-Qing Tang* [1,3*]

[1] *Institute of Neuroscience, Medical College, University of South China, Hengyang, China,* [2] *Institute of Clinical Research, Affiliated Nanhua Hospital, University of South China, Hengyang, China,* [3] *Institute of Clinical Research, the First Affiliated Hospital, University of South China, Hengyang, China*

Correspondence:
Ai-Ping Wang
waiping2011@usc.edu.cn
Xiao-Qing Tang
tangxq-usc@qq.com;
tangxq-usc@usc.edu.cn

† These authors have contributed equally to this work

Backgroud: Chronic restraint stress (CRS) induces depressive-like behaviors in rodents, which involves dysregulation of hippocampal synapse formation and excessive autophagy. Adiponectin has antidepressant activity. Hydrogen sulfide (H_2S) is a novel gasotransmitter. The present work was to investigate whether H_2S antagonizes CRS-induced depressive-like behaviors in rats and to explore whether its potential mechanism involves ameliorated synaptic and autophagic dysregulation by upregulation of adiponectin.

Methods: Depressive-like behavior was analyzed by the tail suspension test (TST), novelty suppressed feeding test (NSFT), and open field test (OFT). The structure of autophagy was observed under transmission electron microscopy. The expressions of adiponectin, beclin1, and sequestosome 1 (p62/SQSTMI) protein in hippocampus were measured by Western blot. The levels of synapsin1 (SYN1) in the hippocampus were calculated by Western blot and immunofluorescence technique.

Results: The behavior experiments, including TST, NSFT, and OFT, showed that NaHS (a donor of H_2S) reduced CRS-induced depressive-like behaviors. NaHS decreased the loss of hippocampal synapse as evidenced by increased the level of SYN1 in the hippocampus of CRS-exposed rats. NaHS rescued CRS-induced excessive hippocampal autophagy as evidenced by declines in the number of autophagosomes and the expression of beclin1 as well as increase in the expression of P62 in the hippocampus of CRS-exposed rats. NaHS upregulated hippocampal adiponectin expression in the CRS-exposed rats. Furthermore, neutralizing adiponectin by Anti-acrp30 reversed the protective response of NaHS to CRS-produced depressive-like behaviors as well as hippocampal synaptic disruption and excessive autophagy.

Conclusion: H_2S mitigates CRS-induced depressive behavior via upregulation of adiponectin, which in turn results in amelioration in hippocampal synapse formation dysfunction and excessive autophagy.

Keywords: adiponectin, chronic restraint stress, depressive-like behavior, hydrogen sulfide, synapse formation, autophagy

INTRODUCTION

Depression is a kind of serious mental disease that was caused by a variety of reasons. Chronic stress is considered as a triggering factor in the pathogenesis of depression (1, 2). It has been reported that chronic restraint stress (CRS) leads to neurological changes and depressive-like behaviors of rodents (3), which is widely applied in animal experiments to study the etiology and pathophysiology of depression (4–6). Hydrogen sulfide (H_2S) is recognized as a neuroprotectant, which plays important roles in the central nervous system (CNS) (7). Our team verified that administration of H_2S antagonizes depressive-like behaviors in streptozotocin-exerted diabetic rats (8). In this study, we will further explore whether H_2S has bioavailability to prevent CRS-induced depressive-like behaviors.

Hippocampus, a critical limbic structure, is associated with mood. It has been confirmed that dysregulation of synapses and excessive autophagy in hippocampus play important roles in major depression disorder (9, 10), and that inhibition in synaptic deficits and excessive autophagy in hippocampus contributes to the antidepressant-like role of ketamine (11, 12). Thus, the present work explored whether this antidepressant-like role of H_2S is involved in regulating hippocampal synapse formation and autophagy.

Adiponectin, as a member of adipokine family, is predominately secreted from adipose tissue (13, 14). Remarkably, adiponectin is detected in human brain and its receptors widely distributes in brain, like hippocampus and cortex (15). It has been reported that adiponectin stimulates hippocampal neurogenesis and neural stem proliferation (16, 17). Adiponectin is also associated with CNS pathologies (18). Accumulative studies reported that adiponectin is decreased in chronic social defeat stress-induced depression (19, 20). In addition, Liu et al. demonstrated that intracranial injection of adiponectin is able to ameliorate depressive-like behaviors in high fat diet-treated mice (19). Furthermore, growing evidences demonstrated that adiponectin regulates synaptic activity and autophagy (21, 22). Therefore, our hypothesis is that hippocampal adiponectin mediates the protective response of H_2S to CRS-induced synaptic dysfunction and excessive autophagy in the hippocampus as well as depressive symptoms.

Our present work reported that H_2S rescued CRS-induced depressive-like behaviors by elevation of hippocampal adiponectin and that suppression in hippocampal synapse loss and autophagy participates in adiponectin-mediated antidepressant efficacy of H_2S in CRS-exposed rats.

MATERIALS AND METHODS

Reagents

Sodium hydrosulfide (NaHS, a donor of H_2S) was obtained from Sigma (Sigma, USA). Acrp30-antibody was purchased from Santa Cruz Biotechnology (California, USA). The primary antibodies of synapsin1, beclin1, and p62/SQSTMI were purchased from Cell Signaling Technology. Bicinchoninic Acid (BCA) Protein Assay Kit was purchased from Beyotime Institute of Biotechnology in Shanghai.

Animals

Animals that were used for all experiments are adult male Sprague-Dawley (SD) rats weighted 200–220 g (Hunan SJA Laboratory Animal Company, Changsha, Hunan, China). They were housed individually in a standard 12 h light/dark cycle and have free approach for food and water. In order to mitigate tense and anxiety of rats and eliminate influences of environmental factors, all rats were allowed to acclimatize themselves to new environment for 7 days before the experiment. This study was carried out in accordance with the recommendations of National Institutes of Health Guide for the Care and use of Laboratory Animals and was approved by the Animal Use and Protection Committee of the University of South China.

Drugs Treatments and Study Design

Respectively measured 1.68 mg or 5.6 mg of NaHS was diluted in phosphate-buffered saline (PBS) to equal concentration of NaHS 30 or 100 μmol/mL. Rats were subjected to CRS as well as injected with 30 or 100 μmol/kg NaHS for 4 weeks. In the fourth week, rats were treated with Anti-acrp30 (1 μg, i.c.v.) at the same time. All behavior tests were performed after 24 h of last injection. There is an interval for 2 days between each behavior test. After all tests were conducted, rats were allowed to have a rest for 1 day. After that, all rats were killed and hippocampus were collected rapidly which then stored at −80°C (**Figure 1**).

Stereotaxic Injection

After anesthetized with 1% sodium pentobarbital (40 mg/kg) delivered through intraperitoneal injection, rats were fixed on a stereotaxic apparatus for operation. The area central on the incision was trimmed and a aseptically cannula was implanted into lateral ventricle by reference to the following coordinates: AP: 1.0 mm, R or L:1.5 mm. For purpose of avoiding drug reflux along the injection track, the needle was drew back halfway and maintained in position for an extra 2 min ahead of being pulled out. After surgery, all rats were injected with penicillin for 3 consecutive days to prevent them from being infected.

Chronic Restraint Stress (CRS) Model

Chronic restraint stress was conducted as previously described (3). Rats were placed in a 50 ml stainless steel pipe for 6 h from 9 a.m. to 15 p.m. This stress was continuous for 28 days.

Tail Suspension Test (TST)

The TST was carried out by reference to which described in a detailed reference (23). Briefly, each subject was tied by taping its tail closely 2 cm from the tip and then suspended in a position of 50 cm above the floor on a hook. Rats were regarded as immobile when they abandoned struggling and remained completely motionless. The time that rats kept immobility during the 6-min test was recorded.

Novelty Suppressed Feeding Test (NSFT)

In light of previously described (24), rats were fasting for 24 h before the test. When the experiment start, rats were placed in a test chamber (50 × 50 × 40 cm) covered with a layer of 2 cm thick wood chips from any of four corners. Food pellets were weighted and then were placed in the center of test chamber.

The time from rats entering into chamber to pick up food with forelimb was defined as latency, which is a key index to reflect the degree of depression. To eliminate the influence of differences in rat appetite on the latency to feed, the rat was reintroduced to their home cage and total food intake in 10 min was recorded.

Open Field Test (OFT)

The open field test (OFT) is applied to analysis the potential impacts of drug used in whole experiments on spontaneous activity. As previously described (25), rats were put in an open test chamber (60 × 60 × 40 cm) with black bottom and walls. Moreover, it is essential to ensure that the chamber was under nature light of brightness uniformity. The rat was placed into the center of test chamber and allowed to explore freely after 2 min adaption. The total distance in 5 min was recorded. Meanwhile, the chamber was cleansed by ethyl alcohol to eliminate effect of smell on spontaneous activity of next subject.

Transmission Electron Microscopy (TEM)

The collected hippocampus tissues were sliced into 1 mm^3 blocks, and were immediately placed in 2% glutaraldehyde overnight for fixation at 4°C. After immersed in 1% osmium tetroxide for 2 h, the blocks were dehydrated using graded ethanol and then embedded in epoxy resin. Next, the blocks were sliced into ultrathin sections (70 nm) using an ultramicrotome (Leica, Germany, EM UC6). Finally, the micrographs were

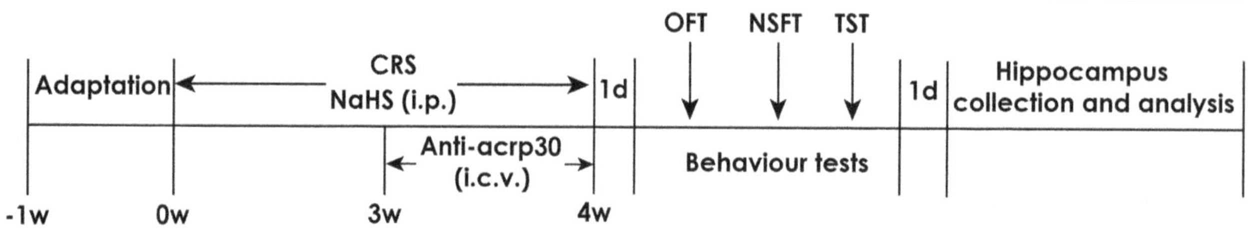

FIGURE 1 | Schematic diagram of the experimental procedures. CRS, chronic restraint stress; TST, tail suspension test; NSFT, novelty suppressed feeding test; OFT, open field test; i.p., intraperitoneal injection; i.c.v., intracerebroventricular injection.

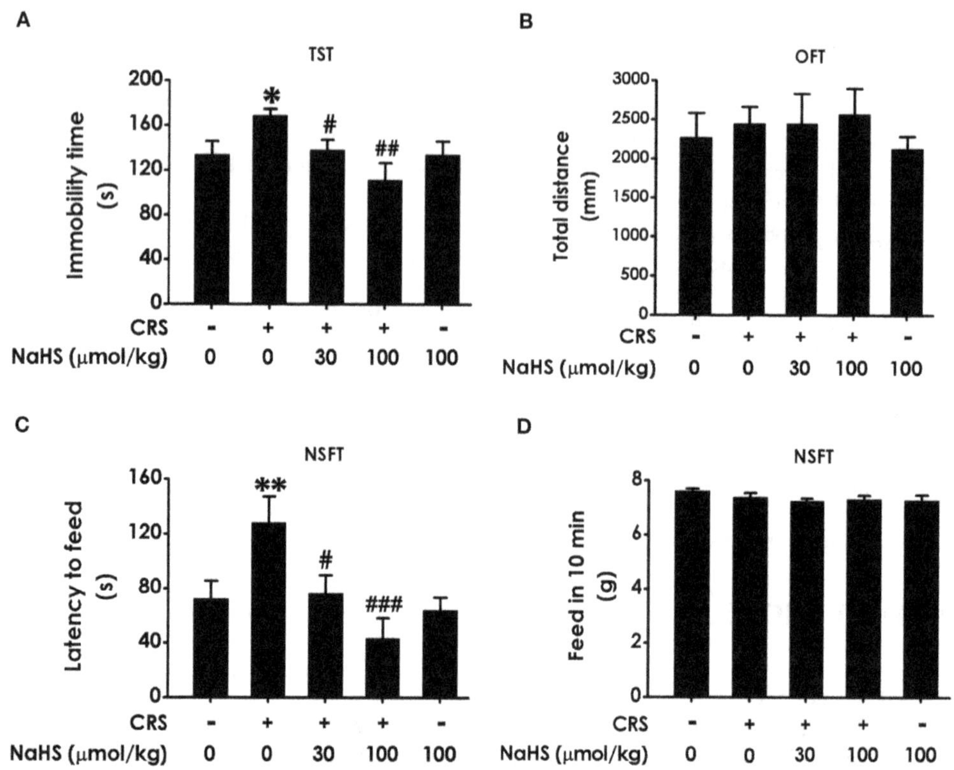

FIGURE 2 | Effect of H_2S on the depressive-like behaviors in CRS-treated rats. SD rats were cotreated with CRS and NaHS (30, 100 μmol/kg, i.p.) for 4 w. Rats were underwent TST **(A)**, OFT **(B)**, and NSFT **(C,D)** to evaluate depressive-like behaviors. Values are expressed as the means ± SEM (*n* = 6–10). $^{*}P < 0.05$, $^{**}P < 0.01$, vs. control group; $^{\#}P < 0.05$, $^{\#\#}P < 0.01$, $^{\#\#\#}P < 0.001$, vs. CRS-treated alone group.

captured under transmission electron microscope (JEOL, Japan, JEM1230).

Western-Blot Analysis

Supernatant were collected of tissue homogenate and total protein concentration was quantified using BCA Protein Assay Kits. After mixed with 5 × loading buffer and heated at 100°C for 5 min, protein lysates were loaded on sodium dodecyl sulfate-polyacrylamide gel for electrophoresis and subsequently transferred onto PVDF membrane using wet transfer system. The blots were blocked using 5% skim milk in TBST buffer (50 mmol/L Tris-HCl, pH 7.5,150 mmol/L NaCl, 0.1% Tween-20) for 2 h and were respectively incubated with primary antibodies against adiponectin, SYN1, beclin1, and P62 (1:1,000), and β-actin (1:2,000) overnight at 4°C. Subsequently, membranes were washed using TBST for 3 × 10 min and were incubated with secondary antibody conjugated to horseradish peroxidase (1:5,000) for 2 h. Finally, protein membranes were washed in the same way and bands were visualized by enhanced chemiluminescence system (BeyoECL Plus kit, Beyotime, P0018). The β-actin was set as a loading control and the signal of immunoblot was analyzed by AlphaImage2200 software.

Immunofluorescence Technique

Paraffin-embedded sections were de-waxed and treated with EDTA contained buffer for antigen retrieval in microwave. Subsequently, sections were coated in autofluorescence eliminator for 5 min before washing. After 3% BSA was applied for 30 min to block nonspecific staining, the primary antibodies were added overnight at 4°C. Sections were washed for 3 × 5 min next day and corresponding secondary antibodies were added for 50 min at room temperature. DAPI was added to staining nuclear for 10 min. After washed in the same way, sections were covered with standard mounting media. Images were captured using microscope (Nikon, Japan, NIKON ECLIPSE C1).

Statistical Analysis

Statistical analysis of all data was conducted using SPSS 18.0 software. All values are exhibited as the mean ± SEM. One-way ANOVA as well as LSD-t are applied to calculate variance as well as to analyze multiple comparisons between groups, respectively. The standard of statistical difference was set at $P < 0.05$.

RESULTS

H_2S Antagonizes CRS-Induced Depressive-Like Behaviors

In TST, treatment with NaHS markedly shorten the immobility time of CRS-exposed rats and NaHS (100 μmol/kg) treated alone didn't affect the immobility time of normal rats (**Figure 2A**), indicating the antidepressive-like action of H_2S. To eliminate the nonspecific motoric effects of NaHS and CRS on behaviors in the TST, the spontaneous activity of

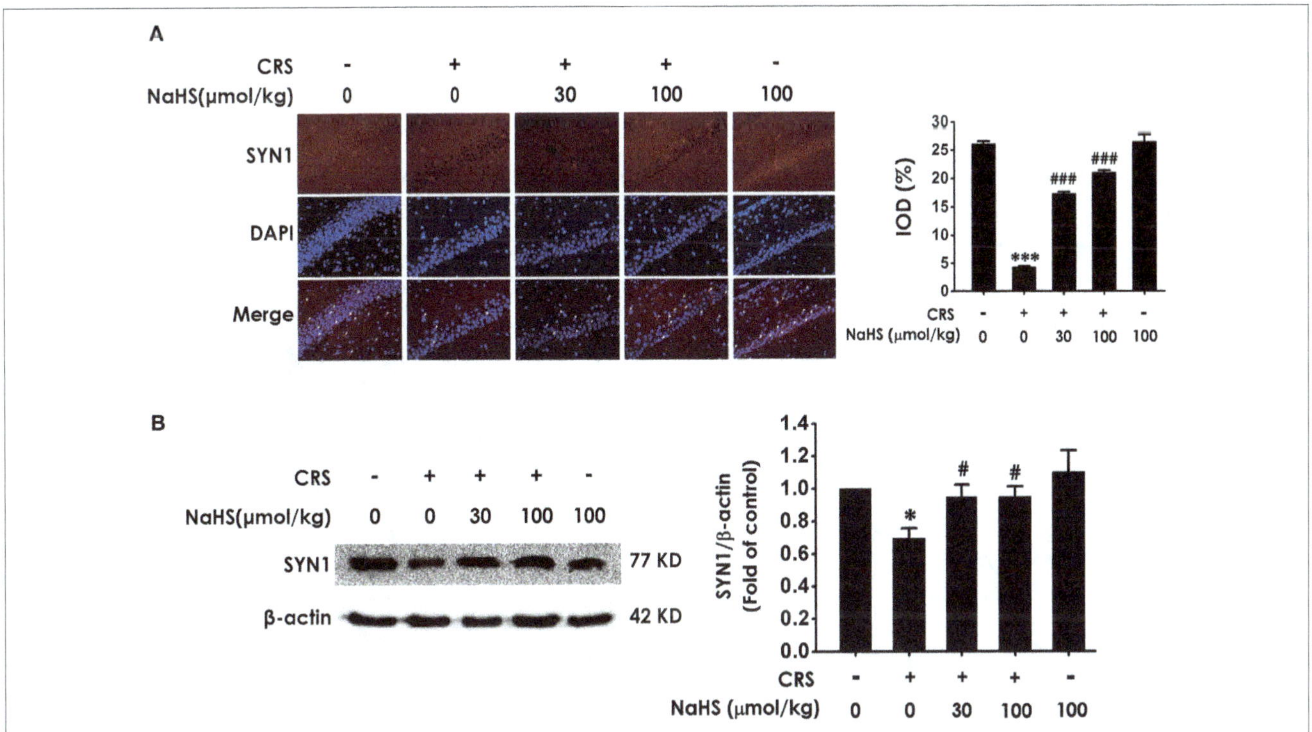

FIGURE 3 | Effects of H_2S on the suppressed synapse formation in the hippocampus of CRS-treated rats. SD rats were cotreated with CRS and NaHS (30, 100 μmol/kg, i.p.) for 4 w. The levels of hippocampal SYN1 were analyzed by immunofluorescence technique [**(A)**, magnification × 400] and western blot **(B)**. β-actin was used as an internal control. Values are expressed as means ± SEM ($n = 3$). $^{*}P < 0.05$, $^{***}P < 0.001$, vs. control group; $^{\#}P < 0.05$, $^{\#\#\#}P < 0.001$, vs. CRS-treated alone group.

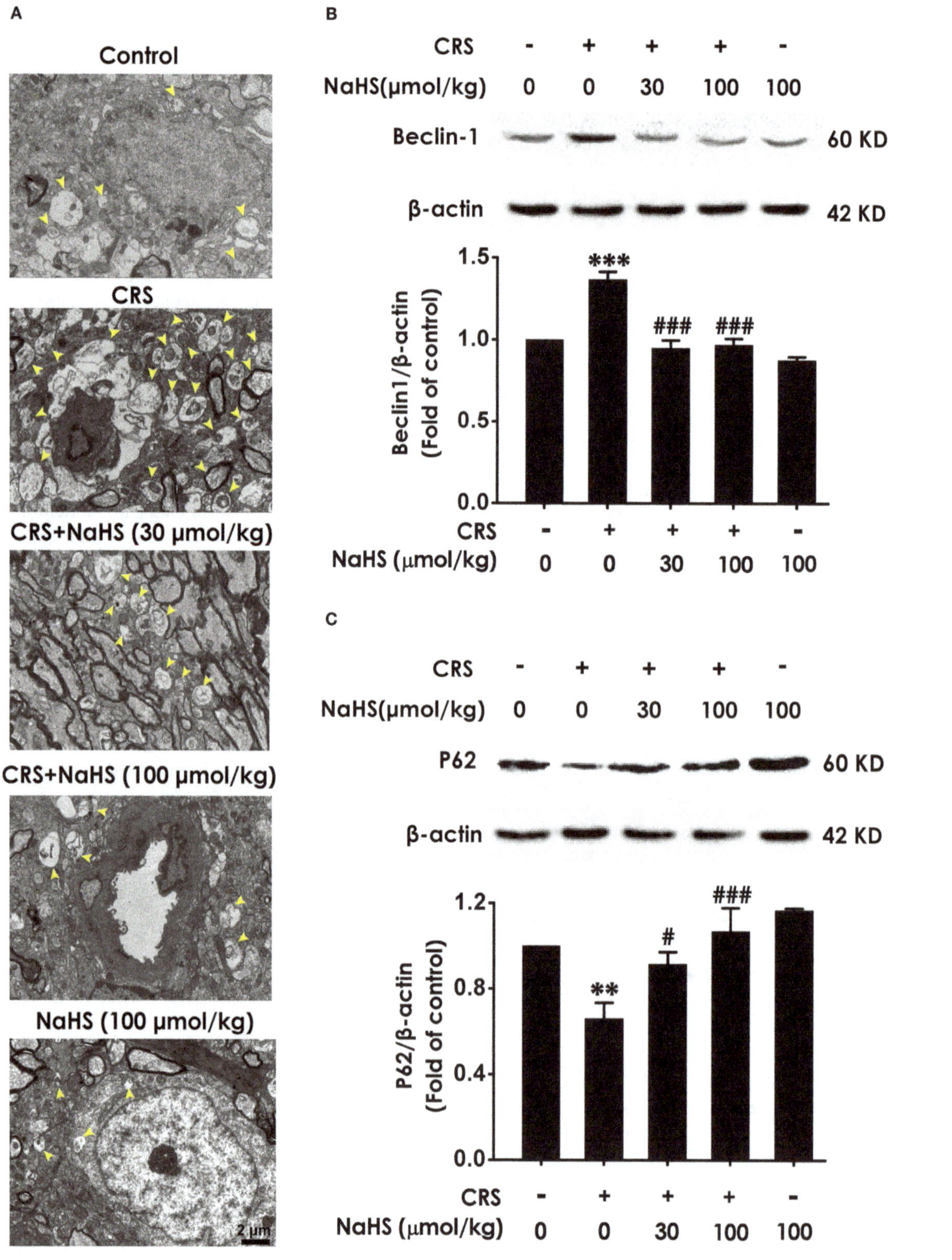

FIGURE 4 | Effect of H_2S on the excessive autophagy in the hippocampus of CRS-exposed rats. SD rats were cotreated with CRS and NaHS (30, 100 μmol/kg, i.p.) for 4 w. The number of hippocampal autophagosomes **(A)** was detected by transmission electron microscopy. The arrowhead marked autophagosomes. The expression of beclin1 **(B)** and P62 **(C)** were detected by western blot and β-actin was used as an internal control. Values are expressed as means ± SEM ($n = 3$). $^{**}P < 0.01$, $^{***}P < 0.001$, vs. control group; $^{\#}P < 0.05$, $^{\#\#\#}P < 0.001$, vs. CRS-treated alone group.

rats were assessed. As shown in **Figure 2B**, treatment with NaHS or STZ alone didn't have any effect on total distance in normal rats, suggesting that alteration in immobility time in TST was not due to the difference in spontaneous activity. In NSFT, the latency to feed in CRS-exposed rats was obviously decreased after administration of NaHS, while NaHS alone didn't change it in normal rats (**Figure 2C**). In this task, the feed in 10 min of each group in their home cage had no significant difference (**Figure 2D**), which excluded the possibility that alteration in the latency to feed was due to the difference in appetite and feeding. These data demonstrated that H_2S alleviates CRS-induced depressive-like behaviors.

H_2S Protects Against CRS-Generated Synaptic Dysfunction in the Hippocampus

Next, we investigated the role of H_2S in synaptic dysfunction induced by CRS in the hippocampus by measuring the expression of hippocampal SYN1. Immunofluorescence analysis exhibited NaHS (30 or 100 μmol/kg, i.p.) obviously rescued CRS-induced decline in hippocampal SYN1-positive cells of rats (**Figure 3A**). Western blot analysis also showed that supplement of NaHS significantly elevated the expression of SYN1 in the hippocampus of CRS-treated rats (**Figure 3B**). In addition, NaHS (100 μmol/kg, i.p.) alone exerted no effect on the level of hippocampal SYN1 (**Figures 3A,B**). These data indicated that H_2S protects against CRS-impaired synapse formation in the hippocampus.

H_2S Suppresses CRS-Exerted Excessive Autophagy in the Hippocampus

To determine wherther the antdepressant-like role of H_2S involves in the change of hippocampal autophagy in CRS-exposed rats, the effects of H_2S on the number of autophagosomes and the expression of beclin1 as well as P62 in the hippocampus of CRS-exposed rats were detected. The number of autophagosomes was accumulated in the hippocampus of CRS-exposed rats, while application of NaHS (30 or 100 μmol/kg, i.p.) dramatically reduced the number of autophagosomes (**Figure 4A**) in the hippocampus. Rats submitted to CRS had an increase in the expression of beclin1 (**Figure 4B**) and a decrease in the expression of P62 (**Figure 4C**), while adminstration of NaHS (30 or 100 μmol/kg/d, i.p.) reversed these changes as indicated by declined expression of beclin1 and elevated expression of P62 in the hippocampus. Meanwhile, NaHS alone didn't alter these autophagic markers in normal rats, which suggested the antagonistic actin of H_2S on CRS-exerted excessive autophagy in the hippocampus.

H_2S Up-Regulates the Expression of Adiponectin in the Hippocampus of CRS-Exposed Rats

To understand the role of adiponectin in H_2S-elicited antidepressant-like activity, we assessed whether H_2S affects the expression of adiponectin in the hippocampus of CRS-exposed rats. CRS-treated group showed a sharply decrease of adiponectin compared to control group. More importantly, treated with NaHS (30 or 100 μmol/kg/d, i.p.) significantly increased the expression of adiponectin in CRS-exposed rats (**Figure 5**). In addition, NaHS alone exerted no effect on adiponectin expression (**Figure 5**). Taken together, H_2S elevated the expression of hippocampus adiponectin in the CRS-treated rats.

Neutralizing Adiponectin Reverses the Antidepressant Response of H_2S in CRS-Exposed Rats

To further examine the mediatory role of adiponectin in H_2S-elicited antidepressant-like effect, we tested whether Anti-acrp30, a neutralizing antibody of adiponectin, reverses the protective action H_2S on CRS-induced depressive-like behaviors. As exhibited in **Figure 6A**, the immobility time in the CRS and NaHS-cotreated rats in TST was sharply increased by administration of Anti-acrp30 (1 μg/d, i.c.v.). The total distance in 5 min in OFT has no significance among five groups (**Figure 6B**), which eliminated the possible impact of Anti-acrp30 on spontaneous activity. In the NSFT, Anti-acrp30 dramatically increased the latency to feed in the cotreatment with NaHS and CRS rats (**Figure 6C**) and the total feed in 10 min has no significant change among all groups (**Figure 6D**). Taken together, these data indicated that inhibition of adiponectin reverses the antidepressant-like function of H_2S in CRS-treated rats.

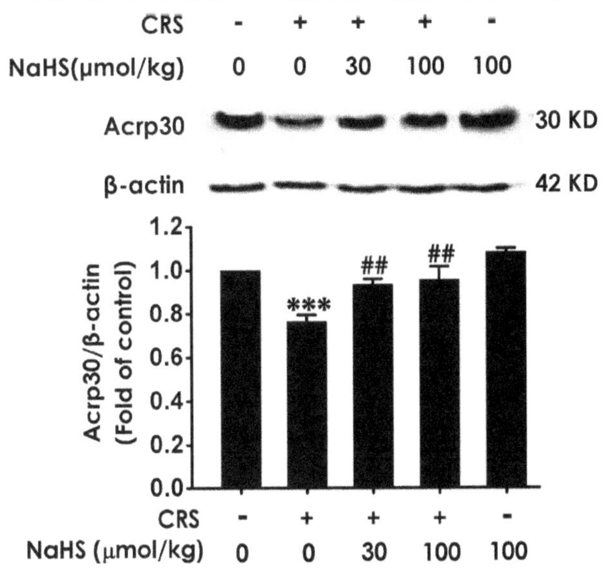

FIGURE 5 | Effect of H_2S on the expression of Adiponectin in the hippocampus of CRS-treated rats. SD rats were cotreated with CRS and NaHS (30, 100 μmol/kg, i.p.) for 4 w. The expression of hippocampal adiponectin (Acrp 30) was measured by western blotting and β-actin was used as an internal control. Values are expressed as means ± SEM ($n = 3$). $^{***}P < 0.001$, vs. control group; $^{\#\#}P<0.01$, vs. CRS-treated alone group.

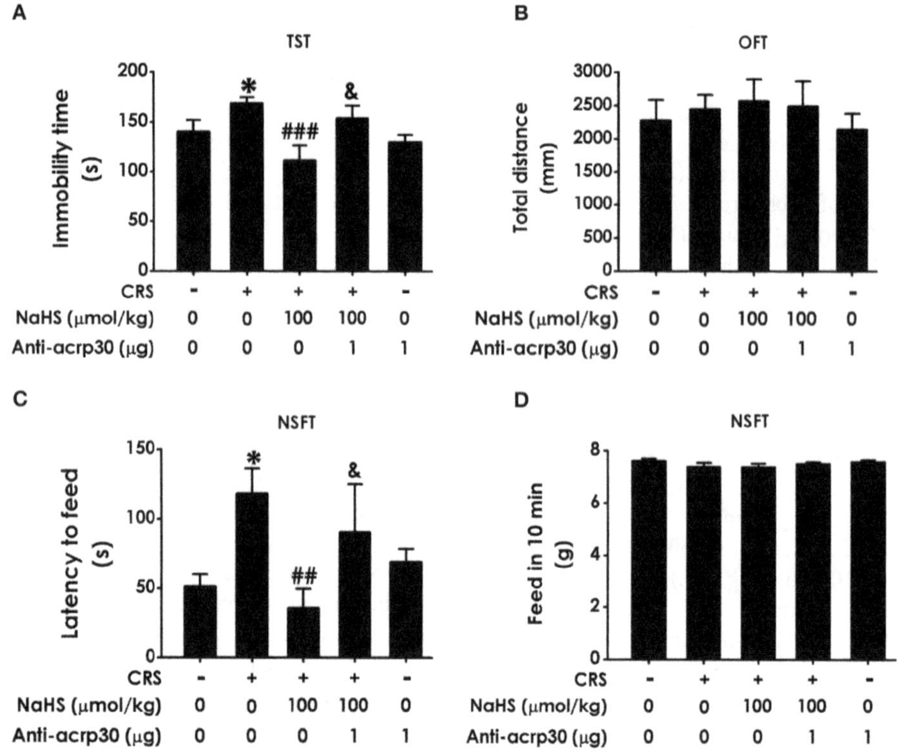

FIGURE 6 | Effect of Anti-acrp30 on H_2S-elicited antidepressant-like function in CRS-exposed rats. After cotreatment with CRS and NaHS (100 μmol/kg, i.p.) for 3 w, SD rats were further co-administrated with Anti-acrp30 (1 μg/d, icv) for 1 w. TST **(A)**, OFT **(B)**, and NSFT **(C,D)** were employed to assess depressive-like behaviors. Values are expressed as means ± SEM (n = 6–10). $^{*}P < 0.05$, vs. control group; $^{\#\#}P < 0.01$, $^{\#\#\#}P < 0.001$, vs. CRS-treated alone group, $^{\&}P < 0.05$, vs. cotreated with CRS and NaHS (100 μmol/kg, i.p.) group.

Neutralizing Adiponectin Abrogates the Ameliorated Effect of H_2S on CRS-Induced Synapse Formation Dysfunction

For the purpose of confirming the functional requirement of adiponectin in the ameliorated role of H_2S in CRS-elicited synaptic dysfunction, we detected the impact of Anti-acrp30 on the expression of hippocampus SYN-1 in the NaHS and CRS-cotreated rats. Immunofluorescence analysis exhibited that Anti-acrp30 (1 μg/d, i.c.v.) sharply prevented NaHS from increasing the level of SYN1-positive cells in the hippocampus of CRS-exposed rats (**Figure 7A**). Western blot analysis also showed that Anti-acrp30 abolished the upregulatory effect of NaHS on the hippocampus SYN1 expression of CRS-treated rats (**Figure 7B**). Moreover, Anti-acrp30 alone didn't change the level of SYN1. These results revealed that neutralizing adiponectin blocks the antagonistic action H_2S in CRS-triggered disruption in hippocampal synapse formation.

Neutralizing Adiponectin Reverses the Inhibitory Role of H_2S in CRS-Exerted Excessive Autophagy

To identify whether adiponectin is indispensable for H_2S-elicited suppression in the hippocampal excessive autophagy of CRS-exposed rats, we detected the impact of Anti-acrp30 on the protection of NaHS against CRS-induced excessive autophagy in the hippocampus. Anti-acrp30 dramatically prevented NaHS from increasing the number of autophagosomes (**Figure 8A**) and the expression of beclin1 (**Figure 8B**) and decreasing the expression of P62 (**Figure 8C**) in the hippocampus of CRS-exposed rats. Additionally, Anti-acrp30 alone exerted no effect on autophagic markers. These data suggested that neutralization of adiponectin reversed the inhibitory action of H_2S in the excessive autophagy of hippocampus driven by CRS.

DISCUSSION

Chronic stress is a triggering factor in the occurrence and progression of depression, which greatly threatened human health. The present work was to explore the antidepressant role of H_2S in CRS-induced depressive-like behaviors and the underlying mechanisms. In this study, we demonstrated that H_2S prevented CRS-induced depression-like behaviors, hippocampal synaptic disorder and excessive autophagy as well as upregulated the expression of hippocampal adiponectin in CRS-exposed rats. Moreover, Neutralization of adiponectin reversed these protective effects of H_2S on CRS-induced depression, disrupted synapse formation, and excessive autophagy. These data uncovered that H_2S antagonizes CRS-induced depressive-like behaviors, involving promotion in hippocampal synapse

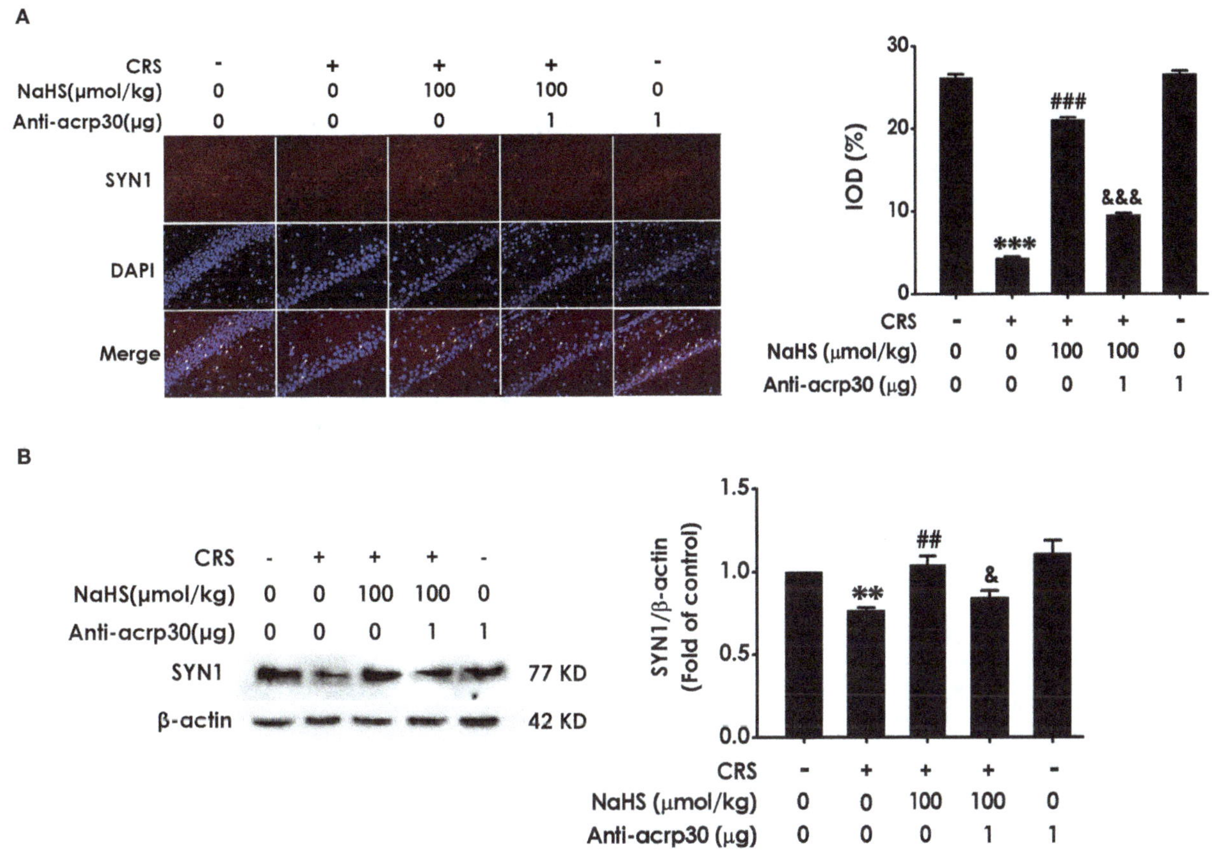

FIGURE 7 | Effect of Anti-acrp30 on H_2S-alleviated synapse formation disorder in CRS-exposed rats. After cotreatment with CRS and NaHS (100 μmol/kg, i.p.) for 3 w, SD rats were further co-administrated with Anti-acrp30 (1 μg/d, icv) for 1 w. The levels of hippocampal SYN1 were analyzed by immunofluorescence technique [**(A)**, magnification × 400] and western blot **(B)**. β-actin was used as an internal control. Values are expressed as means ± SEM ($n = 3$). $^{**}P < 0.01$, $^{***}P < 0.001$, vs. control group; $^{\#\#}P < 0.01$, $^{\#\#\#}P < 0.001$, vs. CRS-treated alone group, $^{\&}P < 0.05$, $^{\&\&\&}P < 0.001$, vs. cotreated with CRS and NaHS (100 μmol/kg, i.p.) group.

formation and suppression in hippocampal excessive autophagy, via upregulation of hippocampal adiponectin.

Chronic restraint stress is a well-established rodent model to simulate depression-like syndrome (3, 26). Hippocampus, which plays important role in depression, is more susceptible to CRS damage (27). H_2S is a new neuromodulator and gas signaling molecules. Several lines evidences proved that physiological concentration of H_2S plays essential roles in central neuron system (28, 29), especially in hippocampus (30). It has reported that H_2S can stay in the blood for more than 1 h and enter the brain through the blood-brain barrier (31). Furthermore, increased level of H_2S in the brain was observed after intraperitoneal injection of H_2S (32). More importantly, our previous study has proved that exogenous administration of H_2S protects against depressive-like behaviors in streptozocin-induced diabetic rats (8). Therefore, it's necessary to investigate the beneficial role of H_2S in CRS-induced depressive-like behaviors. Rats were subjected to CRS for consecutive 28 days and intraperitoneally injected NaHS for 4 weeks simultaneously. Subsequently, depressive-like behaviors were detected by TST, NSFT, and OFT. Consistent with previous study (3), CRS induced depressive-like behaviors. Treatment with NaHS significantly decreased the immobility time in TST of CRS-exposed rats. Meanwhile, OFT showed that there has on statistical difference of total distance among five groups, which excluded the possible influence of NaHS on the spontaneous activity. These data suggested the antidepressant-like role of H_2S in this CRS model. In addition, administration of NaHS reduced the latency to feed in NSFT in CRS-exposed rats and the feed in 10 min has no significant difference among five groups. Taken together, H_2S rescues depressive-like behaviors in CRS-exposed rats.

Synapsin1 (SYN1), as a synapse-associated protein, is expressed in presynaptic membrane and regulates synapse formation (33). Growing studies indicated that alteration of SYN1 is intimately associated with stress-induced depression (34, 35) and that enhancement in SYN1 participates in antidepressant process (36, 37). Autophagy is a maintaining neuronal homeostasis process that transports damaged contents to lysosomes for degradation (38). Previous research found that CRS induces elevated autophagy (39). Furthermore, mTOR signaling in depression is downregulated and this deficiency was effectively rescued by ketamine (40). Therefore, question that

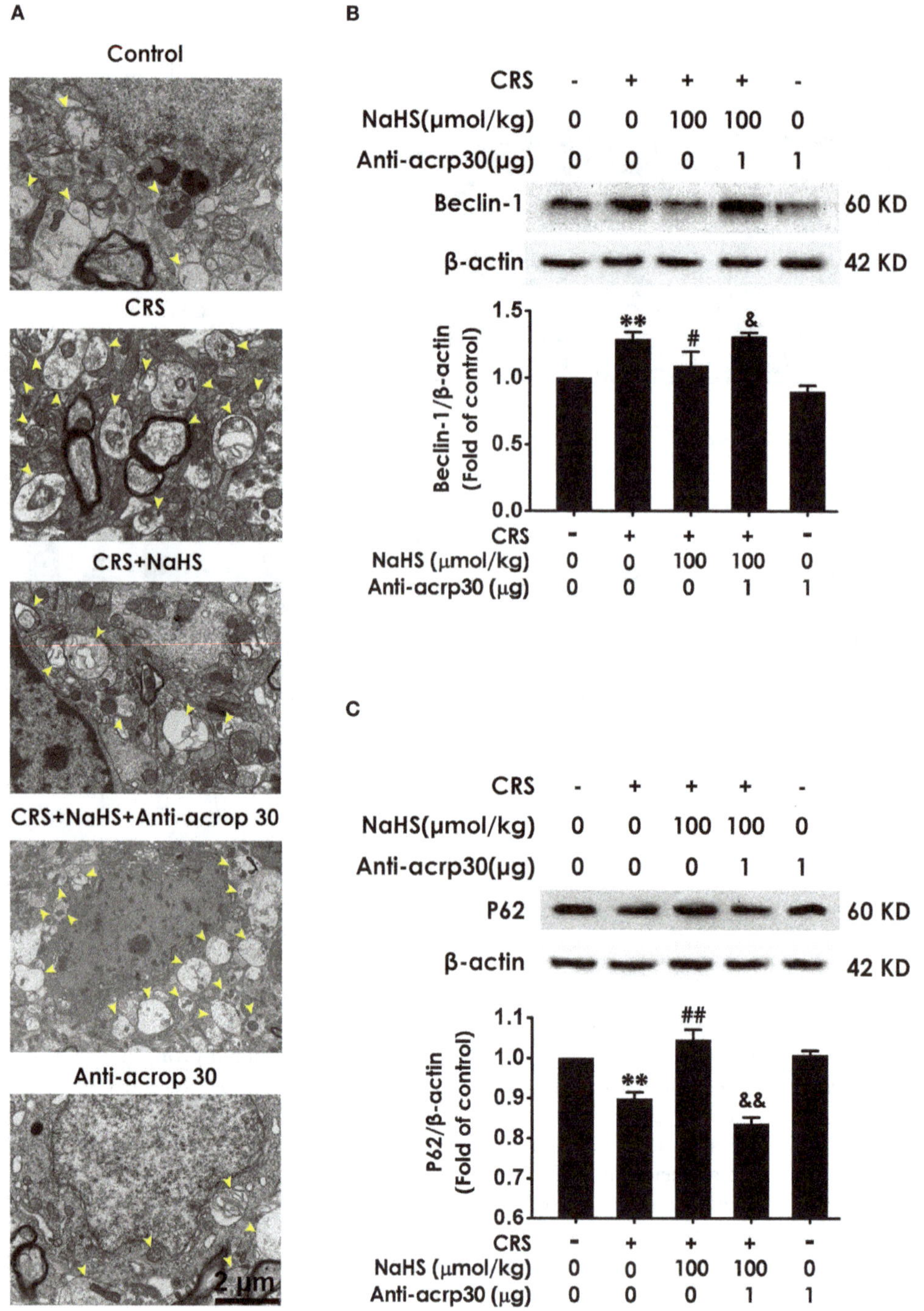

FIGURE 8 | Effect of Anti-acrp30 on H_2S-elicited suppression in CRS-induced excessive hippocampal autophagy. After cotreatment with CRS and NaHS (100 μmol/kg, i.p.) for 3 w, SD rats were further co-administrated with Anti-acrp30 (1 μg/d, icv) for 1 w. The number of hippocampal autophagosomes **(A)** was detected under transmission electron microscopy. The arrowhead marked autophagosomes. The expression of beclin1 **(B)** and P62 **(C)** in the hippocampus were detected by western blot and β-actin was used as an internal control. Values are expressed as means ± SEM ($n = 3$). $^{**}P < 0.01$, vs. control group; $^{\#}P < 0.05$, $^{\#\#}P < 0.01$, vs. CRS-treated alone group, $^{\&}P < 0.05$, $^{\&\&}P < 0.05$, vs. cotreatment with CRS and NaHS (100 μmol/kg, i.p.) group.

the effect of H_2S on CRS-generated synaptic and autophagic dysregulation is necessary to be solved. We found that H_2S exerted antagonistic action in CRS-induced hippocampal synaptic dysfunction indicated by the increased SYN1 level in the hippocampus of CRS-exposed rats. In addition, H_2S attenuated CRS-induced hippocampal autophagic activation as evidenced by decreases in the number of autophagosomes and the expression of beclin1 as well as an increase in the expression of P62 in the hippocampus of CRS-exposed rats. Collectively, these data demonstrated that the protection of H_2S against CRS-caused depressive-like behaviors involves in the ameliorations in synapse formation disorder and excessive autophagy in the hippocampus.

Adiponectin, as a key adipokine, is secreted by adipocytes. It acts an critical role in CNS (41). It has been pointed that major depression disorder patients exhibit declined adiponectin level (42). Liu et al. discovered that inhibition of adiponectin by intracerebroventricular injecting adiponectin neutralizing antibody produces depressive-like behaviors as well as enhances susceptibility to stress, and supplement of adiponectin exerts antidepressant-like effect (19). Recent studies reported that adiponectin mediates the antidepressant-like role of exercise as well as ketamine (16, 43). Our present study showed that H_2S rescued CRS-induced the downregulation of adiponectin in the hippocampus. Further results showed that neutralized adiponectin by Anti-acrp30 reversed the antidepressant-like effect of H_2S in CRS-exposed rats, which demonstrated that adiponectin mediates the protective role of H_2S in CRS-exerted depressive-like behaviors. However, what caused the reduction of hippocampal adiponectin in the CRS model still remains unknown. Liu et al. reported that plasma adiponectin was decreased in chronic social defeat model (19). Even so, further research is needed to dig deeper to find out the change of adiponectin that entered into the brain. In addition, neutralizing adiponectin abrogated H_2S-elicited facilitation in hippocampal synapse formation and suppression in hippocampal excessive autophagy in the CRS-exposed rats. These findings suggested that adiponectin-mediated protective action of H_2S on CRS-induced depressive-like behaviors is via enhancement in hippocampal synapse formation and suppression in hippocampal excessive autophagy.

In conclusion, our work proved that H_2S increases the level of hippocampal adiponectin as a result of promoting hippocampal synapse formation and suppressing hippocampal autophagy in CRS model, and thereby alleviates CRS-induced depression-like behaviors. Taken together, our data further confirmed the antidepressant-like role of H_2S in CRS model and suggested that therapies directed at heightening pharmacological properties of H_2S hold broad applicability for treating depressive disorder.

AUTHOR CONTRIBUTIONS

X-QT and A-PW designed the study. QT, LC, and BL performed experiments. WZ, YY, and PZ conducted the analysis. QT wrote the manuscript and X-QT made necessary modifications to manuscript. All authors reviewed the manuscript.

FUNDING

This work was supported by National Natural Science Foundation of China (81671057, 81371485), the Major Research Topics of the Health and Family Planning Commission of Hunan province (A2017020), and the Key Projects of the Education Department of Hunan province (17A187).

REFERENCES

1. Akil H. Stressed and depressed. *Nat Med.* (2005) 11:116–8. doi: 10.1038/nm0205-116
2. Kessler RC. The effects of stressful life events on depression. *Ann Rev Psychol.* (1997) 48:191–214. doi: 10.1146/annurev.psych.48.1.191
3. Chiba S, Numakawa T, Ninomiya M, Richards MC, Wakabayashi C, Kunugi H. Chronic restraint stress causes anxiety- and depression-like behaviors, downregulates glucocorticoid receptor expression, and attenuates glutamate release induced by brain-derived neurotrophic factor in the prefrontal cortex. *Prog Neuro Psychopharmacol Biol Psychiatry* (2012) 39:112–9. doi: 10.1016/j.pnpbp.2012.05.018
4. Abelaira HM, Reus GZ, Quevedo J. Animal models as tools to study the pathophysiology of depression. *Rev Bras Psiquiatr.* (2013) 35 (Suppl. 2)S112–20. doi: 10.1590/1516-4446-2013-1098
5. Glavin GB, Pare WP, Sandbak T, Bakke HK, Murison, R. Restraint stress in biomedical research: an update. *Neurosci Biobehav Rev.* (1994) 18:223–49.
6. McArthur R, Borsini F. Animal models of depression in drug discovery: a historical perspective. *Pharmacol Biochem Behav.* (2006) 84:436–52. doi: 10.1016/j.pbb.2006.06.005
7. Tan BH, Wong PT, Bian JS. Hydrogen sulfide: a novel signaling molecule in the central nervous system. *Neurochem Int.* (2010) 56:3–10. doi: 10.1016/j.neuint.2009.08.008
8. Tang ZJ, Zou W, Yuan J, Zhang P, Tian Y, Xiao ZF, et al. Antidepressant-like and anxiolytic-like effects of hydrogen sulfide in streptozotocin-induced diabetic rats through inhibition of hippocampal oxidative stress. *Behav Pharmacol.* (2015) 26:427–35. doi: 10.1097/fbp.0000000000000143
9. Kang HJ, Voleti B, Hajszan T, Rajkowska G, Stockmeier CA, Licznerski P, et al. Decreased expression of synapse-related genes and loss of synapses in major depressive disorder. *Nat Med.* (2012) 18:1413–7. doi: 10.1038/nm.2886
10. Jia J, Le W. Molecular network of neuronal autophagy in the pathophysiology and treatment of depression. *Neurosci Bull.* (2015) 31:427–34. doi: 10.1007/s12264-015-1548-2
11. Li N, Lee B, Liu RJ, Banasr M, Dwyer JM, Iwata M, et al. mTOR-dependent synapse formation underlies the rapid antidepressant effects of NMDA antagonists. *Science* (2010) 329:959–64. doi: 10.1126/science.1190287
12. Li N, Liu RJ, Dwyer JM, Banasr M, Lee B, Son H, et al. Glutamate N-methyl-D-aspartate receptor antagonists rapidly reverse behavioral and synaptic deficits caused by chronic stress exposure. *Biol Psychiatry* (2011) 69:754–61. doi: 10.1016/j.biopsych.2010.12.015
13. Hu E, Liang P, Spiegelman BM. AdipoQ is a novel adipose-specific gene dysregulated in obesity. *J Biol Chem.* (1996) 271:10697–703.
14. Scherer PE, Williams S, Fogliano M, Baldini G, Lodish HF. A novel serum protein similar to C1q, produced exclusively in adipocytes. *J Biol Chem.* (1995) 270:26746–9.
15. Kos K, Harte AL, da Silva NF, Tonchev A, Chaldakov G, James S, et al. Adiponectin and resistin in human cerebrospinal fluid and expression of adiponectin receptors in the human hypothalamus. *J Clin Endocrinol Metabol.* (2007) 92:1129–36. doi: 10.1210/jc.2006-1841
16. Yau SY, Li A, Hoo RL, Ching YP, Christie BR, Lee TM, et al. Physical exercise-induced hippocampal neurogenesis and antidepressant effects are mediated by the adipocyte hormone adiponectin. *Proc Natl Acad Sci USA.* (2014) 111:15810–5. doi: 10.1073/pnas.1415219111
17. Zhang D, Guo M, Zhang W, Lu XY. Adiponectin stimulates proliferation of adult hippocampal neural stem/progenitor cells through activation of p38 mitogen-activated protein kinase (p38MAPK)/glycogen synthase kinase 3beta (GSK-3beta)/beta-catenin signaling cascade. *J Biol Chem.* (2011) 286:44913–20. doi: 10.1074/jbc.M111.310052
18. Thundyil J, Pavlovski D, Sobey CG, Arumugam TV. Adiponectin receptor signalling in the brain. *Br J Pharmacol.* (2012) 165:313–27. doi: 10.1111/j.1476-5381.2011.01560.x

19. Liu J, Guo M, Zhang D, Cheng SY, Liu M, Ding J, et al. Adiponectin is critical in determining susceptibility to depressive behaviors and has antidepressant-like activity. *Proc Natl Acad Sci USA.* (2012) 109:12248–53. doi: 10.1073/pnas.1202835109
20. Guo M, Li C, Lei Y, Xu S, Zhao D, Lu XY. Role of the adipose PPARgamma-adiponectin axis in susceptibility to stress and depression/anxiety-related behaviors. *Mol Psychiatry* (2017) 22:1056–68. doi: 10.1038/mp.2016.225
21. Slutsky N, Vatarescu M, Haim Y, Goldstein N, Kirshtein B, Harman-Boehm I, et al. Decreased adiponectin links elevated adipose tissue autophagy with adipocyte endocrine dysfunction in obesity. *Int J Obes.* (2016) 40:912–20. doi: 10.1038/ijo.2016.5
22. Weisz F, Piccinin S, Mango D, Ngomba RT, Mercuri NB, Nicoletti F, et al. The role of adiponectin receptors in the regulation of synaptic transmission in the hippocampus. *Synapse* (2017) 71:e21964. doi: 10.1002/syn.21964
23. Steru L, Chermat R, Thierry B, Simon P. The tail suspension test: a new method for screening antidepressants in mice. *Psychopharmacology* (1985) 85:367–70.
24. Bodnoff SR, Suranyi-Cadotte B, Aitken DH, Quirion R, Meaney MJ. The effects of chronic antidepressant treatment in an animal model of anxiety. *Psychopharmacology* (1988) 95:298–302.
25. Cai L, Yan XB, Chen XN, Meng QY, Zhou JN. Chronic all-trans retinoic acid administration induced hyperactivity of HPA axis and behavioral changes in young rats. *Eur Neuropsychopharmacol.* (2010) 20:839–47. doi: 10.1016/j.euroneuro.2010.06.019
26. Huang P, Li C, Fu T, Zhao D, Yi Z, Lu Q, et al. Flupirtine attenuates chronic restraint stress-induced cognitive deficits and hippocampal apoptosis in male mice. *Behav Brain Res.* (2015) 288:1–10. doi: 10.1016/j.bbr.2015.04.004
27. Conrad CD. Chronic stress-induced hippocampal vulnerability: the glucocorticoid vulnerability hypothesis. *Rev Neurosci.* (2008) 19:395–411.
28. Qu K, Lee SW, Bian JS, Low CM, Wong PT. Hydrogen sulfide: neurochemistry and neurobiology. *Neurochem Int.* (2008) 52:155–65. doi: 10.1016/j.neuint.2007.05.016
29. Hu LF, Lu M, Hon Wong PT, Bian JS. Hydrogen sulfide: neurophysiology and neuropathology. *Antioxi Redox Signal.* (2011) 15:405–19. doi: 10.1089/ars.2010.3517
30. Ando S, Kobayashi S, Waki H, Kon K, Fukui F, Tadenuma T, et al. Animal model of dementia induced by entorhinal synaptic damage and partial restoration of cognitive deficits by BDNF and carnitine. *J Neurosci Res.* (2002) 70:519–27. doi: 10.1002/jnr.10443
31. Li L, Whiteman M, Guan YY, Neo KL, Cheng Y, Lee SW, et al. Characterization of a novel, water-soluble hydrogen sulfide-releasing molecule (GYY4137): new insights into the biology of hydrogen sulfide. *Circulation* (2008) 117:2351–60. doi: 10.1161/circulationaha.107.753467
32. Wei HJ, Xu JH, Li MH, Tang JP, Zou W, Zhang P, et al. Hydrogen sulfide inhibits homocysteine-induced endoplasmic reticulum stress and neuronal apoptosis in rat hippocampus via upregulation of the BDNF-TrkB pathway. *Acta Pharmacol Sin.* (2014) 35:707–15. doi: 10.1038/aps.2013.197
33. De Camilli P, Cameron R, Greengard P. Synapsin I (protein I) a nerve terminal-specific phosphoprotein. I. Its general distribution in synapses of the central and peripheral nervous system demonstrated by immunofluorescence in frozen and plastic sections. *J Cell Biol.* (1983) 96:1337–54.
34. Wu LM, Han H, Wang QN, Hou HL, Tong H, Yan XB, et al. Mifepristone repairs region-dependent alteration of synapsin I in hippocampus in rat model of depression. *Neuropsychopharmacology* (2007) 32:2500–10. doi: 10.1038/sj.npp.1301386
35. Iwata M, Shirayama Y, Ishida H, Kawahara R. Hippocampal synapsin I, growth-associated protein-43, and microtubule-associated protein-2 immunoreactivity in learned helplessness rats and antidepressant-treated rats. *Neuroscience* (2006) 141:1301–13. doi: 10.1016/j.neuroscience.2006.04.060
36. Zhuang F, Li M, Gao X, Wang Y, Wang D, Ma X, et al. The antidepressant-like effect of alarin is related to TrkB-mTOR signaling and synaptic plasticity. *Behav Brain Res.* (2016) 313:158–71. doi: 10.1016/j.bbr.2016.06.057
37. Sarkar A, Kabbaj M. Sex differences in effects of ketamine on behavior, spine density, and synaptic proteins in socially isolated rats. *Biol. Psychiatry* (2016) 80:448–56. doi: 10.1016/j.biopsych.2015.12.025
38. Bredesen DE, Rao RV, Mehlen P. Cell death in the nervous system. *Nature* (2006) 443:796–802. doi: 10.1038/nature05293
39. Wang L, Guo LL, Wang LH, Zhang GX, Shang J, Murao K et al. Oxidative stress and substance P mediate psychological stress-induced autophagy and delay of hair growth in mice. *Arch Dermatol Res.* (2015) 307:171–81. doi: 10.1007/s00403-014-1521-3
40. Denk MC, Rewerts C, Holsboer F, Erhardt-Lehmann A, Turck CW. Monitoring ketamine treatment response in a depressed patient via peripheral mammalian target of rapamycin activation. *Am J Psychiatry* (2011) 168:751–2. doi: 10.1176/appi.ajp.2011.11010128
41. Kadowaki T, Yamauchi T, Kubota N. The physiological and pathophysiological role of adiponectin and adiponectin receptors in the peripheral tissues and CNS. *FEBS Lett.* (2008) 582:74–80. doi: 10.1016/j.febslet.2007.11.070
42. Leo R, Di Lorenzo G, Tesauro M, Cola C, Fortuna E, Zanasi M, et al. Decreased plasma adiponectin concentration in major depression. *Neuroscience Lett.* (2006) 407:211–3. doi: 10.1016/j.neulet.2006.08.043
43. Machado-Vieira R, Gold PW, Luckenbaugh DA, Ballard ED, Richards EM, Henter ID, et al. The role of adipokines in the rapid antidepressant effects of ketamine. *Mol Psychiatry* (2017) 22:127–33. doi: 10.1038/mp.2016.36

4

Yi-nao-jie-yu Prescription Exerts a Positive Effect on Neurogenesis by Regulating Notch Signals in the Hippocampus of Post-stroke Depression Rats

Huiling Tian[1], Xiaoli Li[1], Qisheng Tang[1], Wen Zhang[1], Qingmeng Li[1], Xinyue Sun[1], Ruizhen Zhao[1], Chongyang Ma[2], Haipeng Liu[1], Yushan Gao[2] and Fei Han[1]*

[1] *Department of Encephalopathy, The Third Affiliated Hospital, Beijing University of Chinese Medicine, Beijing, China,*
[2] *Research Institute, Beijing University of Chinese Medicine, Beijing, China*

***Correspondence:**
Xiaoli Li
tigerlxl2002@163.com

Post-stroke depression (PSD) is one of the most frequent complications of stroke. The Yi-nao-jie-yu prescription (YNJYP) is an herbal prescription widely used as a therapeutic agent against PSD in traditional Chinese medicine. Disruption of adult neurogenesis has attracted attention as a potential cause of cognitive pathophysiology in neurological and psychiatric disorders. The Notch signaling pathway plays an important role in neurogenesis. This study investigated the effects of YNJYP on adult neurogenesis and explored its underlying molecular mechanism in a rat model of PSD that is established by middle cerebral artery occlusion and accompanied by chronic immobilization stress for 1 week. At 2, 4, and 8 weeks, depression-like behavior was evaluated by a forced swim test (FST) and sucrose consumption test (SCT). Neurogenesis was observed by double immunofluorescence staining. Notch signals were detected by real-time polymerase chain reaction. The results show that, at 4 weeks, the immobility time in the FST for rats in the PSD group increased and the sucrose preference in the SCT decreased compared with that in the stroke group. Therefore, YNJYP decreased the immobility time and increased the sucrose preference of the PSD rats. Further, PSD interfered with neurogenesis and decreased the differentiation toward neurons of newly born cells in the hippocampal dentate gyrus, and increased the differentiation toward astrocytes, effects that were reversed by YNJYP, particularly at 4 weeks. At 2 weeks, compared with the stroke group, expression of target gene *Hes5* mRNA transcripts in the PSD group decreased, but increased after treatment with YNJYP. At 4 weeks, compared with the stroke group, the expression of Notch receptor *Notch1* mRNA transcripts in the PSD group decreased, but also increased after treatment with YNJYP. Overall, this study indicated that disturbed nerve regeneration, including the increased numbers of astrocytes and decrease numbers of neurons, is a mechanism of PSD, and Notch signaling genes dynamically regulate neurogenesis. Moreover, YNJYP can relieve depressive behavior in PSD rats, and exerts a positive effect on neurogenesis by dynamically regulating the expression of Notch signaling genes.

Keywords: post-stroke depression, Yi-nao-jie-yu prescription, notch signaling, neurogenesis, forced swim test, sucrose consumption test

INTRODUCTION

Post-stroke depression is one of the most frequent complications of stroke, with an estimated prevalence as high as 80% (1). It often takes a chronic course, and is associated with increased morbidity and mortality, and a poorer functional outcome (2–4). Although risk factors, including metabolic factors, impairment of cognitive functions, and social factors, are associated with PSD (5), its pathophysiology remains unclear.

Recently, disruption of adult neurogenesis has attracted attention as a potential cause of cognitive pathophysiology in neurological and psychiatric disorders, such as depression, anxiety, schizophrenia, and bipolar disorder. Numerous studies have demonstrated that stress inhibits neurogenesis in the dentate gyrus (DG) of the hippocampus. Conversely, antidepressants are known to promote adult hippocampal neurogenesis (6). While the regulatory mechanism at the molecular level remains obscure, Notch signaling has been conserved throughout evolution, and plays a fundamental role in neuronal progenitor maintenance and subsequent control of differentiation (7, 8). Gaining a clearer understanding of pathogenesis is essential for the development of better treatments.

The Chinese herbal preparation known as Yi-nao-jie-yu prescription (YNJYP) has been shown to be effective for both body function recovery and the treatment of depression in patients with PSD. In animal studies, the brain damage in PSD model rats was greater than that in stroke model rats, and YNJYP was able to reverse this effect (9). In this study, we hypothesized that disruption of neurogenesis is a pathogenic mechanism of PSD, and that alteration of Notch signaling is the therapeutic mechanism of the beneficial effects of YNJYP at the molecular level. Dynamic changes in neurogenesis and fluctuations in Notch signals were observed in the hippocampus of PSD model rats, and the mechanism of YNJYP for the treatment of PSD was explored.

MATERIALS AND METHODS

Animals

Adult male Sprague-Dawley rats aged 7–9 weeks (300–320 g) were purchased from Vital River Laboratory Animal Technology (No. SCXK2012-0001). Five animals were housed per cage at 23 ± 3°C and a humidity of 45 ± 5%, under a 12-h light/dark cycle (lights on at 8:00 a.m., lights off at 8:00 p.m.), and received standard sterile food and water *ad libitum*. Animals were allowed to acclimatize for 1 week before the study. All procedures were approved and performed according to the guidelines of the Beijing University of Chinese Medicine Animal Care and Use Committee. Experimental protocols were approved by the Animal Experimentation Ethics Committee of Beijing University of Chinese Medicine. Efforts were made to minimize the number of animals used and the suffering of experimental animals.

Combined Middle Cerebral Artery Occlusion and Depression Model

All surgeries, behavioral testing, and histological analysis were performed by a single investigator. Animals were numbered upon arrival at the animal facility, and randomly divided into a sham operation (Sham) group and a surgery group. Left middle cerebral artery occlusion (MCAO) was performed in the surgery group, using a modification of the technique described in our previous study (9). The animals were intraperitoneally anesthetized with sodium pentobarbital (50 mg/kg) for all surgical procedures. Subsequently, MCAO was performed using a monofilament suture with a rounded tip that was introduced into the internal carotid artery carefully and advanced approximately to the origin of the middle cerebral artery. The monofilament was left *in situ*, and withdrawn after 2 h for reperfusion. The temporalis muscle temperature was maintained at 37.0–37.5°C by surface heating until the rats recovered from anesthesia. After recovery from anesthesia, the neurological status of the rats was assessed according to a 5-point scale described by Longa et al. (10). A post-operative care plan was employed to help prevent weight loss and dehydration over the first week after surgery. This included the supply of paracetamol in drinking water (120 mg/kg), sub-cutaneous injections of saline (days 1–3), and provision of soft food. For the first week after surgery, animals were housed in a recovery room where they could be closely monitored. After the seventh day post-surgery, animals were returned to general holding rooms. Additional animals were allocated to longer recovery timepoints to allow for deaths and to ensure enough animals survived up to each timepoint. Data from animals which did not reach their designated endpoint was not included in the analysis.

Finally, a total of 159 rats were used in this study; of these, 27 rats were in the Sham group. The 108 survivors with neurological scores of 1–3 were randomly divided into four groups as follows: stroke group (n=27), PSD group (n = 27), fluoxetine hydrochloride (FXT) group (n = 27), and YNJYP group (n = 27), for further study. Rats were allowed 1 week to recover from the MCAO operation. To establish a PSD model, rats in PSD, FXT, and YNJYP groups were subjected to isolation housing in combination with chronic unexpected mild stress [behavioral restriction: immobilized on wooden shelves, as described by Chen et al. (11), for 2 h at any time of the day, consecutively for 1 week].

YNJYP Preparation and Treatment

Granules of YNJYP were provided by the Pharmacy Department of the Third Affiliated Hospital of Beijing University of Chinese Medicine. Six different Chinese medical herbs were included in the YNJYP: 30 g Manyprickle *Acanthopanax* sp. root, 10 g *Radix curcumae*, 15 g Fructus *Schisandrae chinensis*, 10 g Fructus *Gardeniae* sp., 15 g *Salviae miltiorrhizae*, and 15 g *Rhizoma chuanxiong*. The granules were dissolved in 100 ml of distilled water and maintained at 4°C for further use. Rats in the sham, stroke, and PSD groups were gavaged with 10 ml/kg saline (0.9%).

Abbreviations: BrdU, 5-bromo-2-deoxyuridine; DG, dentate gyrus; FST, forced swim test; FXT, fluoxetine hydrochloride; GFAP, glial fibrillary acidic protein; MCAO, middle cerebral artery occlusion; NeuN, neuronal nuclear antigen; NSC, neural stem cell; PSD, post-stroke depression; SCT, sucrose consumption test; YNJYP, Yi-nao-jie-yu prescription.

Rats in the FXT group were gavaged with 2.33 $mgkg^{-1}day^{-1}$ of FXT (0943A; Patheon France, Jiangsu, People's Republic of China), and the YNJYP rats were gavaged with 9.92 g/kg YNJYP once daily, following the MCAO operation. At 2, 4, or 8 weeks after the simulated stroke, rats were sacrificed after anesthetization for further study.

BrdU Injections

For the analysis of neurogenesis, rats ($n = 3$) in each group received an intraperitoneal injection of 50 mg/kg of the thymidine analog 5-bromo-2-deoxyuridine (BrdU) (b5002; Sigma, St. Louis, MO, USA,), freshly prepared at a concentration of 10 mg/ml dissolved in sterile 0.9% saline solution. The injections were started from the MCAO operation, twice a day for the first 3 days, then twice per week, and finally, once every 8 h for the last 2 days before the rats were sacrificed.

Forced Swim Test

The procedure for the forced swim test (FST) was as described by Veena et al. (12). Rats were subjected to the FST at 2, 4, and 8 weeks. Briefly, animals were subjected to a trial during which they were forced to swim in a plastic bucket (60 cm high, 45 cm in diameter) filled with water (23–25°C) up to a height of 40 cm, so that the rats could not support themselves by touching the bottom with their feet. After 5 min, the rats were removed from the bucket, dried with a towel, and kept warm under a lamp in their home cages. The test was followed by water and food deprivation for 24 h. The analyst was blind to the groups, and recorded the swimming time, during which the rats were swimming along the wall or actively attempting to climb it. A rat was judged as immobile whenever it remained floating passively in the water and made only the movements necessary to keep its nose or head above the water. Rats were counted as mobile if they moved their forepaws or supported themselves by pressing their paws against the wall of the cylinder. After the test, dry towels were used to keep the rats warm and dry them gently.

Sucrose Consumption Test

The sucrose consumption test (SCT) was conducted 2, 4, and 8 weeks after the simulated stroke. Rats were tested for sucrose consumption as described previously (12). Animals were housed individually throughout the test duration, and after water deprivation for 24 h, were presented simultaneously with two bottles in the home cage, one containing a 1% sucrose solution and the other containing standard drinking water, for 60 min. The volumes of water and sucrose-water intake were measured. To prevent a preference for position from affecting the results, the locations of the two bottles (right/left) were switched during this period. The amount of liquid remaining in each bottle was measured at the end of the testing period. The sucrose preference score was expressed as a percentage of total fluid intake.

Double Immunofluorescence Staining

Brains of the three rats in each group that received BrdU injections were fixed in paraformaldehyde after cardiac perfusion. After 24 h, 30% sucrose was added, and after the brains sank to the bottom of the bottle, they were embedded in optimal cutting temperature compound, frozen, and sectioned. Proteinase K was added at 37°C after the brain sections were washed three times with phosphate-buffered saline for 5 min each. Then, 30 min later, the following primary antibodies were added: BrdU (ab115874, mouse, 1:150; Abcam, Cambridge, MA, USA) and nestin (ab92391, rabbit, 1:250; Abcam), BrdU and neuronal nuclear antigen (NeuN) (ab177487, rabbit, 1:1200; Abcam), or BrdU and glial fibrillary acidic protein (GFAP) (16825-1-AP, rabbit, 1:1200; Proteintech, Chicago, IL, USA). After incubation overnight at 4°C, the secondary antibodies tetramethylrhodamine isothiocyanate (ZF-0313, goat anti-rat IgG, 1:200; ZSGB-Bio, Beijing, China) and fluorescein isothiocyanate (ZF-0311, goat anti-rabbit IgG, 1:200; ZSGB-Bio) were added. Following incubation for 2 h at room temperature, 80 μL 4′,6-diamidino-2-phenylindole (bw-d0010; GeneBio, Beijing, China) was added to the sections. A laser scanning confocal microscope (FV1000, Olympus Corporation, Tokyo, Japan) was used to view the hippocampal DG.

Real-Time PCR

The left hippocampus ($n = 6$) was dissected and frozen at −80°C. Total RNA from the hippocampus was isolated using Trizol reagent, according to the manufacturer's protocol (DP405-02; Tiangen Biotech Co., Ltd., Beijing, China). The gene primers were as follows:

Gene	Forward primer	Reverse primer
Notch1	5′-TGGATGCCGCTGA CCTACG-3′	5′-TGGATGCCGCTGACCT ACG-3′
Jagged1	5′-TTAGTAAACGGGATG GGAACAGC-3′	5′-AAGCAACAGACCCAAG CCACT-3′
Hes1	5′-TTGAGCCAACTG AAAACACTGATT- 3′	5′-GTGCTTCACTGTCATTTC CAGAAT-3′
Hes5	5′-GATGCTCAGTCCC AAGGAGAAAA-3′	5′-CCACGAGTAACCCT CGCTGTAGT-3′
GAPDH	5′-CCTTCCGTGTTC CTACCCC-3′	5′-GCCCAGGATGCCC TTTAGTG-3′

The basic protocol for real-time polymerase chain reaction (PCR) was an initial denaturation at 95°C for 30 s, followed by 40 cycles of amplification. For cDNA amplification, cycles consisted of 95°C for 10 s and 60°C for 60 s. The final elongation step was from 60 to 99°C, at a rate of 0.05°C/s. The SYBR green signal was then detected using a real-time PCR machine (ABI7500; Applied Biosystems, Waltham, MA, USA). The PCR products were analyzed by gel electrophoresis and melting curve analysis to confirm specific amplifications. The mRNA expression levels were normalized to those of *GAPDH*. Transcript levels were quantified using the 2-ΔΔCt-value method.

Statistical Analyses

Data were expressed as means±standard deviation, and analyzed using SPSS 20.0 statistical software (IBM, Armonk, NY, USA). Differences between groups were tested using one-way analysis of variance followed by the *post hoc* Fisher's least significant difference test or Kruskal–Wallis test followed by Dunn's test if the data were not normally distributed. Threshold for statistical significance was set to $P < 0.05$.

RESULTS

Effects of YNJYP on the Depressive Behavior of PSD Rats

Depression-like behavior was evaluated by FST and SCT. The immobility time in FST was used to assess the degree of despair in rats and the sucrose preference in the SCT of rats was used to reflect the rat's desire for good things. One way analysis of variance showed a significant difference in the immobility time ($n = 6$; 2 weeks: $F = 3.973$, $P = 0.012$; 4 weeks: $F = 9.054$, $P < 0.001$; 8 weeks: $F = 8.085$, $P < 0.001$; **Figure 1A**) and sucrose preference ($n = 6$; 2 weeks: $F = 12.198$, $P = 0.431$; 4 weeks: $F = 11.875$, $P = 0.039$; 8 weeks: $F = 5.409$, $P = 0.003$; **Figure 1B**) in the 5 groups. At 4 weeks, the immobility time in the FST for rats in the PSD group increased compared with that in the stroke group, and the difference was statistically significant ($P < 0.01$). Interestingly, YNJYP decreased the immobility time of the PSD rats, and at 4 and 8 weeks, the differences were statistically significant ($P < 0.01$ for both, **Figure 1A**). The sucrose preference in the SCT of rats in the PSD group decreased compared with that of rats in the stroke group, and at 4 and 8 weeks, and the differences were statistically significant ($P < 0.01$ for both). However, YNJYP increased the sucrose preference of the PSD rats at 4, and 8 weeks, and the differences were statistically significant ($P < 0.01$ for both, **Figure 1B**).

Neurogenesis

Relationship Between BrdU Labeling and Nestin Immunoreactivity

To observe the proliferation of neural stem cells (NSCs), we performed double-labeling at 2, 4, and 8 weeks with antibodies against BrdU (red), a marker for DNA replication in newly formed cells (13), and nestin (green), a neural progenitor-specific marker (14). **Figures 2A–C** shows that, at 2, 4, and 8 weeks, rats in the stroke group showed an increase in the number of BrdU-labeled (red) newly formed cells and nestin-labeled (green) NSCs in the DG, compared with the sham group. Nestin-positive or BrdU-positive cells could be observed in the PSD, FXT, and YNJYP groups, but only a few cells were positive for both nestin and BrdU. **Figure 2D** shows that the numbers of nestin-positive cells at the observed DG zone of rats in the five groups at 2, 4, and 8 weeks were not statistically significantly different ($F = 2.274$, $P = 0.090$; $F = 2.563$, $P = 0.063$; and $F = 1.314$, $P = 0.292$, respectively). **Figure 2E** shows that the numbers of cells double-positive for nestin and BrdU at the observed DG zone of rats in the five groups at 2, 4, and 8 weeks were not statistically significantly different ($F = 0.754$, $P = 0.565$; $F = 2.086$, $P = 0.113$; and $F = 0.488$, $P = 0.745$, respectively).

Relationship Between BrdU Labeling and NeuN Immunoreactivity

To observe the differentiation of newly formed cells toward neurons, we performed double-labeling with antibodies against BrdU (red) and NeuN (green), a neuron-specific protein (15). **Figures 3A–C** shows that only a few cells double-positive for BrdU and NeuN were observed in rats in the sham, stroke, and PSD groups, but after treatment with FXT or YNJYP more BrdU-positive cells appeared near the DG, and these cells were also NeuN-positive at 2, 4, and 8 weeks. At 2 and 4 weeks, newly formed neurons appeared outside the granule cell layer, and had migrated into the granule cell layer at 8 weeks. **Figure 3D** shows that, compared with the sham group, fewer NeuN-positive cells appeared at the observed DG zone of rats in the stroke group at 2, 4, and 8 weeks, and this difference was statistically significant ($P < 0.01$, $P < 0.01$, and $P < 0.05$, respectively). More NeuN-positive cells appeared in rats in that YNJYP group than in rats in the PSD group, and the difference was statistically significant ($P < 0.05$, $P < 0.05$, and $P < 0.01$, respectively). **Figure 3E** shows that, compared with the sham group, more cells double-positive for NeuN and BrdU appeared at the DG of rats in the stroke

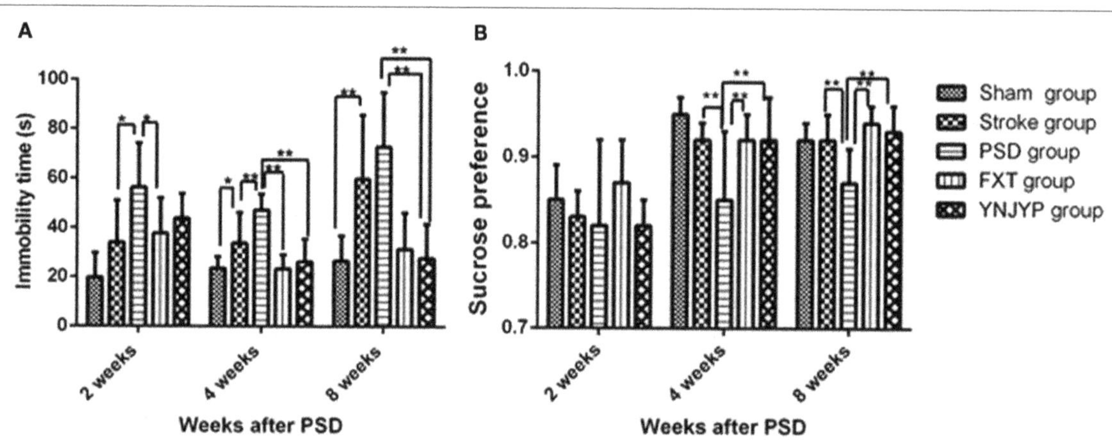

FIGURE 1 | (A) Effect of treatments on the immobility time of PSD rats in the forced swim test. **(B)** Effect of treatments on the sucrose preference of PSD rats in the sucrose consumption test. Data are presented as mean ± standard error of the mean. $n = 6$; $^{*}P < 0.05$, $^{**}P < 0.01$. Sham group, sham operation group; PSD group, post-stroke depression group; FXT group, Fluoxetine hydrochloride capsules group; YNJYP group, Yi-nao-jie-yu prescription group.

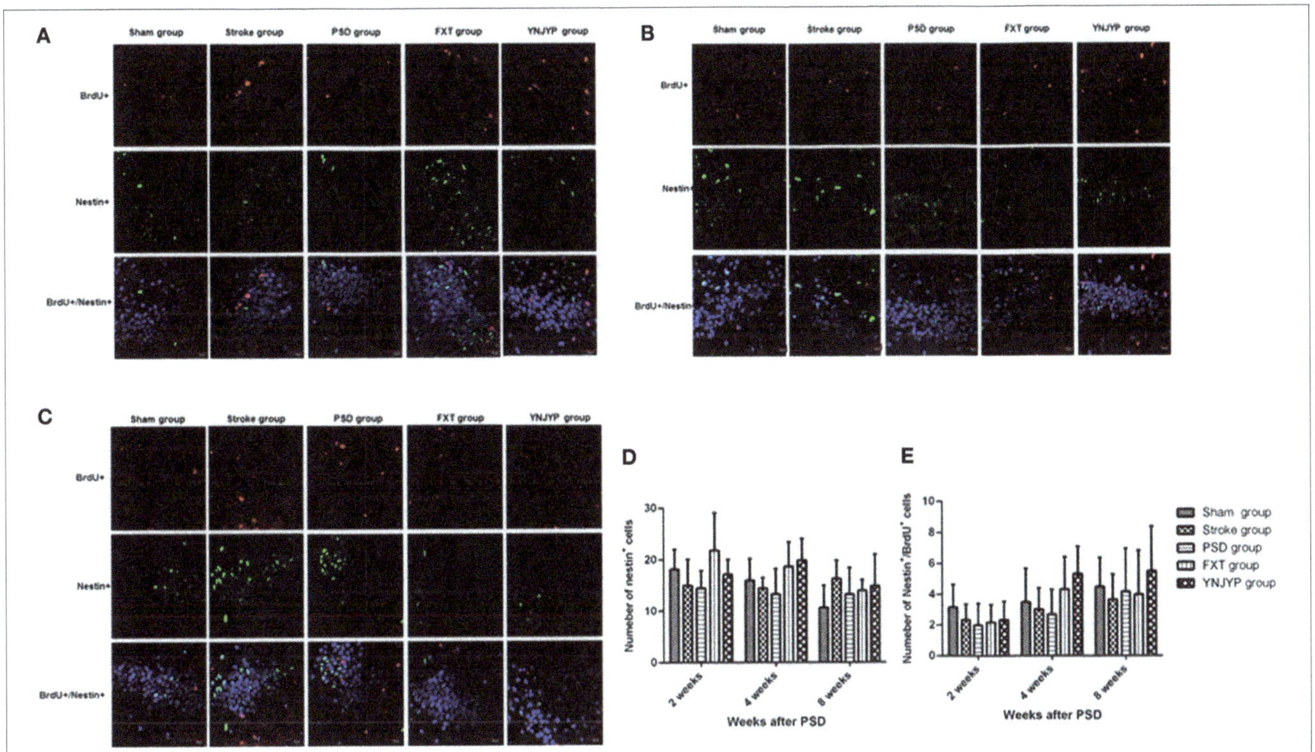

FIGURE 2 | Effects of treatments on neural stem cell proliferation in PSD rats at 2, 4, and 8 weeks post-stroke. To observe the proliferation of neural stem cells (NSCs), newly formed cells were labeled with BrdU (red) and NSCs were labeled with nestin (green) at 2, 4, and 8 weeks post-stroke. Cell nuclei were labeled with 4′,6-diamidino-2-phenylindole (blue). **(A)** At 2 weeks post-stroke. **(B)** At 4 weeks post-stroke. **(C)** At 8 weeks post-stroke. Scale bar = 30 μm. **(D)** The number of nestin-positive cells at the observed dentate gyrus zone (at 2 weeks: $F = 2.274$, $P = 0.090$; at 4 weeks: $F = 2.563$, $P = 0.063$; at 4 weeks: $F = 1.314$, $P = 0.292$). **(E)** The number of cells double-positive for nestin and BrdU appeared at the dentate gyrus (at 2 weeks: $F = 0.754$, $P = 0.565$; at 4 weeks: $F = 2.086$, $P = 0.113$; at 8 weeks: $F = 0.488$, $P = 0.745$). BrdU, 5-bromo-2-deoxyuridine; PSD, post-stroke depression; FXT, fluoxetine hydrochloride capsules; YNJYP, Yi-nao-jie-yu prescription.

group at 2, 4, and 8 weeks, and the difference was statistically significant ($P < 0.01$, $P < 0.01$, and $P < 0.01$, respectively). Further, more cells double-positive for NeuN and BrdU appeared in rats in the YNJYP group than in rats in the PSD group, and the difference was statistically significant ($P < 0.01$, $P < 0.01$, and $P < 0.01$, respectively). These results suggested that more newly formed neurons appeared at the DG after MCAO operation, and YNJYP could increase the number of newly formed neurons at the DG of PSD rats. However, not only the total number of neurons but also the number of newly formed neurons in PSD rats was not statistically significantly different from that of stroke rats. This suggested that the decrease in the number of neurons may be not the key factor for the depressive behavior of PSD rats.

Relationship Between BrdU Labeling and GFAP Immunoreactivity

To observe the differentiation of newly formed cells toward astrocytes, we performed double-labeling with antibodies against BrdU (red) and GFAP (green), an astrocyte-specific marker (16). **Figures 4A–C** shows that more GFAP-positive cells and cells double-positive for GFAP and BrdU appeared at the observed DG zone of the PSD rats than that of rats in the stroke group at 2, 4, and 8 weeks. However, fewer GFAP-positive cells and cells double-positive for GFAP and BrdU appeared at the observed DG zone of rats in the FXT or YNJYP group. At 2 weeks, in rats in the PSD group, astrocytes appeared outside the granule cell layer, and had migrated into the granule cell layer at 4 and 8 weeks. **Figure 4D** shows that the PSD rats showed a statistically significant increase in the number of GFAP positive cells at the observed DG zone at 2 and 4 weeks compared with rats in the stroke group ($P < 0.01$ for both). Both FXT and YNJYP decreased the number of astrocytes at the observed DG zone at 2, 4, and 8 weeks ($P < 0.01$, $P < 0.01$, and $P < 0.01$, respectively). **Figure 4E** shows that the PSD rats showed a statistically significant increase in the number of cells double-positive for GFAP and BrdU at the observed DG zone at 2 and 4 weeks compared with rats in the stroke group ($P < 0.05$, $P < 0.05$, and $P < 0.01$, respectively). Both FXT and YNJYP decreased the number of cells double-positive for GFAP and BrdU at the observed DG zone at 2, 4, and 8 weeks ($P < 0.01$, $P < 0.01$, and $P < 0.01$, respectively). This suggested that the increase in the number of newly formed astrocytes may be the key factor for the depressive behavior of PSD rats.

Notch Signaling Pathway

Real-time PCR was used to measure *Notch1*, *Jagged1*, *Hes1*, and *Hes5* mRNA transcript levels in the hippocampus. Standard curves were generated for the *Notch1*, *Jagged1*, *Hes1*, *Hes5*, and

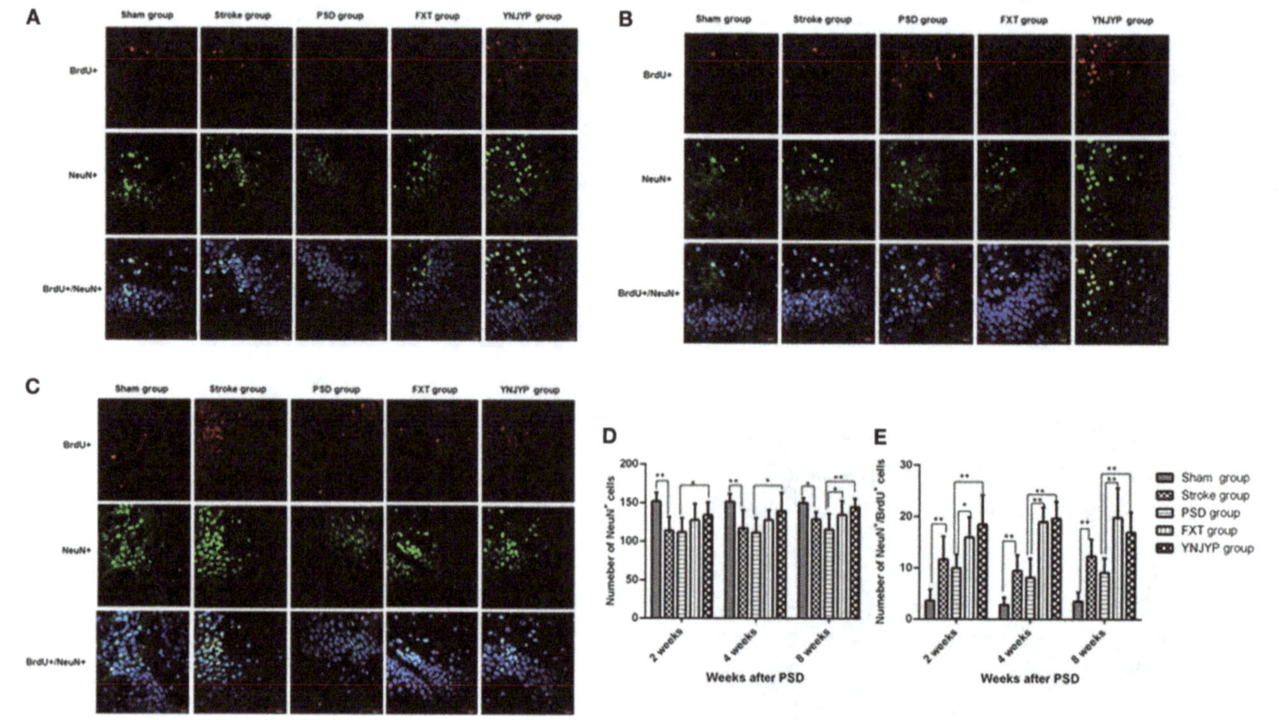

FIGURE 3 | Effects of treatments on differentiation of newly formed cells toward neurons in PSD rats at 2, 4, and 8 weeks post-stroke. To observe the differentiation of newly formed cells toward neurons, recently divided cells were labeled with BrdU (red) and neurons were labeled with NeuN (green) at 2, 4, and 8 weeks. Cell nuclei were labeled with 4′,6-diamidino-2-phenylindole (blue). **(A)** At 2 weeks post-stroke. **(B)** At 4 weeks post-stroke. **(C)** At 8 weeks post-stroke. Scale bar = 30 μm. **(D)** The number of NeuN-positive cells at the observed dentate gyrus zone (at 2 weeks: $F = 5.294$, $P = 0.003$; at 4 weeks: $F = 4.543$, $P = 0.007$, at 8 weeks: $F = 5.543$, $P = 0.002$). **(E)** The number of cells double-positive for NeuN and BrdU at the observed dentate gyrus zone (at 2 weeks: $F = 12.539$, $P = 0.001$; at 4 weeks: $F = 36.158$, $P < 0.001$, at 8 weeks: $F = 17.668$, $P < 0.001$). $n = 6$; $^{*}P < 0.05$, $^{**}P < 0.01$. BrdU, 5-bromo-2-deoxyuridine; PSD, post-stroke depression; FXT, fluoxetine hydrochloride capsules; YNJYP, Yi-nao-jie-yu prescription.

Gapdh genes. Melting curve analysis confirmed no primer dimers in the PCR products.

Notch1 mRNA Transcript Expression in the Hippocampus

Figure 5A shows the *Notch1* mRNA transcript expression in the hippocampus at 2, 4, and 8 weeks ($n = 6$; 2 weeks: $F = 0.413$, $P = 0.797$; 4 weeks: $F = 10.950$, $P < 0.001$; 8 weeks: $F = 12.006$, $P = 0.071$). At 4 weeks, the expression of *Notch1* mRNA transcripts for rats in the PSD group was lower than that for rats in the stroke group ($P < 0.01$), but significantly increased after treatment with FXT or YNJYP ($P < 0.01$). There were no significant differences between the YNJYP and FXT groups ($P > 0.05$). At 2 or 8 weeks, levels of *Notch1* mRNA transcripts of rats in the five groups were not statistically significantly different ($P > 0.05$).

Jagged1 mRNA Transcript Expression in the Hippocampus

Figure 5B shows the *Jagged1* mRNA transcript expression in the hippocampus at 2, 4, and 8 weeks ($n = 6$; 2 weeks: $F = 1.154$, $P = 0.355$; 4 weeks: $F = 3.149$, $P = 0.032$; 8 weeks: $F = 4.582$, $P = 0.007$). At 2 weeks, the levels of *Jagged1* mRNA transcripts of rats in the five groups were not statistically significantly different ($P > 0.05$). At 4 weeks, compared with the sham group, the expression of *Jagged1* mRNA transcripts of rats in the stroke group were higher ($P < 0.01$). *Jagged1* mRNA transcript levels in the YNJYP group were higher than those in the FXT group ($P < 0.05$). At 8 weeks, the expression of *Jagged1* mRNA transcripts in the PSD group was higher than that in the stroke group ($P < 0.01$). There were no statistically significant differences between the YNJYP and PSD groups ($P > 0.05$). These data show that YNJYP was unable to reduce the expression of *Jagged1* mRNA transcripts in the PSD group at 8 weeks.

Hes1 mRNA Transcript Expression in the Hippocampus

Figure 5C shows the *Hes1* mRNA transcript expression in the hippocampus at 2, 4, and 8 weeks ($n = 6$; 2 weeks: $F = 0.113$, $P = 0.977$; 4 weeks: $F = 4.688$, $P = 0.006$; 8 weeks: $F = 2.500$, $P = 0.068$). At 4 weeks, the expression levels of *Hes1* mRNA transcripts of rats in the stroke and PSD groups were similar ($P > 0.05$). After treatment by YNJYP, levels of *Hes1* mRNA transcript expression in the PSD rats increased ($P < 0.01$). At 2 or 8 weeks, levels of *Hes1* mRNA transcripts of rats in the five groups were similar, and showed no statistically significant differences ($P > 0.05$).

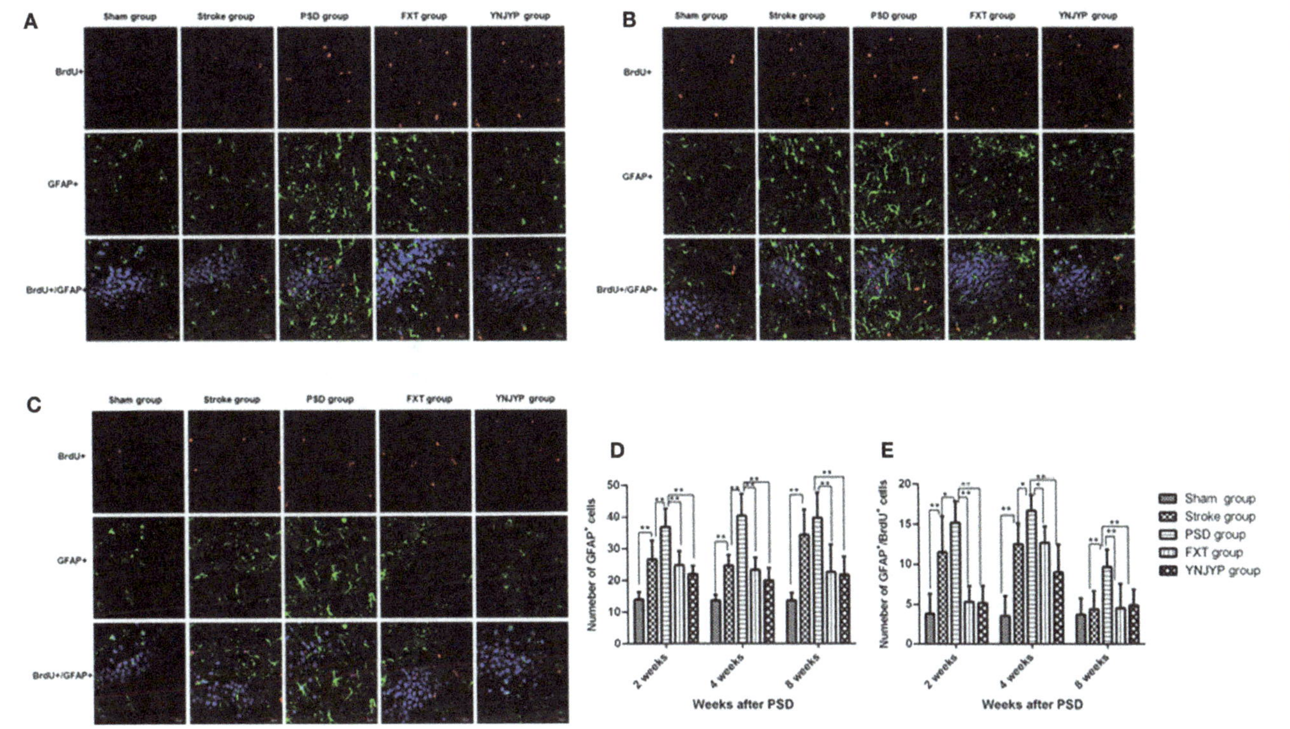

FIGURE 4 | Effects of treatments on differentiation of newly formed cells toward astrocytes in PSD rats at 2, 4, and 8 weeks post-stroke. To observe the differentiation of newly formed cells toward astrocytes, newly formed cells were labeled with BrdU (red) and astrocytes were labeled with GFAP (green) at 2, 4, and 8 weeks. Cell nuclei were labeled with 4′,6-diamidino-2-phenylindole (blue). **(A)** At 2 weeks post-stroke. **(B)** At 4 weeks post-stroke. **(C)** At 8 weeks post-stroke. Scale bar = 30 μm. **(D)** The number of GFAP-positive cells at the observed dentate gyrus zone at 2, 4, and 8 weeks (at 2 weeks: $F = 20.579$, $P < 0.001$; at 4 weeks: $F = 31.673$, $P < 0.001$, at 8 weeks: $F = 13.733$, $P < 0.001$). **(E)** The number of cells double-positive for GFAP and BrdU at the observed dentate gyrus zone (at 2 weeks: $F = 17.182$, $P < 0.001$; at 4 weeks: $F = 22.852$, $P < 0.001$; at 8 weeks: $F = 6.274$, $P = 0.001$). $n = 6$; $^{*}P < 0.05$, $^{*}P < 0.01$. BrdU, 5-bromo-2-deoxyuridine; PSD, post-stroke depression; FXT, fluoxetine hydrochloride capsules; YNJYP, Yi-nao-jie-yu prescription.

Hes5 mRNA Transcript Expression in the Hippocampus

Figure 5D shows the *Hes1* mRNA transcript expression in the hippocampus at 2, 4, and 8 weeks ($n = 6$; 2 weeks: $F = 4.646$, $P = 0.006$; 4 weeks: $F = 3.132$, $P = 0.032$; 8 weeks: $F = 3.358$, $P = 0.025$). At 2 weeks, levels of *Hes5* mRNA transcripts of rats in the PSD group were significantly lower than those in the stroke group ($P < 0.01$). After treatment by FXT or YNJYP, the expression levels of *Hes5* mRNA transcript of rats in the PSD group increased significantly ($P < 0.01$). At 4 weeks, *Hes5* mRNA transcript levels in the YNJYP group were lower than those of the FXT group ($P < 0.05$). At 8 weeks, levels of *Hes5* mRNA transcripts of rats in the five groups were not statistically significantly different ($P > 0.05$).

DISCUSSION

In this study, MCAO was used as a rat model of stroke, and isolation housing combined with chronic immobilization stress was used as a model of post-stroke depression. Compared with the stroke group, PSD rats showed increased immobility time and decreased consumption of sucrose water at 4 weeks. This difference was statistically significant. Therefore, the PSD model used in our study appears to be valid, and at 4 weeks, the PSD-related changes were observed.

According to traditional Chinese medicine, PSD pathogenesis involves kidney deficiency, liver-Qi stagnation, and blood stasis (17). Based on these concepts, YNJYP was created to reinforce the kidneys and regulate the liver-Qi, as well as reduce phlegm and promote blood circulation. It has been proven to be effective for both body function recovery and the antidepressant treatment of patients with PSD. In this study, the effect of YNJYP was evaluated in comparison with FXT, and it proved effective against PSD (18) at 2, 4, and 8 weeks. Our findings demonstrated that YNJYP significantly reversed the depressive behavior of PSD rats in the FST and SCT. However, the therapeutic mechanism underlying the activity of YNJYP remains unclear. Therefore, we explored the mechanism of YNJYP activity by studying neurogenesis and Notch signaling.

Neurogenesis includes the proliferation of NSCs, differentiation (mainly toward neurons and astrocytes), and functional integration of newly formed cells. It is accepted that the proliferation of NSCs and differentiation of the newly formed cells into neurons can contribute to the reversal of depressive behavior and stress-induced cognitive dysfunction. Some newly formed cells that migrate into the granule cell

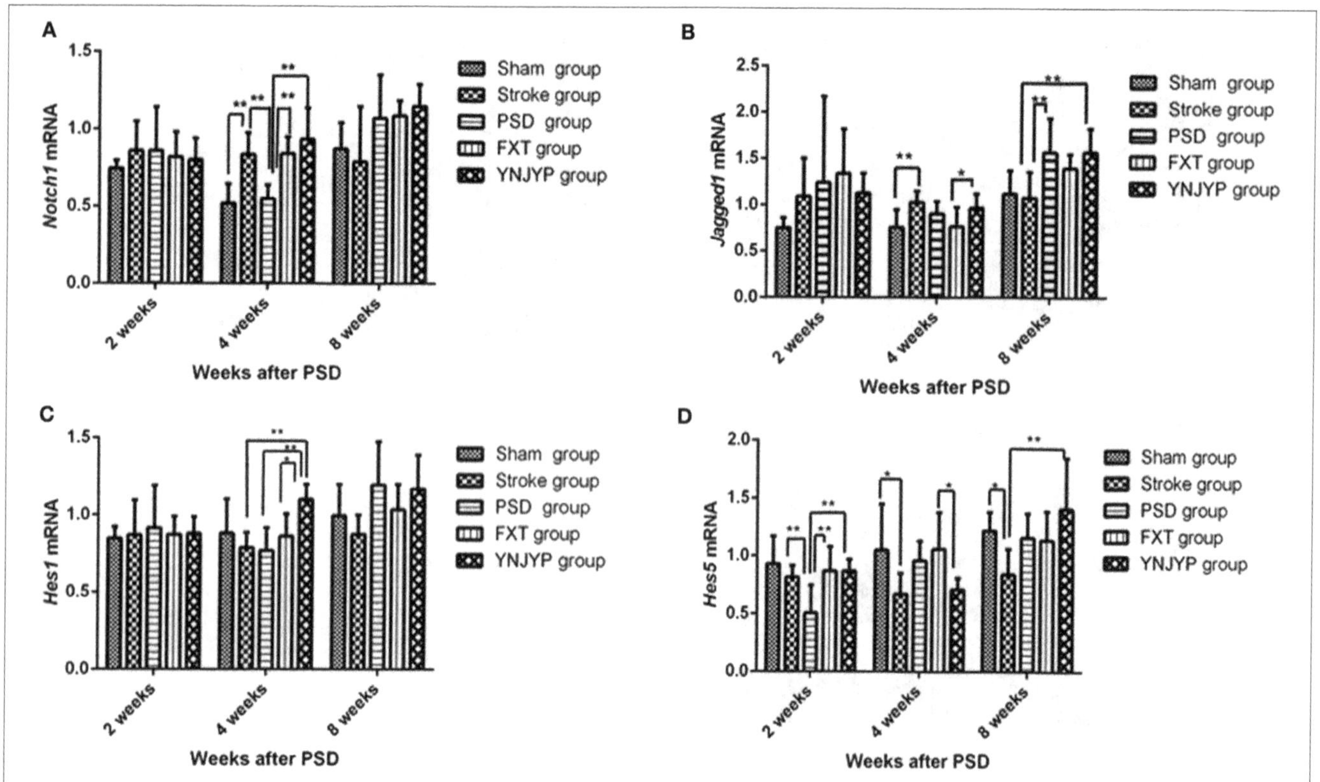

FIGURE 5 | Effects of treatments on the expression levels of *Notch1, Jagged1, Hes1*, and *Hes5* mRNA transcripts in the hippocampus of PSD rats at 2, 4, and 8 weeks post-stroke. Real-time polymerase chain reaction was performed to investigate changes in the expression of *Notch1, Jagged1, Hes1*, and *Hes5* mRNA transcripts in PSD rats and the effects of YNJYP on them ($n = 6$ per group); $^*P < 0.05$, $^{**}P < 0.01$. **(A)** The expression of Notch1 mRNA in rats at 2, 4, and 8 weeks post-stroke ($n = 6$; 2 weeks: $F = 0.413$, $P = 0.797$; 4 weeks: $F = 10.950$, $P < 0.001$; 8 weeks: $F = 12.006$, $P = 0.071$). **(B)** The expression of Jagged1 mRNA in rats at 2, 4, and 8 weeks post-stroke ($n = 6$; 2 weeks: $F = 1.154$, $P = 0.355$; 4 weeks: $F = 3.149$, $P = 0.032$; 8 weeks: $F = 4.582$, $P = 0.007$). **(C)** The expression of Hes1 mRNA in rats at 2, 4, and 8 weeks post-stroke ($n = 6$; 2 weeks: $F = 0.113$, $P = 0.977$; 4 weeks: $F = 4.688$, $P = 0.006$; 8 weeks: $F = 2.500$, $P = 0.068$). **(D)** The expression of Hes5 mRNA of rats at 2, 4, and 8 weeks post-stroke ($n = 6$; 2 weeks: $F = 4.646$, $P = 0.006$; 4 weeks: $F = 3.132$, $P = 0.032$; 8 weeks: $F = 3.358$, $P = 0.025$). PSD, post-stroke depression; FXT, fluoxetine hydrochloride capsules; YNJYP, Yi-nao-jie-yu prescription.

layer are critical for the restoration of function after injury (13). Astrocytes are the most numerous and versatile glial cells in the brain, but some of their functions remain the subject of debate. Some studies have indicated that they are able to regulate neurogenesis in the hippocampus (19), and that they guide the growth and integration of the newly formed neurons (20). Other studies have indicated that excessive differentiation toward astrocytes or hypertrophy results in impaired neurogenesis (21, 22). Neurogenesis in the hippocampus is particularly important in cognitive, affective, and reproductive behaviors, while dysfunctional neurogenic patterns are likely to be involved in mood and psychiatric disorders (23). Stress and depression contribute to decreased neurogenesis, and antidepressant treatment has been shown to ameliorate depression-like behavior and increase neurogenesis (24). 12 found that stress significantly decreased the proliferation and survival of progenitor cells in the hippocampus, which was partially restored following oxotremorine treatment. Apple et al. (23) also found that antidepressant treatment following stroke, which increases neurogenesis, enhanced the proliferation of NSCs and improved their migration toward sites of brain damage.

To understand how YNJYP protected the brain in our present study, neurogenesis in the DG of the hippocampus was observed at 2, 4, and 8 weeks by double immunofluorescence staining. Our observations showed that neurogenesis did occur in the hippocampus, and stroke acted to increase it, which is consistent with previous findings (25, 26). Neurogenesis decreased in the PSD rats compared with the stroke rats, while the depressive behavior of the PSD rats in the FST and SCT was aggravated. We observed that nestin-positive cells or BrdU-positive cells appeared separately, while there were only a few cells double-positive for nestin and BrdU at any of the three timepoints. This observation indicates that, at 2, 4, and 8 weeks post-stroke, the proliferation of NSCs occurred at a low level. At each timepoint, there were a few newly formed neurons (cells double-positive for BrdU and NeuN) in the PSD rats, and many newly formed astrocytes (cells double-positive for BrdU and GFAP), whereas greater numbers of newly formed cells and fewer newly formed astrocytes appeared after treatment with YNJYP. Many astrocytes of rats in the PSD group migrated into the granule cell layer, which may impair the synapses and hinder neurogenesis (22). After treatment with YNJYP, more newly formed neurons migrated to the granule cell layer. At 4 weeks, this phenomenon was much more obvious than at 2 or 8 weeks.

Therefore, the changes observed in our experiment indicated that neurogenesis did occur in the hippocampus. However, PSD reduced neurogenesis in the stroke rats by preventing newly formed cells from differentiating toward neurons and increasing their likelihood of becoming astrocytes. The excessive differentiation toward astrocytes may be the key factor for the depression-like behavior. Interestingly, YNJYP alleviated depressive behavior and dynamically reversed the process of neurogenesis. It was at 4 weeks that YNJYP exerted its most positive effects on neurogenesis.

An important issue raised by this study is the nature of the mechanism at the molecular level. Notch signaling plays an important role during adult neurogenesis. The Notch receptor is activated on binding to the membrane-bound Delta or Serrate ligand present on an adjacent cell. This interaction triggers cleavage of Notch to release a cytoplasmic fragment that enters the nucleus and interacts with the DNA-binding protein, CBF/RBP-J, Suppressor of Hairless, LAG-1, which leads to the transcription of target genes such as *Hairy* and *Enhancer-of-split* (27). Androutsellis-Theotokis et al. (28) found that activation of Notch signaling promotes the growth of nerves and plays a key role in the self-repair process after nerve injury. However, other reports were not consistent with this conclusion, indicating instead that Notch signaling can induce neuronal cell death (29). As previously reported, Notch1 is the most important transmembrane Notch receptor and is required for the maintenance of NSCs in the adult hippocampus (30). Jagged1 is the canonical membrane-bound ligand of Notch signaling, and conditional inactivation of Jagged1 during adult neurogenesis depletes the NSC population and ultimately hinders neurogenesis (31). The transcription factors Hairy/Enhancer-of-split (named *Hes* in mammals) are major downstream targets of Notch signaling. They are essential to regulate neurogenesis, although their roles remain unclear. Some studies indicate that they suppress the transcription of precursor genes, resulting in the inhibition of neuronal differentiation (32). Other studies have reported that Hes1 and Hes5 are essential to promote differentiation (7, 8).

In the present study, we observed fluctuations in *Notch1*, *Jagged1*, *Hes1*, and *Hes5* mRNA transcript levels, and found that, at 2 weeks, compared with the stroke group, expression of *Hes5* in the PSD group was first decreased, but then increased after treatment by FXT or YNJYP, whereas expression levels of the receptor *Notch1* and ligand *Jagged1* were not significantly different among the five groups. Thus, these results support the conclusion that not only Notch signaling, but other signals also participate in the regulation of neurogenesis. At 4 weeks, compared with the stroke group, the expression of *Notch1* and *Hes1* mRNA transcripts in the PSD group decreased, and again increased after treatment with FXT or YNJYP. At 8 weeks, compared with the stroke group, the expression of *Jagged1* mRNA transcripts in the PSD group increased and remained at a high level, even after treatment with FXT or YNJYP. The present study suggests that YNJYP exerts diverse effects on Notch signals at different timepoints, and that other factors also participate in the Notch signaling pathway (33–35).

In summary, this current investigation indicates that YNJYP can alleviate depressive behavior, and exerts a positive effect on neurogenesis by increasing neurogenesis, promoting differentiation toward neurons, and inhibiting differentiation toward astrocytes. At 4 weeks, the effect of YNJYP on neurogenesis was maximum. The beneficial effects of YNJYP treatment may be mediated by the activation of the Notch signaling pathway.

This study identified dynamic effects of YNJYP on adult neurogenesis. We mechanistically explored its effects on Notch signals, both the major Notch receptor and ligand as well as downstream targets of Notch signals, at three timepoints, and found dynamic changes in the levels of these molecules. Understanding the regulatory mechanisms during development may have crucial implications for developing repair therapies for PSD treatment (7). The contributions of other signaling pathways and inhibitors of signal pathways involved in the neuroprotective effects of YNJYP are the subjects of ongoing studies.

AUTHOR CONTRIBUTIONS

HT contributed to the interpretation of results and writing of manuscript; XL and QT contributed to the study design and interpretation of results; WZ and YG analyzed the data; QL, HL and XS conducted the experiments; CM, RZ, and FH reviewed and approved the manuscript.

ACKNOWLEDGMENTS

The authors thank Xin Wang, Kun Hu, Lei Tang, and Houwang Jiang for their helpful discussion and advice on animal experiments. This work was funded by grants from the National Natural Science Foundation of China (No. 81673930, XL), Beijing National Natural Science Foundation of China (No. 7142100, XL), and Beijing University of Chinese Medicine (No. 2017-JYB-XS-121, HT).

REFERENCES

1. Yang RR, Lu BC, Li T, Du YF, Wang X, Jia YX. The relationship between high sensitivity C-reactive protein at admission and post stroke depression: a 6-month follow-up study. *Int J Geriatr Psychiatry* (2015) 24:231–9. doi: 10.1002/gps.4315
2. Gillen R, Tennen H, McKee TE, Gernert-Dott P, Affleck G. Depressive symptoms and history of depression predict rehabilitation efficiency in stroke patients. *Arch Phys Med Rehab.* (2001) 82:1645–49. doi: 10.1053/apmr.2001.26249
3. Williams LS, Ghose SS, Swindle RW. Depression and other mental health diagnoses increase mortality risk after ischemic stroke. *Am J Psychiatry* (2004) 161:1090–5. doi: 10.1176/appi.ajp.161.6.1090
4. Cheng SY, Zhao YD, Li J, Chen XY, Wang RD, Zeng JW. Plasma levels of glutamate during stroke is associated with development

of post-stroke depression. *Psychoneuroendocrinol* (2014) 47:126–35. doi: 10.1016/j.psyneuen.2014.05.006
5. Wang X, Li YH, Li MH, Lu J, Zhao JG, Sun XJ, et al. Glutamate level detection by magnetic resonance spectroscopy in patients with post-stroke depression. *Eur Arch Psychiatry Clin Neurosci.* (2012) 262:33–8. doi: 10.1007/s00406-011-0209-3
6. Jun H, Hussaini SM, Rigby MJ, Jang MH. Functional role of adult hippocampal neurogenesis as a therapeutic strategy for mental disorders. *Neural Plast.* (2012) 10:1–20. doi: 10.1155/2012/854285
7. Roy M, Pear WS, Aster JC. The multifaceted role of Notch in cancer. *Curr Opin Genet Dev.* (2007) 17:52–9. doi: 10.1016/j.gde.2006.12.001
8. Lewis J, Hanisch A, Holder M. Notch signaling, the segmentation clock, and the patterning of vertebrate somites. *J Biol.* (2009) 44:44–50. doi: 10.1186/jbiol145
9. Tian HL, Li XL, Tang QS, Li X, Li QM, Gao YS. The effects of Yinao Jieyu decoction on the behaviors and damages of pathology in hippocampal CA1 area of rats with post-stroke depression. *Chi J Info TCM.* (2017) 24:49–53.
10. Longa EZ, Weinstein PR, Carlson S, Cummins R. Reversible middle cerebral artery occlusion without craniectomy in rats. *Stroke* (1989) 20:84–91. doi: 10.1161/01.STR.20.1.84
11. Chen JX, Li W, Zhao X, Xu HY, Wang ZF, Yue GX, et al. Effects of three Chinese formulas on BDNF, TrkB in rat cortex and hippocampus with chronic immobilization stress. *Chi J Pathophysiol.* (2007) 23:1296–300.
12. Veena J, Srikumar BN, Mahati K, Raju TR, Rao BS. Oxotremorine treatment restores hippocampal neurogenesis and ameliorates depression-like behavior in chronically stressed rats. *Psychopharmacology* (2011) 217:239–53. doi: 10.1007/s00213-011-2279-3
13. Jin KL, Minami MB, Lan JQ, Mao MO, Batteur S, Simon RP, et al. Neurogenesis in dentate subgranular zone and rostral subventricular zone after focal cerebral ischemia in the rat. *Proc Natl Acad Sci USA.* (2001) 98:4710–5. doi: 10.1073/pnas.081011098
14. Lagace DC, Whitman MC, Noonan MA, Ables JL, DeCarolis NA. Dynamic contribution of nestin-expressing stem cells to adult neurogenesis. *J Neurosci.* (2007) 27:12623–9. doi: 10.1523/JNEUROSCI.3812-07.2007
15. Gusel'nikova VV, Korzhevskiy DE. NeuN as a neuronal nuclear antigen and neuron differentiation marker. *Acta Nat.* (2015) 7:42–7.
16. Takizawa T, Gudla PR, Guo L, Lockett S, Misteli T. Allele-specific nuclear positioning of the monoallelically expressed astrocyte marker GFAP. *Genes Dev.* (2008) 102:489–98. doi: 10.1101/gad.1634608
17. Li X, Tang QS, Hou XJ, Luo B. Changes in brain monoamine neurotransmitters of rats with post-stroke depression and the interventional effect of Chinese herb of YinaoJieyu prescription. *Chi J Clin Rehab.* (2006) 10:49–51.
18. Fruehwald S, Gatterbauer E, Rehak P, Baumhack U. Early fluoxetine treatment of post-stroke depression: a three-month double-blind placebo-controlled study with an open-label long-term follow up. *J Neurol.* (2003) 250:347–51. doi: 10.1007/s00415-003-1014-3
19. Zhao YN, Zhang Q, Shao X, Ouyang LF, Wang X, Zhu K, et al. Decreased glycogen content might contribute to chronic stress induced atrophy of hippocampal astrocyte volume and depression-like behavior in rats. *Sci Rep.* (2017) 7:43192–8. doi: 10.1038/srep43192
20. Cotter D, MacKay D, Landau S, Kerwin R, Everall I. Reduced glial cell density and neuronal size in the anterior cingulate cortex in major depressive disorder. *Arch Gen Psychiatry* (2001) 58:545–53. doi: 10.1001/archpsyc.58.6.545
21. Chen Y, Swanson RA. Astrocytes and brain injury. *J Cereb Blood Flow Metabol.* (2003) 23:137–49. doi: 10.1097/01.WCB.0000044631.80210.3C
22. Robinson C, Apgar C, Shapiro LA. Astrocyte hypertrophy contributes to aberrant neurogenesis after traumatic brain injury. *Neural Plast.* (2016) 10:1–10. doi: 10.1155/2016/1347987
23. Apple DM, Fonseca RS, Kokovay E. The role of adult neurogenesis in psychiatric and cognitive disorders. *Brain Res.* (2017) 1655:270–6. doi: 10.1016/j.brainres.2016.01.023
24. Mahar A, Bambico I, Mechawar FR, Nobrega N. Stress, serotonin and hippocampal neurogenesis in relation to depression and antidepressant effects. *Neurosci Biobehav Rev.* (2014) 38:173–92. doi: 10.1016/j.neubiorev.2013.11.009
25. Kee NJ, Preston E, Wojtowicz JM. Enhanced neurogenesis after transient global ischemia in the dentate gyrus of the rat. *Exp Brain Res.* (2001) 136:313–20. doi: 10.1007/s002210000591
26. Lang UE, Beglinger C, Schweinfurth N, Walter M, Borgwardt S. Nutritional aspects of depression. *Cell Physiol Biochem.* (2015) 37:1029–43. doi: 10.1159/000430229
27. Cheng YC, Huang YC, Ye TH. Deltex1 is inhibited by the Notch–Hairy/E(Spl) signaling pathway and induces neuronal and glial differentiation. *Neural Dev.* (2015) 10:1–15. doi: 10.1186/s13064-015-0055-5
28. Androutsellis-Theotokis A, Leker RR, Soldner F, Hoeppner DJ, Ravin R, Poser SW, et al. Notch signalling regulates stem cell numbers *in vitro* and *in vivo*. *Nature* (2006) 442:823–6. doi: 10.1038/nature04940
29. Arumugam TV, Cheng YL, Choong Y. Evidence that gamma-secretase-mediated Notch signaling induces neuronal cell death via the nuclear factor-kappaB-Bcl-2-interacting mediator of cell death pathway in ischemic stroke. *Mol Pharmacol.* (2011) 10:23–31. doi: 10.1124/mol.111.071076
30. Ables JL, Carolis NA, Johnson MA. Notch1 is required for maintenance of the reservoir of adult hippocampal stem cells. *J Neurosci.* (2010) 30:10484–92. doi: 10.1523/JNEUROSCI.4721-09.2010
31. Alfonso L, Guillermo O. Jagged1 is necessary for postnatal and adult neurogenesis in the dentate gyrus. *Dev Biol.* (2014) 388:11–21. doi: 10.1016/j.ydbio.2014.02.004
32. Zhao C, Deng W, Gage FH. Mechanisms and functional implications of adult neurogenesis. *Cell* (2008) 132:645–60. doi: 10.1016/j.cell.2008.01.033
33. Alvarez-Buylla BA, Lim DA. For the long run: maintaining germinal niches in the adult brain. *Neuron* (2004) 41:683–6. doi: 10.1016/S0896-6273(04)00111-4
34. Doe CQ. Neural stem cells: balancing self-renewal with differentiation. *Development* (2008) 135:1575–87. doi: 10.1242/dev.014977
35. Fuentealba LC, Obernier K, Alvarez-Buylla A. Adult neural stem cells bridge their niche. *Cell Stem Cell.* (2012) 10:698–708. doi: 10.1016/j.stem.2012.05.012

5

Review of Abnormal Self-Knowledge in Major Depressive Disorder

Yixue Lou [1,2,3]*, Yi Lei* [1,3*]*, Ying Mei* [1,3]*, Paavo H. T. Leppänen* [2] *and Hong Li* [1,3]

[1] *College of Psychology and Sociology, Shenzhen University, Shenzhen, China,* [2] *Faculty of Education and Psychology, University of Jyväskylä, Jyväskylä, Finland,* [3] *Center for Neurogenetics, Shenzhen Institute of Neuroscience, Shenzhen, China*

***Correspondence:**
Yi Lei
yutian@szu.edu.cn

Background: Major depressive disorder (MDD) is an affective disorder that is harmful to both physical and mental health. Abnormal self-knowledge, which refers to abnormal judgments about oneself, is a core symptom of depression. However, little research has summarized how and why patients with MDD differ from healthy individuals in terms of self-knowledge.

Objective: To gain a better understanding of MDD, we reviewed previous studies that focused on the behavioral and neurological changes of self-knowledge in this illness.

Main Findings: On the behavioral level, depressed individuals exhibited negative self-knowledge in an explicit way, while more heterogeneous patterns were reported in implicit results. On the neurological level, depressed individuals, as compared with non-depressed controls, showed abnormal self-referential processing in both early perception and higher cognitive processing phases during the Self-Referential Encoding Task. Furthermore, fMRI studies have reported aberrant activity in the medial prefrontal cortex area for negative self-related items in depression. These results revealed several behavioral features and brain mechanisms underlying abnormal self-knowledge in depression.

Future Studies: The neural mechanism of implicit self-knowledge in MDD remains unclear. Future research should examine the importance of others' attitudes on the self-concept of individuals with MDD, and whether abnormal self-views may be modified through cognitive or pharmacological approaches. In addition, differences in abnormal self-knowledge due to genetic variation between depressed and non-depressed populations remain unconfirmed. Importantly, it remains unknown whether abnormal self-knowledge could be used as a specific marker to distinguish healthy individuals from those with MDD.

Conclusion: This review extends our understanding of the relationship between self-knowledge and depression by indicating several abnormalities among individuals with MDD and those who are at risk for this illness.

Keywords: major depressive disorder, self-knowledge, abnormality, behavioral abnormality, neurological abnormality

INTRODUCTION

Major depressive disorder (MDD) is a complicated affective disease characterized by abnormal clinical symptoms, including neurovegetative dysfunction (appetite or sleep disturbances), cognitive dissonance (inappropriate guilt, feelings of worthlessness), aberrant psychomotor activities (agitation or retardation) (1), and elevated suicide risk (2, 3). According to the World Health Organization, there are approximately 350 million people suffering from depression worldwide (4). In a recent survey, the proportion of years lived with disability (YLDs) caused by MDD was 4.2%, approximately 34.1 million of the total YLDs (5). Thus, MDD is thought to be a major global cause of disease burden and human suffering (5–7).

Abnormal perception and understanding of the self is a core symptom of MDD (1). This includes abnormal processes and/or representations involved in being aware of the self, abnormal knowledge about the self, and/or abnormal judgments about the self (National Institute of Mental Health; NIMH). As a sub-construct of perception and understanding of the self, self-knowledge, which refers to the ability to make judgments about one's current cognitive or emotional internal states, traits, and/or abilities (NIMH), is also impaired in individuals with MDD (8–11). For instance, individuals with MDD, unlike non-depressed healthy individuals, often exhibit negative self-evaluation, inappropriate self-blame, and excessive self-criticism (8, 12).

Although researchers have increasingly begun exploring abnormal self-knowledge in depression, few have compared existing findings in a single study. To enable a better understanding of how and why patients with MDD differ from healthy individuals in terms of self-knowledge, the current review focused on previous studies that examined behavioral patterns and brain mechanisms underlying abnormal self-knowledge in depression. Both explicit and implicit self-knowledge, which reflect conscious and unconscious self-views respectively, were discussed. Various abnormalities such as abnormal brain responses and aberrant neural circuits were illustrated. Furthermore, the present review pointed out some possible directions for future clinical studies (see **Figure 1**).

LITERATURE

Literature Review

A search of previous studies published between January 1960 and August 2018 was conducted using the databases Web of Science and PubMed. Self-knowledge is defined as a construct that includes self-evaluation, self-esteem, and self-reference. Thus, the search terms were designed as follows: "depression AND self-evaluation," OR "depression AND self-esteem," OR "depression AND self-reference." Search filters were set for publications written in English. Empirical research and reviews that examined the role of self-evaluation, self-attitude, self-view, self-reference, and/or self-esteem in MDD were found.

Eligibility Criteria

We screened for inclusion based on titles and abstracts, and again using full text. To be included, previous studies had to focus on behavioral and neurological changes of self-knowledge in MDD. All publications had to be reported on clinical populations currently or previously diagnosed with MDD, or populations who were currently in a depressive episode, regardless of gender and age. Conference abstracts were excluded if they were not published in a scientific journal. Publications were also excluded if they were published in a language other than English (see **Supplementary Figure 1**).

PARADIGMS

The majority of the research conformed to one of two methods. Specifically, these were explicit and implicit research paradigms.

Explicit Paradigms

Explicit methods are used to assess individuals' self-attitudes by using self-reported measures such as direct self-evaluation. The most commonly used explicit methods are the Self-Referential Encoding Task (SRET) (13) and self-reported questionnaires (14, 15).

Self-Referential Encoding Task, SRET

The self-referential encoding task (SRET) was designed to examine one's self-attitude (13, 16). Theoretically, individuals are more sensitive to information that is encoded as strongly related to oneself (17). Thus, self-related stimuli commonly display better recall and recognition performance, when compared to other-related stimuli (18). In the SRET, researchers present participants with positive and negative personality trait words, and ask them to decide whether each trait describes themselves (self-related condition), a familiar other (other-related condition) (19–22), or a socially desirable trait (semantic encoding condition; see **Figure 2**) (10, 23). After the judgment, the participants were asked to recall or recognize all the trait words that had been presented to them.

Individuals with positive self-attitudes, such as feelings of self-value, commonly endorse more positive traits relative to negative traits as self-describing, and show better recall and recognition rates of these words (18). Conversely, negative self-attitudes, such as feelings of worthlessness in individuals with MDD, often lead to more endorsement of negative traits and, in turn, better memory performance of these words (18, 24).

Other Explicit Approaches

Direct self-report questionnaires are often used in studies of depressive self-knowledge. For instance, researchers have used the Rosenberg Self-Esteem Scale (RSES) to measure explicit self-esteem in depression (15). In addition, the self-worth subscale of the World Assumption Scale (25) and the self-acceptance subscale of the Scales of Psychological Well-Being (26) are used to assess explicit self-attitude in depression. Moreover, the Beck Depression Inventory (BDI), which is commonly used to measure the depressive state, also

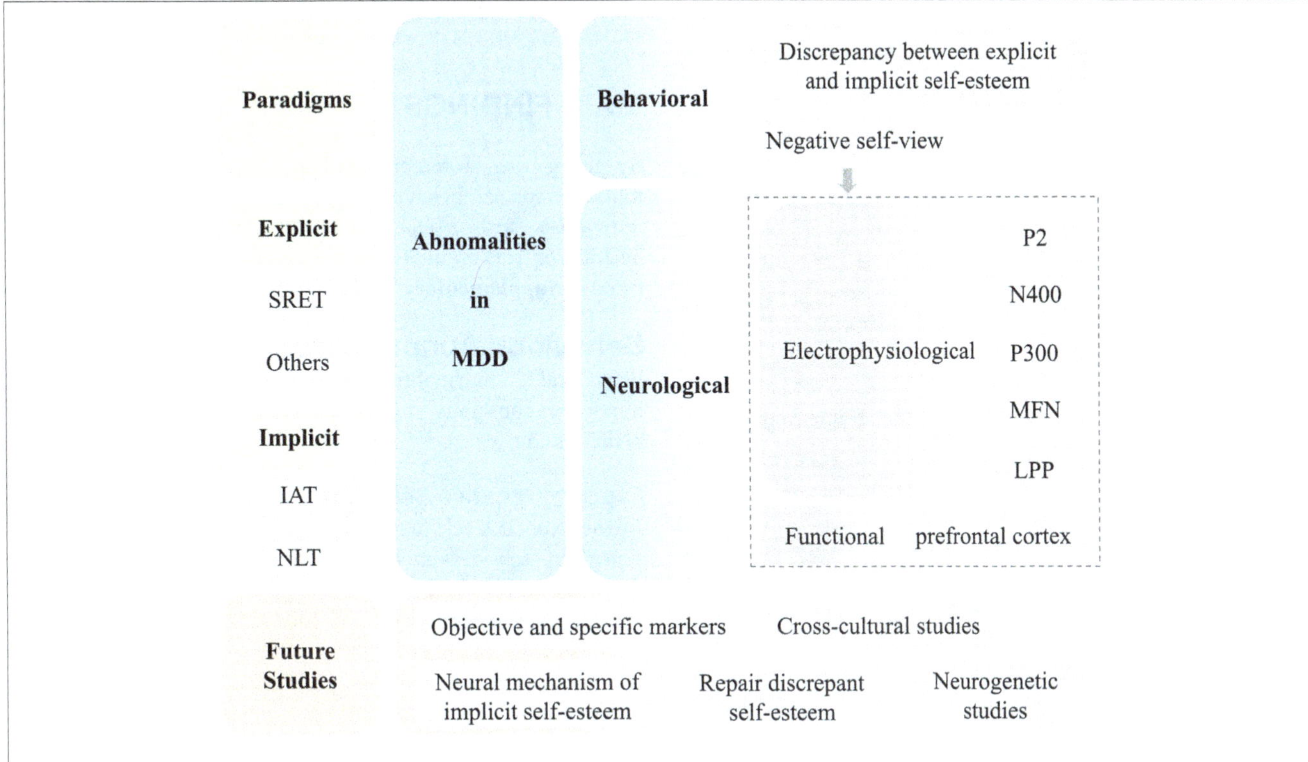

FIGURE 1 | Framework of the current review.

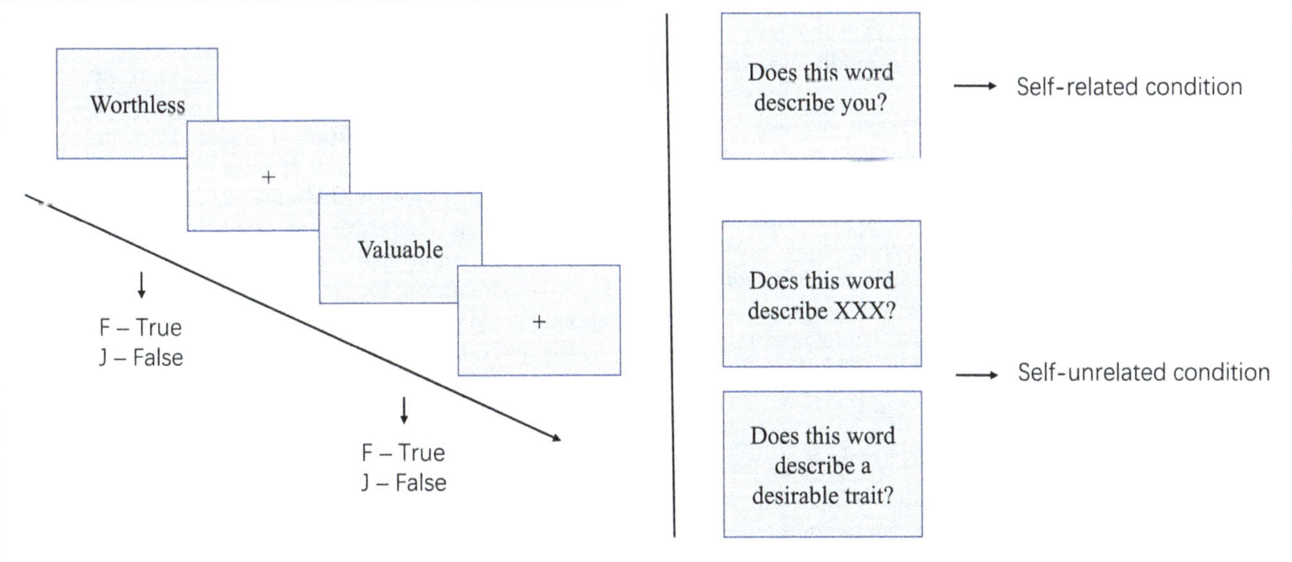

FIGURE 2 | Illustration of the self-referential encoding task (SRET).

contains self-evaluation factors, such as the self-blame factor, in its items (14).

Implicit Paradigms

The efficacy of explicit methods is debated by some researchers for the following reasons. First, according to cognitive theory, the self-concept involves automatic processes that occur without reflection and/or logical reasoning accessible within the conscious mind (27). Second, direct self-appraisal might be affected by social desirability and cultural differences (28, 29). In brief, explicit methods may not accurately reflect a person's real attitude about him/herself (30, 31). Thus, implicit paradigms were introduced into self-knowledge studies (32–34). The most commonly used implicit paradigms are the Implicit

TABLE 1 | Illustration of the self-evaluation Implicit Association Task (sIAT).

Task	Categorization	Stimulus	Key-press
Compatible	Self-related/unrelated words	Self	F
		Other	J
	Personality trait words	Valuable	F
		Worthless	J
Incompatible	Self-related/unrelated words	Self	F
		Other	J
	Personality trait words	Valuable	J
		Worthless	F

Association Test (IAT) (35, 36) and the Name-Letter Test (NLT) (37, 38).

Implicit Association Task, IAT

The self-evaluation IAT (sIAT) is a paradigm that has been commonly used to examine implicit self-attitudes of depression (39, 40). In the sIAT, it is assumed that information that is compatible with one's implicit attitude would be better processed as compared to that which is incompatible (36). Thus, participants are asked to complete two types of categorization (compatible and incompatible) by using a two key-press system. In the compatible condition, self-related stimulus words (e.g., one's own name or date of birth) shared the same key with "valuable" personality trait words (e.g., competent), while self-unrelated words (e.g., other's name or non-meaningful date) shared another key with "worthless" personality trait words (e.g., unsuccessful). The incompatible condition was reverse coded (34, 41, 42) (**Table 1**).

Differences in reaction times (RTs) and accuracy (ACC) between compatible and incompatible conditions were analyzed. Typically, the condition that is congruent with one's implicit self-attitude should show better performance when compared to the incongruent one. For instance, individuals with positive self-bias should demonstrate a faster and more accurate response in the compatible condition, relative to the incompatible condition (43, 44), while the negative self-attitude found in depression should lead to an opposite pattern.

Name-Letter Test, NLT

The name-letter test (NLT) has also been used in previous studies to measure implicit self-attitudes (38, 45–47). In the NLT, researchers presented participants with the 26 letters of the alphabet one-by-one, and asked them to judge the attractiveness or likability of each letter, relying on their first, intuitive reaction (48). According to the name letter effect, one's initial is thought to be highly associated with the self (49, 50). Thus, under the influence of positive self-bias, non-depressed individuals should show a rational preference toward their initials relative to other letters, even though they are generally unaware of this effect (38). However, an opposite pattern may be true for individuals with MDD (33).

The name letter effect has been shown to be a cross-cultural phenomenon, since it has also been reported in Thai, Japanese, and Korean studies (51–53). Thus, the NLT qualifies as an indirect assessment of self-attitude in depression (33).

MAIN FINDINGS

By using the aforementioned paradigms, researchers have found abnormal behavioral patterns and brain responses in individuals with MDD, when compared to non-depressed, healthy controls. Evaluation of the quality of included studies was listed in **Supplementary Table 1**.

Behavioral Abnormalities

Behavioral abnormalities include explicit/conscious and implicit/unconscious behaviors that have been observed in depression.

Explicit: Negative Self-View

At the explicit level, previous behavioral research has revealed a negative self-view in depression, as compared with a non-depressed healthy population. For instance, healthy individuals typically exhibit positive attitudes about themselves (54–57). For instance, they often attribute themselves with more positive, rather than negative, personality traits (54, 58), so that their self-esteem may be protected (18, 59). However, individuals with depression typically demonstrate an abnormally negative self-view (1, 60, 61).

For instance, under the influence of negative self-knowledge, individuals with MDD show less positive self-bias, less self-confidence, and lower self-esteem (62–65), as well as excessive self-criticism, negative self-evaluation, inappropriate self-blame, and shame (8, 12, 66–68). This negative self-representation has been associated with greater self-reported depression (69, 70), poor and slower recovery from a major depressive episode (71, 72), and higher probability of suicide attempt (73, 74). In addition, individuals with higher self-esteem may exhibit sudden improvements in depressive symptomatology even without treatment (75), while lower self-esteem is thought to be a prospective risk factor for depressive symptoms from young adulthood to old age (76–78).

In the SRET, individuals with depression, relative to healthy controls, endorsed more negative trait words as self-described, and showed faster response, better recall performance, and increased recognition rate for these words (9, 23, 79, 80). In a longitudinal study Derry and Kuiper (13), found that such negative self-bias might be a specific symptom in currently depressed patients, since the recall rate of negative self-related words decreased after recovery from the illness.

Implicit: Discrepancy Between Explicit and Implicit Self-Esteem

Although a large number of studies have indicated a lower self-attitude in MDD, relative to healthy individuals, at an explicit level (8–10, 20), more heterogeneous patterns have been reported in implicit studies (34, 36, 41, 42, 81).

For instance, when using the IAT and/or NLT to measure implicit self-esteem (ISE) and RSES to assess explicit self-esteem (ESE), some researchers have observed both low ESE and ISE in currently depressed individuals (39, 40, 42) and chronically depressed individuals with early onset (33), relative to never depressed healthy controls. However, more researchers have reported a normal ISE combined with a lower ESE in individuals with current depression (41, 42, 82–85), previous depression (41), remitted depression (11, 39, 86), and chronic depression with late onset (33), when compared to non-depressed individuals. Some researchers have even observed higher ISE and lower ESE in current depression (83, 85, 87) and previous depression (34, 82).

The discrepancy between explicit and implicit self-esteem, especially the combination of low ESE and high ISE, is thought to be associated with internalizing problems such as affective disorders (88–92). For major depression, such a discrepancy seems to be more severe in depressed individuals with suicidal ideation relative to those without such ideation (42). Moreover, depressed patients with congruent self-esteem, compared to those with incongruent self-esteem, exhibited better recovery from the illness throughout antidepressant treatment (93).

Neurological Abnormalities

Neurological abnormalities include abnormal electrophysiological responses and aberrant functional neural activities. These abnormalities were all detected using the SRET.

Abnormal Electrophysiological Response

To explore the brain mechanism of negative self-knowledge in depression, electroencephalography (EEG) technology was used in conjunction with the SRET. By collecting the event-related potentials (ERPs) during the SRET, researchers attempted to identify the key ERP components that are involved in negative self-referent processing in MDD.

For instance, Shestyuk and Deldin (62) observed increased P2 component, which was quantified as a positive peak in the 200- to 300-ms time window poststimulus, in individuals with depression while processing negative, relative to positive, self-referential items. The opposite, however, was true for the non-depressed healthy controls. A recent study reported decreased N400 amplitude, which was measured as mean voltage of the ERP average between 350–500 ms, in individuals with depression, as compared with healthy controls, in negative self-referent processing (9). Regarding the latter component, Poulsen et al. (94) found an attenuated or absent MFN response between 260 ms and 480 ms in depression, relative to non-depressed controls, when specifically endorsing negative trait descriptors. However, in a recent study, depressed individuals were found to exhibit enhanced MFN for both positive and negative endorsement (95). Consistently, an attenuated P300 response from 300- to 600- ms was observed in both of these two studies (94, 95). Concerning the more delayed late positive potential (LPP), larger LPP amplitudes were detected following negative vs. positive endorsement in depressed adults (62, 96), depressed adolescents (8), and young girls who were vulnerable to depression (97), when compared to healthy controls.

In these studies, the P2 component is thought to be related to automatic semantic processes (98). Thus, an increased P2 reflects a stronger automatic attentional capture and orientation in patients with depression under the negative, relative to positive, self-related condition (62). The N400 component was interpreted to be influenced by semantic memories about the self, and could be reduced by greater association of the stimuli with a preceding self-related context (99, 100). Therefore, this result indexed a congruent pattern between negative semantic memories and the self-concept in individuals with depression (9). In addition, the MFN is thought to be associated with early cognitive evaluation during self-referential processing (95). The altered MFN response may reflect abnormal self-evaluation among clinically depressed individuals. The greater P300, which is evoked by a saliency effect of self-referential information and positive affect (101), was attenuated in depression. One possible interpretation is that it was possibly associated with a chronically negative self-view in this population (95). Last, an increased LPP amplitude, which is associated with effortful encoding (102), indicates that individuals with depression engage more cognitive effort in processing self-related negative, relative to positive, items (62).

In all, in the time domain, abnormal self-knowledge in depression could be reflected in early phases of self-related processing, such as automatic attention and orientation toward negative self-descriptive items (62). Retrieval of negative memories about the self could also be involved (9). For later phases of self-referential processing, an attenuated bonding between positive affect and the self may be associated with negative self-view in depression (95). Furthermore, depressed individuals seem to engage more cognitive effort in negative, instead of positive, self-reference (62).

Abnormal Functional Neural Activities

The high spatial resolution of functional MRI technology makes it possible for researchers to determine abnormal brain activities in depression during the SRET. Several fMRI studies, thus, have suggested that the prefrontal cortex and its sub-regions might be abnormal in individuals with MDD (103). The prefrontal cortex is thought to play an important role in self-referential processing (104). In particular, dysfunction within the medial prefrontal cortex (mPFC) and in the circuits that connect the mPFC to other cortical and limbic structures is responsible for the cognitive dissonance found in depression (103).

For instance, the cortical midline structures (CMS), such as the mPFC, are critical for self-referential processing in healthy individuals (17, 105), adult patients (106–108), and adolescent patients with MDD (109). However, aberrant activity in the mPFC was reported in depression when compared to healthy controls (17, 23, 106). Additionally, Yoshimura et al. (108) found that individuals with depression, relative to healthy controls, exhibited hyperactivity in the mPFC and the rostral anterior cingulate cortex (rostral ACC) during self-referential processing of negative personality traits; such activity was shown to be associated with depressive symptoms (108).

Furthermore, abnormal activities of other sub-regions of the prefrontal cortex were also observed during the processing of self-related negative stimuli in depression (10, 23). For instance, by using the SRET, researchers found significantly higher activation of the central mPFC and significantly lower activation of the dorsal mPFC in depression, relative to healthy controls, during the self-referential condition (10). Local connectivity of the dorsal mPFC was also reduced during self-reflection in depressed adolescents (109). The activity of the dorsolateral prefrontal cortex (dlPFC) was also involved in self-referential processing in depression, but was absent in healthy controls (23). In addition, a meta-analysis revealed hyperactivation in the ventromedial prefrontal cortex (vmPFC) within major depression during resting state, which was discussed as a neural reflection of self-referential processing (110).

Therefore, aberrant activity of the prefrontal cortex and its sub-regions could index the abnormal brain activity that is a hallmark of depression, specifically during the processing of self-referential stimuli. In particular, hyperactivity in the mPFC during negative self-referential processing could possibly even be associated with the severity of depressive symptoms.

DISCUSSION

According to previous studies, abnormal self-knowledge, which is commonly found in MDD, is mainly reflected in abnormal behaviors and abnormal neurological responses during self-evaluation, self-esteem, and/or self-referential processing.

At the behavioral level, abnormal self-knowledge could be indexed by a negative explicit self-view (13, 80) and discrepant self-esteem, which involves relatively higher implicit self-esteem and lower explicit self-esteem (11, 33, 34, 111). Furthermore, a greater discrepancy between implicit and explicit self-esteem is related to more severe MDD, or a higher possibility of being affected by the illness (42, 111).

At the neurological level, several abnormalities have been found during abnormal self-referential processing, by using electrophysiological technology (8, 9, 62) and fMRI technology (10, 108, 112, 113). For instance, for abnormal electrophysiological processing, enhanced P2 and LPP and decreased N400 amplitudes were all detected in depression, relative to non-depressed controls, in the SRET. For aberrant brain activities, higher activation of the central mPFC, lower activation of the dorsal mPFC (10), and aberrant activity of the dlPFC (23) during self-referential processing can also distinguish MDD, as well as indicate the severity of symptoms.

By using the indexes above, researchers and clinicians could distinguish patients with MDD and non-depressed individuals more objectively and effectively. However, caution should be exercised for several reasons. First, some of the studies involved limited samples and poor replications. For instance, abnormalities in P2 and LPP amplitude in MDD were reported in a study with 17 patients with current depression, 17 patients with remitted depression, and 18 controls, and abnormalities of N400s were reported in a study including 16 patients with MDD and 16 controls. Considering this issue, larger samples are needed to confirm changes of electrophysiological response during depressive self-referential processing.

Second, abnormal self-knowledge is only one component of MDD, despite being a core feature. Behavioral abnormalities may not be sensitive and specific for MDD, since they are affected by non-clinical factors such as personality traits (114–117). Thus, more evidence is needed to confirm the behavioral abnormalities identified in the current review.

Third, although we reviewed various investigations that focused on abnormal self-knowledge in depression, a classical review is relatively less objective compared with a systematic meta-analysis.

FUTURE STUDIES

In the exploration of self-knowledge in depression, there are still many unanswered questions. First, although the discrepancy between explicit and implicit self-esteem in depression has been confirmed by several previous studies (11), and the neural mechanism of explicit self-esteem has been richly explored (8, 10, 23, 108), little is known about the neural basis of implicit self-esteem in depression, suggesting the need for further research.

Second, it remains unclear whether the pattern of self-knowledge in patients with depression would be different in a cross-cultural context. For instance, collectivism of eastern Asia, relative to individualism in Western culture, allows individuals to view themselves as dynamic entities that are continually defined by their social context and relationships (118). Thus, in Eastern cultures, judgment by important others about oneself, which is currently ignored in self-related studies, plays a critical role in the quality of one's self-view (119). Indeed, the development of self-knowledge relies not only on one's reflection of the self, but also on how important others evaluate the individual (22, 58, 119–121).

Third, some previous neurogenetic research explored the association between different gene types and abnormal self-knowledge in depression, and found that the serotonin transporter promoter polymorphism (5-HTTLPR) played a crucial role in susceptibility to developing depression (122). In a recent study, Ma et al. (21) reported a modulation effect of the 5-HTTLPR polymorphism in brain activities associated with negative self-knowledge in depression. It was suggested that the s allele of 5-HTTLPR could possibly be a risk factor for individuals vulnerable to depression (21). However, differences in abnormal self-knowledge due to genetic variation between healthy and depressed populations remains unconfirmed, calling for further research.

Fourth, to repair discrepant self-esteem found in depression, which involves low explicit and high implicit self-esteem, the development of cognitive and/or medical approaches is needed to enhance explicit self-attitudes. A previous study indicated that depression can be prevented or reduced by interventions that improve explicit self-esteem (123–126). For example, researchers have utilized positive self-images (127) and mindfulness (128, 129) to realize an improvement of both explicit and implicit self-esteem. It is possible that these methods can also be used to diminish the discrepancy of self-esteem found in depression. Furthermore, since the s allele of 5-HTTLPR may elevate the risk of developing depression (21), it is reasonable to consider whether the use of selective serotonin reuptake inhibitors (SSRIs) could enhance self-satisfaction (130–132).

Finally, to conquer complex diseases such as MDD, the National Institute of Mental Health (NIMH) has raised the importance of identifying clinically useful biomarkers and behavioral indicators that predict change across the trajectory of illnesses (19). However, the most fundamental challenge is to identify these diseases effectively. In the diagnosis of MDD, the most commonly used measurements are structured interviews and/or depression inventories (133), which are relatively subjective and require researchers to be professionally trained. To facilitate the identification of objective criteria for MDD diagnosis, it must be determined whether abnormal self-knowledge can be used as an objective and specific marker for identifying MDD. For this purpose, patterns of abnormal self-knowledge should be compared between MDD and other mental disorders, such as bipolar disorder.

CONCLUSION

MDD is a main cause of disease burden worldwide (6, 7), and abnormal self-knowledge is one of the cardinal symptoms of this disorder. Through a review of previous studies that measured abnormal self-knowledge in individuals with clinical MDD, several abnormalities that distinguish patients with MDD as well as those at risk of the illness were revealed. We also pointed out several possible directions for future clinical studies based on previous findings. Overall, this review extends our understanding of the relationship between self-knowledge and depression.

AUTHOR CONTRIBUTIONS

YLo wrote the paper. YLe supervised the review and assisted in paper revision. YM assisted in paper revision. PL assisted in paper revision. HL assisted in paper writing and funding supports. All authors were involved in revising the manuscript critically for important intellectual content and approved the final version of the manuscript.

FUNDING

This work was supported by the Shenzhen Peacock Plan [Grant No. KQTD2015033016104926] and the Guangdong Pearl River Talents Plan Innovative and Entrepreneurial Team [Grant No. 2016ZT06S220].

REFERENCES

1. Fava M, Kenneth KS. Major depressive disorder. *Neuron.* (2000) 28:335. doi: 10.1016/S0896-6273(00)00112-4
2. Chesney E, Goodwin GM, Fazel S. Risks of all-cause and suicide mortality in mental disorders: a meta-review. *World Psychiatry Offic J World Psychiatr Assoc.* (2014) 13:153. doi: 10.1002/wps.20128
3. Klonsky ED, May AM, Saffer BY. Suicide, suicide attempts, and suicidal ideation. *Ann Rev Clin Psychol.* (2016) 12:307. doi: 10.1146/annurev-clinpsy-021815-093204
4. Smith K. Mental health: a world of depression. *Nature.* (2014) 515:181. doi: 10.1038/515180a
5. Vos T, Abajobir AA, Abbafati C, Abbas KM, Abate KH, Abd-Allah F, et al. Global, regional, and national incidence, prevalence, and years lived with disability for 328 diseases and injuries for 195 countries, 1990-2016: a systematic analysis for the Global Burden of Disease Study 2016. *Lancet.* (2017) 390:1211–59. doi: 10.1016/S0140-6736(17)32154-2
6. Lozano R, Naghavi M, Foreman K, Lim S, Shibuya K, Aboyans V, et al. Years lived with disability (YLDs) for 1160 sequelae of 289 diseases and injuries 1990–2010: a systematic analysis for the Global Burden of Disease Study 2010. *Lancet.* (2012) 380:2163–96. doi: 10.1016/s0140-6736(12)61729-2
7. Murray CJ, Vos T, Lozano R, Naghavi M, Flaxman AD, Michaud C, et al. Disability-adjusted life years (DALYs) for 291 diseases and injuries in 21 regions, 1990-2010: a systematic analysis for the Global Burden of Disease Study 2010. *Lancet.* (2012) 380:2197–223. doi: 10.1016/s0140-6736(12)61689-4
8. Auerbach RP, Stanton CH, Proudfit GH, Pizzagalli DA. Self-referential processing in depressed adolescents: a high-density event-related potential study. *J Abnorm Psychol.* (2015) 124:233–45. doi: 10.1037/abn0000023
9. Kiang M, Farzan F, Blumberger DM, Kutas M, McKinnon MC, Kansal V, et al. Abnormal self-schema in semantic memory in major depressive disorder: evidence from event-related brain potentials. *Biol Psychol.* (2017) 126:41–7. doi: 10.1016/j.biopsycho.2017.04.003
10. Li Y, Li M, Wei D, Kong X, Du X, Hou X, et al. Self-referential processing in unipolar depression: distinct roles of subregions of the medial prefrontal cortex. *Psychiatry Res.* (2017) 263:8–14. doi: 10.1016/j.pscychresns.2017.02.008
11. Smeijers D, Vrijsen JN, van Oostrom I, Isaac L, Speckens A, Becker ES, et al. Implicit and explicit self-esteem in remitted depressed patients. *J Behav Ther Exp Psychiatry.* (2017) 54:301–6. doi: 10.1016/j.jbtep.2016.10.006
12. Auerbach RP, Ho M, Kim JC. Identifying cognitive and interpersonal predictors of adolescent depression. *J Abnorm Child Psychol.* (2014) 42:913–24. doi: 10.1007/s10802-013-9845-6
13. Derry PA, Kuiper NA. Schematic processing and self-reference in clinical depression. *J Abnorm Psychol.* (1981) 90:286. doi: 10.1037/0021-843X.90.4.286
14. Beck AT, Steer RA, Brown GK. Beck depression inventory - second edition manual. *Psihologijski Mjerni Instrumenti.* (1996) 93:88.
15. Rosenberg M. *Society and the Adolescent Self-Image (rev. ed.).* Princeton, NJ: Princeton University Press (1965).
16. Ramel W, Goldin PR, Eyler LT, Brown GG, Gotlib IH, McQuaid JR. Amygdala reactivity and mood-congruent memory in individuals at risk for depressive relapse. *Biol Psychiatry.* (2007) 61:231–9. doi: 10.1016/j.biopsych.2006.05.004
17. Northoff G, Heinzel A, De GM, Bermpohl F, Dobrowolny H, Panksepp J. Self-referential processing in our brain–a meta-analysis of imaging studies on the self. *Neuroimage.* (2006) 31:440–57. doi: 10.1016/j.neuroimage.2005.12.002
18. Caudek C. Individual differences in cognitive control on self-referenced and other-referenced memory. *Conscious Cogn.* (2014) 30:169–83. doi: 10.1016/j.concog.2014.08.017
19. Auerbach RP, Bondy E, Stanton CH, Webb CA, Shankman SA, Pizzagalli DA. Self-referential processing in adolescents: Stability of behavioral and ERP markers. *Psychophysiology.* (2016) 53:1398–406. doi: 10.1111/psyp.12686

20. Ji JL, Grafton B, MacLeod C. Referential focus moderates depression-linked attentional avoidance of positive information. *Behav Res Ther.* (2017) 93:47–54. doi: 10.1016/j.brat.2017.03.004
21. Ma Y, Li B, Wang C, Shi Z, Sun Y, Sheng F, et al. 5-HTTLPR polymorphism modulates neural mechanisms of negative self-reflection. *Cereb Cortex.* (2014) 24:2421–9. doi: 10.1093/cercor/bht099
22. Yang J, Xu X, Chen Y, Shi Z, Han S. Trait self-esteem and neural activities related to self-evaluation and social feedback. *Sci Rep.* (2016) 6:20274. doi: 10.1038/srep20274
23. Lemogne C, le Bastard G, Mayberg H, Volle E, Bergouignan L, Lehericy S, et al. In search of the depressive self: extended medial prefrontal network during self-referential processing in major depression. *Soc Cogn Affect Neurosci.* (2009) 4:305–12. doi: 10.1093/scan/nsp008
24. Caudek C, Monni A. Do you remember your sad face? *Roles Negat Cogn Style Sad Mood Memory.* (2013) 21:891. doi: 10.1080/09658211.2013.765893
25. Janoffbulman R. Assumptive worlds and the stress of traumatic events: applications of the schema construct. *Soc Cogn.* (1989) 7:113–36. doi: 10.1521/soco.1989.7.2.113
26. Ryff CD, Keyes C. The structure of psychological well-being revisited. *J Pers Soc Psychol.* (1995) 69:719–27. doi: 10.1037/0022-3514.69.4.719
27. Franck E, De Raedt R, Dereu M, Van den Abbeele D. Implicit and explicit self-esteem in currently depressed individuals with and without suicidal ideation. *J Behav Ther Exp Psychiatry.* (2007) 38:75–85. doi: 10.1016/j.jbtep.2006.05.003
28. Kitayama S, Uchida Y. Explicit self-criticism and implicit self-regard: Evaluating self and friend in two cultures. *J Exp Soc Psychology.* (2003) 39:476–82. doi: 10.1016/S0022-1031(03)00026-X
29. Yamaguchi S, Greenwald AG, Banaji MR, Murakami F, Chen D, Shiomura K, et al. Apparent universality of positive implicit self-esteem. *Psychol Sci.* (2007) 18:498–500. doi: 10.1111/j.1467-9280.2007.01928.x
30. Kim YH, Chiu CY, Peng S, Cai H, Tov W. Explaining east-west differences in the likelihood of making favorable self-evaluations: the role of evaluation apprehension and directness of expression. *J Cross Cult Psychol.* (2010) 41:62–75. doi: 10.1177/0022022109348921
31. Kudo E, Numazaki M. Explicit and direct self-serving bias in Japan. *J Cross Cult Psychol.* (2003) 34:511–21. doi: 10.1177/0022022103256475
32. Grundy JG, Benarroch MF, Lebarr AN, Shedden JM. Electrophysiological correlates of implicit valenced self-processing in high vs. *Low Self Esteem Individ Soc Neurosci.* (2015) 10:100–12. doi: 10.1080/17470919.2014.965339
33. Randenborgh AV, Pawelzik M, Quirin M, Kuhl J. Bad roots to grow: deficient implicit self-evaluations in chronic depression with an early onset. *J Clin Psychol.* (2016) 72:580–90. doi: 10.1002/jclp.22275
34. Roberts JE, Porter A, Vergara-Lopez C. Implicit and explicit self-esteem in previously and never depressed individuals: Baseline differences and reactivity to rumination. *Cogn Ther Res.* (2015) 40:164–72. doi: 10.1007/s10608-015-9732-2
35. Greenwald AG, Mcghee DE, Schwartz JL. Measuring individual differences in implicit cognition: the implicit association test. *J Personal Soc Psychol.* (1998) 74:1464. doi: 10.1037/0022-3514.74.6.1464
36. Greenwald AG, Nosek BA, Banaji MR. Understanding and using the implicit association test: I. An improved scoring algorithm *J Personal Soc Psychol.* (2003) 85:197. doi: 10.1037/0022-3514.85.2.197
37. Greenwald AG, Banaji MR. Implicit social cognition: attitudes, self-esteem, and stereotypes. *Psychol Rev.* (1995) 102:4–27. doi: 10.1037/0033-295X.102.1.4
38. Nuttin JM. Narcissism beyond Gestalt and awareness: the name letter effect. *Eur J Soc Psychol.* (1985) 15:353–61. doi: 10.1002/ejsp.2420150309
39. Risch AK, Buba A, Birk U, Morina N, Steffens MC, Stangier U. Implicit self-esteem in recurrently depressed patients. *J Behav Ther Exp Psychiatry.* (2010) 41:199–206. doi: 10.1016/j.jbtep.2010.01.003
40. Romero N, Sanchez A, Vázquez C, Valiente C. Explicit self-esteem mediates the relationship between implicit self-esteem and memory biases in major depression. *Psychiatry Res.* (2016) 242:336–44. doi: 10.1016/j.psychres.2016.06.003
41. Franck E, De Raedt R, De Houwer J. Activation of latent self-schemas as a cognitive vulnerability factor for depression: the potential role of implicit self-esteem. *Cogn Emot.* (2008) 22:1588–99. doi: 10.1080/02699930801921271
42. Franck E, De Raedt R, De HJ. Implicit but not explicit self-esteem predicts future depressive symptomatology. *Behav Res Ther.* (2007) 45:2448. doi: 10.1016/j.brat.2007.01.008
43. Fleischhauer M, Strobel A, Diers K, Enge S. Electrophysiological evidence for early perceptual facilitation and efficient categorization of self-related stimuli during an Implicit Association Test measuring neuroticism. *Psychophysiology.* (2014) 51:142–51. doi: 10.1111/psyp.12162
44. Wu L, Gu R, Cai H, Zhang J. Electrophysiological evidence for executive control and efficient categorization involved in implicit self-evaluation. *Soc Neurosci.* (2016) 11:153–63. doi: 10.1080/17470919.2015.1044673
45. Hoorens V, Takano K, Franck E, Roberts JE, Raes F. Initial and noninitial name-letter preferences as obtained through repeated letter rating tasks continue to reflect (different aspects of) self-esteem. *Psychol Assess.* (2015) 27:905. doi: 10.1037/pas0000092
46. Jones JT, Pelham BW, Mirenberg MC, Hetts JJ. Name letter preferences are not merely mere exposure: implicit egotism as self-regulation. *J Exp Soc Psychol.* (2002) 38:170–7. doi: 10.1006/jesp.2001.1497
47. Stieger S, Burger C. More complex than previously thought: new insights into the optimal administration of the initial preference task. *Self Ident.* (2013) 12:201–16. doi: 10.1080/15298868.2012.655897
48. Koole SL, Dijksterhuis A, Van KA. What's in a name: implicit self-esteem and the automatic self. *J Personal Soc Psychol.* (2001) 80:669. doi: 10.1037/0022-3514.80.4.669
49. Fischer C, Dailler F, Morlet D. Novelty P3 elicited by the subject's own name in comatose patients. *Clin Neurophysiol Offic J Int Feder Clin Neurophysiol.* (2008) 119:2224. doi: 10.1016/j.clinph.2008.03.035
50. Koole SL, Pelham BW. On the nature of implicit self-esteem: the case of the Name Letter Effect. In: Spencer S, Fein S, Zanna MP, editors. *Motivated Social Perception: The Ontario Symposium.* Hillsdale: NJ: Lawrence Erlbaum (2003), p. 93–116.
51. Fujii T. Does the name-letter effect emerge in Korea? *Japan J Res Emot.* (2015) 23:32–7. doi: 10.4092/jsre.23.32
52. Hoorens V, Nuttin JM, Herman IE, Pavakanun U. Mastery pleasure versus mere ownership: a quasi-experimental cross-cultural and cross-alphabetical test of the name letter effect. *Eur J Soc Psychol.* (1990) 20:181–205. doi: 10.1002/ejsp.2420200302
53. Kitayama S, Karasawa M. Implicit self-esteem in Japan: name letters and birthday numbers. *Personal Soc Psychol Bull.* (1997) 23:736–42. doi: 10.1177/0146167297237006
54. Chen Y, Zhong Y, Zhou H, Zhang S, Tan Q, Fan W. Evidence for implicit self-positivity bias: an event-related brain potential study. *Exp Brain Res.* (2014) 232:985–94. doi: 10.1007/s00221-013-3810-z
55. Mezulis AH, Abramson LY, Hyde JS, Hankin BL. Is there a universal positivity bias in attributions? A meta-analytic review of individual, developmental, and cultural differences in the self-serving attributional bias. *Psychol Bull.* (2004) 130:711–47. doi: 10.1037/0033-2909.130.5.711
56. Pahl S, Eiser JR. Valence, comparison focus and self-positivity biases: does it matter whether people judge positive or negative traits? *Exp Psychol.* (2005) 52:303. doi: 10.1027/1618-3169.52.4.303
57. Watson LA, Dritschel B, Obonsawin MC, Jentzsch I. Seeing yourself in a positive light: brain correlates of the self-positivity bias. *Brain Res.* (2007) 1152:106. doi: 10.1016/j.brainres.2007.03.049
58. Zhou A, Li S, Herbert C, Xia R, Xu K, Xu Q, et al. Perspective taking modulates positivity bias in self-appraisals: behavioral and event-related potential evidence. *Soc Neurosci.* (2013) 8:326. doi: 10.1080/17470919.2013.807873
59. Leary MR. Motivational and emotional aspects of the self. *Ann Rev Psychol.* (2007) 58:317. doi: 10.1146/annurev.psych.58.110405.085658
60. Brand-Gothelf A, Yoeli-Bligh N, Gilboa-Schechtman E, Benaroya-Milshtein N, Apter A. Perceptions of self, mother and family and behavior of prepubertal depressed children. *Eur Psychiatry.* (2015) 30:69–74. doi: 10.1016/j.eurpsy.2014.05.005
61. Ruehlman LS, West SG, Pasahow RJ. Depression and evaluative schemata. *J Personal.* (2010) 53:46–92. doi: 10.1111/j.1467-6494.1985.tb00888.x

62. Shestyuk AY, Deldin PJ. Automatic and strategic representation of the self in major depression: trait and state abnormalities. *Am J Psychiatry.* (2010) 167:536–44. doi: 10.1176/appi.ajp.2009.06091444
63. Shestyuk AY, Deldin PJ, Brand JE, Deveney CM. Reduced sustained brain activity during processing of positive emotional stimuli in major depression. *Biol Psychiatry.* (2005) 57:1089–96. doi: 10.1016/j.biopsych.2005.02.013
64. Tripković I, Roje R, Krnić S, Nazor M, Karin Ž, Capkun V. (2015). Depression and self-esteem in farly adolescence. *Centr Eur J Public Health.* 23:166–9. doi: 10.21101/cejph.a4017
65. Watson LA, Dritschel B, Jentzsch I, Obonsawin MC. Changes in the relationship between self-reference and emotional valence as a function of dysphoria. *Br J Psychol.* (2008) 99:143–52. doi: 10.1348/000712607X248689
66. Alexander B, Brewin CR, Vearnals S, Wolff G, Leff J. An investigation of shame and guilt in a depressed sample. *Psychol Psychother Theor Res Pract.* (2011) 72:323–38. doi: 10.1348/000711299160031
67. Braet C, Wante L, Van Beveren ML, Theuwis L. Is the cognitive triad a clear marker of depressive symptoms in youngsters? *Eur Child Adolesc Psychiatry.* (2015) 24:1261. doi: 10.1007/s00787-015-0674-8
68. Thew GR, Gregory JD, Roberts K, Rimes KA. The phenomenology of self critical thinking in people with depression, eating disorders, and in healthy individuals. *Psychol Psychother.* (2017) 90:751–69. doi: 10.1111/papt.12137
69. Gara MA, Woolfolk RL, Allen LA. Social cognitive complexity and depression: cognitive complexity moderates the correlation between depression self-ratings and global self-evaluation. *J Nerv Mental Dis.* (2002) 190:670. doi: 10.1097/00005053-200210000-00003
70. Orchard F, Reynolds S. The combined influence of cognitions in adolescent depression: biases of interpretation, self-evaluation, and memory. *Br J Clin Psychol.* (2018) 57:420–35. doi: 10.1111/bjc.12184
71. Gildengers AG, Houck PR, Mulsant BH, Dew MA, Aizenstein HJ, Jones BL, et al. Trajectories of treatment response in late-life depression: psychosocial and clinical correlates. *J Clin Psychopharmacol.* (2005) 25(4 Suppl. 1):S8. doi: 10.1097/01.jcp.0000161498.81137.12
72. Woolfolk RL, Gara MA, Ambrose TK, Williams JE, Allen LA, Irvin SL, et al. Self-complexity and the persistence of depression. *J Nerv Ment Dis.* (1999) 187:393–9. doi: 10.1097/00005053-199907000-00001
73. Hur JW, Kim WJ, Kim YK. The mediating effect of psychosocial factors on suicidal probability among adolescents. *Arch Suicide Res.* (2011) 15:327–36. doi: 10.1080/13811118.2011.615701
74. Wetzel RD, Reich T. The cognitive triad and suicide intent in depressed in-patients. *Psychol Rep.* (1989) 65:1027–32. doi: 10.2466/pr0.1989.65.3.1027
75. Kelly MA, Roberts JE, Bottonari KA. Non-treatment-related sudden gains in depression: the role of self-evaluation. *Behav Res Ther.* (2007) 45:737–47. doi: 10.1016/j.brat.2006.06.008
76. Orth U, Robins RW, Roberts BW. Low self-esteem prospectively predicts depression in adolescence and young adulthood. *J Personal Soc Psychol.* (2008) 95:695–708. doi: 10.1037/0022-3514.95.3.695
77. Orth U, Robins RW, Widaman KF, Conger RD. Is low self-esteem a risk factor for depression? Findings from a longitudinal study of Mexican-origin youth. *Dev Psychol.* (2014) 50:622–33. doi: 10.1037/a0033817
78. Steiger AE, Allemand M, Robins RW, Fend HA. Low and decreasing self-esteem during adolescence predict adult depression two decades later. *J Pers Soc Psychol.* (2014) 106:325–38. doi: 10.1037/a0035133
79. Disner SG, Shumake JD, Beevers CG. Self-referential schemas and attentional bias predict severity and naturalistic course of depression symptoms. *Cogn Emot.* (2017) 31:632–44. doi: 10.1080/02699931.2016.1146123
80. Dobson KS, Shaw BF. Specificity and stability of self-referent encoding in clinical depression. *J Abnorm Psychol.* (1987) 96:34. doi: 10.1037/0021-843X.96.1.34
81. De Houwer J. What are implicit measures and why are we using them? *Rwwiers.* (2006) 11–28. doi: 10.4135/9781412976237.n2
82. Gemar MC, Segal ZV, Sagrati S, Kennedy SJ. Mood-induced changes on the implicit association test in recovered depressed patients. *J Abnorm Psychol.* (2001) 110:282. doi: 10.1037/0021-843X.110.2.282
83. Kesting ML, Mehl S, Rief W, Lindenmeyer J, Lincoln TM. When paranoia fails to enhance self-esteem: explicit and implicit self-esteem and its discrepancy in patients with persecutory delusions compared to depressed and healthy controls. *Psychiatry Res.* (2011) 186:197–202. doi: 10.1016/j.psychres.2010.08.036
84. Lemmens LH, Roefs A, Arntz A, van Teeseling HC, Peeters F, Huibers MJ. The value of an implicit self-associative measure specific to core beliefs of depression. *J Behav Ther Exp Psychiatry.* (2014) 45:196–202. doi: 10.1016/j.jbtep.2013.10.006
85. Raedt RD, Schacht R, Franck E, Houwer JD. Self-esteem and depression revisited: implicit positive self-esteem in depressed patients? *Behav Res Ther.* (2006) 44:1017–28. doi: 10.1016/j.brat.2005.08.003
86. van Tuijl LA, Glashouwer KA, Bockting CL, Tendeiro JN, Penninx BW, de Jong PJ. Implicit and explicit self-esteem in current, remitted, recovered, and comorbid depression and anxiety Disorders: the NESDA study. *PLoS ONE.* (2016) 11:e0166116. doi: 10.1371/journal.pone.0166116
87. Jabben N, de Jong PJ, Kupka RW, Glashouwer KA, Nolen WA, Penninx BW. Implicit and explicit self-associations in bipolar disorder: a comparison with healthy controls and unipolar depressive disorder. *Psychiatry Res.* (2014) 215:329–34. doi: 10.1016/j.psychres.2013.11.030
88. Creemers DHM, Scholte RHJ, Engels RCME, Prinstein MJ, Wiers RW. Damaged self-esteem is associated with internalizing problems. *Front Psychol.* (2013) 4:152. doi: 10.3389/fpsyg.2013.00152
89. Dimaro LV, Roberts NA, Moghaddam NG, Dawson DL, Brown I, Reuber M. Implicit and explicit self-esteem discrepancies in people with psychogenic nonepileptic seizures. *Epilepsy Behav.* (2015) 46:109–17. doi: 10.1016/j.yebeh.2015.03.032
90. Leeuwis FH, Koot HM, Creemers DH, van Lier PA. Implicit and explicit self-esteem discrepancies, victimization and the development of late childhood internalizing problems. *J Abnor Child Psychol.* (2015) 43:909–19. doi: 10.1007/s10802-014-9959-5
91. Schröder-Abé M, Rudolph A, Schütz A. High implicit self-esteem is not necessarily advantageous: discrepancies between explicit and implicit self-esteem and their relationship with anger expression and psychological health. *Eur J Pers.* (2007) 21:319–39. doi: 10.1002/per.626
92. Valiente C, Cantero D, Vazquez C, Sanchez A, Provencio M, Espinosa R. Implicit and explicit self-esteem discrepancies in paranoia and depression. *J Abnorm Psychol.* (2011) 120:691–9. doi: 10.1037/a0022856
93. Eberl C, Winkler I, Pawelczack S, Tröbitz E, Rinck M, Becker ES, et al. Self-esteem consistency predicts the course of therapy in depressed patients. *PLoS ONE.* (2018) 13:e0199957. doi: 10.1371/journal.pone.0199957
94. Poulsen C, Luu P, Crane SM, Quiring J, Tucker DM. Frontolimbic activity and cognitive bias in major depression. *J Abnorm Psychol.* (2009) 118:494–506. doi: 10.1037/a0015920
95. Waters AC, Tucker DM. Principal components of electrocortical activity during self-evaluation indicate depressive symptom severity. *Soc Cogn Affect Neurosci.* (2016) 11:1335–43. doi: 10.1093/scan/nsw046
96. Dainer-best J, Trujillo LT, Schnyer DM, Beevers CG. Sustained engagement of attention is associated with increased negative self-referent processing in major depressive disorder. *Biol Psychol.* (2017) 129:231–41. doi: 10.1016/j.biopsycho.2017.09.005
97. Speed BC, Nelson BD, Auerbach RP, Klein DN, Hajcak G. Depression risk and electrocortical reactivity during self-referential emotional processing in 8 to 14 year-old girls. *J Abnorm Psychol.* (2016) 125:607–19. doi: 10.1037/abn0000173
98. West WC, Holcomb PJ. Imaginal, Semantic, and Surface-Level Processing of Concrete and Abstract Words: An Electrophysiological Investigation. *J. Cogn. Neurosci.* (2000) 12:1024–37. doi: 10.1162/08989290051137558
99. Kutas M, Federmeier KD. Thirty years and counting: finding meaning in the N400 component of the event-related brain potential (ERP). *Ann Rev Psychol.* (2011) 62:621. doi: 10.1146/annurev.psych.093008.131123
100. White KR, Crites SL, Taylor JH, Corral G. Wait, what? Assessing stereotype incongruities using the N400 ERP component. *Soc Cogn Affect Neurosci.* (2009) 4:191. doi: 10.1093/scan/nsp004
101. Yang J, Hong L, Jiang Q, Qinglin Z. Effects of self evaluation on late ERP components. *自然科学进展 Natural in progress.* (2007) B07:106–9.
102. Naumann E, Bartussek D, Diedrich O, Laufer ME. Assessing cognitive and affective information processing functions of the brain by means of the late positive complex of the event-related potential. *J Psychophysiol.* (1992) 63:285–98.

103. Drevets WC, Price JL, Furey ML. Brain structural and functional abnormalities in mood disorders: implications for neurocircuitry models of depression. *Brain Struct Funct.* (2008) 213:93–118. doi: 10.1007/s00429-008-0189-x
104. Morel N, Villain N, Rauchs G, Gaubert M, Piolino P, Landeau B, et al. Brain activity and functional coupling changes associated with self-reference effect during both encoding and retrieval. *PLoS ONE.* (2014) 9:e90488. doi: 10.1371/journal.pone.0090488
105. Gillihan SJ, Farah MJ. Is self special? A critical review of evidence from experimental psychology and cognitive neuroscience. *Psychol Bull.* (2005) 131:76–97. doi: 10.1037/0033-2909.131.1.76
106. Grimm S, Ernst J, Boesiger P, Schuepbach D, Hell D, Boeker H, et al. Increased self-focus in major depressive disorder is related to neural abnormalities in subcortical-cortical midline structures. *Hum Brain Mapp.* (2009) 30:2617–27. doi: 10.1002/hbm.20693
107. Mor N, Winquist J. Self-focused attention and negative affect: a meta-analysis. *Psychol Bull.* (2002) 128:638. doi: 10.1037/0033-2909.128.4.638
108. Yoshimura S, Okamoto Y, Onoda K, Matsunaga M, Ueda K, Suzuki S, et al. Rostral anterior cingulate cortex activity mediates the relationship between the depressive symptoms and the medial prefrontal cortex activity. *J Affect Disord.* (2010) 122:76–85. doi: 10.1016/j.jad.2009.06.017
109. Bradley KA, Colcombe S, Henderson SE, Alonso CM, Milham MP, Gabbay V. Neural correlates of self-perceptions in adolescents with major depressive disorder. *Dev Cogn Neurosci.* (2016) 19:87–97. doi: 10.1016/j.dcn.2016.02.007
110. Kuhn S, Gallinat J. Resting-state brain activity in schizophrenia and major depression: a quantitative meta-analysis. *Schizophr Bull.* (2013) 39:358–65. doi: 10.1093/schbul/sbr151
111. Pavlickova H, Turnbull OH, Bentall RP. Discrepancies between explicit and implicit self-esteem and their relationship to symptoms of depression and mania. *Psychol Psychother Theor Res Prac.* (2014) 87:311–23. doi: 10.1111/papt.12015
112. Grimm S, Boesiger P, Beck J, Schuepbach D, Bermpohl F, Walter M, et al. Altered negative BOLD responses in the default-mode network during emotion processing in depressed subjects. *Neuropsychopharmacology.* (2009) 34:932. doi: 10.1038/npp.2008.81
113. Masten CL, Eisenberger NI, Borofsky LA, Mcnealy K, Pfeifer JH, Dapretto M. Subgenual anterior cingulate responses to peer rejection: a marker of adolescents' risk for depression. *Dev Psychopathol.* (2011) 23:283. doi: 10.1017/s0954579410000799
114. Moritz D, Roberts JE. Self-other agreement and metaperception accuracy across the Big Five: examining the roles of depression and self-esteem. *J Personal.* (2017) 86:296–307. doi: 10.1111/jopy.12313
115. Ranjith G, Farmer A, Mcguffin P, Cleare AJ. Personality as a determinant of social functioning in depression. *J Affect Disord.* (2005) 84:73–6. doi: 10.1016/j.jad.2004.10.008
116. Roberts SB, Kendler KS. Neuroticism and self-esteem as indices of the vulnerability to major depression in women. *Psychol Med.* (1999) 29:1101–9. doi: 10.1017/S0033291799008739
117. Schmitz N, Kugler J, Rollnik J. On the relation between neuroticism, self-esteem, and depression: results from the National Comorbidity Survey. *Comprehens Psychiatry.* (2003) 44:169–76. doi: 10.1016/S0010-440X(03)00008-7
118. Chiao JY, Harada T, Komeda H, Li Z, Mano Y, Saito D, et al. Neural basis of individualistic and collectivistic views of self. *Hum Brain Mapp.* (2009) 30:2813–20. doi: 10.1002/hbm.20707
119. Bosson JK, Brown RP, Zeigler-Hill V, Swann WB. Self-enhancement tendencies among people with high explicit self-esteem: the moderating role of implicit self-esteem. *Self Identity.* (2003) 2:169–87. doi: 10.1080/15298860309029
120. Leary MR, Tambor ES, Terdal SK, Downs DL. Self-esteem as an interpersonal monitor: the sociometer hypothesis. *J Pers Soc Psychol.* (1995) 68:270–4. doi: 10.1037/0022-3514.68.3.518
121. Pfeifer JH, Lieberman MD, Dapretto M. "I Know You Are But What Am I?!": neural bases of self- and social knowledge retrieval in children and adults. *J Cogn Neurosci.* (2007) 19:1323–37. doi: 10.1162/jocn.2007.19.8.1323
122. Hauser J, Leszczynska A, Samochowiec J, Czerski PM, Ostapowicz A, Chlopocka M, et al. Association analysis of the insertion/deletion polymorphism in serotonin transporter gene in patients with affective disorder. *Eur Psychiatry J Assoc Eur Psychiatr.* (2003) 18:129. doi: 10.1016/S0924-9338(03)00026-9
123. Dinger U, Ehrenthal JC, Nikendei C, Schauenburg H. Change in self-esteem predicts depressive symptoms at follow-up after intensive multimodal psychotherapy for major depression. *Clin Psychol Psychother.* (2017) 24:1040–6. doi: 10.1002/cpp.2067
124. Orth U, Robins RW. Understanding the Link between low self-esteem and depression. *Curr Direct Psychol Sci.* (2013) 22:455–60. doi: 10.1177/0963721413492763
125. Sowislo JF, Orth U. Does low self-esteem predict depression and anxiety? A meta-analysis of longitudinal studies. *Psychol Bull.* (2013) 139:213–40. doi: 10.1037/a0028931
126. Wegener I, Geiser F, Alfter S, Mierke J, Imbierowicz K, Kleiman A, et al. Changes of explicitly and implicitly measured self-esteem in the treatment of major depression: evidence for implicit self-esteem compensation. *Comprehensive Psychiatry.* (2015) 58:57–67. doi: 10.1016/j.comppsych.2014.12.001
127. Hulme N, Hirsch C, Stopa L. Images of the self and self-esteem: do positive self-images improve self-esteem in social anxiety? *Cogn Behav Ther.* (2012) 41:163. doi: 10.1080/16506073.2012.664557
128. Keng SL, Seah STH, Tong EMW, Smoski M. Effects of brief mindful acceptance induction on implicit dysfunctional attitudes and concordance between implicit and explicit dysfunctional attitudes. *Behav Res Ther.* (2016) 83:1–10. doi: 10.1016/j.brat.2016.05.004
129. Remmers C, Topolinski S, Koole SL. Why being mindful may have more benefits than you realize: Mindfulness improves both explicit and implicit mood regulation. *Mindfulness.* (2016) 7:829–37. doi: 10.1007/s12671-016-0520-1
130. Di SM, Norbury R, Harmer CJ. Short-term antidepressant administration reduces negative self-referential processing in the medial prefrontal cortex in subjects at risk for depression. *Mol Psychiatry.* (2012) 17:503–10. doi: 10.1038/mp.2011.16
131. Dubini A, Bosc M, Polin V. Noradrenaline-selective versus serotonin-selective antidepressant therapy: differential effects on social functioning. *J Psychopharmacol.* (1997) 11:17–23.
132. Matthews SC, Simmons AN, Strigo IA, Arce E, Stein MB, Paulus MP. Escitalopram attenuates posterior cingulate activity during self-evaluation in healthy volunteers. *Psychiatry Res.* (2010) 182:81–7. doi: 10.1016/j.pscychresns.2010.02.003
133. Beck AT, Ward CH, Mendelson M, Mock J, Erbaugh J. An inventory for measuring depression. *Arch General Psychiatry.* (1961) 4:561–71. doi: 10.1001/archpsyc.1961.01710120031004

6

Childhood Trauma and Sleep Among Young Adults With a History of Depression: A Daily Diary Study

Jessica L. Hamilton [1], Ryan C. Brindle [2], Lauren B. Alloy [3] and Richard T. Liu [4]*

[1] Department of Psychiatry, University of Pittsburgh, Pittsburgh, PA, United States, [2] Department of Psychology and Neuroscience Program, Washington and Lee University, Lexington, VA, United States, [3] Department of Psychology, Temple University, Philadelphia, PA, United States, [4] Department of Psychiatry and Human Behavior, Alpert Medical School of Brown University, Providence, RI, United States

***Correspondence:**
Jessica L. Hamilton
hamiltonjl2@upmc.edu

Child maltreatment and sleep disturbances are particularly prevalent among individuals with a history of depression. However, the precise relation between child maltreatment and sleep within this population is unclear. The present study evaluated childhood maltreatment and trauma as a predictor of sleep duration and insomnia symptoms among young adults with prior depression. A total of 102 young adults (18–22; 78% female) with a history of clinical or subclinical depression completed an in-person visit with diagnostic interviews and questionnaires of childhood trauma (maltreatment and general trauma), and 2 weeks of daily assessments of sleep and depressive symptoms using internet-capable devices. Using multilevel modeling, we found that only childhood emotional neglect significantly predicted higher levels of insomnia symptoms over the 2 weeks, controlling for daily depression. Neither childhood maltreatment nor trauma predicted sleep duration. Our findings highlight a unique relationship between emotional neglect and insomnia symptoms among individuals with a depression history that, given prior research, may potentially play a role in depression recurrence and represent a potential treatment target.

Keywords: depression, child maltreatment, emotional neglect, insomnia, sleep

INTRODUCTION

Childhood trauma is highly prevalent in depression, with over half of individuals with depression endorsing childhood abuse and neglect (1). Meta-analyses indicate that individuals exposed to childhood maltreatment are not only more likely to develop depression, but also experience depression that has a more severe, chronic, and treatment-resistant course [e.g., (1–3)]. Although all types of childhood maltreatment can have lasting consequences, research highlights a distinct relationship between emotional maltreatment and depression, such that emotional abuse and neglect more strongly predict depression course and severity than physical or sexual abuse (1, 3). Given the increased risk of chronic, recurrent depression among those exposed to childhood maltreatment, it is critical to identify potential mechanisms through which childhood maltreatment, particularly emotional abuse and neglect, may confer risk for future depression.

Importantly, sleep disturbance may be one critical mechanism through which individuals exposed to maltreatment are vulnerable for recurrent depressive episodes. Indeed, sleep complaints are among the most common residual symptoms of depression (4, 5). In particular, shorter sleep duration and difficulty initiating and maintaining sleep (i.e., insomnia symptoms) robustly predict depression recurrence (6–8), and are associated with increased risk of suicide (9).

Although research has only recently explored the long-term effects of childhood adversity on sleep in adulthood [for a review see (10)], studies indicate that childhood maltreatment and trauma contributes to poor sleep among adults decades later, even after taking into account intermediate life stress and depression [e.g., (11, 12)]. Further, a recent study of young adults undergoing the college transition prospectively evaluated the impact of specific subtypes of childhood trauma, including emotional, physical, and sexual abuse and neglect, on changes in sleep across the transition (13). This study found that only childhood emotional neglect predicted current psychological distress and subsequent decreases in sleep quality over 6 months later among young adults (13), thereby highlighting a unique relationship between childhood emotional neglect and poor sleep in the context of transitional life stress.

Although childhood maltreatment, and specifically emotional neglect, is associated with both sleep and depression, it remains unclear to what extent childhood trauma contributes to current sleep (duration and insomnia) among clinical populations (e.g., among young adults with a depression history), which may provide valuable information for intervention. Examining the effects of maltreatment and sleep *within* a group of individuals with former depression may yield critical information regarding individual differences in risk, and identify a potential mechanism through which individuals with childhood maltreatment are at heightened risk of recurrent depressive episodes. Given that sleep is a modifiable risk factor, it may represent a potential treatment target for prevention of recurrence among those exposed to child maltreatment and trauma. To date, however, most research has generally relied on retrospective recall of sleep quality over a significant stretch of time (e.g., 6 months), which, in addition to inherent limitations in temporal resolution, could potentially be confounded by current psychological distress.

Thus, as an initial step along this line of empirical inquiry, the present study evaluated the effects of childhood maltreatment on current sleep among young adults with a history of depression. Specifically, we evaluated *both* childhood maltreatment (emotional abuse, emotional neglect, physical abuse, sexual abuse) and general childhood trauma as predictors of sleep duration and insomnia symptoms reported over 2-week daily assessments. Although we hypothesized all forms of childhood maltreatment to be positively associated with insomnia symptoms and shorter sleep duration, we expected a more robust prospective relationship for emotional maltreatment with sleep given prior research indicating a unique role for emotional maltreatment (13). Thus, we expected that emotional abuse and neglect would be the most robust prospective predictors of sleep disturbance (duration, insomnia symptoms), after controlling for current depressive and anxiety symptoms.

METHOD

Participants and Procedure

Participants included young adults (n = 102) who participated in the Stress and Emotion study. To participate in the study, participants had to have (1) history of a major or subthreshold depression episode (but not current depression or bipolar disorder), (2) fluency in written and spoken English, and, (3) 18–22 years of age. This sample was selected to ensure sufficient variability of study constructs (i.e., fluctuations in sleep and depressive symptoms) to examine risk for *future* (but not current) depression among those most vulnerable (14). Following a clinical diagnostic interview with trained diagnosticians and informed consent [see (15) for full recruitment procedures], participants completed a baseline assessment with questionnaires about childhood maltreatment, childhood trauma, and an interview about negative life events that occurred in the past 4 weeks. For the next 2 weeks, participants completed daily diary assessments using internet-capable devices (between 6 p.m. and 12 a.m.,) of sleep (sleep/wake times and insomnia symptoms) and current depressive symptoms. This 2-week period was selected to provide a snapshot into participants' sleep and mood, which would provide better representation of individuals' habitual sleep and mood than 1 week without considerably adding participant burden. This study received ethical approval from the Temple University Institutional Review Board.

In the present study, participants on average were 19.86 years old (SD = 1.17 years), 78% were female, and 70% self-identified as Caucasian, 15% as African American/biracial, 15% as Asian, and 7% also as Hispanic/Latino. Over 20% identified as lesbian, gay, or bisexual, or "Something else/Other," and 44% of participants reported maternal education of "some college or less" [used as a proxy for socioeconomic status]. In terms of clinical history, 76 participants (74.5%) met criteria for past major depressive disorder (MDD) and 26 (25.5%) for subthreshold depression, which has a similar course and impairment as MDD (16). The average age of onset of clinical or subclinical depression was 15.62 years (SD = 3.31 years).

Measures

Childhood Trauma

To assess childhood trauma, we included two questionnaires that assess specific subtypes of childhood abuse and neglect [Childhood Trauma Questionnaire- CTQ; (17)] and more general childhood traumatic experiences [Trauma History Questionnaire-THQ; (18)].

The CTQ is a 28-item measure that assesses the severity of five subtypes of childhood maltreatment, including emotional abuse (EA), emotional neglect (EN), physical abuse (PA), physical neglect (PN), and sexual abuse (SA). Each subscale consists of five items asking participants to select the extent to which each item is true ("never true" to "very often true"). Higher scores indicate more maltreatment in each domain. The CTQ only examines the extent of maltreatment and does not assess the exact timing or duration. The CTQ has demonstrated excellent psychometric test properties in clinical and non-clinical samples (17, 19).

For more general trauma, participants completed the 24-item Trauma History Questionnaire (THQ), and individuals endorsed the occurrence and age of onset for traumatic events that occurred in their lives in three categories: crime-related (n = 4 items), general disaster, and trauma (n = 13), and physical and sexual experiences (n = 7). Endorsed events are summed in each category. To separately evaluate the impact of more general childhood trauma on sleep, the current study only included events ($n = 17$) in the domains of crime-related (i.e., "Has anyone ever attempted to or succeed in breaking into your home while you were there?") and general disaster and trauma (i.e., "Have you ever seen someone seriously injured or killed?") that occurred prior to age 18.

Recent Interpersonal Stressors

To account for the effects of recent negative interpersonal events, participants completed the Life Events Scale (LES) and Interview [LEI; (20)], which includes 100 major and minor life events (e.g., school, work, finances, family, peer, and, romantic relationships). Per the gold standard approach for assessing life events (21), participants were interviewed for objective indicators of the occurrence of events to reduce potential biases in event reporting. Events categorized as negative and interpersonal ($n = 44$) were included in the present study. The LES and LEI have demonstrated excellent reliability and validity (20).

Anxiety Symptoms

To control for the effects of anxiety on current sleep problems, participants completed the Beck Anxiety Inventory [BAI; (22)]. It is a 21-item measure of anxiety symptoms, and has demonstrated acceptable reliability (22).

Daily Depressive Symptoms

In the daily diary, participants reported on daily depressive symptoms using the eight-item PROMIS-Depression-Short Form [SF; (23)], which does not include any sleep items. The PROMIS-Depression-SF also has been found to have sound psychometric properties (23, 24), with $\alpha = 0.90$ in the present study.

Daily Sleep Duration and Insomnia

Also in the daily diary, participants reported the time (hour and minutes) that they went to bed and woke up in the morning, which was used to calculate an estimate of sleep duration. In addition, participants completed three items from the Insomnia Severity Index [ISI; (25, 26)], which assesses the extent of difficulty falling and staying asleep. These items are on a 5-point scale, ranging from 0 (none) to 4 (very severe). The sum of these three items reflected daily insomnia symptoms.

Statistical Analyses

To better understand the impact of demographic characteristics [race/ethnicity, gender, socioeconomic status (maternal education)] and depression history (clinical vs. subclinical) on experiences of child maltreatment and sleep, we conducted *t*-tests. Given the sample breakdown, race was dichotomized as "Minority" (African American/Black, biracial, Asian, Native American, or Other) and "Non-Minority" (White/Caucasian), and maternal education (proxy for SES) was dichotomized as "Higher" ("College graduate" or more) or "Lower" ("Some college" or lower).

To test the association of childhood trauma with daily-reported insomnia symptoms and sleep duration, we conducted multilevel modeling in Mplus 7.0 (27) with full information maximum likelihood to estimate parameters for missing data. Specifically, our model had two levels of data, including level 1 (within-person) of daily sleep and depressive symptoms and level 2 (between person) of childhood maltreatment and trauma. For analyses, childhood maltreatment subtypes (emotional abuse, neglect, physical abuse, sexual abuse) and general trauma were entered simultaneously as level 2 (between-person) predictors. The outcomes for all analyses were daily sleep parameters of insomnia symptoms and sleep duration [level 1(within-person) variables]. Due to multicollinearity, physical neglect was evaluated separately. For all analyses, we covaried for concurrent daily depressive symptoms (level 1) and between-person (level 2) variables of recent negative interpersonal stressors, anxiety symptoms, and demographic variables (gender, age, race, SES, and prior depression diagnosis).

RESULTS

Table 1 presents descriptives and bivariate correlations of primary study variables. There were several significant differences of maltreatment by demographic information (gender, race/ethnicity, SES). First, we found that women were more likely to report childhood sexual abuse than men ($t = 2.33$, $p = 0.01$), but there were no other differences on other trauma types or sleep. In addition, minority individuals were more likely to report emotional neglect ($t = 3.63$, $p < 0.001$), physical neglect ($t = 2.28$, $p = 0.03$), and physical abuse ($t = 4.83$, $p < 0.001$) than non-minority individuals. By socioeconomic status (maternal education), there were significant differences for physical abuse ($t = 3.33$, $p = 0.001$) and sexual abuse ($t = 2.14$, $p = 0.04$), and marginal differences in emotional abuse ($t = 1.75$, $p = 0.08$) and emotional neglect ($t = 1.88$, $p = 0.06$). The direction of these relationships was such that individuals with lower socioeconomic status reported more maltreatment. In terms of clinical history, individuals with a major compared to subthreshold depression history were only more likely to experience sexual abuse ($t = 2.33$, $p = 0.01$). There were no other significant differences for other forms of child maltreatment (*t*'s < 1.11) or general trauma ($t = 0.93$, $p = 0.36$). Importantly, there were no differences on sleep duration or insomnia symptoms by gender, race/ethnicity, SES, or clinical history.

Child Maltreatment and General Trauma With Insomnia Symptoms and Sleep Duration

Consistent with hypotheses for insomnia symptoms, results indicated there was a significant association between childhood emotional neglect with insomnia symptoms over the 2-week period, such that young adults who experienced more childhood emotional neglect reported higher levels of insomnia symptoms over 2 weeks (**Table 2**). Of note, this was found after covarying for current daily depressive symptoms, recent interpersonal life stress, baseline anxiety symptoms, other forms of childhood abuse and neglect, and demographic characteristics (race, gender, age, SES). Importantly, there were no significant effects of other

TABLE 1 | Descriptive statistics and bivariate correlations of primary study variables.

Measure	1	2	3	4	5	6	7	8	9
1. Childhood EA	–								
2. Childhood EN	0.55	–							
3. Childhood PA	0.21	0.32	–						
4. Childhood PN	0.19	0.53	0.37	–					
5. Childhood SA	0.39	0.19	0.06	0.09	–				
6. General Childhood Trauma	0.04	−0.03	0.01	0.06	0.04	–			
7. Daily Depressive Symptoms	0.15	0.26	0.03	0.20	0.13	−0.03	–		
8. Daily Sleep Duration	−0.01	−0.06	−0.11	0.04	0.04	0.05	−0.23	–	
9. Insomnia	0.24	0.34	0.13	0.06	0.06	−0.02	0.22	−0.15	–
Mean	12.11	9.37	5.79	6.11	5.52	1.08	10.95	7.79	1.59
SD	2.99	3.98	1.18	1.79	2.32	1.25	3.10	0.86	1.34

Correlations > |0.20| are statistically significant ($p < 0.05$). Mean levels of daily depressive symptoms and sleep are reported. EA, Emotional abuse; EN, Emotional Neglect; PA, Physical Abuse; PN, Physical Neglect; SA, Sexual Abuse.

TABLE 2 | Fixed effects of childhood trauma on sleep in young adulthood.

Variable	Insomnia symptoms			Sleep duration		
	B	***SE***	***t***	***B***	***SE***	***t***
BETWEEN-PERSON						
Intercept	2.63	2.30	1.14	7.38	1.68	4.39***
MDD	0.30	0.28	1.07	−0.11	0.20	−0.55
Sex	0.23	0.31	0.75	−0.15	0.23	−0.67
Age	−0.15	0.11	−1.37	0.05	0.08	0.68
Race	−0.32	0.34	−0.94	0.08	0.25	0.33
SES	−0.29	0.26	−1.09	0.13	0.19	0.68
Anxiety	0.01	0.01	0.68	< 0.01	0.01	−0.05
Recent Stress	0.10	0.05	2.11*	−0.03	0.04	−0.08
Child Trauma						
EA	< −0.01	0.06	−0.09	< 0.01	0.04	0.07
EN	0.10	0.04	2.37*	−0.02	0.03	−0.81
PA	0.02	0.12	0.18	−0.06	0.09	−0.66
SA	0.04	0.06	0.62	0.04	0.05	0.88
THQ	−0.07	0.07	−0.97	−0.05	0.05	−0.98
Within–person						
Depression Symptoms	0.006	0.02	0.38	<0.01	0.02	0.05

**$p < 0.05$; ** $p < 0.01$; *** $p < 0.001$. B represents the unstandardized coefficient. MDD, Major Depressive Disorder (Coded as 0, None; 1, Present); Sex coded as 0, male; 1, female; Race coded as 0, minority; 1, minority; SES coded as 0, lower; 1, higher. EA, Emotional abuse; EN, Emotional Neglect; PA, Physical Abuse; SA, Sexual Abuse; THQ, Trauma History Questionnaire.*

childhood maltreatment [physical neglect or abuse (emotional, physical, and sexual)] or general childhood trauma.

In contrast to our hypotheses, there were no significant effects of childhood maltreatment or trauma on sleep duration (**Table 2**). This indicates that the effect of childhood emotional neglect was specific to insomnia symptoms, as there were no main effect of emotional neglect on sleep duration in young adults with prior depression.

DISCUSSION

Childhood trauma can have long-lasting effects on physical and mental health. Although research has consistently linked childhood trauma with depression and, more recently, sleep in adulthood (12, 13), this is the first study to evaluate the relationship between specific subtypes of childhood trauma and sleep in young adulthood among individuals with a depression history. Specifically, we evaluated childhood abuse (emotional, physical, sexual), neglect (physical and emotional), and general childhood trauma (total of crime, environmental, danger) as predictors of insomnia symptoms and sleep duration reported over a 2-week period using a daily diary design.

Overall, our results indicated that childhood emotional neglect uniquely predicted insomnia symptoms among young adults with prior depression, even after accounting for other forms of childhood maltreatment and traumatic experiences, current depressive, and anxiety symptoms, and a range of demographic features that could impact this relationship (gender, race, SES, and depression history). In addition, in contrast to our hypotheses, our results were specific to emotional neglect and insomnia symptoms, as no form of childhood trauma predicted sleep duration. Thus, our results highlight a distinct relationship between emotional neglect during childhood and difficulties initiating and/or maintaining sleep as young adults, which is important given that emotional neglect is one of the most prevalent forms of maltreatment (28). Importantly, given that all individuals had a prior depression history, this is a clinical sample of individuals who are most vulnerable to both childhood trauma exposure and sleep disturbance. This suggests that the effects of emotional neglect on insomnia symptoms may indicate individual differences of future risk for depression recurrence, which is important for identifying sleep as a potential treatment target to improve outcomes and prevent depression recurrence among those with a history of emotional neglect.

Although we hypothesized that emotional neglect would predict both insomnia symptoms and shorter sleep duration, there are several possibilities why childhood emotional neglect may specifically contribute to insomnia symptoms compared to sleep duration and other forms of trauma. Specifically, emotional neglect is a distinct form of maltreatment characterized by the *absence* or *omission* of emotional or psychological support (i.e., child ignored, unresponsive parenting) compared to other types of maltreatment, such as emotional and physical abuse, which are more active acts of *commission*. Further, emotional neglect is described as a pattern of interactions between the caregiver and child rather than specific events or experiences that are *tangible*, such as absence of physical resources (e.g., food). Thus, emotional neglect may uniquely contribute to difficulty in understanding their emotional experiences (29), and impaired biological and cognitive regulation of emotions and perceived stress (30–32). Consequently, emotional neglect may contribute to emotional and social isolation throughout development and into adulthood (31). Given research on the effect of loneliness and both social and emotional isolation on sleep disturbance in adulthood (33, 34), it could be that emotional neglect deprives individuals the emotional safety required for restorative sleep (35), and heighten psychophysiological arousal. Insomnia is characterized by physiological, cognitive, and affective hyperarousal (36); thus, emotional neglect may specifically contribute to insomnia symptoms. Importantly, our study found evidence for the relationship of emotional neglect and insomnia even after taking into account the effect of current interpersonal stressors, which also significantly predict prospective insomnia symptoms. However, it is important for future research to explore the relationship between childhood emotional neglect and current socio-emotional isolation, and empirically evaluate the underlying psychosocial and biological mechanisms linking emotional neglect and sleep disturbance.

Although our study demonstrated the continuing effect of trauma on insomnia symptoms among individuals with depression histories, it is important to note several important directions of future research based on limitations of the current study. For one, it is difficult to disentangle the directionality of these relationships, and it is possible that sleep disturbance preceded the trauma and depression. Given research on the intergenerational transmission of trauma (37) and continuous cycle of abuse (38), it is possible that maltreated individuals have parents who also experienced childhood trauma. Parental experience of trauma could impact neurodevelopmental pathways that contribute to sleep disturbance and depression (39), as well as limited parenting ability to promote sleep hygiene and habits (40). Although we did not assess parental trauma or assess sleep prior to maltreatment exposure, our study did find demographic differences in the experience of emotional neglect by race and socioeconomic status, with minority and lower income individuals reporting more emotional neglect and other forms of maltreatment. However, we did not find any demographic differences in sleep duration or insomnia symptoms. This suggests that despite differences in exposure, reported sleep was less affected by these factors. However, this may indicate individual protective factors that could influence the relationships observed in the study. For instance, it is important to consider to what extent individual and contextual protective factors, such as individual resilience (41), parental sleep monitoring (42), or social support (43), may buffer the effects of maltreatment, which could provide more direct and modifiable targets for intervention.

Our study should be considered in the context of several other limitations, which may influence generalizability and provide critical directions for future research. In particular, this study relied on daily self-reported sleep rather than behaviorally assessed sleep parameters (e.g., actigraphy), which limits our ability objectively to assess sleep duration. Thus, it is possible that emotional neglect (and other forms of maltreatment) may impact sleep duration, but our measure captured *time in bed*, which may not be the most accurate representation of time spent asleep. Further, our study did not assess other sleep domains that could be impacted by child maltreatment (e.g., sleep onset latency, nighttime awakenings). Furthermore, given the high rates of comorbidity of PTSD and depression, particularly among maltreated individuals (44), it is important to recognize that the current study did not assess post-traumatic symptoms or nightmare-related sleep disturbance. It is very possible that individuals with maltreatment histories have post-traumatic symptoms or nightmares related to the trauma that could contribute to the current findings (45). Thus, future research and clinical practice should focus on better understanding whether nightmares and other post-traumatic symptoms, such as hypervigilance, contribute to the relationship observed between childhood emotional neglect and insomnia symptoms in young adulthood.

In addition, we utilized self-report retrospective measures of childhood trauma. Given the length of time that could have elapsed since the trauma, it is possible that individuals may not accurately recall trauma. It is important to note that our study used a prospective daily diary design, which temporally distinguished the timing of childhood maltreatment and sleep assessments. Although this is a strength of the study, it should be noted that it is possible that the 2 weeks captured by the study presents a relatively brief observational period of the association between maltreatment and sleep patterns. Therefore, it is important for future research to carefully consider and incorporate multiple methods and informants to the assessment of maltreatment and sleep. Specifically, though the current study used trauma measures that are widely-used and well-validated (18, 19), clinical interviews would provide more specific information about the maltreatment, including timing, duration, and severity, which may influence the relationships observed in the study. Relatedly, our sample included mostly women and individuals with a history of depression, which limited our ability to test gender differences in these relationships, which is important to consider in future research. In addition, it is unclear the extent to which our findings apply to non-clinical samples (i.e., those without depression) or individuals with later-onset depression. However, given that our sample experienced relatively young first depression onset (15–16 years old), the young adults in this sample may represent a particularly vulnerable group for both sleep disturbance and childhood adversity. Consequently, the fact that we identified emotional neglect as a unique predictor of insomnia symptoms *within* this vulnerable group highlights the importance of examining individual differences within clinical populations.

Importantly, our study provides new insight and preliminary evidence of a distinct relationship between childhood trauma and sleep in young adulthood. Specifically, our findings highlight a unique relationship between childhood emotional neglect and insomnia symptoms among individuals with a history of depression, which may provide important targets of treatment to prevent depression recurrence.

AUTHOR CONTRIBUTIONS

JH designed the study, collected the data, and conducted the analyses. JH and RB wrote the initial draft of the manuscript. LA and RL provided substantive revisions to the manuscript.

FUNDING

This work was supported by grants from the National Institutes of Health to JH (F31MH106184, T32HL082610), RB (F32 HL137227), LA (R01MH079369, R01MH101168), and RL (R01 MH101138).

REFERENCES

1. Nelson J, Klumparendt A, Doebler P, Ehring T. Childhood maltreatment and characteristics of adult depression: meta-analysis. *Br J Psychiatry* (2017) 210:96–104. doi: 10.1192/bjp.bp.115.180752
2. Nanni V, Uher R, Danese A. Childhood maltreatment predicts unfavorable course of illness and treatment outcome in depression: a meta-analysis. *Am J Psychiatry* (2012) 169:141–51. doi: 10.1176/appi.ajp.2011.11020335
3. Norman RE, Byambaa M, De R, Butchart A, Scott J, Vos T. The long-term health consequences of child physical abuse, emotional abuse, and neglect: a systematic review and meta-analysis. *PLoS Med.* (2012) 9:1001349. doi: 10.1371/journal.pmed.1001349
4. Judd LL, Rapaport MH, Paulus MP, Brown JL. Subsyndromal symptomatic depression: a new mood disorder? *J Clin Psychol.* (1994) 55:18–28.
5. Tsuno N, Besset A, Ritchie K. Sleep and depression. *J Clin Psychiatry* (2005) 66:1254–69. doi: 10.4088/JCP.v66n1008
6. Baglioni C, Battagliese G, Feige B, Spiegelhalder K, Nissen C, Voderholzer U, et al. Insomnia as a predictor of depression: a meta-analytic evaluation of longitudinal epidemiological studies. *J Affect Disord.* (2011) 135:10–9. doi: 10.1016/j.jad.2011.01.011
7. Franzen PL, Buysse DJ. Sleep disturbances and depression: risk relationships for subsequent depression and therapeutic implications. *Dialog Clin Neurosci.* (2008) 10:473–81. doi: 10.1177/0263775816657084
8. Zhai L, Zhang H, Zhang D. Sleep duration and depression among adults: a meta-analysis of prospective studies. *Depress Anxiety* (2015) 32:664–70. doi: 10.1002/da.22386
9. Bernert RA, Joiner TE. Sleep disturbances and suicide risk: a review of the literature. *Neuropsychiatr Dis Treat.* (2007) 3:735–43. doi: 10.2147/NDT.S1248
10. Kajeepeta S, Gelaye B, Jackson CL, Williams MA. Adverse childhood experiences are associated with adult sleep disorders: a systematic review. *Sleep Med.* (2015) 16:320–30. doi: 10.1016/j.sleep.2014.12.013
11. Baiden P, Fallon B, den Dunnen W, Boateng GO. The enduring effects of early-childhood adversities and troubled sleep among Canadian adults: a population-based study. *Sleep Med.* (2015) 6:760–7. doi: 10.1016/j.sleep.2015.02.527
12. Brindle RC, Cribbet MR, Samuelsson LB, Gao C, Frank E, Krafty R, et al. The relationship between childhood trauma and poor sleep health in adulthood. *Psychosom Med.* (2018) 80:200–7. doi: 10.1097/PSY.0000000000000542
13. John- Henderson NA, Williams SE, Brindle RC, Ginty AT. Changes in sleep quality and levels of psychological distress during the adaptation to university: the role of childhood adversity. *Br J Psychol.* (2018) 109:694–707 doi: 10.1111/bjop.12314
14. Burcusa SL, Iacono WG. Risk for recurrence in depression. *Clin Psychol Rev.* (2007) 27:959–85. doi: 10.1016/j.cpr.2007.02.005
15. Hamilton JL, Alloy, L. B. (2017). Physiological Markers of Interpersonal Stress Generation in Depression. *Clin Psychol Sci,* 5:911–29. doi: 10.1177/2167702617720211
16. Kessler RC, Zhao S, Blazer DG, Swartz M. Prevalence, correlates, and course of minor depression and major depression in the National Comorbidity Survey. *J Affect Disord.* (1997) 45:19–30. doi: 10.1016/S0165-0327(97)00056-6
17. Bernstein DP, Stein JA, Newcomb MD, Walker E, Pogge D, Ahluvalia T, et al. Development and validation of a brief screening version of the childhood trauma questionnaire. *Child Abuse Negl.* (2003) 27:169–90. doi: 10.1016/S0145-2134(02)00541-0
18. Hooper LM, Stockton P, Krupnick JL, Green BL. Development, use, and psychometric properties of the trauma history questionnaire. *J Loss Trauma* (2011) 16:258–83. doi: 10.1080/15325024.2011.572035
19. Scher CD, Stein MB, Asmundson GC, McCreary DR, Forde DR. The childhood trauma questionnaire in a community sample: psychometric properties and normative data. *J Trauma Stress* (2001) 14:843–57. doi: 10.1023/A:1013058625719
20. Safford SM, Alloy LB, Abramson LY, Crossfield AG. Negative cognitive style as a predictor of negative life events in depression-prone individuals: a test of the stress generation hypothesis. *J Affect Disord.* (2007) 99:147–54. doi: 10.1016/j.jad.2006.09.003
21. Hammen C. Stress and depression. *Annu Rev Clin Psychol.* (2005) 1:293–319. doi: 10.1146/annurev.clinpsy.1.102803.143938
22. Beck AT, Epstein N, Brown G, Steer RA. An inventory for measuring clinical anxiety: psychometric properties. *J Consult Clin Psychol.* (1988) 56:893–7. doi: 10.1037/0022-006X.56.6.893
23. Pilkonis PA, Choi SW, Reise SP, Stover AM, Riley WT, Cella D, et al. Item banks for measuring emotional distress from the patient-reported outcomes measurement information system (PROMIS(R): depression, anxiety, and anger. *Assessment* (2011) 18:263–83. doi: 10.1177/1073191111411667
24. Olino TM, Yu L, McMakin DL, Forbes EE, Seeley JR, Lewinsohn PM, et al. Comparisons across depression assessment instruments in adolescence and young adulthood: an item response theory study using two linking methods. *J Abnorm Child Psychol.* (2013) 41:1267–77. doi: 10.1007/s10802-013-9756-6
25. Morin CM. *Insomnia: Psychological Assessment and Management.* New York, NY: Guilford Press (1993).

26. Bastien CH, Vallieres A, Morin CM. Validation of the insomnia severity index as an outcome measure for insomnia research. *Sleep Med.* (2000) 2:297–307. doi: 10.1016/S1389-9457(00)00065-4
27. Muthén LK, Muthén BO. *Mplus User's Guide.* 6th ed. Los Angeles, CA: Muthén and Muthén (2007).
28. Edwards VJ, Holden GW, Felitti VJ, Anda RF. Relationship between multiple forms of childhood maltreatment and adult mental health in community respondents: results from the adverse childhood experiences study. *Am J Psychiatry* (2003) 160:1453–60. doi: 10.1176/appi.ajp.160.8.1453
29. Jessar A, Hamilton JL, Flynn M, Abramson LY, Alloy LB. Emotional clarity as a mechanism linking emotional neglect and depressive symptoms during early adolescence. *J Early Adolesc.* (2017) 37:414–32. doi: 10.1177/0272431615609157
30. Bruce J, Fisher PA, Pears KC, Levine S. Morning cortisol levels in preschool-aged foster children: differential effects of maltreatment type. *Dev Psychobiol.* (2009) 51:14–23. doi: 10.1002/dev.20333
31. Repetti R, Taylor S, Seeman T. Risky family social environments and physical and mental health of the offspring. *Psychol Bull.* (2002) 128:330–66. doi: 10.1037/0033-2909.128.2.330
32. Wright MO, Crawford E, Del Castillo D. Childhood emotional maltreatment and later psychological distress among college students: the mediating role of maladaptive schemas. *Child Abuse Negl.* (2009) 33:59–68. doi: 10.1016/j.chiabu.2008.12.007
33. Cacioppo JT, Hawkley LC, Berntson CG, Ernst JM, Gibbs AC, Stickgold R, et al. Do lonely days invade nights? Potential social modulation of sleep efficiency. *Psychol Sci.* (2002) 13:384–7. doi: 10.1111/j.0956-7976.2002.00469.x
34. Matthews T, Danese A, Gregory A, Caspi A, Moffitt T, Arseneault L. Sleeping with one eye open: loneliness and sleep quality in young adults. *Psychol Med.* (2017) 47:2177–86. doi: 10.1017/S0033291717000629
35. Hawkley LC, Cacioppo JT. Loneliness matters: a theoretical and empirical review of consequences and mechanisms. *Ann Behav Med.* (2010) 40:218–27. doi: 10.1007/s12160-010-9210-8
36. Levenson JC, Kay DB, Buysse DJ. The pathophysiology of insomnia. *Chest* (2015) 147:1179–92. doi: 10.1378/chest.14-1617
37. Zuravin S, McMillen C, DePanfilis D, Riley-Curtiss C. The intergenerational cycle of child maltreatment: continuity versus discontinuity. *J Interpers Violence* (1996) 11:315–34. doi: 10.1177/088626096011003001
38. Merrick MT, Guinn AS. Child abuse and neglect: breaking the intergenerational link. *Am J Public Health* (2018) 108:1117–8. doi: 10.2105/AJPH.2018.304636
39. Buss C, Entringer S, Moog NK, Toepfer P, Fair DA, Simhan HN, et al. Intergenerational transmission of maternal childhood maltreatment exposure: implications for fetal brain development. *J Am Acad Child Adolesc Psychiatry* (2017) 56:373–82. doi: 10.1016/j.jaac.2017.03.001
40. Zalewski M, Cyranowski JM, Cheng Y, Swartz HA. Role of maternal childhood trauma on parenting among depressed mothers of psychiatrically ill children. *Depress Anxiety* (2013) 30:792–9. doi: 10.1002/da.22116
41. Wingo AP, Wrenn G, Pelletier T, Gutman AR, Bradley B, Ressler KJ. Moderating effects of resilience on depression in individuals with a history of childhood abuse or trauma exposure. *J Affect Disord.* (2010) 126:411–4. doi: 10.1016/j.jad.2010.04.009
42. Short MA, Gradisar M, Wright H, Lack LC, Dohnt H, Carskadon MA. Time for bed: parent-set bedtimes associated with improved sleep and daytime functioning in adolescents. *Sleep* (2011) 34:797–800. doi: 10.5665/SLEEP.1052
43. Sperry DM, Widom CS. Child abuse and neglect social support, and psychopathology in adulthood: a prospective investigation. *Child Abuse Negl.* (2013) 37:415–25. doi: 10.1016/j.chiabu.2013.02.006
44. Flory JD, Yehuda R. Comorbidity between post-traumatic stress disorder and major depressive disorder: alternative explanations and treatment considerations. *Dialog Clin Neurosci.* (2015) 17:141–50.
45. Harvey AG, Jones C, Schmidt DA. Sleep and posttraumatic stress: a review. *Clin Psychol Rev.* (2003) 23:377–407. doi: 10.1016/S0272-7358(03)00032-1

7

An Improved Model of Physical and Emotional Social Defeat: Different Effects on Social Behavior and Body Weight of Adolescent Mice by Interaction With Social Support

Man Li[1,2,3,4], *Hang Xu*[4,5] *and Weiwen Wang*[4,5]*

[1] Department of Psychology, Tianjin Normal University, Tianjin, China, [2] Academy of Psychology and Behavior, Tianjin Normal University, Tianjin, China, [3] Center of Collaborative Innovation for Assessment and Promotion of Mental Health, Tianjin, China, [4] CAS Key Laboratory of Mental Health, Institute of Psychology, Beijing, China, [5] Department of Psychology, University of Chinese Academy of Sciences, Beijing, China

***Correspondence:**
Weiwen Wang
wangww@psych.ac.cn

Social stress is a prevalent etiological environmental factor that can affect health, especially during adolescence. Either experiencing or witnessing a traumatic event during adolescence can increase the risk of psychiatric disorders, such as PTSD. The present study attempted to establish an improved social stress model to better distinguish the effects of physical and emotional social stress on the behavior and physiology of adolescent mice. In addition, we investigated how social support affected these stress-induced changes in social behavior. On PND 28, male littermates were exposed to either physical stress (PS) or emotional stress (ES), afterwards, half of them were paired-housed and the others were singly housed. The PS exposed mice were directly confronted with a violent aggressor using the social defeat stress (SDS) paradigm for 15 min/trial (with the total of 10 trials randomly administered over a week), while the ES exposed mice were placed in a neighboring compartment to witness the PS procedure. Our results indicate that both stressors induced an effective stress response in adolescent mice, but PS and ES had differential influence in the context of relevant social anxiety/fear and social interaction with peers. Additionally, social support following stress exposure exerted beneficial effects on the social anxiety/fear in ES exposed mice, but not on PS exposed mice, suggesting that the type of stressor may affect the intervention efficacy of social support. These findings provide extensive evidence that physical and emotional stressors induce different effects. Moreover, ES exposed mice, rather than PS exposed mice, seemed to benefit from social support. In summary, the study suggests that this paradigm will be helpful in investigating the effects of psychological intervention for the treatment of stress-related psychiatric disorders.

Keywords: adolescent, physical stress, emotional stress, social behavior, social support

INTRODUCTION

Adolescence, a transition period between childhood and adulthood, is a critical period for the development of social psychology and the brain (1, 2). During this period, an individuals' social relations experience a transition from family-oriented to peer-, school-, and environment-directed relations, showing strong interest in and sensitivity to social information, such as social interaction, novelty seeking, etc. (3). Concomitant with social behavioral manifestations in adolescence, the structure and function of the social brain, which refers to the network of brain regions underlying social emotion and cognition, especially the prefrontal cortex and subcortical pathways, undergo profound and rapid developmental changes (4). These constitute the unique neurobehavioral characteristics of adolescents, that also increase their vulnerability to a variety of social stressors (5, 6). For instance, it has been indicated that a variety of negative social experiences, including peer bullying, abuse, etc., can act as substantial stressors in the adolescent group (7, 8) and intimately relate to the onset of psychiatric disorders, such as PTSD, depression, etc. (9–11).

It is not only experiencing traumatic events, but also witnessing such events that can increase the risk of psychiatric disorders, such as PTSD. Previous studies showed that approximately 25–30% of individuals who witnessed a traumatic event might develop PTSD and other forms of mental disorders, including depression (12, 13). In animal studies, it has also been observed that exposing mice to both physical stress (e.g., foot shocks) and emotional stress (e.g., witnessing foot shocks) induced conditional fear memory, a core symptom of PTSD (14, 15). Although the foot-shock model is useful for investigating the effects of PS and ES, it is a rather severe stressor and is difficult to translate to the human context. Peer bullying, on the other hand, is a common stressor in children and adolescents, shown to be highly predictive of subsequent psychopathology, such as PTSD (16–18). Such types of socially stressful experiences in humans can be simulated by the social defeat stress (SDS) model in rodents, typically by the "resident-intruder" paradigm. It has been proven that this model can effectively induce emotional and cognitive alterations relevant to symptoms of a patient with stress-related psychiatric disorders, such as PTSD and depression (19). The protocol of SDS often includes two stages: first, the experimental subjects (the "intruders") are directly exposed to the aggressive subjects (the "resident") to induce PS for a short time (usually, 5–15 min); afterwards, they are separated by a transparent, perforated divider to maintain sensory contact for a period of time (e.g., the remainder of the day, or 30 min, etc.) (13, 19, 20;), thereby inducing further emotional stress in the defeated animal. However, the model can be adapted to include a pure ES group composed of animals that witness the social defeat of others. Warrant et al. observed that mice in both PS and ES groups showed a smaller weight gain, decreased social interaction and increased anxiety-like behaviors in the elevated-plus maze (EPM) test after 7 days of stress exposure (20). Miao et al. also found that pregnant mice exhibited decreased sucrose preference and spent less time in the open arms of the EPM after witnessing the defeat of their mates (21). However, as mentioned above, the PS animals are in fact exposed to both PS (in the first stage of SDS), and ES (in the second stage of SDS). Therefore, it is difficult to distinguish between the separate effects of PS and ES on behavior and physiology. Due to a common etiological stressor, it is necessary to develop an improved PS and ES model to further clarify the effects of the two types of stressors.

There is extensive evidence that social support is an important factor affecting the consequences of stress. Substantive social support is known to be a protective factor decreasing or preventing the detrimental effects of stress, especially under conditions of severe stress (22). In animal research, isolation-housing after SDS induces prolonged behavioral and physiological alterations, including reduced sucrose preference, cognitive impairment, enhanced anxiety-like behavior in the EPM test, social avoidance, enhanced locomotor activity in the open field test and an increased heart rate, etc.(23–25). Intriguingly, these effects were substantially reduced in animals that were group-housed after SDS. These studies clearly indicate that social relations and/or social support can play an important role in reducing the effect of stress. However, not all studies have reached this conclusion and some have even indicated that social relationships might act as a new stressor, under certain conditions (26, 27). Moreover, it remains to be explored whether social support has a similar effect in PS- and ES-exposed animals.

As social stress is an important etiological factor in the (mental) health of adolescents, the present study aimed to establish an improved model on the basis of classical social defeat stress, to better distinguish the effects of PS and ES on social behavior. We also investigated the role of social support in these effects.

MATERIALS AND METHODS

Animals

Male offspring of C57BL/6J mice (Beijing Vital River Laboratory Animal Technology Co., Ltd) obtained at weaning (postnatal day, PND21) from our in-house breeding program (Center for Experimental Animal Research, Institute of Psychology, Chinese Academy of Sciences) were used as intruders. From PND21 to PND28, male siblings were housed in groups of 2-4 mice per cage, with free access to water and food. Male CD-1 mice (Beijing Vital River Laboratory Animal Technology Co., Ltd) were used as residents and housed singly until 3–4 months of age. All mice were bred and housed under standard conditions [12:12 h light-dark cycle with lights on at 07:00 a.m.; the room temperature was $20 \pm 2°C$].

Experimental procedures were performed with the approval of the Institutional Review Board of the Institute of Psychology, Chinese Academy of Health Guide for the Care and Use of Laboratory Animals.

Physical and Emotional Stress Procedures

The stress cage (L × W × H: 45 × 30 × 17.5 cm) was divided into three equal chambers (L × W × H: 45 × 10 × 11 cm) with transparent perforated Plexiglas boards (**Figure 1A**). Appropriate selection of aggressive CD-1 male mice is critical

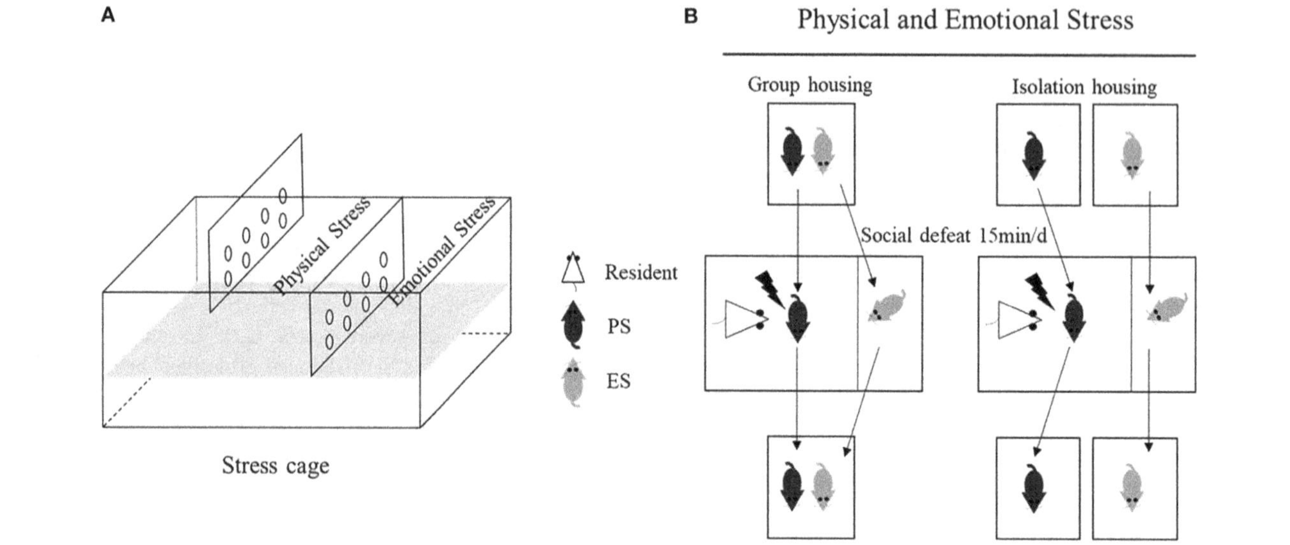

FIGURE 1 | Schematic representation of the stress cage **(A)**, and the physical and emotional stress process **(B)**.

for the successful application of physical and emotional stress. Therefore, CD-1 mice were selected as aggressors (residents) based on the following standards: attack latency shorter than 10 s and multiple or continuous violent attacks for three consecutive days. Additionally, prior to the stress test, the resident CD-1 mice were placed in the stress cage for at least 3 days to enhance their territorial behavior.

On PND28, male litters were assigned to physical stress (PS, $n = 14$) or emotional stress (ES, $n = 14$) groups. As the social relationship (e.g., familiar or unfamiliar) is an important factor of modulating the intensity of emotional stress (28, 29), littermates were paired into PS and ES groups. PS mice were directly placed in the stress cage, where they experienced physical aggression by a CD-1 resident for 15 min, similar to the "resident-intruder" paradigm described previously (30, 31); meanwhile, the ES littermates witnessed the social defeat process in the adjacent chamber (**Figure 1B**). After each social defeat exposure, the PS and ES mice were returned to their home cages; half of them were housed in pairs, and the others were singly housed. PS mice faced different residents each time and a total of 10 randomized social defeats over 1 week were performed, to maintain the stress effect (32). The stress submission was performed in the morning or the afternoon of a given day, according to a randomized defeat time and frequency and two defeats were administered on three randomly selected days over 1 week, with one defeat on the remaining 4 days. During the entire stress period, mice in the control (CON) group were placed in the same cage while the residents were C57BL/6J mice and were separated by the dividers in the stress cages, to avoid direct physical contact. No aggressive behavior occurred during these control sessions.

Body weight was recorded before the social defeat and after the last social defeat protocol. The behavioral tests were conducted 24 h after the last social defeat stress.

Behavioral Tests

Three-Chamber Social Approach Test

A modification of the sociability and social novelty preference test was used to reflect the level of social interest and the ability to recognize new social objects (33). The testing apparatus was a three-chamber rectangular arena (L × W × H: 60 × 40 × 20 cm, made of white Plexiglas), that was divided into three equal zones by two transparent Plexiglas partitions. There was a channel that could be closed and opened (8 × 8 cm) at the bottom of the partition to allow the mouse to move between chambers (**Supplementary Figure 1**). The distance traveled and the time spent in each zone, were automatically recorded by infrared video tracking and analysis in the dark condition (EthoVision XT with Social Interaction Module; Noldus Information Technology).

The test consisted of three stages. After each stage, the mouse was returned to the home cage. There was a 5 min interval between each stage.

In the first stage, the shuttle channel was closed. The mouse was placed in the middle chamber and allowed to explore for 10 min. The distance traveled in the middle zone was recorded to assess the locomotor activity. The second stage was the social interaction test. Two unfamiliar C57BL/6J males that had no prior contact with the subject mice were placed in the wire cage (L × W × H: 20 × 10 × 10 cm) in the corner of each interaction zone. The shuttle channels were opened, and the experimental mouse was placed in the same starting position, in the middle zone and allowed to explore freely for 10 min. The third stage was the new social object recognition test. To avoid the influence of position preference, a new strange mice was placed in the wire cage on one side where the experimental mouse spent the least amount of time in the second stage. Afterwards, the mouse was placed in the middle zone at the same starting position and allowed to explore freely for 10 min. The chambers of the testing apparatus were cleaned with 75% ethanol to prevent olfactory interference with subsequent tests.

The time spent in each zone was recorded. The social interaction (SI) was calculated as (time spent in the two interaction zones)/(time in the middle zone). The new social object recognition was calculated as (time spent in the new object zone)/(total time spent in the interaction zone), which also reflects the level of social working memory.

Social Avoidance

The next day after the three-chamber social approach tests, social avoidance was tested as described previously (19, 30). In brief, mice were placed in an arena (L × W × H: 40 × 40 × 20 cm) that contained an interaction zone (L × W: 20 × 14 cm) at one end of the arena with a small, metallic mesh cage (L × W × H: 8 × 8 × 8 cm) in the middle. The time spent in the interaction zone was initially monitored for 150 s in the absence of a CD-1 mouse, followed by another 150 s in the presence of a CD-1 mouse in the small cage, which was automatically recorded by an infrared behavior tracking and analysis system (EthoVision XT with Social Interaction Module; Noldus Information Technology). The social avoidance ratio was calculated as (time in the interaction zone with CD-1)/(time in the interaction zone without CD-1). After each test, the arena was cleaned with 75% ethanol to prevent olfactory interference with subsequent tests.

Statistical Analysis

Results are expressed as the mean ± SEM. The analysis was performed using the GraphPad Prism6 software (USA). The weight data and the behavioral data for locomotor activity, social interaction ratio, working memory and social avoidance were analyzed using a two-way ANOVA. Following significant results from the analysis of variance, an LSD analysis was used as the *post hoc* test. The significance level was defined as a $p < 0.05$.

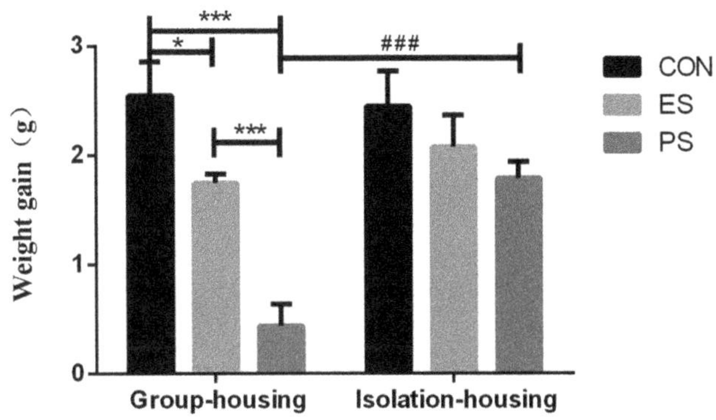

FIGURE 2 | Effects of stress and housing conditions on the bodyweight gain. The results are expressed as the mean ± S.E.M ($n = 7$ per group). $^{***}p < 0.001$, $^{**}p < 0.01$, $^{*}p < 0.05$ indicate the p-value for the differences among CON, PS, and ES mice. $^{\#\#\#}p < 0.001$ corresponds to the difference between housing conditions in the PS group.

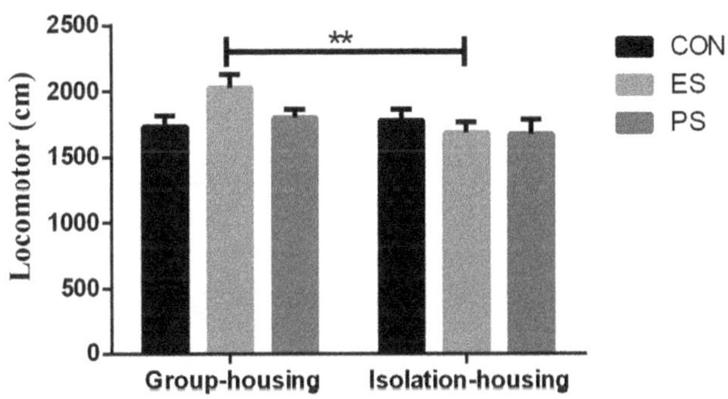

FIGURE 3 | Effects of stress and housing conditions on locomotor activity. The results are expressed as the mean ± S.E.M ($n = 7$ per group), with $^{**}p < 0.01$ for the difference between housing conditions in the ES group.

RESULTS

Effects of Stress and Rearing Condition on Body Weight Gain

As shown in **Figure 2**, the two-way ANOVA indicated significant main effects of stress ($F_{(2,37)} = 16.45$, $p < 0.001$) and housing conditions ($F_{(1,37)} = 7.68$, $p < 0.05$) as well as stress × housing condition interaction ($F_{(2,37)} = 4.67$, $p < 0.05$). The *post hoc* analysis showed that both PS and ES significantly reduced the bodyweight gain under the group housing condition compared to the controls ($p < 0.05$) and the PS mice experienced the least weight gain. However, isolation housing increased the bodyweight gain significantly in PS mice compared to the group housing condition ($p < 0.001$).

Effects of Stress and Housing Conditions on Locomotor Activity

As shown in **Figure 3**, there were marginally significant main effects of housing conditions ($F_{(1,37)} = 3.86$, $p = 0.058$), but not of stress ($F_{(2,37)} = 1.08$, $p = 0.35$) or of stress × housing condition interaction ($F_{(2,37)} = 2.56$, $p = 0.091$). The *post hoc* analysis indicated that mice in the group housing condition in the ES group exhibited significantly increased locomotor activity compared to those in the ES isolation housing condition ($p < 0.01$).

Effects of Stress and Housing Conditions on Social Interaction

The social interaction performance is shown in **Figure 4**. There were significant main effects of stress (time: $F_{(2,37)} = 40.78$, $p < 0.001$; ratio: $F_{(2,37)} = 43.64$, $p < 0.001$) and housing conditions (time: $F_{(1,37)} = 4.35$, $p < 0.05$; ratio: $F_{(1,37)} = 5.58$, $p < 0.05$) but not of stress × housing conditions interaction (time: $F_{(2,37)} = 0.51$, $p = 0.60$; ratio: $F_{(2,37)} = 0.46$, $p = 0.63$). The *post hoc* analysis revealed that only mice that experienced physical stress showed a significant reduction in social interaction in both the group and isolation housing conditions ($p < 0.05$). Although the interaction between the housing condition and stress was not significant, the mice housed in isolation had a more pronounced reduction of social interaction in the PS group ($p < 0.05$).

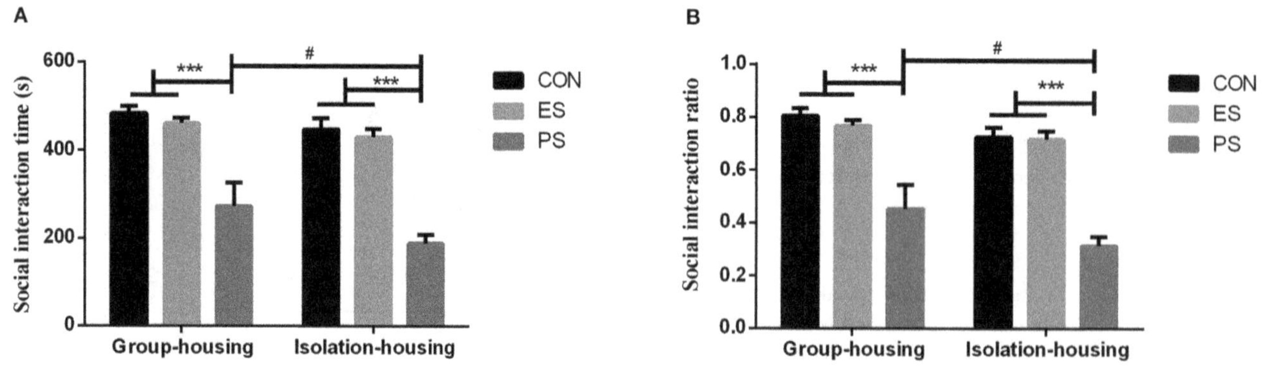

FIGURE 4 | Effects of stress and housing conditions on social interaction time **(A)** and ratio **(B)**. The results are expressed as the mean ± S.E.M ($n = 7$ per group). The social interaction time is calculated as a sum of the time spent in the two interaction zones. The social interaction ratio was defined as (time spent in the two interaction zones)/(time in the middle zone) × 100%. ***$p < 0.001$, compared to controls; #$p < 0.05$ for the difference between housing conditions in the PS group.

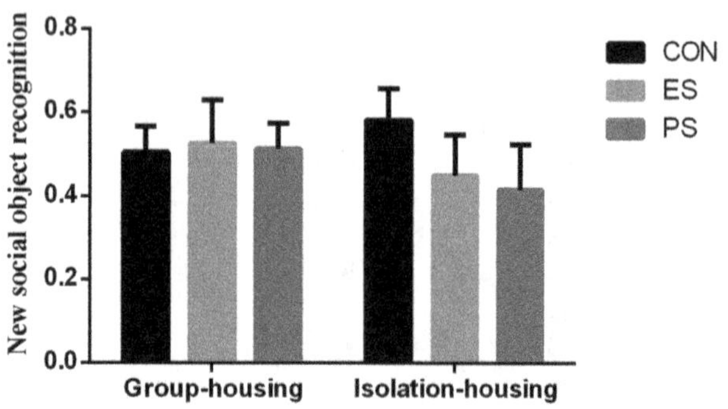

FIGURE 5 | Effects of stress and housing conditions on new social object recognition. The results are expressed as the mean ± S.E.M ($n = 7$ per group). New social object recognition was calculated as (time spent in the new object zone)/(total time spent in the interaction zone) × 100%.

Effects of Stress and Housing Conditions on New Social Object Recognition

The result of new social object recognition is shown in **Figure 5**. There were no main effects of stress ($F_{(2,37)} = 0.28$, $p = 0.76$) or housing conditions ($F_{(1,37)} = 0.06$, $p = 0.80$), nor of stress × housing condition interaction ($F_{(2,37)} = 0.47$, $p = 0.63$), indicating that neither stress nor the housing condition influenced the new social object recognition in our experiment.

Effects of Stress and Housing Conditions on Social Avoidance

As shown in **Figure 6**, there were significant main effects of stress (time: $F_{(2,35)} = 16.26$, $p < 0.001$; ratio: $F_{(2,35)} = 27.48$, $p < 0.001$) and stress × housing condition interaction on the social avoidance ratio ($F_{(2,35)} = 3.34$, $p < 0.05$). However, effects of the housing conditions (time: $F_{(1,35)} = 0.05$, $p = 0.83$; ratio: $F_{(1,35)} = 0.14$, $p = 0.71$) and stress × housing condition interaction on social avoidance time ($F_{(2,35)} = 2.54$, $p = 0.091$) were not significant. The *post hoc* analysis revealed that both ES and PS mice exhibited a lower social avoidance ratio (**Figure 6B**) compared to the controls under isolation housing conditions ($p < 0.05$). However, only PS mice showed significant social avoidance under the group housing conditions ($p < 0.05$).

DISCUSSION

In the presents study, we aimed to develop an improved social stress model to better distinguish the effects of PS and ES. Reduced weight gain in mice exposed to PS or ES compared to the control mice, suggested that both stressors indeed induced a substantial stress response in adolescent mice. We also found that PS and ES exerted differential effects on social behaviors. Finally, we found that social support had different effects on the stress induced changes in social behavior. These results suggest that our paradigm is indeed an effective adolescent stress model that mimics the complex effects of social environmental factors on adolescent development.

Social avoidance primarily reflects a state of anxiety or fear in the context of defeat and this behavioral phenotype bears relevance for posttraumatic stress disorders, such as social phobia (19, 34). Our present study demonstrated that both PS and ES significantly increased social avoidance to previously stressful context, compared to the corresponding controls under the isolation housing condition; while only the PS, but not ES mice showed a lower social avoidance ratio, compared to that of ES mice under group housing conditions. As mentioned above, mice exposed to a social defeat in previous studies suffered compound physical and emotional social stress (19, 20). We found that "pure" physical stress and emotional social defeat can also induce contextual social avoidance, a behavioral phenotype relevant to posttraumatic stress disorder through experiencing or witnessing a traumatic event. Additionally, a more significantly decreased social avoidance ratio was observed in PS-exposed mice, indicating that physical stress had greater effects than those of emotional stress.

In contrast to social avoidance, social interaction reflects a more general social interest (35). We found that only PS exposed mice showed lower social interaction behaviors with

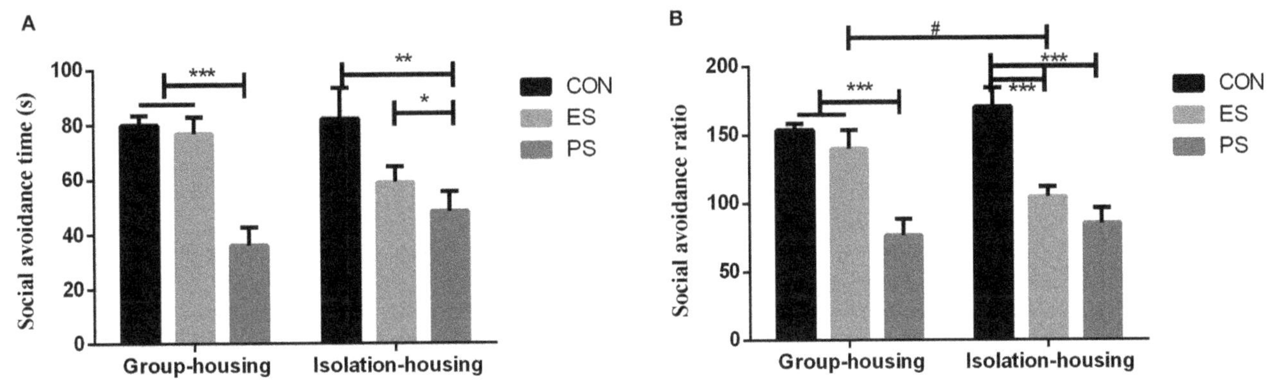

FIGURE 6 | Effects of stress and housing conditions on the social avoidance time **(A)** and ratio **(B)**. The results are expressed as the mean ± S.E.M ($n = 7$ per group). The social avoidance time is calculated as time in the interaction zone with CD-1. The social avoidance ratio is calculated as (time in the interaction zone with CD-1 mice)/(time in the interaction zone without CD-1 mice) × 100%. $^{***}p < 0.001$, $^{**}p < 0.01$, $^{*}p < 0.05$, the differences among CON, PS and ES mice. $^{\#}p < 0.05$, the difference between housing conditions in the ES group.

peers, including lower interaction time and ratio with other mice, suggesting that physical social stress induced a more generalized impairment in their social behavior. Previous studies reported that physical stress induced a more extensive and robust influence on the social behavior of animals than that of emotional stress (20, 36). However, in these studies, PS was somehow conflated with ES exposure, while here we further demonstrated that pure physical social stress could impair social behavior, while only emotional social stress did not cause a general decrease in social interest. Additionally, there were no differences in the new social object recognition task between groups, suggesting that impaired social interaction could not be attributed to a reduced recognition ability. Mice in different groups also exhibited similar locomotor activity, further excluding the potential effects of less contact with peers on the evaluation of social interest in the social interaction test.

The protective effects of social support on trauma and related psychiatric disorders have been extensively reported (20, 29, 37). Partially consistent with previous studies, we also found that some of the changes induced by adolescent PS and ES were moderated by the housing conditions, isolation or group housing. For example, in the social avoidance paradigm, PS induced a lower time and ratio in the interaction area, with effects being unaffected by the housing conditions, while the social avoidance behaviors seen in ES mice were only observed in the isolation housing conditions. Similarly, the PS induced reduction in social interest was independent of the housing conditions. In other words, the protective effect of social support seems to be limited to the ES-exposed mice. Although the exact reasons for this differential effect of social support are unclear, several factors might be involved. First, only the PS group exhibited an impairment of general social interest as manifested by a decreased social interaction time and ratio. Thus, we can speculate that PS exposed mice may be less capable of effectively using social support. To verify this possibility, the daily social behaviors of group-housed PS exposed mice with cage mates, need to be investigated further in the future. Moreover, the lack of social contact is closely related to loneliness, a psychological stress that can cause a variety of behavioral and physiological changes (38, 39). Additionally, as our data showed, PS induced more severe deficits than ES did and it can be speculated that social support may not provide sufficient protection to the more severe consequences of PS. In summary, this suggested that lower availability of social support to physically stressed subjects may contribute to weakened beneficial effects in a social environment. Therefore, improving individual social support utilization is a critical issue.

Our results showed that exposure to PS or ES reduced weight gain in mice compared to the control mice, a result consistent with previous studies (40, 41). Warren et al. also found that both PS and ES reduced weight gain (20, 42, 43). Somewhat surprisingly, in PS-exposed mice, isolation housing increased body-weight gain compared to that observed in the group housing conditions. It is currently unclear why this occurred. As mentioned above, PS decreased social interactions with peers. There may be a compensatory mechanism, whereby the mice exposed to PS decreased play behavior with cage mates and increased their food intake, due to an increased basal metabolic response (43).

CONCLUSION

In the present study, we developed an improved social defeat stress model that could help us further discriminate between the different effects of physical and emotional stress. We found this model to be an effective adolescent social stress model, of inducing alterations in experience-relevant social anxiety/fear and general social interaction. Importantly, these alterations were differentially affected by social support conditions after the stressful experience, depending on the type of stressor. These findings provide important evidence regarding the response to physical and emotional stressors, interacting with psychological interventions. We are confident that the model will be beneficial for understanding stress-related psychopathology.

AUTHOR CONTRIBUTIONS

WW designed the research; ML and HX performed the research, acquired and analyzed the data; ML, HX, and WW drafted, revised, and wrote the paper.

FUNDING

This work was supported by the National Natural Science Foundation of China (Grant No. 81471122 and 31470988), the Chinese Academy of Sciences (Grant No. KJZD-EW-L04), the Philosophy and Social Sciences Planning Foundation of Tianjin (Grant No. TJJXQN17-003), the doctoral fund of Tianjin Normal university (Grant No.043-135202WW1713), the Department of Psychology and the Beijing Key Laboratory of Behavior and Mental Health, the Chinese Academy of Sciences (KJZD-EW-L04) and the CAS Key Laboratory of Mental Health, Institute of Psychology.

ACKNOWLEDGMENTS

This work was supported by the National Natural Science Foundation of China (Grant No. 81471122 and 31470988), the Chinese Academy of Sciences (Grant No. KJZD-EW-L04), the Philosophy and Social Sciences Planning Foundation of Tianjin (Grant No. TJJXQN17-003), the doctoral fund of Tianjin Normal university (Grant No.043-135202WW1713), and the CAS Key Laboratory of Mental Health, Institute of Psychology.

REFERENCES

1. Spear LP. The adolescent brain and age-related behavioral manifestations. *Neurosci Biobehav Rev.* (2000) 24:417–63. doi: 10.1016/S0149-7634(00)00014-2
2. Burnett S, Sebastian C, Cohen Kadosh K, Blakemore SJ. The social brain in adolescence: evidence from functional magnetic resonance imaging and behavioural studies. *Neurosci Biobehav Rev.* (2011) 35:1654–64. doi: 10.1016/j.neubiorev.2010.10.011
3. McCormick C, Green M. From the stressed adolescent to the anxious and depressed adult: investigations in rodent models. *Neuroscience* (2013) 249:242–57. doi: 10.1016/j.neuroscience.2012.08.063
4. Crews F, He J, Hodge C. Adolescent cortical development: a critical period of vulnerability for addiction. *Pharmacol Biochem Behav.* (2007) 86:189–99. doi: 10.1016/j.pbb.2006.12.001
5. Vidal J, de Bie J, Granneman RA, Wallinga AE, Koolhaas JM, Buwalda B. Social stress during adolescence in Wistar rats induces social anxiety in adulthood without affecting brain monoaminergic content and activity. *Physiol Behav.* (2007) 92:824–30. doi: 10.1016/j.physbeh.2007.06.004
6. Vidal J, Buwalda B, Koolhaas JM. Differential long-term effects of social stress during adolescence on anxiety in Wistar and wild-type rats. *Behav Proces.* (2011) 87:176–82. doi: 10.1016/j.beproc.2011.03.004
7. Gladstone GL, Parker GB, Malhi GS. Do bullied children become anxious and depressed adults?: a cross-sectional investigation of the correlates of bullying and anxious depression. *J Nerv Mental Dis.* (2006) 194:201–8. doi: 10.1097/01.nmd.0000202491.99719.c3
8. Bourke CH, Neigh GN. Behavioral effects of chronic adolescent stress are sustained and sexually dimorphic. *Hormones Behav.* (2011) 60:112–20. doi: 10.1016/j.yhbeh.2011.03.011
9. Hammen C. Adolescent depression: stressful interpersonal contexts and risk for recurrence. *Curr Direct Psychol Sci.* (2009) 18:200–4. doi: 10.1111/j.1467-8721.2009.01636.x
10. Eiland L, Ramroop J, Hill MN, Manley J, McEwen BS. Chronic juvenile stress produces corticolimbic dendritic architectural remodeling and modulates emotional behavior in male and female rats. *Psychoneuroendocrinology* (2012) 37:39–47. doi: 10.1016/j.psyneuen.2011.04.015
11. Kovalenko IL, Galyamina AG, Smagin DA, Michurina TV, Kudryavtseva NN, Enikolopov G. Extended effect of chronic social defeat stress in childhood on behaviors in adulthood. *PLoS ONE* (2014) 9:e917623. doi: 10.1371/journal.pone.0091762
12. Yehuda R, Resnick H, Kahana B, Giller EL. Long-Lasting Hormonal Alterations to Extreme Stress in humans: normative or maladaptive? *Psychosom Med.* (1993) 55:287–97.
13. Patki G, Salvi A, Liu H, Salim S. Witnessing traumatic events and post-traumatic stress disorder: insights from an animal model. *Neurosci Lett.* (2015) 600:8–32. doi: 10.1016/j.neulet.2015.05.060
14. Endo Y, Shiraki K. Behavior and body temperature in rats following chronic foot shock or psychological stress exposure. *Physiol Behav.* (2000) 71:263–8. doi: 10.1016/S0031-9384(00)00339-5
15. Pijiman FTA, Wolterink G, Van Ree JM. Physical and emotional stress have differential effects on preference for saccharine and open field behaviour in rats. *Behav Brain Res.* (2003) 139:131–8. doi: 10.1016/S0166-4328(02)00124-9
16. Rossow I, Lauritzen G. Shattered childhood: a key issue in suicidal behavior among drug addicts? *Addiction* (2001) 96:227–40. doi: 10.1080/09652140020020955
17. Hamilton LD, Newman ML, Delville CL, Delville Y. Physiological stress response of young adults exposed to bullying during adolescence. *Physiol behav.* (2008) 95:617–24. doi: 10.1016/j.physbeh.2008.09.001
18. Pelkonen M, Marttunen M, Kaprio J, Huurre T, Aro H. Adolescent risk factors for episodic and persistent depression in adulthood. A 16-year prospective follow-up study of adolescents. *J Affect Disord.* (2008) 106:123–31. doi: 10.1016/j.jad.2007.06.001
19. Golden SA, Covington HEIII, Berton O, Russo SJ. A standardized protocol for repeated social defeat stress in mice. *Nat Protocols* (2011) 6:1183–91. doi: 10.1038/nprot.2011.361
20. Warren BL, Vialou VF, Iñiguez SD, Alcantara LF, Wright KN, Feng J, et al. Neurobiological sequelae of witnessing stressful events in adult mice. *Biol Psychiatry* (2013) 73:7–14. doi: 10.1016/j.biopsych.2012.06.006
21. Miao Z, Mao FB, Liang JL, Szyf MS, Wang Y, Sun ZS. Anxiety-related behaviours associated with microRNA-206-3p and BDNF expression in pregnant female mice following psychological social stress. *Mol Neurobiol.* (2018) 55:1097–111. doi: 10.1007/s12035-016-0378-1
22. Stevens NR, Gerhart J, Goldsmith RE, Heath NM, Chesney SA, Hobfoll SE. Emotion regulation difficulties, low social support, and interpersonal violence mediate the link between childhood abuse and posttraumatic stress symptoms. *Behav Ther.* (2013) 44:152–61. doi: 10.1016/j.beth.2012.09.003

23. Nakayasu T, Ishii K. Effects of pair-housing after social defeat experience on elevated plus-maze behavior in rats. *Behav Proces.* (2008) 78:477–80. doi: 10.1016/j.beproc.2008.02.007
24. Lehmann ML, Herkenham M. Environmental enrichment confers stress resiliency to social defeat through an infralimbic cortex-dependent neuroanatomical pathway. *J Neurosci.* (2011) 31:6159–73. doi: 10.1523/JNEUROSCI.0577-11.2011
25. McQuaid RJ, Audet MC, Jacobson-Pick S, Anisman H. Environmental enrichment influences brain cytokine variations elicited by social defeat in mice. *Psychoneuroendocrinology* (2013) 38:987–96. doi: 10.1016/j.psyneuen.2012.10.003
26. McQuaid RJ, Audet MC, Jacobson-Pick S, Anisman H. The differential impact of social defeat on mice living in isolation or groups in an enriched environment: plasma corticosterone and monoamine variations. *Int J Neuropsychopharmacol.* (2013) 16:351–63. doi: 10.1017/S1461145712000120
27. McCormick CM, Hodges TE, Simone JJ. Peer pressures: social instability stress in adolescence and social deficits in adulthood in a rodent model. *Dev Cogn Neurosci.* (2015) 11:2–11. doi: 10.1016/j.dcn.2014.04.002
28. Watanabe S. Empathy and reversed empathy of stress in mice. *PLoS ONE* (2011) 6:e23357. doi: 10.1371/journal.pone.0023357
29. Patki G, Solanki N, Salim S. Witnessing traumatic events causes severe behavioral impairments in rats. *Int J Neuropsychopharmacol.* (2014) 17:2017–29. doi: 10.1017/S1461145714000923
30. Zhang F, Yuan SN, Shao F, Wang WW. Adolescent social defeat induced alterations in social behavior and cognitive flexibility in adult mice: effects of developmental stage and social condition. *Front Behav Neurosci.* (2016) 10:149. doi: 10.3389/fnbeh.2016.00149
31. Xu H, Wang J, Zhang K, Zhao M, Ellenbroek B, Shao F, et al. Effects of adolescent social stress and antidepressant treatment on cognitive inflexibility and Bdnf epigenetic modifications in the mPFC of adult mice. *Psychoneuroendocrinology* (2018) 88:92–101. doi: 10.1016/j.psyneuen.2017.11.013
32. Parihar VK, Hattiangady B, Kuruba R, Shuai B, Shetty AK. Predictable chronic mild stress improves mood, hippocampal neurogenesis and memory. *Mol Psychiatry* (2011) 16:171–83. doi: 10.1038/mp.2009.130
33. Moy SS, Nadler JJ, Perez A, Barbaro RP, Johns JM, Magnuson TR, et al. Sociability and preference for social novelty in five inbred strains: an approach to assess autistic-like behavior in mice. *Genes Brain Behav.* (2004) 3:287–302. doi: 10.1111/j.1601-1848.2004.00076.x
34. Lagace DC, Donovan MH, DeCarolis NA, Farnbauch LA, Malhotra S, Berton O, et al. Adult hippocampal neurogenesis is functionally important for stress-induced social avoidance. *Proc Natl Acad Sci USA.* (2010) 107:4436–41. doi: 10.1073/pnas.0910072107
35. Sheth SKS, Li Y, Shaw CA. Is exposure to aluminium adjuvants associated with social impairments in mice? A pilot study. *J Inorgan Biochem.* (2018) 181:96–103. doi: 10.1016/j.jinorgbio.2017.11.012
36. Warren BL, Sial OK, Alcantara LF, Greenwood MA, Brewer JS, Rozofsky JP, et al. Altered gene expression and spine density in nucleus accumbens of adolescent and adult male mice exposed to emotional and physical stress. *Dev Neurosci.* (2014) 36:250–60. doi: 10.1159/000362875
37. Clapp JD, Beck JG. Understanding the relationship between PTSD and social support: The role of negative network orientation. *Behav Res Ther.* (2009) 47:237–44. doi: 10.1016/j.brat.2008.12.006
38. Hawkley LC, Thisted RA, Cacioppo JT. Loneliness predicts reduced physical activity: cross-sectional & longitudinal analyses. *Health Psychol.* (2009) 28:354–63. doi: 10.1037/a0014400
39. Lukkes JL, Mokin MV, Scholl JL, Forster GL. Adult rats exposed to early-life social isolation exhibit increased anxiety and conditioned fear behavior, and altered hormonal stress responses. *Hormones Behav.* (2009) 55:248–56. doi: 10.1016/j.yhbeh.2008.10.014
40. Berton O, McClung CA, Dileone RJ, Krishnan V, Renthal W, Russo SJ, et al. Essential role of BDNF in the mesolimbic dopamine pathway in social defeat stress. *Science* (2006) 311:864–8.
41. Krishnan V, Han MH, Graham DL, Berton O, Renthal W, Russo SJ, et al. Molecular adaptations underlying susceptibility and resistance to social defeat in brain reward regions. *Cell* (2007) 131:391–404. doi: 10.1016/j.cell.2007.09.018
42. Wood SK, Walker HE, Valentino RJ, Bhatnagar S. Individual differences in reactivity to social stress predict susceptibility and resilience to a depressive phenotype: role of corticotropin-releasing factor. *Endocrinology* (2010) 151:1795–805. doi: 10.1210/en.2009-1026
43. Sial OK, Warren BL, Alcantara LF, Parise EM, Bolanos-Guzman CA. Vicarious social defeat stress: bridging the gap between physical and emotional stress. *J Neurosci Methods* (2016) 258:94–103. doi: 10.1016/j.jneumeth.2015.10.012

8

Paeoniflorin Ameliorates Chronic Stress-Induced Depression-Like Behaviors and Neuronal Damages in Rats via Activation of the ERK-CREB Pathway

Xiaoming Zhong [1†], *Guanze Li* [1], *Fengmei Qiu* [2†] *and Zhen Huang* [1*]

[1] Department of Chinese Medical Resources, College of Pharmacy, Zhejiang Chinese Medical University, Hangzhou, China,
[2] Pharmacy Teaching Experiment Centre, College of Pharmacy, Zhejiang Chinese Medical University, Hangzhou, China

***Correspondence:**
Zhen Huang
huangzhen@zcmu.edu.cn

† These authors have contributed equally to this work

Neuronal damage is related to the onset and treatment of depressive disorders. Antidepressant-like effects have been elicited by paeoniflorin on animal models. The aim of this study is to demonstrate whether the neuroprotective effect of paeoniflorin on rats suffered from chronic unpredictable mild stress (CUMS) was regulated by the ERK-CREB signaling pathway. Results showed that paeoniflorin not only ameliorated depressive-like behavior with low locomotor activity and prolonged immobility duration in our forced swimming test but also reduced sucrose consumption. Paeoniflorin treatment decreased the degree of neuronal damage in the hippocampus of the model rats. Conversely, it markedly increased the mRNA levels of ERK1, ERK2, and CREB and the levels of ERK, p-ERK, CREB, and p-CREB protein expression in the hippocampus. Blockade of the ERK-CREB axis with the ERK-specific inhibitor U0126 repressed the neuroprotective and antidepressant-like effects of paeoniflorin on rats in the setting of chronic-mild-stress and abolished the recoveries of p-ERK mediated by paeoniflorin treatment. Thus, paeoniflorin possibly exerted a neuroprotective effect modulated by the ERK-CREB signaling pathway on CUMS-induced hippocampal damage in rats.

Keywords: neuroprotection, paeoniflorin, chronic mild stress, ERK-CREB pathway, U0126

INTRODUCTION

As announced by the World Health Organization, over 300 million people suffered from depressive disorders, accounting for 4.4% of the world's population in 2015. Depression is listed as the single largest contributor to global disability (1), but its mechanism and exact therapeutic drugs remain unclear.

Peony is the root of *Paeonia lactiflora* Pall., which is used to treat depression in many prescriptions of traditional Chinese medicine, including "Danggui Shaoyao San" and "Xiaoyao powder" (2–6). The total glycoside extraction of peony and its main active component paeoniflorin exert remarkable antidepressant-like effects in multiple animal models with depressive disorders (7–14). Paeoniflorin has neuroprotective effects related to depression in animal models except the CUMS model (15–18).

Pathological studies have shown neuronal damage in the hippocampus contributes to the etiology of depression and antidepressants can reverse such damage. Hippocampal atrophy is observed in patients with depressive disorders (19, 20) and changes to hippocampus are possibly caused by declined neuronal damage (21, 22). In studies on intracellular signal transduction in depression, the extracellular signal-regulated kinase–cyclic adenosine monophosphate response element binding protein (ERK-CREB) pathway plays a crucial role in the pathological change and treatment of depression, thereby regulating the growth, proliferation, and differentiation of hippocampal nerve cells, meanwhile this pathway has an important learning and memory effect on the synaptic plasticity in the brain (23, 24). However, studies have not yet to elucidate whether the ERK-CREB pathway mediates the neuroprotective effect of paeoniflorin. In the current study, the potential neuroprotection of paeoniflorin and its effect on the ERK-CREB pathway in rats with induced CUMS were assessed.

MATERIALS AND METHODS

Drugs and Reagents

The primary antibodies against ERK (4696), p-ERK (4370), CREB (9104S), p-CREB (9198), and GAPDH (5174) were purchased from Cell Signaling Technology. The secondary antibodies, namely, goat anti-rabbit IRDye® 680CW and goat anti-mouse IRDye® 680RD, were obtained from LI-COR Biosciences, USA. TaKaRa MiniBEST Universal RNA extraction kit (Cat.9767), Prime ScriptTM RT Master Mix (Cat.RR036A), and SYBR® Premix Ex *Taq* (Cat.RR420A) were procured from TaKaRa, Japan. Whole cell lysis assay (KGP250/KGP2100) and BCA protein quantitative kit were obtained from KeyGen Biotech (China) and Beijing ComWin Biotech Co., Ltd. (China), respectively. The specific primers of target genes and GAPDH (Shanghai Shenggong Co., China) were used. Paeoniflorin (purity $\geq$ 98%) was acquired from Huaxia Center for Certified Reference Materials (Guizhou, China, 201110). For intraperitoneal injection, paeoniflorin was dissolved in saline to the desired concentration (30 and 60 mg/kg) on the day of the test. In the present study, paeoniflorin was injected i.p. 1 h once daily before the test.

Animals

Male Sprague Dawley rats (160–200 g) were purchased from the Animal Center of Zhejiang Chinese Medical University (SCXK2013-0016). Rats were bred at room temperature (24 $\pm$ 1°C), humidity (50 $\pm$ 10%), and day and night for 12 h, eating and drinking freely. They were bred to acclimate for 1 week before the CUMS procedures were facilitated. The laboratory animals were used according to requirements of the Ethical Committee on Laboratory Animals, Zhejiang Chinese Medical University, and experimental methods conformed to principles for protection of laboratory animals.

Preparation of Model and Treatment

The rats were assigned to seven groups at random: control group (saline), CUMS group (saline), CUMS plus U0126 group, CUMS plus 30 mg/kg paeoniflorin group, CUMS plus 30 mg/kg paeoniflorin plus U0126 group, CUMS plus 60 mg/kg paeoniflorin, and CUMS plus 60 mg/kg paeoniflorin plus U0126 group. In the last week of CUMS, 1 μL/min U0126 was injected in the lateral ventricle once per day for 5 min. The CUMS process was carried out as described in existing literature (13) with minor modification. The rats with CUMS were exposed to varying stressors once a day for 5 weeks. These stressors included food or water deprivation for 24 h, tail nipped at 1 cm from the tip of the tail for 1 min, restraint stress for 2 h, 5 min of exposure to 45 or 4°C, and continuous illumination for 24 h. Control rats received no stimulus. Paeoniflorin and saline were injected i.p. at the same volume before each stressor was used one time per day for 5 consecutive weeks.

Sucrose Preference Consumption Test

Sucrose preference index was detected after 5 weeks of CUMS treatment in accordance with previously described methods but with slight modifications (13). As a pretest, the rats were trained to adapt to 1% sucrose solution, which were bred individually to each rat in two bottles. After 24 h, one of the solution was converted to purified water for 24 h. Then after deprivation of water and feeding stuff for 12 h, the rats were free to obtain 1% sucrose and purified water in two bottles which were exchanged in 1 h. After 2 h, the weight of solution in every bottle was measured, and the consumed weight and rate of sucrose preference was calculated.

Locomotor Activity Test

The locomotor activity was detected by an open-field test with slight modification (25, 26). Briefly, the test was carried out with the OFT-100 mouse and rat opening activity experiment system with a box (length of side, 100 cm), which was separated into 9 squares with weak light. The rats were individually placed at the center, and the total movement distances and the central time were recorded for 5 min with the system. The floor of the box was cleaned with water and 75% alcohol before each trial.

Forced Swimming Test (FST)

The duration of immobility in the test was quantified by the method of Porsolt et al. (27, 28) with slightly different points. The test was performed in the FST-100 system with a transparent cylinder whose diameter was 21 cm, containing 35 cm of water with temperature at 25 $\pm$ 1°C. In brief, each rat was arranged to swim for 15 min, and then carried back to house. After 24 h, the rats were individually put in the cylinders to swim. The duration of immobility of each rat was detected for 5 min in the same system described above.

Nissl Staining Test

The rats were sacrificed, 24 h after exposed to the last stressor of CUMS procedures. Each whole brain was rapidly dissected from the rats and flushed in ice-cold saline. The right hippocampi were separated on ice bath, immediately stored in liquid nitrogen for western blot and RT-PCR analysis. The left cerebral hemisphere was embedded in glue, and 6 μm of serial sections were performed in the coronal plane. Nissl staining were employed to observe the morphology of hippocampus and count the amount of normal nerve cells in hippocampus CA3 by microscopy. The nerve cells in hippocampal CA3 were numbered with Image-Pro Plus 6.0 software, obtaining the five-vision average to the section of the nerve cell number.

ERK1, ERK2, and CREB mRNA Expression Levels Determined by RT-PCR

The mRNA levels were measured using SYBR RT-PCR analysis. Hippocampus samples stored in liquid nitrogen were weighed, and the extraction of total RNA was using the TaKaRa MiniBEST Universal RNA extraction kit. The total RNA was reverse-transcribed into complementary DNA with the PrimeScript™ RT Master Mix and amplified in a PCR machine. The primers of the target genes and GAPDH were used, as described as follows: ERK1 F: 5′-GGGCCAAGCTTTTCCCAAA−3′ and R: 5′- AGC CACTGGTTCATCTGTCG−3′; ERK2 F: 5′- ATCTTAAATTGG TCAGGACAAGGG−3′ and R: 5′- CTCGGAACGGCTCAA AGGAG−3′; CREB F: 5′- CTGAGGAGCTTGTACCACCG−3′ and R: 5′- CTGCTGGCATGGATACCTGG−3′; GAPDH F: 5′-ACAGCAACAGGGTGGTGAC−3′ and R: 5′- TTTGAGGG TGCAGCGAACTT−3′. Real-time quantitative PCR analysis was performed with a SYBR® Premix Ex Taq by using 7500 Real-Time PCR System with the following profile: 2 min hold at 50°C, 10 min hold at 95°C, 40 cycles of 15 s at 95°C, and 1 min at 60°C. 7500 Sequence Detection software 2.3 was used for data analysis. The relative expression levels of target genes were normalized against the level of GAPDH in the same cDNA by using the relative quantification method ($2^{-\Delta\Delta CT}$).

ERK, p-ERK, CREB, and p-CREB Protein Levels Detected by Western Blot

Total protein was isolated by the whole cell lysis assay and analyzed with the BCA protein quantitative kit. The proteins were separated using 10% SDS-PAGE gel and then transferred to PVDF membranes. After blocked in 5% BSA, membranes were incubated with primary antibodies (GAPDH, ERK, p-ERK, CREB, and p-CREB antibodies, 1:1000 dilution) overnight at 4°C and then exposed to the secondary antibodys (1:15000 dilution) for 1 h. Protein expression levels were quantified with Odyssey infrared scanning system software and normalized against the level of GAPDH protein as an internal control according to the previous study (29).

Statistical Analysis

Statistical analyses were performed by SPSS 20.0. All values were presented as the mean ± SEM. Comparison between two groups was done with *t*-test or Mann–Whitney *U*-test. $P < 0.05$ was considered statistically significant.

RESULTS

Effects of Paeoniflorin and U0126 on Sucrose Preference Index

The results are presented in **Figure 1**. *Post-hoc* analysis showed that the rate of sucrose preference markedly differed from each group. Exposure to CUMS significantly reduced rat sucrose consumption ($P < 0.01$ vs. control group). Paeoniflorin (30 and 60 mg/kg) markedly increased sucrose consumption in CUMS rats ($P < 0.05$, $P < 0.01$); this effect was reversed by U0126 ($P < 0.05$ when U0126 combined with 60 mg/kg paeoniflorin). Moreover, U0126 itself further decreased sucrose consumption in CUMS rats ($P < 0.01$).

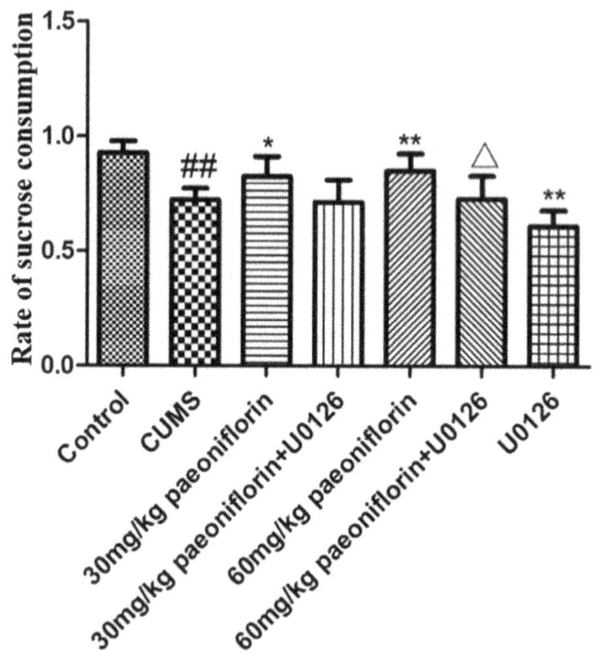

FIGURE 1 | Effects of paeoniflorin on the sucrose preference index in CUMS-exposed rats ($n = 8$). ##$P < 0.01$ vs. control, *$P < 0.05$, **$P < 0.01$ vs. model group; $^{\Delta}P < 0.05$ vs. 60 mg/kg paeoniflorin group.

Effects of Paeoniflorin and U0126 on Locomotor Activity

The total distance and the central time markedly differed among groups. *Post-hoc* analysis indicated that chronic stressors significantly reduced the total distance and the central time ($P < 0.01$), compared with the normal rats. The CUMS rats treated with paeoniflorin had an increase of the total distance and the central time vs. CUMS group ($P < 0.05$, $P < 0.01$). The U0126 group was not statistically different with the CUMS group but manifested a decrease. The paeoniflorin groups plus U0126 had a decrease of the total distance and the central time, compared with the paeoniflorin groups ($P < 0.05$, $P < 0.01$), as shown in **Figure 2**.

Effect of Paeoniflorin and U0126 on Duration of Immobility in FST

The result is depicted in **Figure 3**. CUMS group significantly increased the duration of immobility ($P < 0.01$) in comparison with the controls. Conversely, paeoniflorin groups reduced the total immobility time ($P < 0.05$, $P < 0.01$), and the U0126 group

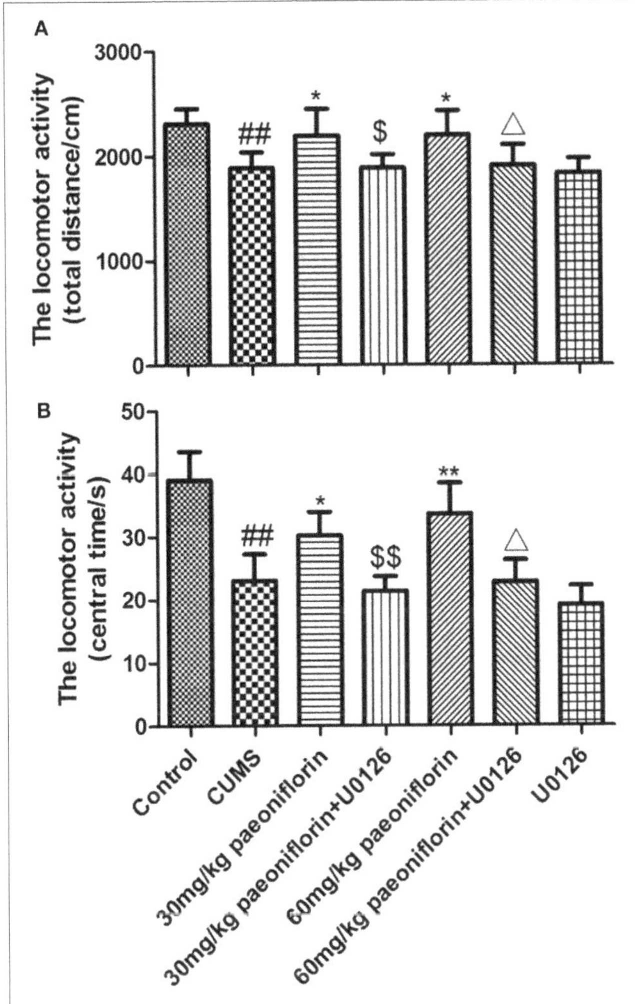

FIGURE 2 | Effects of paeoniflorin on total distance **(A)** and central time **(B)** of locomotor activity in CUMS-exposed rats ($n = 8$). ##$P < 0.01$ vs. control; *$P < 0.05$, **$P < 0.01$ vs. model group; \$$P < 0.05$, \$\$$P < 0.01$ vs. 30 mg/kg paeoniflorin group; △$P < 0.05$ vs. 60 mg/kg paeoniflorin group.

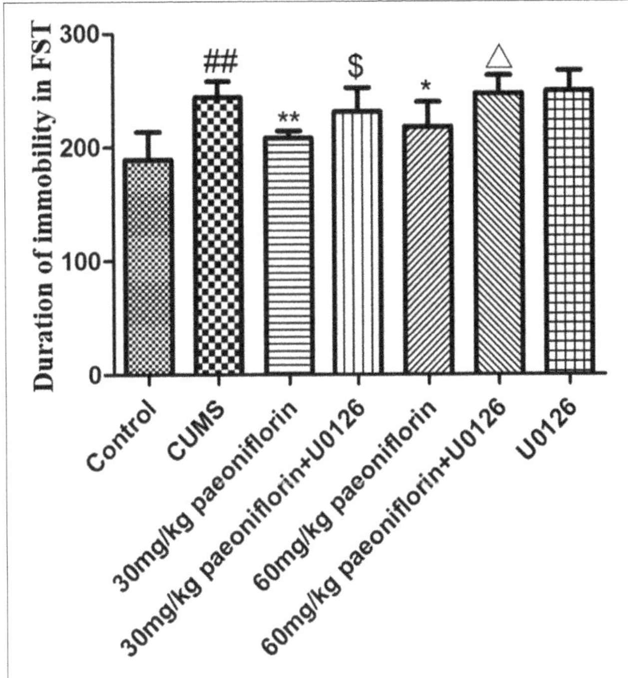

FIGURE 3 | Effect of paeoniflorin on the duration of immobility of CUMS-exposed rats in FST ($n = 8$). ##$P < 0.01$ vs. control; *$P < 0.05$, **$P < 0.01$ vs. model group; \$$P < 0.05$ vs. 30 mg/kg paeoniflorin group; △$P < 0.05$ vs. 60 mg/kg paeoniflorin group.

showed no statistical difference, though the immobility time increased. Furthermore, paeoniflorin plus U0126 groups reduced the total immobility time vs. the paeoniflorin groups ($P < 0.05$).

Effect of Paeoniflorin and U0126 on Morphology and Number of Neuron in Hippocampus CA3

Hippocampal neurons were arranged orderly, and the Nissl substance was clear and dyed deeply in control rats (**Figure 4A**). In CUMS-induced rats, the hippocampal neurons were disordered and loose, and the Nissl substance was shallow-dyed and partly dissolved (**Figure 4B**). The U0126 group showed hippocampal nerve nucleus pyknosis, loose and disordered arrangement, austenite-shallow dye, and the degree of cell damage was similar to CUMS group (**Figure 4G**). The paeoniflorin groups indicated that hippocampal neurons manifested a mild disorder, partial nucleus pyknosis, austenite-shallow dye, and reduced cell damage vs. CUMS rats (**Figures 4C,E**). Compared with the paeoniflorin groups, the paeoniflorin plus U0126 groups aggravated cell damage (**Figures 4D,F**). The number of hippocampal neurons in hippocampal CA3 area was significantly reduced in the model group ($P < 0.01$) vs. control group, while paeoniflorin treatment recovered it in CUMS rats ($P < 0.05$, $P < 0.01$), and the U0126 group showed no significance. Compared with the 60 mg/kg paeoniflorin group, the number of hippocampal neurons in hippocampal CA3 area was significantly reduced in the 60 mg/kg paeoniflorin plus U0126 group ($P < 0.05$), as illustrated in **Figure 4H**.

Effects of Paeoniflorin on ERK1, ERK2, and CREB mRNA Expression Levels in Hippocampus

CUMS significantly decreased the levels of ERK1, ERK2, and CREB mRNA in the hippocampus (73.6, 67.3, and 86.2%, respectively) in comparison with the controls ($P < 0.05$, $P < 0.01$). The CUMS-induced rats administrated with paeoniflorin at various doses possessed a higher ERK1, ERK2, and CREB mRNA levels in the hippocampus, compared with the CUMS-exposed rats ($P < 0.05$, $P < 0.01$), as shown in **Figure 5**.

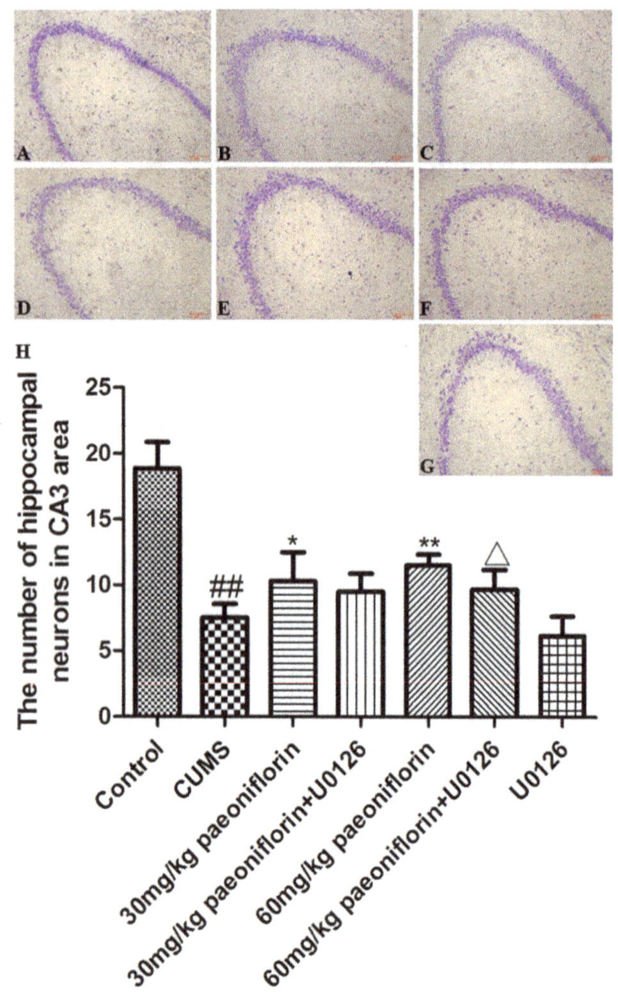

FIGURE 4 | Effect of paeoniflorin on the morphology and number of hippocampal neurons in CUMS-exposed rats ($n = 8$). **(A)** control group, **(B)** CUMS group, **(C)** CUMS plus 30 mg/kg paeoniflorin group, **(D)** CUMS plus 30 mg/kg paeoniflorin plus U0126 group, **(E)** CUMS plus 60 mg/kg paeoniflorin, **(F)** CUMS plus 60 mg/kg paeoniflorin plus U0126 group, **(G)** CUMS plus U0126 group. **(H)** Effect of paeoniflorin on the number of hippocampal neurons. $^{\#\#}P < 0.01$ vs. control; $^{*}P < 0.05$, $^{**}P < 0.01$ vs. model group; $^{\Delta}P < 0.05$ vs. 60 mg/kg paeoniflorin group.

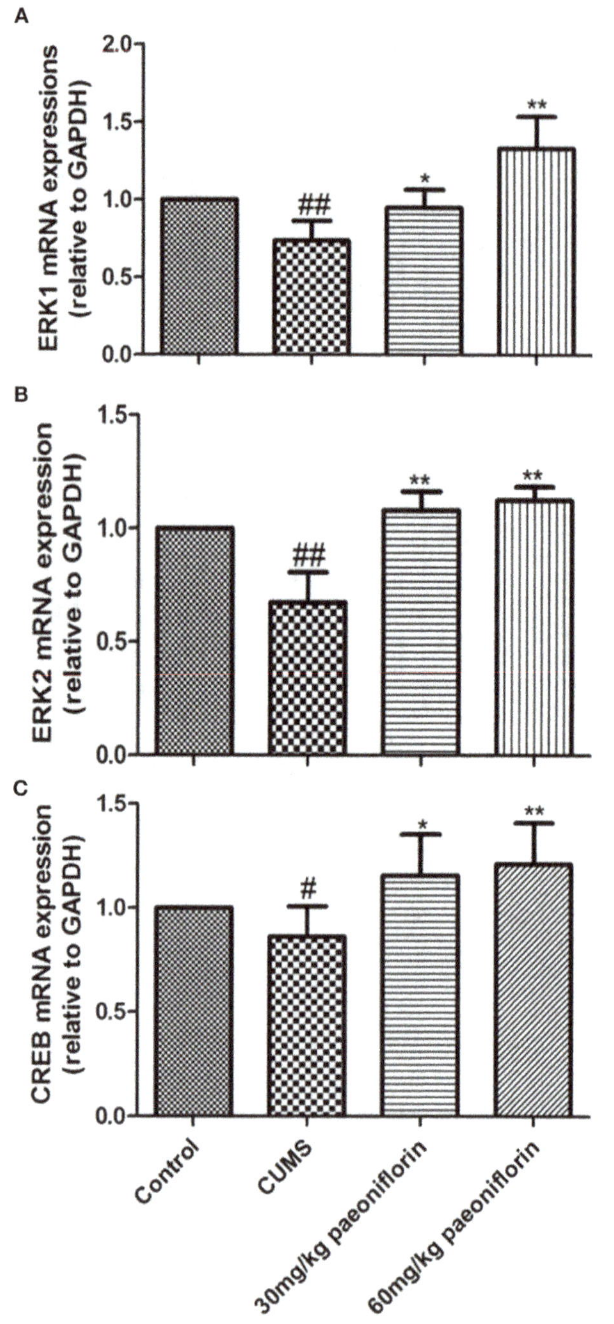

FIGURE 5 | Effects of Paeoniflorin on ERK1 **(A)**, ERK2 **(B)**, and CREB **(C)** mRNA Expression Levels in Hippocampus ($n = 8$). $^{\#}P < 0.05$, $^{\#\#}P < 0.01$ vs. control; $^{*}P < 0.05$, $^{**}P < 0.01$ vs. model group.

Effects of Paeoniflorin and U0126 on ERK, p-ERK, CREB, and p-CREB Protein Levels in Hippocampus

The results are shown in **Figure 6**. CUMS markedly decreased ERK and p-ERK protein expression levels in comparison with the control group. Paeoniflorin treatment at two doses significantly improved the expression levels of ERK and p-ERK protein compared with the CUMS-exposed rats ($P < 0.01$), while the change of p-ERK protein was prevented by the U0126. Moreover, CREB and p-CREB protein levels in the hippocampus were significantly different among groups. CUMS induced a significant decrease in the CREB and p-CREB protein ($P < 0.01$) levels, as compared with the control rats. Treatment with various dose of paeoniflorin significantly attenuated the decrease in protein levels ($P < 0.05$ and $P < 0.01$, respectively), and U0126 significantly enhanced the decrease of the p-CREB protein level ($P < 0.01$) vs. the rats with CUMS. Paeoniflorin treatment plus U0126, was not statistically significant on the levels of CREB and p-CREB protein, compared with the paeoniflorin treatment in the hippocampus.

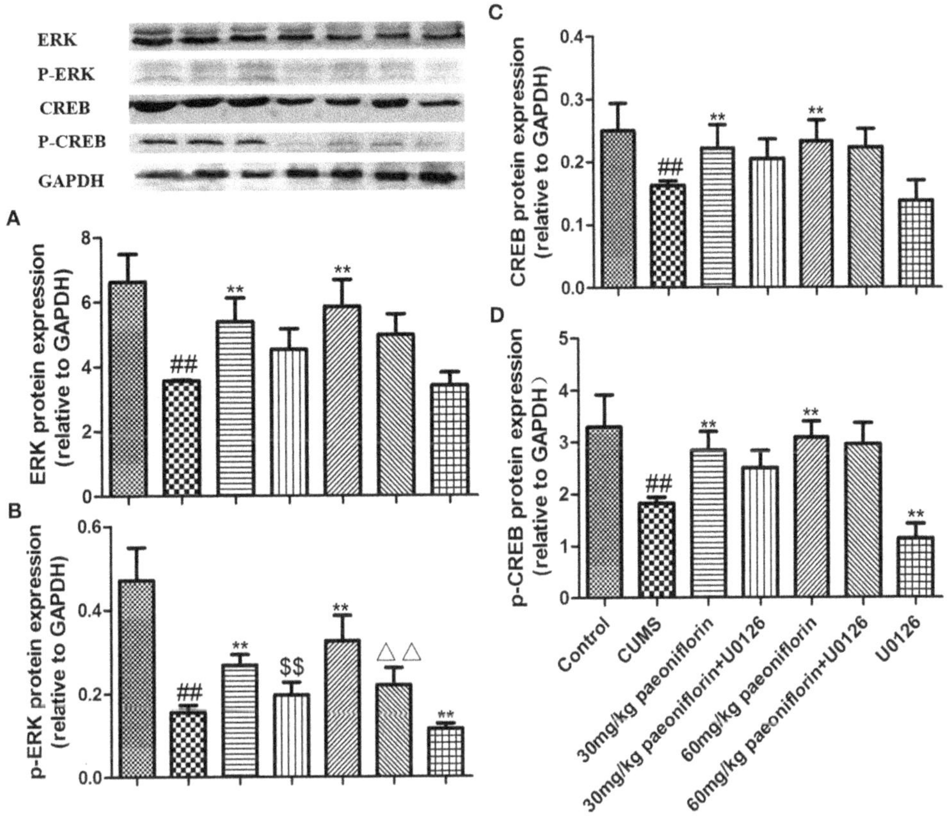

FIGURE 6 | Effects of paeoniflorin on ERK **(A)**, p-ERK **(B)**, CREB **(C)**, and p-CREB **(D)** protein expression levels in the hippocampus of CUMS-exposed rats ($n = 8$). ##$P < 0.01$ vs. control; **$P < 0.01$ vs. model group; $$P < 0.01$ vs. 30 mg/kg paeoniflorin group; $^{\Delta\Delta}P < 0.05$ vs. 60 mg/kg paeoniflorin group.

DISCUSSION

Depression has become a hot spot in medical studies (30–32). The active ingredients of traditional Chinese medicine as well as the structure-activity relationship were especially researched on. The total glycoside fraction of peony exerted remarkable antidepressant-like effects in CUMS models of depression (10, 33). In the present study, paeoniflorin could clearly increase the sugar preference index, total movement distance, and the central movement time and reduce the immobility time in FST of CUMS model rats, which indicated that paeoniflorin could ameliorate the depression-like behaviors. Additionally, paeoniflorin could reduce the structural damage in the hippocampus and improve the pathological injury of brain tissues in the rats with CUMS by the Nissl staining experiment, prompting the antidepressant effects of paeoniflorin.

Based on the previous activity screening experiments, the present study clarified regulation mechanism of signaling pathway of paeoniflorin in rats with CUMS. Our previous researches (18) revealed that total glycoside fraction of peony could clearly increase BDNF protein and gene expression levels in the hippocampus of the CUMS rats and the cortisone-induced depression model rats. In fact, the neuroprotective effects of BDNF were based on the process that BDNF combined with TrkB to initiate multiple signaling pathways. The ERK-CREB signaling pathway possesses an important effect in mediating cell reaction procedures and participates in various physiological effects, such as signal transmission and identification between cells, and cell growth and development. The phosphorylation of ERK can activate its downstream signaling molecule CREB expression, which has been proposed to partly response to the expression of most cAMP-regulated genes, including BDNF. The subsequent release of target proteins can promote neuronal survival, thereby exerting antidepressant effects (34). Our experiment selected ERK-CREB signaling pathway as a breakthrough point, used specific inhibitor U0126 to block the pathway, and observed the spontaneous activities and the change of the key molecular effects of the signaling pathway in rats with CUMS. Based on the RT-PCR and Western blot experiments, paeoniflorin could markedly increase the ERK1, ERK2, and CREB mRNA expression levels and the ERK, p-ERK, CREB, and p-CREB protein expression levels in the hippocampus of CUMS-exposed rats, while the activation of p-ERK protein by paeoniflorin in model rats could be blocked by U0126. Futhermore, U0126 repressed the neuroprotective and antidepressant-like effects of paeoniflorin on rats in the setting of CUMS. This research indicated that the neuroprotection of paeoniflorin may play a role of antidepressant by activating the ERK-CREB pathway. This signaling pathway is also activated by multiple anti-depressant drugs, such as Xingnao Jieyu Decoction, memantine, and so on (34, 35), which suggests that the ERK-CREB pathway plays a key role in the treatment of depression.

In summary, paeoniflorin could alleviate the depression of rats with CUMS and ameliorate the pathological injury of nerve cells in the hippocampus, indicating that the antidepressant effect and protective effect of paeoniflorin on hippocampal nerve cells might be mediated by ERK-CREB signaling pathway, which are the downstream pathway of BDNF. However, understanding a signaling pathway is inadequate to study the pathogenesis of depression. We should seek other effective multiple signaling pathways involved in the pathogenesis of depression and explore cross connections and interactions among various pathways.

NOMENCLATURE

Resource Identification Initiative

The antibodies against ERK: Cell Signaling Technology Cat# 4696, RRID:AB_390780.
The antibodies against p-ERK: Cell Signaling Technology Cat# 4370, RRID:AB_2315112.
The antibodies against CREB: Cell Signaling Technology Cat# 9104S, RRID:AB_10691832.
The antibodies against p-CREB: Cell Signaling Technology Cat# 9198, RRID:AB_2561044.
The antibodies against GAPDH: Cell Signaling Technology Cat# 5174, RRID:AB_10622025.

AUTHOR CONTRIBUTIONS

XZ contributed to data collection and drafted the article. GL contributed to preparation of animal models and medicine administration. FQ contributed to coordination of experiments, data collection, and statistical analysis. ZH designed the study and revised the manuscript for important intellectual content. All authors contributed to and approved the final manuscript, and agreed to be accountable for all aspects of the work.

FUNDING

This project was supported by the Zhejiang education department research project (Y201328806), the Zhejiang Provincial Natural Science Foundation of China (LQ14H280005, Q14H280023), and the National Natural Science Foundation of China (81573643, 81503274).

REFERENCES

1. World Health Organization. *Depression and Other Common Mental Disorders: Global Health Estimates*. (2017). Available online at: http://www.who.int/mental_health/management/depression/prevalence_global_health_estimates/en/
2. Kim SH, Han J, Seog DH, Chung JY, Kim N, Hong Park Y, et al. Antidepressant effect of Chaihu-Shugan-San extract and its constituents in rat models of depression. *Life Sci.* (2005) 76:1297–306. doi: 10.1016/j.lfs.2004.10.022
3. Kasper S, Pail G. Milnacipran: a unique antidepressant? *Neuropsychiatr Dis Treat.* (2010) 6:23–31. doi: 10.2147/NDT.S11777
4. Huang Z, Mao QQ, Zhong XM, Li ZY, Qiu FM, Ip SP. Mechanistic study on the antidepressant-like effect of Danggui-Shaoyao-San, a Chinese herbal formula. *Evid Based Complement Altern Med.* (2012) 10:1155–61. doi: 10.1155/2012/173565
5. Cao GP, Gui D, Fu LD, Guo ZK, Fu WJ. Anxiolytic and neuroprotective effects of the Traditional Chinese Medicinal formulation Dan-zhi-xiao-yao-san in a rat model of chronic stress. *Mol Med Rep.* (2016) 14:1247–54. doi: 10.3892/mmr.2016.5382
6. Wang X, Ye XL, Liu XB, Luo J, Zeng N. Research status of antidepressant effect of Xiaoyaosan. *Chin J Exp Tradit Med Form.* (2018) 24:277–86. doi: 10.13422/j.cnki.syfjx.20181144
7. Mao QQ, Huang Z. Research progress on therapeutic mechanism of depression treated by traditional chinese medicine. *Zhongguo Zhong Yao Za Zhi* (2007) 32:877–80.
8. Mao QQ, Huang Z, Ip S, Che C. Antidepressant-like effect of ethanol extract from *Paeonia lactiflora* in mice. *Phytother Res.* (2008) 22:1496–9. doi: 10.1002/ptr.2519
9. Mao QQ, Ip SP, Tsai SH, Che CT. Antidepressant-like effects of peony glycosides in mice. *J Ethnopharmacol.* (2008) 119:272–5. doi: 10.1016/j.jep.2008.07.008
10. Mao QQ, Ip SP, Ko KM, Tsai SH, Xian YF, Che CT. Effects of peony glycosides on mice exposed to chronic unpredictable stress: further evidence for antidepressant-like activity. *J Ethnopharmacol.* (2009) 124:316–20. doi: 10.1016/j.jep.2009.04.019
11. Mao QQ, Ip SP, Ko KM, Tsai SH, Zhao M, Che CT. Peony glycosides protect against corticosterone-induced neurotoxicity in PC12 cells. *Cell Mol Neurobiol.* (2009) 29:643–7. doi: 10.1007/s10571-009-9357-7
12. Mao QQ, Ip SP, Xian YF, Hu Z, Che CT. Anti-depressant-like effect of peony: a mini-review. *Pharm Biol.* (2012) 50:72–7. doi: 10.3109/13880209.2011.602696
13. Qiu FM, Zhong XM, Mao QQ, Huang Z. Antidepressant-like effects of paeoniflorin on the behavioural, biochemical, and neurochemical patterns of rats exposed to chronic unpredictable stress. *Neurosci Lett.* (2013) 541:209–13. doi: 10.1016/j.neulet.2013.02.029
14. Qiu FM, Zhong XM, Mao QQ, Huang Z. The antidepressant-like effects of paeoniflorin in mouse models. *Exp Ther Med.* (2013) 5:1113–6. doi: 10.3892/etm.2013.925
15. Xiao L, Wang YZ, Liu J, Luo XT, Ye Y, Zhu XZ. Effects of paeoniflorin on the cerebral infarction, behavioral and cognitive impairments at the chronic stage of transient middle cerebral artery occlusion in rats. *Life Sci.* (2005) 78:413–20. doi: 10.1016/j.lfs.2005.04.069
16. Zhong SZ, Ge QH, Li Q, Qu R, Ma SP. Peoniflorin attentuates Abeta((1-42))-mediated neurotoxicity by regulating calcium homeostasis and ameliorating oxidative stress in hippocampus of rats. *J Neurol Sci.* (2009) 280:71–8. doi: 10.1016/j.jns.2009.01.027
17. Mao QQ, Zhong XM, Feng CR, Pan AJ, Li ZY, Huang Z. Protective effects of paeoniflorin against glutamate-induced neurotoxicity in PC12 Cells via antioxidant mechanisms and Ca2+ antagonism. *Cell Mol Neurobiol.* (2010) 30:1059–66. doi: 10.1007/s10571-010-9537-5
18. Mao QQ, Zhong XM, Qiu FM, Li ZY, Huang Z. Protective effects of paeoniflorin against corticosterone-induced neurotoxicity in PC12 cells. *Phytother Res.* (2012) 26:969–73. doi: 10.1002/ptr.3673
19. Nguyen L, Kakeda S, Katsuki A, Sugimoto K, Otsuka Y, Ueda I, et al. Relationship between VEGF-related gene polymorphisms and brain morphology in treatment-naïve patients with first-episode major depressive disorder. *Eur Arch Psychiatry Clin Neurosci* (2018). doi: 10.1007/s00406-018-0953-8. [Epub ahead of print].
20. Taylor WD, Deng Y, Boyd BD, Donahue MJ, Albert K, McHugo M, et al. Medial temporal lobe volumes in late-life depression:

effects of age and vascular risk factors. *Brain Imaging Behav.* (2018). doi: 10.1007/s11682-018-9969-y. [Epub ahead of print].

21. Zhu XL, Chen JJ, Han F, Pan C, Zhuang TT, Cai YF, et al. Novel antidepressant effects of Paeonol alleviate neuronal injury with concomitant alterations in BDNF, Rac1 and RhoA levels in chronic unpredictable mild stress rats. *Psychopharmacology* (2018) 235:2177–219. doi: 10.1007/s00213-018-4915-7.
22. Fan C, Song Q, Wang P, Li Y, Yang M, Liu B, et al. Curcumin protects against chronic stress-induced dysregulation of neuroplasticity and depression-like behaviors via suppressing IL-1β pathway in rats. *Neuroscience* (2018) 392:92–106. doi: 10.1016/j.neuroscience.2018.09.028
23. Connor SA, Hoeffer CA, Klann E. Fragile X mental retardation protein regulates heterosynaptic plasticity in the hippocampus. *Learn Mem.* (2011) 4:207–20. doi: 10.1101/lm.2043811
24. Adams JP, Sweatt JD. Molecular psychology: roles for the ERK MAP kinase cascade in memory. *Annu Rev Pharrnacol Toxicol.* (2002) 42:135–63. doi: 10.1146/annurev.pharmtox.42.082701.145401
25. Cox BM, Alsawah F, McNeill PC, Galloway MP, Perrine SA. Perrine, neurochemical, hormonal, and behavioral effects of chronic unpredictable stress in the rat. *Behav Brain Res.* (2011) 220:106–11. doi: 10.1016/j.bbr.2011.01.038
26. Shin JY, Shin JW, Ha SK, Kim Y, Swanberg KM, Lee S, et al. Radix polygalae extract attenuates PTSD-like symptoms in a mouse model of single prolonged stress and conditioned fear possibly by reversing BAG1. *Exp Neurobiol.* (2018) 27:200–9. doi: 10.5607/en.2018.27.3.200
27. Huang Z, Zhong XM, Li ZY, Feng CR, Pan AJ, Mao QQ. Curcumin reverses corticosterone-induced depressive-like behavior and decrease in brain BDNF levels in rats. *Neurosci Lett.* (2011) 493:145–8. doi: 10.1016/j.neulet.2011.02.030
28. Porsolt RD, Bertin A, Jalfre M. Behavioral despair in mice: a primary screening test for antidepressant. *Arch Int Pharmacodyn Ther.* (1977) 229:327–36.
29. Zhu YP, Xi SH, Li MY, Ding TT, Liu N, Cao FY, et al. Fluoride and arsenic exposure affects spatial memory and activates the ERK/CREB signaling pathway in offspring rats. *Neurotoxicology* (2017) 59:56–64. doi: 10.1016/j.neuro.2017.01.006
30. Yeh TC, Kao LC, Tzeng NS, Kuo TB, Huang SY, Chang CC, et al. Heart rate variability in major depressive disorder and after anti-depressant treatment with agomelatine and paroxetine: findings from the Taiwan Study of Depression and Anxiety (TAISDA). *Prog Neuropsychopharmacol Biol Psychiatry* (2015) 64:60–7. doi: 10.1016/j.pnpbp.2015.07.007
31. Lenze EJ, Mulsant BH, Blumberger DM, Karp JF, Newcomer JW, Anderson SJ, et al. Efficacy, safety, and tolerability of augmentation pharma-cotherapy with aripiprazole for treatment-resistant depression in late life: a randomised, double-blind, placebo-controlled trial. *Lancet Psychiat.* (2015) 386:2404–12. doi: 10.1016/S0140-6736(15)00308-6
32. Lemini C, García-Albor E, Cruz-López B, Matamoros-Trejo G, Martínez-Mota L. Differential effect of the 17 beta-aminoestrogens prolame, butolame and pentolame in anxiety and depression models in rats. *Prog Neuropsychopharmacol Biol Psychiatry* (2016) 64:102–8. doi: 10.1016/j.pnpbp.2015.07.013
33. Mao QQ, Xian YF, Ip SP, Tsai SH, Che CT. Long-term treatment with peony glycosides reverses chronic unpredictable mild stress-induced depressive-like behavior via increasing expression of neurotrophins in rat brain. *Behav Brain Res.* (2010) 2:171–7. doi: 10.1016/j.bbr.2010.02.026
34. Li T, Wang D, Zhao B, Yan Y. Xingnao Jieyu decoction ameliorates poststroke depression through the BDNF/ERK/CREB pathway in rats. *Evid Based Complement Altern Med.* (2018) 2018:5403045. doi: 10.1155/2018/5403045
35. Takahashi K, Nakagawasai O, Nemoto W, Kadota S, Isono J, Odaira T, et al. Memantine ameliorates depressive-like behaviors by regulating hippocampal cell proliferation and neuroprotection in olfactory bulbectomized mice. *Neuropharmacology* (2018) 137:141–55. doi: 10.1016/j.neuropharm.2018.04.013

9

Minocycline Attenuates Stress-Induced Behavioral Changes via its Anti-inflammatory Effects in an Animal Model of Post-traumatic Stress Disorder

Wei Wang [1], Rui Wang [1], Jingjing Xu [1], Xiaqing Qin [1], Hong Jiang [1], Arslan Khalid [1], Dexiang Liu [1], Fang Pan [1], Cyrus S. H. Ho [2] and Roger C. M. Ho [2]*

[1] *Department of Medical Psychology and Ethics, School of Basic Medical Sciences, Shandong University, Jinan, China,*
[2] *Department of Psychological Medicine, Yong Loo Lin School of Medicine, National University of Singapore, Singapore, Singapore*

Correspondence:
Dexiang Liu
liudexiang@sdu.edu.cn

Accumulating evidences have suggested that anxiety-like behavior and impairment of learning and memory are key symptoms of post-traumatic stress disorder (PTSD), and pharmacological treatment can ameliorate anxiety and cognitive impairments. Recent studies have shown that minocycline exhibits anxiolytic effects. The aims of the present study were to determine whether minocycline administration would alter anxiety-like behavior and cognitive deficits induced by inescapable foot shock (IFS) and to explore the underlying mechanisms. Male Wistar rats were exposed to the IFS protocol for a period of 6 days to induce PTSD. The PTSD-like behavior was tested using the open field test, elevated plus maze test, and Morris water maze test. The effects of minocycline on pro-inflammatory cytokines, activation of microglia, and NF-κB in the PFC and hippocampus were also examined. Treatment with minocycline significantly reversed the IFS induced behavioral and cognitive parameters (impaired learning and memory function) in stressed rats. Additionally, IFS was able to increase pro-inflammatory cytokines, activate microglia, and enhance NF-κB levels, while minocycline significantly reversed these alterations. Taken together, our results suggest that the anxiolytic effect of minocycline is related to its ability to decrease the levels of pro-inflammatory cytokines and inhibit activation of microglia and NF-κB in the PFC and hippocampus.

Keywords: post-traumatic stress disorder, inescapable foot shock, microglia, minocycline, pro-inflammatory cytokines, NF-κB

INTRODUCTION

Post-traumatic stress disorder (PTSD) is one of the "trauma- and stressor-related disorders," and its diagnostic criteria include exposure to extreme traumatic events, recurrent and intrusive traumatic memories, avoidance of traumatic event-related stimuli, cognitive impairment, negative emotions, hyper-aroused state, hyper-vigilance, clinical distress, and social impairment (1). PTSD is a global health issue and has a serious negative impact on individuals and society, the prevalence of PTSD is high and it substantially increases the risk of other psychiatric morbidities as well as medical disorders (2–4). Although the current studies have identified the molecular, neurochemical and genetic abnormalities associated with of PTSD (5), prevention and treatment of PTSD are limited (4, 6).

Based on the diagnostic criteria, stress is strongly associated with PTSD. Stress is implicated in the etiology and pathogenesis of a number of psychiatric disorders including major depressive disorder and anxiety disorders (7). Previous research has demonstrated that different types of stress have a close association with inflammatory activities in the central nervous system (CNS) (8) and peripheral circulation (9). Several studies have demonstrated that the levels of peripheral pro-inflammatory cytokines or other inflammatory markers were elevated in patients suffering from PTSD (10–12). Furthermore, studies based on the rodent models of PTSD found increased levels of cytokines in different neuroanatomical areas (13–15). These cytokines coordinate communication between neurons, microglia and astrocytes and alter the neuroendocrine and neurochemical processes, which lead to ultimate changes in behavior (16). Although, the cytokines in the CNS can travel to the peripherial circulation, the major cells that producing pro-inflammatory cytokines are microglia (17). As resident macrophages in the CNS, chronic, and severe stress can trigger the transition of microglia from a resting state to a pro-inflammatory state and produce a "cytokine storm" that can disrupt the homeostasis of the brain (18). The above studies prompted researchers to consider a new therapeutic avenue for PTSD by inhibiting the activation of microglia. Nuclear factor kappa B (NF-κB) is a transcription factor of inflammation, which translocates into the nucleus and is able to up-regulate the expression of pro-inflammatory immune response genes, including tumor necrosis factor (TNF)-α, interleukin (IL)-1β, and IL-6 (19). Inhibition of this pathway might be a potential treatment for PTSD.

It was recently reported that minocycline, the semi-synthetic tetracycline, can serve as a versatile drug for the treatment of inflammatory diseases (20), as well as psychiatric disorders (21). Accumulating evidence has shown that minocycline exhibits its potential anti-inflammatory and immune-modulatory effects in the CNS. In addition, previous studies have shown that minocycline administration is able to improve anxiety-like behavior and cognitive impairment (22–25). The beneficial effects of minocycline might partly be attributed to its ability to down-regulate pro-inflammatory cytokines (20, 21), attenuate the activation of microglia (26) and selectively inhibit the polarization of microglia toward the M1 phenotype (27). In addition, previous studies have suggested that minocycline can be a potential treatment for PTSD experienced by rodents (14). However, the cellular and molecular mechanism of minocycline remains unknown.

In the present study, rats were exposed to a 6 days inescapable foot shock (IFS) protocol followed by subsequent behavioral assessments. The levels of pro-inflammatory cytokines, activation of microglia and NF-κB in the prefrontal cortex (PFC) and hippocampus were evaluated. We hypothesized that minocycline could exert a therapeutic effect in the rat model of PTSD, and it might exhibit a neuroprotective function through anti-inflammatory effects by down-regulating the activation of microglia and NF-κB in the PFC and hippocampus. This study evaluated minocycline as a potential therapeutic agent for PTSD.

MATERIALS AND METHODS

Animals and Drug Treatment

Eight-weeks-old male Wistar rats weighing 190–210 g were purchased from the Animal Center of Shandong University. A total of 40 rats were housed in a controlled environment (12 h day/night cycle, 23 ± 2°C) with free access to water and food. The research procedures were approved by the Animal Ethics Committee of Shandong University.

Minocycline was dissolved in saline, and the rats were intragastrically administered with minocycline (Biottoped, China) at the dosage of 40 mg/kg/d, which were based on the methods of previous studies (25, 28). Based on the established protocol, the rats received a single dose of minocycline or vehicle 30 min before receiving daily foot shock for a total of 6 times in 6 days.

Experimental Design

Animals were randomly divided into four experimental groups: control, PTSD alone, minocycline alone and PTSD + minocycline, with 10 rats per group. After 1 week adaptation, animals were exposed to daily foot shock for 6 days (day 8–13). Then all animals were conducted with the open field (OF) test (day 14), elevated plus maze (EPM) test (day 15), Morris water maze (MWM) train (day 16–20), and test (day21) in a sequential manner. Following the behavioral tests, animals were decapitated or anesthetized for tissue preparation (day 22).

The IFS Procedure

The IFS-exposed rats received foot shocks twice a day with a break of more than 4 h in-between foot shocks, and the procedure continued for 6 days. Rats in the IFS-exposed groups were placed in a dark foot-shock box and received 15 spaced shocks (3 mA, 2 s) in 30 min with a variable shock interval. Rats in the two unexposed groups were placed into the box for 30 min without electric shock.

Behavioral Test

The Open Field (OF) Test

The OF test was used to assess exploratory activities and anxiety-like behavior in an open box (29). The open field is a square wooden box with a base of 50 cm^2 and a wall height of 50 cm, and the bottom was divided equally into 25 blocks with markers. Before each trial, the arena surface was cleaned with 75% ethanol, the rats were placed in the center of the apparatus, and the subsequent activities were recorded by a camera for 5 min. All behavioral data were counted by two independent experimenters. The evaluation of behavioral data included horizontal locomotion (the number of three limbs crossing the line), duration of time spent in the central area, rearing frequency (two forepaws lifting from the ground), and grooming frequency (licking or scratching).

The Elevated Plus Maze (EPM) Test

The EPM test was designed to test the animal's anxiety-like behavior by examining the duration of time spent and frequency of entries in the open arms and closed arms (30). The device is elevated 50 cm from the floor and has two open arms and two closed arms (surrounded on three sides by walls 18 cm in height) connected by a square platform. The animals were placed in the center area with their heads facing the open arm, and trajectory of the rat was recorded for 5 min with video tracking software (SMART 2.5, Spain). The device was cleaned with 75% ethanol before each trial. The percentage of time spent in the open arms and the frequency of entering the open arms were calculated.

The Morris Water Maze (MWM) Test

The MWM test was designed to assess learning and memory function through training and testing in a circular pool (31). The round water maze (120 cm in diameter) was divided into four quadrants, and a platform was hidden 1 cm below the surface of the water. Rats were trained to search for the platform four times a day for 5 days, and they were tested on the sixth day with the platform removed. The escape latency (time taken to find the platform) in the training day and the percentage of time spent and entry frequency in the target quadrant (the quadrant where the platform was placed) in the testing day were recorded by video tracking software (SMART 2.5, Spain).

Biochemical Determination

Tissue Preparation

For western blotting, enzyme-linked immunosorbent assay (ELISA), and real-time PCR, rats were decapitated, and the brains were immediately removed from the rats. The PFC and hippocampus were separated on ice and frozen at −80°C. For immunohistochemistry (IHC), Rats were anesthetized with pentobarbital sodium (50 mg/kg) and transcardially perfused with 0.9% saline and then 4% paraformaldehyde dissolved in PBS. Then the brains were removed and post-fixed in 4% paraformaldehyde for 24 h at 4°C.

ELISA

The samples were weighed and then homogenized completely in phosphate-buffered solution (PBS). After centrifugation (1,000 × g, 10 min) of the homogenates at 4°C, supernatants were collected and stored at −80°C. The concentrations of TNF-α, IL-1β, and IL-6 were detected following the instruction of ELISA kits (Tianjin Anoric Bio-technology, Co., Ltd, China).

IHC

The tissues were dehydrated in a graded series of ethanol, cleared in xylene and embedded in paraffin blocks. The blocks of tissue were sectioned serially at 5 μm using a microtome. After the tissues were mounted on the slide, deparaffinated and rehydrated, they were immersed in sodium citrate for antigen retrieval using a microwave oven (medium power for 6 min, 4 times). The sections were treated with 3% H_2O_2 for 10 min and washed three times with PBS. These sections were blocked with 5% bovine serum albumin (BSA) in PBS for 30 min and incubated overnight with the primary antibody Iba-1 (ab5076, 1:400, Abcam) at 4°C. After three PBS washes, these sections were incubated with biotinylated-conjugated rabbit anti-goat IgG secondary antibody for 30 min at 37°C. After three PBS washes, sections were treated with SABC for 30 min at 37°C and then washed three times with PBS. A DAB kit was used for chromogenic detection, and the sections were then stained with haematoxylin and mounted. The images were captured by an OLYMPUS microscope.

RNA Extraction and Real-Time PCR

Total RNA was isolated from the PFC and hippocampus of rats using RNAprep Pure Tissue Kit (Tiangen Biotech Co., Ltd, China) following the manufacturer's instructions. The RNA was quantified and analyzed for the absorbance ratios A260/280 nm using a nano-400 (Hangzhou Allsheng Instruments Co.,Ltd, China). 1 μg RNA was reverse-transcribed into first-strand cDNA using the FastKing RT kit (Tiangen Biotech Co., Ltd, China) with random primer. RT-PCR was performed using a Biorad system (Bio-Rad Laboratories, USA) with SYBR Green. Each PCR was performed in triplicate to a final solution volume of 20:10 μl of SuperReal PreMix Plus, 1 μl of diluted cDNA products, 0.6 μl of each paired primer, and 7.8 μl of RNase-free water. Protocols were as follows: initial denaturation for 15 min at 95°C, followed by 40 cycles denaturation for 10 s at 95°C, and extension for 30 s at 60°C. Last cycle for dissociation of SYBR Green probe was 15 s at 95°C, 30 s at 56°C, and 15 s at 95°C. Primer pairs for quantitative real-time PCR were as follows: Iba1, 5′- CTTCAGCTCTAGATG GGTCTTGG−3′ (sense) and 5′- AAGAGAGGTTGGATGGGA TCAAC−3′ (anti-sense),GAPDH, 5′- ACCAGCTTCCCATTC TCAGC−3′ (sense) and 5′- GAAGGTCGGTGTGAACGGAT-3′(anti-sense). The mRNA levels of the Iba1 were calibrated against GAPDH mRNA and the fold difference between groups was calculated by the $2^{-\Delta\Delta Ct}$ method (32).

Western Blotting

The samples were mixed with RIPA and PMSF (Beyotime, China) and homogenized on ice. The dissolved proteins were centrifuged at 10,000 × g for 10 min at 4°C, and the supernatants were collected for further detection. The concentrations were determined using a BCA protein assay kit (Beyotime, China). Samples containing 30 μg protein were loaded on a polyacrylamide gel (5% stacking gel, 10% resolving gel), run at 80 mv for electrophoresis, and then electrophoretically transferred to PVDF membranes (Bio-Rad, USA) at 200 mA for 1.5 h. Membranes were blocked with 5% milk in TBST for 1 h and then incubated overnight with the primary antibody, NF-κB (1:2,000, ab32536, Abcam, USA). GAPDH (1:10,000, Beyotime, China) was used as an internal control. After three TBS washes, the membranes were incubated with a horseradish peroxidase-conjugated secondary antibody, sheep anti-rabbit IgG (1:8,000, Beyotime, China) for 1 h. After washing three times with TBST, the membranes were incubated with chemiluminescence substrates (Millipore Corp, USA) for 3 min and exposed to X-ray film. The gray value was quantified by ImageJ 1.50i software (NIH).

Statistical Analysis

Quantitative data were presented as the mean ± SEM. In most cases, two-way ANOVA was used for statistical analysis, and multiple comparisons of individual groups were performed using Fisher's LSD test. Differences were considered statistically significant if the p value was <0.05. For the MWM test, the average escape latency in the first 5 days of training among different groups was evaluated by three-way repeated-measures ANOVA.

RESULTS

Effects of Minocycline in the OF Test

For the duration of time spent in the central area, two-way ANOVA revealed a significant effect for IFS treatment [$F_{(1, 36)} = 4.621$, $p < 0.05$, **Figure 1B**], no effect was observed for minocycline-treatment and IFS-minocycline interaction. There was no effect was observed in the total number of crossing (**Figure 1A**), rearing (**Figure 1C**), and grooming (**Figure 1D**) in different groups. Fisher's LSD test confirmed that IFS-exposed rats showed a marked decrease in the time spent in the central area when compared with the control group ($p < 0.01$), and the central time of IFS-exposed rats treated with minocycline was significantly greater than that of IFS-exposed rats treated with vehicle ($p < 0.05$).

Effects of Minocycline in the EPM Test

In terms of open-arm entries, two-way ANOVA revealed a significant effect for minocycline treatment [$F_{(1, 36)} = 6.806$, $p < 0.05$, **Figure 2A**] and an IFS-minocycline interaction [$F_{(1, 36)} = 5.801$, $p < 0.05$]. For the duration of time spent in open arms, there were no significant differences between groups (**Figure 2B**). Fisher's LSD test confirmed that IFS caused a significant reduction in the open arm entries ($p < 0.01$) compared with the control group. In addition, the IFS-exposed rats treated with minocycline exhibited a remarkable increase in the open-arm entries ($p < 0.05$) compared with the IFS-exposed rats treated with vehicle.

Effects of Minocycline in the MWM Test

As shown in **Figure 3A**, three-way repeated-measures ANOVA revealed that escape latency of the four groups reduced over the 5 days training period [$F_{(4, 24)} = 122.562$, $p < 0.001$], and there was no interaction between days, IFS exposure and minocycline treatment [$F_{(4, 24)} = 1.481$, $p > 0.05$]. There was no IFS-minocycline interaction, day-IFS interaction and day-minocycline interaction [$F_{(1, 6)} = 3.403$, $p > 0.05$, $F_{(4,24)} = 0.593$, $p > 0.05$, $F_{(4,24)} = 1.316$, $p > 0.05$, respectively]. The IFS-exposed group had a longer escape latency during the training day on day 2 and day 3, while there was no significant difference between these groups.

As shown in **Figure 3B**, the IFS-exposed rats had fewer entries in the target quadrant compared with the control group, while treatment with minocycline increased the number of entries of the IFS-exposed rats compared to IFS-exposed rats treated

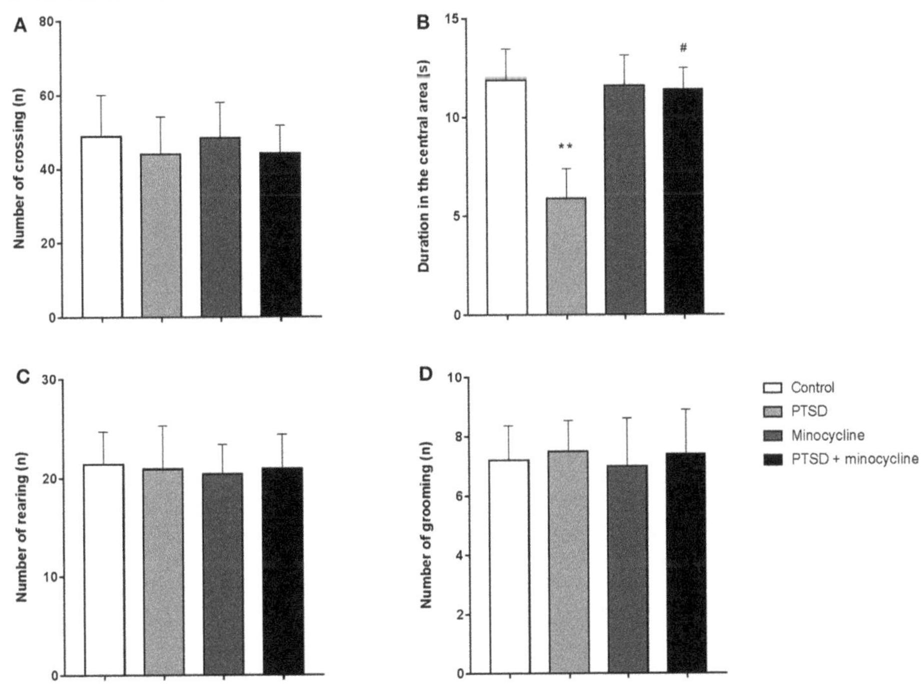

FIGURE 1 | The effects of minocycline on the OF test. **(A)** The number of crossings in the open field. **(B)** Time spent in the central area of the apparatus. **(C)** The number of rearing events in the device. **(D)** The number of grooming events in the facility. The results are expressed as the mean ± SEM, $n = 10$, ** $p < 0.01$ vs. control; # $p < 0.05$ vs. PTSD.

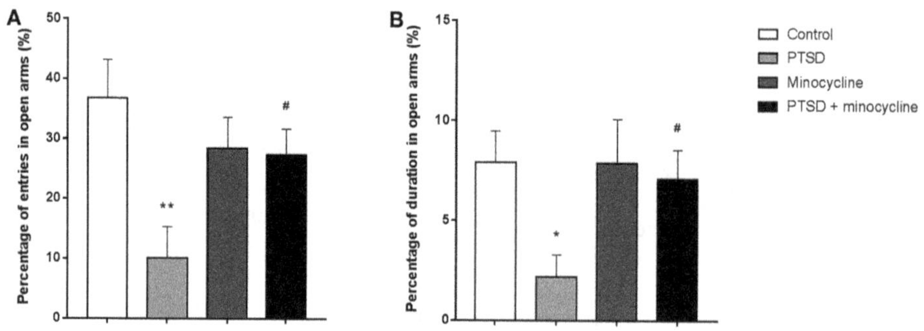

FIGURE 2 | The effects of minocycline on the EPM test. **(A)** The percentage of entries in open arms. **(B)** The percentage of duration of time spent in open arms. The results are expressed as the mean ± SEM, n = 10, * $p < 0.05$, ** $p < 0.01$ vs. control; # $p < 0.05$ vs. PTSD.

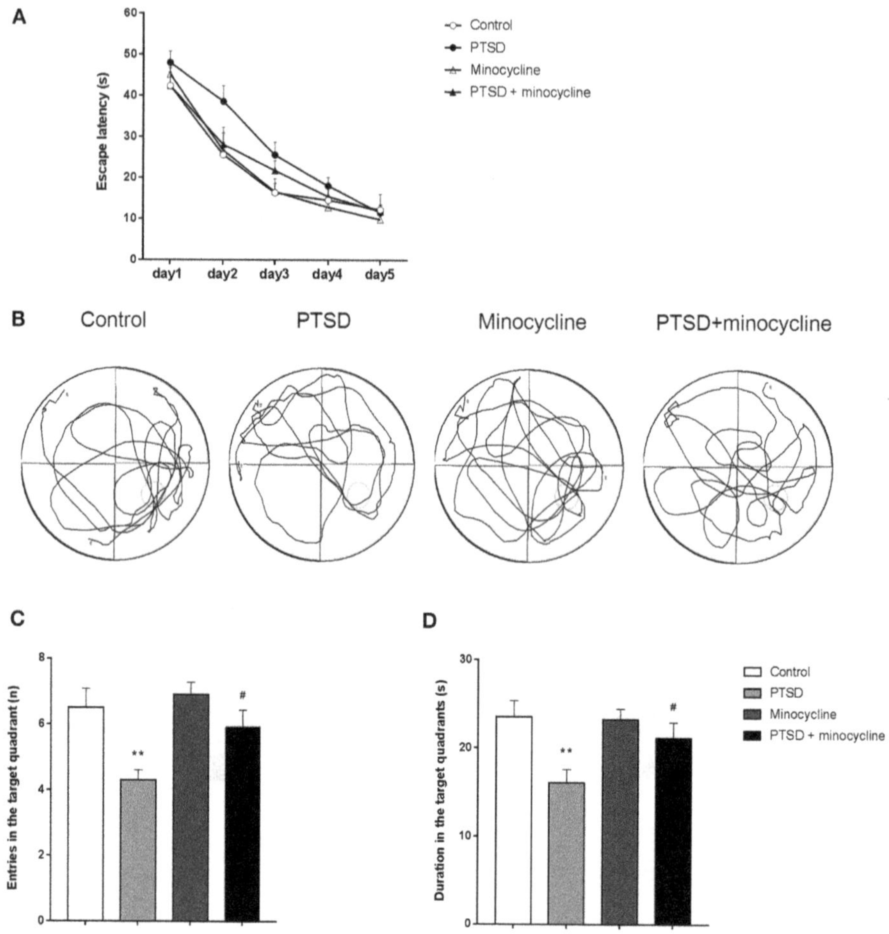

FIGURE 3 | The effects of minocycline on the MWM test. **(A)** Average escape latency on the training day, taking into account the times of three sessions (excepted for the session starting in the target quadrant) per day. **(B)** One of the representative trajectories of the four groups in the water maze on the sixth day within 1 min (origination is opposite to the target quadrant). **(C)** Number of entries to the target quadrant on the sixth day of testing. **(D)** Duration of time spent in the target quadrant on the testing day. The results are expressed as the mean ± SEM, $n = 10$, ** $p < 0.01$ vs. control; # $p < 0.05$ vs. PTSD.

with vehicle. In terms of entries in the target quadrant, two-way ANOVA revealed significant differences for IFS exposure [$F_{(1, 36)} = 12.06$, $p < 0.01$, **Figure 3C**] and minocycline treatment [$F_{(1, 36)} = 4.712$, $p < 0.05$]. In terms of duration in the target quadrant, two-way ANOVA revealed a significant difference for IFS exposure [$F_{(1, 36)} = 8.892$, $p < 0.01$, **Figure 3D**]. Fisher's LSD test confirmed that IFS-exposed rats showed a significant decrease in the number of entries ($p < 0.01$) and duration ($p < 0.01$) in the target quadrant compared with the control group, and administration of minocycline remarkably increased the

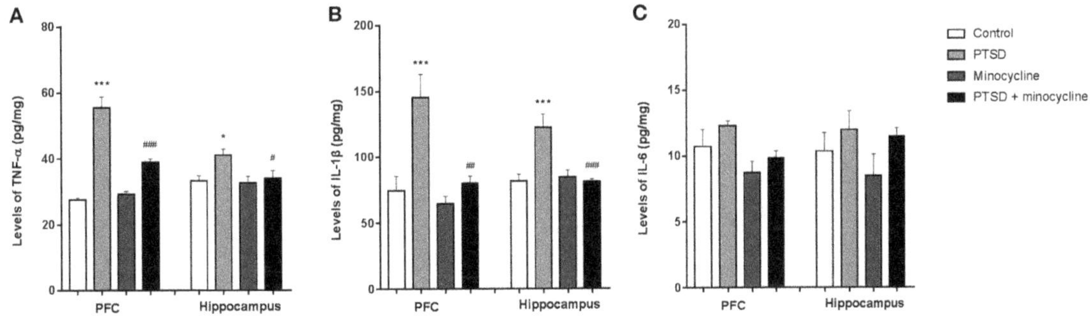

FIGURE 4 | Effects of minocycline on pro-inflammatory cytokines in the PFC and hippocampus. **(A)** The levels of TNF-α in the PFC and hippocampus. **(B)** The levels of IL-1β in the PFC and hippocampus. **(C)** The levels of IL-6 in the PFC and hippocampus. The concentrations of cytokines in the tissue were detected by ELISA. The results are expressed as the mean ± SEM, $n = 4$, * $p < 0.05$, *** $p < 0.001$ vs. control; # $p < 0.05$, ## $p < 0.01$, ### $p < 0.001$ vs. PTSD.

number of entries ($p < 0.05$) and duration ($p < 0.05$) in the target quadrant compared with the vehicle treatment in IFS-exposed rats.

Effects of Minocycline on Pro-inflammatory Cytokines in the PFC and Hippocampus

As shown in **Figure 4A**, in the levels of TNF-α in the PFC, two-way ANOVA revealed a significant effect for IFS exposure [$F_{(1, 12)} = 105.9$, $p < 0.001$], minocycline treatment [$F_{(1, 12)} = 16.41$, $p < 0.01$] and an IFS-minocycline interaction [$F_{(1, 12)} = 24.59$, $p < 0.001$]. In the levels of TNF-α in the hippocampus, two-way ANOVA revealed a significant effect for the IFS exposure [$F_{(1, 12)} = 5.139$, $p < 0.05$]. Fisher's LSD test confirmed that the IFS-exposed group showed a significant increase in the levels of TNF-α in the PFC ($p < 0.001$) and hippocampus ($p < 0.05$) compared with the control group. The levels of TNF-α in the PFC ($p < 0.001$) and hippocampus ($p < 0.05$) of IFS-exposed rats treated with minocycline were markedly lower than that of IFS-exposed vehicle treated rats.

As shown in **Figure 4B**, in the levels of IL-1β in the PFC and hippocampus, two-way ANOVA revealed a significant effect for IFS exposure [$F_{(1, 12)} = 14.84$, $p < 0.01$ and $F_{(1,12)} = 8.83$, $p < 0.05$, respectively], a minocycline treatment effect [$F_{(1, 12)} = 11.45$, $p < 0.01$ and $F_{(1,12)} = 9.348$, $p < 0.01$, respectively] and an IFS-minocycline interaction [$F_{(1, 12)} = 6.158$, $p < 0.05$ and $F_{(1,12)} = 12.47$, $p < 0.01$, respectively]. Fisher's LSD test confirmed that IFS-exposed rats exhibited a significant increase in the levels of IL-1β in the PFC ($p < 0.001$) and hippocampus ($p < 0.001$) compared with control rats, and minocycline-treated IFS rats exhibited a significant decrease in the levels of IL-1β in the PFC ($p < 0.01$) and hippocampus ($p < 0.001$) compared with IFS-exposed rats treated with vehicle.

As shown in **Figure 4C**, in the levels of IL-6 in the PFC, two-way ANOVA revealed a significant difference for minocycline administration [$F_{(1, 12)} = 6.874$, $p < 0.05$]. In the levels of IL-6 in the hippocampus, no effect was observed between groups.

Effects of Minocycline on the Activation of Microglia in the PFC and Hippocampus

In the number of microglia in the PFC, two-way ANOVA revealed a significant effect for IFS exposure [$F_{(1, 36)} = 16.9$, $p < 0.001$, **Figure 5A**] and an IFS-minocycline interaction [$F_{(1, 36)} = 9.878$, $p < 0.01$]. In the number of microglia in the DG, CA1 and CA3 of hippocampus, two-way ANOVA revealed a significant effect for IFS stress [$F_{(1, 36)} = 6.861$, $p < 0.05$, $F_{(1, 36)} = 0.4354$, $p > 0.05$, $F_{(1, 36)} = 19.2$, $p < 0.001$, respectively, **Figure 5B**] and a minocycline treatment effect [$F_{(1, 36)} = 4.199$, $p < 0.05$, $F_{(1, 36)} = 0.08328$, $p > 0.05$, $F_{(1, 36)} = 2.232$, $p > 0.05$, respectively]. Fisher's LSD test confirmed that IFS-exposed rats showed a significant increase in microglia number in the PFC ($p < 0.001$), DG ($p < 0.01$), and CA3 ($p < 0.001$) compared with the control rats, and the microglia number in the PFC ($p < 0.01$) and DG ($p < 0.05$) of minocycline-treated IFS-exposed rats was remarkably less than that of IFS-exposed vehicle-treated rats.

For the relative level of mRNA of Iba1 in the PFC, two-way ANOVA showed a significant effect for IFS exposure [$F_{(1, 8)} = 19.61$, $p < 0.01$, **Figure 5D**] and a minocycline treatment effect [$F_{(1, 8)} = 7.598$, $p < 0.05$]. For the relative level of mRNA of Iba1 in the hippocampus, two-way ANOVA showed a significant effect for IFS exposure [$F_{(1, 8)} = 10.93$, $p < 0.05$, **Figure 5E**]. Fisher's LSD test confirmed that IFS-exposed rats exhibited a significant increase in the relative level of mRNA of Iba1 in the PFC ($p < 0.01$) and hippocampus ($p < 0.05$) compared with the control rats, and the relative level of mRNA of Iba1 in the PFC ($p < 0.05$) of minocycline-treated IFS-exposed rats was significantly less than that of IFS-exposed vehicle-treated rats.

Effects of Minocycline on NF-κB in the PFC and Hippocampus

For the levels of p65 in the PFC and hippocampus, two-way ANOVA showed a significant effect for IFS exposure [$F_{(1, 8)} = 9.398$, $p < 0.05$, **Figure 6A** and $F_{(1, 8)} = 5.877$, $p < 0.05$, **Figure 6B**, respectively], a minocycline treatment effect [$F_{(1, 8)} = 15.73$, $p < 0.01$ and $F_{(1, 8)} = 7.192$, $p < 0.05$, respectively] and an IFS-minocycline interaction [$F_{(1, 8)} = 16.04$, $p < 0.01$ and $F_{(1, 8)} = 8.038$, $p < 0.05$, respectively]. Fisher's LSD test confirmed that

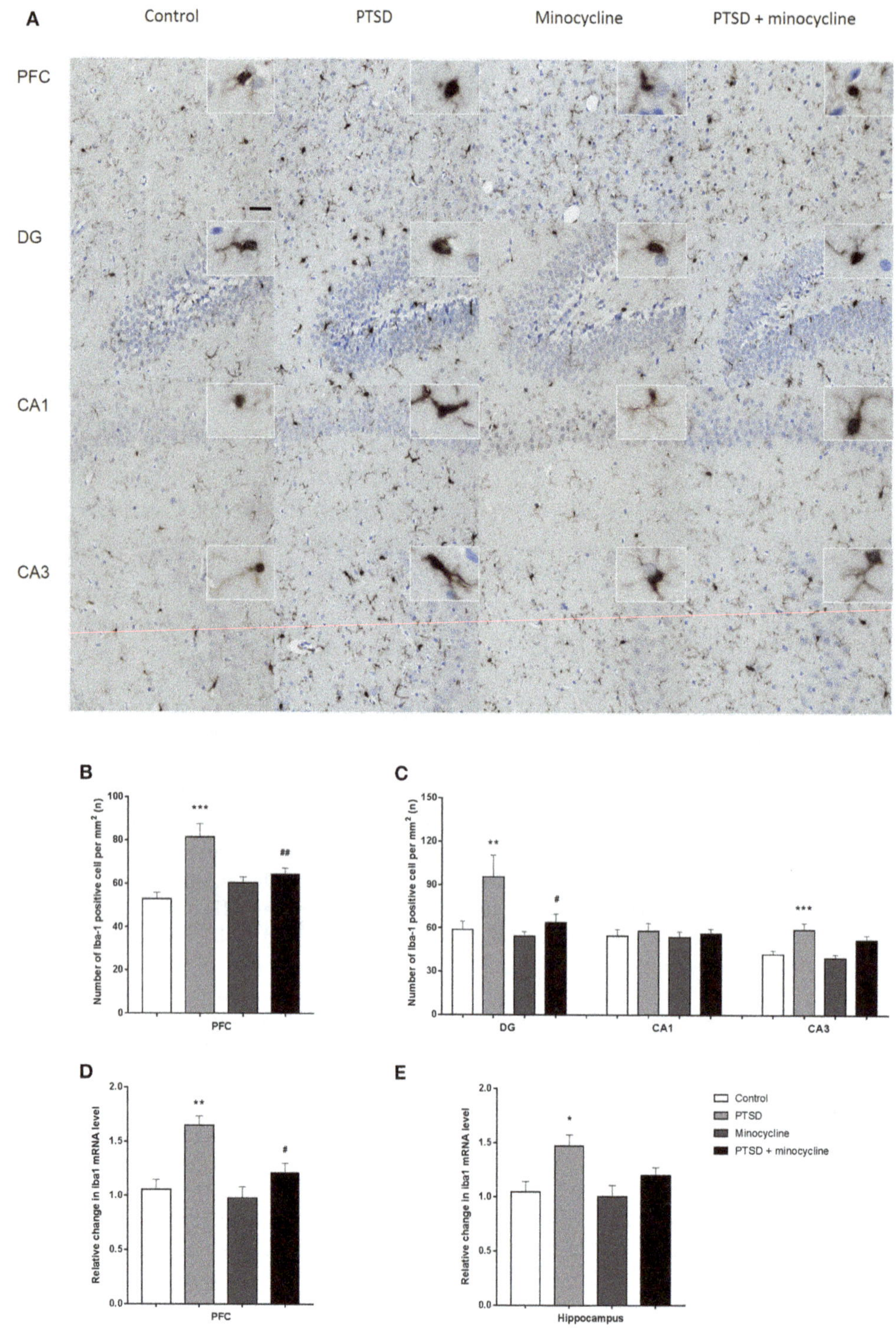

FIGURE 5 | The effects of minocycline on microglial activation in the PFC and hippocampus. **(A)** One of the representative images of the PFC, DG, CA1, and CA3 of the hippocampus in the four groups. **(B)** The number of Iba-1-positive cells in the PFC. **(C)** The number of Iba-1-positive cells in the region of DG, CA1, and CA3 in the hippocampus. **(D)** Relative changes of the Iba1 mRNA levels in the PFC. **(E)** Relative changes of the Iba1 mRNA levels in the hippocampus. The results are expressed as the mean ± SEM. The number of Iba-1-positive cells was manually calculated from 10 sections of three rats of each group by ImageJ, and the relative levels of Iba1 mRNA were detected from three rats in different groups, $^{*}p < 0.05$, $^{**}p < 0.01$, $^{***}p < 0.001$ vs. control; $^{\#}p < 0.05$, $^{\#\#}p < 0.01$ vs. PTSD. Scales bars = 50 µm.

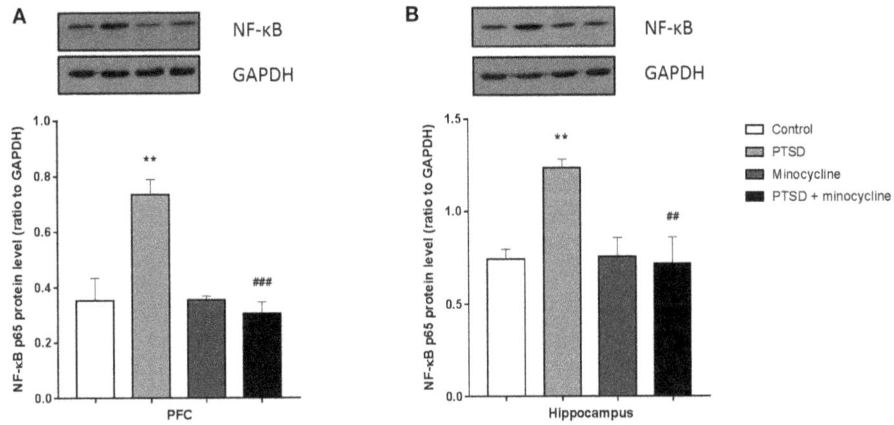

FIGURE 6 | The effect of minocycline on the expression of NF-κB in the PFC and hippocampus. **(A)** The levels of p65 in the PFC. **(B)** The levels of p65 in the hippocampus. The protein levels were detected by western blotting, and each value was normalized to GAPDH. The results are expressed as the mean ± SEM, and the blot shown is one of 3 independent experiments, $^{**}p < 0.01$ vs. control; $^{\#\#}p < 0.01$, $^{\#\#\#}p < 0.001$ vs. PTSD.

the IFS-exposed rats showed a significant increase in the levels of p65 in the PFC ($p < 0.01$) and hippocampus ($p < 0.01$) compared with the control group, and minocycline significantly reduced the levels of p65 in the PFC ($p < 0.01$) and hippocampus ($p < 0.01$) compared to vehicle treatment in IFS-exposed rats.

DISCUSSION

The present study demonstrated that the 6 days IFS protocol was able to induce PTSD-like behavior, as evidenced by anxiety-like behavior in the OF test and the EPM test, as well as impairment of learning and memory in the MWM test. The behavioral changes were accompanied by a significant increase in the production of pro-inflammatory cytokines and activation of microglia and NF-κB in the PFC and hippocampus in the stressed animals. However, treatment with minocycline was able to reverse these behavioral alterations, and the neuroprotective effects of minocycline might be exerted through its anti-inflammatory properties via the NF-κB signaling pathway.

In the present study, we examined the effects of minocycline on the anxiety-like behaviors and learning and memory functioning in a rat model of PTSD induced by IFS. The OF test is designed to measure spontaneous activity and anxiety-like behaviors. The results of the OF test revealed that IFS induced anxiety-like behavior and did not affect spontaneous movement, while minocycline was able to attenuate anxiety-like behaviors, as indicated by the increased time spent in the central area. These results suggested that minocycline has an anxiolytic effect in a model of IFS, which is consistent with previous studies (22, 23, 33). The EPM is widely used to (22, 23, 33). The EPM is widely used to measure anxiety-like behavior in rodents, and it was validated pharmacological agent. Utilizing the IFS model of PTSD, administration of minocycline significantly reduced the IFS-induced anxiety-like behaviors, as evidenced by the increase in number of entries and duration of time spent in the open arms of the EPM. The MWM test assesses spatial learning and memory function in rodents. Our results showed that IFS caused impairment in spatial learning and memory, as shown by an increased latency in reaching the platform and reduced duration of time and frequency of entry in the target quadrant, which were reversed by the treatment with minocycline. These results were consistent with previous studies in rodents suggesting that with previous studies in rodents suggesting that minocycline is beneficial for cognitive functions Anxiety and cognitive impairment are common symptoms of PTSD and other psychiatric disorders, especially stressor-related disorders. However, the underlying mechanism of PTSD is not well understood. Our previous studies and other researchers noted that the hypothalamic-pituitary-adrenocortical (HPA) axis was involved in the response to stress, which manifested by enhanced negative feedback inhibition of the HPA axis (34) and excessive expression of corticotrophin-releasing factor receptor in the hypothalamus, amygdala and PFC (35). Furthermore, other studies have indicated that inflammation is a crucial mediator of the responses to various stressors and may lead to anxiety-like behavior and cognitive impairments. Previous studies have found that pro-inflammatory cytokines were increased in rodent models of PTSD and patients suffering from PTSD. For example, studies on rodent models of PTSD indicated higher levels of the pro-inflammatory cytokines in the hippocampus and PFC (14, 36, 37). A meta-analysis reported that the levels of IL-6, IL-1β, TNF-α and interferon-γ were up-regulated in patients with PTSD compared with controls (38). Our results also indicated the protein levels of TNF-α, IL-1β, and IL-6 were increased in the PFC and hippocampus. The microglia act as the resident macrophages in the brain and produce pro/anti-inflammatory cytokines. We also examined the relative levels of mRNA and protein of Iba-1, a marker of microglia, in the PFC and hippocampus. The qPCR and IHC results indicated that IFS increased the level of mRNA of iba-1, the number of Iba-1-positive cells and changed the morphology of the microglia from hyper-ramified to amoeboid shape in the PFC and hippocampus. Consistent with our results, Sun et al. also found up-regulation of Iba-1 in the CA1 and CA3 regions of the hippocampus in the animal model of PTSD induced by single prolonged stress (36). Similarly, other studies also reported that various stressors could induce microglial activation in different animal models (39–42). These increased microglial responses are likely part of the neuroinflammatory responses in which microglial activation is the major cellular response to CNS dysfunction. The presence of morphological and immunological findings suggests a potential role for microglia and neuroinflammation in the pathogenesis of the PTSD. It is well known that NF-κB is a crucial regulator of immunological processes. O'Donovan et al. found an up-regulation of target genes of NF-κB in patients suffering from PTSD compared with non-PTSD controls (43). Pace et al. analyzed the circulating peripheral mononuclear cells of child abuse victims with PTSD and reported greater NF-κB signaling activity in female childhood abuse victims with PTSD than non-PTSD controls (44). In addition, a model of PTSD induced by predator scent stress was found to be associated with overexpression of NF-κB in the hippocampus (45). Our results also suggested that NF-κB was activated in the brains of rats subjected to IFS. Pyrrolidine dithiocarbamate, an inhibitor of NF-κB, was found to normalize anxiety-like behavior, as well as startle response and startle habituation in rodents (45). Si et al. indicated that NF-κB activity in the basolateral amygdala was essential for memory reconsolidation and may be a potential target for pharmacological treatment for PTSD (46). Since the NF-κB is a critical factor in neuroinflammation, an inhibitor of NF-κB signaling might attenuate PTSD symptoms by down-regulating inflammation.

The choices for pharmacological treatment for PTSD are limited, although selective serotonin reuptake inhibitors (SSRI) are the mainstay treatment. In addition, aspirin and brufen were used in clinical trials to reduce neuroinflammation in patients suffering from PTSD (5). Our findings demonstrated that administration of minocycline significantly reduced the levels of pro-inflammatory cytokines and the activation of microglia and NF-κB in a rat model of PTSD induced by IFS. Previous studies have reported that a single dose of minocycline had a potential effect of preventing the deterioration of behavior and exaggeration of neuroinflammation (14). Similarly, a longer injection of minocycline also attenuated single prolonged stress-induced anxiety-like behavior (36). In addition, minocycline was able to improve cognitive deficits in a cerebral microvascular amyloid model (47). Minocycline has been found to inhibit the activation of microglia *in vivo* (26). Moreover, researchers have suggested that minocycline can selectively inhibit microglia polarization to the pro-inflammatory state (27). Furthermore, previous studies indicated that minocycline affected the mRNA and protein expression of NF-κB in microglia (27). In the present study, our results suggested that treatment with minocycline was able to inhibit the NF-κB pathway, attenuate neuroinflammation and alleviate IFS-induced behavioral disturbances in rats.

In conclusion, our study demonstrated that a 6 days IFS protocol was able to induce PTSD-like behavior, elevate pro-inflammatory cytokines and activate the microglia and NF-κB in the PFC and hippocampus, which suggested that neuroinflammation is involved in the response to stress. Minocycline can attenuate these behavioral and molecular alterations, suggesting that minocycline might be a potential pharmacological agent for the treatment of PTSD. Although minocycline has been considered a safe antibiotic and anti-inflammatory agent for humans, further clinical trials are required to assess its therapeutic efficacy in clinical population with PTSD.

AUTHOR CONTRIBUTIONS

WW performed the major experiments, data analysis, and wrote the manuscripts. RW, JX, XQ, HJ, and AK established the biophysical model, DL and FP designed this study. DL, CH, and RH revised the paper.

ACKNOWLEDGMENTS

We thank H.-R Wu for help with immunohistochemistry; D.-Q Xin, X.-L Chu for advice on behavioral tests.

REFERENCES

1. American Psychiatric Association. *Diagnostic and Statistical Manual of Mental Disorders : DSM-IV-TR*. 4th ed. text revision. American Psychiatric Association (2013). Available online at: http://ci.nii.ac.jp/ncid/BA47976780 (Accessed November 1, 2017).
2. Amos T, Stein DJ, Ipser JC. Pharmacological interventions for preventing post-traumatic stress disorder (PTSD). *Cochrane Database Syst Rev.* (2014) CD006239. doi: 10.1002/14651858.CD006239.pub2
3. Pacella ML, Hruska B, Delahanty DL. The physical health consequences of PTSD and PTSD symptoms: a meta-analytic review. *J Anxiety Disord.* (2013) 27:33–46. doi: 10.1016/j.janxdis.2012.08.004
4. Sareen J. Posttraumatic stress disorder in adults: impact, comorbidity, risk factors, and treatment. *Can J Psychiatry* (2014) 59:460–7. doi: 10.1177/070674371405900902
5. Yehuda R, Hoge CW, McFarlane AC, Vermetten E, Lanius RA, Nievergelt CM, et al. Post-traumatic stress disorder. *Nat Rev Dis Primer* (2015) 1:nrdp201557. doi: 10.1038/nrdp.2015.57
6. Jayatunge RM, Pokorski M. Post-traumatic stress disorder: a review of therapeutic Role of meditation interventions. In: *Advances in Experimental Medicine and Biology*. New York, NY: Springer (2018). p. 1–7. doi: 10.1007/5584_2018_167
7. Lupien SJ, McEwen BS, Gunnar MR, Heim C. Effects of stress throughout the lifespan on the brain, behaviour and cognition. *Nat Rev Neurosci.* (2009) 10:434–45. doi: 10.1038/nrn2639
8. Lu Y, Ho CS, Liu X, Chua AN, Wang W, McIntyre RS, Ho RC. Chronic administration of fluoxetine and pro-inflammatory cytokine change in a rat model of depression. *PloS ONE* (2017) 12:e018670. doi: 10.1371/journal.pone.0186700
9. Grippo AJ, Scotti M-AL. Stress and neuroinflammation. *Inflamm Psychiatry* (2013) 28:20–32. doi: 10.1159/000343965
10. Känel RV, Hepp U, Kraemer B, Traber R, Keel M, Mica L, Schnyder U. Evidence for low-grade systemic proinflammatory activity in patients with posttraumatic stress disorder. *J Psychiatr Res.* (2007) 41:744–52. doi: 10.1016/j.jpsychires.2006.06.009
11. Michopoulos V, Powers A, Gillespie CF, Ressler KJ, Jovanovic T. Inflammation in fear- and anxiety-based disorders: PTSD, GAD, and beyond. *Neuropsychopharmacology* (2017) 42:254–70. doi: 10.1038/npp.2016.146
12. Speer K, Upton D, Semple S, McKune A. Systemic low-grade inflammation in post-traumatic stress disorder: a systematic review. *J Inflamm Res.* (2018) 11:111–21. doi: 10.2147/JIR.S155903

13. Jones ME, Lebonville CL, Barrus D, Lysle DT. The role of brain interleukin-1 in stress-enhanced fear learning. *Neuropsychopharmacology* (2015) 40:1289–96. doi: 10.1038/npp.2014.317
14. Levkovitz Y, Fenchel D, Kaplan Z, Zohar J, Cohen H. Early post-stressor intervention with minocycline, a second-generation tetracycline, attenuates post-traumatic stress response in an animal model of PTSD. *Eur Neuropsychopharmacol* (2015) 25:124–32. doi: 10.1016/j.euroneuro.2014.11.012
15. Wilson CB, McLaughlin LD, Ebenezer PJ, Nair AR, Dange R, Harre JG, et al. Differential effects of sertraline in a predator exposure animal model of post-traumatic stress disorder. *Front Behav Neurosci* (2014) 8:256. doi: 10.3389/fnbeh.2014.00256
16. Camacho-Arroyo I, López-Griego L, Morales-Montor J. the role of cytokines in the regulation of neurotransmission. *Neuroimmunomodulation* (2009) 16:1–12. doi: 10.1159/000179661
17. Kettenmann H, Hanisch UK, Noda M, Verkhratsky A. Physiology of microglia. *Physiol Rev.* (2011) 91:461–553. doi: 10.1152/physrev.00011.2010
18. Clark IA, Vissel B. The meteorology of cytokine storms, and the clinical usefulness of this knowledge. *Semin Immunopathol.* (2017) 39:505–16. doi: 10.1007/s00281-017-0628-y
19. Irwin MR, Cole SW. Reciprocal regulation of the neural and innate immune systems. *Nat Rev Immunol.* (2011) 11:625–32. doi: 10.1038/nri3042
20. Garrido-Mesa N, Zarzuelo A, Gálvez J. Minocycline: far beyond an antibiotic. *Br J Pharmacol.* (2013) 169:337–52. doi: 10.1111/bph.12139
21. Dean OM, Datafranco J, Giorlando F, Berk M. Minocycline: therapeutic potential in psychiatry. *Cns Drugs* (2012) 26:391. doi: 10.2165/11632000-000000000-00000
22. Dansie LE, Phommahaxay K, Okusanya AG, Uwadia J, Huang M, Rotschafer SE, et al. Long-lasting effects of minocycline on behavior in young but not adult Fragile X mice. *Neuroscience* (2013) 246:186–98. doi: 10.1016/j.neuroscience.2013.04.058
23. Shigemori T, Sakai A, Takumi T, Itoh Y, Suzuki H. Altered microglia in the amygdala are involved in anxiety-related behaviors of a copy number variation mouse model of autism. *J Nippon Med Sch.* (2015) 82:92–9. doi: 10.1272/jnms.82.92
24. Singh A, Kumar A. Microglial inhibitory mechanism of coenzyme Q10 against Aβ (1-42) induced cognitive dysfunctions: possible behavioral, biochemical, cellular, and histopathological alterations. *Front Pharmacol.* (2015) 6:268. doi: 10.3389/fphar.2015.00268
25. Giri PK, Lu Y, Lei S, Li W, Zheng J, Lu H, et al. Pretreatment with minocycline improves neurogenesis and behavior performance after midazolam exposure in neonatal rats. *Neuroreport* (2018) 29:153–9. doi: 10.1097/WNR.0000000000000937
26. Tikka T, Fiebich BL, Goldsteins G, Keinänen R, Koistinaho J. Minocycline, a tetracycline derivative, is neuroprotective against excitotoxicity by inhibiting activation and proliferation of microglia. *J Neurosci.* (2001) 21:2580–8. doi: 10.1523/JNEUROSCI.21-08-02580.2001
27. Kobayashi K, Imagama S, Ohgomori T, Hirano K, Uchimura K, Sakamoto K, et al. Minocycline selectively inhibits M1 polarization of microglia. *Cell Death Dis.* (2013) 4:e525. doi: 10.1038/cddis.2013.54
28. Soczynska JK, Mansur RB, Brietzke E, Swardfager W, Kennedy SH, Woldeyohannes HO, et al. Novel therapeutic targets in depression: Minocycline as a candidate treatment. *Behav Brain Res.* (2012) 235:302–17. doi: 10.1016/j.bbr.2012.07.026
29. Prut L, Belzung C. The open field as a paradigm to measure the effects of drugs on anxiety-like behaviors: a review. *Eur J Pharmacol.* (2003) 463:3–33. doi: 10.1016/S0014-2999(03)01272-X
30. Walf AA, Frye CA. The use of the elevated plus maze as an assay of anxiety-related behavior in rodents. *Nat Protoc* (2007) 2:322. doi: 10.1038/nprot.2007.44
31. Morris R. Developments of a water-maze procedure for studying spatial learning in the rat. *J Neurosci Methods* (1984) 11:47–60. doi: 10.1016/0165-0270(84)90007-4
32. Livak KJ, Schmittgen TD. Analysis of relative gene expression data using real-time quantitative PCR and the 2–ΔΔCT Method. *Methods* (2001) 25:402–8. doi: 10.1006/meth.2001.1262
33. Neigh GN, Karelina K, Glasper ER, Bowers SLK, Zhang N, Popovich PG, DeVries AC. Anxiety following cardiac arrest/Cpr: exacerbated by stress and prevented by minocycline. *Stroke J Cereb Circ.* (2009) 40:3601. doi: 10.1161/STROKEAHA.109.564146
34. Daskalakis NP, Lehrner A, Yehuda R. Endocrine aspects of post-traumatic stress disorder and implications for diagnosis and treatment. *Endocrinol Metab Clin North Am.* (2013) 42:503. doi: 10.1016/j.ecl.2013.05.004
35. Li C, Liu Y, Yin S, Lu C, Liu D, Jiang H, et al. Long-term effects of early adolescent stress: dysregulation of hypothalamic–pituitary–adrenal axis and central corticotropin releasing factor receptor 1 expression in adult male rats. *Behav Brain Res.* (2015) 288:39–49. doi: 10.1016/j.bbr.2015.04.007
36. Sun R, Zhang Z, Lei Y, Liu Y, Lu C, Rong H, et al. Hippocampal activation of microglia may underlie the shared neurobiology of comorbid posttraumatic stress disorder and chronic pain. *Mol Pain* (2016) 12:1744806916679166. doi: 10.1177/1744806916679166
37. Wilson CB, McLaughlin LD, Nair A, Ebenezer PJ, Dange R, Francis J. Inflammation and oxidative stress are elevated in the brain, blood, and adrenal glands during the progression of post-traumatic stress disorder in a predator exposure animal model. *PLOS ONE* (2013) 8:e76146. doi: 10.1371/journal.pone.0076146
38. Passos IC, Vasconcelos-Moreno MP, Costa LG, Kunz M, Brietzke E, Quevedo J, et al. Inflammatory markers in post-traumatic stress disorder: a systematic review, meta-analysis, and meta-regression. *Lancet Psychiatry* (2015) 2:1002–12. doi: 10.1016/S2215-0366(15)00309-0
39. Hinwood M, Morandini J, Day TA, Walker FR. Evidence that microglia mediate the neurobiological effects of chronic psychological stress on the medial prefrontal cortex. *Cereb Cortex* (2012) 22:1442–54. doi: 10.1093/cercor/bhr229
40. Kreisel Merzel T, Frank M, Licht T, Reshef R, Zidon O, Baratta MV, et al. Dynamic microglial alterations underlie stress-induced depressive-like behavior and suppressed neurogenesis. (2013) 19:155. doi: 10.1038/mp.2013.155
41. Réus GZ, Fries GR, Stertz L, Badawy M, Passos IC, Barichello T, et al. The role of inflammation and microglial activation in the pathophysiology of psychiatric disorders. *Neuroscience* (2015) 300:141–54. doi: 10.1016/j.neuroscience.2015.05.018
42. Tian L, Hui CW, Bisht K, Tan Y, Sharma K, Chen S, et al. Microglia under psychosocial stressors along the aging trajectory: Consequences on neuronal circuits, behavior, and brain diseases. *Prog Neuropsychopharmacol Biol Psychiatry* (2017) 79:27–39. doi: 10.1016/j.pnpbp.2017.01.007
43. O'Donovan A, Sun B, Cole S, Rempel H, Lenoci M, Pulliam L, et al. Transcriptional control of monocyte gene expression in post-traumatic stress disorder. *Dis Markers* (2011) 30:123–32. doi: 10.3233/DMA-2011-0768
44. Pace TWW, Wingenfeld K, Schmidt I, Meinlschmidt G, Hellhammer DH, Heim CM. Increased peripheral NF-κB pathway activity in women with childhood abuse-related posttraumatic stress disorder. *Brain Behav Immun.* (2012) 26:13–7. doi: 10.1016/j.bbi.2011.07.232
45. Cohen H, Kozlovsky N, Matar MA, Zohar J, Kaplan Z. The characteristic long-term upregulation of hippocampal NF-κB complex in PTSD-like behavioral stress response is normalized by high-dose corticosterone and pyrrolidine dithiocarbamate administered immediately after exposure. *Neuropsychopharmacology* (2011) 36:2286. doi: 10.1038/npp.2011.118
46. Si J, Yang J, Xue L, Yang C, Luo Y, Shi H, et al. Activation of NF-κB in basolateral amygdala is required for memory reconsolidation in auditory fear conditioning. *PLoS ONE* (2012) 7:e43973. doi: 10.1371/journal.pone.0043973
47. Fan R, Xu F, Previti ML, Davis J, Grande AM, Robinson JK, et al. Minocycline reduces microglial activation and improves behavioral deficits in a transgenic model of cerebral microvascular amyloid. *J Neurosci.* (2007) 27:3057–63. doi: 10.1523/JNEUROSCI.4371-06.2007

10

Short Term Intrarectal Administration of Sodium Propionate Induces Antidepressant-Like Effects in Rats Exposed to Chronic Unpredictable Mild Stress

Jianguo Li [1,2], Luwen Hou [3], Cui Wang [3], Xueyang Jia [3], Xuemei Qin [2,3]* and Changxin Wu [1]*

[1] Laboratory for Microbiome Sciences, Institute of Biomedical Sciences, Shanxi University, Taiyuan, China, [2] Key Laboratory of Chemical Biology and Molecular Engineering of Ministry of Education, Shanxi University, Taiyuan, China, [3] Modern Research Center for Traditional Chinese Medicine, Shanxi University, Taiyuan, China

***Correspondence:**
Jianguo Li
lijg@sxu.edu.cn
Xuemei Qin
qinxm@sxu.edu.cn

Depression has been correlated with metabolic disorders, and the gut microbiota and its metabolites have been reported to be key factors affecting metabolic disorders. Several metabolites generated by the gut microbiota have been reported to exert antidepressant-like effects, including the short chain fatty acid (SCFA) butyrate. However, recent work has suggested that the abundance of butyrate is not significantly changed in neither human nor experimental animals with depression, and butyrate has been reported to decrease upon the administration of prebiotics with antidepressant-like effects. Supplementation of endogenous metabolites that are unchanged in depression may induce additional metabolic disorders and may lead to poorer clinical outcomes. However, the endogenous metabolites that are imbalanced in depression may include several antidepressant candidates that could circumvent these problems. In this study, we used GC-MS spectrometry to study the fecal metabolome of rats under Chronic Unpredictable Mild Stress (CUMS). We carried out static and dynamic metabolomics analyses to identify the differential metabolites between the CUMS rats and control rats. We identified propionic acid, rather than butyric acid, as a differential metabolite of the CUMS rats. Consistent with this, a 1-week intrarectal administration of sodium propionate (NaP, the salt form of propionic acid) induced antidepressant-like effects and partially rebalanced the plasma metabolome. The antidepressant-like effects of NaP were correlated with differential rescue of neurotransmitters in the prefrontal cortex, which may be achieved through the reduction of catabolism of noradrenaline, tryptophan and dopamine, rather than serotonin. These findings support NaP as a potential candidate in fighting depression by administering an endogenous metabolite.

Keywords: propionate, antidepressant-like, metabolomics, Analysis of variance (ANOVA) Simultaneous Component Analysis, neurotransmitter

INTRODUCTION

Depression is a widespread psychiatric disorder that is characterized by persistent depressive mood and anhedonia (1). Although the pathophysiology of depression is not yet completely understood, several hypotheses have been put forward, including lack of monoaminergic neurotransmitters, hyperactivity of the hypothalamic- pituitary-adrenal axis, chronic low-grade inflammation, and others (1, 2). Metabolic disorder was recently reported to be a novel feature of depression (3). Imbalanced metabolic states were observed in the serum (4), liver (5), and gut (6) of depressed patients and in experimental animals (7). In addition, restoring the metabolic state of these in experimental animal models has been associated with improvement of depression (8, 9), and several endogenous metabolites have been identified as potential biomarkers for depression (10–13).

The gut microbiota and its metabolites have also been reported to be important factors affecting depression (7, 14, 15). Fecal transplantation from depressed patients can transfer depressive symptoms to recipient animals (5, 16). Gut metabolites were correlated with a distinct liver metabolome in depressed mice (5), and it has been suggested that some metabolites have the potential to alleviate depression (17). One gut metabolite, butyrate, was reported to have antidepressant-like effects (18–20). However, there is little variation in the abundance of butyrate in the serum, liver, or gut of depressed individuals compared to healthy controls (21, 22). Moreover, supplementation with prebiotics that exhibit antidepressant-like effects decreased the abundance of butyrate in cecum of experimental animals (23), suggesting that butyrate may instead act to worsen depression symptoms. Therefore, caution should be taken when selecting an endogenous metabolite as an antidepressant candidate. To avoid inducing additional metabolome imbalances, candidate endogenous metabolites must therefore be evaluated for any potential influence on the depressed metabolic state before their antidepressant-like effects are investigated. Metabolites that typically show a reduced abundance in depression provide an alternative shortcut in the selection of endogenous metabolites as antidepressant candidates (21–24).

Metabolomics has been shown to be a powerful tool in searching for disease-specific metabolites (25, 26). LC-MS, GC-MS, and NMR are three of the most popular analytical platforms for metabolomics investigations (27, 28). Due to the sophisticated library of metabolite standards and the excellent coverage of non-polar small compounds, GC-MS spectrometry has been widely applied in metabolomics studies of drug pharmacology and disease pathophysiology (29, 30). Dozens of reports have used metabolomics to investigate the imbalanced metabolic state and the differential metabolites associated with depression (31–34). However, most of the current studies are limited to static metabolomics of cross-sectional data, which ignore the complicated dynamic development of depression (35).

Dynamic metabolomics was developed to overcome the above limitations of static metabolomics (36–38). Analysis of variance (ANOVA) Simultaneous Component Analysis (ASCA), one dynamic metabolomics strategy, accounts for time, phenotype, and the interactions between time and phenotype; divides metabolomics data into effect matrices; and reveals time-dependent trends through separate multivariate study of these effect matrices (39, 40). ASCA-based dynamic metabolomics has been successfully applied to evaluate the metabolic effects of energy-restricted intervention (41), to provide urinary metabolic profiling of a rat model of postnatal stress (42), and to evaluate the effect of amyloid peptide on hippocampal and serum metabolism (43).

This study uses GC-MS spectrometry and a combination of static and dynamic metabolomics data analysis to study the typical gut metabolites of rats with depression-like behaviors. Propionic acid was observed by both static and dynamic metabolomics data analysis, and intervention with NaP (the salt form of propionic acid) was carried out to study the effects of propionic acid on depression.

MATERIALS AND METHODS

Animals and Reagents

Male Sprague-Dawley rats (weighing 200 ± 10 g) were purchased from Beijing Vital River Laboratories Co. (SCXK (Jing) 2011-2012). Rats were housed 10 per cage with free access to water and food, under controlled feeding conditions of temperature (25±1°C), humidity (45 ± 15%), and light (lights on at 8:00 a.m., 12-h day/night switch). Rats were allowed a 1-week adaption to the new environment before further experiments. The rats were randomly assigned into two groups: the Control group, and the CUMS group. The Control group contained 10 rats. The CUMS group contained 40 rats, and the success of CUMS modeling was evaluated by behavior tests at the fourth week. The rats without typical depressive-like behaviors were excluded (25% of the CUMS group). The successful modeled rats were then randomly separated into three groups: the CUMS group, the PBS group (CUMS+PBS administration), the NaP group (CUMS+NaP administration). The rats in each group were then filtered by the outliers of experimental results, and six rats per group was finally selected. The experimental results for each group were then backtracked. All experimental procedures were approved by the Committee on Animal Research and Ethics of Shanxi University.

Neurotransmitter standards: 5-hydroxytryptamine (5-HT), Kynurenine (KYN), 3-methoxytyramine (3-MT), gamma-aminobutyric acid (GABA), 3,4-dihydroxyphenylacetic acid (DOPAC), norepinephrine (NE), 5-hydroxyindole acetic acid (5-HIAA), Tryptophan (TRP), 3-hydroxykynurenine (3-HK), 3-hydroxyanthranilic acid (3-HAA), were purchased from Sigma-Aldrich (St. Louis, MO, USA). Dopamine (DA) was acquired from Dr. Ehrenstorfer GmbH (Augsburg, Germany). Homovanillic acid (HVA) and the derivatization reagent dansyl chloride were purchased from Tokyo Chemical Industry Co. Ltd. (Tokyo, Japan). Formic acid, acetone, methanol and acetonitrile (LC-MS grade) were obtained from Merck (Darmstadt, Germany). Standards for short chain fatty acids (SCFAs, acetic acid, propionic acid, butyric acid) were purchased from Sigma-Aldrich (St. Louis, MO, USA). All solvents were HPLC grade or above.

Chronic Unpredictable Mild Stress (CUMS) Model

CUMS modeling was performed with a previously described protocol (44). Briefly, rats were individually housed and subjected to no more than 4 of the following stressors every day in a random order for 5 weeks: swimming in 4°C water for 5 min, foot-shock for 2 min, tail clamp for 2 min, subject to noise for 3 h, water deprivation for 24 h, food deprivation for 24 h, subject to a temperature of 45°C for 5 min. The above stressors were imposed separately, and each rat received no more than one stressor simultaneously. If a rat received a stressor of water deprivation or food deprivation, no more stressor was imposed to this rat at the same day. Every five rats of the control group was housed together, and received none of the above mentioned stressors. Fecal samples were collected with metabolic cage every week. After the experiment, rats were sacrificed after ethyl carbamate anesthesia. Blood samples were acquired through the arteria cruralis. EDTA anticoagulant-treated blood samples were centrifuged at 4°C, 3,000 rpm for 15 min, and the supernatants were split into three aliquots and stored at −80°C.

NaP Administration

NaP was administrated intrarectally every day for 1 week from the beginning of the 5th week (**Figure 1A**). To reduce variation between individuals, each rat in the NaP group received 1 mL of NaP (200 mmol/L) in PBS (pH 7.4), while rats in the PBS group received an equal volume of PBS.

Behavioral Tests

Body Weight Measurement

The body weights of rats in both of the CUMS group and the control group were measured at 9 a.m. on days 0, 7, 14, 21, 28, 35, and 42 of the CUMS model.

Sucrose Preference Test (SPT)

Exposure to 1% sucrose solution for 24 h was carried out before SPT to avoid neophobia. To test for sucrose preference, each rat was provided with a bottle containing a 1% sucrose solution and a second bottle containing tap water for 4 h. Consumption of sucrose and water were recorded. The sucrose preference rate was calculated as: sucrose consumption (g)/ (sucrose consumption (g) + water consumption (g)).

Open-Field Test (OPT)

OPTs were performed once a week in a custom-made black metal cage (100 ×100 × 40 cm), with the bottom divided into 25 equal sectors by white stripes. To avoid influence of confounding factors (the environment and animals' emotional and physical state, etc.), OPT was performed in the morning of the same day of the weeks during the CUMS modeling. Each rat was gently placed into the central square and monitored for 5 min. The immobility time, grooming time, rearing counts, and crossing counts were recorded. The bottom of the open field was cleaned before each OPT.

GC-MS Spectrometry

GC-MS spectrometry was conducted as previously described (44), with some modifications. Briefly, 200 mg of dried feces was homogenized in 500 μL water, and 400 μL acetonitrile was added into the centrifuged supernatant to precipitate protein. The second supernatants were then thoroughly dried under nitrogen and re-suspended in 30 μL Pyridine-methoxy amino acid salt solution (15 mg/mL). The solution was subsequently incubated at 70°C for 1 h, 50 μL of N,O-bis(trimethylsilyl)trifluoroacetamide (including 1% trimethylchlorosilane) was added to the solution, and the samples were incubated at 40°C for 1.5 h. One microliter of each analyte was injected in a (10:1) split mode into a trace gas chromatograph coupled with a Polyris Q Ion Trap mass spectrometer (Thermo Fisher Scientific, MA, USA). Separation of the ECF derivatives was conducted with a DB-5MS capillary column (30 m × 250 μm i.d., 0.25 μm film thickness, Agilent J & W Scientific, CA, USA). Helium was employed as carrier gas at a constant flow rate of 1.0 mL/min. The oven temperature was first held at 80°C for 3 min, ramped to 140°C at a speed of 7°C/min, held at 140°C for 4 min, ramped to 180°C at a speed of 4°C/min, held at 180°C for 6 min, then ramped to 280°C at a speed of 5°C/min, held at 280°C for 2 min. The mass data were collected in a full scan mode from m/z 50 to 650. Compounds were identified by comparison of mass spectra with the standards in National Institute of Standards and Technology (NIST) library (version 2.0). The Human Metabolome Database (HMDB) (http://www.hmdb.ca) was employed for further reference. The identified metabolites were validated with commercially available analytical standards. The raw GC-MS result files were converted into Net-CDF format and processed using XCMS with default settings.

Quantitation of Neurotransmitters and SCFAs

Simultaneous UHPLC-ESI-MS/MS quantitation of 12 neurotransmitters in the prefrontal cortex (PFC) of rats was carried out as previously described (45) with some modifications. Briefly, 30–50 mg of the PFC was homogenized and precipitated with methanol, the supernatants were dried under nitrogen and reconstituted with the initial mobile phase. UHPLC-ESI-MS/MS was performed on a Thermo Scientific Dionex Ultimate 3000 RSLC system combined with a Thermo Q Exactive Orbitrap mass spectrometer. The analytes were separated with a Thermo Hypersill GOLD (2.1 × 100 mm, 1.7 μm) column. The mobile phase consisting of phases A [water: formic acid (99.9: 0.1, v/v)] and B [acetonitrile: formic acid (99.9: 0.1, v/v)] was applied with a gradient elution at a flow rate of 0.3 mL/min: linear increase from 0 to 20% B in 3 min; hold at 60% B for 3 min; linear increase from 60 to 80% B in 4 min; linear increase from 80 to 95% B in 3 min; hold at 95% B for 4 min. ESI-MS/MS conditions were set as follows: gas temperature 350°C, sheath gas flow rate 46, capillary voltage 3000 V, nebulizer pressure 35 ps. MS acquisitions were performed in PRM (Parallel Reaction Monitoring, also known as Targeted-MS/MS) mode. The calibration curves for each

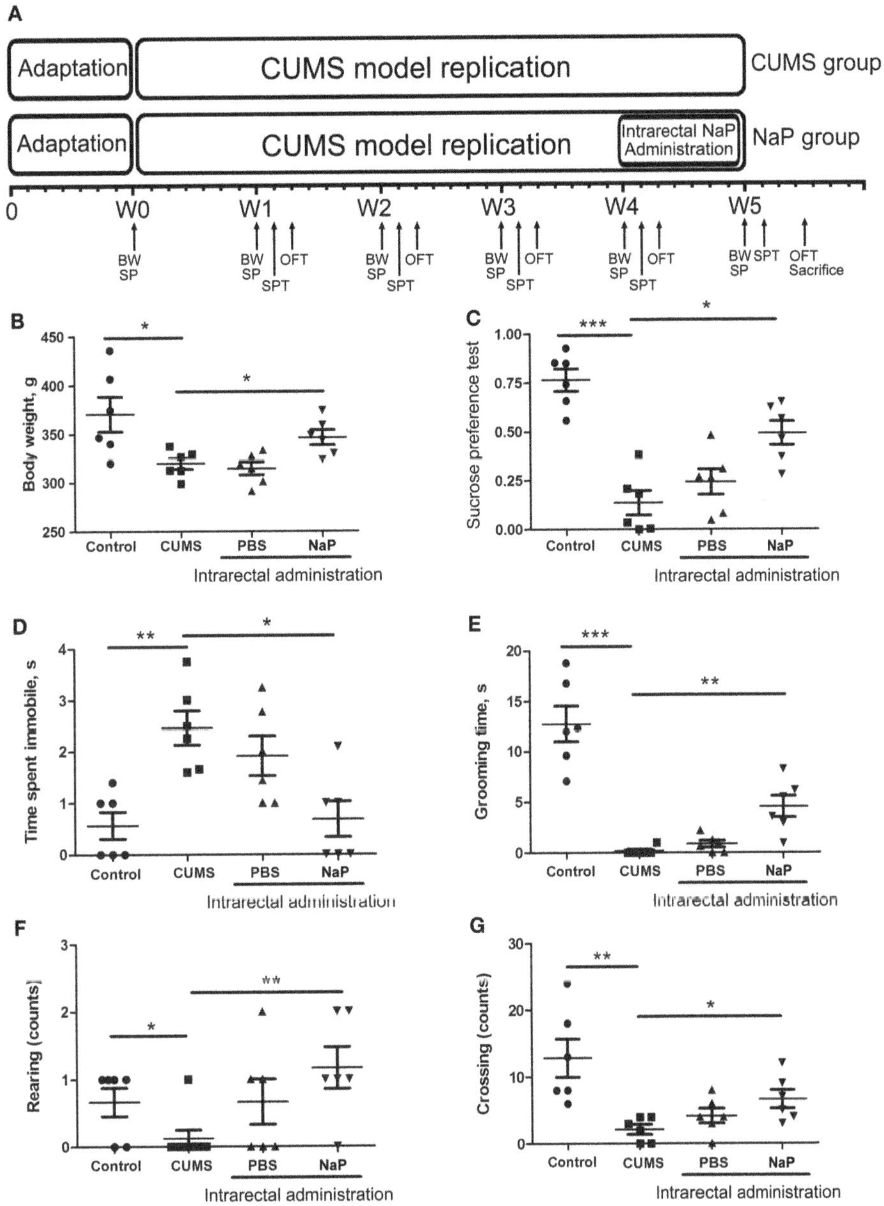

FIGURE 1 | Experimental procedures **(A)** and results of behavioral tests **(B–G)** in this study. The rats were randomly assigned into two groups: the Control group, and the CUMS group. The Control group contained 10 rats. The CUMS group contained 40 rats, and the success of CUMS modeling was evaluated by behavior tests at the fourth week. The successful modeled rats were then randomly separated into three groups: the CUMS group, the PBS group (CUMS+PBS administration), the NaP group (CUMS+NaP administration). The rats in each group were then filtered by the outliers of experimental results, and six rats per group was finally selected. The experimental results for each group were then backtracked. CUMS modeling was performed over 5 weeks (W1–W4), and intrarectal administration of NaP was carried out during the last week (W5). Body weight **(B)**, sucrose preference rate **(C)**, and indices of OFT **(D–G)** were measured for CUMS and control animals every week during this period, and the measurements in the fifth week are shown. BW, body weight; SP, sample collection; SPT, sucrose preference test; OFT, open field test. One-way ANOVA was used to determine the statistical significance of differences between groups. $^{*}p < 0.05$, $^{**}p < 0.01$, and $^{***}p < 0.001$.

analyte were obtained by linear regression analysis with 1/x2 weighting factor, which contained 10 data points covering a linear range of 0.02–20 ng. Data acquisition and analysis were performed with Thermo Xcalibur 2.2 software. Simultaneous UHPLC-ESI-MS/MS quantitation of SCFAs were performed as previously described (46).

Data Analysis

Static Metabolomics

The GC-MS spectrometry generated data was introduced to SIMCA-P 13.0 (Umetrics AB, Umea, Sweden) for static multivariate analysis. Principal component analysis (PCA) was used to explore the natural separation of metabolomes between

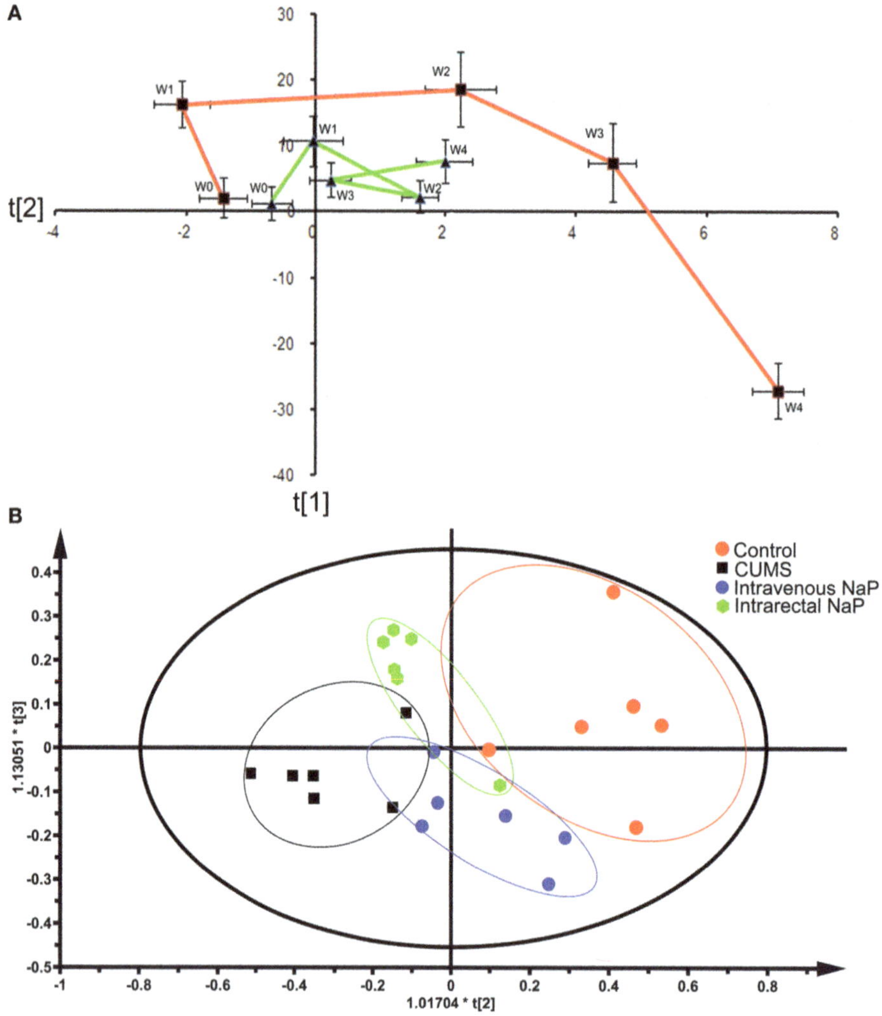

FIGURE 2 | PCAs of the fecal metabolomes for the time-coursed trajectories **(A)** and the effects of NaP administration **(B).** For the time-coursed metabolomics trajectories analysis, dots represent the average metabolic status, and bar lines indicate the standard deviations of PC1 (horizontal axis) and PC2 (longitudinal axis) in the PCA model. The red and green lines represent the CUMS and the control groups, respectively. For the PCA plots of the effects of NaP administration, the red dots represent the control animals, the black dots represent the CUMS animals, the green dots represent the CUMS animals that received intrarectal administration of NaP, and the blue dots represent the CUMS animals that received intravenous administration of NaP with the same dose of the intrarectal administration group.

the study groups. Orthogonal Projection to latent structure-discriminate analysis (OPLS-DA) was used to investigate the difference between groups by incorporating known classification information. The results were presented with S-Plot, in which each plot represented one metabolite ion. The distance of a plot from the origin represented the contribution of the corresponding metabolite to the separation. Metabolites with Variable Importance in Projection (VIP) values greater than 1 in the established OPLS-DA model and $P < 0.05$ in an independent-samples t-test were considered to be differential metabolites contributing to the separation of the study groups.

Dynamic Metabolomics

The metabolomic datasets from all five time points of the CUMS model (**Figure 1A**) were combined, peak aligned and then introduced to the MetaboAnalyst web portal (40). The combined dataset was normalized to constant sum, transformed with log transformation and Pareto scaling before further analysis. ASCA was applied to split the original dataset into subsets describing the variations of phenotypes, the variations of time, and their interactions. SPE (Squared Prediction Error) and Leverage were proposed to evaluate the fitness of the ASCA model. SPE (derived from residuals) was used to test the fitness of a model for the metabolite. Leverage (derived from loadings) was used to evaluate the importance of a metabolite to the model. Variables with high Leverage values and low SPE values were considered to have significant contributions to the model.

Group data were expressed as mean ±S.E.M. Statistical analyses were performed with independent t-test in SPSS 22.0 (Chicago, USA), and values of $P < 0.05$ were considered statistically significant.

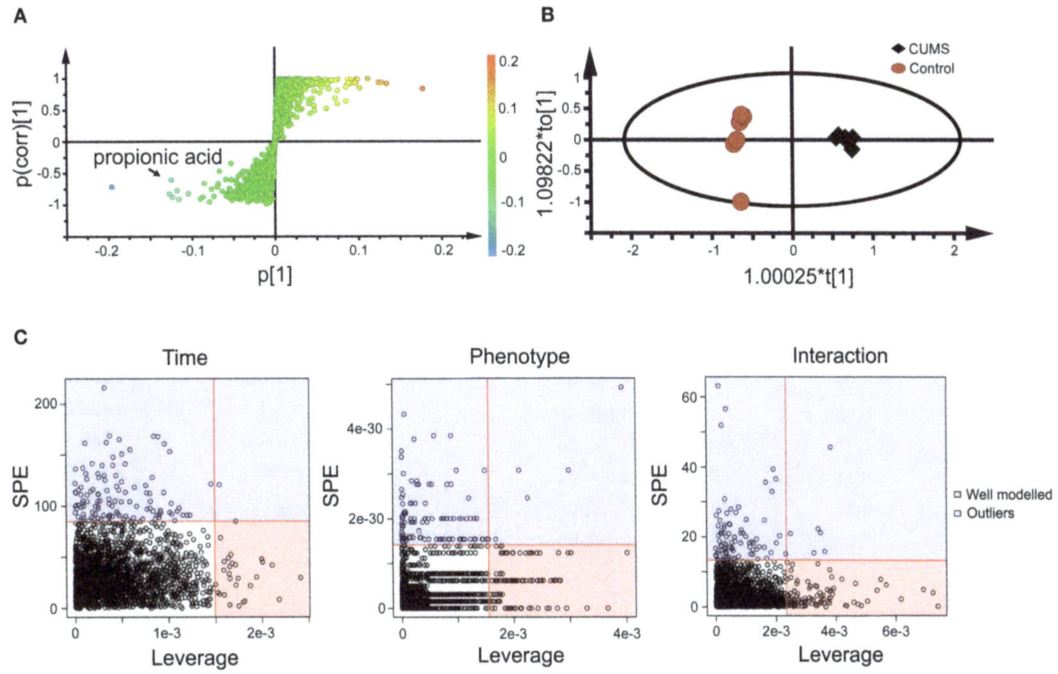

FIGURE 3 | Static **(A,B)** and dynamic **(C)** metabolomics analyses of the fecal metabolomes collected in the 5th week of CUMS modeling. S-Plot **(A)** and OPLS-DA plot **(B)** were used to visualize the static metabolomics analysis. Metabolites with VIP>1 and $p < 0.05$ were considered to be differential metabolites. Only propionic acid was labeled in the S-plot; please refer to **Table 1** for detailed information on all differential metabolites identified via the static metabolomics analysis. ASCA **(C)** was used to analyze in the dynamic metabolomics data. Metabolites with a high leverage value and a low SPE value were considered to be differential metabolites (the well-modeled group); please refer to **Table 2** for detailed information on all of the differential metabolites identified via ASCA dynamic metabolomics analysis.

RESULTS

Data Acquisition Quality and Model Validations for the Metabolomics Data Analyses

Quality controls (QCs) were used to evaluate the performance of the analytical system and to monitor the robustness of sample preparation and the stability of instrument analysis. QCs for the GC-MS spectrometry were prepared by pooling equal aliquots of fecal samples. The first five QCs were tested before the analysis to stabilize the analytical system, and the acquired results were removed prior to data processing. Tight clustering of the QCs in PCA scores was observed (**Supplementary Figure 1**), suggesting a good reproducibility of the metabolomics experiments.

Model validations for static and dynamic metabolomics were also performed. For the static metabolomic analysis, a validation plot for the arrangement analysis of the selected PLS-DA model was generated (**Supplementary Figure 2**). The resulting correlation ($R^2 = 0.553$) demonstrated that the selected model could explain 55.3% of the total variables in the static metabolomics data, while the observed $Q^2 = 0.838$ suggested that the model had good predictive power. A permutation-based significance test was performed to validate the model selected for the ASCA dynamic metabolomics analysis. Significance levels of $P < 0.05$ for the phenotype, the time, and the interaction between phenotype and time were observed (**Supplementary Figure 3B**), demonstrating an acceptable fitness of the selected model for ASCA analysis.

CUMS Model Induced Depression-Like Phenotypes

CUMS is a widely accepted method for modeling depression in experimental animals (8, 18, 47–49), and there is growing evidence for correlations between depression and the serum or urine metabolome (31, 50). To further investigate the correlation between the gut metabolome and depression, we replicated the CUMS rat model and monitored changes in behavioral indices and neurotransmitters in the PFC (**Figure 1A**). Compared to the healthy controls, CUMS rats suffered a significant decrease in body weight (**Figure 1B**) and sucrose preference rate (**Figure 1C**) in the fifth week. In parallel, OFTs showed significant variations in behavioral indices including immobility time, grooming time, rearing counts, and crossing counts in the fifth week (**Figure 1D–G**). We also observed significant decreases in several neurotransmitters (including 5-HT, 5-HIAA, NE, DA, TRP, 3-HAA, 3-HK) in the PFC of CUMS rats (**Figure 4**). These results suggested that the CUMS model was successfully replicated.

Metabolomic Trajectory Analysis Revealed Distinct Fecal Metabolomes in CUMS Rats

Metabolomic trajectory may represent the dynamics of host responses to environmental changes. To investigate the dynamic changes in the gut metabolome during the development of

TABLE 1 | Typical fecal metabolites of the CUMS rats.

Metabolite	VIP	*P*
Lactic acid	1.22	1.00E-02
Succinic acid	1.42	3.35E-04
Glutaric acid	1.72	1.00E-04
Methionine	2.45	1.87E-05
Threonine	3.10	2.99E-05
Proline	3.23	7.10E-04
Leucine	3.45	3.89E-04
Valine	3.89	1.56E-03
Glycine	4.65	6.22E-04
Serine	5.02	1.23E-05
Isoleucine	5.05	1.94E-05
Alanine	5.87	1.22E-04
Glycerol	6.24	4.65E-04
Aspartic acid	6.33	8.73E-04
Propionic acid	6.55	2.32E-05

VIP, variable importance in projection.

TABLE 2 | Typical metabolites identified by the ASCA dynamic metabolomics analysis.

Model	Metabolite	Leverage	SPE
Time	Lactic acid	2.00E-03	4.79E+00
	Valeric acid	2.11E-03	4.18E+00
	Glycerol	1.55E-03	6.91E+00
	Isoleucine	1.59E-03	3.71E+00
	Serine	1.75E-03	2.08E+00
	Valine	. 1.65E-03	4.06E+00
Phenotype	Lactic acid	2.30E-03	3.65E-30
	Acetic acid	2.41E-03	1.23E-30
	Hexanoic acid	1.96E-03	6.16E-31
	Phosphoric acid	2.49E-03	6.16E-31
	Succinic acid	2.15E-03	6.16E-31
	Valeric acid	2.22E-03	1.23E-30
	Malic acid	2.04E-03	6.16E-31
	Glycerol	2.29E-03	6.16E-31
	Glycine	1.93E-03	6.16E-31
	Valine	1.79E-03	7.70E-31
	Sarcosine	2.94E-03	6.16E-31
	Serine	1.74E-03	1.54E-31
	Threonine	1.74E-03	3.08E-31
	Alanine	2.83E-03	6.16E-31
	Aspartic acid	1.62E-03	1.54E-31
	Pyrimidine	1.86E-03	1.23E-30
Interaction	Lactic acid	3.02E-03	9.26E-01
	Propanoic acid	2.60E-03	1.77E+00
	Valeric acid	3.13E-03	5.92E+00
	Malic acid	3.04E-03	7.22E+00
	Glycerol	3.35E-03	5.81E+00
	Leucine	2.38E-03	3.79E-01
	Glycine	2.48E-03	1.44E+00
	Pyrimidine	2.83E-03	2.01E+00
	Serine	2.60E-03	2.22E-01
	Threonine	2.52E-03	1.23E+00
	Methionine	6.91E-03	5.02E+00
	Valine	2.48E-03	8.39E+00
	Sarcosine	3.23E-03	1.87E+00

depression, fecal metabolomic datasets generated from the first five time points (W0–W4) of the CUMS model (**Figure 1A**) were analyzed with PCA. The mean scores of the first two principal components (PCs) of PCA were used to infer the time-course trajectories of fecal metabolome. We observed dramatically different paths of CMUS animals and healthy controls (**Figure 2A**). The CUMS rats exhibited a large response, while those of the control groups clustered tightly during the time course. This distinct metabolomic trajectory of the CUMS rats indicates a possible correlation between the gut metabolome and depression. A further investigation of this relationship will be significant in providing a clearer understanding of the pathophysiology of depression. Because the three-way high-dimensional dataset (multi-variables, multi-subjects and multi-time points)), time-resolved metabolomics is too complex to investigate using any single method. To reach a more objective conclusion, we therefore carried out static and dynamic metabolomics data analysis from multiple perspectives in subsequent experiments.

Static Metabolomics Analysis Observed Propionic Acid as a Differential Metabolite of the CUMS Rats

Within the 2,511 spectral features generated from the fecal metabolome of all five time points of CUMS animals, 45 metabolites were putatively validated (**Supplementary Table 1**). Static metabolomics analysis was carried out based on the dataset generated from the rats with successful replicated CUMS model (at the fifth week of treatment) and the corresponding healthy controls. S-Plot (**Figure 3A**) and OPLS-DA (**Figure 3B**) analyses were applied to identify differential metabolites differentiating the CUMS rats and the healthy controls. A total of 15 differential metabolites were identified (**Table 1**), including 2 fatty acids, 2 diatomic fatty acids, 10 amino acids, and glycerol. Interestingly, propionic acid was the only SCFA differentiating the gut metabolome of the CUMS rats from that of the healthy controls, while no changes were observed in acetic acid or butyric acid. These findings suggested that propionic acid is a differential metabolite in the fecal metabolome of the depression-like animal model.

ASCA Dynamic Metabolomics Analysis Confirms Propionic Acid as a Differential Metabolite of CUMS Rats

To further validate the findings of static metabolomics analysis, we carried out ASCA dynamic metabolomics analysis. ASCA analysis split the multilevel, time-coursed metabolomic datasets into subsets describing the variations between rats of the CUMS group and the control group, the variations along time-scale, and their interactions. The metabolomic datasets were normalized

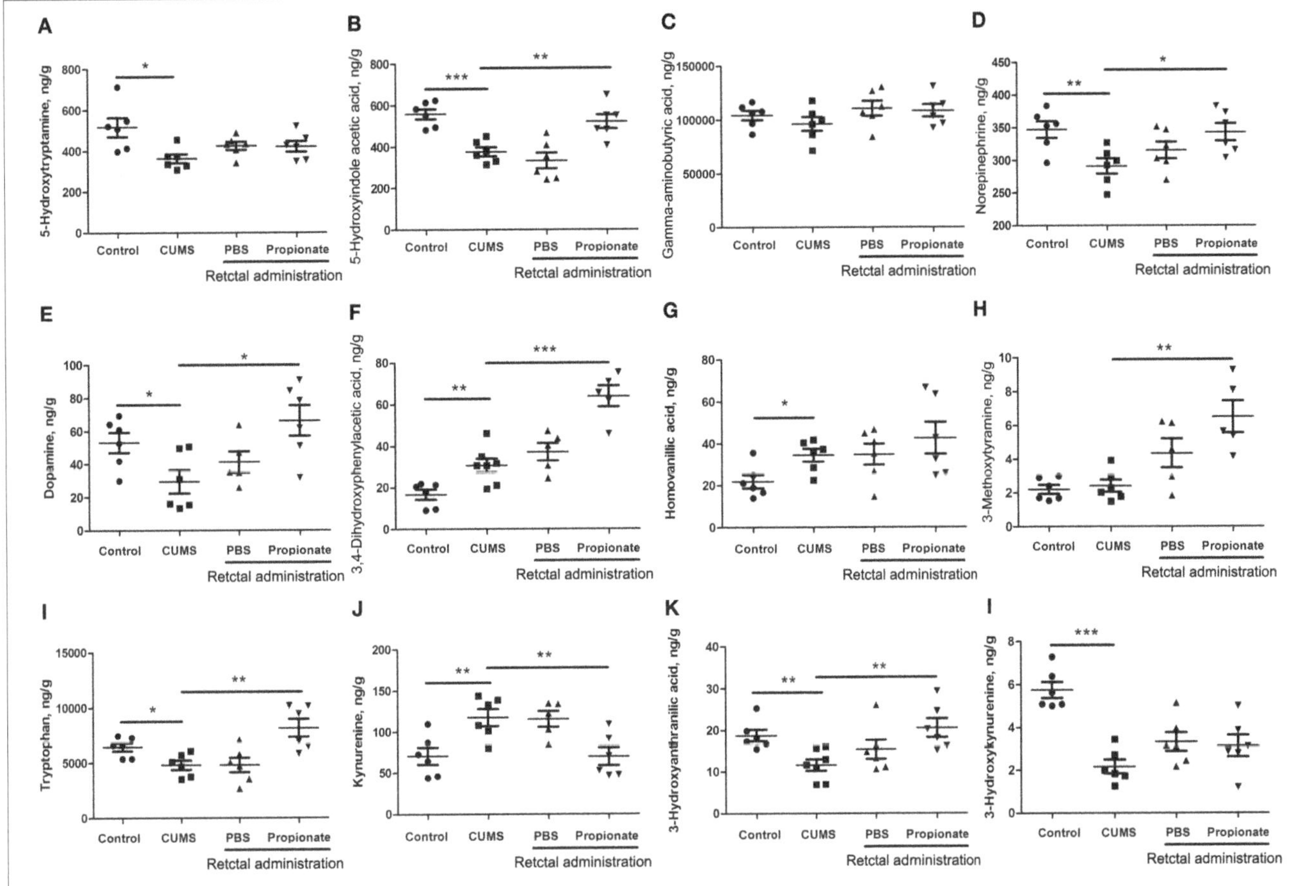

FIGURE 4 | The abundance of neurotransmitters in the prefrontal cortex of rats exposed to CUMS and NaP. UHPLC ESI MS/MS was used to quantify neurotransmitters in the plasma collected in the 5th week of the CUMS animals. 5-HT **(A)**, 5-HIAA **(B)**, GABA **(C)**, NE **(D)**, DA **(E)**, DOPAC **(F)**, HVA **(G)**, 3-MT **(H)**, TRP **(I)**, KYN **(J)**, 3-HAA **(K)**, 3-HK **(L)** were quantified. One-way ANOVA was used to determine the statistical significance of differences between groups. $^{*}p < 0.05$, $^{**}p < 0.01$, and $^{***}p < 0.001$.

before further investigations (**Supplementary Figure 3A**). We observed an excellent fitness of the model selected for the ASCA analysis, with high significance levels ($p < 0.05$) of phenotype, time and their interactions generating from a permutation test (**Supplementary Figure 3B**). Leverage/SPE was used to identify significant spectrometric features associated with a specific factor. Features with high Leverage values and low SPE values were included in the "well-modeled" group in the ASCA analysis. In all, 15 metabolites were identified from the greatly altered (and well-modeled) features over time, phenotype or their interactions (**Figure 3C**, see details in **Table 2** and **Supplementary Table 2**). This analysis, like the static metabolomics analysis, identified propionic acid as a significant metabolite discriminating the CUMS rats and the healthy controls. To validate the findings from metabolomics analyses, we then determined the abundance of SCFAs in plasma. Propionic acid was the only SCFA with significantly changed abundance in the plasma of the CUMS rats (**Figure 5**). The collective findings from both the static and the dynamic metabolomics analyses led us to hypothesize that propionic acid may play a role in the pathophysiology of depression.

Short-Term Intrarectal Administration of NaP Induces Antidepressant-Like Effects

Because we had identified and validated propionic acid as a typical fecal metabolite of the CUMS rats using static and dynamic metabolomics analysis and because the abundance of propionic acid was decreased in the plasma of CUMS rats, we next investigated the role of NaP (the salt form of propionic acid) in the pathophysiology of depression. To do this, we introduced NaP to the CUMS rats via intrarectal administration. A 1-week intrarectal administration of NaP rescued the loss of body weight and sucrose preference phenotypes of the CUMS rats (**Figures 1B,C**). The administration of NaP also rescued the behavioral indices in the OFT (**Figures 1D–G**) and restored plasma levels of propionic acid (**Figure 5**). In addition, NaP administration partially rescued the imbalanced plasma metabolomes of CUMS rats (**Figure 2B**). These results suggested that intrarectal administration of NaP has short-term antidepressant-like effects.

Neurotransmitter imbalance in the central nervous system has been associated with depression (51, 52). To further investigate the effects of NaP administration, we next determined the

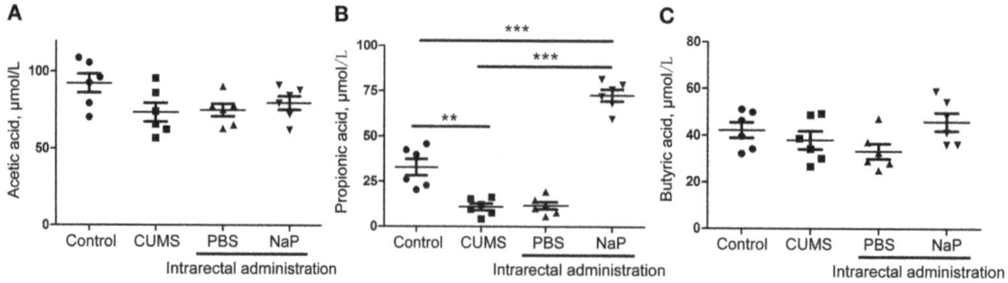

FIGURE 5 | Quantitation of SCFAs in the plasma of rats at the 5th week of CUMS modeling. UHPLC-ESI-MS/MS was used for simultaneous quantitation of acetic acid **(A)**, propionic acid **(B)**, and butyric acid **(C)** from plasma of the control group, the CUMS group, the intrarectal PBS group, and the intrarectal NaP group. One-way ANOVA was used to determine the statistical significance of differences between groups. $^{**}p < 0.01$, and $^{***}p < 0.001$.

abundance of several neurotransmitters in the PFC of the CUMS rats (**Figure 4**). The decreased levels of NE, DA, TRP, 5-HIAA, and 3-HAA in the PFC of CUMS rats were restored by short term intrarectal NaP administration, but decreased 5-HT and 3-HK were not. Among the metabolites of DA, the increased abundance of DOPAC by CUMS was further up-regulated by NaP administration, but the abundance of HVA was not significantly changed, and the unchanged levels of 3-MT were significantly up-regulated. Because neurotransmitter metabolism has been correlated with the pathophysiology of depression (53) and with the antidepressant-like effects of endogenous metabolites (24), we then examined the effects of NaP administration on the turnover of the depression associated neurotransmitters (**Table 3**). The increased turnover of TRP to KYN (calculated as KYN/TRP) by CUMS was significantly down-regulated by NaP administration, while the increased turnover of DA to HVA (calculated as HVA/DA) was also restored by NaP administration; the unchanged turnover of 5-HT to 5-HIAA (calculated as 5-HIAA/5-HT) was not significantly influenced by NaP administration. In addition, the decreased turnover of KYN to 3-HK was significantly up-regulated by NaP administration. These results suggest that short-term intrarectal administration of NaP selectively restores the metabolism of neurotransmitters in the PFC of CUMS rats.

TABLE 3 | Turnover of neurotransmitters in the PFC of rats under CUMS and intrarectal NaP administration.

	Control	CUMS	Intrarectal administration	
			PBS	NaP
5-HIAA/5-HT	1.11	1.04	0.98	1.28
KYN/TRP	0.011	0.0245***	2.41E-02	0.00878###
3-HAA/KYN	0.0029	2.60E-03	2.30E-03	2.50E-03
3-HK/KYN	0.092	0.02**	2.87E-02	0.0465#
HVA/DA	0.43	1.59*	1.44	0.49#
DOPAC/DA	0.31	1.51**	1.46	0.98
3-MT/DA	0.043	0.095***	1.03E-01	1.05E-01

**Significance value from Student-t-test between the Control group and the CUMS group.*
$^{*}P < 0.05$, $^{**}P < 0.01$, $^{***}P < 0.001$.
#Student-t-test between the CUMS group and NaP administration group.
$\#P < 0.05$, $\#\#\#P < 0.001$.

DISCUSSION

In the present study, propionic acid was identified by both static and dynamic metabolomics analyses as a differential metabolite in the fecal metabolome of CUMS rats. A 1-week intrarectal administration of NaP (the salt form of propionic acid) induced antidepressant-like effects, which reversed the depression-like behavior and selectively restored neurotransmitter levels in the PFC. These findings provide support for NaP as a promising potential alternative in fighting against depression using an endogenous metabolite.

Several endogenous metabolites have been reported to have antidepressant-like effects with distinctive action mechanisms (24, 54–57). The anti-depressant-like effects of lactate was reported to be associated with serotonin receptor trafficking, astrocyte function, neurogenesis, nitric oxide synthesis, and cAMP signaling (24). Agmatine has been reported to attenuate depression-like symptoms by modulating the nitrergic signaling pathway (54, 58). Oleoylethanolamide may exert its antidepressant-like effects through the regulation of brain-derived neurotrophic factor (BDNF) levels in the hippocampus and PFC, via antioxidant defenses, and by normalizing the hyperactivity of the hypothalamic-pituitary-adrenal (HPA) axis (55). One SCFA, butyrate, was also reported to have antidepressant-like effects with a multi-faced mechanism, including up-regulating the concentration of 5-HT in the brain, increasing the expression of BDNF and restoring blood-brain barrier impairments (18), acting as histone deacetylase inhibitor (HDACi) to influence microglial activation (56) or gene expression in the hippocampus (59), or acting as an N-Methyl-D-aspartate receptor (NMDA) enhancer (19).

Although butyrate administration induced antidepressant-like effects, the abundance of butyrate (or butyric acid) was not significantly changed in depressed animal models (5) or humans (58) in previous reports or in the present study (**Figure 5**). Supplementation of these unchanged endogenous metabolites may lead to poorer outcomes for depression by inducing additional metabolome imbalance, due to the close associations between depression and metabolic disorders in serum (4), liver

(5), feces (7), and the central nervous system (60). Nevertheless, another SCFA, propionic acid, was greatly altered in the feces and the plasma of our animal model with depression-like behaviors, which is consistent with a previous report (61). It was also reported that prebiotics with antidepressant-like effects may raise the abundance of propionate and reduce the abundance of butyrate in the cecum of animals with depression-like behaviors (23). Taken together, this study and previous work suggest that propionate may be a better candidate endogenous metabolite for antidepressant than butyrate.

The PFC is a key brain area that is responsible for working memory and emotional regulation (62). The antidepressant-like effects of NaP in this study are correlated with the levels of several neurotransmitters in the PFC. Neurotransmitter imbalance in the PFC is one of the classical pathophysiologies of depression (52, 63) and is associated with the effects of antidepressants (64). Accordingly, we found that NaP exerts antidepressant-like effects through selective rescue of neurotransmitter levels in the PFC. Intrarectal administration of NaP completely restored the levels of depression-associated neurotransmitters in the PFC, except 5-HT (**Figure 4A**). This is quite different from the observed effect of butyrate, which up-regulated the levels of 5-HT (18). Although the decreased 5-HT was not affected in this study, another neurotransmitter, NE, was completely rescued by short-term NaP administration (**Figure 4D**). It has been reported that NE is responsible for the quick onset effects of antidepressants (65), while 5-HT is correlated with the late-onset anti-depression effects of the neurotransmitter reuptake inhibitors (66). It is thus reasonable to hypothesize that the short-term, NaP-induced, quick-onset, antidepressant-like effects were correlated with the recovery of NE in the PFC of the CUMS rats.

The altered function of TRP metabolic pathway has been proposed as one of the crucial links between neurotransmitter dysregulation and the aberrant immune function associated with depression (67). Consistent with a previous report (68), we observed increased TRP turnover in the CUMS rats in this study, which increased the accumulation of KYN and further increased the production of several neurotoxic metabolites such as 3-HK (**Figure 4I**). In addition, NaP administration reduced the turnover of TRP by decreasing the production of KYN and its neurotoxic metabolites, which is consistent with the reported antidepressant effects of glycyrrhizic acid (69) and ketamine (70).

DA is another important neurotransmitter that is partially responsible for the anhedonia of depression. The decreased DA in the CUMS rats was rescued by NaP administration in this study, and the increased total catabolism of DA, as indicated by the ratio of HVA/DA (71) was decreased by NaP administration (**Table 3**). This is consistent with the reported antidepressant effects of paroxetine (72) and fluvoxamine (73). It is difficult to elucidate the major DA catabolism pathway that is affected by NaP administration, because the ratios of DOPAC/DA and 3-MT/DA were not significantly changed. NaP administration may decrease the up-regulated DA catabolism by exerting week effects on both the MAO (monoamine oxidase)-dependent oxidative pathway (DOPAC/DA) and the COMT (catechol-O-methyltransferase)-dependent methylation pathway (3-MT/DA) (74). These results may therefore suggest that NaP exerts its antidepressant-like effects partially by decreasing the turnover of DA.

As a limitation of this study, OPT is insufficient to some extent to represent the depressive-like behaviors. However, the CUMS modeling in this study was also supported by sucrose preference rate and neurotransmitters quantitation, representing key features of depression of anhedonia and neurotransmitters depletion, respectively. More behavior tests are needed to obtain more solid results in future similar studies. Another limitation of this study is lack of behavior data of the rats after NaP administration, which is valuable to evaluate the duration of the antidepressant-like effects. Future similar studies should pay attention on this point.

In conclusion, the present study demonstrated that propionic acid is a differential metabolite in CUMS rats via static and dynamic metabolomics analyses. Furthermore, we found that short term intrarectal administration of NaP induced antidepressant-like effects, possibly by up-regulating the abundance of NE and down-regulating the turnover of TRP and DA in the PFC of the CUMS rats. Future clinical investigations will be required to validate NaP as a novel endogenous metabolite antidepressant candidate.

ETHICS STATEMENT

This study was carried out in accordance with the recommendations of UFRN protocol No. 034/2014. The protocol was approved by the Committee on Animal Research and Ethics of Shanxi University.

AUTHOR CONTRIBUTIONS

JL and XQ conception and design. JL, CWa, CWu and LH analysis and interpretation. JL, XJ, and XQ drafting the manuscript for important intellectual content.

FUNDING

This work was supported by the National Natural Science Foundation of China (No. 31570346).

SUPPLEMENTARY MATERIAL

Supplementary Figure 1 | PCA scores plot of the QCs and fecal samples within the run analyzed in GC-MS for evaluation of the data acquisition quality. QCs were prepared through pooling equal aliquots of fecal samples. The first five QCs were tested before the analysis to stabilize the analytical system, and the acquired results were removed prior to data processing. PCA analysis was carried out with SIMCA-P 13.0 (Umetrics AB, Umea, Sweden) after total area normalization. Each dot represents one sample (green) or one QC (red).

Supplementary Figure 2 | Model validation plot of the static metabolomics data. The validation analysis was performed through pair-wise comparison of the fecal metabolomes from the CUMS group and the healthy control group at the 5th week of CUMS modeling. A 200 permutation was applied for the validation analysis.

Supplementary Figure 3 | Data normalization **(A)** and model validation **(B)** of the dynamic metabolomics data. The effect of data normalization was shown **(A)**. Model validations were performed through permutations, as demonstrated by significance levels of $p < 0.05$ for the phenotype, time, and the interaction between phenotype and time.

Supplementary Table 1 | Metabolites identified from fecal metabolome of rats in this study.

Supplementary Table 2 | Typical metabolites identified by the ASCA dynamic metabolomics analysis.

REFERENCES

1. Seo J, Wei J, Qin L, Kim Y, Yan Z, Greengard P. Cellular and molecular basis for stress-induced depression. *Mol Psychiatry* (2017) 22:1440–47. doi: 10.1038/mp.2016.118
2. Keller J, Gomez R, Williams G, Lembke A, Lazzeroni L, Murphy G, et al. HPA axis in major depression: cortisol, clinical symptomatology and genetic variation predict cognition. *Mol Psychiatry* (2017) 22:527–36. doi: 10.1038/mp.2016.120
3. Vancampfort D, Stubbs B, Mitchell A, De Hert M, Wampers M, Ward P, et al. Risk of metabolic syndrome and its components in people with schizophrenia and related psychotic disorders, bipolar disorder and major depressive disorder: a systematic review and meta-analysis. *World Psychiatry* (2015) 14:339–47. doi: 10.1002/wps.20252
4. Ali-Sisto T, Tolmunen T, Toffol E, Viinamaki H, Mantyselka P, Valkonen-Korhonen M, et al. Purine metabolism is dysregulated in patients with major depressive disorder. *Psychoneuroendocrinology* (2016) 70:25–32. doi: 10.1016/j.psyneuen.2016.04.017
5. Li B, Guo K, Zeng L, Zeng B, Huo R, Luo Y, et al. Metabolite identification in fecal microbiota transplantation mouse livers and combined proteomics with chronic unpredictive mild stress mouse livers. *Transl Psychiatry* (2018) 8:34. doi: 10.1038/s41398-017-0078-2
6. Dash S, Clarke G, Berk M, Jacka F. The gut microbiome and diet in psychiatry: focus on depression. *Curr Opin Psychiatry* (2015) 28:1–6. doi: 10.1097/YCO.0000000000000117
7. Yu M, Jia H, Zhou C, Yang Y, Zhao Y, Yang M, et al. Variations in gut microbiota and fecal metabolic phenotype associated with depression by 16S rRNA gene sequencing and LC/MS-based metabolomics. *J Pharm Biomed Anal.* (2017) 138:231–9. doi: 10.1016/j.jpba.2017.02.008
8. Gao X, Cui J, Zheng X, Li Z, Choi Y, Zhou Y, et al. An investigation of the antidepressant action of xiaoyaosan in rats using ultra performance liquid chromatography-mass spectrometry combined with metabonomics. *Phytother Res.* (2013) 27:1074–85. doi: 10.1002/ptr.4805
9. Li J, Zhang S, Wang W, Cheng K, Guo H, Rao C, et al. Potential antidepressant and resilience mechanism revealed by metabolomic study on peripheral blood mononuclear cells of stress resilient rats. *Behav Brain Res.* (2017) 320:12–20. doi: 10.1016/j.bbr.2016.11.035
10. Zheng P, Fang Z, Xu X, Liu M, Du X, Zhang X, et al. Metabolite signature for diagnosing major depressive disorder in peripheral blood mononuclear cells. *J Affect Disord.* (2016) 195:75–81. doi: 10.1016/j.jad.2016.02.008
11. Lin L, Chen X, Liu R. Novel urinary metabolite signature for diagnosing postpartum depression. *Neuropsychiatr Dis Treat.* (2017) 13:1263–70. doi: 10.2147/NDT.S135190
12. Zheng P, Chen J, Huang T, Wang M, Wang Y, Dong M, et al. A novel urinary metabolite signature for diagnosing major depressive disorder. *J Proteome Res.* (2013) 12:5904–11. doi: 10.1021/pr400939q
13. Zhang W, Zhang X. A novel urinary metabolite signature for non-invasive post-stroke depression diagnosis. *Cell Biochem Biophys.* (2015) 72:661–7. doi: 10.1007/s12013-014-0472-9
14. Winter G, Hart R, Charlesworth R, Sharpley C. Gut microbiome and depression: what we know and what we need to know. *Nat Rev Neurosci.* (2018) 29:629–43. doi: 10.1515/revneuro-2017-0072
15. Cepeda M, Katz E, Blacketer C. Microbiome-gut-brain axis: probiotics and their association with depression. *J Neuropsychiatry Clin Neurosci.* (2017) 29:39–44. doi: 10.1176/appi.neuropsych.15120410
16. Zheng P, Zeng B, Zhou C, Liu M, Fang Z, Xu X, et al. Gut microbiome remodeling induces depressive-like behaviors through a pathway mediated by the host's metabolism. *Mol Psychiatry* (2016) 21:786–96. doi: 10.1038/mp.2016.44
17. Cryan J, Dinan T. Mind-altering microorganisms: the impact of the gut microbiota on brain and behaviour. *Nat Rev Neurosci.* (2012) 13:701–12. doi: 10.1038/nrn3346
18. Sun J, Wang F, Hong G, Pang M, Xu H, Li H, et al. Antidepressant-like effects of sodium butyrate and its possible mechanisms of action in mice exposed to chronic unpredictable mild stress. *Neurosci Lett.* (2016) 618:159–66. doi: 10.1016/j.neulet.2016.03.003
19. Valvassori S, Resende W, Budni J, Dal-Pont G, Bavaresco D, Reus G, et al. Sodium butyrate, a histone deacetylase inhibitor, reverses behavioral and mitochondrial alterations in animal models of depression induced by early- or late-life stress. *Curr Neurovasc Res.* (2015) 12:312–20. doi: 10.2174/1567202612666150728121121
20. Wei Y, Melas P, Wegener G, Mathe A, Lavebratt C. Antidepressant-like effect of sodium butyrate is associated with an increase in TET1 and in 5-hydroxymethylation levels in the Bdnf gene. *Int J Neuropsychopharmacol.* (2014) 18:pyu032. doi: 10.1093/ijnp/pyu032
21. Liu C, Wu Y, Feng G, Gao X, Zhou Y, Hou W, et al. Plasma-metabolite-biomarkers for the therapeutic response in depressed patients by the traditional Chinese medicine formula Xiaoyaosan: a 1H NMR-based metabolomics approach. *J Affect Disord.* (2015) 185:156–63. doi: 10.1016/j.jad.2015.05.005
22. Gao X, Zheng X, Li Z, Zhou Y, Sun H, Zhang L, et al. Metabonomic study on chronic unpredictable mild stress and intervention effects of Xiaoyaosan in rats using gas chromatography coupled with mass spectrometry. *J Ethnopharmacol.* (2011) 137:690–9. doi: 10.1016/j.jep.2011.06.024
23. Burokas A, Arboleya S, Moloney R, Peterson V, Murphy K, Clarke G, et al. Targeting the microbiota-gut-brain axis: prebiotics have anxiolytic and antidepressant-like effects and reverse the impact of chronic stress in mice. *Biol Psychiatry* (2017) 82:472–87. doi: 10.1016/j.biopsych.2016.12.031
24. Carrard A, Elsayed M, Margineanu M, Boury-Jamot B, Fragniere L, Meylan E, et al. Peripheral administration of lactate produces antidepressant-like effects. *Mol Psychiatry* (2016). 23:392–9. doi: 10.1038/mp.2016.179
25. Calvani R, Miccheli A, Capuani G, Tomassini Miccheli A, Puccetti C, Delfini M, et al. Gut microbiome-derived metabolites characterize a peculiar obese urinary metabotype. *Int J Obes Lond.* (2010) 34:1095–8. doi: 10.1038/ijo.2010.44
26. Dumas M, Kinross J, Nicholson J. Metabolic phenotyping and systems biology approaches to understanding metabolic syndrome and fatty liver disease. *Gastroenterology* (2014) 146:46–62. doi: 10.1053/j.gastro.2013.11.001
27. Wishart D. Emerging applications of metabolomics in drug discovery and precision medicine. *Nat Rev Drug Discov.* (2016) 15:473–84. doi: 10.1038/nrd.2016.32
28. Amberg A, Riefke B, Schlotterbeck G, Ross A, Senn H, Dieterle F, et al. NMR and MS methods for metabolomics. *Methods Mol Biol.* (2017) 1641:229–58. doi: 10.1007/978-1-4939-7172-5_13
29. Cobbold S, Chua H, Nijagal B, Creek D, Ralph S, McConville M. Metabolic Dysregulation induced in plasmodium falciparum by dihydroartemisinin and other front-line antimalarial drugs. *J Infect Dis.* (2016) 213:276–86. doi: 10.1093/infdis/jiv372
30. Murfitt S, Zaccone P, Wang X, Acharjee A, Sawyer Y, Koulman A, et al. Metabolomics and lipidomics study of mouse models of type 1 diabetes highlights divergent metabolism in purine and tryptophan metabolism prior to disease onset. *J Proteome Res.* (2018) 17:946–60. doi: 10.1021/acs.jproteome.7b00489
31. Zheng P, Wang Y, Chen L, Yang D, Meng H, Zhou D, et al. Identification and validation of urinary metabolite biomarkers for major depressive disorder. *Mol Cell Proteomics* (2013) 12:207–14. doi: 10.1074/mcp.M112.021816
32. Nedic Erjavec G, Konjevod M, Nikolac Perkovic M, Svob Strac D, Tudor L, Barbas C, et al. Short overview on metabolomic approach and

redox changes in psychiatric disorders. *Redox Biol.* (2018) 14:178–86. doi: 10.1016/j.redox.2017.09.002

33. Lan M, McLoughlin G, Griffin J, Tsang T, Huang J, Yuan P, et al. Metabonomic analysis identifies molecular changes associated with the pathophysiology and drug treatment of bipolar disorder. *Mol Psychiatry* (2009) 14:269–79. doi: 10.1038/sj.mp.4002130
34. Maes M, Nowak G, Caso J, Leza J, Song C, Kubera M, et al. Toward omics-based, systems biomedicine, and path and drug discovery methodologies for depression-inflammation research. *Mol Neurobiol.* (2016) 53:2927–35. doi: 10.1007/s12035-015-9183-5
35. Tian J, Peng G, Gao X, Zhou Y, Xing J, Qin X, et al. Dynamic analysis of the endogenous metabolites in depressed patients treated with TCM formula Xiaoyaosan using urinary 1H NMR-based metabolomics. *J Ethnopharmacol.* (2014) 158(Pt A):1–10. doi: 10.1016/j.jep.2014.10.005
36. Krycer J, Yugi K, Hirayama A, Fazakerley D, Quek L, Scalzo R, et al. Dynamic metabolomics reveals that insulin primes the adipocyte for glucose metabolism. *Cell Rep.* (2017) 21:3536–47. doi: 10.1016/j.celrep.2017.11.085
37. Cinquemani E, Laroute V, Cocaign-Bousquet M, de Jong H, Ropers D. Estimation of time-varying growth, uptake and excretion rates from dynamic metabolomics data. *Bioinformatics* (2017) 33:i301–10. doi: 10.1093/bioinformatics/btx250
38. Kowalski G, De Souza D, Burch M, Hamley S, Kloehn J, Selathurai A, et al. Application of dynamic metabolomics to examine *in vivo* skeletal muscle glucose metabolism in the chronically high-fat fed mouse. *Biochem Biophys Res Commun.* (2015) 462:27–32. doi: 10.1016/j.bbrc.2015.04.096
39. Smilde A, Jansen J, Hoefsloot H, Lamers R, van der Greef J, Timmerman M. ANOVA-simultaneous component analysis ASCA: a new tool for analyzing designed metabolomics data. *Bioinformatics* (2005) 21:3043–8. doi: 10.1093/bioinformatics/bti476
40. Xia J, Sinelnikov I, Han B, Wishart D. MetaboAnalyst 3.0–making metabolomics more meaningful. *Nucleic Acids Res.* (2015) 43:W251–7. doi: 10.1093/nar/gkv380
41. Zheng H, Lorenzen J, Astrup A, Larsen L, Yde C, Clausen M,et al. Metabolic effects of a 24-week energy-restricted intervention combined with low or high dairy intake in overweight women: an nmr-based metabolomics investigation. *Nutrients* (2016) 8:108. doi: 10.3390/nu8030108
42. Tomassini A, Vitalone A, Marini F, Pratico G, Sciubba F, Bevilacqua M, et al. 1H NMR-based urinary metabolic profiling reveals changes in nicotinamide pathway intermediates due to postnatal stress model in rat. *J Proteome Res.* (2014) 13:5848–59. doi: 10.1021/pr500748r
43. Du Y, Zheng H, Xia H, Zhao L, Hu W, Bai G, et al. Early effect of amyloid beta-peptide on hippocampal and serum metabolism in rats studied by an integrated method of NMR-based metabolomics and ANOVA-simultaneous component analysis. *Biomed Res Int.* (2017) 2017:3262495. doi: 10.1155/2017/3262495
44. Tian J, Liu C, Xiang H, Zheng X, Peng G, Zhang X, et al. Investigation on the antidepressant effect of sea buckthorn seed oil through the GC-MS-based metabolomics approach coupled with multivariate analysis. *Food Funct.* (2015) 6:3585–92. doi: 10.1039/c5fo00695c
45. Zhao L, Zheng S, Su G, Lu X, Yang J, Xiong Z, et al. *In vivo* study on the neurotransmitters and their metabolites change in depressive disorder rat plasma by ultra high performance liquid chromatography coupled to tandem mass spectrometry. *J Chromatogr B Analyt Technol Biomed Life Sci.* (2015) 988:59–65. doi: 10.1016/j.jchromb.2015.02.029
46. Goettel M, Niessner R, Pluym N, Scherer G, Scherer M. A fully validated GC-TOF-MS method for the quantification of fatty acids revealed alterations in the metabolic profile of fatty acids after smoking cessation. *J Chromatogr B Analyt Technol Biomed Life Sci.* (2017) 1041-2:141–50. doi: 10.1016/j.jchromb.2016.12.035
47. Willner P, Towell A, Sampson D, Sophokleous S, Muscat R. Reduction of sucrose preference by chronic unpredictable mild stress, and its restoration by a tricyclic antidepressant. *Psychopharmacology* (1987) 93:358–64. doi: 10.1007/BF00187257
48. Hou X, Hu Z, Zhang D, Lu W, Zhou J, Wu P, et al. Rapid antidepressant effect of hydrogen sulfide: evidence for activation of mTORC1-TrkB-AMPA receptor pathways. *Antioxid Redox Signal.* (2017) 27:472–88. doi: 10.1089/ars.2016.6737
49. Zhang Y, Yuan S, Pu J, Yang L, Zhou X, Liu L, et al. Integrated metabolomics and proteomics analysis of hippocampus in a rat model of depression. *Neuroscience* (2018) 371:207–20. doi: 10.1016/j.neuroscience.2017.12.001
50. Quinones M, Kaddurah-Daouk R. Metabolomics tools for identifying biomarkers for neuropsychiatric diseases. *Neurobiol Dis.* (2009) 35:165–76. doi: 10.1016/j.nbd.2009.02.019
51. Vaishnav K, Eric JN. Linking molecules to mood: new insight into the biology of depression. *Am. J. Psychiatry* (2010) 167:1305–1320. doi: 10.1176/appi.ajp.2009.10030434
52. Nutt D. Relationship of neurotransmitters to the symptoms of major depressive disorder. *J Clin Psychiatry* (2008) 69(Suppl. E1):4–7. doi: 10.1007/springerreference_116852
53. Ashok AH, Marques TR, Jauhar S, Nour MM, Goodwin GM, Young AH, et al, The dopamine hypothesis of bipolar affective disorder: the state of the art and implications for treatment. *Mol Psychiatry* (2017) 22:666–79. doi: 10.1038/mp.2017.16
54. Zomkowski AD, Hammes L, Lin J, Calixto JB, Santos AR, and Rodrigues AL. Agmatine produces antidepressant-like effects in two models of depression in mice. *Neuroreport* (2002) 13:387–91. doi: 10.1097/00001756-200203250-00005
55. Jin P, Yu H, Tian L, Zhang F, Quan ZS. Antidepressant-like effects of oleoylethanolamide in a mouse model of chronic unpredictable mild stress. *Pharmacol Biochem Behav.* (2015) 133:146–54. doi: 10.1016/j.pbb.2015.04.001
56. Wang P, Zhang Y, Gong Y, Yang R, Chen Z, Hu W, et al. Sodium butyrate triggers a functional elongation of microglial process via Akt-small RhoGTPase activation and HDACs inhibition. *Neurobiol Dis.* (2018) 111:12–25. doi: 10.1016/j.nbd.2017.12.006
57. Schroeder F, Lin C, Crusio W, Akbarian S. Antidepressant-like effects of the histone deacetylase inhibitor, sodium butyrate, in the mouse. *Biol Psychiatry* (2007) 62:55–64. doi: 10.1016/j.biopsych.2006.06.036
58. Taksande B, Faldu D, Dixit M, Sakaria J, Aglawe M, Umekar M, et al. Agmatine attenuates chronic unpredictable mild stress induced behavioral alteration in mice. *Eur J Pharmacol.* (2013) 720:115–20. doi: 10.1016/j.ejphar.2013.10.041
59. Yamawaki Y, Fuchikami M, Morinobu S, Segawa M, Matsumoto T, Yamawaki S. Antidepressant-like effect of sodium butyrate HDAC inhibitor and its molecular mechanism of action in the rat hippocampus. *World J Biol Psychiatry* (2012) 13:458–67. doi: 10.3109/15622975.2011.585663
60. Liu L, Zhou X, Zhang Y, Liu Y, Yang L, Pu J, et al. The identification of metabolic disturbances in the prefrontal cortex of the chronic restraint stress rat model of depression. *Behav Brain Res.* (2016) 305:148–56. doi: 10.1016/j.bbr.2016.03.005
61. Chen J, Zhou C, Liu Z, Fu Y, Zheng P, Yang D, et al. Divergent urinary metabolic phenotypes between major depressive disorder and bipolar disorder identified by a combined GC-MS and NMR spectroscopic metabonomic approach. *J Proteome Res.* (2015) 14:3382–9. doi: 10.1021/acs.jproteome.5b00434
62. Minton G, Young A, McQuade R, Fairchild G, Ingram C, Gartside S. Profound changes in dopaminergic neurotransmission in the prefrontal cortex in response to flattening of the diurnal glucocorticoid rhythm: implications for bipolar disorder. *Neuropsychopharmacology* (2009) 34:2265–74. doi: 10.1038/npp.2009.53
63. Belzung C, Willner P, Philippot P, Depression: from psychopathology to pathophysiology. *Curr Opin Neurobiol.* (2015) 30:24–30. doi: 10.1016/j.conb.2014.08.013
64. Artigas F. Developments in the field of antidepressants, where do we go now? *Eur Neuropsychopharmacol.* (2015) 25:657–70. doi: 10.1016/j.euroneuro.2013.04.013
65. Costi S, Van Dam N, Murrough J. Current status of ketamine and related therapies for mood and anxiety disorders. *Curr Behav Neurosci Rep.* (2015) 2:216–25. doi: 10.1007/s40473-015-0052-3
66. Liu B, Liu J, Wang M, Zhang Y, Li L. From serotonin to neuroplasticity: evolvement of theories for major depressive disorder. *Front Cell Neurosci.* (2017) 11:305. doi: 10.3389/fncel.2017.00305
67. Chaves Filho A, Lima C, Vasconcelos S, de Lucena D, Maes M, Macedo D. IDO chronic immune activation and tryptophan metabolic pathway: A potential pathophysiological link between depression and obesity. *Prog Neuropsychopharmacol Biol Psychiatry* (2018) 80:234–49. doi: 10.1016/j.pnpbp.2017.04.035

68. Teraishi T, Hori H, Sasayama D, Matsuo J, Ogawa S, Ota M. 13C-tryptophan breath test detects increased catabolic turnover of tryptophan along the kynurenine pathway in patients with major depressive disorder. *Sci Rep.* (2015) 5:15994. doi: 10.1038/srep15994
69. Wang B, Lian Y, Dong X, Peng W, Liu L, Su W. Glycyrrhizic acid ameliorates the kynurenine pathway in association with its antidepressant effect. *Behav Brain Res.* (2018) 353:250–7. doi: 10.1016/j.bbr.2018.01.024
70. Wang N, Yu H, Shen X, Gao Z, Yang C, Yang J. The rapid antidepressant effect of ketamine in rats is associated with down-regulation of pro-inflammatory cytokines in the hippocampus. *Ups J Med Sci.* (2015) 120:241–48. doi: 10.3109/03009734.2015.1060281
71. Lorenc-Koci E, Lenda T, Antkiewicz-Michaluk L, Wardas J, Domin H, Smialowska M. Different effects of intranigral and intrastriatal administration of the proteasome inhibitor lactacystin on typical neurochemical and histological markers of Parkinson's disease in rats. *Neurochem Int.* (2011) 58:839–49. doi: 10.1016/j.neuint.2011.03.013
72. Miura H, Kitagami T, Ozaki N. Suppressive effect of paroxetine, a selective serotonin uptake inhibitor, on tetrahydrobiopterin levels and dopamine as well as serotonin turnover in the mesoprefrontal system of mice. *Synapse* (2007) 61:698–706. doi: 10.1002/syn.20407
73. Miura H, Qiao H, Kitagami T, Ohta T, Ozaki N. Fluvoxamine, a selective serotonin reuptake inhibitor, suppresses tetrahydrobiopterin levels and dopamine as well as serotonin turnover in the mesoprefrontal system of mice. *Psychopharmacology* (2005) 177:307–14. doi: 10.1007/s00213-004-1959-7
74. Antkiewicz-Michaluk L, Michaluk J, Mokrosz M, Romanska I, Lorenc-Koci E, Ohta S. Different action on dopamine catabolic pathways of two endogenous 1,2,3,4-tetrahydroisoquinolines with similar antidopaminergic properties. *J Neurochem.* (2001) 78:100–8. doi: 10.1046/j.1471-4159.2001.00391.x

11

The Interaction of TPH2 and 5-HT2A Polymorphisms on Major Depressive Disorder Susceptibility in a Chinese Han Population

Jiarun Yang [1], Xueyan Zhao [1], Jingsong Ma [1], Zhengxue Qiao [1], Xiuxian Yang [1], Erying Zhao [1], Bo Ban [2], Xiongzhao Zhu [3], Depin Cao [4], Yanjie Yang [1]* and Xiaohui Qiu [1]**

[1] Department of Medical Psychology, Institute of Public Health, Harbin Medical University, Harbin, China, [2] Department of Endocrinology, Affiliated Hosptial of Jining Medical University, Jining, China, [3] Medical Psychological, Institute of the Second Xiangya Hospital of Central South University, Changsha, China, [4] Department of Medical Education Management, Harbin Medical University, Harbin, China

***Correspondence:**
Yanjie Yang
yanjie1965@163.com
Depin Cao
caodp211@163.com
Xiaohui Qiu
qiuxiaohui@foxmail.com

Purpose: TPH2 and 5-HT2A appear to play vital roles in the homeostatic regulation of serotonin levels in the brain, their genetic variations may lead to impaired homeostatic regulation of serotonin resulting in abnormal levels of serotonin in the brain, thus predisposing individuals to MDD. However, research studies have yet to confirm which gene-gene interaction effect between TPH2 and 5-HT2A polymorphisms results in increased susceptibility to MDD.

Methods: A total of 565 participants, consisting of 278 MDD patients and 287 healthy controls from the Chinese Han population, were recruited for the present study. Six single nucleotide polymorphisms (SNPs) of TPH2/5-HT2A were selected to assess their interaction by use of a generalized multifactor dimensionality reduction method.

Results: A-allele carriers of rs11178997 and rs120074175 were more likely to suffer from MDD than T-allele carriers of rs11178997, or G-allele carriers of rs120074175. The interaction between TPH2 (rs120074175, rs11178997) and 5-HT2A (rs7997012) was considered as the best multi-locus model upon the MDD susceptibility.

Conclusions: Our data identified an important effect of TPH2 genetic variants (rs11178997 and rs120074175) upon the risk of MDD, and suggested that the interaction of TPH2/5-HT2A polymorphism variants confer a greater susceptibility to MDD in Chinese Han population.

Keywords: major depressive disorder, TPH2, 5-HT2A, gene-gene interaction, polymorphisms

INTRODUCTION

Major depressive disorder (MDD) is a frequently occurring mental disorder with a strikingly high rate of relapses, and has become the leading cause of years lived with disability worldwide according to data compiled by the World Health Organization. Patients suffering with MDD struggle with severe role impairment (1) and most suffer from suicidal ideation, suicidal intent or suicidal attempts (2). Genetic factors have been found to be an important contributor to MDD (3), and inheritance can increase the risk of developing MDD by 40–70% (4).

Previous studies have provided strong evidence that serotonergic transmission is altered in MDD (5), and have identified polymorphism variants that are associated with deficits in the transmission of serotonin, which are believed to be involved in the pathophysiology of MDD (6). Polymorphism of the tryptophan hydroxylase-2 (TPH2) gene is one such example. TPH2 is the rate-limiting enzyme for the synthesis of serotonin in the brain (7). Functional polymorphisms of the TPH2 gene have been found to affect serotonin synthesis capacity and serotonin neurotransmission (8, 9), and several TPH2 gene polymorphisms have been confirmed to be associated with MDD. The first report of the association between TPH2 and MDD was published by Zill et al. (10). Subsequently, rs120074175 (1463G/A), a functional polymorphism variant of TPH2, which was shown to attenuate the synthesis of serotonin by ~80%, was also associated with MDD (8). A meta-analysis also showed that TPH2 rs4570625 (-703G/T) has strong epidemiological credibility for an involvement with MDD (11). In addition, the association of MDD and a haplotype block including rs4570625 and rs11178997 (473T/A) was confirmed (12). Collectively, these findings strongly indicated that TPH2 polymorphisms may play an important role in the development of MDD. In spite of the fact that TPH2 polymorphisms could result in the attenuation of serotonin synthesis, the genetic variation of TPH2 in isolation is unlikely to lead to a high risk of MDD (13, 14).

Interestingly, one research study suggested that the risk imposed by TPH2 may be modulated by the serotonin 2A receptor (5-HT2A) (15), an important regulator of the serotonin signaling (16). Multiple animal studies have confirmed that 5-HT2A binding is associated with serotonin levels (17, 18). In addition, changes in 5-HT2A binding levels have also been identified in different regions of the brain in depressed individuals (19, 20). Some genetic studies have also shown the association of 5-HT2A polymorphisms and MDD; for example, rs6311, rs6313, rs7997012 (21–23). 5-HT2A variants were identified as showing specific associations with MDD.

MDD is a polygenic disease; in other words, there are multiple and partially overlapping sets of MDD susceptibility genes which interact with each other, thus predisposing individuals to the development of MDD (24). Over recent years, genetic studies have identified numerous genetic variants implicated in MDD. However, results arising from the analyses of single markers have often been inconsistent, and for many candidate SNPS, results could not be replicated (25). Gene–gene interaction analysis is a promising method that can reveal susceptibility genes and their interaction, and has been confirmed as a particularly important method for revealing the molecular mechanisms of complex human diseases, such as MDD (26).

Based on the earlier observations, TPH2 and 5-HT2A appear to play vital roles in the homeostatic regulation of serotonin levels in the brain. Furthermore, TPH2 and 5-HT2A genetic variations may lead to impaired homeostatic regulation of serotonin resulting in abnormal levels of serotonin in the brain for long periods of time, thus predisposing individuals to MDD. However, research studies have yet to confirm what gene–gene interaction effect between TPH2 and 5-HT2A results in increased susceptibility to MDD.

The purpose of the present study was thus to investigate the specific interaction between the TPH2 and 5-HT2A genes and whether this mechanism contributes to susceptibility for MDD. SNPs selected in this study are not only associated with MDD but also associated with its gene expression (8, 27–29). Resultant data will contribute to a better understanding of MDD and genetic predisposition, and will assist in further interpreting the role of serotonin in susceptibility for MDD.

MATERIALS AND METHODS

Subjects

In total, 278 MDD patients, and 287 healthy controls, were recruited for the present study. All subjects were from the Chinese Han population, and were living in the same geographical area in the north of China. MDD patients were diagnosed according to the criteria for MDD described in the Fourth Edition of Diagnostic and Statistical Manual of Mental Disorders (DSM-IV). The 24-item Hamilton Rating Scale for Depression (HAMD) was used to evaluate all patients. Our inclusion criteria required that subjects had a HAMD score of 21 or higher, and had not received antidepressant treatment for 1 month preceding assessment. Our exclusion criteria included: (1) a history of brain organic mental disorders or other mental disorders; (2) a family history of genetic disorders; (3) individuals with mental retardation or dementia; and (4) individuals recently receiving blood transfusion treatment. All psychiatrists involved in patient diagnosis were specifically trained using the Structured Clinical Interview for DSM-IV disorders (SCID-I). Each patient was interviewed independently by at least two psychiatrists. Written informed consent was obtained from all participants and the study was approved by the Research Ethics Committee of Harbin Medical University, China.

DNA Isolation and Genotyping

Venous blood was taken from all participants and DNA isolated from EDTA-anticoagulated blood samples using the AxyPrep™ Blood Genomic DNA Minprep Kit (Axygen, Union City, CA, USA). Primer Premier 5.0 software was used to design the primers for polymerase chain reaction (PCR) amplification and final primers were evaluated using NCBI-BLAST (https://blast.ncbi.nlm.nih.gov/Blast.cgi). Primer sequences are given in **Table 1**.

DNA samples (TPH2: rs4570625, rs120074175, rs11178997; 5-HT2A: rs7997012, rs6311, rs6313) were genotyped using PCR TaqMan assays and read on an ABI PRISM 7900 Sequence Detection System (Applied Biosystems, Foster City, CA, USA). PCR amplicons were sequenced and purified using an ABI 3730 DNA Sequencer.

Statistical Analysis

The Hardy–Weinberg equilibrium test was carried out for all SNP loci and an independent-samples *t*-test was used to estimate differences in age distribution between case and control groups. The chi-square test was used to investigate differences in categorical variables, such as gender or differences in the distribution of genotype. A $p < 0.05$(two-tailed) was considered

TABLE 1 | The primers sequence for SNPs of TPH2 and 5-HT2A.

Gene	SNP ID	Polymorphisms	Location	Primer sequence (5′→ 3′)
TPH2	rs4570625	G/T	5′Regulatory region	F: 5′-AGTAGAGAGAAAAACCACAAGAGTATT-3′ R: 5′-CATTGCCTCAAGCATTTATCA-3′
	rs11178997	A/T	5′Regulatory region	F: 5′-TCCTTTTATCTATCCCTCGTACCAA-3′ R: 5′-GGTCCTGCACCACATTTTCA-3′
	rs120074175	A/G	Coding region	F: 5′-TGAGGCAATGGATATCTTGATTACC-3′ R: 5′-GCACTGCTGAATGCTTAAACCA-3′
5-HT2A	rs7997012	A/G	Intron region	F: 5′-CTAACCTCATGTCACCTCACA-3′ R: 5′-ATGTTGCAAACAATGGGCCAG-3′
	rs6311	T/C	5′Regulatory region	F: 5′-ATGGCCTTTTGTGCAGATTCC-3′ R: 5′-AGAGTTATCACCACAGACGTG-3′
	rs6313	T/C	Intron region	F: 5′-GCTACAAGTTCTGGCTTAGAC-3′ R: 5′-TGAAGTAAGGAGAGACACGAC-3′

as statistically significant. SPSS 19.0 software was used for all statistical analysis.

Haplotype analysis was performed using Haploview software (version 4.2) and analyzed differences in haplotype frequencies between case and control groups. Gene-gene interactions were tested using generalized multifactor dimensionality reduction (GMDR) software (version v0.7) and default parameters. In the configuration file, 10-fold cross-validation (CV) was defined and threshold ratio set at 1.0. The analysis was performed ten times using ten different random number seeds. The results were averaged to avoid spurious outcomes due to chance division of the data. Age and gender were regarded as covariates. The best gene–gene interaction model was selected based upon the values arising from CV consistency and accuracy testing. Interaction graphs and dendrograms were used to help interpret a multi-locus model of disease susceptibility.

RESULTS

Participant characteristics are shown in **Table 2**. In total, our study incorporated 565 participants, including 278 MDD patients and 287 healthy controls. There were 74 males (26.6%) and 204 females (73.4%) in the MDD group, and 83 males (28.9%) and 204 females (71.1%) in the control group. The mean age of MDD cases and controls was 42.79 years and 41.90 years, respectively. There was no statistically significant difference between cases and controls in terms of either gender or age distribution (gender: $p = 0.378$, age: $p = 0.542$). The HAMD score of the MDD group ranged from 21 to 58 points.

The genotype distributions of TPH2 and 5-HT2A polymorphisms conformed to the Hardy–Weinberg equilibrium and the results of our single marker analysis are presented in **Table 3**. Significant differences in genotypic and allelic distributions between cases and controls were confirmed at locus rs11178997 ($p = 0.000$ for both genotype and allele) and rs120074175 ($p = 0.000$ for both genotype and allele) of the TPH2 gene; after Bonferroni correction, these differences remained significant. Odds ratio analysis showed that A-allele carriers of rs11178997 and rs120074175 were more likely to suffer from MDD than T-allele carriers of rs11178997, or

TABLE 2 | The characteristics of participants.

Variables	MDD ($n = 278$)	Control ($n = 287$)	p-value
Sex(males/females)	74/204	83/204	0.542
Age(mean ± SD)	42.79 ± 12.21	41.90 ± 11.93	0.378
HAMD score(mean ± SD)	30.38 ± 6.58	5.93 ± 5.76	

G-allele carriers of rs120074175 (rs11178997: OR = 1.637, 95%CI: 1.290–2.078; rs120074175: OR = 7.909, 95%CI: 5.987–10.447). Differences in the distribution of rs6311 and rs6313 of the 5-HT2A gene were observed only in terms of genotype (rs6311: $p = 0.029$; rs6313: $p = 0.049$), but after Bonferroni correction, these differences were not significant. We did not identify an association between MDD and the other SNPs tested (TPH2:rs4570625, 5-HT2A: rs7997012).

Haplotype frequencies in case and control groups were estimated by Haploview software (version 4.2) and our results are shown in **Table 4**. Strong Linkage Disequilibrium (LD) was observed between the 5-HT2A rs6311 and rs6313 ($D' = 1.0$, $r^2 = 0.979$), but the 5-HT2A rs6311-rs6313 haplotypes were not associated with MDD.

GMDR was used to detect the interaction effects of six TPH2/5-HT2A SNPs in MDD susceptibility. The results of gene-gene interaction models, using age and gender as covariates, are given in **Table 5**. In total, 1,000 replications were used to determine the empirical p-value of prediction accuracy using the permutation test. Significant 2-locus to 6-locus gene-gene interaction models were observed ($p < 0.001$). The interaction between TPH2 (rs120074175, rs11178997) and 5-HT2A (rs7997012) showed a CV consistency of 10/10 and a testing accuracy of 81.86%, and this was therefore considered as the best multi-locus model. The testing accuracy of all multi-locus models was higher than the accuracy of the best single locus model. This result suggested there was an interaction effect of TPH2 and 5-HT2A upon MDD susceptibility.

An interaction graph and an interaction dendrogram were created in order to interpret the relationship between the six SNPs tested. As shown in **Figure 1**, we found that rs11178997 and rs120074175 both had strong independent

TABLE 3 | Genotypic and allelic distributions of TPH2 and 5-HT2A polymorphisms of MDD patients and controls.

Gene	SNP	Sample	Genotype (%)			p	Allele (%)		p	Odds ratio (95%CI)
TPH2	rs4570625		GG	TG	TT		G	T		
		Case	73 (26.3)	131 (47.1)	74 (26.6)	0.129	277 (49.8)	279 (50.2)	0.079	1.233
		Control	55 (19.2)	146 (50.9)	86 (29.9)		256 (44.6)	318 (55.4)		(0.976–1.558)
	rs11178997		AA	AT	TT		A	G		
		Case	93 (33.5)	170 (61.1)	15 (5.4)	**0.000***	356 (64.0)	200 (36.0)	**0.000***	1.637
		Control	135 (47.0)	29 (10.1)	123 (42.9)		299 (52.1)	275 (47.9)		(1.290–2.078)
	rs120074175		AA	AG	GG		A	T		
		Case	207 (74.5)	48 (17.2)	23 (8.3)	**0.000***	462 (83.1)	94 (16.9)	**0.000***	7.909
		Control	108 (37.6)	4 (1.4)	175 (61.0)		220 (38.3)	354 (61.7)		(5.987–10.447)
5-HT2A	rs7997012		AA	AG	GG		A	G		
		Case	22 (7.9)	106 (38.1)	150 (54.0)	0.247	150 (27.0)	406 (73.0)	0.257	1.167
		Control	13 (4.5)	112 (39.0)	162 (56.5)		138 (24.0)	436 (76.0)		(0.893–1.526)
	rs6311		TT	CT	CC		T	C		
		Case	82 (29.5)	128 (46.0)	68 (24.5)	**0.029**	292 (52.5)	264 (47.5)	0.662	1.053
		Control	65 (22.6)	164 (57.2)	58 (20.2)		294 (51.2)	280 (48.8)		(0.834–1.330)
	rs6313		TT	CT	CC		T	C		
		Case	79 (28.4)	129 (46.4)	70 (25.2)	**0.049**	287 (51.6)	269 (48.4)	0.847	1.023
		Control	65 (22.6)	163 (56.8)	59 (20.6)		293 (51.0)	281 (49.0)		(0.810–1.292)

Bolded indicates statistically significant ($p < 0.05$).
**indicates the difference was still significant after Bonferroni correction.*

TABLE 4 | Haplotype-based association analysis results.

Gene	Haplotype	Case ratios	Control ratios	χ^2	p
5-HT2A	TT	0.516	0.510	0.037	0.847
	CC	0.475	0.488	0.191	0.662

effects (rs11178997, 27.41%; rs120074175, 26.51%). The strongest redundant interaction occurred between rs120074175 and rs11178997 in the TPH2 gene with an entropy of−15.00%. Rs120074175 also had a redundant interaction with rs6311 andrs6313, while rs11178997 had a redundant interaction with the other four SNPs. The interactions between other SNPs were relatively independent.

DISCUSSION

Serotonin has been proven to be involved in the pathogenesis of MDD (6), although the precise role of the serotonin system in MDD is still under debate (5, 30). TPH2 and 5-HT2A are key regulators of central serotonin transmission, and are considered as potential risk genes for MDD. Aberrant genes are known to predispose subjects to depression (31), although the validation of MDD susceptibility genes, including TPH2 and 5-HT2A, its interaction is unclear leading to the need for further investigations of the potential gene-gene interaction effects played by the key regulators of serotonin system in MDD susceptibility.

In the present study, we attempted to verify the relationship of TPH2 variants (rs4570625, rs120074175, and rs11178997) and 5-HT2A variants (rs7997012, rs6311, and rs6313) with MDD by evaluating their single and interaction effects upon MDD susceptibility in a Chinese Han population. The results of the present study not only suggested the important effect of the TPH2 gene upon the risk of MDD, but also provided preliminary evidence that the interaction between TPH2 and 5-HT2A polymorphism variants may influence MDD susceptibility. To the best of our knowledge, this is the first report to investigate TPH2/5-HT2A interaction effects upon the risk of MDD. In addition, our results suggested that the impaired homeostatic regulation of serotonin may predispose individuals to MDD.

In single-locus association analysis, we observed significant differences in genotypic and allelic distribution with the rs11178997 and rs120074175 TPH2 variants. The number of A-allele individuals for rs11178997/rs120074175 was significantly greater in the MDD group than in the control group, which revealed that A-allele carriers of rs11178997 and rs120074175 were more likely to suffer from MDD with a 1.637-fold and a 7.909-fold increased risk, respectively, compared to non-carriers. This result suggested that the TPH2 gene might play a major role in MDD, particularly the rs11178997 TPH2 polymorphism, which had the most independent effect. Previous studies have found that both the rs11178997 (27) and the rs120074175 (8) polymorphism affected the transcriptional activity of TPH2, thereby influencing serotonin production. Papers by Van Den Bogaert et al. and Cichonet al. have, respectively reported an association between rs11178997 and unipolar or bipolar affective disorder (32, 33),while Zhang et al.

TABLE 5 | The best gene-gene interaction models obtained by GMDR.

Locus no.	Best model	Testing accuracy (%)	CV consistency	*p* value
1	TPH2(rs120074175)	74.91	9/10	<0.001
2	TPH2(rs120074175,rs11178997)	81.18	10/10	<0.001
3	TPH2(rs120074175,rs11178997), 5-HT2A(rs7997012)	81.86	10/10	<0.001
4	TPH2(rs4570625,rs120074175,rs11178997), 5-HT2A(rs6311)	77.10	5/10	<0.001
5	TPH2(rs4570625,rs120074175,rs11178997), 5-HT2A(rs7997012, rs6311)	77.93	10/10	<0.001
6	TPH2(rs4570625,rs120074175,rs11178997), 5-HT2A(rs7997012, rs6311,rs6313)	77.90	10/10	<0.001

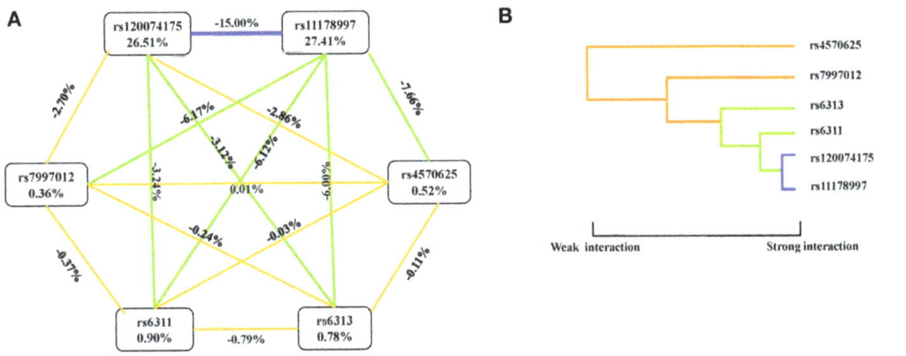

FIGURE 1 | Interaction graphs and dendrograms. **(A)** Interaction graphs. The percentage at the bottom of each SNP represents its interaction entropy, and the percentage on the line represents the percentage of interaction entropy between two SNPs. The golden line indicates additivity, while the blue or green lines indicate redundancy interaction. **(B)** Interaction dendrograms. The golden line represents additivity, while the blue line represents redundancy interaction. The shorter the dendrograms arm, the stronger the interaction.

reported an association of rs120074175 with unipolar major depression (8).

An earlier review suggested that the pathophysiology of depression might result, at least in part, from the direct dysregulation of brain 5-HT2A neurotransmission or indirectly from the dysfunction of other neurotransmitter systems that are under the control of 5-HT2A (34). Some existing studies have attempted to explore the association between the 5-HT2A SNPs and MDD (35–37), but few of these have met with success (38, 39). After Bonferroni correction, our current data showed no association of three 5-HT2A SNPs (rs7997012, rs6311, rs6313) with MDD at either the single-locus or haplotypic level. The inconsistency in our data may have arisen due to sample sizes, different ethnicities, and different definitions of disease; however, the negative results of the single marker analyses do not preclude the fact that the 5-HT2A gene variation has a minor effect upon MDD susceptibility (40). A recent study found that 5-HT2A mRNA levels in the peripheral blood mononuclear cells of MDD patients may have been associated with the severity of depression and the duration of illness in an Iranian population (41).

GMDR analysis can improve the predictive power of genetic association with MDD (42), and has been used to investigate gene-gene interaction in other biological pathways. GMDR is a non-parametric and genetic model for detecting and characterizing non-linear interactions among discrete genetic attributes that are sensitive to the detection of high-order interactions (43). Our GMDR results indicated potential gene-gene interactions between TPH2 and 5-HT2A with significant 2-locus to 6-locus interaction models, which confer a greater susceptibility to MDD. The best TPH2/5-HT2A interaction model was a 3-locus model (TPH2: rs120074175, rs11178997; 5-HT2A: rs7997012) using age and gender as covariates, which had a higher testing accuracy than the multi-locus interaction model of the single TPH2 gene. Identifying interaction between TPH2 and 5-HT2A is likely to contribute to a better understanding of genetic predisposition to MDD. In addition, we also found that both rs11178997 and rs120074175 have greater independent effects in terms of TPH2/5-HT2A interaction, which was far stronger than some other MDD susceptibility genes (44), and there was a strong redundant interaction between these variants, suggesting that TPH2 polymorphism may play vital roles in interaction.

Furthermore, previous research has suggested that the biological interaction between TPH2 and 5-HT2A is involved in the development of MDD. An animal study showed, using a TPH2 decrease-of-function model, gave rise to increased 5-HT2A binding in some brain regions (18). Another animal study observed that long-term activation of the 5-HT2A receptor induced an increase in TPH2 gene expression, TPH2 activity, and serotonin levels (15). These findings suggest that concurrent TPH2 and 5-HT2A variations may develop into long-term abnormal serotonin levels, thus predisposing individuals to MDD.

In interpreting the results of the current study, it is important to consider the following limitations. Firstly, in the current study, the geographic region and ethnic origin were strictly controlled to reduce the potential effects of population stratification; consequently, our data need to be further verified in other ethnicities and geographical regions. Secondly, our sample size was relatively small with only 565 subjects (case: 278, control: 287), although our study still possessed a *post-hoc* power of 0.99 to detect a moderate (0.5) effect size at the 0.05 significance level (two-tailed). Thirdly, SNPs were chosen in this study with more evidence that they are associated with MDD. The interaction of other TPH2/5-HT2A SNPs, which are potentially associated with MDD, was not investigated in the present study. It is therefore necessary to perform further investigations to better understand the role of interaction between TPH2 and 5-HT2A polymorphisms in MDD susceptibility.

CONCLUSION

For the first time, this study reports the interaction of serotonin-related genes, TPH2 and 5-HT2A, upon MDD susceptibility in a Chinese Han population. Our data identified an important effect of TPH2 gene variants (rs11178997 and rs120074175) upon the risk of MDD, and suggested that the interaction of TPH2/5-HT2A polymorphism variants confer a greater susceptibility to MDD. The present study also provided preliminary evidence that the interaction of TPH2 and 5-HT2A polymorphism variants may influence the susceptibility to MDD in a Chinese Han population, and suggested that impaired serotonin homeostatic regulation may be a risk factor for MDD.

ETHICS STATEMENT

This study was carried out in accordance with the recommendations of the Ethics Committee of Harbin Medical University with written informed consent from all subjects. All subjects gave written informed consent in accordance with the Declaration of Helsinki. The protocol was approved by the Ethics Committee of Harbin Medical University.

AUTHOR CONTRIBUTIONS

JY and YY designed the study. XQ, XY, and ZQ participated in the acquisition of data, which were analyzed by XuZ and JM. JY and XuZ wrote the article. BB, XiZ, and DC critically reviewed it. All authors assisted in the revision process, and gave approval for the final version of the article to be published.

FUNDING

This research was supported by the National Natural Science Foundation of China [81773536] to YY.

REFERENCES

1. Kessler RC, Bromet EJ. The epidemiology of depression across cultures. *Annu Rev Public Health.* (2013) 34:119–38. doi: 10.1146/annurev-publhealth-031912-114409
2. Avenevoli S, Swendsen J, He JP, Burstein M, Merikangas KR. Major depression in the national comorbidity survey-adolescent supplement: prevalence, correlates, and treatment. *J Am Acad Child Adolesc Psychiatry.* (2015) 54:37–44 e32. doi: 10.1016/j.jaac.2014.10.010
3. Sullivan PF, Neale MC, Kendler KS. Genetic epidemiology of major depression: review and meta-analysis. *Am J Psychiatry.* (2000) 157:1552–62. doi: 10.1176/appi.ajp.157.10.1552
4. Zubenko GS, Zubenko WN, Spiker DG, Giles DE, Kaplan BB. Malignancy of recurrent, early-onset major depression: a family study. *Am J Med Genet.* (2001) 105:690–9. doi: 10.1002/ajmg.1554
5. Andrews PW, Bharwani A, Lee KR, Fox M, Thomson JA Jr. Is serotonin an upper or a downer? The evolution of the serotonergic system and its role in depression and the antidepressant response. *Neurosci Biobehav Rev.* (2015) 51:164–88. doi: 10.1016/j.neubiorev.2015.01.018
6. Belmaker RH, Agam G. Major depressive disorder. *N Engl J Med.* (2008) 358:55–68. doi: 10.1056/NEJMra073096
7. Walther DJ, Peter JU, Bashammakh S, Hortnagl H, Voits M, Fink H, et al. Synthesis of serotonin by a second tryptophan hydroxylase isoform. *Science.* (2003) 299:76. doi: 10.1126/science.1078197
8. Zhang X, Gainetdinov RR, Beaulieu JM, Sotnikova TD, Burch LH, Williams RB, et al. Loss-of-function mutation in tryptophan hydroxylase-2 identified in unipolar major depression. *Neuron.* (2005) 45:11–6. doi: 10.1016/j.neuron.2004.12.014
9. Jacobsen JP, Siesser WB, Sachs BD, Peterson S, Cools MJ, Setola V, et al. Deficient serotonin neurotransmission and depression-like serotonin biomarker alterations in tryptophan hydroxylase 2 (Tph2) loss-of-function mice. *Mol Psychiatry.* (2012) 17:694–704. doi: 10.1038/mp.2011.50
10. Zill P, Baghai TC, Zwanzger P, Schule C, Eser D, Rupprecht R, et al. SNP and haplotype analysis of a novel tryptophan hydroxylase isoform (TPH2) gene provide evidence for association with major depression. *Mol Psychiatry.* (2004) 9:1030–6. doi: 10.1038/sj.mp.4001525
11. Gao J, Pan Z, Jiao Z, Li F, Zhao G, Wei Q, et al. TPH2 gene polymorphisms and major depression–a meta-analysis. *PLoS ONE.* (2012) 7:e36721. doi: 10.1371/journal.pone.0036721
12. Zhou Z, Roy A, Lipsky R, Kuchipudi K, Zhu G, Taubman J, et al. Haplotype-based linkage of tryptophan hydroxylase 2 to suicide attempt, major depression, and cerebrospinal fluid 5-hydroxyindoleacetic acid in 4 populations. *Arch Gen Psychiatry.* (2005) 62:1109–18. doi: 10.1001/archpsyc.62.10.1109
13. Angoa-Perez M, Kane MJ, Briggs DI, Herrera-Mundo N, Sykes CE, Francescutti DM, et al. Mice genetically depleted of brain serotonin do not display a depression-like behavioral phenotype. *ACS Chem Neurosci.* (2014) 5:908–19. doi: 10.1021/cn500096g
14. Hammer C, Degenhardt F, Priebe L, Stutz AM, Heilmann S, Waszak SM, et al. A common microdeletion affecting a hippocampus- and amygdala-specific isoform of tryptophan hydroxylase 2 is not associated with affective disorders. *Bipolar Disord.* (2014) 16:764–8. doi: 10.1111/bdi.12207
15. Naumenko VS, Tsybko AS, Bazovkina DV, Popova NK. Implication of 5-HT2A receptors in the genetic mechanisms of the brain 5-HT system autoregulation. *Mol Biol (Mosk).* (2012) 46:416–22. doi: 10.1134/S0026893312020100
16. Smith RM, Papp AC, Webb A, Ruble CL, Munsie LM, Nisenbaum LK, et al. Multiple regulatory variants modulate expression of 5-hydroxytryptamine 2A receptors in human cortex. *Biol Psychiatry.* (2013) 73:546–54. doi: 10.1016/j.biopsych.2012.09.028

17. Pinborg LH, Adams KH, Yndgaard S, Hasselbalch SG, Holm S, Kristiansen H, et al. [18F]altanserin binding to human 5HT2A receptors is unaltered after citalopram and pindolol challenge. *J Cereb Blood Flow Metab.* (2004) 24:1037–45. doi: 10.1097/01.WCB.0000126233.08565.E7
18. Jorgensen CV, Jacobsen JP, Caron MG, Klein AB, Knudsen GM, Mikkelsen JD. Cerebral 5-HT2A receptor binding, but not mGluR2, is increased in tryptophan hydroxylase 2 decrease-of-function mice. *Neurosci Lett.* (2013) 555:118–22. doi: 10.1016/j.neulet.2013.08.073
19. Rosel P, Arranz B, San L, Vallejo J, Crespo JM, Urretavizcaya M, et al. Altered 5-HT(2A) binding sites and second messenger inositol trisphosphate (IP(3)) levels in hippocampus but not in frontal cortex from depressed suicide victims. *Psychiatry Res.* (2000) 99:173–81. doi: 10.1016/S0925-4927(00)00076-7
20. Rosel P, Arranz B, Urretavizcaya M, Oros M, San L, Navarro MA. Altered 5-HT2A and 5-HT4 postsynaptic receptors and their intracellular signalling systems IP3 and cAMP in brains from depressed violent suicide victims. *Neuropsychobiology.* (2004) 49:189–95. doi: 10.1159/000077365
21. Jokela M, Lehtimaki T, Keltikangas-Jarvinen L. The influence of urban/rural residency on depressive symptoms is moderated by the serotonin receptor 2A gene. *Am J Med Genet B Neuropsychiatr Genet.* (2007) 144B:918–22. doi: 10.1002/ajmg.b.30555
22. Brezo J, Bureau A, Merette C, Jomphe V, Barker ED, Vitaro F, et al. Differences and similarities in the serotonergic diathesis for suicide attempts and mood disorders: a 22-year longitudinal gene-environment study. *Mol Psychiatry.* (2010) 15:831–43. doi: 10.1038/mp.2009.19
23. Kamata M, Suzuki A, Yoshida K, Takahashi H, Higuchi H, Otani K. Genetic polymorphisms in the serotonergic system and symptom clusters of major depressive disorder. *J Affect Disord.* (2011) 135:374–6. doi: 10.1016/j.jad.2011.08.027
24. Lopizzo N, Bocchio Chiavetto L, Cattane N, Plazzotta G, Tarazi FI, Pariante CM, et al. Gene-environment interaction in major depression: focus on experience-dependent biological systems. *Front Psychiatry.* (2015) 6:68. doi: 10.3389/fpsyt.2015.00068
25. Cardon LR, Bell JI. Association study designs for complex diseases. *Nat Rev Genet.* (2001) 2:91–9. doi: 10.1038/35052543
26. Moore JH. A global view of epistasis. *Nat Genet.* (2005) 37:13–4. doi: 10.1038/ng0105-13
27. Scheuch K, Lautenschlager M, Grohmann M, Stahlberg S, Kirchheiner J, Zill P, et al. Characterization of a functional promoter polymorphism of the human tryptophan hydroxylase 2 gene in serotonergic raphe neurons. *Biol Psychiatry.* (2007) 62:1288–94. doi: 10.1016/j.biopsych.2007.01.015
28. Preuss N, Salehi B, van der Veen JW, Shen J, Drevets WC, Hodgkinson C, et al. Associations between prefrontal gamma-aminobutyric acid concentration and the tryptophan hydroxylase isoform 2 gene, a panic disorder risk allele in women. *Int J Neuropsychopharmacol.* (2013) 16:1707–17. doi: 10.1017/S1461145713000254
29. Ruble CL, Smith RM, Calley J, Munsie L, Airey DC, Gao Y, et al. Genomic structure and expression of the human serotonin 2A receptor gene (HTR2A) locus: identification of novel HTR2A and antisense (HTR2A-AS1) exons. *BMC Genet.* (2016) 17:16. doi: 10.1186/s12863-015-0325-6
30. Albert PR, Benkelfat C. The neurobiology of depression–revisiting the serotonin hypothesis. II Genetic, epigenetic and clinical studies. *Philos Trans R Soc Lond B Biol Sci.* (2013) 368:20120535. doi: 10.1098/rstb.2012.0535
31. Wurtman RJ. Genes, stress, and depression. *Metabolism.* (2005) 54(5 Suppl. 1):16–9. doi: 10.1016/j.metabol.2005.01.007
32. Van Den Bogaert A, Sleegers K, De Zutter S, Heyrman L, Norrback KF, Adolfsson R, et al. Association of brain-specific tryptophan hydroxylase, TPH2, with unipolar and bipolar disorder in a Northern Swedish, isolated population. *Arch Gen Psychiatry.* (2006) 63:1103–10. doi: 10.1001/archpsyc.63.10.1103
33. Cichon S, Winge I, Mattheisen M, Georgi A, Karpushova A, Freudenberg J, et al. Brain-specific tryptophan hydroxylase 2 (TPH2): a functional Pro206Ser substitution and variation in the 5'-region are associated with bipolar affective disorder. *Hum Mol Genet.* (2008) 17:87–97. doi: 10.1093/hmg/ddm286
34. Guiard BP, Di Giovanni G. Central serotonin-2A (5-HT2A) receptor dysfunction in depression and epilepsy: the missing link? *Front Pharmacol.* (2015) 6:46. doi: 10.3389/fphar.2015.00046
35. Gu L, Long J, Yan Y, Chen Q, Pan R, Xie X, et al. HTR2A-1438A/G polymorphism influences the risk of schizophrenia but not bipolar disorder or major depressive disorder: a meta-analysis. *J Neurosci Res.* (2013) 91:623–33. doi: 10.1002/jnr.23180
36. Jin C, Xu W, Yuan J, Wang G, Cheng Z. Meta-analysis of association between the−1438A/G (rs6311) polymorphism of the serotonin 2A receptor gene and major depressive disorder. *Neurol Res.* (2013) 35:7–14. doi: 10.1179/1743132812Y.0000000111
37. Tan J, Chen S, Su L, Long J, Xie J, Shen T, et al. Association of the T102C polymorphism in the HTR2A gene with major depressive disorder, bipolar disorder, and schizophrenia. *Am J Med Genet B Neuropsychiatr Genet.* (2014) 165B:438–55. doi: 10.1002/ajmg.b.32248
38. Petit AC, Quesseveur G, Gressier F, Colle R, David DJ, Gardier AM, et al. Converging translational evidence for the involvement of the serotonin 2A receptor gene in major depressive disorder. *Prog Neuropsychopharmacol Biol Psychiatry.* (2014) 54:76–82. doi: 10.1016/j.pnpbp.2014.04.013
39. Cao S, Li H, Lou L, Xie Z, Zhao X, Pang J, et al. Association study between 5-HT2A and NET gene polymorphisms and recurrent major depression disorder in Chinese Han population. *Pak J Pharm Sci.* (2015) 28:1101–8.
40. Lin E, Chen PS, Chang HH, Gean PW, Tsai HC, Yang YK, et al. Interaction of serotonin-related genes affects short-term antidepressant response in major depressive disorder. *Prog Neuropsychopharmacol Biol Psychiatry.* (2009) 33:1167–72. doi: 10.1016/j.pnpbp.2009.06.015
41. Amidfar M, Kim YK, Colic L, Arbabi M, Mobaraki G, Hassanzadeh G, et al. Increased levels of 5HT2A receptor mRNA expression in peripheral blood mononuclear cells of patients with major depression: correlations with severity and duration of illness. *Nord J Psychiatry.* (2017) 71:1–10. doi: 10.1080/08039488.2016.1276624
42. Roetker NS, Yonker JA, Lee C, Chang V, Basson JJ, Roan CL, et al. Multigene interactions and the prediction of depression in the Wisconsin Longitudinal Study. *BMJ Open.* (2012) 2:e000944. doi: 10.1136/bmjopen-2012-000944
43. Ma J, Xiao H, Yang Y, Cao D, Wang L, Yang X, et al. Interaction of tryptophan hydroxylase 2 gene and life events in susceptibility to major depression in a Chinese Han population. *J Affect Disord.* (2015) 188:304–9. doi: 10.1016/j.jad.2015.07.041
44. Li Z, Zhang Y, Wang Z, Chen J, Fan J, Guan Y, et al. The role of BDNF, NTRK2 gene and their interaction in development of treatment-resistant depression: data from multicenter, prospective, longitudinal clinic practice. *J Psychiatr Res.* (2013) 47:8–14. doi: 10.1016/j.jpsychires.2012.10.003

12

Long-Lasting Sex-Specific Effects Based On Emotion- and Cognition-Related Behavioral Assessment of Adult Rats After Post-Traumatic Stress Disorder From Different Lengths of Maternal Separation

*Rucui Yang[1], Haoran Sun[1], Yani Wu[1], Guohua Lu[2], Yanyu Wang[2], Qi Li[3], Jin Zhou[4], Hongwei Sun[2] and Lin Sun[2]**

[1]Department of Clinical Medicine, Weifang Medical University, Weifang, China, [2]Department of Psychology, Weifang Medical University, Weifang, China, [3]Department of Psychiatry and Centre for Reproduction Growth and Development, University of Hong Kong, Hong Kong, Hong Kong, [4]College of Pharmacy, Weifang Medical University, Weifang, China

Correspondence:
Lin Sun,
linsun2013@wfmc.edu.cn

Adverse early life stress is a major cause of vulnerability to various mental disorders in adulthood, including post-traumatic stress disorder (PTSD). Recent studies have suggested that early life stress can help the body adapt optimally when faced with stressful trauma in adult life. An interaction may exist between early life stress (e.g., childhood trauma) and vulnerability to PTSD. This study aimed to evaluate emotion-related behaviors and verify the long-lasting effects of cognitive aspects of PTSD after exposure to severe adverse early life stress, such as long-term separation. Adverse early life stress was simulated by subjecting rats to 3 or 6 consecutive hours of maternal separation (MS) daily, from postnatal day (PND) 2 to PND 14. Single-prolonged stress (SPS) was simulated on PND 80 to imitate other adulthood stresses of PTSD with gender divisions (M-MS3h-PTSD, F-MS3h-PTSD, M-MS6h-PTSD, F-MS6h-PTSD, M-PTSD, and F-PTSD). After the MS and PTSD sessions, behavioral tests were conducted to assess the effectiveness of these treatments, which included an open field test (OFT), elevated plus maze test (EPMT), water maze test (WMT), and forced swimming test (FST) to detect anxiety-like behavior (OFT and EPMT), memory behavior (WMT), and depressive behavior (FST). The M-MS3h-PTSD group had fewer time entries into the open arms of EPMT than the F-MS3h-PTSD group, and the M-MS6h-PTSD group demonstrated fewer up-right postures in the OFT than the F-MS6h-PTSD group. The M-MS3h-PTSD group exhibited more exploratory behavior than the M-MS6h-PTSD and M-PTSD groups in the OFT. Less exploratory behavior was observed in the F-MS3h-PTSD group than in the F-MS6h-PTSD group, which demonstrated significantly increased freezing times in the FST compared to the F-PTSD group. The WMT revealed significant differences in learning and memory performance between the M-MS3h-PTSD group and other treatment groups, which were not found in the female rats. These findings demonstrate that an early stressful experience, such as MS, may be involved in helping the body adapt optimally when faced with additional trauma in adulthood, although mild early life stress might benefit learning and memory among males.

Keywords: maternal separation (MS), early-life stress, post-traumatic stress disorder (PTSD), single prolonged stress (SPS), gender difference, behavioral test

INTRODUCTION

Studies have found that regions of the brain that are especially susceptible to stress during the first 7 years of life (1–3) are involved in detecting and responding to threats and in regulating stress responses. Modifying this system is one of the primary ways human brains are shaped by early adversity (4). For instance, studies on children raised in orphanages—where they lack proper social and maternal support—have reported lasting adverse effects on cognitive functioning and increased risk for psychiatric disorders (5, 6). Epidemiological studies have indicated that adverse early life events can increase one's risk of developing psychopathology in adulthood (7). Although child abuse is a serious social problem in most countries, an understanding of various types of separations and corresponding gender differences in adulthood remains unclear.

Early postnatal stress animal models have been developed due to the high prevalence and serious consequences of early stress in humans. Rats exposed to early-life stresses, such as maternal separation (MS) during lactation, serve as good models for studying the effects that neglect has in early life (8). The use of animal models to induce early life stress is common when studying long-term consequences of stress (9). Researchers have performed MS in various ways, such as different lengths of separation; some authors separated animals for 3h (10) every day, whereas others separated them from 4h (11) or 6h (12). Only a few papers have compared different lengths of MS (13, 14).

Post-traumatic stress disorder (PTSD) is a highly disabling condition observed in individuals following exposure to severe emotional or physically life-threatening traumatic events (12), compounded by genetic and environmental factors (15). Early life stress and its associated changes in several hormonal states induce structural alterations. These alterations then induce disorders of brain functions throughout life (16). A focus on reliance has been largely ignored in relevant genetic and environmental interaction studies, referring to a dynamic pattern of positive adaptation despite experiencing significant trauma or adversity (17). Early environmental events exert enduring effects on behavioral parameters related to coping with stress, and animal models of stress represent an invaluable tool for investigating the complex relationship between brain development and stress (18, 19). In this study, the MS model was used to mimic early life stress and a potential influencing factor of PTSD.

Repeated MS is thought to increase animals' sensitivity to stress (9). Some studies have confirmed that the interaction of perinatal exposure to adversity with individual genetic liabilities may increase an individual's vulnerability to psycho- and physiopathology throughout life (20). However, other studies have cited data supplementing other reports, questioning whether early life stress is always detrimental later in life (21–23). Adolescence is a life period during which behavioral development is particularly susceptible to social influences. Stressful social events during this time have been found to alter and canalize behavior in an adaptive fashion or enhance specific types of cognitive performance, such that earlier influences on behavioral development are complemented and modified (23, 24). Macrì and Würbel proposed that perinatal low-to-moderate stressful situations could induce "protective" effects in adulthood; however, severely stressful situations can result in detrimental effects. Although several studies have demonstrated that as a case of early handling, brief daily separation from the mother during the neonatal phase can attenuate the effects of chronic stress on inducing hypothalamic-pituitary-adrenal (HPA) axis reactivity (25), these effects in animal models of PTSD have not been examined.

The aim of the present study was to compare the functional consequences of the PTSD model after MS at either 3h or 6h every day over a wide range of behaviors, which were either emotion-related (anxiety and depression) or learning-related (e.g., memory) in adulthood. The PTSD model after MS in rats imitates orphans or left-behind children exposed to a traumatic event (or events), as it alters vulnerability to psychiatric disorders and cognitive deficits in adult life. The sex of rats was considered because sexual differences in enduring early-life stress could induce rodents' alterations in neurogenesis (26).

MATERIALS AND METHODS

Animals

Pregnant Sprague–Dawley (SD) rats were bred at our animal facility and randomly selected from the Animal Center of Weifang Medical University. The day of birth was recorded as postnatal day (PND) 0. Pups were subjected to either MS or animal-facility-reared treatment (27). Rats were divided into 4 groups: control, no MS, MS 3h, and MS 6h per day from PND 2 to PND 14. After that, the pups were weaned and kept with rats of the same sex, from which 7 male pups and 7 female pups were randomly selected from the groups that we mentioned before. The rest were removed to ensure an equal number of males and females per litter. The 56 animals (220–350g at the end of the experiment) were housed in a limited-access rat facility with 7 rats per polycarbonate cage at a constant room temperature (22 +/−2°C), humidity (55 ± 15%), and an artificial light-dark cycle of 12h (08:00–20:00/20:00–08:00). We performed model-building tasks at 13:00 and 16:00, after animals had reached adulthood.

These experiments were designed to minimize the number of the animals used and were conducted in line with National Institutes of Health Guidelines (Use of Laboratory Animals) and ethical standards, including ethics committee approval as well as consent procedure. Experiments were approved by the Animal Care and Use Committee of Weifang Medical University.

Maternal Separation

Litters were randomly assigned to be reared under animal-facility-rearing conditions or undergo MS. Animals were randomly divided into 8 groups and their behavioral parameters were recorded separately: male control group (M-Control, n = 7), male rats with PTSD (M-PTSD, n = 7), male rats with 3h MS and PTSD (M-MS3h-PTSD, n = 7), male rats with 6h MS and PTSD (M-MS6h-PTSD, n = 7), female control group (F-Control, n = 7), female rats with PTSD (F-PTSD, n = 7), female rats with 3h MS and PTSD (F-MS3h-PTSD, n = 7), and female rats with 6h MS and PTSD (F-MS6h-PTSD, n = 7). In the F/M-MS3h-PTSD groups, litters were separated from their dams for 3h (9:00–12:00) each day (10, 19). In the F/M-MS6h-PTSD groups, litters were separated from their dams for 6h (9:00–15:00) each day (PND 2-PND 14). During separation, each dam was removed from its maternity cage and placed into an identical cage until the end of the separation period. The pups were then removed from the nest, placed in an incubator (30°C with humidity 55 ± 15%), and transferred to an adjacent room to eliminate influences of the dams' odor and sounds. At the end of the separation period, pups were returned to their maternity cages and reunited with the dams. Pups without MS in the F/M-PTSD groups were left with the dams.

The Establishment of PTSD Model

Single prolonged stress (SPS) procedures were similar to previous experiments (28), conducted in three stages. Animals were immobilized for 2h (IMO 2h). Rats were then immediately subjected to a 20-min forced swim (FS 20min). After removal, they were dried and allowed 15 min to recover (Rest 15min) under a heating lamp before being exposed to diethyl ether until loss of consciousness. The SPS procedure refers to the application of the three stressors and a 7-day quiescent period (28). The quiescent period is critical for developing behavioral and PTSD-like physiological abnormalities after SPS (29). Behavioral experiments were generally performed approximately 7 days after establishing the PTSD model.

EXPERIMENTAL PROCEDURES

All animals underwent all behavioral experiments, which were conducted sequentially with the same sequences: 1) open field test (OFT), 2) elevated plus maze test (EPMT), 3) water maze test (WMT), and 4) forced swimming test (FST) (**Figure 1**). This sequence was selected based on the principle of preference for light-pressure and general requirements for the operation of animal experiments (30, 31).

Anxiety-Like Behavior

Open field test. The chamber was a box without a lid (100 × 100 × 50 cm) consisting of a black floor and walls. Incandescent bulbs installed on the ceiling were used for illuminating the box. Each rat was transported from the colony room to the OFT room on the day of OFT. At the beginning of the experiment, the animals were placed gently in the corner and allowed to explore the chamber freely for 5 min, and upright numbers were recorded at the same time. Automated image analysis software (SMART 3.0, Panlab SL; Barcelona, Spain) was used for recording time spent in central areas, which evaluated the anxiety-like behavior. The open field was cleaned with ethanol after each test.

Elevated plus maze test. The EPMT is commonly used to score PTSD-like anxiogenic behavior in rats by exploiting the conflict between rats' innate fear of open spaces versus their desire to explore novel environments (32). The elevated plus maze was 50 cm above the floor and consisted of two open arms (50 cm × 10 cm) and two enclosed arms (50 cm × 10 cm × 40 cm) with an open roof extending from a center platform (10 cm × 10 cm). The structures were arranged so the two open arms were opposite each other. All the rats were placed gently in the central platform, facing the closed arm and allowed to explore the area freely for 5 min. After each test the maze was wiped with ethanol. A video camera was positioned above the apparatus to record each animal's behavior, namely

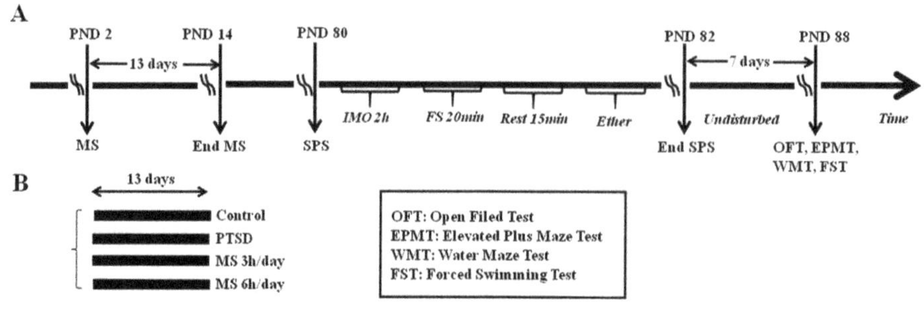

FIGURE 1 | (A) The process diagram of the experiment. SPS was conducted in three stages. Rats were immobilized for 2h (IMO 2 h), forced to swim for 20 min (FS 20 min), allowed to recover with a heating lamp for 15 min, and then exposed to diethyl ether until loss of consciousness (Ether). Rats were then returned to their home cages and left undisturbed for 7 days until the experimental manipulations. **(B)** The experiment included the control group (n = 14), PTSD group without MS (n = 14), PTSD-treated with prior 3h MS (n = 14), PTSD-treated with prior 6h MS (n = 14) or simply 'Control,' 'PTSD,' 'MS3h-PTSD' and 'MS6h-PTSD', respectively. Behavior experiments included OFT, EPMT, WMT and FST.

the following parameters: the number of open arm entries and the time spent in the open arms. An entry was counted when a rat's four paws entered a closed or open arm. The shorter the time spent in open arms, the higher the rat's anxiety.

Learning and Memory Behavior

Water maze test. The WMT can be used for measuring spatial navigation learning and memory in rats (33). We utilized a 160-cm-diameter pool filled with water to a depth of 30 cm and maintained at 23 ± 1°C. The pool had a 20×20 cm escape platform, which was hidden 1 cm below the water surface in the center of one quadrant of the pool. The platform was in the same location during the training session, and the order of start locations was quasi-random. Four prominent shapes were placed on the poor's wall (one per quadrant: square, heart, triangle and moon), and the water was changed daily. Rats were placed in the pool and allowed to search for the platform for 90 s. The rat was guided to the platform and allowed to remain there for 20 s to recognize the location if it did not find the platform after 90 s. Rats were subjected to four sequential trials each day at an interval of 30 s, during which the rat was placed in its home cage in a different room. The training session lasted 4 days. The probe trial was performed on day 5, when the platform was removed. The escape latency time required for the rat to find and climb onto the platform was recorded. Each training session was recorded by a video camera mounted above the center of the tank, and movement data was analyzed using SMART 3.0.

Depressive Behavior

Forced swimming test. The FST is a test used for measuring depression-like behavior in rodents (31, 34). On the first day, we placed rats individually into a cylindrical tank composed of a transparent Plexiglas cylinder (diameter: 20 cm; height: 46 cm) to a depth of 36 cm filled with warm water (23–24°C) for 15 min (pretest session) in order to adapt to the apparatus better. At the same time on the following day, the rats were put into the cylinders for 5 min, after which they were removed from the cylinder, returned to their home cage and dried with a towel. Each rat assumed an immobile posture after being placed in the water, defined as the state in which rats made only the movements necessary to keep their head above the surface of water (35). The duration of each rat's immobility at 5 min on the second day was scored using videotapes by a trained observer who was blind to the experimental conditions. Water in the tank was guaranteed to be changed after each trial. We referred to the process of Jong-Ho Lee et al., and Lanwei Hou et al. (11, 36) during this test.

An overview of the experimental procedure is displayed in **Figure 1**.

STATISTICAL ANALYSIS

Data were expressed as mean ± standard error. We deleted the values with the largest difference in each group to ensure the credibility of the data, so the final quantity is 6. The OFT, EPMT, probe test of WMT, and FST results were analyzed using analysis of variance (ANOVA) with Tukey. Independent-samples t-test was used for the comparison of gender difference. A repeated-measures multivariate analysis of variance (MANOVA) was conducted to analyze of WMT escape latencies using SPSS statistical software (Version 22.0, SPSS, Inc.; Chicago, IL, USA) at a significance level of $p < .05$ and values are means ± standard error.

RESULTS

Analysis of Anxiety-Like Behavior

The F-MS3h-PTSD group demonstrated less upright time than the F-MS6h-PTSD rats ($F(3,20) = 3.88$, $p = .025$; Post hoc test: $p = .017$). The M-MS3h-PTSD and F-MS3h-PTSD rats showed no obvious gender differences between upright times (**Figure 2A**). Rats in the F-PTSD and F-MS6h-PTSD group exhibited significantly more upright time in the OFT apparatus than the M-PTSD and M-MS6h-PTSD rats ($t = 7.432$, $p < .001$; $t = 6.154$, $p < .001$; **Figure 2D**, **F**). In other cases there was no gender difference (**Figure 2C**, **E**, **I**, **G**, **K** and **L**). The M-MS6h-PTSD group and F-MS6h-PTSD group had less upright numbers and time spent in the central squares compared with their control groups ($F(3,20) = 3.97$, $p = .023$, Post hoc test: $p = .026$; $F(3,20) = 3.59$, $p = .032$, Post hoc test: $p = .028$), (**Figure 2A**, **G**). The tracking images is shown in the figure (**Figure 2M**).

The numbers of entries into the open arms in EPMT were not significantly different between the M-MS3h-PTSD and M-MS6h-PTSD groups and the M-PTSD group on PND 88; the same results were found in the females. The M-PTSD rats had less time entering the open arms when compared to the control group; however, the female rats suggested no significant differences between entering the open arms or the opposite side (**Figure 3A**). The female rats had more upright postures of OFT and time entering the open arms of the EPMT than the male rats with MS and PTSD (**Figure 2F**, **Figure 3K**). The results of time spent in the open arms in the M-MS3h-PTSD and M-MS6h-PTSD groups were not significantly different from the M-PTSD group, and no difference was found between the F-MS3h-PTSD and F-MS6h-PTSD groups and the F-PTSD group (**Figure 3G**). Rats in the M-MS3h-PTSD group spent significantly less time in the open arms of the EPMT than the F-MS3h-PTSD group ($t = 2.936$, $p = .015$; see **Figure 3K**). In other cases there was no gender difference (**Figure 3C–F**, **I** and **L**). The tracking images was shown in the figure (**Figure 3M**).

No significant difference between the groups was found when there were no gender differences in upright numbers of OFT and time spent in open arms of EPMT (**Figure 2B**, **Figure 3G**). There were statistically significant differences between the control groups and the experimental groups in the time spent in central squares of OFT (MS3h-PTSD: $p = .021$; MS6h-PTSD: $p = .007$) and number of entries into open arms of EPMT (PTSD: $p = .003$; MS3h-PTSD: $p = .008$; MS6h-PTSD: $p = .006$), (**Figure 2H**, **Figure 3B**). When consider time and gender, no difference was found about time spent in open arms (**Figure 3H**). Detailed data information can be found in the **Supplementary Material**.

Analysis of Learning and Memory Behavior

A repeated MANOVA was used to analyze the mean latency of each group in finding the platform during initial spatial learning with

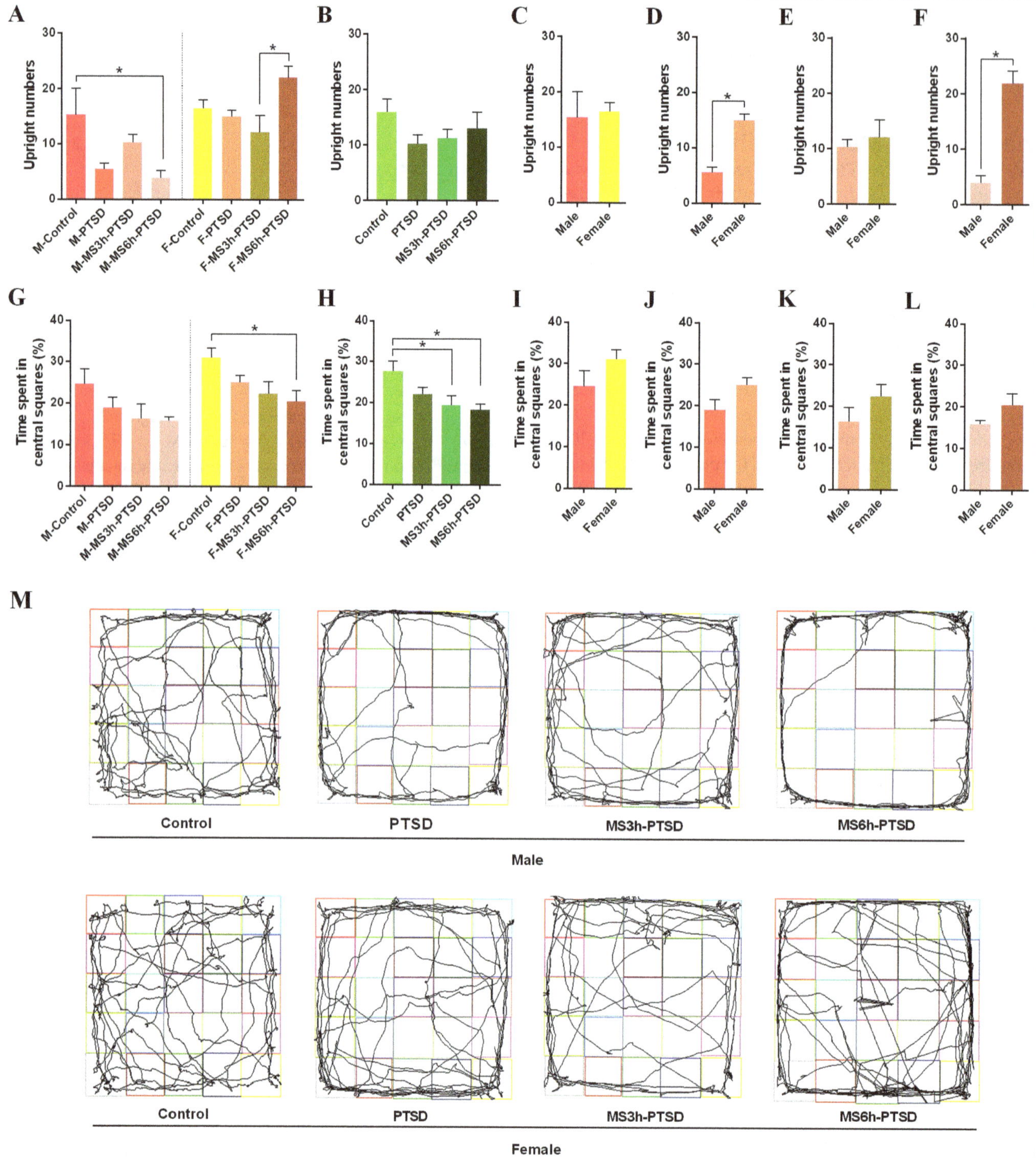

FIGURE 2 | Anxiety-related effect that MS had from PND 2 to PND 14 after subjecting the animals to the SPS as a PTSD model process in adulthood. **(A)** and **(B)**: Upright numbers in the OFT. **(G)** and **(H)**: Time spent in central squares (%). **(A)** and **(G)**: Divided by gender and time difference of MS. **(B)** and **(H)**: Divided by time difference of MS. **(C)**, **(D)**, **(E)**, **(F)**, **(I)**, **(J)**, **(K)** and **(L)**: Gender difference. **(M)**: Representative video tracking images during 5 min in the OFT. Values are means ± standard error. *$p < .05$ was statistically significant.

treatment and test days across different genders and separation time of MS. In male rats, the interaction was statistically significant between treatment and time ($F(9,207) = 10.92$, $p < .001$). The results showed that the separate effect that the treatment had was significant from day 1 to day 3 (**Figure 4A**). On day 1, the control groups spent less time finding the platform compared to other groups (PTSD: $p = .014$; MS3h-PTSD: $p = .008$; MS6h-PTSD: $p = .003$). On day 2, the PTSD and MS6h-PTSD groups demonstrated

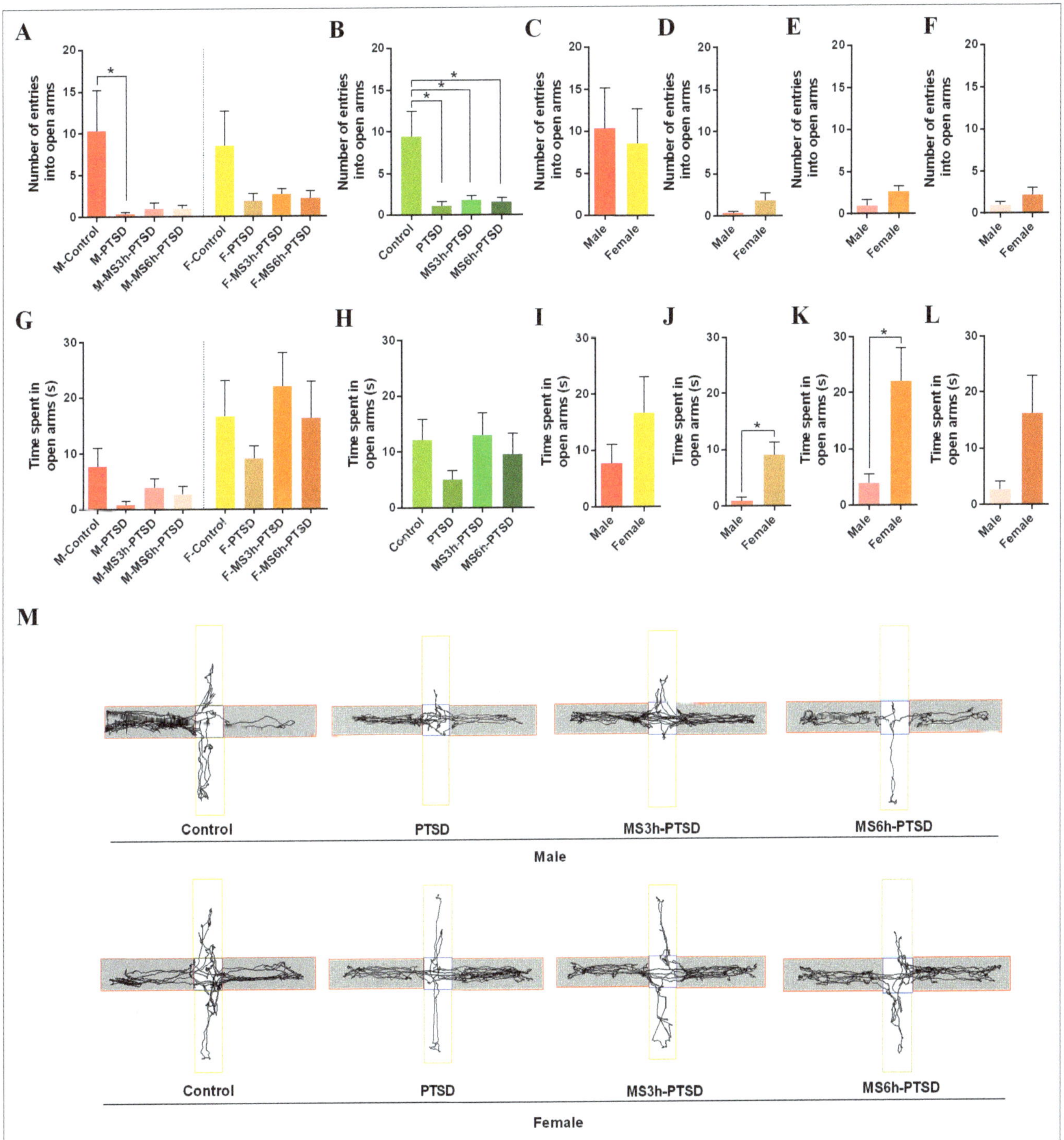

FIGURE 3 | Anxiety-related effect that MS had from PND 2 to PND 14 after subjecting the animals to the SPS as a PTSD model process in adulthood. **(A)** and **(B)**: Number entering in open arms in the EPMT. **(G)** and **(H)**: Time spent in open arms (s) in the EPMT. **(A)** and **(G)**: Divided by gender and time difference of MS. **(B)** and **(H)**: Divided by time difference of MS. **(C)**, **(D)**, **(E)**, **(F)**, **(I)**, **(J)**, **(K)** and **(L)**: Gender difference. **(M)**: Representative video tracking images during 5 min in the EPMT. Values are means ± standard error. *$p < .05$ was statistically significant.

more time compared to the control ($p = .001$; $p = .007$) and MS3h-PTSD ($p < .001$; $p < .001$) groups. On day 3, the MS3h-PTSD group used less time compared to the control ($p = .003$) and PTSD ($p = .003$) groups. However, there were no striking differences on day 4 between any of the treatment groups. In female rats the interaction between treatment and time was statistically significant ($F(9,207) = 12.73$, $p < .001$). Further analysis of the female groups showed that the separate effects of treatment was significant on day 1, day 3 and day 4 (**Figure 4B**). On day 1, the control group used significantly fewer time compared to the rest groups (PTSD:

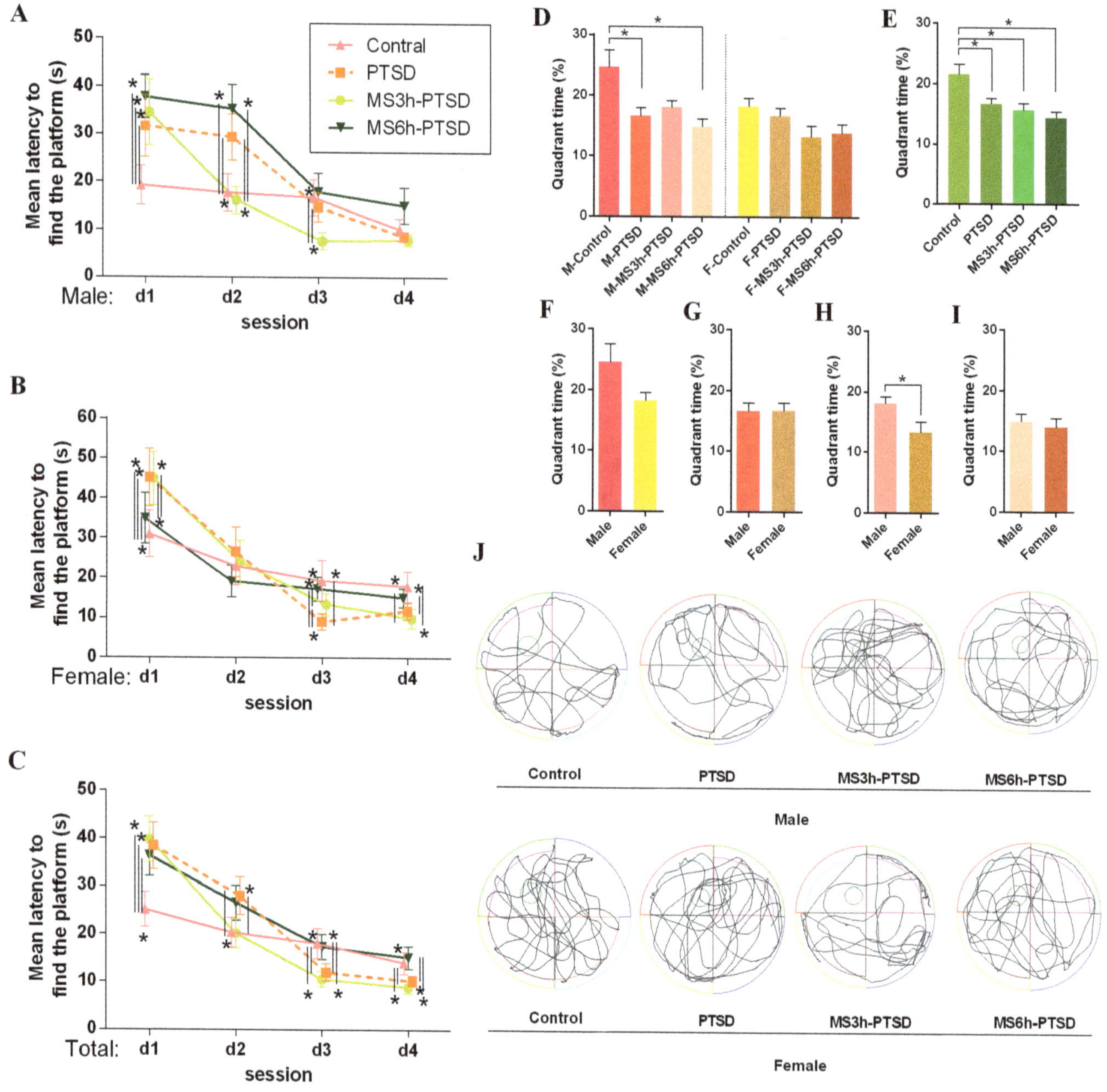

FIGURE 4 | Learning and memory-related effect that MS had from PND 2 to PND 14 after subjecting the animals to the process of SPS as a PTSD model in adult age. **(A)**, **(B)** and **(C)**: Mean latency to find the platform (s) in the spatial learning test in the WMT. **(D)** and **(E)**: Quadrant time (%) of probe test in the WMT. **(D)**: Divided by gender and time difference of MS. **(E)**: Divided by time difference of MS. **(F)**, **(G)**, **(H)** and **(I)**: Gender difference. **(J)**: Representative video tracking images of probe test in the WMT. Values are means ± standard error. $^{*}p < .05$ was statistically significant.

$p = .002$; MS3h-PTSD: $p < .001$; MS6h-PTSD: $p = .028$) apart from that MS6h-PTSD group had significantly less time compared to the PTSD ($p = .004$) and MS3h-PTSD group ($p = .001$). No striking difference was found on day 2 between any of the groups. On day 3, the PTSD group spent less time compared to other groups (Control: $p = .024$; MS3h-PTSD: $p = .021$; MS6h-PTSD: $^{*}p < .001$), and the MS3h-PTSD group used less time compared to the MS6h-PTSD group ($p = .006$). On day 4, the MS3h-PTSD group used less time compared to the control group ($p = .001$) as well as the MS6h-PTSD group ($p = .010$), and the MS6h-PTSD group used significantly more time compared to the PTSD group ($p < .001$). When we explored rats controlling for gender difference, the interaction was statistically significant between treatment and time ($F(9,423) = 16.16$, $p < .001$). The separate effects of treatment were significant from day 1 to day 4 (**Figure 4C**). On day 1, the control group used less time compared to other groups (PTSD: $p < .001$; MS3h-PTSD: $p < .001$; MS6h-PTSD: $p < .001$). On day 2, the PTSD group used more time compared to the control group ($p = .005$) and the MS3h-PTSD group ($p < .001$). On day 3, the control group required more time compared to the PTSD group ($p = .017$) and the MS3h-PTSD group ($p = .003$), and the MS6h-PTSD group used more time compared to the PTSD group ($p = .027$) and the MS3h-PTSD group ($p = .005$). On day 4, the control and MS6h-PTSD groups used more time respectively compared to the PTSD group ($p = .045$, $p = .036$) and the MS3h-PTSD group ($p = .001$, $p = .010$).

The separate effect that the test day had from day 1 to day 4 was significant in all treatments no matter if the rats were male (Control: $p = .001$; PTSD: $p = .003$; MS3h-PTSD: $p = .001$; MS6h-PTSD: $p < .001$), female (Control: $p = .003$; PTSD: $p < .001$; MS3h-PTSD: $p < .001$; MS6h-PTSD: $p = .001$) or from the group without gender difference (Control: $p < .001$; PTSD: $p < .001$; MS3h-PTSD: $p < .001$; MS6h-PTSD: $p = .000$), suggesting that the groups' learning ability improved after the treatment test.

The results of the probe test revealed gender differences between rats in the MS3h group and the PTSD group; additionally, the M-MS3h-PTSD rats showed a higher spatial preference for the target quadrant than the F-MS3h-PTSD rats ($F(5,66) = 2.72$, $p = .034$). No significant differences were found between treatments (**Figure 4D**). A higher proportion of M-Control could be seen, compared with the M-PTSD and M-MS6h-PTSD groups, with significant differences ($p = .014$, $p = .002$; **Figure 4D**). When male and female rats were studied together without gender difference in WMT, the control groups required more quadrant time compared with rats in other groups, while there were no significant differences among the experimental groups (**Figure 4E**). The gender difference here is not significant (**Figure 4F, G, H** and **J**) and the tracking images was shown in the figure (**Figure 4J**). Detailed data information can be found in the **Supplementary Material**.

Analysis of Depressive Behavior

The F-MS3h-PTSD group showed more immobility than the F-PTSD group ($F(3,20) = 8.49$, $p = .001$; Post hoc test: $p = .001$) and no immobility difference in male rats (**Figure 5A**). No gender differences were found in terms of immobility between the MS3h-PTSD groups and MS6h-PTSD groups (**Figure 5A**). The F-MS3h-PTSD groups had more immobility time compared to the F-Control rats ($F(3,20) = 8.49$, $p = .002$). No significant differences emerged in depressive-like behavior between the MS3h-PTSD, MS6h-PTSD, and PTSD groups when there was no gender distinction (**Figure 5B**). The gender difference here is not significant (**Figure 5C, D, E** and **F**). Detailed data information can be found in the **Supplementary Material**.

DISCUSSION

Several lines of evidence have showed that in stressful contexts under MS conditions, physiological systems prepare themselves more efficiently (11). MS changes can be regarded as adaptive modifications. If animals are raised in stressful environments early, the nervous system, immune systems, and the endocrine system will

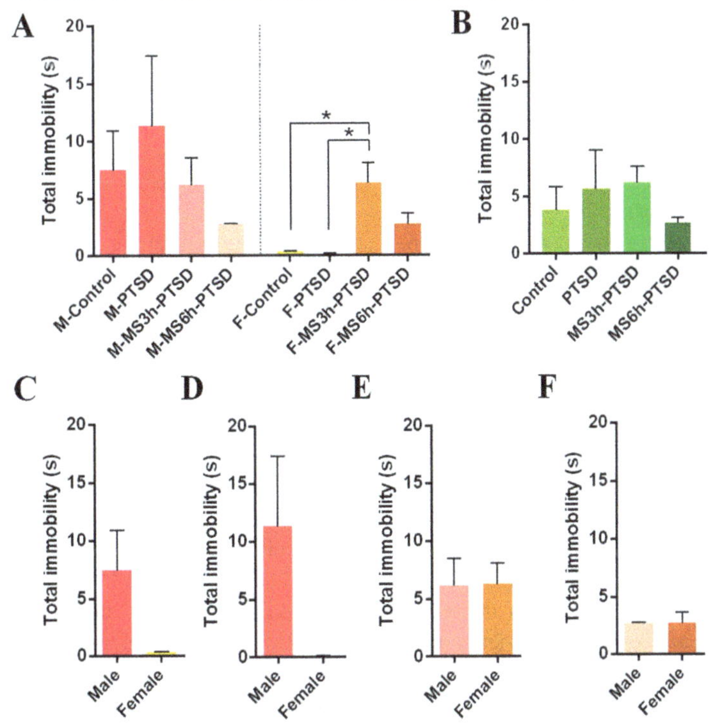

FIGURE 5 | Depression-related effect that MS had from PND 2 to PND 14 after subjecting the animals to the process of SPS as a PTSD model in adult age. **(A)** and **(B)**: Total immobility(s) in the FST. **(A)**: Divided by gender and time difference of MS. **(B)**: Divided by time difference of MS. **(C)**, **(D)**, **(E)**, and **(F)**: Gender difference. Values are means ± standard error. *$p < .05$ was statistically significant.

be altered to cope with stressful conditions later (26, 37). This finding differs from previous theories positing that early adverse experiences represent a risk element for developing anxiety disorders. In this research, we performed MS 3h or MS 6h daily from PND 2 to PND 14 to mimic adverse early life stress along with the SPS process to mimic secondary stress in adulthood, resulting in PTSD.

The impacts of MS on the rats' neurobehavioral development remain ambiguous as a result of the varying patterns observed by researchers. Some have shown that the impacts of MS depend on separation conditions (e.g., length and time of separation, gender, environmental conditions such as ambient temperature, and genetic background) (38, 39). Care must be taken when implementing MS, as pups are affected by their mothers' odor or sounds; thus, it is important to ensure complete separation to guarantee the accuracy of results. In this study, pups were removed from the nest and placed into a 30°C incubator. As one source of error, unscheduled husbandry of cages may lead to high levels of ammonia, which cannot be neglected (40). Results cannot be tied directly to a poor early social environment if pups lose body warmth, because temperature might play a role, hence the recommendation for an incubator to avoid hypothermia (41). These observations show that long-term effects can be influenced by distinct MS conditions. The length and time of day when maternal separation occurs carries significant implications for these effects. In this experiment, differences in daily separation time (3h or 6h per day) and gender were studied. Female rats with 6h MS showed less anxiety than those with 3h PTSD. Increased sensitivity of the pituitary gland to exogenous corticotrophin-releasing hormone administration and the impaired negative feedback regulation of the HPA axis in male rats could explain this phenomenon. We can postulate that the previously mentioned adaptations might be useless in non-stressful conditions, which could lead to neuropsychiatric-like disorders or behavioral impairments. This finding could explain inconsistent conclusions. Potential behavioral consequences, as well as the mechanisms underlying this effect, will require future research.

Several animal models of PTSD, such as those involving social stress and predator stress, have been proposed. These animal models fail to demonstrate the most consistent neuroendocrinologic characteristic observed in PTSD patients, namely enhanced inhibition of the HPA axis, although they present behavioral alterations like PTSD (42–44). The SPS model, proposed by Liberzon et al., replicates the specific neuroendocrinologic abnormalities observed in PTSD patients (45), for example, enhanced glucocorticoid negative feedback. A recent 'dismantling' study that employed different components of SPS (i.e., two of three stressors) was compared to the effect of full SPS (involving restraint, forced swim, and ether exposure); only those rats that were exposed to the full procedure exhibited deficits in retention of extinction memories—a mechanism which was thought to contribute to an inability to retain new safe memories and prevent trauma recovery (46). Rats exposed to SPS in this study suggested enhanced inhibition of the HPA system. We used this classical animal model to establish severe PTSD-mimicking trauma in adults who had experienced early stress in their childhood.

In the present study, rats that withdrew from the SPS test exhibited a significant reduction in exploratory activity, such as upright posturing during the OFT (47). Anxiety-like behavior and locomotor activity were evaluated *via* EPMT (48). The increased time spent in the closed arms during a 5-min session was indicative of high anxiety-like behaviors (49). The less time the rats spent in open arms, the more anxious and less curious they were. Although the OFT and EPMT can detect the degree of anxiety, the OFT is suited to measuring spontaneous activity, whereas the EPMT is suited to explore animals' reactions to novelty in new and different environments. Gender differences were found in adult rats that had experienced MS before PTSD: male rats had significantly fewer upright numbers and less time in open arms in the OFT or EPMT. Female rats with MS 3h were more likely to enter the open arms in the EPMT. Male rats with less locomotor activities, which experienced severely adverse early life conditions (MS 6h), were more likely than female rats to exhibit anxious emotions after the second trauma in adulthood. The female rats showed less anxiety-like behavior and were more curious when subjected to severe early stress (MS 6h). Early adverse experience thus affected males more intensely, despite the fact that that compared to men, women have a higher prevalence of anxiety disorders. We thought the contradiction between these consequences might be attributable to species-specific differences, especially when studying sex differences in the susceptibility to early adverse conditions (50). The timing of estrogen in females should also be considered, as it may influence hormones and neurotransmitters. Anxiety-like behavior has been found to be directly related to certain hormone levels. León Rodríguez and Dueñas et al. found that females rats that experienced maternal separation from their mothers (6h per day, PND 1 - 21) displayed decreased levels of anxiety and impulsive behavior and were more active than their stressed male counterparts, consistent with our findings (51). Wang et al. employed repeated MS (one daily period of 4h from PND 1 to 21) and found no significant gender differences in anxiety or locomotor activity in the OFT, regardless of age (52). Some studies suggested that MS could exacerbate the result of exposure to a PTSD model in exploration activities, at least in male animals. Prut et al. discovered anxiety-like behavior in MS male rats, as determined by the time spent in the central area in OFT, which implied aggravation of the anxiety-like degree (i.e., increase of movement time in the surrounding area) when exposed to dangerous environments; however, this impact was not observed in females. Our study revealed no significant differences between the experimental group regarding anxiety as represented by the time entering the central area of the OFT regardless of gender or treatment. We suspect that early life stress might not always contribute to unpredictable traumatic events experienced in adulthood. The OFT material and the different MS operations may have been susceptible to the smell of the rats, which could have influenced the final results.

Spatial learning data from the WMT showed that the M-MS3h-PTSD group had significantly lower mean latency when locating the platform on the second and third test day compared to the rats in the M-MS6h-PTSD group; this result implies that MS for the 3 h/day from PND 2 to 14 slightly strengthened spatial learning in the male adult rats, in line with prior research. This might be because mild early stress was more conducive to spatial learning. A previous study found that 24h maternal separation in PND 9 improved spatial learning (53) but found no significant gender difference in the spatial learning test. Our conclusions differ from those of other studies, and we suspect that this may be due to differences in the design of the experiment, which means that the results of MS are different from the results of PTSD after the MS, although the effects of possible experimental errors need to be taken into account. Our results suggest that the M-MS6h-PTSD group had poor performances in the spatial navigation learning; although the differences did not have statistical significance, the trend is still there. We suspect that 6h of MS could model the impacts of early life stress in cognitive dysfunction during adulthood and might lead to additional general learning deficits later in life. Longer MS could also result in dystrophy, which affects brain size, volume, activity, and the number of brain cells. Research has shown that early adverse experiences resulting from MS 6h could reduce cell proliferation in the dentate gyros of the hippocampus, hinder acquisition of spatial learning (54, 55), lead to neuronal cell death, and eventually cause memory impairment (56). Over time, all male rat groups showed enhanced spatial learning after 4 days' training in this study, but no significant differences appeared in the rats' ultimate learning ability in any group. Interactions between an individual genetic profile and the early environment, such as MS, could be involved in adaptive programming, which could amplify responsiveness in animals. Severely adverse early life conditions in female rats (MS6h) affected the spatial learning of the subject, which spent significantly less time on mean latency to find the platform on the first training day and more time on the third and fourth day, suggesting that MS 6 h/day from PND 2 to 14 slightly disrupted spatial learning in adult female rats. A similar situation was found on the third and fourth training days without gender difference. Xiu-Min Sun et al. found behavioral results of the WMT indicating that the rats' memory and spatial learning ability were impaired by early life stress. Our study found that the spatial probe test showed no significant differences among the MS3h-PTSD, MS6h-PTSD and PTSD groups, implying that rats who experienced trauma early in life and then experienced a second trauma in adulthood do not suffer from effects on spatial memory. Charles V Vorhees and Michael T Williams offered that the number of times an animal floats could be reduced by proper water temperature (57); thus, a more stable temperature would be better during the experimental process.

Immobility is a sign of increased depression-like behavior (49). Female rats that experienced PTSD gave evidence of lower levels of depression when subjected to the FST. This pattern was evidenced by the increased proportion of immobility latencies compared with the F-MS3h-PTSD group, suggesting that female rats that experienced mild early stress (MS 3h) prior to PTSD exhibited more depression-like behavior than the F-PTSD group. These findings were consistent with a study from Hesong Liu, Gaurav Patki et al., which found that experiencing early-life maternal stress causes depression-like behavior later in adulthood for PND 60. This research was found in male and female rats, implying no gender difference in this behavior (58). A difference was found in depression in female rats; differences in experimental design, control group, strain differences, or a combination of these factors might cause such discrepancies, these may also explain the high standard deviation of male rats in the blank control group and the PTSD group.

Our study utilized emotion- and cognition-related behavioral assessments of adult rats following induced post-traumatic stress disorder after various lengths of maternal separation to explore the impact of MS on PTSD as well as the effects of different MS periods. Whether the aforementioned adaptations are useful in non-stressful environments remains unknown, although we will continue to explore this potential effect as well as the underlying mechanisms that may result from relevant treatments.

CONCLUSIONS

This study demonstrated that, with early life stress, female rats that showed less anxiety are more resilient to second stress in adulthood compared with male rats. Although there were signs of reduced anxiety in rats with early MS trauma compared with animals with only PTSD, they were not significant. Apart from that, male rats with slight MS exhibited better spatial learning than those exposed to severe MS. In terms of depression, female rats that experienced mild MS showed no adaptation to trauma but exhibited increased depression-like emotions. Although different results were obtained with different MS intensities, our data suggest that under several circumstances, early life stress could be adaptive in some respects, especially in spatial learning. This feature could play a role in predicting the emotional and cognitive outcomes of left-behind children who experience trauma in adulthood.

ETHICS STATEMENT

Our study followed the conventional requirements of experimental operation and was approved by the ethics committee of Weifang Medical University.

AUTHOR CONTRIBUTIONS

LS, RY, HRS and YW designed the study. RY, HRS and YW collected the data. RY analyzed data and drafted the manuscript. GL, YW, QL, JZ, HWS and LS reviewed the manuscript. All authors contributed to and approved the final manuscript.

FUNDING

This research was supported by the Youth Natural Science Foundation of Shandong Province (ZR2017QH001), the science and technology foundation program of the colleges and universities of Shandong province (J17KB096), and the research award foundation program for outstanding young scientists of Shandong province (BS2014YY043), and the Students' Research Fund of Weifang Medical University.

REFERENCES

1. Jensen SK, Dickie EW, Schwartz DH, Evans CJ, Dumontheil I, Paus T, et al. Effect of early adversity and childhood internalizing symptoms on brain structure in young men. *JAMA Pediatr* (2015) 169(10):938–46. doi: 10.1001/jamapediatrics.2015.1486
2. Lyons-Ruth K, Pechtel P, Yoon SA, Anderson CM, Teicher MH. Disorganized attachment in infancy predicts greater amygdala volume in adulthood. *Behav Brain Res* (2016) 308:83–93. doi: 10.1016/j.bbr.2016.03.050
3. Teicher MH, Anderson CM, Ohashi K, Khan A, McGreenery CE, Bolger EA, et al. Differential effects of childhood neglect and abuse during sensitive exposure periods on male and female hippocampus. *Neuroimage* (2018) 169:443–52. doi: 10.1016/j.neuroimage.2017.12.055
4. Teicher MH, Samson JA, Anderson CM, Ohashi K. The effects of childhood maltreatment on brain structure, function and connectivity. *Nat Rev Neurosci* (2016) 17(10):652–66. doi: 10.1038/nrn.2016.111
5. Rutter M, Sonuga-Barke EJ, Castle JI. Investigating the impact of early institutional deprivation on development: background and research strategy of the English and Romanian Adoptees (ERA) study. *Monogr Soc Res Child Dev* (2010) 75(1):1–20. doi: 10.1111/j.1540-5834.2010.00548.x
6. Kokubo M, Toya S, Amano I, Takatsuru Y. Early-life stress induces motor coordination dysfunction in adult mice. *J Physiol Sci* (2018) 68(5):663–9. doi: 10.1007/s12576-017-0580-6
7. Teicher MH. Childhood trauma and the enduring consequences of forcibly separating children from parents at the United States border. *BMC Med* (2018) 16(1):146. doi: 10.1186/s12916-018-1147-y
8. Nylander I, Roman E. Is the rodent maternal separation model a valid and effective model for studies on the early-life impact on ethanol consumption? *Psychopharmacology (Berl)* (2013) 229(4):555–69. doi: 10.1007/s00213-013-3217-3
9. Gross CM, Flubacher A, Tinnes S, Heyer A, Scheller M, Herpfer I, et al. Early life stress stimulates hippocampal reelin gene expression in a sex-specific manner: evidence for corticosterone-mediated action. *Hippocampus* (2012) 22(3):409–20. doi: 10.1002/hipo.20907
10. Dimatelis JJ, Vermeulen IM, Bugarith K, Stein DJ, Russell VA. Female rats are resistant to developing the depressive phenotype induced by maternal separation stress. *Metab Brain Dis* (2016) 31(1):109–19. doi: 10.1007/s11011-015-9723-8
11. Banqueri M, Mendez M, Arias JL. Behavioral effects in adolescence and early adulthood in two length models of maternal separation in male rats. *Behav Brain Res* (2017) 324:77–86. doi: 10.1016/j.bbr.2017.02.006
12. Sun XM, Tu WQ, Shi YW, Xue L, Zhao H. Female-dependent impaired fear memory of adult rats induced by maternal separation, and screening of possible related genes in the hippocampal CA1. *Behav Brain Res* (2014) 267:111–8. doi: 10.1016/j.bbr.2014.03.022
13. Pierce AN, Ryals JM, Wang R, Christianson JA. Vaginal hypersensitivity and hypothalamic-pituitary-adrenal axis dysfunction as a result of neonatal maternal separation in female mice. *Neuroscience* (2014) 263:216–30. doi: 10.1016/j.neuroscience.2014.01.022
14. Freund N, Thompson BS, Denormandie J, Vaccarro K, Andersen SL. Windows of vulnerability: maternal separation, age, and fluoxetine on adolescent depressive-like behavior in rats. *Neuroscience* (2013) 249:88–97. doi: 10.1016/j.neuroscience.2013.06.066
15. Sullivan EV, Pfefferbaum A, Swan GE, Carmelli D. Heritability of hippocampal size in elderly twin men: equivalent influence from genes and environment. *Hippocampus* (2001) 11(6):754–62. doi: 10.1002/hipo.1091
16. Gershon A, Sudheimer K, Tirouvanziam R, Williams LM, O'Hara R. The long-term impact of early adversity on late-life psychiatric disorders. *Curr Psychiatry Rep* (2013) 15(4):352. doi: 10.1007/s11920-013-0352-9
17. Kim-Cohen J, Turkewitz R. Resilience and measured gene-environment interactions. *Dev Psychopathol* (2012) 24(4):1297–306. doi: 10.1017/S0954579412000715
18. O'Malley D, Dinan TG, Cryan JF. Neonatal maternal separation in the rat impacts on the stress responsivity of central corticotropin-releasing factor receptors in adulthood. *Psychopharmacology (Berl)* (2011) 214(1):221–9. doi: 10.1007/s00213-010-1885-9
19. de Melo SR, de David Antoniazzi CT, Hossain S, Kolb B. Neonatal stress has a long-lasting sex-dependent effect on anxiety-like behavior and neuronal morphology in the prefrontal cortex and hippocampus. *Dev Neurosci* (2018) 40(2):93–103. doi: 10.1159/000486619
20. Sanchez MM, Ladd CO, Plotsky PM. Early adverse experience as a developmental risk factor for later psychopathology: evidence from rodent and primate models. *Dev Psychopathol* (2001) 13(3):419–49 doi: 10.1017/S0954579401003029
21. Frankenhuis WE, Del Giudice M. When do adaptive developmental mechanisms yield maladaptive outcomes? *Dev Psychol* (2012) 48(3):628–42. doi: 10.1037/a0025629
22. Fuentes S, Daviu N, Gagliano H, Garrido P, Zelena D, Monasterio N, et al. Sex-dependent effects of an early life treatment in rats that increases maternal care: vulnerability or resilience? *Front Behav Neurosci* (2014) 8:56. doi: 10.3389/fnbeh.2014.00056
23. Mittal C, Griskevicius V, Simpson JA, Sung S, Young ES. Cognitive adaptations to stressful environments: When childhood adversity enhances adult executive function. *J Pers Soc Psychol* (2015) 109(4):604–21. doi: 10.1037/pspi0000028
24. Sachser N, Hennessy MB, Kaiser S. Adaptive modulation of behavioural profiles by social stress during early phases of life and adolescence. *Neurosci Biobehav Rev* (2011) 35(7):1518–33. doi: 10.1016/j.neubiorev.2010.09.002
25. Oines E, Murison R, Mrdalj J, Gronli J, Milde AM. Neonatal maternal separation in male rats increases intestinal permeability and affects behavior after chronic social stress. *Physiol Behav* (2012) 105(4):1058–66. doi: 10.1016/j.physbeh.2011.11.024
26. Korosi A, Naninck EF, Oomen CA, Schouten M, Krugers H, Fitzsimons C, et al. Early-life stress mediated modulation of adult neurogenesis and behavior. *Behav Brain Res* (2012) 227(2):400–9. doi: 10.1016/j.bbr.2011.07.037
27. Meaney MJ, Aitken DH, Viau V, Sharma S, Sarrieau A. Neonatal handling alters adrenocortical negative feedback sensitivity and hippocampal type II glucocorticoid receptor binding in the rat. *Neuroendocrinology* (1989) 50(5):597–604. doi: 10.1159/000125287
28. George SA, Stout SA, Tan M, Knox D, Liberzon I. Early handling attenuates enhancement of glucocorticoid receptors in the prefrontal cortex in an animal model of post-traumatic stress disorder. *Biol Mood Anxiety Disord* (2013) 3(1):22. doi: 10.1186/2045-5380-3-22
29. Knox D, George SA, Fitzpatrick CJ, Rabinak CA, Maren S, Liberzon I. Single prolonged stress disrupts retention of extinguished fear in rats. *Learn Mem* (2012) 19(2):43–9. doi: 10.1101/lm.024356.111
30. Xiong GJ, Yang Y, Wang LP, Xu L, Mao RR. Maternal separation exaggerates spontaneous recovery of extinguished contextual fear in adult female rats. *Behav Brain Res* (2014) 269:75–80. doi: 10.1016/j.bbr.2014.04.015
31. Jiang Y, Wang Y, Sun X, Lian B, Sun H, Wang G, et al. Short- and long-term antidepressant effects of ketamine in a rat chronic unpredictable stress model. *Brain Behav* (2017) 7(8):e00749. doi: 10.1002/brb3.749
32. Jin S, Zhao Y, Jiang Y, Wang Y, Li C, Zhang D, et al. Anxiety-like behaviour assessments of adolescent rats after repeated maternal separation during early life. *Neuroreport* (2018) 29(8):643–9. doi: 10.1097/WNR.0000000000001010
33. Santin LJ, Rubio S, Begega A, Arias JL. Effects of chronic alcohol consumption on spatial reference and working memory tasks. *Alcohol* (2000) 20(2):149–59. doi: 10.1016/S0741-8329(99)00070-1
34. Álvarez-Suárez P, Banqueri M, Vilella M, Méndez M, Arias JL. The effect of recording interval length on behavioral assessment using the forced swimming test. *Revista Iberoamericana de Psicología y Salud* (2015) 6(2):90–5. doi: 10.1016/j.rips.2015.04.004
35. Lee JH, Kim HJ, Kim JG, Ryu V, Kim BT, Kang DW, et al. Depressive behaviors and decreased expression of serotonin reuptake transporter in rats that experienced neonatal maternal separation. *Neurosci Res* (2007) 58(1):32–9. doi: 10.1016/j.neures.2007.01.008
36. Hou L, Qi Y, Sun H, Wang G, Li Q, Wang Y, et al. Applying ketamine to alleviate the PTSD-like effects by regulating the HCN1-related BDNF. *Prog Neuropsychopharmacol Biol Psychiatry* (2018) 86:313–21. doi: 10.1016/j.pnpbp.2018.03.019
37. Banqueri M, Mendez M, Arias JL. Impact of stress in childhood: psychobiological alterations. *Psicothema* (2017) 29(1):18–22. doi: 10.7334/psicothema2016.264
38. Kosten TA, Lee HJ, Kim JJ. Early life stress impairs fear conditioning in adult male and female rats. *Brain Res* (2006) 1087(1):142–50. doi: 10.1016/j.brainres.2006.03.009

39. Farkas J, Reglodi D, Gaszner B, Szogyi D, Horvath G, Lubics A, et al. Effects of maternal separation on the neurobehavioral development of newborn Wistar rats. *Brain Res Bull* (2009) 79(3-4):208-14. doi: 10.1016/j.brainresbull.2008.12.011
40. Koontz JM, Kumsher DM, Kelly R, 3rd, Stallings JD. Effect of 2 bedding materials on ammonia levels in individually ventilated cages. *J Am Assoc Lab Anim Sci* (2016) 55(1):25-8.
41. Pinheiro RM, de Lima MN, Portal BC, Busato SB, Falavigna L, Ferreira RD, et al. Long-lasting recognition memory impairment and alterations in brain levels of cytokines and BDNF induced by maternal deprivation: effects of valproic acid and topiramate. *J Neural Transm (Vienna)* (2015) 122(5):709-19. doi: 10.1007/s00702-014-1303-2
42. Stein MB, Yehuda R, Koverola C, Hanna C. Enhanced dexamethasone suppression of plasma cortisol in adult women traumatized by childhood sexual abuse. *Biol Psychiatry* (1997) 42(8):680-6. doi: 10.1016/S0006-3223(96)00489-1
43. Yehuda R. Biology of posttraumatic stress disorder. *J Clin Psychiatry* (2001) 62(Suppl 17):41-6.
44. Yehuda R. Neuroendocrine aspects of PTSD. *Psychiatric Annals* (2005) 33(1):30-36. doi: 10.3928/0048-5713-20030101-06
45. Liberzon I, Lopez JF, Flagel SB, Vazquez DM, Young EA. Differential regulation of hippocampal glucocorticoid receptors mRNA and fast feedback: relevance to post-traumatic stress disorder. *J Neuroendocrinol* (1999) 11(1):11-7. doi: 10.1046/j.1365-2826.1999.00288.x
46. Pitman RK, Rasmusson AM, Koenen KC, Shin LM, Orr SP, Gilbertson MW, et al. Biological studies of post-traumatic stress disorder. *Nat Rev Neurosci* (2012) 13(11):769-87. doi: 10.1038/nrn3339
47. Casu MA, Pisu C, Sanna A, Tambaro S, Spada GP, Mongeau R, et al. Effect of delta9-tetrahydrocannabinol on phosphorylated CREB in rat cerebellum: an immunohistochemical study. *Brain Res* (2005) 1048(1-2):41-7. doi: 10.1016/j.brainres.2005.04.053
48. Myers B, Greenwood-Van Meerveld B. Divergent effects of amygdala glucocorticoid and mineralocorticoid receptors in the regulation of visceral and somatic pain. *Am J Physiol Gastrointest Liver Physiol* (2010) 298(2):G295-303. doi: 10.1152/ajpgi.00298.2009
49. Liu H, Atrooz F, Salvi A, Salim S. Behavioral and cognitive impact of early life stress: insights from an animal model. *Prog Neuropsychopharmacol Biol Psychiatry* (2017) 78:88-95. doi: 10.1016/j.pnpbp.2017.05.015
50. Diehl LA, Silveira PP, Leite MC, Crema LM, Portella AK, Billodre MN, et al. Long lasting sex-specific effects upon behavior and S100b levels after maternal separation and exposure to a model of post-traumatic stress disorder in rats. *Brain Res* (2007) 1144:107-16. doi: 10.1016/j.brainres.2007.01.084
51. Leon Rodriguez DA, Duenas Z. Maternal separation during breastfeeding induces gender-dependent changes in anxiety and the GABA-A receptor alpha-subunit in adult wistar rats. *PLoS One* (2013) 8(6):e68010. doi: 10.1371/journal.pone.0068010
52. Wang Q, Li M, Du W, Shao F, Wang W. The different effects of maternal separation on spatial learning and reversal learning in rats. *Behav Brain Res* (2015) 280:16-23. doi: 10.1016/j.bbr.2014.11.040
53. Lehmann J, Pryce CR, Bettschen D, Feldon J. The maternal separation paradigm and adult emotionality and cognition in male and female Wistar rats. *Pharmacol Biochem Behav* (1999) 64(4):705-15. doi: 10.1016/S0091-3057(99)00150-1
54. Oitzl MS, Workel JO, Fluttert M, Frosch F, De Kloet ER. Maternal deprivation affects behaviour from youth to senescence: amplification of individual differences in spatial learning and memory in senescent Brown Norway rats. *Eur J Neurosci* (2000) 12(10):3771-80. doi: 10.1046/j.1460-9568.2000.00231.x
55. Zhang L, Li B, Zhao W, Chang YH, Ma W, Dragan M, et al. Sex-related differences in MAPKs activation in rat astrocytes: effects of estrogen on cell death. *Brain Res Mol Brain Res* (2002) 103(1-2):1-11. doi: 10.1016/S0169-328X(02)00130-4
56. Baek SB, Bahn G, Moon SJ, Lee J, Kim KH, Ko IG, et al. The phosphodiesterase type-5 inhibitor, tadalafil, improves depressive symptoms, ameliorates memory impairment, as well as suppresses apoptosis and enhances cell proliferation in the hippocampus of maternal-separated rat pups. *Neurosci Lett* (2011) 488(1):26-30. doi: 10.1016/j.neulet.2010.10.074
57. Vorhees CV, Williams MT. Morris water maze: procedures for assessing spatial and related forms of learning and memory. *Nat Protoc* (2006) 1(2): 848-58. doi: 10.1038/nprot.2006.116
58. Liu H, Patki G, Salvi A, Kelly M, Salim S. Behavioral effects of early life maternal trauma witness in rats. *Prog Neuropsychopharmacol Biol Psychiatry* (2018) 81:80-7. doi: 10.1016/j.pnpbp.2017.10.013

13

Alterations of DNA Methylation at GDNF Gene Promoter in the Ventral Tegmental Area of Adult Depression-Like Rats Induced by Maternal Deprivation

Yi Zhang[1], *Lei Wang*[1], *Xin Wang*[1], *Yuting Wang*[1,2], *Chuting Li*[1] *and Xiongzhao Zhu*[1*]

[1] *Medical Psychological Center, The Second Xiangya Hospital, Central South University, Changsha, China,* [2] *Department of Clinical Psychology, Maternal and Child Health Hospital of Hunan Province, Changsha, China*

Correspondence:
Xiongzhao Zhu
xiongzhaozhu@csu.edu.cn

Objective: To study the expression and DNA methylation of the Glial cell line-derived neurotrophic factor (GDNF) gene in the development of depression-like behaviors in rats experiencing maternal deprivation stress in early life.

Methods: Newborn SD rats were randomly assigned to a normal control group (NOR) or maternal deprivation group (MD). An open field test (OPT), sucrose preference test (SPT), and a forced swimming test (FST) were used to evaluate rats' behaviors. Protein, mRNA, and methylation levels were measured by ELISA/Western blot, real-time PCR, and BiSulfte Amplicon sequencing PCR, respectively.

Results: MD rats had significantly shorter total distance and more fecal pellets in OPT, a lower sucrose preference rate in SPT, and a longer immobility time in FST than NOR rats. Compared with NOR rats, MD rats showed a significantly higher plasma corticosterone (CORT) level. The levels of plasma dopamine (DA) and the GDNF were significantly lower in the MD rats than in NOR rats. In the ventral tegmental area (VTA) tissues, MD rats had a significantly higher level of methylation at the GDNF gene promoter than NOR rats. The expression of the GDNF mRNA and protein were significantly lower in MD rats than in NOR rats. The total distance was significantly correlated with plasma DA and GDNF, the DNA methylation level at the GDNF promoter and the GDNF mRNA level in the VTA. Fecal pellets showed a significant correlation with plasma CORT. The sucrose preference rate was significantly correlated with plasma DA, the DNA methylation level at the GDNF promoter and the GDNF mRNA level in the VTA. Immobility time showed a significant correlation with the plasma DA, the plasma GDNF and the GDNF mRNA level in the VTA.

Conclusion: up-regulation of DNA methylation at the GDNF gene promotor and the subsequent down-regulation of the GDNF gene expression in the VTA, may be involved in the development of depression-like behaviors in rats experiencing MD in early life.

Keywords: maternal deprivation, depression, GDNF, DNA methylation, ventral regimental area

INTRODUCTION

Major depressive disorder (MDD) is a common psychiatric disorder with a lifetime prevalence of 3–17% (1). MDD is characterized by anhedonia, a depressive mood, and psychomotor retardation. Previous studies on the etiology, suggest that MDD is multifactorial and involves both genetic and environmental factors. Epidemiological studies demonstrated that early life stress is associated with the stress-related psychopathologies in later life, including depression (2, 3). However, the effect of early life adversity on depression is poorly understood, particularly, the influences of both the genetic and environmental factors.

The monoamine hypothesis proposes that MDD may be caused by the dysregulation of monoaminergic neurotransmitters in the central nervous system (CNS) including serotonin, dopamine (DA), and norepinephrine. Among them, dopamine is most abundant in the CNS and the body of dopaminergic neurons is mainly located in the ventral tegmental area (VTA) and projected to almost the entire brain (4), involved in the regulation of cognition, motivation, reward, reinforcement behavior, and emotions (5–7). Numerous studies have observed the deficiency of the dopaminergic system in patients with MDD (8–10). In addition, early life adversity influences the development of the dopaminergic system, followed by an impairment of its structures and functions (11–13).

The accumulated evidence revealed that the glial cell line-derived neurotrophic factor (GDNF) can promote the survival of dopamine neurons (14, 15). Kumar et al. (16) found that the GDNF can regulate the postnatal developments and adult functions of the dopamine system. It has been demonstrated that an exogenous increase of the GDNF level in the CNS, could increase the number of adult dopamine neurons or its terminals in the dorsal striatum. In addition, the GDNF can increase dopamine levels and augment dopamine release and re-uptake in the striatum (15). Moreover, the epigenetic status of the GDNF in the nucleus accumbens, is thought to be associated with the susceptibility and adaptation to chronic stressful events, and DNA hypermethylation in the promoter of the GDNF gene, which reduces the expression of the GDNF, and has been revealed to determine the behavioral responses to chronic stress (17).

To further investigate the epigenetic mechanisms of early life stress induced depression and to better characterize the role of the GDNF, maternal deprivation (MD), a well-known paradigm reflecting early life stress, was employed in this study to establish an animal model. The sucrose preference, open field, and forced swimming test were adopted to obtain behavioral data. The levels of CORT, DA, and the GDNF in plasma were measured, while the DNA methylation and expression of the GDNF gene in the VTA, were monitored to determine the relationship between biomarkers and the behavioral consequences.

Abbreviations: CNS, central nervous system; CORT, corticosterone; DA, dopamine; ELISA, Enzyme-linked immunosorbent assay; FST, forced swimming test; GDNF, glial cell line-derived neurotrophic factor; HPA, hypothalamic-pituitary-adrenal; MDD, major depressive disorder; MD, maternal deprivation group; OFT, open Field Test; PND, postnatal day; SD, Sprague-Dawley; SPT, sucrose preference test; VTA, ventral tegmental area.

MATERIALS AND METHODS

Animal and Design

Pregnant Sprague-Dawley rats (SLAC Laboratory Animal Inc., Shanghai, China) were housed individually and checked daily until delivery. The date of birth of the litter was labeled as postnatal day 0 (PND 0). On PND 1, newborn males were randomly assigned into two groups: (1) the maternally deprived stress group (MD, $N = 20$): these rats were exposed to maternally deprived manipulation from PND1 to PND14; (2) the normal control group (NOR, $N = 20$): these rats were not exposed to any stress conditions. The behavior of rats was measured on the 10th week by a sucrose preference, open field, and forced swimming test. The experiment schedule is shown in **Figure 1**. The experimental animal protocol was approved by the Animal Ethics Committee of Central South University. All rats were housed with water and food available *ad libitum* on a 12 h light/dark cycle (lights on 7:00–19:00 h).

Maternal Deprivation (MD)

The MD paradigm was designed as previously described (18). Briefly, litters were deprived from dams for 6 h daily from PND 1 to PND 14 (the deprivations assigned at 9:00–15:00). To block communication among littermates, pups were placed individually in a single cell (8 × 8 × 14 cm for each cell) and covered with dry sawdust. At the end of the deprivation period, litters were returned to their maternal cages. All experiments were carried out in a temperature-controlled room (30°C).

Open Field Test (OFT)

The open-field test was conducted within a rectangular area (50 × 83 × 56 cm) as previously described (18). At the start of the test, animals were placed at the center of the arena and were allowed to crawl freely. The behavior of rodents was monitored for 5 min, by a video camera mounted on the ceiling above the center of the arena (Ethovision 1.50, Noldus IT, Wageningen, Netherlands). The total distance, vertical counts, percentage of central distance, and fecal pellets were recorded by the computerized tracking system to assess locomotor activity, exploration, and anxiety levels, respectively. After each trial, the box was thoroughly cleaned with 75% ethanol.

Sucrose Preference Test (SPT)

The SPT was conducted as previously described (18). Rats were kept individually and given free access to two bobbles of water. On the first day, two bottles of tap water were placed in every cage. One bottle of tap water was replaced with a 1.5% sucrose solution on the second day. On the third day, rats were deprived of water for 23-h, and then a bottle of 1.5% sucrose water and a bottle of tap water were given to the rats at a random location in the cage for the last 1-h. The consumption amount of total water and a 1.5% sucrose agent were determined in the last 1-h. The sucrose preference rate was calculated according to the following equation: sucrose preference rate = sucrose intake (g)/[(sucrose intake (g) + tap water intake (g)].

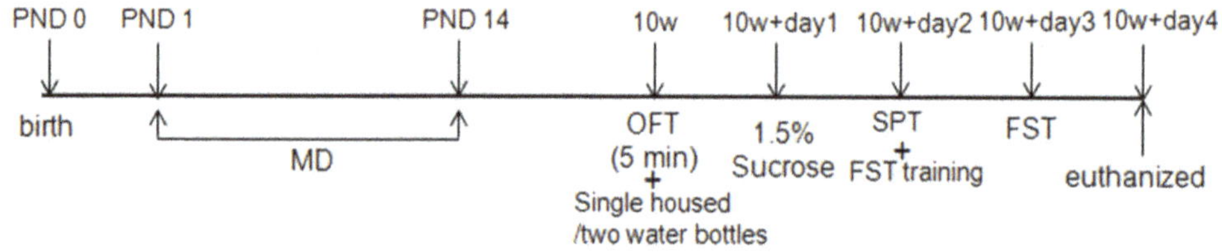

FIGURE 1 | Experiment schedule. OFT, open-field test; SPT, sucrose preference test; FST, forced swimming test; PND, postnatal day; SD rats were assigned to two groups: the normal control group (NOR) and the maternal deprivation stress group (MD).

Forced Swimming Test (FST)

Rats were placed in an open cylindrical container (35 × 32 cm) with water of 29 cm depth and a temperature of 24 ± 1°C, and the experiment was conducted as previously described (18). There was a 15-min practice round before the day of the test. At the same time on the following day, rats were placed in the swimming container individually for a 6-min test. The activities of rats were record by a video camera. When the rat floated without struggling and kept its head above the water, the time spent was defined as the immobility time. The immobility time was recorded in the last 5 min in a 6-min test to assess behavioral despair.

Enzyme-Linked Immunosorbent Assay (ELISA)

Animals were euthanized with an overdose of pentobarbital on the next day of the behavioral test. Blood was collected into EDTA (ethylenediaminetetraacetic acid) tubes via cardiac puncture under deep anesthesia. The plasma was collected by centrifugation of the blood at 1,500 rpm for 5 min at 4°C and kept at −80°C until testing. The concentration of CORT, DA, and the GDNF in plasma was detected using a Corticosterone EIA Kit (Cayman, Germany), Rat dopamine, DA ELISA kit (R&D, USA) and a Rat GDNF ELISA kit (Sigma, USA) following the manufacturers manual instructions, respectively.

Real-Time Reverse Transcription Quantitative PCR (qRT-PCR)

According to the rat brain in stereotaxic coordinates, the whole ventral tegmental area (VTA) tissue was immediately collected after blood collection. The total RNA was isolated from the dissected brain tissue according to the standard Trizol (Life Technologies) protocol. q*RT-PCR* was performed as previously described (18). The sequencing primers were ttcaagccaccatcaaaagac and gtagcccaaacccaagtcagt for the GDNF, cacccgcgagtacaaccttc (Forward) and cccatacccaccatcacacc (reverse) for β-actin. The data analysis was performed using the comparative ΔΔCT method. β-actin mRNAs were used as internal control.

Western Blot

The VTA tissues were homogenized in ice-cold homogenization buffer containing protein and phosphatase inhibitors and a Western blot was performed as previously described (18). Antibodies for the GDNF protein were purchased from Abcam (Cambridge, MA, USA). To control for loading efficiency, the blots were stripped and reprobed with a β-actin antibody. Proteins were normalized to β-actin.

DNA Isolation and DNA Methylation Analysis

Genomic DNA was isolated from the VTA tissues using a proteinase K/phenol-chloroform extraction method and dissolved in TE buffer. CpG islands in the promoter of the GDNF gene were selected: (1) 200 bp minimum in length; (2) 50% or higher GC content; and (3) 0.60 or higher ratio of observed/expected dinucleotides. Two regions including CpG islands were finally selected and sequenced. Both CpG islands are highly conserved in mice, rats, and humans. BiSulfte Amplicon sequencing PCR was used for quantitative methylation analysis. The methylation level at each CpG site was calculated as the percentage of the methylated cytosines over the total tested cytosines. The average methylation level was calculated.

Statistical Analysis

Data were analyzed using the statistical software SPSS 17.0 and expressed as mean ± S.D. The Students' *t*-test was used to detect a statistical significance between two groups. Correlations between biomarkers and behavioral indexes were analyzed using the Pearson correlation. A $p < 0.05$ was considered as significant.

RESULTS

The Long-Term Effect of Maternal Deprivation on Rats' Behaviors in Adulthood

In open field test, the total distance was significantly shorter in MD rats than in NOR rats ($t = -3.75$, $p = 0.001$; **Figure 2A**). The number of fecal pellets in MD rats was significantly more than in NOR rats ($t = 2.34$, $p = 0.03$; **Figure 2B**). While there was no significant difference of vertical counts ($t = -0.63$, $p = 0.54$; **Figure 2C**) and the percentage of central distance ($t = -1.42$, $p = 0.17$; **Figure 2D**) between the MD group and the NOR group.

In the sucrose preference test, the sucrose preference rate was significantly lower in MD rats than in NOR rats ($t = -3.45$, $p = 0.002$; **Figure 2E**).

In the forced swimming test, MD rats showed significantly longer immobility time than NOR rats ($t = 2.53$, $p = 0.02$; **Figure 2F**).

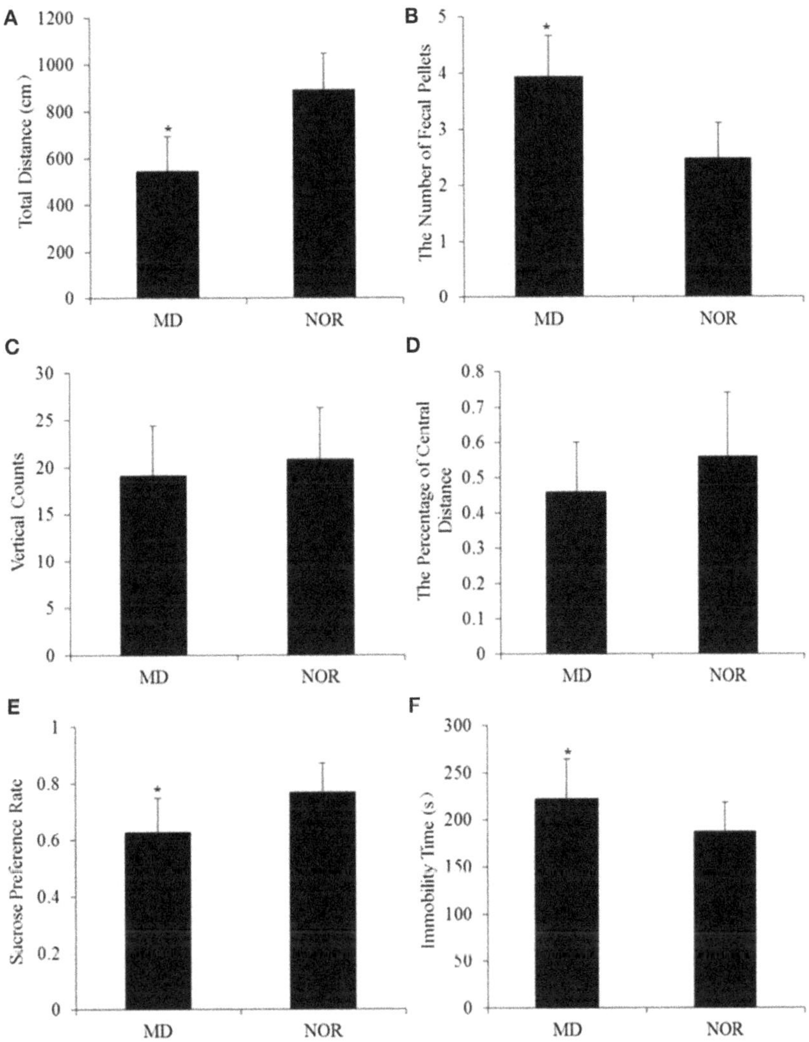

FIGURE 2 | Maternal deprivation (MD)-induced behavioral changes in adult rats. **(A)** Total Distance in the open field test. **(B)** The number of fecal pellets in the open field test. **(C)** Vertical counts in the open field test. **(D)** The percentage of central distance in the open field test. **(E)** Sucrose preference rate in the sucrose preference test. **(F)** Immobility time in the forced swimming test. $^*p < 0.05$ vs. the normal control (NOR) group.

The Long-Term Effect of Maternal Deprivation on CORT, DA, and GDNF Level in Plasma of Adult Rats

The concentration of the plasma CORT in MD rats was significantly higher than that in NOR rats ($t = 3.17$, $p = 0.01$; **Figure 3A**). While compared with the NOR group, there were significantly lower levels of DA ($t = -3.45$, $p = 0.006$; **Figure 3B**) and the GDNF ($t = -2.27$, $p = 0.047$; **Figure 3C**) in the plasma of the MD group rats.

The Long-Term Effect of Maternal Deprivation on DNA Methylation of the GDNF Gene Promotor, the GDNF mRNA, and Protein in the VTA of Adult Rats

The methylation levels of CpG sites within the GDNF promoter were measured and the results revealed a significantly higher percentage of methylated clones in the VTA of MD rats compared with NOR rats ($t = 6.55$, $p < 0.001$; **Figure 3D**) Concomitantly, The expression of the GDNF mRNA ($t = -3.81$, $p = 0.003$; **Figure 3E**) and protein ($t = -2.61$, $p = 0.026$; **Figure 3F**) in the VTA of MD rats were both significantly lower than that in NOR rats. Furthermore, the GDNF mRNA expression is negatively correlated with the methylation at the gene promoter ($r = -0.64$, $p < 0.05$).

The Correlation Between Behavior Indexes and Biomarkers

The total distance significantly correlated with the plasma DA level ($r = 0.74$, $p < 0.01$), the plasma GDNF level ($r = 0.61$, $p < 0.05$), the DNA methylation level at the GDNF promoter ($r = -0.66$, $p < 0.05$) and the GDNF mRNA level ($r = 0.769$, $p < 0.01$) in the VTA. The number of fecal pellets showed a significant correlation with the plasma CORT ($r = -0.75$, $p < 0.01$). The

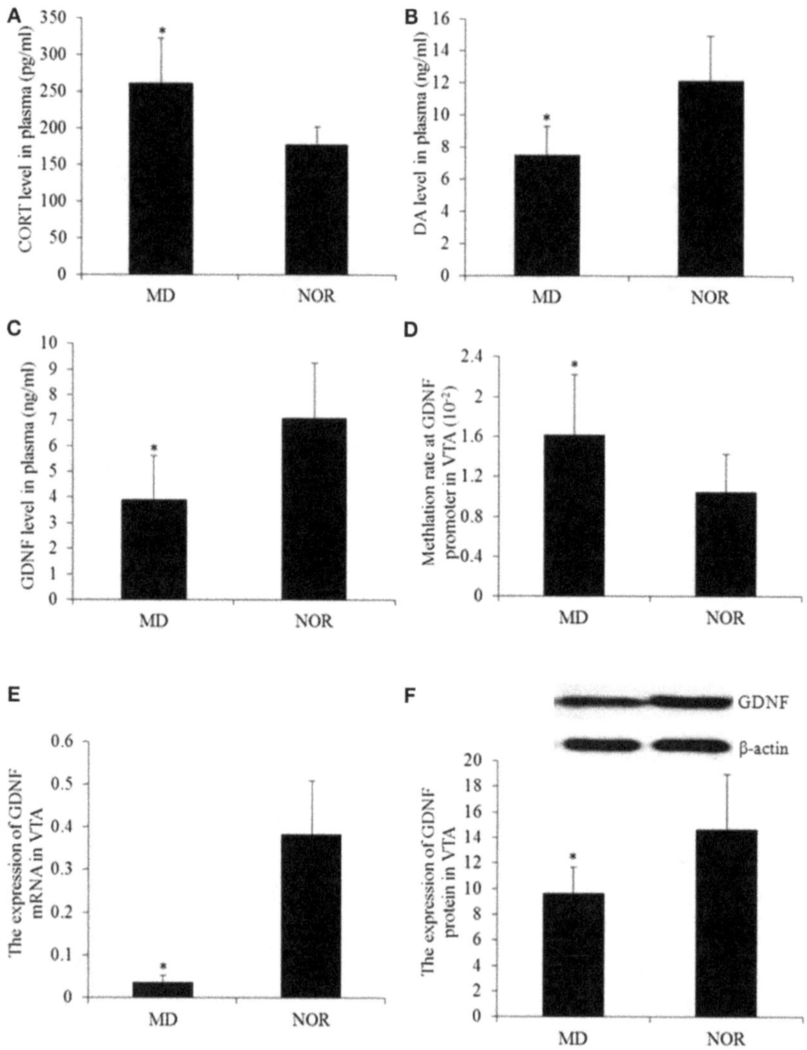

FIGURE 3 | Corticosterone (CORT), Dopamine (DA), and the Glial cell line-derived neurotrophic factor (GDNF) gene expression and methylation. **(A)** Plasma CORT concentration. **(B)** Plasma DA concentration. **(D)** Plasma GDNF concentration. **(D)** The total methylation level at the GDNF promoter in the ventral tegmental area (VTA) tissue. **(E)** The GDNF mRNA level in the VTA tissue. **(F)** Western blot of the GDNF expression in the VTA tissues. *$p < 0.05$ vs. the NOR group.

sucrose preference rate was significantly correlated with the plasma DA level ($r = 0.65$, $p < 0.05$), the DNA methylation level at the GDNF promoter ($r = -0.67$, $p < 0.05$) and the GDNF mRNA level ($r = 0.71$, $p < 0.05$) in the VTA. Immobility time showed a significant correlation with the plasma DA level ($r = -0.58$, $p < 0.05$), the plasma GDNF level ($r = -0.61$, $p < 0.05$) and the GDNF mRNA level ($r = -0.68$, $p < 0.05$) in the VTA (**Table 1**).

DISCUSSION

Anhedonia is one of the core symptoms of MDD (19), and was examined in this study using a sucrose preference test. Results showed that MD significantly decreased the sucrose preference rate. The behavioral despair in MD rats were reflected by the increased immobility time during the forced swimming test (20). Our findings suggest that early life maternal deprivation has a long-term effect on rodent behaviors and induce depressive-like behaviors in adult rats. The locomotor activity, exploration, and anxiety level were reflected by the total distance, vertical counts, percentage of central distance and fecal pellets in the open field test, respectively. In this study, early life maternal deprived rats showed a significantly shorter total distance and more fecal pellets. The results indicate that MD increased anxiety-like behaviors and decreased locomotor activity, which is consistent with the psychomotor retardation and anxiety in depressive patients. Altogether, these results indicate that early life maternal deprivation has a long-term effect on rats' behaviors and induce depression- and anxiety-like behavior in adulthood, which is similar as our previous studies (3, 13, 21).

Previous studies have shown that the hypothalamic-pituitary-adrenal (HPA) axis is involved in individual experiences of psychological stress (22). Corticosterone (CORT), as a glucocorticoid, is widely used to reflect an individual stress response. In this study, rats exposed to early life maternal

TABLE 1 | Correlation between biomarkers and behavioral indexes (r).

		Total distance	Fecal pellets	Sucrose preference rate	Immobility time
In plasma	CORT	−0.09	0.75**	−0.38	0.42
	DA	0.74**	−0.19	0.65*	−0.58*
	GDNF	0.61*	−0.20	−0.09	−0.61*
In VTA	Methylation level of GDNF promoter	−0.66*	0.38	−0.67*	0.45
	GDNF mRNA level	0.77**	−0.16	0.71*	−0.68*
	GDNF Protein level	0.54	−0.24	0.16	−0.41

*$p < 0.05$, **$p < 0.01$.

deprivation stress still had a significantly higher level of plasma CORT in adulthood, indicating that early life stress can induce long-term high levels of CORT. This result is consistent with previous studies, that indicate that early life adversity affects the individual HPA axis and induces an aberrant stress coping style in individuals. Furthermore, the plasma CORT level showed a significant correlation with anxiety-like behaviors, which suggests that CORT levels not only reflect individuals in a status of stress, but also reflects an individual's high level of anxiety.

Dopamine is an important neurotransmitter in the brain, which is closely related to stress-induced depression. Many studies have found that early life stress can induce abnormal changes in the dopaminergic system (18, 23). In the current study, maternal deprivation stress significantly reduced plasma dopamine concentration. When the dopaminergic system in the CNS is damaged, such as the dopaminergic neuron, the secretion of the dopamine and the blood that enters through the blood-brain barrier both decrease. Therefore, low levels of dopamine in the blood reflect the abnormality of the central dopamine system to some extent. In addition, the level of plasma dopamine was significantly correlated with the rate of sucrose preference, immobility time and the total distance in MD rats, suggesting that maternal deprivation stress-induced depression-like behaviors may be closely related to the inactivation of the dopamine system.

It has been found that the GDNF plays a crucial role in the nutritional support of central dopaminergic neurons and can promote the development and repair of dopaminergic neurons (24). Human and animal studies have shown that high expression of the GDNF can promote the growth of transplanted dopaminergic neurons and alleviate the damage of the dopaminergic system induced by psychological stress (25, 26). In this study, maternal deprivation stress down-regulated the plasma GDNF level, and the expression of the GDNF mRNA and protein in the VTA. The expression of the GDNF mRNA in the VTA was significantly correlated with anhedonia, despair, and locomotor activity, suggesting that the GDNF is associated with maternal deprivation-induced depression-like behaviors. A recent study has demonstrated that the GDNF is important for the pathogenesis of depression, such as the decrease of the GDNF protein and mRNA expression in the serum and hippocampus of depressive individuals (27). According to previous studies on the effect of the GDNF on dopaminergic neurons, it was suggested that early life stress down-regulates the expression of the GDNF gene in the VTA, subsequently impair the nutritional effect of the GDNF on the growth and function maintenance of dopaminergic neurons, destroy the repairing effect of the GDNF on the damaged dopaminergic neurons, which finally leads to the onset of depression-like behavior.

Increasing evidence suggests that aberrant transcription regulation, such as the epigenetic regulation of some critical genes in the brain, is a key component in the pathophysiology of depression (28, 29). DNA methylation of genes could trigger the development of depression symptoms in response to psychological stress (30–33). The results in this study showed that MD rats had a high level of DNA methylation at the promoter of the GDNF gene in the VTA which may down-regulate the expression of the GDNF gene. Furthermore, the methylation level of the GDNF gene correlated with anhedonia and locomotor activity, suggesting that a high level of DNA methylation in the GDNF gene in the VTA, may be one of the regulatory mechanisms of maternal deprivation-induced adult depression in rats. A study by Uchida et al. (17) showed that epigenetic regulation of the GDNF promoter in the NAc is associated with the susceptibility and the adaptation responses to chronic stress. Collectively these data indicate that long-term changes in the GDNF expression, induced by early life maternal deprivation, may be the underlying factor that increases the probability of developing psychopathology later in life.

In conclusion, up-regulation of the DNA methylation at the GDNF gene promotor and the subsequent down-regulation of the GDNF gene expression in the VTA, may be involved in the development of depression-like behaviors in rats experiencing maternal deprivation in early life.

AUTHOR CONTRIBUTIONS

YZ, LW, XW, and YW performed the experiments, data analysis, and prepared the manuscript. YZ, LW, XZ, and CL designed the study, revised the manuscript, and approved the final version.

FUNDING

This work was supported by National Natural Science Foundation of China (Nos. 81671341, 81701333) and Hunan Provincial Natural Science Foundation China (No. 2017JJ3439).

REFERENCES

1. Richards D. Prevalence and clinical course of depression: a review. *Clin Psychol Rev.* (2011) 31:1117–25. doi: 10.1016/j.cpr.2011.07.004
2. Berg L, Rostila M, Hjern A. Parental death during childhood and depression in young adults - a national cohort study. *J Child Psychol Psychiat.* (2016) 57:1092. doi: 10.1111/jcpp.12560
3. Zhang Y, Wang Y, Lei H, Wang L, Xue L, Wang X, et al. Optimized animal model to mimic the reality of stress-induced depression in the clinic. *BMC Psychiatry* (2017) 17:171. doi: 10.1186/s12888-017-1335-x
4. Beckstead RM, Domesick VB, Nauta WJ. Efferent connections of the substantia nigra and ventral tegmental area in the rat. *Brain Res.* (1979) 175:191–217. doi: 10.1016/0006-8993(79)91001-1
5. Nieoullon A, Coquerel A. Dopamine: a key regulator to adapt action, emotion, motivation and cognition. *Curr Opin Neurol.* (2003) 16:S3–9.
6. Perkins KA, Lerman C, Grottenthaler A, Ciccocioppo MM, Milanak M, Conklin CA, et al. Dopamine and opioid gene variants are associated with increased smoking reward and reinforcement due to negative mood. *Behav Pharmacol.* (2008) 19:641–9. doi: 10.1097/FBP.0b013e32830c367c
7. Wise RA. Dopamine, learning and motivation. *Nat Rev Neurosci.* (2004) 5:483–94. doi: 10.1038/nrn1406
8. Dunlop BW, Nemeroff CB. The role of dopamine in the pathophysiology of depression. *Arch Gen Psychiatry* (2007) 64:327–37. doi: 10.1001/archpsyc.64.3.327
9. Ruhe HG, Mason NS, Schene AH. Mood is indirectly related to serotonin, norepinephrine and dopamine levels in humans: a meta-analysis of monoamine depletion studies. *Mol Psychiatry* (2007) 12:331–59. doi: 10.1038/sj.mp.4001949
10. Li Z, He Y, Tang J. Molecular imaging of striatal dopamine transporters in major depression—a meta-analysis. *J Affect Disord.* (2015) 174:137–43. doi: 10.1016/j.jad.2014.11.045
11. Rentesi G, Antoniou K, Marselos M. Early maternal deprivation-induced modifications in the neurobiological, neurochemical and behavioral profile of adult rats. *Behav Brain Res.* (2013) 244:29–37. doi: 10.1016/j.bbr.2013.01.040
12. Kunzler J, Braun K, Bock J. Early life stress and sex-specific sensitivity of the catecholaminergic systems in prefrontal and limbic regions of Octodon degus. *Brain Struct Funct.* (2015) 220:861–8. doi: 10.1007/s00429-013-0688-2
13. Bai M, Zhu X, Zhang L, Zhang Y, Xue L, Wang Y, et al. Divergent anomaly in mesocorticolimbic dopaminergic circuits might be associated with different depressive behaviors, an animal study. *Brain Behav.* (2017) 7:e00808. doi: 10.1002/brb3.808
14. Lin LF, Doherty DH, Lile JD, Bektesh S, Collins F. GDNF: a glial cell line-derived neurotrophic factor for midbrain dopaminergic neurons. *Science* (1993) 260:1130–2. doi: 10.1126/science.8493557
15. Chermenina M, Schouten P, Nevalainen N, Johansson F, Orädd G, Strömberg I. GDNF is important for striatal organization and maintenance of dopamine neurons grown in the presence of the striatum. *Neuroscience* (2014) 270:1–11. doi: 10.1016/j.neuroscience.2014.04.008
16. Kumar A, Kopra J, Varendi K, Porokuokka LL, Panhelainen A, Kuure S, et al. GDNF overexpression from the native locus reveals its role in the nigrostriatal dopaminergic system function. *PLoS Genet.* (2015) 11:e1005710. doi: 10.1371/journal.pgen.1005710
17. Uchida S, Hara K, Kobayashi A, Otsuki K, Yamagata H, Hobara T, et al. Epigenetic status of in the ventral striatum determines susceptibility and adaptation to daily stressful events. *Neuron* (2011) 69:359–72. doi: 10.1016/j.neuron.2010.12.023
18. Zhang Y, Wang Y, Wang L, Bai M, Zhang X, Zhu X. Dopamine receptor D2 and associated microRNAs are involved in stress susceptibility and resistance to escitalopram treatment. *Int J Neuropsychopharmacol.* (2015) 18:1–10. doi: 10.1093/ijnp/pyv025
19. Wong ML, Licinio L. Research and treatment approaches to depression. *Nat Rev Neurosci.* (2001) 2:343–51. doi: 10.1038/35072566
20. Porsolt RD, Le Pichon M, Jalfre M. Depression: a new animal model sensitive to antidepressant treatments. *Nature* (1977) 266:730–2. doi: 10.1038/266730a0
21. Bai M, Zhang L, Zhu X, Zhang Y, Zhang S, Xue L. Comparison of depressive behaviors induced by three stress paradigms in rats. *Physiol Behav.* (2014) 131:81–6. doi: 10.1016/j.physbeh.2014.04.019
22. Ushijima K, Morikawa T, To H, Higuchi S, Ohdo S. Chronobiological disturbances with hyperthermia and hypercortisolism induced by chronic mild stress in rats. *Behav Brain Res002E* (2006) 173:326–30. doi: 10.1016/j.bbr.2006.06.038
23. Zhu X, Peng S, Zhang S, Zhang X. Stress-induced depressive behaviors are correlated with par-4 and drd2 expression in rat striatum. *Behav Brain Res.* (2011) 223:329–35. doi: 10.1016/j.bbr.2011.04.052
24. Enomoto H. Regulation of neural development by glial cell line-derived neurotrophic factor family ligands. *Anat Sci Int.* (2005) 80:42–52. doi: 10.1111/j.1447-073x.2005.00099.x
25. Mendez I, Dagher A, Hong M, Hebb A, Gaudet P, Law A, et al. Enhancement of survival of stored dopaminergic cells and promotion of graft survival by exposure of human fetal nigral tissue to glial cell line—derived neurotrophic factor in patients with Parkinson's disease. *J Neurosurg.* (2000) 92:863–9. doi: 10.3171/jns.2000.92.5.0863
26. Ostenfeld T, Tai YT, Martin P, Déglon N, Aebischer P, Svendsen CN. Neurospheres modified to produce glial cell line-derived neurotrophic factor increase the survival of transplanted dopamine neurons. *J Neurosci Res.* (2002) 69:955–65. doi: 10.1002/jnr.10396
27. Lin PY, Tseng PT. Decreased glial cell line-derived neurotrophic factor levels in patients with depression: a meta-analytic study. *J Psychiatr Res.* (2015) 63:20–7. doi: 10.1016/j.jpsychires.2015.02.004
28. Tsankova N, Renthal W, Kumar A, Nestler EJ. Epigenetic regulation in psychiatric disorders. *Nat Rev Neurosci.* (2007) 8:355–67. doi: 10.1038/nrn2132
29. Krishnan V, Nestler EJ. The molecular neurobiology of depression. *Nature* (2008) 455:894–902. doi: 10.1038/nature07455
30. Weaver IC, Cervoni N, Champagne FA, D'Alessio AC, Sharma S, Seckl JR, et al. Epigenetic programming by maternal behavior. *Nat Neurosci.* (2004) 7:847–54. doi: 10.1038/nn1276
31. Fyffe SL, Neul JL, Samaco RC, Chao HT, Ben-Shachar S, Moretti P, et al. Deletion of Mecp2 in Sim1-expressing neurons reveals a critical role for MeCP2 in feeding behavior, aggression, and the response to stress. *Neuron* (2008) 59:947–58. doi: 10.1016/j.neuron.2008.07.030
32. Jakobsson J, Cordero MI, Bisaz R, Groner AC, Busskamp V, Bensadoun JC, et al. KAP1-mediated epigenetic repression in the forebrain modulates behavioral vulnerability to stress. *Neuron* (2008) 60:818–31. doi: 10.1016/j.neuron.2008.09.036
33. LaPlant Q, Vialou V, Covington HE III, Dumitriu D, Feng J, Warren BL, et al. Dnmt3a regulates emotional behavior and spine plasticity in the nucleus accumbens. *Nat Neurosci.* (2010) 13:1137–43. doi: 10.1038/nn.2619

14

SiNiSan Ameliorates the Depression-Like Behavior of Rats that Experienced Maternal Separation Through 5-HT1A Receptor/CREB/BDNF Pathway

Kerun Cao[1], *Chongkun Shen*[1], *Yumei Yuan*[2], *Shasha Bai*[3], *Lei Yang*[3], *Lili Guo*[4], *Rong Zhang*[3*] *and Yafei Shi*[1*]

[1] School of Fundamental Medical Science, Guangzhou University of Chinese Medicine, Guangzhou, China, [2] Shenzhen Baoan Hospital of Chinese Medicine, Shenzhen, China, [3] Institute of Clinical Pharmacology, Guangzhou University of Chinese Medicine, Guangzhou, China, [4] Third Affiliated Hospital of Henan University of Chinese Medicine, Henan University of Chinese Medicine, Zhengzhou, China

***Correspondence:**
Rong Zhang
550267658@qq.com
Yafei Shi
446750173@qq.com

Background: Early adverse life stress is an important dangerous factor in the development of psychiatric disorders, particularly depression. Available clinical antidepressant agents, such as fluoxetine, [a selective serotonin reuptake inhibitor (SSRI)], are unsatisfactory because of their side effects. SiNiSan (SNS) is a classic Chinese medicine prescription regarded to disperse stagnated liver qi to relieve qi stagnation. Therefore, this study was designed to detect the effects and molecular mechanism of SNS treatment in rats subjected to maternal separation (MS).

Method: Male neonatal Wistar rats were divided into six groups including control + ddH_2O, MS + ddH_2O, MS + fluoxetine (5 g/kg), MS + SNS -low dose (2.5 g/kg), MS + SNS -medium dose (5 g/kg), MS + SNS -high dose (10 g/kg). The volume of drugs and ddH2O in each group are according to the weight of rats every day (10 mL/kg). Each group comprised 16 pups with 8 young and 8 adult pups. Except for the control group, all MS groups were separated from their mothers for 4 h/day from 9:00 to 13:00 during postnatal days (PNDs) 1 to 21. After MS, the six groups were intragastrically administered with ddH2O, fluoxetine, and different doses of SNS until PND 28 (for young pups) and PND 56 (for adult pups). The pups were weighed every day, and depression-like behavior was assessed by sucrose preference test, open field test, and forced swimming test. Serotonin 1A (5-HT1A) receptor, phosphorylated protein kinase A (p-PKA) substrate, cAMP response element-binding protein (CREB), p-CREB and brain-derived neurotrophic factor (BDNF) in the hippocampus were examined by Western blot, and *in situ* 5-HT1A receptor expression was measured by IHC.

Results: Young and adult MS rats exhibited depression-like behavior. However, the depression-like behavior was ameliorated by SNS in both age groups. The levels of 5-HT1A receptor, p-CREB, and BDNF in the hippocampus were reduced in young and adult MS rats. SNS treatment significantly up-regulated the expression of 5-HT1A receptor, p-CREB, and BDNF in the hippocampus of adult MS rats. However, few significant effects on the protein expression were observed in the young MS rats.

Conclusion: MS in infancy could develop depression-like behavior in young and adult. SNS treatment may perform antidepressant effects on young and adult MS rats through the BDNF/PKA/CREB pathway.

Keywords: SiNiSan, early life stress, depression, brain-derived neurotrophic factor, serotonin 1A receptor

INTRODUCTION

Adverse stress in early life is an important dangerous factor for suffering from many types of mental disease, such as depression, posttraumatic stress disorder, and schizophrenia. Several reports have shown that adversity in early life is closely related to the occurrence and development of depression, which is likely to be accompanied with impulsive, suicidal, and self-injurious behavior (1, 2). Maternal separation (MS) in rats, which temporarily deprives pups from their mothers to a new environment during lactation, has been established as a model to replicate early life adversity in animal experiments (3). MS has been suggested to induce depression-like behavior in rodents, such as behavioral despair during forced swimming test (FST) and anhedonia in sugar water preference test (4, 5). In addition, MS could trigger anxiety-like behavior in the open field test (OFT) (6). On one hand, for juvenile and adult rats, postnatal MS procedure could downregulate new born cells in the hippocampus and granule cells in the dentate gyrus of the hippocampus. Thus, MS may affect the development and neuroplasticity in the hippocampus of rats (7). These results indicate that the emotions and behavior of individuals could be significantly affected by postnatal MS in the long term.

The change in the serotonin system has been demonstrated to be closely related with mental disorders, but this relationship needs further investigation (8, 9). Serotonin 1A (5-HT1A) receptor is closely related to emotional disorders. Moreover, the brain-derived neurotrophic factor (BDNF) has been increasingly investigated for depression in animal models. BDNF is generally distributed in the hippocampus and participates in neurogenesis and development of the hippocampus. Previous study showed that the expression of BDNF in the hippocampus of rats that experienced postnatal MS declined with age but increased in the medial prefrontal cortex for normal rats. BDNF significantly decreased in these two regions during the early adulthood of rats (10). A systematic review of the change in BDNF expression using the social isolation model of rats revealed that BDFN could be downregulated in the hippocampus by stress during postnatal period but not altered in the cerebral cortex (11). Another study has reported the correlation of serotonin and BDNF and showed that these molecules played to some extent crucial roles in neuroplasticity and were associated with certain neurological diseases, especially during aging (12). Furthermore, the relative signaling pathways of BDNF caused by early life stress have been studied to explore the mechanism of depression and antidepressants. BDNF and CREB/BDNF signaling pathways, including the expression of BDNF, phospho-cAMP response element-binding protein (CREB) (pCREB), phospho-ERK1/2, phospho-Protein kinase B (AKT), and TrkB (a receptor of BDNF), were downregulated in the cerebral hippocampus of depression models that underwent stress (13, 14). Moreover, numerous studies have shown certain correlation between CREB and the pathogenesis of depression as well as the mechanism of antidepressants. CREB, which is regarded as a crucial transcription factor, could be activated by various signaling pathways. Protein kinase A (PKA), which is the upstream signal for CREB, may be associated with the pathogenesis of depression. Several studies have reported that the disorder of adenosine cyclophosphate (cAMP)-PKA-CREB-BDNF signaling pathway in the hippocampus of animals could be involved in the pathophysiological process of depression (15, 16).

Monoamine-based antidepressants, such as selective serotonin reuptake inhibitors (SSRIs), are frequently used for depression. However, SSRIs, such as fluoxetine, are unsatisfactory for depression because of their side effects, such as delayed onset of ~6–8 weeks after taking the medicine and the insensitivity for the drug by some patients (17, 18). In traditional Chinese medicine, the primary pathogenesis of depression is emotional upset and stagnation of qi in the liver. Depression belongs to melancholia in traditional Chinese medicine, and the treatment should be based on soothing the liver and relieving depression. SiNiSan comes from the Treatise on Febrile Diseases, and is mainly used to regulate the liver-qi. This compound is considered the most fundamental formula on soothing the liver and resolving depression. Moreover, several animal experiments have demonstrated the effects of SiNiSan on depressive behavior, such as recovering the loss of weight, anhedonia in sucrose preference test (SPT), and low activity in OFT for CUMS models (19). However, few studies have focused on the effect of SiNiSan treatment for depression triggered by early life adversity through the signaling pathway of 5-HT1A receptor/CREB/BDNF. Although these findings have indicated the depression-like behavior caused by postnatal MS and the effect of SiNiSan on depression, the effect of SiNiSan on depression induced by postnatal MS in young and adult rats is rarely investigated.

In the present study, we explored the effect of SiNiSan treatment on young and adult Wistar rats maternally separated during early development by behavioral tests and expression detection of several relative proteins in the 5-HT1A receptor/CREB/BDNF signaling pathway. The results provided valid evidence for the clinical use of SiNiSan on depressive patients who experienced MS during childhood.

MATERIALS AND METHODS

Animals

The 20 Wistar pregnant rats with 16-day gestation were bought from the Experimental Animal Center in Guangzhou University of Chinese Medicine and housed in a controlled environment. All animals were raised on a 12 h light/12 h dark cycle (lights on at 19:00) and with free access to food and water. The environmental conditions were maintained at 22°C and relative humidity of 40–70%. All pregnant rats produced ~8–10 pups per dam, and 91 male pups were selected from all 20 dams for the experiment. At the end of molding at postnatal day (PND) 21, the male pups were randomly divided into six groups based on the weight, namely, control group (non-MS), model group (MS administration), positive group (fluoxetine treatment), low-dose SNS treatment (SNS-L), medium-dose SNS treatment (SNS-M), and high-dose SNS treatment (SNS-H). All experimental procedures strictly followed the guidelines of the International Association for the Use of Animals in Research and permitted by the Committee of Animal Experiment Ethics Review in Guangzhou University of Chinese Medicine.

Maternal Separation

The day of birth was regarded as PND 0. The groups, except the control, were all maternally separated from PND 1 to PND 21, while the control group was undisturbed. This procedure was according to the method employed in a previous study (10). One male pup from each litter was randomly left in the cage with his mother, and marked as the control group (NMS group). The rest of the male pups were separated from their mothers to another room from PND 1 to PND 21 for 4 h per day (from 10:00 to 14:00). In addition, cotton was laid on the bottom plate of the pup cage to keep the pups warm from PND 1 to PND 10. During the separation, pups from the same litters were placed in the same pup cage but isolated from each other by several hardboards to avoid contact. After weaning at PND 21, the medicine group was administered with medicine intervention. All male rats underwent behavioral test during young stage (PND 22–28) and adult stage (PND 50–55) and sacrificed to gather complete brains and hippocampus for Western blot (WB) test and immunohistochemistry (IHC) at PND 28 and PND 56.

Drug Treatment

SNS is composed of four Chinese medicinal herbs, namely, Zhigancao, Zhishi, Chaihu, and Shaoyao with equal ratio at 1:1:1:1. SNS was bought from the First Affiliated Hospital of Guangzhou University of Chinese Medicine. The herbs were ground into coarse powder and soaked in ten times volume of ddH_2O more than the herb for 60 min. After boiling by strong fire, the herbs were heated by slow fire for 40 min. After cooling, the decoction was filtered using several layers of gauze to collect the colature concentrated to 1 g/mL of raw drug by a rotary evaporator. The Quality Control of Sinisan was performed by HPLC. It was performed on an Agilent Technologies 1260 Infinity system with a 1260 DAD VL detector at 240 nm. Kromasil Cl8 (250 mm × 4.6 mm, 5 μm) column was used and the temperature was set at 30°C. The mobile phase was consisted of acetonitrile (A) and water containing 0.1% phosphoric acid (B). A linear gradient elution program was used as follows: 0–10 min, 0%–10% A; 10–20 min, 20%–25% A; and 20–28 min, 25%–29% A, 28–40 min, 29%–40% A , 40–50 min, 40%–55% A, 50–60 min, 55%–73% A. The flow rate was set at 1.0 mL· min^{-1}. The injection volume was 10 μL (**Supplementary Materials**). Considering low dose as an equivalent dose, the low dose was calculated from the equivalent dose coefficient conversion on people and rats. The low, medium, and high doses of SNS were 0.25, 0.5, and 1 g/mL, respectively. Fluoxetine was bought from the First Affiliated Hospital of Guangzhou University of Chinese Medicine and dissolved in ddH_2O to 0.5 mg/mL, which also depended on the equivalent dose coefficient conversion on people and rats. After molding at PND 22, the groups were intragastrically intervened by ddH_2O, fluoxetine, and different doses of SNS rats until PND 28 (young rats) and PND 56 (adult rats). The process time points are shown in **Figure 1**.

Behavioral Test

Body Weight (BW)

The change in BW was compared with the baseline data measured at PND 21 to evaluate the impact of MS on the food preference. The data were recorded per day and measured on PNDs 21, 28, 35, 42, 49, and 56 to observe the weight variation and alteration in BW gain (**Figure 2**, **Table 1**).

Sucrose Preference Test

The preference of sucrose intake by the male rats was evaluated by the decrease in the consumption of sucrose water. This behavior has been considered as an indicator of anhedonia, which usually appears in depression (5, 6). All rats were exercised to adapt to 1% sucrose solution during the period of adaptation. For the first 2 days, the rats were provided two bottles of 1% sucrose solution for 24 h, and then one bottle of water and one 1% sucrose solution for the second 24 h with an exchange of bottles at half time. Then, following a 24 h period of food and water deprivation, all rats placed in individual cages were tested simultaneously with two pre-weighed bottles, one bottle of sucrose (1% w/v) and the other water, for 2 h. The two bottles were exchanged one time at the middle time. After the test, the bottles of 1% sucrose solution and water were reweighted and recorded to calculate the liquid consumption. Sucrose preference was calculated from the following formula as applied in previous studies: Sucrose preference = {Sucrose consumption (g)/[Sucrose consumption (g) + water consumption (g)]} × 100. SPT was measured on PND 24 and PND 54 per rat (20). Anhedonia was presented by reduced sucrose preference.

Open Field Test

General curiosity and detective activity of each rat were detected to assess the anxiety-like behavior during OFT as described in previous studies (6). The open field apparatus consisted of a 100×100 cm square space with black walls and black baseplate (The Spontaneous Activity Open Field, Guangzhou Feidi Biotechnology Co. LTD). Each rat was carefully placed at the center of the open field floor and allowed to move independently and explore freely for 3 min. To evaluate the ability of the rats to adapt to a new environment and the detective activities, the time and distance spent in the central

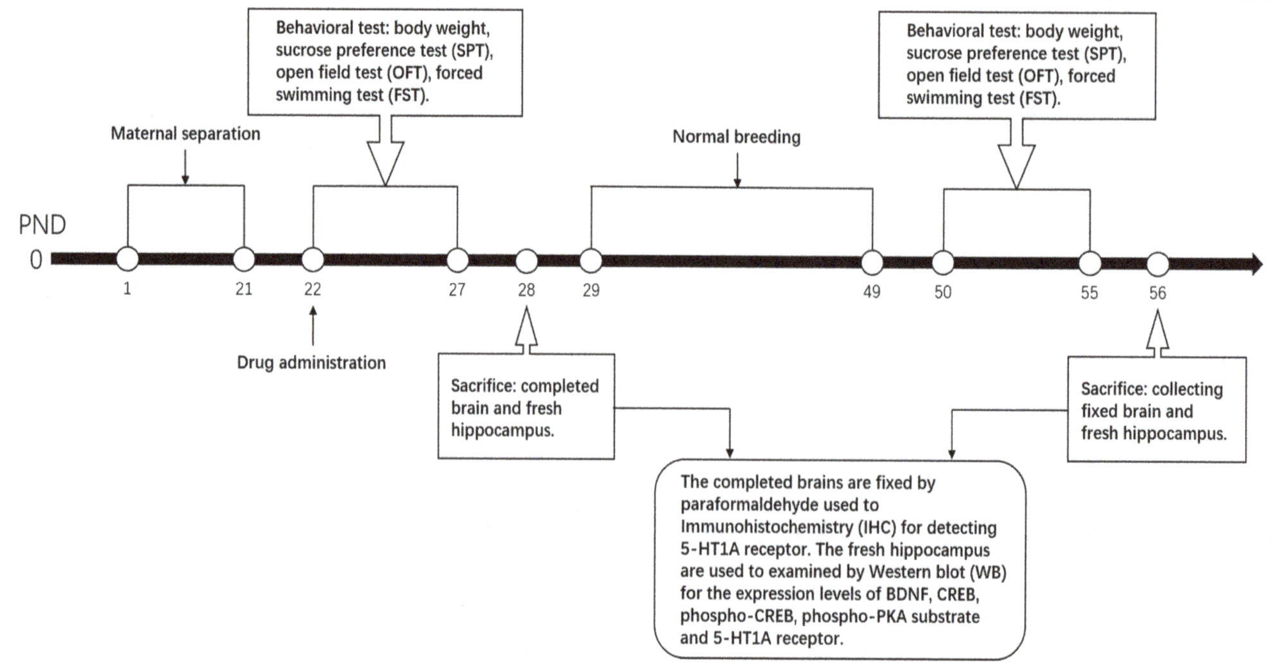

FIGURE 1 | Process time points. The process time points are shown by the timeline.

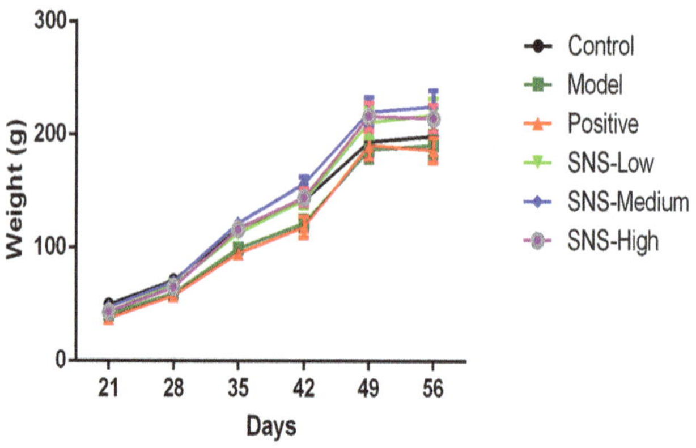

FIGURE 2 | Effects of SNS on the changes in body weight (BW). The effect of SNS on the changes in the BWs of MS male rats during PND21–26 was expressed in the graph. The weights on PND 21, 35, 42, 49, and 56 are presented as means ± SEM.

area were traced and recorded. These parameters are considered indices of locomotor activity. After each test, 75% ethyl alcohol was used to clean the urine and feces left behind by the other rats which could produce odor signals that would interfere the next rats to be tested. OFT was performed on PNDs 22 and 51.

Forced Swimming Test

The FST, especially for young rats, was originally described in a previous study (21). The rats were placed in a plexiglass cylinder with a diameter of 30 cm and a height of 50 cm. The cylinder was filled with ~30 cm of water at 23–26°C such that the rats could not touch the bottom of the cylinder. On the first day for exercise, the animals underwent a 15-min pre-test swim. After the pretest, the rats were immediately removed from the cylinder and mildly dried with a towel. After completely dried, the rats were returned to their home cages. On the second day after the pre-test, the rats were placed in a water-filled cylinder for the test, and the behavior was recorded by videotape for 5 min. The water in the cylinder was changed after each rat had been tested. After the test swim was completed, the rats were dried similarly as that during the pre-test. Then, the rats were returned to their cages until they were dried.

Biochemical Assays

Western Blot Analysis

The rats in the six groups were sacrificed on PNDs 28 and 56. The animals were anesthetized with an injection of 10% chloral hydrate (0.35 mL/100 g, i.p.). Then, all rats were sacrificed by decapitation. Six rats per group were administered decollation to gather the fresh hippocampus from the brain. The hippocampus was quickly frozen in liquid nitrogen and then transferred to an −80°C refrigerator for the WB, which was performed as follows. The samples were homogenized with RIPA lysis buffer (strong) which was added with protease inhibitor cocktail for protein extraction at a proportion of 1:100. Then, the supernatant was collected after centrifugation at 12,000 rpm under 4°C for 15 min. The total protein content was determined using BCA assay. After the quantitative determination and addition of loading buffer for the total protein content, the proteins of each sample in the Eppendorf tube were denatured in water at 100°C for 5 min. Subsequently, protein samples were fractionated through

TABLE 1 | The effects of SNS on weight increase of MS male rats (g).

	PND28	PND35	PND42	PND49	PND56
Control	21.64 ± 1.00	66.73 ± 1.85*	92.43 ± 3.34	147.40 ± 3.09	152.31 ± 2.62
Model	18.24 ± 0.80	58.36 ± 2.77	80.72 ± 5.32	148.80 ± 8.97	152.86 ± 8.57
Positive	19.98 ± 1.13	57.82 ± 2.98	81.13 ± 7.36	149.88 ± 8.04	145.74 ± 6.90
SNS-low	23.98 ± 1.76	68.69 ± 2.81*	98.46 ± 6.67*	168.73 ± 11.21	175.69 ± 12.14
SNS-medium	22.51 ± 2.06	71.88 ± 2.11*	107.47 ± 6.23**	175.68 ± 9.74	180.53 ± 10.93
SNS-high	21.81 ± 1.30	70.62 ± 2.40*	99.03 ± 6.56*	172.36 ± 8.66	170.64 ± 8.61

*The body weights of all male rats were weighed per day from PND 21 after MS. The data of PND 21 were used as the starting point. Weight gain was measured on weeks 1, 2, 3, 4, and 5 at the age of PND 28, 35, 42, and 56. Differences were analyzed by one-way ANOVA with Fisher's LSD. Data are presented as means ±SEM. *P < 0.05, **P < 0.01 compared with the model group (statistically significant).*

12% SDS-polyacrylamide gel electrophoresis. The proteins of samples were electro-transferred onto polyvinylidene difluoride membranes with constant current at 300 mA for 75 min. The membranes were blocked with 5% bull serum albumin-TBST for 3 h at room temperature. Protein expression was detected by incubation with rabbit polyclonal primary antibodies against BDNF (1:1,500), CREB (1:1,000), pCREB(1:1,000), pPKA substrate (1:1,000), 5-HT1A receptor (1:1,000), and rat polyclonal primary antibody GAPDH (1:5,000) at 4°C overnight. After incubation with the primary antibody, the membranes were incubated with goat anti-rabbit HRP-conjugated IgG (1:3000–5,000) and goat anti-rat HRP-conjugated IgG (1: 5,000) at room temperature for 1 h. All antibodies were dissolved in 0.5% blocking reagent. The bound antibodies were expressed using an enhanced chemiluminescence reagent by ECL kit (BIO-RAD Molecular Imager™ XRS+) and quantified using Image Lab™ software. The experiments were performed four times with four samples per group. In the WB analysis, GAPDH was used as loading control to normalize the levels of target protein detected. The mean optical density value of each protein band relative to that of the GAPDH band from the same sample was calculated.

Immunohistochemistry (IHC)

After sacrificing on PNDs 28 and 56, two rats from each group were administered with 4% paraformaldehyde solution perfusion to collect the complete brain samples. The samples were stored in the perfusion solution for IHC. Briefly, IHC was performed such that the fixed brain tissue with 4% paraformaldehyde solution was separated from the hippocampus, that is, 1.30–5.30 mm from the bregma. Then, the brain samples were dehydrated thrice for 30 min using different concentrations of ethyl alcohol (70, 90, 96, and 100%) and xylene and set in paraffin. After dewaxing by xylene twice for 8 min, ethanol (70, 80, 95, and 100%) for 5 min, and distilled water for 3 min, the sections were put into citrate buffer solution (0.01 M pH 6.0) and heated in a microwave oven. The slides were blocked using 6.5% BSA for 30 min at room temperature (RT) and incubated in a first rabbit anti-5-HT1A receptor polyclonal IgG (1:500) at 4°C overnight. After washing thrice in 0.05 M PBS for 5 min at RT, the sections were incubated with a secondary goat anti-rabbit IgG (1:1,000) for 1 h at RT and incubated in an avidin—biotin—peroxidase complex for 1 h. Finally, the sections were dehydrated by serial rinsing with alcohol, dewaxed in dimethyl and benzene, and cover-slipped. Results were scanned by 3D HISTECH Pannoramic 250, MADE IN Hungary.

Statistical Analysis

Statistical significance was assessed using one-way ANOVA followed by Fisher's least significant difference (LSD) analysis with $P < 0.05$ as statistically significant. SPSS was used for statistical analysis. Data were expressed as means ± standard error of the mean (SEM).

RESULTS

Effects of SNS on Body Weight

Several variations in BW of the male rats were observed from PND 21 to PND 56. The BWs of all male rats were weighed per day from PND 21 after MS. The lower BW was shown in the model group than the control group after MS. The BWs of the MS male rats presented relatively slow weight gain compared with the control group. However, the three groups administered with SNS showed more rapid increase in BW in a dose-dependent manner from PND 42 to PND 56 than model group (**Figure 2**). MS significantly restrained the increase in weight of these male rats on PND 35. The weight gain of the MS male rats was markedly decreased compared with the control rats from PND 21 to PND 35 ($P < 0.05$). Meanwhile, compared with the model group, the male rats in the three SNS-treated groups gained more weight on PND 35 ($P < 0.05$). In addition, from PND 21 to PND 42, the BWs of the three SNS-treated groups significantly increased compared with the model group (SNS-L and SNS-H, $P < 0.05$; SNS-M, $P < 0.01$). Moreover, no significant differences were observed among the six groups from PND 21 to PND 28, 49, and 56 (**Table 1**).

Effects of SNS on Anhedonia

SPT was performed for 2 h on PND 28 and PND 56 for the young and adult stages, respectively, to evaluate depression-like behavior. MS contributed to anhedonia in both stages. SNS-H and SNS-L treatments alleviated the depressive behavior in young and adult MS male rats. Among the young MS male rats, specific consumption of 1% sugar water in the model group was markedly reduced compared with the control group ($P < 0.05$). However, data from the SNS-H group showed significantly reversed results compared with MS rats without

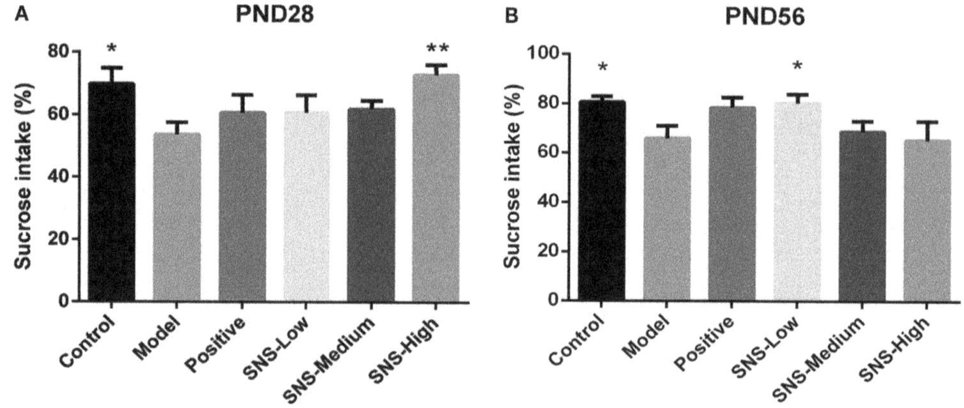

FIGURE 3 | Effects of SNS on the anhedonia of MS male rats during the sucrose preference test (SPT). The animals were examined by the reduction of 1% sucrose consumption on PND 28 **(A)** and PND 56 **(B)**. The values were analyzed by one-way ANOVA with Fisher's least significant difference (LSD) from 6 young rats and 5 adult rats per group. Data are expressed as means ± SEM. $^*P < 0.05$, $^{**}P < 0.01$ vs. model (statistically significant).

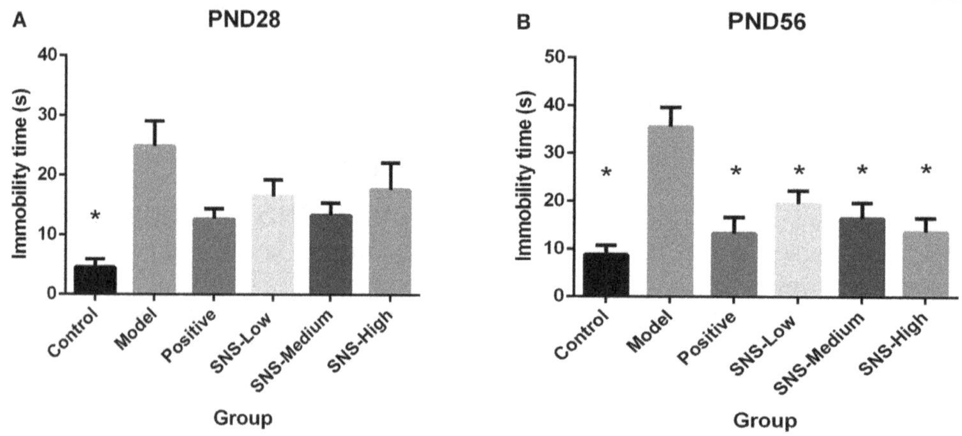

FIGURE 4 | Effects of SNS on the behavioral despair of MS male rats during the forced swimming test (FST). The rats were assessed by immobility time on PND 28 **(A)** and PND 56 **(B)**. Data were analyzed by one-way ANOVA with Fisher's LSD from 6 young rats and 5 adult rats per group and expressed as means ± SEM. $^*P < 0.05$ vs. model (statistically significant).

treatment ($P < 0.01$) (**Figure 3A**). Compared with the control group, specific consumption of 1% sugar water of the adult male rats in the model group was significantly decreased ($P < 0.05$). Nevertheless, SNS-L treatment on the MS male rats markedly increased the consumption of 1% sugar water compared with the model group ($P < 0.05$) (**Figure 3B**).

Effects of SNS on Behavioral Despair

FST was used to assess the depression-like behaviors on PND 28 and PND 56 for the young and adult stages, respectively. All male rats underwent FST for 5 min after a 15 min pre-test session on the day before. MS induced behavioral despair on both stages. However, medication administration did not affect this depressive behavior during FST for young MS male rats, but relief of behavioral despair was observed for adult MS male rats. On PND 28, the immobility time of the MS male rats in the model group was significantly augmented compared with the control male rats ($P < 0.05$). However, only reduced immobility time was observed in the MS male rats in all drug intervention groups, compared with the MS male rats in the model group, but without statistical significance (**Figure 4A**). The immobility duration of the adult male rats in the model group was markedly increased compared with that in the control group ($P < 0.05$), but significant decrease in immobility time was observed in the MS male rats in all drug intervention groups ($P < 0.05$) (**Figure 4B**).

Effects of SNS on Anxiety-Like Behavior

OFT was performed on PND 28 and 56 to evaluate the anxiety-like behavior. MS induced anxiety-like behavior in the MS adult male rats during OFT, and fluoxetine mitigated this behavior. The results showed that the central region time and distance of young male rats had no marked differences among the six groups, only a decreasing tendency was observed in the model group

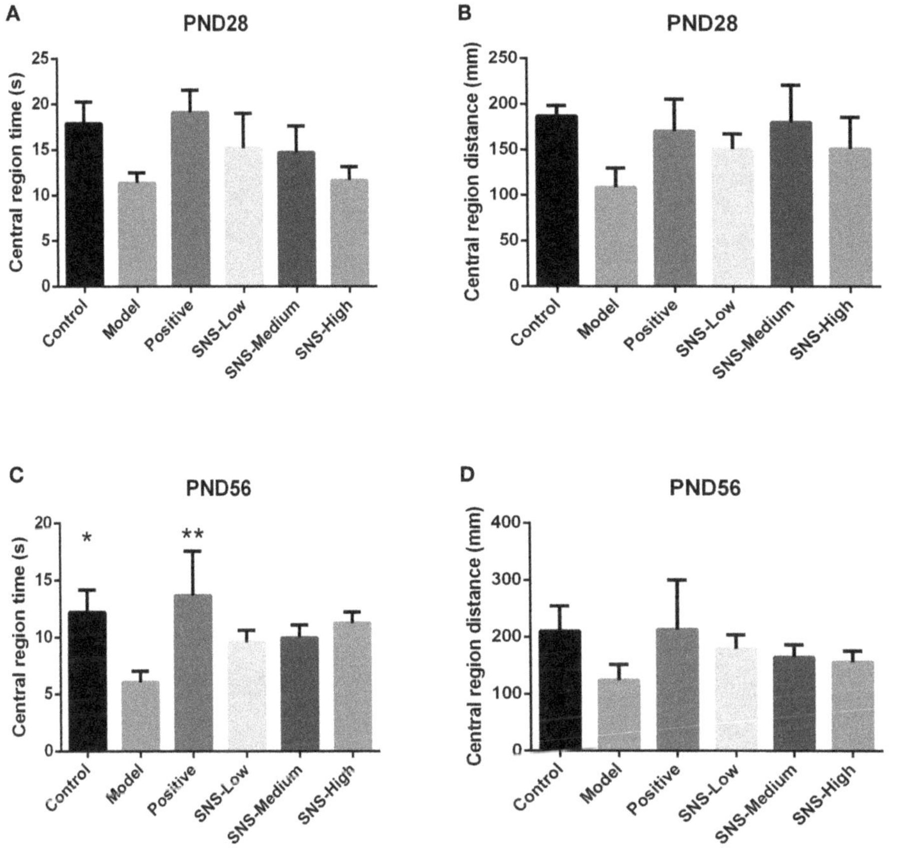

FIGURE 5 | Effects of SNS on the anxiety-like behavior of MS male rats. The animals were evaluated by the time spent at the central region on PND 28 **(A)** and PND 56 **(C)** and the distance within the central region on PND 28 **(B)** and PND 56 **(D)** in the open field test (OFT). Data were analyzed by one-way ANOVA with Fisher's LSD from 5 to 8 rats per group and are shown as means ± SEM. **P* < 0.05 and ***P* < 0.01 vs. model (statistically significant).

vs. the control group and increased in the positive, SNS-L, SNS-M, and SNS-H groups vs. the model group (**Figures 5A,B**). For the adult male rats during OFT, the MS rats in the model group exhibited significant decline in the central region time compared with the control rats, and comparing with MS rats in model group the data from MS rats treated by fluoxetine were significantly reversed ($P < 0.05$, **Figure 5C**). However, significant differences were not found in the central region distance in the adult male rats, which only showed a trend similar to that in the central region time (**Figure 5D**).

Impact of SNS on 5-HT1A Receptor by Immunohistochemistry

The expression of 5-HT1A receptor in the CA1 region of the hippocampus of the male rats was detected by IHC (**Figure 5**). MS triggered the decrease in 5-HT1A receptor expression in the CA1 region in the hippocampus of young (PND 28) and adult (PND 56) male rats compared with control rats without MS. However, the expression was upregulated by SNS treatment on MS rats compared with model group. The results show that the expression of 5-HT1A receptor was slightly reduced in the CA1 of hippocampus of the male rats subjected to MS at PND 28 compared with control rats. This phenomenon was reversed by fluoxetine and medium and high SNS doses compared with MS rats but no treatment (**Figure 6**). On PND 56, the expression of 5-HT1A receptor was obviously downregulated by MS in the CA1 region of hippocampus of adult male rats compared with control group. The downregulation of 5-HT1A receptor expression in the CA1 in the hippocampus of adult male rats subjected to MS was reversed by fluoxetine and SNS treatment compared with model group (**Figure 7**).

Impact of SNS on BDNF Signal Pathway at PND28

The results indicated that, compared with the young male rats in the control group, the expression of pCREB (**Figure 8D**) and BDNF (**Figure 8B**) in the cerebral hippocampus of MS rats was significantly downregulated ($P < 0.05$), but without statistical significance for the medication treatment groups compared with the model group. The expression of 5-HT1A receptor in the cerebral hippocampus of young male rats in the model group was downregulated by MS compared with that in the control group, but fluoxetine and SNS administration reversed this downregulation, compared with the MS rats in the

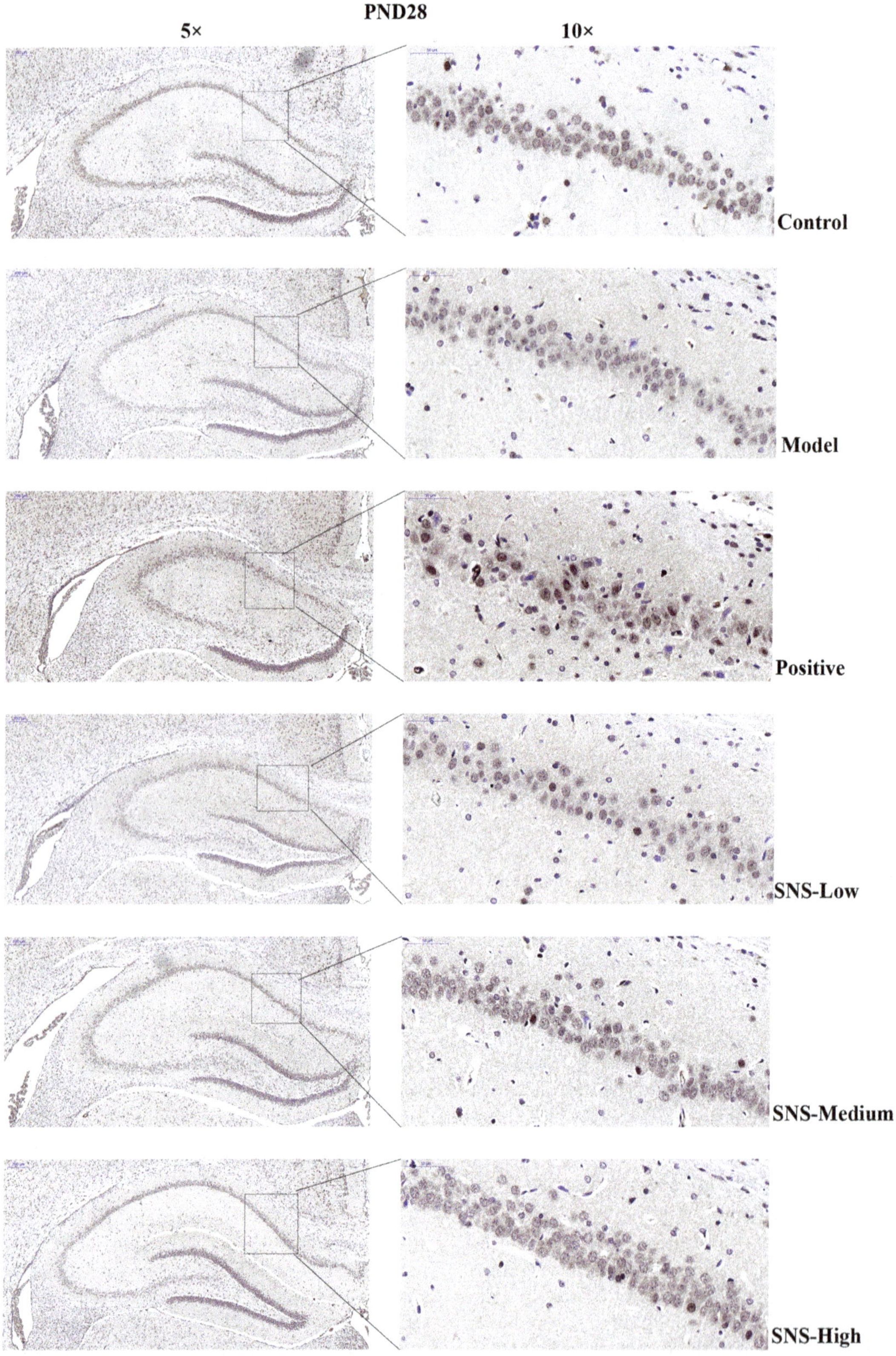

FIGURE 6 | Change in the hippocampal 5-HT1A receptor expression of rats on PND 28 by immunohistochemistry (IHC). The effects of SNS treatment on 5-HT1A receptor expression in the CA1 area of cerebral hippocampus of MS male rats on PND28 as shown by IHC. Scale bar = 50 μm.

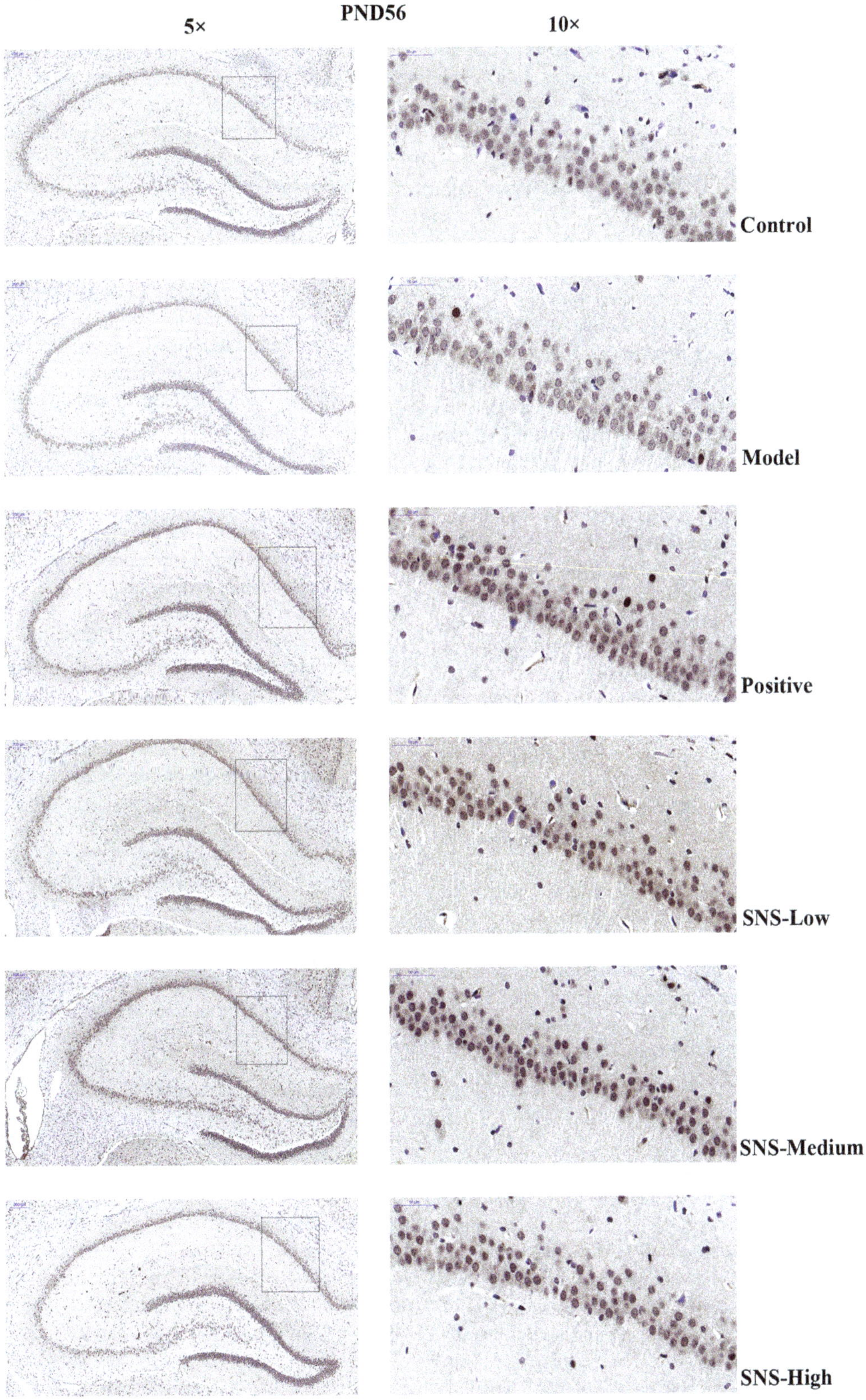

FIGURE 7 | Change in the expression of hippocampal 5-HT1A receptor of rats on PND 56 by IHC. The effects of SNS treatment on 5-HT1A receptor expression in the CA1 area of cerebral hippocampus of MS male rats on PND56 as shown by IHC. Scale bar = 50 μm.

model group. These results are without statistical significance (**Figure 8F**). Nevertheless, the expression of CREB (**Figure 8C**) and pPKA substrate in the cerebral hippocampus of adult male rats (**Figure 8E**) showed no marked differences among the groups. In addition, the bands of these proteins are expressed in **Figure 8A**.

Impact of SNS on BDNF Signal Pathway at PND56

The results of CREB/BDNF signal pathway of cerebral hippocampus in adult male rats were analyzed (**Figure 8**). CREB/BDNF signal pathway in the cerebral hippocampus of adult male rats was downregulated by MS compared with control rats, and SNS treatment reversed this downregulation on MS rats compared with the MS rats in model group. The results showed that the expression of 5-HT1A receptor was significantly decreased in the cerebral hippocampus of adult MS male rats in the model group compared with the control group, and SNS treatment markedly reversed the downregulation compared with the MS rats in the model group (**Figure 9F**). No significant differences were found in the expression of CREB in the cerebral hippocampus of adult male rats between the control and model groups. However, fluoxetine and low SNS dose administration significantly upregulated CREB expression of MS rats compared with MS rats in the model group ($P < 0.05$, $P < 0.01$; **Figure 9C**). One-way ANOVA demonstrated that the expression of pCREB in the cerebral hippocampus of adult male rats was markedly decreased in the model group compared with control group, which was significantly reversed by low and medium doses SNS compared with the MS rats in model group ($P < 0.05$; **Figure 9D**). The expression of pPKA substrate in the cerebral hippocampus of adult male rats was downregulated in the MS rats in the model group vs. the control group but upregulated in the MS rats administered with medication vs. the untreated MS rats in model group (**Figure 9E**). MS markedly reduced the expression of BDNF in the cerebral hippocampus of adult male rats compared with the control rats. Meanwhile, low and medium doses of SNS significantly upregulated the BDNF expression compared with the MS rats in the model group ($P < 0.05$; **Figure 9B**). All protein bands are shown in **Figure 9A**.

DISCUSSION

In present study, we manifested several attractive findings on the antidepressant effect of SNS treatment from the results of behavior and molecular level in depressive rats. The MS paradigm used for the animal model of depression in this study has been considered as a classic depressive model for early life stress on rats (22). Our study was aimed to illustrate the effects of SNS on depression-like behavior of both young and adult rats that experienced MS during the postnatal period. Moreover, we further detected the relative proteins of potential signaling pathway involved in the mechanism of depressive symptoms and the antidepressant effect of SNS. Thus, the results might present a new discovery that may guide the clinical medication for new therapy for depression caused by trauma during childhood.

Antidepressant Effect of SNS

In our study, the BW was measured from PND 21 pre-treatment and throughout the whole experiment. The weights of the MS rats presented a lower trend than normal rats and MS rats administered with SNS from PND 21 to PND 56. However, fluoxetine exerted no effects on weight in MS rats (**Figure 2**). From the BW gain of rats with the baseline at PND 21, MS reduced the BW gain at PNDs 28, 35, 42, 49, and 56, but SNS treatment reversed this process. However, compared with the MS group, the fluoxetine group exhibited no increasing trend in the BW gain, although significant statistical difference was only observed on PND 35 (**Table 1**). The results showed that SNS could improve the loss of weight in MS rats during the growth stage until adulthood, which showed that the MS rats could develop some symptoms, such as eating less and losing weight, whereas SNS might ameliorate this appetite and nutrition condition in MS rats. The result on weight was consistent with several studies which have indicated that the postnatal MS could reduce the weight gain compared with normal breast-feeding in rats and caused under nutrition accompanied with the damage to insulin-like growth factor-1 (IGF-1) levels and growth and alteration of the hippocampus (23, 24). Meanwhile, a recent study manifested the effect of SNS on the psychological stress and stress-related nonalcoholic fatty liver disease. The results indicated that the SNS group administered with long-term chronic restraint stress showed a significant increase in BW gain compared with the stress group (25). However, the absence of effect of fluoxetine on the loss of weight in MS rats may be attributed to the enhanced satiety for food and restrain hunger-related pathways, as previously reported (26).

SPT and FST are usually applied to rats to evaluate depression-like behavior and antidepressant effect. The effect of SNS on mental disorders and chronic stress-related diseases, such as depression, has been already demonstrated in some studies, but age specificity was not mentioned (27, 28). Our results indicated that young and adult MS rats exhibited anhedonia during SPT as shown by the reduced sucrose consumption and behavioral despair during FST as shown by augmented immobility time. The effect of fluoxetine and SNS on depression-like behavior could be observed in young (PND 28) and adult (PND 56) MS rats. Fluoxetine and SNS treatment resulted in increased sucrose consumption during SPT and reduced immobility time during FST, when compared with the untreated MS rats. For the young rats, only high SNS dose significantly improved anhedonia during SPT, which was observed in the low dose group for adult rats (**Figure 3**). During FST, although all SNS and fluoxetine groups showed significantly higher immobility time compared with the MS group in adult rats, SNS and fluoxetine increased the immobility time of young MS rats but without statistical significant difference (**Figure 4**). However, no significant difference was found between the SNS and fluoxetine groups in all rats. These findings illustrated that SNS could take effect on depression-like behaviors depending on the doses and duration of treatment for rats that experienced early life stress, such as MS. In addition, the reason why the effect of fluoxetine on depression-like behaviors only emerged in adult rats presented by FST might due to its side-effect, such as

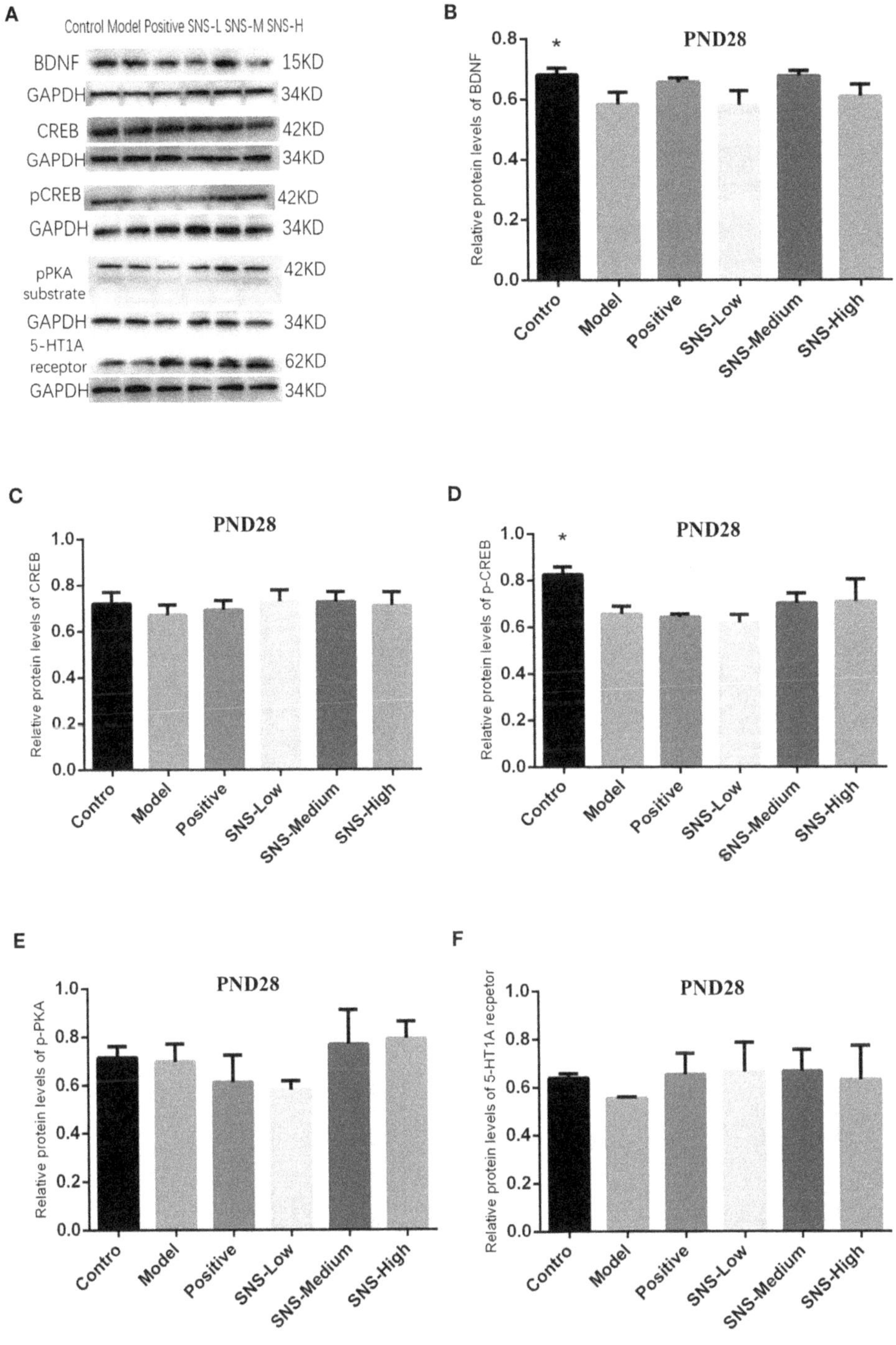

FIGURE 8 | Impacts of SNS on the expression of 5-HT1A receptor/CREB/BDNF in MS rats on PND 28. Impacts of SNS treatments on the 5-HT1A receptor/CREB/BDNF signaling in the cerebral hippocampus of MS male rats on PND 28. The bands of protein in the hippocampus of each group tested by Western blot (WB) are shown in **(A)**. Differences were analyzed by one-way ANOVA with Fisher's LSD. The results are presented as means ± SEM. The relative protein levels of the brain-derived neurotrophic factor (BDNF) **(B)**, cAMP-response element binding protein (CREB) **(C)**, phospho-CREB (pCREB) **(D)**, phospho-protein kinase A (pPKA) substrate **(E)**, and serotonin 1A (5-HT1A) receptor **(F)** in the cerebral hippocampus of young (PND28) male rats of each group (n = 4) were detected by WB. *P < 0.05 compared with the model group.

delayed onset time (29). Nevertheless, only a few studies have focused on the onset time of SNS treatment on mental disorders, especially for emotional diseases induced by early life stress. This investigation is needed to be the next step to provide evidence for clinical medication. In addition, no statistical differences were found on the time and distance spent during

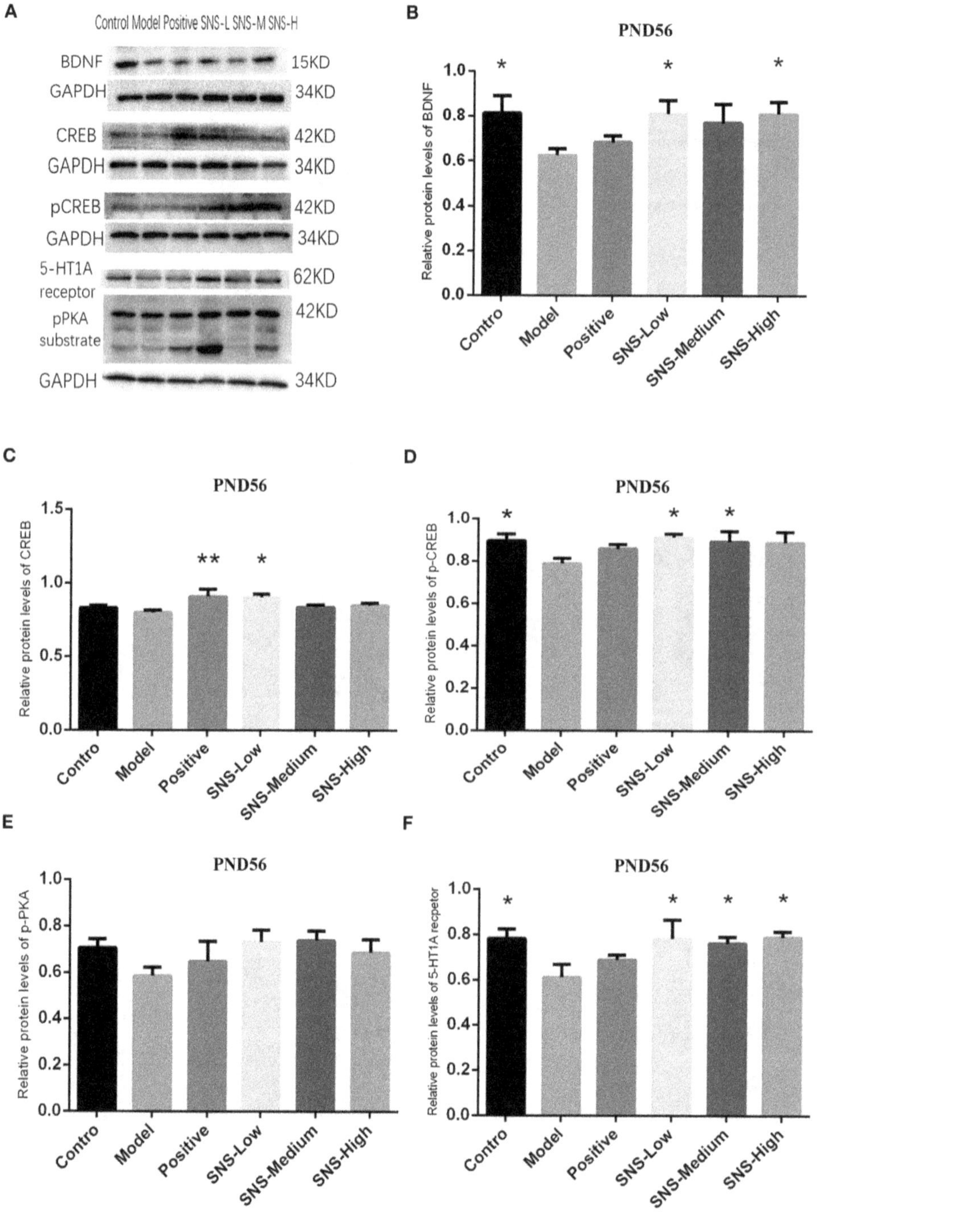

FIGURE 9 | Impacts of SNS on the expression of 5-HT1A receptor/CREB/BDNF in MS rats on PND56. Impacts of SNS treatments on the 5-HT1A receptor/CREB/BDNF signaling in the cerebral hippocampus of MS male rats on PND 56. The bands of protein in the hippocampus of each group tested by WB are shown in **(A)**. Differences were analyzed by one-way ANOVA with Fisher's LSD. The results are shown as means ± SEM. The relative protein levels of BDNF **(B)**, CREB **(C)**, pCREB **(D)**, pPKA substrate **(E)**, and 5-HT1A receptor **(F)** expression in the cerebral hippocampus of adult (PND56) male rats of each group ($n = 4$) were assessed by WB. $^{*}P < 0.05$, $^{**}P < 0.01$ compared with the model group.

OFT between MS and normal rats for young rats but with decreasing trend. However, for adult rats, the time, rather than distance spent, at the central area were significantly decreased by MS. Meanwhile, although SNS treatment increased the time and distance spent at the central area in the young and adult rats, no statistical difference was found in the improvement of anxious symptom for the fluoxetine group, which showed marked increase in these two indicators (**Figure 5**) During OFT, no statistical differences were found probably because of the insufficient sample size. Therefore, our results during OFT could indicate that the impact of MS on anxiety-like behavior might emerge from the young stage to the adult stage, and SNS could alleviate this symptom to some extent. Only a few studies have focused on the effect of SNS to mitigate the depression-like behavior of young rats. Nevertheless, a previous study reported that modified SNS treatment (from PND 24 to PND 51) relatively improved the depression-like behavior of adolescent rats maternally deprived from PND 1 to PND21, followed by chronic unpredictable stress from PND 24 to PND 51. The improvement was observed in weight assessment, SPT, OFT, and the level of hypothalamic pituitary adrenal (HPA) axis (30). Similar to the present study, several previous studies illustrated the antidepressant effect of SNS and its active ingredients on chronic unpredictable stress rats expressed by behavioral tests, such as SPT, FST, OFT, or tail suspension test, during adulthood. SNS could improve anhedonia, behavioral despair, and anxiety-like behavior of adult rats (31–33). Therefore, SNS may be used to treat emotional diseases, especially the depression caused by early life adversity.

Role of PKA/CREB/BDNF Pathway on Antidepressant of SNS

The BDNF plays an important role on neurogenesis, neuroplasticity, and nerve cell survival in the hippocampus, which is closely associated with the pathogenesis of depression and involved in the mechanism of antidepressant (34–36). Previous studies showed that the PKA-CREB-BDNF pathway and the phosphorylation of PKA and CREB proteins in the hippocampus could be downregulated by CUMS, whereas the expression of these proteins was normalized by traditional Chinese prescription or its active ingredient (37). Moreover, the role of 5-HT1A receptor, as a crucial receptor of serotonin system regarded as the major mechanism of mood modification under stress, has been previously reported. The 5HT1A receptor played an important role in the neurogenesis and synapse formation probably by activating certain signaling pathways and may be linked to a certain deficit in behavior and cognition (38). Thus, we paid attention to the alterations in 5-HT1AR and BDNF, as well as the relative protein on the relative pathway (including the pPKA substrate, CREB, and pCREB), influenced by SNS treatment on MS-induced depressive rats. In the present study, SNS administration influenced the 5-HT1A receptor/pPKA substrate/CREB/BDNF signaling pathway in the cerebral hippocampus of MS rats on PND 28 (young) and PND 56 (adult) as shown by the measured expression of the 5HT1A receptor, pPKA substrate, CREB, pCREB, and BDNF protein.

First, at PND 28, the IHC results showed that the expression of 5-HT1A receptor in the hippocampal CA1 area was reduced by postnatal MS but reversed by fluoxetine and high dose SNS (**Figure 6**). Moreover, MS also downregulated the hippocampal expression of the 5-HT1A receptor, CREB, pCREB, and BDNF protein. However, statistical significant difference was found only on pCREB and BDNF, compared with the control rats, as shown by the WB test. Although SNS upregulated the hippocampal expression of 5-HT1A receptor, CREB, pCREB and BDNF protein, compared with untreated MS rats, no significant differences were observed among these proteins (**Figure 8**). One previous study suggested that MS could impair the synaptogenesis with decreased spine formation and maturation during the early development of brain in postnatal period. This phenomenon may be mediated by downregulating the BDNF/ERK signaling pathway and may produce certain impairment of hippocampal-dependent learning ability (39). The impairment of MS on the function of cerebral hippocampus, which is as a crucial region involving the mechanism of depression, may emerge during the early development of rats. Thus, the evidence provided in (39) is consistent with our findings, that is, postnatal MS could impair the pCREB/BDNF expression in the hippocampus of MS-induced depressive rats emerging in early development. Thus, during the young stage, MS reduced the hippocampal phosphorylation of CREB such that enough transcription of BDNF gene could not be activated. Thus, the depression-like behavior caused by postnatal MS accompanied alterations in the BDNF upstream signaling pathway in young rats. However, although SNS or fluoxetine treatment did not significantly mitigate the 5HT1A receptor-pPKA substrate-CREB-pCREB-BDNF pathway in the hippocampus of MS rats, compared with the model group, medium and high SNS doses partly restored the expression of 5-HT1A receptor, CREB, pCREB, and BDNF (**Figure 8**). Only a few studies have investigated the antidepressant effect of SNS on the BDNF relative signaling pathway for MS-induced depressive rats during young stage at PND 28. The present results on young rats may indicate that the impairment of 5HT1A receptor-pPKA substrate-CREB-pCREB-BDNF pathway could not be completely recovered by SNS and fluoxetine for only 1 week treatment, although the depressive symptoms were alleviated by high SNS dose for a week. This result could account for the delayed onset of the antidepressant drug for at least 2 weeks of drug administration. This phenomenon was also reported by a previous study on the effect of active components in SNS for chronic stress induced-depression (40).

Then, up to the adulthood of rats at PND 56, the expression of 5-HT1A receptor in the hippocampal CA1 area was downregulated by MS during early life but reversed by fluoxetine and SNS treatment in IFC (**Figure 7**). Furthermore, we found that 5-HT1A receptor, phosphor-CREB, and BDNF expression were significantly downregulated by postnatal MS in adult rats, and the expression of CREB and pPKA substrate was reduced only with downtrend compared with the non-MS group, as shown by WB analysis. After drug treatment for 5 weeks, SNS significantly restored the expression of 5-HT1A receptor, CREB, pCREB, and BDNF expression and slightly upregulated the pPKA substrate expression in the MS adult rats but without dose specificity. In addition, fluoxetine slightly upregulated these proteins, except for CREB with significant difference compared with the model rats (**Figure 9**). Thus, MS during early life could generate long-term impacts on the expression of upstream relative protein of BDNF in the hippocampus of rats during adulthood, which coincided with their depression-like behavior. SNS treatment on the MS rats may improve the pCREB/BDNF pathway, which is activated by increased 5-HT1A receptor for adult rats that experienced early life stress. A recent study has illustrated that CREB/BDNF signaling pathway was involved in the mechanism of antidepressant effect. The increased ratio of p-CREB/CREB and mBDNF/proBDNF expression in the hippocampus might contribute to the therapeutic effects on the lipopolysaccharide-intervention rats (41). In addition, similar to the present results, the results from an assay showed that MS could trigger the depression-like behavior accompanied with downregulated CREB/BDNF expression and mRNA level of BDNF (42). Moreover, several studies have stated that antidepressant administration, including physical and Chinese herbs, mitigated depressive behavior by increasing 5HT1A receptor-mediated cAMP/PKA/CREB pathway in the hippocampus of rats that underwent chronic stress for adults, in accordance with our results on MS adult rats (43, 44). A previous research on the effect of SNS treatment on the depression caused by chronic stress also showed that the SNS administration group had significantly higher expression of 5-HT1A receptor than the model group (45). *In vitro* study on the antidepressant mechanism demonstrated that Jiawei SNS exhibited nerve protection and antidepressant effect by upregulating the expression of CREB and pCREB on PC12 cell stressed by corticosterone and glutamate (46). Therefore, our results indicated that the depression-like behaviors in the young and adult rats which experienced early life stress could be alleviated different doses of SNS by regulating the 5-HT1A receptor/CREB/BDNF signaling pathway. However, whether pPKA substrate could be significantly altered under MS and SNS treatment could not be observed just with the trend on PND 56, probably because the antibody we applied was a substrate protein instead of the original pPKA. The substrate protein of pPKA contained the pCREB that was activated

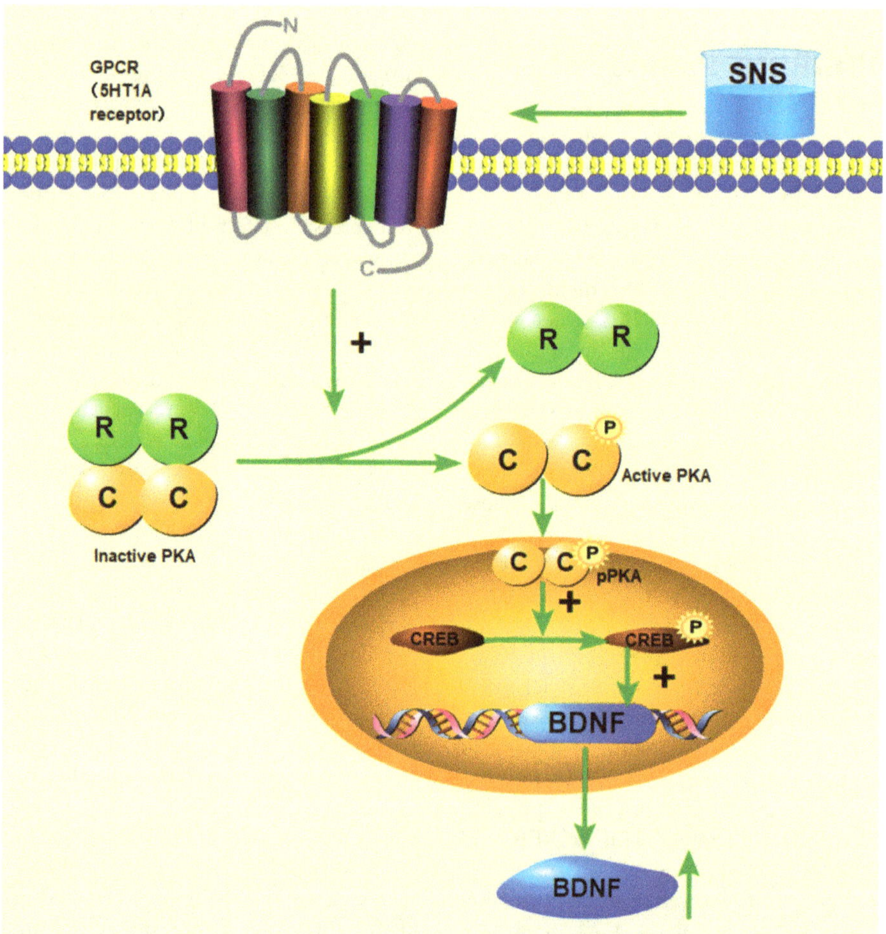

FIGURE 10 | Abridged general view of the potential pathway for the effect of SNS. The mechanism of antidepressant effect for SNS is illustrated. SNS upregulated the 5-HT1A receptor expression, which in turn activated the phosphorylation of PKA. The activation of pPKA mediated the phosphorylation of CREB. Then, pCREB transcribed the expression of the BDNF gene, upregulated the production of BDNF to benefit the hippocampal neurogenesis, and alleviated the mental disorders closely related to the hippocampus.

by pPKA. Therefore, to some degree, the significant change on pCREB may reflect the effect of MS/SNS on the pPKA substrate. This phenomenon needs further verification by co-immunoprecipitation in our next study. The above results show that the antidepressant effect of SNS on maternal separation rats may work through upregulating the 5-HT1A receptor expression which in turn activated the phosphorylation of PKA. The activation of pPKA mediated the phosphorylation of CREB. Then, pCREB transcribed the expression of the BDNF gene, upregulated the production of BDNF to benefit the hippocampal neurogenesis, and alleviated the mental disorders closely related to the hippocampus (**Figure 10**).

CONCLUSION

In summary, our study still needs to further expound the mechanism of onset time and concentration of SNS on MS models, especially on the pPKA/CREB/BDNF pathway mediated by 5-HT1A receptor and the impacts on the hippocampal neurogenesis. The results showed the positive effects of SNS on the MS-induced depression-like behavior. The present study elucidated the antidepressant effect of traditional Chinese medicine SNS for depression, which may be used for young and adult individuals who have experienced adversity in early life. Importantly, our data first illustrated that the regulation of the hippocampal 5-HT1A receptor/CREB/BDNF pathway may contribute to the antidepressant effect of SNS. Therefore, our findings may provide evidence and clinical guidance to formulate an effective therapy for children and adults undergoing depression caused by stress during early life adversity.

ETHICS STATEMENT

All experimental procedures were followed the guidelines of the International Association for the Use of Animals in Research and approved by the Committee of Animal experiment ethics review in Guangzhou University of Chinese Medicine.

AUTHOR CONTRIBUTIONS

YS: designed the study; KC, CS, SB, LY, YY, and LG: performed the experiments; KC and RZ: analyzed the data; KC: wrote the manuscript.

FUNDING

This work was supported by the National Natural Science Foundation of China (No. 81573912) and the Project for Developing High-level University of Guangzhou University of Chinese Medicine (No. A1-AFD018171Z11032).

REFERENCES

1. Brodsky BS, Oquendo M, Ellis SP, Haas GL, Malone KM, Mann JJ. The relationship of childhood abuse to impulsivity and suicidal behavior in adults with major depression. *Am J Psychiatry.* (2001) 158:1871–7. doi: 10.1176/appi.ajp.158.11.1871
2. Teicher MH. Childhood trauma and the enduring consequences of forcibly separating children from parents at the United States border. *BMC Med.* (2018) doi: 10.1186/s12916-018-1147-y
3. Hall FS. Social deprivation of neonatal, adolescent and adult rats has distinct neurochemical and behavioral consequences. *Crit Rev Neurobiol.* (1998) 12:129–62. doi: 10.1615/CritRevNeurobiol.v12.i1-2.50
4. Amini-Khoei H, Mohammadi-Asl A, Amiri S, Hosseini MJ, Momeny M, Hassanipour M, et al. Oxytocin mitigated the depressive-like behaviors of maternal separation stress through modulating mitochondrial function and neuroinflammation. *Prog Neuropsychopharmacol Biol Psychiatry.* (2017) doi: 10.1016/j.pnpbp.2017.02.022
5. Zhang Y, Zhu X, Bai M, Zhang L, Xue L, Yi J. Maternal deprivation enhances behavioral vulnerability to stress associated with miR-504 expression in nucleus accumbens of rats. *PLoS ONE.* (2013) 8:e69934. doi: 10.1371/journal.pone.0069934
6. Bondar NP, Lepeshko AA, Reshetnikov VV. Effects of early-life stress on social and anxiety-like behaviors in adult mice: sex-specific effects. *Behav Neurol.* (2018) 2018:1538931. doi: 10.1155/2018/1538931
7. Oreland S, Nylander I, Pickering C. Prolonged maternal separation decreases granule cell number in the dentate gyrus of 3-week-old male rats. *Int J Dev Neurosci.* (2010) 28:139–44. doi: 10.1016/j.ijdevneu.2009.12.005
8. Baumgarten HG, Grozdanovic ZŽ. Anatomy of central serotoninergic projection systems. In: Van de Kar LDŽ, editor. *Serotoninergic Neurons and 5-HT Receptors in the CNS.* New York, NY: Springer (1997) pp. 41–89.
9. Lambás-Señas L, Mnie-Filali O, Certin V, Faure C, Lemoine L, Zimmer L, et al. Functional correlates for 5-HT1A receptors in maternally deprived rats displaying anxiety and depression-like behaviors. *Prog Neuro-Psychopharmacol Biol Psychiatry.* (2008) 33:262–8. doi: 10.1016/j.pnpbp.2008.11.017
10. Wang Q, Shao F, Wang W. Maternal separation produces alterations of forebrain brain-derived neurotrophic factor expression in differently aged rats. *Front Mol Neurosci.* (2015). 8:49. doi: 10.3389/fnmol.2015.00049
11. Murínová J, Hlaváčová N, Chmelová M, Riečanský I. The evidence for altered BDNF expression in the brain of rats reared or housed in social isolation: a systematic review. *Front Behav Neurosci.* (2017) 11:101. doi: 10.3389/fnbeh.2017.00101
12. Mattson MP, Maudsley S, Martin B. BDNF and 5-HT: a dynamic duo in age-related neuronal plasticity and neurodegenerative disorders. *Trends Neurosci.* (2004) 27:589–94. doi: 10.1016/j.tins.2004.08.001
13. Wang H, Zhao Y, Wang YJ, Song L, Wang JL, Huang C, et al. Antidepressant-like effects of tetrahydroxystilbene glucoside in mice: involvement of BDNF signaling cascade in the hippocampus. *CNS Neurosci Ther.* (2017) 23:627–36. doi: 10.1111/cns.12708
14. Liao L, Zhang XD, Li J, Zhang ZW, Yang CC, Rao CL, et al. Pioglitazone attenuates lipopolysaccharide-induced depression-like behaviors, modulates NF-κB/IL-6/STAT3, CREB/BDNF pathways and central serotonergic neurotransmission in mice. *Int Immunopharmacol.* (2017) 49:178–86. doi: 10.1016/j.intimp.2017.05.036

15. Pliakas AM, Carlson RR, Neve RL, Konradi C, Nestler EJ, Carlezon WA. Altered responsiveness to cocaine and increased immobility in the forced swim test associated with elevated cAMP response element-binding protein expression in nucleus accumbens. *J Neurosci.* (2001) 21:7397–403. doi: 10.1523/JNEUROSCI.21-18-07397.2001
16. Wang C, Guo J, Guo R. Effect of XingPiJieYu decoction on spatial learning and memory and cAMP-PKA-CREB-BDNF pathway in rat model of depression through chronic unpredictable stress. *BMC Complement Altern Med.* (2017) 17:73. doi: 10.1186/s12906-016-1543-9
17. Uher R, Mors O, Rietschel M, Rajewska-Rager A, Petrovic A, Zobel A, et al. Early and delayed onset of response to antidepressants in individual trajectories of change during treatment of major depression: a secondary analysis of data from the Genome-Based Therapeutic Drugs for Depression (GENDEP) study. *J Clin Psychiatry.* (2011) 72:1478. doi: 10.4088/JCP.10m06419
18. Trivedi MH, Rush AJ, Wisniewski SR, Nierenberg AA, Warden D, Ritz L, et al. Evaluation of outcomes with citalopram for depression using measurement based care in STAR*D: implications for clinical practice. *Am J Psychiatry.* (2006)163:28–40. doi: 10.1176/appi.ajp.163.1.28
19. Junling L, Kai X, Tian W, Xiaoxing X, Jinglu Y, Huihui Z, et al. Current progress of Sini powder in depression. *Glob Tradit Chin Med.* (2017) 1:1. doi: 10.3969/J.issn.1674-1749.2017.01.038
20. Willner P, Towell A, Sampson D, Sophokleous S, Muscat R. Reduction of sucrose preference by chronic unpredictable mild stress, and its restoration by a tricyclic antidepressant. *Psychopharmacology.* (1987) 93:358–64. doi: 10.1007/BF00187257
21. Detke MJ, Lucki I. Detection of serotonergic and noradrenergic antidepressants in the rat forced swimming test: the effects of water depth. *Behav Brain Res.* (1996) 73:43–6. doi: 10.1016/0166-4328(96)00067-8
22. Tractenberg SG, Levandowski ML, de Azeredo LA, Orso R, Roithmann LG, Hoffmann ES, et al. (2016) An overview of maternal separation effects on behavioral outcomes in mice: evidence from a four-stage methodological systematic review. *Neurosci Biobehav Rev.* 68:489–503. doi: 10.1016/j.neubiorev.2016.06.021
23. de Almeida Magalhães T, Correia D, de Carvalho LM, Damasceno S, Brunialti Godard AL. Maternal separation affects expression of stress response genes and increases vulnerability to ethanol consumption. *Brain Behav.* (2018) 8:e00841. doi: 10.1002/brb3.841
24. Figueiredo ÍL, Frota PB, da Cunha DG, da Silva Raposo R, Canuto KM, de Andrade GM, et al. Prolonged maternal separation induces undernutrition and systemic inflammation with disrupted hippocampal development in mice. *Nutrition.* (2016) 32:1019–27. doi: 10.1016/j.nut.2016.02.016
25. Cheng F, Ma C, Wang X, Zhai C, Wang G, Xu X, et al. Effect of traditional Chinese medicine formula SiNiSan on chronic restraint stress-induced nonalcoholic fatty liver disease: a rat study. *BMC Complement Altern Med.* (2017) 17:203. doi: 10.1186/s12906-017-1707-2
26. da Silva AI, Braz GRF, Silva SCA, Pedroza AADS, de Lima-Júnior NC, Silva TLA, et al. Body composition, biochemical, behavioral and molecular alterations in overfed rats after chronic exposure to SSRI. *Behav Brain Res.* (2018) 356:62–70. doi: 10.1016/j.bbr.2018.08.007
27. Shen X, Zhao Z, Luo X, Wang H, Hu B, Guo Z. Systems pharmacology based study of the molecular mechanism of SiNiSan formula for application in nervous and mental diseases. *Evid Based Complement Alternat Med.* (2016) 2016:9146378. doi: 10.1155/2016/9146378
28. Wang YT, Tan QR, Sun LL, Cao J, Dou KF, Xia B, et al. Possible therapeutic effect of a Traditional Chinese medicine, SiNiSan, on chronic restraint stress related disorders. *Neurosci Lett.* (2009) 449:215–9. doi: 10.1016/j.neulet.2008.10.100
29. Iñiguez SD, Alcantara LF, Warren BL, Riggs LM, Parise EM, Vialou V, et al. Fluoxetine exposure during adolescence alters responses to aversive stimuli in adulthood. *J Neurosci.* (2014) 34:1007–21. doi: 10.1523/JNEUROSCI.5725-12.2014
30. Guo LL, Shi YF, Sang F, Yuan YM, Wu HM. Effect of maternal deprivation following with chronic unpredictable stress on behavior and HPA axis in adolescent rats and intervention of modified Sini San. *Trad Chinese Drug Res Clin Pharmacol.* (2016) 27:4. doi: 10.1937/jissn.1003-9783.2016.04.004
31. Chang HS, Liang JC, Sun JN, Wang QG, Li J. Effect of effective fraction of Sini powder on mouse model of behavioral despair and medical depression. *J Beijing Univ Traditional Chinese Med.* (2006) 29:7.
32. Chang HS, Wang QG, Shi RB, Jin Yan. Effects of the active components of Sini powder on the behavior and cerebral monoamine neurotransmitters in the rat model of depressive chronic stress. *J Beijing Univ TCM.* (2003) 26:5.
33. Li M, Xu XD. Effect of Sini Powder on behavior and neurotransmitter of rat with chronic stress-induced depression. *J Changchun Univ Tradit Chin Med.* (2014) 30:8. doi: 10.13463/j.cnki.cczyy.2014.04.006
34. Djalali S, Höltje M, Grosse G, Rothe T, Stroh T, Grosse J, et al. Effects of brain-derived neurotrophic factor (BDNF) on glial cells and serotonergic neurones during development. *J Neurochem.* (2005) 92:616–27. doi: 10.1111/j.1471-4159.2004.02911.x
35. Phillips C. Brain-derived neurotrophic factor, depression, and physical activity: making the neuroplastic connection. *Neural Plast.* (2017) 2017:7260130. doi: 10.1155/2017/7260130
36. Björkholm C, Monteggia LM. BDNF - a key transducer of antidepressant effects. *Neuropharmacology.* (2016) 102:72–9. doi: 10.1016/j.neuropharm.2015.10.034
37. Liu Z, Qi Y, Cheng Z, Zhu X, Fan C, Yu SY. The effects of ginsenoside Rg1 on chronic stress induced depression-like behaviors, BDNF expression and the phosphorylation of PKA and CREB in rats. *Neuroscience.* (2016) 322:358–69. doi: 10.1016/j.neuroscience.2016.02.050
38. Rojas PS. What do we really know about 5-HTReceptor signaling in neuronal cells? *Front Cell Neurosci.* (2016) 10:272. doi: 10.3389/fncel.2016.00272
39. Ohta KI, Suzuki S, Warita K, Kaji T, Kusaka T, Miki T. Prolonged maternal separation attenuates BDNF-ERK signaling correlated with spine formation in the hippocampus during early brain development. *J Neurochem.* (2017) 141:179–94. doi: 10.1111/jnc.13977
40. Jin Y, Wang QG, Shi RB, et al. Influence of active components of Sini powder on the expression of 5-HT1A receptor mRNA in the cortex and hippocampus of the rat model of depression induced by chronic stressors. *J Beijing Univ TCM.* (2004) 27:4.
41. Li DD, Xie H, Du YF, Long Y, Reed MN, Hu M, et al. Antidepressant-like effect of zileuton is accompanied by hippocampal neuroinflammation reduction and CREB/BDNF upregulation in lipopolysaccharide-challenged mice. *J Affect Disord.* (2018) 227:672–80. doi: 10.1016/j.jad.2017.11.047
42. Bian Y, Yang L, Wang Z, Wang Q, Zeng L, Xu G. Repeated three-hour maternal separation induces depression-like behavior and affects the expression of hippocampal plasticity-related proteins in C57BL/6N mice. *Neural Plast.* (2015) 2015:627837. doi: 10.1155/2015/627837
43. Kim MH, Leem YH. Chronic exercise improves repeated restraint stress-induced anxiety and depression through 5HT1A receptor and cAMP signaling in hippocampus. *J Exerc Nutrition Biochem.* (2014) 18:97–104. doi: 10.5717/jenb.2014.18.1.97
44. Wang XL, Gao J, Wang XY, Mu XF, Wei S, Xue L, et al. Treatment with Shuyu capsule increases 5-HT1AR level and activation of cAMP-PKA-CREB pathway in hippocampal neurons treated with serum from a rat model of depression. *Mol Med Rep.* (2018) 17:3575–82. doi: 10.3892/mmr.2017.8339
45. Yu Q, Jin GL. Impacts of three Chinese herbal compound on the 5-HT1A receptor gene expression of liver qi stagnation model rat induced by chronic stress. *Beijing J Tradit Chin Medi.* (2008). 27:1. doi: 10.16025/J.1674-1307.2008.01.030
46. Yan C, Wu LL, Pan Y, Song Q, Ran CL, Liu SK. The effect of Jiaweisinisan on cAMP response element binding protein and phosphorylation in PC12 cells injured by Corticosterone and Glutamate. *Chinese Pharmacol Bull.* (2009) 25:270–4.

15

Altered Brain Function in Drug-Naïve Major Depressive Disorder Patients With Early-Life Maltreatment: A Resting-State fMRI Study

Zhexue Xu[1,2†], Jing Zhang[1†], Di Wang[3†], Ting Wang[4], Shu Zhang[5], Xi Ren[2], Xiaolei Zhu[7], Atsushi Kamiya[7], Jiliang Fang[6] and Miao Qu[1,2*]*

[1] Department of Neurology, Xuan Wu Hospital Capital Medical University, Beijing, China, [2] Department of Neurology, Third Affiliated Hospital, Beijing University of Chinese Medicine, Beijing, China, [3] Department of Clinical Psychology, Beijing Anding Hospital, Beijing, China, [4] Nanjing Municipal Hospital of Traditional Chinese Medicine, Nanjing, China, [5] Department of Neurology, Fengtai Integrated Chinese and Western Medicine Hospital of Beijing, Beijing, China, [6] Department of Radiology, Guang' anmen Hospital China Academy of Chinese Medical Sciences, Beijing, China, [7] Department of Psychiatry and Behavioral Sciences, Johns Hopkins University School of Medicine, Baltimore, MD, United States

***Correspondence:**
Miao Qu
qumiaotcm@126.com
Jiliang Fang
fangmgh@163.com

†These authors contributed equally to this work.

Childhood Maltreatment (CM) is an important risk factor for major depressive disorder (MDD). Previous studies using emotional task-state functional magnetic resonance (task-state fMRI) found that altered brain function in prefrontal-limbic regions was the key neuropathological mechanism in adult MDD patients with experience of early-life maltreatment. However, to the best of our knowledge, there is no published study investigating brain function in MDD patients with CM experience using resting-state fMRI (rs-fMRI). In present study, we aimed to detect altered resting-state brain activity in MDD patients with CM experience, and identify significantly activated brain regions, which may provide new insights into the neural mechanism underlying the relationship between MDD and CM experience. The results showed MDD patients with CM experience were associated with increased amplitude of low-frequency fluctuation (ALFF) and altered function connection (FC) in the prefrontal cortex, when compared to MDD patients without CM. Of note, left frontal middle gyrus (LFEG) was found as a specific brain region which differentiates MDD patients with CM from patients without CM. These results suggest that rs-fMRI is a useful method in studying the correlation between MDD and CM experience and altered function of LFEG in resting-state may explain the correlation between MDD and CM experience.

Keywords: major depressive disorder, childhood maltreatment, resting state, fMRI, prefrontal-limbic system

INTRODUCTION

Major depressive disorder (MDD) has become the single largest contributor to nonfatal health loss globally in 2015 (1). The causality of MDD is heterogeneous. Although stress, poor family relationship and social support in adulthood have been thoroughly studied as environmental risks for MDD, unpleasant psychical or physical experiences during childhood were often overlooked. Childhood maltreatment (CM) has recently gained greater attention because it may confer susceptibility to depression in later-life. Clinical evidence from retrospective and prospective cohort studies suggests that CM could markedly increase the risk of MDD (2–5). Furthermore, it has been reported that approximately 65% of chronically depressed patients have a history of CM, which is associated with more relapses and heightened therapy resistance (6, 7). Therefore, it is important to identify the neural mechanisms underlying the impact of CM on MDD pathophysiology, for pursuing early intervention and mechanism-based treatment strategies.

CM has been proved to affect brain function and development in MDD patients (8–11). Task- and resting-state functional magnetic resonance imaging (fMRI) has been wildly used to non-invasively evaluate functional brain activity for identification of specific brain regions and neural circuits associated with disease conditions. Previous studies using emotional task-state Fmri (12–15) showed altered activation of prefrontal-limbic regions, including ventromedial prefrontal cortex (vmPFC), anterior cingulate cortex (ACC), amygdale and hippocampus, in MDD patients with CM.

Nonetheless, to our best knowledge, resting-state brain function in MDD patients with CM still remains to be investigated. In the present study, we utilized rs-fMRI to examine the neuropathological mechanisms of drug-naïve MDD with CM experience. We hypothesize that altered blood oxygenation level dependency (BOLD) in certain brain regions may be correlated with CM experience in MDD patients and these brain areas may include subregions of the prefrontal-limbic system, which has previously been reported to be associated with MDD patients with CM using task-state fMRI.

METHODS

Participants

Fifteen MDD patients with CM and fifteen patients without CM were recruited from the outpatient clinic of Xuanwu Hospital Capital Medical University, Third Affiliated Hospital of Beijing University of Chinese Medicine, and Beijing Anding Hospital. All of the patients were diagnosed with modified structure clinical interview for DSM-V (16) by two senior clinical psychiatrists, and were rated with a 17-item Hamilton depression scale (HAMD). All MDD patients were drug-naïve and in their first episode of illness. These patients were right-handed and would be excluded if they had another major psychiatric illness, neurological illness, head injury, alcohol or drug abuse. CM was assessed by a short form childhood trauma questionnaire (CTQ-SF) (17).

Seventeen age-, gender- and education-matched healthy controls (HC) were recruited from community-based advertising through flyers posted at hospital and university campuses. They were also interviewed with the Structured Clinical Interview for DSM-V. All HC were right-handed, free of depression and any other psychiatric or neurological illness and had no history of head injury, alcohol or drug abuse.

Data Acquisition

T1-weighted and resting-state fMRI data were acquired using a 3T Siemens Trio scanner (Magnetom Allegra, Siemens, Erlangen, Germany) in the Beijing Guang' anmen Hospital China Academy of Chinese Medical Sciences. The scanning sessions included the following: (i) three-dimensional T1-weighted whole-brain images: 3D-MPRAGE sequence, Repetition Time (TR)/Echo Time (TE) = 2300/3ms, 176 sagittal slices. (ii) Rs-fMRI scans contain 180 functional volumes, using a T2-weigthed Echo Planar Imaging sequence, TR/TE = 2,000/30 ms, flip angle = 90°, acquisition matrix = 64 × 64 axial slices = 40, thickness/gap = 3/0 mm, Voxel size: 3.0 × 3.0 × 3.0mm (3), Field of view = 210 × 210 mm. During the scanning, subjects laid supine in the scanner with their heads fixed with foam pads to decrease head motion. They were informed to close their eyes but remain awake, and a simple inquiry was conducted to exclude any sleeping periods.

Pre-Processing

Image preprocessing and statistical analysis were performed using the Data Processing Assistant for Resting-state fMRI (DPARSF, http://www.rfmri.org/DPARSF) toolkits (18), Resting State fMRI Data Analysis Toolkit 1.8 version (REST, https://www.nitrc.org/projects/rest/) (19) and SPM8 software (SPM8, http://www.fil.ion.ucl.ac.uk/spm/) (20).

Images were drafted by REST and BrainNet Viewer toolkit. Data pre-processing was performed by DPARSF toolkits. The steps were as follows: (i) Raw DICOM data were converted to the NifTI format; (ii) To allow for instrumental stabilization of the initial signal, first 10 images were discarded; (iii) Images were slice-timing and 3D motion corrected for head motions, we excluded images if patients' and HC's head movement data in translational and rotational planes i.e. exceeded 2mm or 2° and 1mm or 1°; (iv) Images were normalized based on the Montreal Neurological Institute (MNI) Space with Smoothing Method (Full Width at Half Maximum, FWHM 4mm); (v) rs-fMRI data were processed with linear detrending and band-pass filtering.

ALFF and FC Analysis

After pre-processing, very low-frequency drift and high-frequency noise was first filtered (band-pass, 0.01~0.08Hz), and then a Fast Fourier Transform (FFT) was used to convert the frequency domain. This averaged square root was termed Amplitude of Low-Frequency Fluctuation (ALFF) at the given voxel (21). Furthermore, in order to eliminate the physiological signals, fractional ALFF (fALFF) was also performed. In the following FC analysis, according to our present results and referenced by previous CM task-fMRI study results (22), the left orbital part of inferior frontal gyrus, left anterior cingulated and paracingulate gyri, left middle frontal gyrus and left inferior parietal, extending to supramarginal and angular gyri, were chosen as a region of interest (ROI). After, seed-to-voxel functional connectivity was performed.

Statistical Analysis

Subjects' demographic information, including age, gender, education level, and their matched HC groups were analyzed by One-way ANCOVA. Gender related differences were detected by Chi-square tests. ALFF, fALFF and FC results were performed in correlation with CM scale using Pearson Correlation.

The statistical significance level was set at $p < 0.05$. All statistical tests were performed using SPSS 18.0 (SPSS Inc., IL, USA).

The technologists who performed fMRI data analysis were blind to the subjects. Significant brain activation in the whole brain was computed using one-sample t-test in REST (Threshold $p < 0.05$) for every group. Voxel-wise group comparisons were detected with two-sample t-test (AlphaSim correction $p < 0.01$; continuous voxels > 16). The precise anatomical position in the brain, with statistical significance on the corresponding MNI coordinate, was identified using the Viewer in REST. Voxel-wise FC analyses revealed the Pearson correlation coefficients between the seeds and the rest of the whole brain areas. Fisher r-to-z transformation were used to transform FC values into z-values. The group differences in the functional connectivity (AlphaSim correction $p < 0.01$; continuous voxels > 16) were disclosed using two sample t-tests.

RESULTS

Demographic and Clinical Characteristics of the Study Group

MDD patients (n = 15 MDD with CM and n = 15 MDD without CM) and matched HC (n = 17) participated in this study. As a subject in MDD without CM group was excluded for a big head motion, there were 14 subjects in MDD without CM group in practice. The demographic information, HAMD scores, and CM scores for these groups were shown in **Table 1**. There were no statistical differences in age, gender, and years of education between the groups. The MDD with or without CM showed higher HAMD scores compared to those in matched HC (MDD with CM: 26.33 ± 7.99; MDD without CM: 24.14 ± 4.88, HC: 1.06 ± 1.19, $p < 0.01$), whereas no significant difference in HAMD scores between CM and without CM groups was observed. MDD with CM had a higher CM score than MDD without CM and HC (MDD with CM: 63.33 ± 4.03; MDD without CM: 31.16 ± 5.63, HC: 30.83 ± 4.02, $p < 0.01$), and there was no significant difference found between MDD without CM and HC.

ALFF and fALFF Analysis

Intergroup differences of results from ALFF analysis were shown in **Table 2**. Compared to HC group, MDD with CM showed increased ALFF in the left orbital part of inferior frontal gyrus (-45, 18, -9. BA47/38), left middle frontal gyrus (-36, 39, 21. BA10/9/46), left medial of superior frontal gyrus (-3, 48, 33. BA9), left supplementary motor area (-3, -3, 75. BA6), left anterior cingulated and paracingulate gyri (-3, 45, 9. BA32), left supramarginal gyrus (-60, -27, 39. BA1/2), left inferior parietal, extending to supramarginal and angular gyri (-45, -48, 57. BA40/7), right orbital part of middle frontal gyrus (48, 51, -6. BA47/10/45), right triangular part of inferior frontal gyrus (51, 33, 18. BA46) and right dorsolateral part of superior frontal gyrus (21, 48, 36. BA9/8) (**Figure 1**). Increased ALFF in MDD without CM, compared to HC group, was observed in left triangular part of inferior frontal gyrus (-48, 48, 3. BA10/46/47), left middle frontal gyrus (-24, 51, 36. BA9), left inferior parietal, extending to supramarginal and angular gyri (-45, -51, 48. BA40/39), left precuneus (-6, -72, 57. BA7), left middle occipital gyrus (-27, -96, 12. BA19), right orbital part of inferior frontal gyrus (54, 42, -6. BA10/47/45), right medial part of superior frontal gyrus (18, 66, 12. BA10/9/6/8), right supplementary motor area (3, -6, 72. BA6), right precuneus (3, -66, 45. BA7), right angular (57, -60, 24. BA39) and right temporal role: superior temporal gyrus (45, 18, -15. BA38/47/34/28) (**Figure 2**).

Compared to MDD without CM, increased ALFF was observed in the left frontal middle frontal gyrus (-27, 48, 12. NS), left cerebellum (-33, -75, -39. NS) and right cerebellum (39, -78, -39. NS) in MDD with CM (**Figure 3**).

Intergroup differences detected in fALFF analysis were shown in **Table 3**. Compared to HC group, MDD with CM showed increased fALFF in left cuneus (-9, -84, 18. BA19) (**Figure 4**). Increased fALFF in MDD without CM, compared to HC group, was observed in left middle temporal gyrus (-54, -57, 9. BA39) (**Figure 4**).

FC Analysis

Intergroup differences observed in FC analysis were shown in **Table 4**. Left middle frontal gyrus where ALFF was significantly changed between MDD with CM, compared with MDD without CM, was taken as ROI. The left anterior cingulated and paracingulate gyri, left orbital part of inferior frontal gyrus and left inferior parietal, extending to supramarginal and angular gyri where ALFF was altered in MDD with CM and MDD without CM, when compared to HC, were also taken as ROIs.

In MDD with CM group, positive FC was observed between left middle frontal gyrus and left precentral gyrus (-45, -6, -60.

TABLE 1 | Demographic and psychological data of MDD with CM, MDD patients without CM and controls.

	MDD with CM	MDD without CM	Control	χ^2/ F	P-value
No. of subjects	15	14	17		
Gender (M/F)	6/9	5/9	7/10	$\chi^2 = 0.10$	$p = 0.95$
Age, years (mean, SD)	28.33 ± 5.81	32.36 ± 6.23	28.94 ± 5.92	$F = 1.90$	$p = 0.16$
Education, years (mean, SD)	16.13 ± 3.09	16.14 ± 3.11	16.18 ± 2.81	$F = 0.001$	$p = 0.99$
HAMD score (mean, SD)	26.33 ± 7.99	24.14 ± 4.88	1.06 ± 1.19	$F = 110.84$	$p < 0.01$
CM score (mean, SD)	63.33 ± 4.03	31.16 ± 5.63	30.83 ± 4.02	$F = 97.71$	$p < 0.01$

MDD, Major Depressive Disorder; HAMD, Hamilton Depression Rating Scales; Age, Education and HAMD score adopted one-way ANOVA; CM, Childhood Maltreatment. There is no difference between MDD with CM and MDD without CM in HAMD scores (p = 0.82, Bonferroni corrected). MDD with CM had significant differences with MDD without and Control in CM scores respectively (p < 0.01, Bonferroni corrected), and there is no significant difference between MDD without CM and HC (p = 0.90, Bonferroni corrected).

TABLE 2 | The comparison of ALFF in MDD with CM, MDD patients without CM and controls (AlphaSim-corrected, $p < 0.01$).

Brain areas			BA	Voxels	MNI			*T*-scores	Correlation r&p
Hemisphere	Region	Label			x	y	z		
(Abuse > HC)									
Left	Frontal	Inferior frontal gyrus, orbital part	47/38	34	-45	18	-9	4.88	r=-0.06 p=0.81
		Middle frontal gyrus	10/9/46	131	-36	39	21	4.27	r=-0.1 p=0.71
		Superior frontal gyrus, medial	9	16	-3	48	33	3.75	r=-0.09 p=0.74
		Supplementary motor area	6	29	-3	-3	75	3.63	NS
	Cingulate	Anterior cingulated and paracingulate gyri	32	59	-3	45	9	4.76	r=-0.09 p=0.74
	Parietal	Supramarginal gyrus	1/2	20	-60	-27	39	4.87	r=-0.11 p=0.69
		Inferior parietal, extending to supramarginal and angular gyri	40/7	100	-45	-48	57	4.61	r=-0.08 p=0.77
Right	Frontal	Middle frontal gyrus, orbital part	47/10/45	42	48	51	-6	4.57	r=-0.09 p=0.73
		Inferior frontal gyrus, triangular part	46	18	51	33	18	3.39	r=-0.10 p=0.70
		Superior frontal gyrus, dorsolateral	9/8	24	21	48	36	3.66	r=-0.08 p=0.75
(NS-Abuse > HC)									
Left	Frontal	Inferior frontal gyrus, triangular part	10/46/47	100	-48	48	3	7.58	NS
		Middle frontal gyrus	9	34	-24	51	36	4.11	NS
	Parietal	Inferior parietal, extending to supramarginal and angular gyri	40/39	217	-45	-51	48	5.70	NS
		Precuneus	7	19	-6	-72	57	3.73	NS
	Occipital	Middle occipital gyrus	19	16	-27	-96	12	4.73	NS
Right	Frontal	Inferior frontal gyrus, orbital part	10/47/45	28	54	42	-6	3.70	NS
		Superior frontal gyrus, medial	10/9/6/8	411	18	66	12	6.35	NS
		Supplementary motor area	6	41	3	-6	72	4.68	NS
	Parietal	Precuneus	7	26	3	-66	45	4.38	NS
		Angular	39	21	57	-60	24	3.75	NS
	Temporal	Temporal pole: superior temporal gyrus	38/47/34/28	51	45	18	-15	4.85	NS
(Abuse > NS-Abuse)									
Left	Frontal	Middle frontal gyrus	NS	19	-27	48	12	3.79	NS
	Cerebelum		NS	43	-33	-75	-39	4.12	NS
Right	Cerebelum		NS	27	39	-78	-39	4.03	NS

ALFF, amplitude of low frequency fluctuation; MDD, Major Depressive Disorder; Abuse, MMD patients with CM; NS-Abuse, MDD patients without CM; HC, matched healthy controls; MNI, Montreal Neurological Institute; x, y and z, coordinates of primary peak locations in the MNI space.; Correlation, the correlation between ALFF and CM scales.

BA6), and negative FC was observed in right medial of superior frontal gyrus (6, 51, 33. BA10). The left anterior cingulated and paracingulate gyri had positive FC with left parahippocampal gyrus (-24, -6, -36. BA36) and right triangular part of inferior frontal gyrus (33, 18, 27. NS). Negative FC was observed in right superior parietal gyrus (39, -51, 57, BA40). Left orbital part of inferior frontal gyrus had positive FC with left triangular part of inferior frontal gyrus (-24, 30, 6. NS) and negative FC was observed in left medial of superior frontal gyrus (-3, 66, 0. BA10) and right medial of superior frontal gyrus (9, 42, 48. BA8). The left inferior parietal, extending to supramarginal and angular gyri, had positive FC with left Fusiform gyrus (-39, -57, -12. BA19). Negative FCs were found in left inferior temporal gyrus (-48, -3, -42. BA20), left paracentral lobule (-9, -33, 60. BA19), and right middle frontal gyrus (45, 57, 6. BA19) (**Figure 5**).

In MDD without CM, positive FC was observed between left middle frontal gyrus and left inferior temporal gyrus (-48, -24, -27. BA20), left middle temporal gyrus (-60, -39, -6. BA21), whereas negative FC was observed in left fusiform gyrus (-27, -51, -15. BA19) and right fusiform gyrus (24, -48, -15. BA19). The left inferior parietal, extending to supramarginal and angular gyri, had positive FC with right inferior temporal gyrus (66, -45, -9. BA20). Negative FC was found in left precentral gyrus (-54, 0, 24. BA19) (**Figure 5**).

Correlation between Brain Functional Alteration

Pearson Correlation showed that FC alteration between the left inferior, extending to supramarginal and angular gyri, and right middle frontal gyrus, had a positive correlation with CM scale ($r = 0.68$, $p < 0.01$). All details are shown in **Table 2, 3, 4**.

DISCUSSION

The current study has investigated the impact of maltreatment during early-life in MDD patients by examining functional activation and connectivity during resting state. To the best of our knowledge, this is the first study that visualizes the whole brain ALFF profiles of MDD with CM during spontaneous brain activity using rs-fMRI. Moreover, FC also has been adopted to detect special brain connectivity. The purpose of this study is to elucidate the mechanism of brain function underlying correlations between MDD and CM experience, based on ALFF

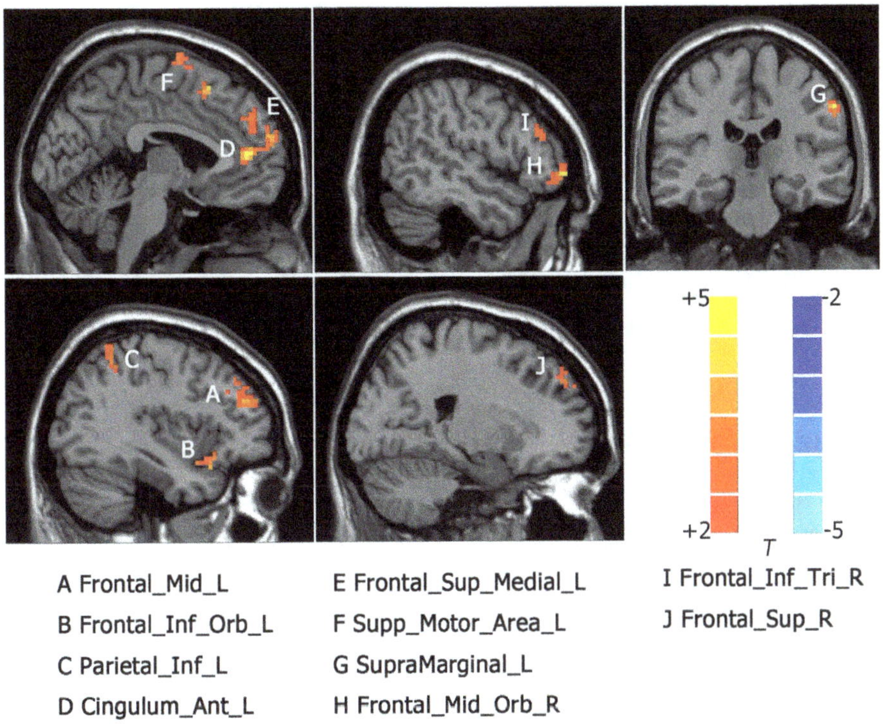

FIGURE 1 | Activated brain regions showed by rs-fMRI using method of Amplitude of Low-Frequency Fluctuation (ALFF) in MDD patients with childhood maltreatment (CM) compared with the health control (HC). A: Frontal_Mid_L, left middle frontal gyrus; B: Frontal_Inf_Orb_L, left inferior frontal gyrus, orbital part; C: Parietal_Inf_L, left inferior parietal, but supramarginal and angular gyri; D: Cingulum_Ant_L, left anterior cingulated and paracingulate gyri; E: Frontal_Sup_Medial_L, left superior frontal gyrus, medial; F: Supp_Motor_Area_L, left supplementary motor area; G: SupraMarginal_L, left supramarginal gyrus; H: Frontal_Mid_Orb_R, right superior frontal gyrus, medial orbital; I: Frontal_Inf_Tri_R, right inferior frontal gyrus, triangular part. J: Frontal_Sup_R, right superior frontal gyrus, dorsolateral.

and FC results. We also aimed to discover distinct brain regions which could differentiate MDD patients with CM experience from patients without CM.

Firstly, we found that under scan of rs-fMRI, compared with HC, MDD patients with CM had enhanced ALFF in prefrontal-limbic regions, left orbital part of inferior frontal gyrus, right orbital part of middle frontal gyrus, which is similar to the results from previous task-state fMRI studies in MDD with CM (23, 24). In MDD patients without CM, compared with HC, increased ALFF only in the right orbital part of inferior frontal gyrus was found. A depressive patient who had CM experience had more activated OFC than MDD without CM in resting state. Furthermore, brain activity in the right dorsolateral prefrontal cortex (DLPFC) was increased in MDD with CM, but not in MDD without CM. DLPFC had been targeted in transcranial magnetic therapy for MDD. DLPFC is involved in emotional process during the suppression stage, and increased FC was reported in vmPFC (25) and orbitofrontal cortex (OFC) (26). OFC is considered anatomically synonymous with the vmPFC (27–29). The orbitofrontal cortex (OFC) is well-known as a key region for regulating emotion, and any damage in OFC would result in changes in emotion, personality, behavior, and social conduct (30). The loss of volume of OFC was reported in MDD (31, 32). In the present study, both increased OFC and DLPFC were found in MDD with CM. In addition, both precuneus and angular were activated, which play great role in depression (33).

Our results show that ALFF of left anterior cingulated and paracingulate gyri, which belong to the ACC of limbic system, was increased in MDD with CM, whereas no increased ALFF in any subregion of limbic system was detected in MDD without CM. Previous studies indicated that people with CM had a smaller ACC volume than those without CM (34, 35). Task-state fMRI studies demonstrated that vmPFC/ACC activation plays key roles in processing fear, appraising negative emotions and regulating emotional responses *via* the limbic system (36–39). Thus, hyperactivity of ACC may underlie fear dysregulation in MDD with CM, compared with patients without CM. Although abnormal function of amygdale (40) and hippocampus (41) are reportedly associated with MDD and CM, we found no alteration in ALFF in the amygdale and hippocampus. Interestingly, altered ALFF in these brain regions in MDD patients with CM was reported using negative emotional discrimination under task-state fMRI (13, 42, 43). The discrepancy between the results may be explained by the following reasons: for the amygdale, vmPFC have direct white matter fiber projection to the amygdale (44, 45) and have a top-down, inhibitory effect on

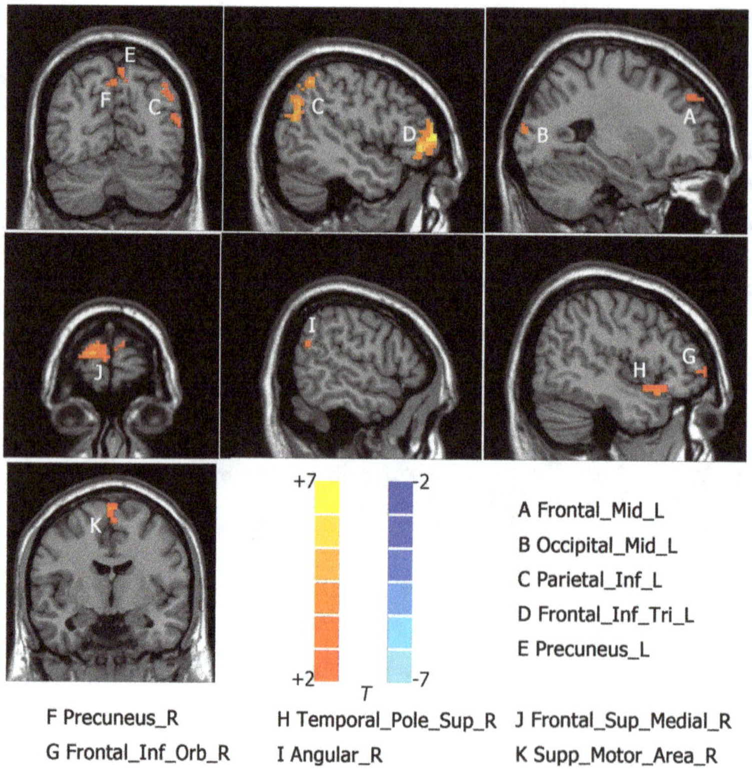

FIGURE 2 | Activated brain regions showed by rs-fMRI using method of ALFF in MDD patients without CM compared with the HC. A: Frontal_Mid_L, left middle frontal gyrus; B: Occ:pital_Mid_L, left middle occipital gyrus; C: Parietal_Inf_L, left inferior parietal, but supramarginal and angular gyri; D: Frontal_Inf_Tri_L; left inferior frontal gyrus, triangular part, E: Precuneus_R, left precuneus; F: Precuneus_R, right precuneus; G: Frontal_Inf_Orb_R, right inferior frontal gyrus, orbital part; H Temporal_Pole_Sup_R, right temporal role: superior temporal gyrus; I: Angular_R, right angular; J: Frontal_Sup_Medial_R, right superior frontal gyurs, medial; K: Supp_Motor_Area_R, right supplementary motor area.

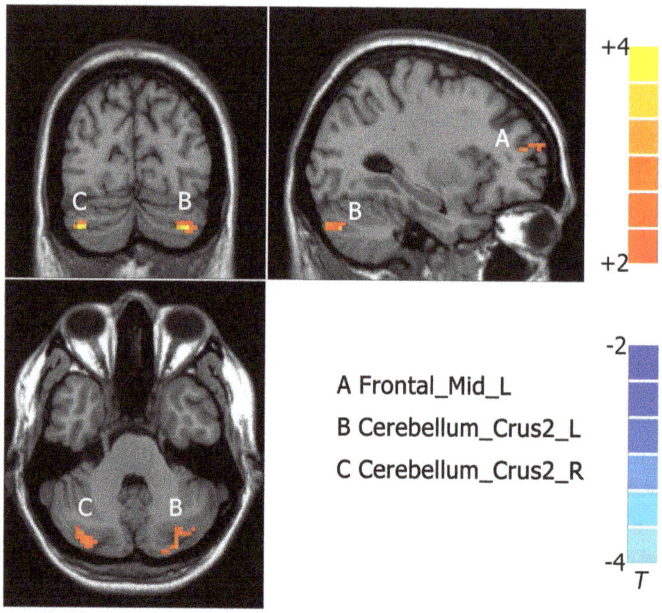

FIGURE 3 | Activated brain regions showed by rs-fMRI using method of ALFF in MDD patients with CM compared with patients without CM. A: Frontal_Mid_L, left middle frontal gyrus; B: Cerebelum_Crus2_L, left cerebellum; C: Cerebelum_Crus2_R, right cerebellum.

TABLE 3 | The comparison of fALFF in MDD with CM, MDD patients without CM and controls (AlphaSim-corrected, p < 0.01).

Brain areas			BA	Voxels	MNI			*T*-scores	Correlation r&p
Hemisphere	**Region**	**Label**			**x**	**y**	**z**		
(Abuse > HC)									
Left	Parietal	Cuneus	19	27	-9	-84	18	17.79	r=-0.16 p=0.57
(NS-Abuse > HC)									
Left	Temporal	Middle temporal gyrus	39	16	-54	-57	9	26.75	NS
(Abuse > NS-Abuse)									
NS	NS		NS	NS	NS	NS	NS	NS	NS

fALFF, fractional amplitude of low frequency fluctuation; MDD, Major Depressive Disorder; Abuse, MMD patients with CM; NS-Abuse, MDD patients without CM; HC, matched healthy controls; MNI, Montreal Neurological Institute; x, y and z, coordinates of primary peak locations in the MNI space.; Correlation, the correlation between ALFF and CM scales.

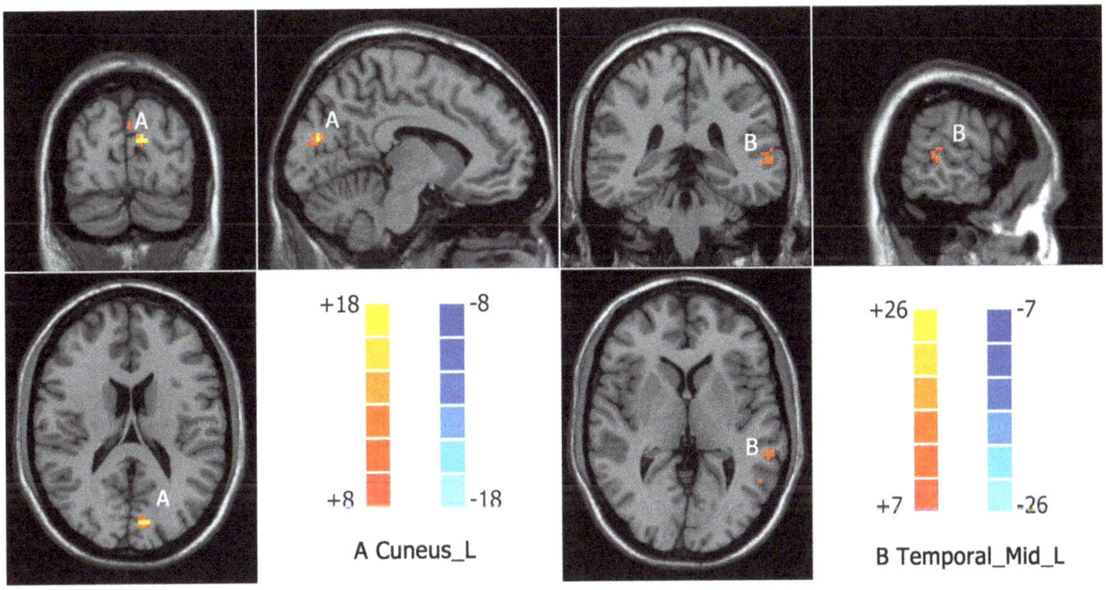

FIGURE 4 | Increased fALFF in MDD patients with CM and patients without CM compared with healthy controls(HC). A: Cuneus_L, left cuneus; B: Temporal_Mid_L, left middle temporal gyrus.

the amygdale, because OFC and ACC were both found to have increased ALFF in our study, thus the function of amygdale might be inhibited by OFC; as for the hippocampus, relative to the prefrontal cortex (PFC), it matures earlier from perceptive of evolution, thus the hippocampus is less vulnerable to CM experience (23, 46). Moreover, other factors, such as limited sample number, different states (rest instead of task), and different measurements (task activation vs. amplitude), may also affect the difference.

Secondly, our FC study showed that the left inferior frontal gyrus (orbital part) had increased FC with left inferior frontal gyrus (triangular part), and decreased FCs with bilateral superior medial frontal gyrus. Also, the left anterior cingulated, paracingulate gyri had increased FC with left parahippocampal gyrus, and decreased FC with right superior parietal gyrus in MDD with CM, compared with HC, whereas no FC was observed in these ROIs in MDD without CM. Our results also revealed the dysfunction of OFC in MDD with CM, which was consistent with previous FC studies showing increased connection between sub-regions within the orbital and prefrontal cortex (47–49), specific brain areas playing critical roles in MDD's aberrant networks. Our results showed that the anterior cingulated and paracingulate gyri had decreased FC with superior parietal gyrus, and had increased FC with parahippocampal gyrus, which was similar to results from previous research (50). Given that ACC was a key node in default-mode network and the parahippocampal gyrus essentially involved in memory encoding, aberrant connectivity in MDD with CM may be involved in episodic memory related to experience of CM.

Lastly, after comparing the ALFF between MDD patients with CM and without CM, notably, altered ALFF in the left middle frontal gyrus (LMFG) and cerebellum was unexpectedly detected in MDD with CM compared to those

TABLE 4 | The comparison of functional connectivity in MDD with CM, MDD patients without CM to HC (AlphaSim-corrected, p < 0.01).

Regions of interest	Brain areas			BA	Voxels	MNI			*T*-scores	*z*-scores	Correlation r&p
	Hemisphere	Region	Label			x	y	z			
(*Abuse* > HC)											
Left middle frontal gyrus	Left	Frontal	Precentral gyrus	6	19	-45	-6	-60	4.11	0.21	r=-0.09 p=0.72
Left anterior cingulated and paracingulate gyri	Left		Parahippocampal gyrus	36	19	-24	-6	-36	4.95	0.16	r=-0.07 p=0.78
	Right	Frontal	Inferior frontal gyrus, triangular part	NS	25	33	18	27	3.41	0.13	r=-0.23 p=0.40
Left inferior frontal gyrus, orbital part	Left	Frontal	Inferior frontal gyrus, triangular part	NS	21	-24	30	6	3.51	0.21	r=0.23 p=0.39
Left inferior parietal, extending to supramarginal and angular gyri	Left		Fusiform gyrus	19	21	-39	-57	-12	4.273	0.12	r=0.03 p=0.53
(HC > *Abuse*)											
Left middle frontal gyrus	Right	Frontal	Superior frontal gyrus, medial	10	28	6	51	33	3.59	0.05	r=0.11 p=0.67
Left anterior cingulated and paracingulate gyri	Right	Parietal	Superior parietal gyrus	40	28	39	-51	57	3.90	0.45	r=0.15 p=0.59
Left inferior frontal gyrus, orbital part	Left	Frontal	Superior frontal gyrus, medial	10	32	-3	66	0	3.66	0.11	r=0.25 p=0.35
	Right	Frontal	Superior frontal gyrus, medial	8	28	9	42	48	5.01	0.25	r=0.25 p=0.36
Left inferior parietal, extending to supramarginal and angular gyri	Left	Temporal	Inferior temporal gyrus	20	28	-48	-3	-42	4.07	0.07	r=0.06 p=0.82
	Left		Paracentral lobule	6	20	-9	-33	60	3.92	0.14	r=-0.29 p=0.27
	Right	Frontal	Middle frontal gyrus	19	10	45	57	6	3.69	0.05	r=0.68 p<0.01
(*NS-Abuse* > HC)											
Left middle frontal gyrus	Left	Temporal	Inferior temporal gyrus	20	21	-48	-24	-27	3.69	0.20	NS
	Left	Temporal	Middle temporal gyrus	21	28	-60	-39	-6	4.28	0.19	NS
Left inferior parietal, but supramarginal and angular gyri	Right	Temporal	Inferior temporal gyrus	20	20	66	-45	-9	3.29	0.16	NS
(HC > NS-Abuse)											
Left middle frontal gyrus	Left		Fusiform gyrus	19	17	-27	-51	-15	4.26	0.15	NS
	Right		Fusiform gyrus	19	68	24	-48	-15	5.04	0.16	NS
Left inferior parietal, but extending to supramarginal and angular gyri	Left		Precentral gyrus	19	9	-54	0	24	3.84	0.16	NS

MDD, Major Depressive Disorder; Abuse, MMD patients with CM; NS-Abuse, MDD patients without CM; HC, matched healthy controls; MNI, Montreal Neurological Institute; x, y and z, coordinates of primary peak locations in the MNI space. Correlation, the correlation between FC and CM scales.

without CM. MFG is a part of frontal lobe which has advanced cognitive function and participates in integrating emotion and information from the internal and external environment, and extracting episodic memory (51, 52). LMFG is located in dorsolateral prefrontal cortex, which has inhibitive (53) and recalling (54) function in psychological disease. LMFG may play a role in extracting unpleasant memory of early-life CM experience, especially memory of disagreeable verbal information, and impaired LMFG function may affect MDD onset. As for cerebellum, its volume declines in patients with MDD (55) and is involved in the modulation of emotional processing and may act as 'emotional pacemaker' (56) in MDD. Thus, MDD patients with CM may have a greater increase in brain activity in recalling past sufferings and emotional experience, than patients without CM.

CONCLUSION

Our study revealed altered resting-state brain activation in drug-naïve MDD patients with CM experience. The approach using

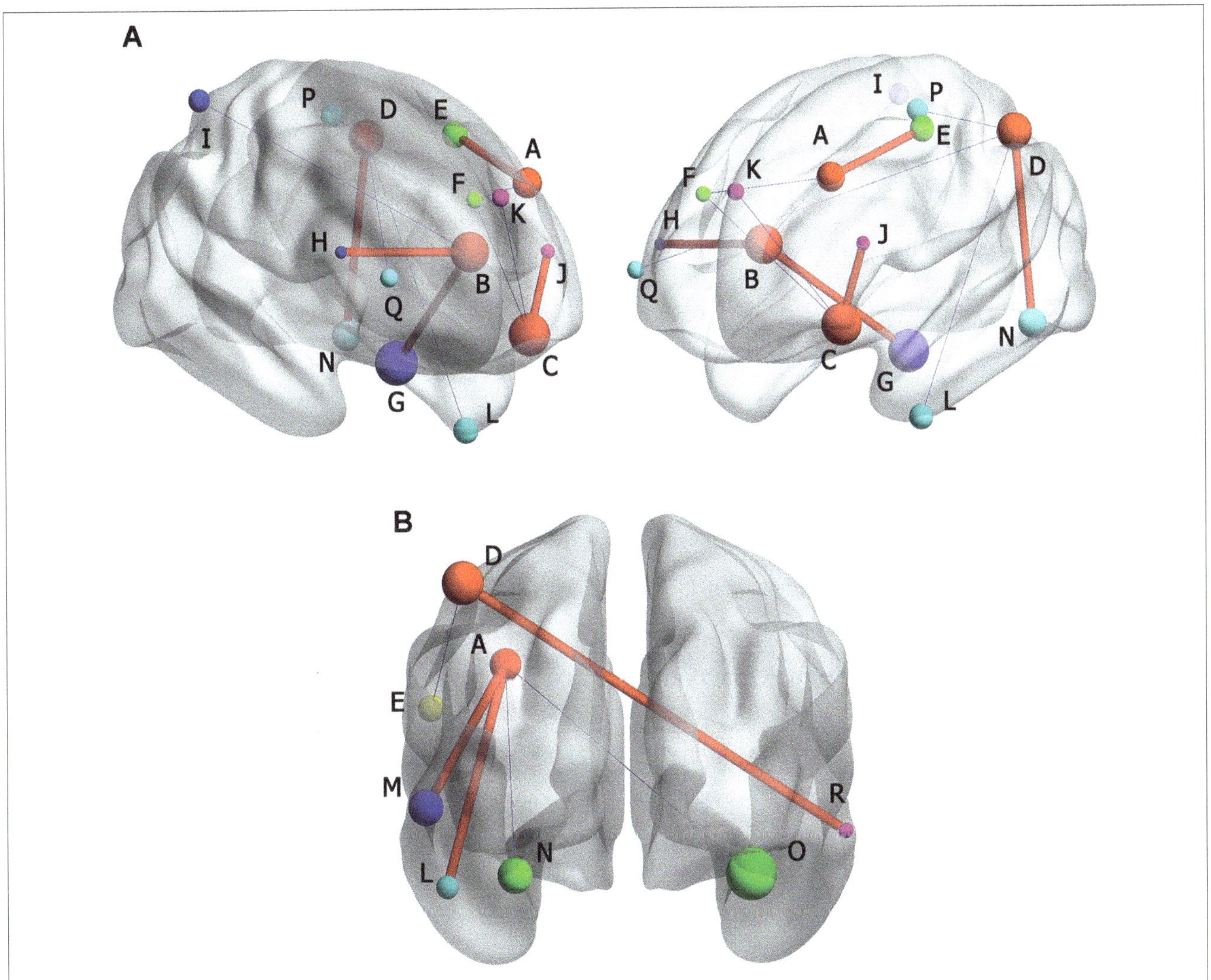

FIGURE 5 | (A) Brain functional connectivity (FC) of rs-fMRI in MDD without CM compared with HC. **(B)** FC in MDD patients with CM compared with HC. Size of balls represent the t-scores of every brain regions; the blue thin edge represents the negative FC and the red bold edge represents the positive FC between different brain regions; A: left middle frontal gyrus; B: left anterior cingulated and paracingulate gyri; C: left inferior frontal gyrus, orbital part; D: left inferior parietal, but supramarginal and angular gyri; E: left precentral gyrus; F: right superior frontal gyrus, medial; G: left parphippocampal gyrus; H: right inferior frontal gyrus, triangular part; I: right superior parietal gyrus; J: left inferior frontal gyrus, triangular part; K: left superior frontal gyrus, medial; L: left inferior temporal gyrus; M: left middle temporal gyrus; N: left fusiform gyrus; O: right fusiform gyrus; P: left paracentral lobule; Q: right middle frontal gyrus; R: right inferior temporal gyrus.

rs-fMRI may be useful to investigate neural mechanisms into how CM affects developmental trajectory of brain maturation, leading to MDD in the later life.

LIMITATIONS

There are two major limitations. Firstly, for Chinese patients with traditional conservative concept in sex, it is difficult to collect any information regarding sex abuse during their childhood. Secondly, CM contains heterogeneous conditions that include emotional abuse, sex abuse, physical abuse, emotional neglect, and physical neglect. We did not separately analyze our results depending on the subtypes of CM in MDD patients due to limited sample number. These limitations will be a line with future inquiry being pursued by our group.

ETHICS STATEMENT

This study was approved by the Ethical Committee at the Third Affiliated Hospital of Beijing University of Chinese Medicine (protocol number: 2015BZHYLL0140). In accordance with the Declaration of Helsinki, all subjects were given written informed consent.

AUTHOR CONTRIBUTIONS

ZX, JZ and DW participated in the design of the study, conducted the analyses, and wrote the manuscript. SZ collected the clinical information and performed the HAMD assessment. TW helped with the design and coordination of the study and wrote the manuscript. XR participated in fMRI data collection. XZ and AK contributed to interpretation of the data and drafting the manuscript. MQ and JF conceived and coordinated the design of the study, and wrote the manuscript. All authors read and approved the final manuscript.

FUNDING

This work was supported by the National Natural Science Foundation of China (Grant No. 81573905) and Excellent Project of Beijing Municipal Science and Technology Commission (Grant No. Z141107002514080).

REFERENCES

1. WHO. *Depression and other common mental disorders: global health estimates*. World Health Organization (2017).
2. Anda RF, Whitfield CL, Felitti VJ, Chapman D, Edwards VJ, Dube SR, et al. Adverse childhood experiences, alcoholic parents, and later risk of alcoholism and depression. *Psychiatr Serv* (2002) 53:1001–9. doi: 10.1176/appi.ps.53.8.1001
3. Scott KM, Smith DR, Ellis PM. Prospectively ascertained child maltreatment and its association with DSM-IV mental disorders in young adults. *Arch Gen Psychiatry* (2010) 67:712–9. doi: 10.1001/archgenpsychiatry.2010.71
4. Green JG, McLaughlin KA, Berglund PA, Gruber MJ, Sampson NA, Zaslavsky AM, et al. Childhood adversities and adult psychiatric disorders in the national comorbidity survey replication I: associations with first onset of DSM-IV disorders. *Arch Gen Psychiatry* (2010) 67:113–23. doi: 10.1001/archgenpsychiatry.2009.186
5. Danese A, Moffitt TE, Harrington H, Milne BJ, Polanczyk G, Pariante CM, et al. 27. Adverse childhood experiences predict adult risk factors for age-related disease: depression, inflammation, and clustering of metabolic risk markers. *Brain Behav Immun* (2009) 23:S32–S32. doi: 10.1016/j.bbi.2009.06.032
6. Keller MB, Lavori PW, Mueller TI, Endicott J, Coryell W, Hirschfeld RM, et al. Time to recovery, chronicity, and levels of psychopathology in major depression: A 5-year prospective follow-up of 431 subjects. *Arch Gen Psychiatry* (1992) 49(10):809–16. doi: 10.1001/archpsyc.1992.01820100053010
7. Wiersma JE, Hovens JG, van Oppen P, Giltay EJ, van Schaik DJ, Beekman AT, et al. The importance of childhood trauma and childhood life events for chronicity of depression in adults. *J Clin Psychiatry* (2009) 70(7):983–9. doi: 10.4088/JCP.08m04521
8. Danese A, McEwen BS. Adverse childhood experiences, allostasis, allostatic load, and age-related disease. *Physiol Behav* (2012) 106:29–39. doi: 10.1016/j.physbeh.2011.08.019
9. Ito Y, Teicher MH, Glod CA, Harper D, Magnus E, Gelbard HA. Increased prevalence of electrophysiological abnormalities in children with psychological, physical, and sexual abuse. *J Neuropsychiatry Clin Neurosci* (1993) 5:401–8. doi: 10.1176/jnp.5.4.401
10. Schiffer F, Teicher MH, Papanicolaou AC. Evoked potential evidence for right brain activity during the recall of traumatic memories. *J Neuropsychiatry Clin Neurosci* (1995) 7:169–75. doi: 10.1176/jnp.7.2.169
11. Teicher MH. Scars that won't heal: the neurobiology of child abuse. *Sci Am* (2002) 286:68–75. doi: 10.1038/scientificamerican0302-68
12. Fonzo GA, Flagan TM, Sullivan S, Allard CB, Grimes EM, Simmons AN, et al. Neural functional and structural correlates of childhood maltreatment in women with intimate-partner violence-related posttraumatic stress disorder. *Psychiatry Res* (2013) 211:93–103. doi: 10.1016/j.pscychresns.2012.08.006
13. Dannlowski U, Kugel H, Huber F, Stuhrmann A, Redlich R, Grotegerd D, et al. Childhood maltreatment is associated with an automatic negative emotion processing bias in the amygdala. *Hum Brain Mapp* (2013) 34:2899–909. doi: 10.1002/hbm.22112
14. De Bellis MD, Keshavan MS, Spencer S, Hall J. N-Acetylaspartate concentration in the anterior cingulate of maltreated children and adolescents with PTSD. *Am J Psychiatry* (2000) 157:1175–77. doi: 10.1176/appi.ajp.157.7.1175
15. Opel N, Redlich R, Zwanzger P, Grotegerd D, Arolt V, Heindel W, et al. Hippocampal atrophy in major depression: a function of childhood maltreatment rather than diagnosis? *Neuropsychopharmacology* (2014) 39:2723–31. doi: 10.1038/npp.2014.145
16. American Psychiatric Association. *Diagnostic and statistical manual of mental disorders*, 5th Edition. American Psychiatric Publishing (2013). doi: 10.1176/appi.books.9780890425596
17. Bernstein DP, Stein JA, Newcomb MD, Walker E, Pogge D, Ahluvalia T, et al. Development and validation of a brief screening version of the childhood trauma questionnaire. *Child Abuse Negl* (2003) 27:169–90. doi: 10.1016/S0145-2134(02)00541-0
18. Chao-Gan Y, Yu-Feng Z. DPARSF: A MATLAB toolbox for "pipeline" data analysis of resting-state fMRI. *Front Syst Neurosci* (2010) 4:13. doi: 10.3389/fnsys.2010.00013
19. Song XW, Dong ZY, Long XY, Li SF, Zuo XN, Zhu CZ, et al. REST: a toolkit for resting-state functional magnetic resonance imaging data processing. *PloS one* (2011) 6:e25031. doi: 10.1371/journal.pone.0025031
20. Xia M, Wang J, Yong H. BrainNet viewer: a network visualization tool for human brain connectomics. *PloS one* (2013) 8:e68910. doi: 10.1371/journal.pone.0068910
21. Zou QH, Zhu CZ, Yang Y, Zuo XN, Long XY, Cao QJ, et al. An improved approach to detection of amplitude of low-frequency fluctuation (ALFF) for resting-state fMRI: fractional ALFF. *J Neurosci Methods* (2008) 172:137–41. doi: 10.1016/j.jneumeth.2008.04.012
22. Teicher MH, Samson JA, Anderson CM, Ohashi K. The effects of childhood maltreatment on brain structure, function and connectivity. *Nat Rev Neurosci* (2016) 17:652. doi: 10.1038/nrn.2016.111
23. Hart H, Lim L, Mehta MA, Simmons A, Mirza KAH, Rubia K. Altered fear processing in adolescents with a history of severe childhood maltreatment: an fMRI study. *Psychol Med* (2018) 48:1092–101. doi: 10.1017/S0033291716003585
24. Wang L, Paul N, Stanton SJ, Greeson JM, Smoski MJ. Loss of sustained activity in the ventromedial prefrontal cortex in response to repeated stress in individuals with early-life emotional abuse: implications for depression vulnerability. *Front Psychol* (2013) 4:320. doi: 10.3389/fpsyg.2013.00320
25. Koenigs M, Grafman J. The functional neuroanatomy of depression: distinct roles for ventromedial and dorsolateral prefrontal cortex. *Behav Brain Res* (2009) 201:239–43. doi: 10.1016/j.bbr.2009.03.004
26. Frodl T, Bokde AL, Scheuerecker J, Lisiecka D, Schoepf V, Hampel H, et al. Functional connectivity bias of the orbitofrontal cortex in drug-free patients with major depression. *Biol Psychiatry* (2010) 67:161–7. doi: 10.1016/j.biopsych.2009.08.022
27. Phillips LH, MacPherson S, Della Sala S. Age, cognition and emotion: the role of anatomical segregation in the frontal lobes. In J Grafman (Ed.), *Handbook of Neuropsychology: the frontal lobes*. Amsterdam: Elsevier Science (2002) p. 73–97.
28. Gorka AX, Hanson JL, Radtke SR, Hariri AR. Reduced hippocampal and medial prefrontal gray matter mediate the association between reported childhood maltreatment and trait anxiety in adulthood and predict sensitivity to future life stress. *Biol Mood Anxiety Disord* (2014) 4:12–12. doi: 10.1186/2045-5380-4-12
29. Chugani HT, Behen ME, Muzik O, Juhász C, Nagy F, Chugani DC, et al. Local brain functional activity following early deprivation: a study of

postinstitutionalized Romanian orphans. *Neuroimage* (2001) 14:1290–301. doi: 10.1006/nimg.2001.0917

30. Kringelbach ML, Rolls ET. The functional neuroanatomy of the human orbitofrontal cortex: evidence from neuroimaging and neuropsychology. *Prog Neurobiol* (2004) 72:341–72. doi: 10.1016/j.pneurobio.2004.03.006
31. Lacerda AL, Keshavan MS, Hardan AY, Yorbik O, Brambilla P, Sassi RB, et al. Anatomic evaluation of the orbitofrontal cortex in major depressive disorder. *Biol Psychiatry* (2004) 55:353–8. doi: 10.1016/j.biopsych.2003.08.021
32. Ballmaier M, Toga AW, Blanton RE, Sowell ER, Lavretsky H, Peterson J, et al. Anterior cingulate, gyrus rectus, and orbitofrontal abnormalities in elderly depressed patients: an MRI-based parcellation of the prefrontal cortex. *Am J Psychiatry* (2004) 161:99. doi: 10.1176/appi.ajp.161.1.99
33. Cheng W, Rolls ET, Qiu J, Yang D, Ruan H, Wei D, et al. Functional connectivity of the precuneus in unmedicated patients with depression. *Biol Psychiatry: Cogn Neurosci Neuroimag* (2018) 12:1040–9. doi: 10.1016/j.bpsc.2018.07.008
34. Cohen RA, Grieve S, Hoth KF, Paul RH, Sweet L, Tate D, et al. Early life stress and morphometry of the adult anterior cingulate cortex and caudate nuclei. *Biol Psychiatry* (2006) 59:975–82. doi: 10.1016/j.biopsych.2005.12.016
35. Jensen SK, Dickie EW, Schwartz DH, Evans CJ, Dumontheil I, Paus T, et al. Effect of early adversity and childhood internalizing symptoms on brain structure in young men. *Jama Pediatr* (2015) 169:938–46. doi: 10.1001/jamapediatrics.2015.1486
36. Phelps EA, Delgado MR, Nearing KI, Ledoux JE. Extinction learning in humans: role of the amygdala and vmPFC. *Neuron* (2004) 43:897–905. doi: 10.1016/j.neuron.2004.08.042
37. Milad MR, Quirk GJ, Pitman RK, Orr SP, Fischl B, Rauch SL, et al. A role for the human dorsal anterior cingulate cortex in fear expression. *Biol Psychiatry* (2007) 62:1191–4. doi: 10.1016/j.biopsych.2007.04.032
38. Hänsel A, Känel RV. The ventro-medial prefrontal cortex: a major link between the autonomic nervous system, regulation of emotion, and stress reactivity? *Biopsychosoc Med* (2008) 2:21–21. doi: 10.1186/1751-0759-2-21
39. Etkin A, Egner T, Kalisch R. Emotional processing in anterior cingulate and medial prefrontal cortex. *Trends Cogn Sci* (2011) 15:85–93. doi: 10.1016/j.tics.2010.11.004
40. Yuan H, Young KD, Phillips R, Zotev V, Misaki M, Bodurka J, et al. Resting-state functional connectivity modulation and sustained changes after real-time functional magnetic resonance imaging neurofeedback training in depression. *Brain Connect* (2014) 4:690. doi: 10.1089/brain.2014.0262
41. Macqueen G, Frodl T. The hippocampus in major depression: evidence for the convergence of the bench and bedside in psychiatric research? *Mol Psychiatry* (2011) 16:252. doi: 10.1038/mp.2010.80
42. McCrory EJ, De Brito SA, Sebastian CL, Mechelli A, Bird G, Kelly PA, et al. Heightened neural reactivity to threat in child victims of family violence. *Curr Biol* (2011) 21:R947–R948. doi: 10.1016/j.cub.2011.10.015
43. Grant MM, Cannistraci C, Hollon SD, Gore J, Shelton R. Childhood trauma history differentiates amygdala response to sad faces within MDD. *J Psychiatr Res* (2011) 45:886–95. doi: 10.1016/j.jpsychires.2010.12.004
44. Sah P, Faber ES, Lopez DAM, Power J. The amygdaloid complex: anatomy and physiology. *Physiol Rev* (2003) 83:803–34. doi: 10.1152/physrev.00002.2003
45. Holland PC, Gallagher M. Amygdala-frontal interactions and reward expectancy. *Curr Opin Neurobiol* (2004) 14:148–55. doi: 10.1016/j.conb.2004.03.007
46. Lupien SJ, McEwen BS, Gunnar MR, Heim C. Effects of stress throughout the lifespan on the brain, behaviour and cognition. *Nature Reviews Neuroscience* (2009) 10:434–45. doi: 10.1038/nrn2639
47. Price JL, Drevets WC. Neurocircuitry of mood disorders. *Neuropsychopharmacology* (2010) 35:192. doi: 10.1038/npp.2009.104
48. Pizzagalli DA. Frontocingulate dysfunction in depression: toward biomarkers of treatment response. *Neuropsychopharmacology* (2011) 36:183–206. doi: 10.1038/npp.2010.166
49. Hamani C, Mayberg H, Stone S, Laxton A, Haber S, Lozano AM. The subcallosal cingulate gyrus in the context of major depression. *Biol Psychiatry* (2011) 69:301–8. doi: 10.1016/j.biopsych.2010.09.034
50. van der Werff SJ, Pannekoek JN, Veer IM, van Tol MJ, Aleman A, Veltman DJ, et al. Resting-state functional connectivity in adults with childhood emotional maltreatment. *Psychol Med* (2013) 43:1825–36. doi: 10.1017/S0033291712002942
51. Frith CD, Frith U. Interacting minds—a biological basis. *Science* (1999) 286:1692–5. doi: 10.1126/science.286.5445.1692
52. Liang MJ, Zhou Q, Yang KR, Yang XL, Fang J, Chen WL, et al. Identify changes of brain regional homogeneity in bipolar disorder and unipolar depression using resting-state fMRI. *PloS one* (2013) 8:e79999. doi: 10.1371/journal.pone.0079999
53. Heitzeg MM, Nigg JT, Hardee JE, Soules M, Steinberg D, Zubieta JK, et al. Left middle frontal gyrus response to inhibitory errors in children prospectively predicts early problem substance use. *Drug Alcohol Depend* (2014) 141:51–7. doi: 10.1016/j.drugalcdep.2014.05.002
54. Manenti R, Cotelli M, Robertson IH, Miniussi C. Transcranial brain stimulation studies of episodic memory in young adults, elderly adults and individuals with memory dysfunction: a review. *Brain Stimul* (2012) 5:103–9. doi: 10.1016/j.brs.2012.03.004
55. Frodl TS, Koutsouleris N, Bottlender R, Born C, Jäger M, Scupin I, et al. Depression-related variation in brain morphology over 3 years: effects of stress? *Arch Gen Psychiatry* (2008) 65:1156. doi: 10.1001/archpsyc.65.10.1156
56. Minichino A, Bersani FS, Trabucchi G, Albano G, Primavera M, Delle Chiaie R, et al. The role of cerebellum in unipolar and bipolar depression: a review of the main neurobiological findings. *Riv Psichiatr* (2014) 49:124–31. doi:10.1708/1551.16907.

16

Dysfunction of Pre-Attentive Visual Information Processing in Drug-Naïve Women, But Not Men, During the Initial Episode of Major Depressive Disorder

Xiuxian Yang[1†], Qihe Wang[1†], Zhengxue Qiao[1], Xiaohui Qiu[1], Dong Han[1], Xiongzhao Zhu[2], Congpei Zhang[3] and Yanjie Yang[1]*

[1] Department of Medical Psychology, Public Health Institute of Harbin Medical University, Harbin, China, [2] Medical Psychological Institute, Second Xiangya Hospital, Central South University, Changsha, China, [3] The First Special Hospital of Harbin, Harbin, China

***Correspondence:**
Yanjie Yang
yanjie1965@163.com

[†]These authors have contributed equally to this work

Women are twice as likely as men to develop depression. Few studies have explored gender difference in cognitive function of patients with MDD. The gender difference in the pre-attentive information processing of MDD patients is still poorly understood. To examine the gender differences in change detection, 30 medication-free MDD patients (15 women) and 30 age and education matched controls (15 women) were recruited. The deviant-standard reverse oddball paradigm (50 ms/150 ms) was used to obtain the visual mismatch negativity (vMMN) in first episode MDD patients. Compared to men with MDD, women with MDD showed a significantly decreased increment vMMN, while no gender difference in decrement vMMN was found. The increment vMMN amplitude in MDD women was smaller than in healthy women, whereas no difference was found in decrement vMMN. Neither increment nor decrement vMMN differed between MDD men and healthy men. The mean amplitude of increment vMMN was not correlated with symptoms of MDD in MDD patients and MDD women. To conclude, the dysfunction of visual information processing existed at pre-attentive stage in MDD women.

Keywords: pre-attentive processing, gender, major depressive disorder, visual mismatch negativity, cognitive function

INTRODUCTION

Major depressive disorder (MDD) is one of the most common mood disorders and is a leading cause of disability worldwide (1). Women are twice as likely as men to suffer from MDD at some point in their life (2, 3). Moreover, depressed women experience more symptoms associated with MDD, and with greater severity, including sadness and somatic pain, compared to men (4, 5).

Although numerous studies have been conducted to explore the gender differences in the presentation and features of MDD, gender differences in cognitive function have been paid less attention. Several studies reported that cognitive functions were affected differently in depressed women compared to their male counterparts. The event-related potentials (ERPs) were widely used to measure the cognitive functions of some physical or mental stimuli. These potentials can be extracted from the ongoing electroencephalogram by filtering and signal averaging. P300, N170, MMN are all the ERP components which have been explored in cognitive function studies. Studies reported higher posterior P300 amplitude (reflect orientation of attention) in depressed patients, especially in women, indicating that the cognitive functions (e.g. automatic orientation of attention and controlled orientation of attention, response resolution, and working memory) of depressed women are more serious than those of depressed men (6–8). In addition, depressed women scored significantly lower in tests involving cognitive interference threshold (Stroop III) and visual recall (Rey-Osterreith Complex Figure Test) compared to depressed men (9), thus implying a more severe cognitive dysfunction in depressed women.

Pre-attentive information processing is the early stage of cognition which is essential for perception and cognition in humans. It is necessary for either survival or social skills development to filter information from pre-attentive processing to attentive processing (10). In addition, pre-attentive information processing provides effective basements for successful processing of advanced cognitive function such as task-relevant information (11). Moreover, the impairment of pre-attentive information processing may underline the clinical symptoms of some mental diseases (12, 13) and may regulate deficiencies in more complex cognitive processing (14). Hence, pre-attentive information processing has been widely used to study cognitive function in psychiatric patients (15).

Pre-attentive automatic detection can be indexed using visual mismatch negativity (vMMN), which reflects the difference waves between the ERPs elicited by deviant (presented infrequently) and standard (presented frequently) stimuli (16). The memory template was formed by the standard stimulus input repeatedly, when the deviant stimuli input against the template, the vMMN was generated. VMMN is a negativity deflection in the temporal-occipital electrodes during 150 ms and 350 ms after the deviant stimulus input. It can be produced by many different types of visual stimuli such as duration (17), color (18), motion direction (19), and facial expression (20). Importantly, vMMN has been explored in psychiatric and neural diseases, including Alzheimer's disease (21), schizophrenia (22), and MDD (17, 20), indicating that vMMN can reflect the dysfunction of detecting the automatic changes of visual stimuli in patients with these diseases. Interestingly, reports on vMMN in patients with MDD have only been found in recent years. For example, Chang et al. found the amplitudes of vMMN decreased in MDD patients, reflecting a deficit in pre-attentive expression processing (20). In their study, the facial stimuli lasted for a period of time in the center of the screen, so it was difficult for participants to ignore facial expressions, although they were task-independent. Therefore, the vMMN in this study may not be a memory-comparison-base vMMN, which reflects automatic memory-based change. In support of the latter hypothesis, using a deviant-standard reverse paradigm, Qiu et al. reported that vMMNs which elicited by deviant duration were decreased in MDD patients. Obviously, the cognitive function of change detection in visual modality impaired in patients with MDD, however, the aforementioned studies matched patients and controls with gender, a direct interaction between depression and gender remains unknown.

Gender differences in automatic change detection in healthy participants have been explored and obtained inconclusive results so far. Using the traditional oddball paradigm, Langrova et al. found no gender differences in direction vMMN amplitudes (23), whereas our previous study reported that the amplitude of duration vMMN increased in males compared to females (24). The different findings may attribute to changes in previous research methods. The vMMN in Langrova et al.'s study was observed by traditional oddball paragram in which the vMMN is obtained by subtracting the ERP waveforms elicited by standard stimuli from that elicited by deviant stimuli (23), and hence the vMMN may have confounded low-level physical differences between deviants and standards. On the other hand, the standard stimuli are presented more frequently than the deviant stimuli in these studies, that is to say neuronal processing of the standard stimuli would likely have more refractory effects than those processing the deviant stimuli. Thus, the vMMN may not properly reflect the pre-attentive memory-based change detection because of the compound of refractory effect between the standard and deviant stimuli. Furthermore, our brain may process information differently for different physical properties of the stimuli (direction in Langrova vs. duration in Yang) (23).

In order to clarify gender differences in pre-attentive information processing in MDD patients, it is essential to obtain vMMN based on memory comparison. Schroger and Wolff designed a paradigm in which an equal-probability sequence protocol as a control condition to obtain a memory-comparison-base MMN (25). In particular, a deviant-standard-reverse oddball paradigm was introduced by Jacobsen and Schroger in which two stimuli were counterbalanced as standard or deviant in two separate blocks. And they found that the MMNs obtained under the deviant-standard inversion condition was similar to that observed under the control condition from the equal probability sequence, so they proposed to use the deviant-standard-reverse paradigm to obtain the memory-comparison-base MMN (26). In addition, it has reported that deviant stimuli could elicit memory-comparison-base MMN using the deviant-standard-reverse method with a "safe" presentation probability of 15% (27). Moreover, our previous studies have found that the visual and auditory pre-attentive information processing impaired in MDD patients by the reverse oddball paradigm with a presentation probability of 20% (17, 28). Therefore, we still employed the reverse oddball paradigm to acquire the memory-comparison-base vMMN in this study.

Based on the above studies, we hypothesized that the impairment of pre-attentive information processing was more severe in MDD women compared to MDD men. Therefore, the aim of the present study was to explore whether gender differences exist in the pre-attentive information processing among MDD patients, meanwhile to examine whether duration vMMN correlated with depressive symptoms.

METHODS

Participants

Participants included 30 patients with MDD and 30 healthy controls. All participants had normal hearing and normal or corrected to normal vision. They were given a detailed procedure of the study, and written consent was approved and obtained by the Ethics Committee of the Harbin Medical University. The participants completing the experiment were paid seven dollars.

The MDD group consisted of 15 men and 15 women, which were recruited from the First Affiliated Hospital of Harbin Medical University. They all received structured interviews with the Diagnostic and Statistical Manual for Mental Illness (fourth edition, DSM-IV) to identify MDD. Before the ERP recording, all patients were interviewed by two psychiatrists to confirm the first episode and with no treatment. The 17-item Hamilton Rating Scale of Depression (HRSD-17) and the 14-item Hamilton Anxiety Rating scale (HAMA) were used to evaluate the severity of depression and anxiety respectively. Twenty out of the 30 MDD patients appeared anxiety symptoms. Patients were excluded if they had any other axis-I mental disorders.

The healthy controls (15 males and 15 females) were recruited from the Physical Examination Center in the First Affiliated Hospital of Harbin Medical University. The Structured Clinical Interview for DSM-IV (SCID) was also used to exclude any psychiatric disease, neurological illness, alcohol or drug abuse, and medications known to affect the test. HRSD-17 and HAMA were measured in control group as well. Education level and age matched between controls and patients. And the participants with traumatic brain injury and intellectual impairment were excluded in both groups.

An overall ANOVA with group and gender as between-subject factor was conducted to analyze age, education, depression score (HRSD-17), and anxiety score (HAMA) in MDD group and healthy control group. The main effect of group was found in depression score and anxiety score. No gender effect was found in age, education, depression score, and anxiety score. The interactions of Group × Gender on age, education, depression, and anxiety severity were not significant (**Table 1**).

Stimuli and Procedure

Participants sat in a sound attenuated, electrically shielded dark room and were focused on a black cross presented in the center of a white screen with luminance of 56 cd/m^2. The black cross was displayed continuously throughout the stimulus blocks. Response hands were counterbalanced across participants. As shown in **Figure 1**, at the beginning of the experiment, the cross was presented 1,000 ms. Occasionally, the cross become bigger or smaller randomly (mean frequency: 12/min). Two solid black squares (1/1 cm) were presented 50 or 150 ms at the same time in the periphery with a visual angle of 3.8° × 4.0°. The stimulus onset asynchrony (SOA) was fixed at 600 ms. When the peripheral squares were appeared, the cross was simultaneously presented with unchanged size. The duration of the bigger or smaller cross was 150 ms. Upon resizing of the cross, participants were requested to ignore the peripheral stimuli. And they pressed the left or the right button accordingly within 800 ms when the cross became "big" or "small." Participants were inquired whether they noticed changes of the peripheral squares after finishing the experiment. No participant reported awareness of these changes.

Our experiment included two conditions: decrement deviant (50 ms duration) with a 150 ms standard (A) and increment deviant (150 ms duration) with a 50 ms standard (B). The decrement MMN was obtained by subtracting the ERP of decrement deviant in (A) from the ERP of the 50 ms presented as a standard in (B). Similarly, the increment MMN was calculated by subtracting the ERP of increment deviant in (B) from the ERP of 150 ms presented as a standard in (A). Under the two blocking conditions, the exposure probability of deviation (20%) and standard stimulus (80%) was equal, and the blocking order between subjects was balanced. Each block included six experimental sequences of 150 trials. In each condition, the stimuli were presented in pseudorandom manner with two or more standard stimuli before each deviant stimulus.

EEG Recording

EEG readings were recorded continuously with a Neuroscan 40-electrode cap (NuAmps amplifier) including channels based on the International 10-20 system. The horizontal EOG was recorded by two electrodes placed on the outer canthi of both eyes and vertical EOG was recorded by another two electrodes placed above and below the right eye. vMMNs were recorded by the electrode sites O1, O2, and Oz placed on

TABLE 1 | An overall ANOVA of demographic characteristic in MDD group and healthy control group (M, SD).

Group	Age (year)	Education (year)	Anxiety	Depression
MDD patients				
MDD men	40.95, 10.38	8.47, 5.08	14.69, 5.60	24.93, 4.65
MDD women	41.96, 9.91	8.53, 4.97	15.37, 6.56	25.67, 4.19
Healthy controls				
Healthy men	41.19, 10.50	8.47,4.24	2.08, 0.96	1.95, 0.72
Healthy women	41.27, 9.76	9.13,4.63	2.58, 1.12	2.16, 0.85
Group effect	F = 0.009, P = 0.925	F = 0.060, P = 0.807	F = 547.971, P = 0.000	F = 1.732.082, P = 0000
Gender effect	F = 0.269, P = 0.606	F = 0.090, P = 0.766	F = 0.003, P = 0.957	F = 1.511, P = 0.224
Group × Gender	F = 1.297, P = 0.263	F = 0.060, P = 0.807	F = 0.146, P = 0.704	F = 0.771, P = 0.384

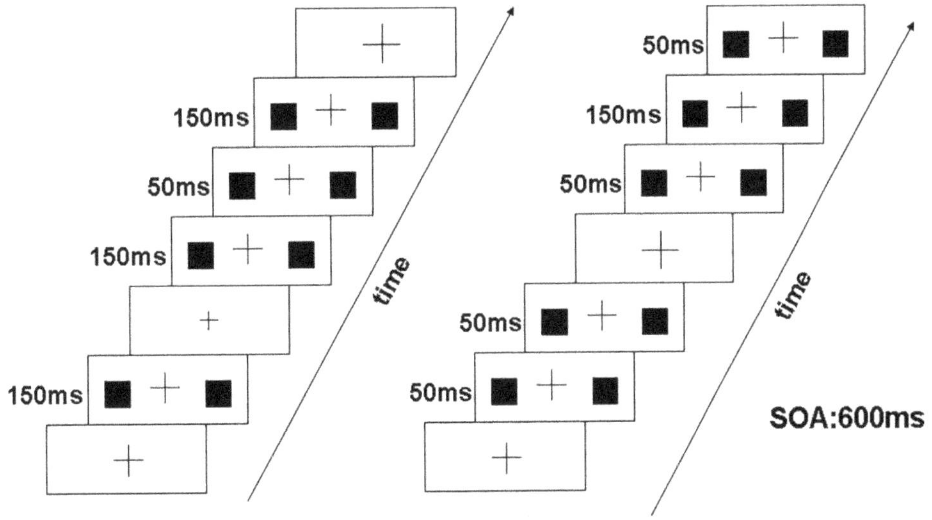

FIGURE 1 | Visual stimuli consisted of two solid black squares (1 cm × 1 cm) presented simultaneously for 50 ms or 150 ms in the periphery. The left panel illustrates deviant stimuli at 50 ms and standard stimuli at 150 ms, and right panel illustrates deviant stimuli at 150 ms and standard stimuli at 50 ms.

the occipital. The reference electrode was put on the tip of the nose. The impedances of all electrodes were less than 5 kΩ throughout the experiment and the sampling rate was 500 Hz/channel.

After correcting EOG artifact with the method of Gratton (29), the EEG was segmented to 500 ms including 100 ms pre-stimulus and 400 ms time locked to stimuli onset. We rejected the trials with artifacts greater than ±100 μV and the trails in which the participant responded. The EEG segments were averaged respectively for the deviant and standard stimuli and the averaged ERP data were digitally filtered with a band-pass filter at 1–30 Hz, 24 dB/octave. In MDD group, the numbers of accepted/rejected epochs for each stimulus were 83/4 and 332/13 (deviant, standard in 50 ms deviant condition), and 84/3 and 324/12 (deviant, standard in 150 ms deviant condition), respectively. In control group, the numbers of accepted/rejected epoch for each stimulus were 87/5 and 333/15 (deviant, standard in 50 ms deviant condition), and 86/4 and 329/11 (deviant, standard in 150 ms deviant condition), respectively.

Data Analysis

The software Statistical Package for the Social Sciences (version 18.0 for Windows) was used to conduct statistical analyses. Repeated measures ANOVA with group and gender as between-subject factors were used to analyze the performance data (reaction times, correct rate). The mean amplitudes of the vMMN were measured during the time window of 150–300 ms. All the analysis were conducted on the average amplitudes of O1, O2, and OZ. Group and gender were used as the factors between the subjects, hem or location (O1/OZ/O2) were used as the factors within the subjects for 2*2 ANOVA. The Greenhouse-Geisser procedure was used to correct the statistical probability. Tukey's honestly significantly different (HSD) test was used as a *post-hoc* test. A *p*-value of < 0.05 was considered statistically significant.

RESULTS

Behavioral Performance

For detecting cross changes in the center of the screen, responses were scored as hit if the correct button was pressed within 150 to 800 ms after target onset. For accuracy rate, the main effect of group and gender on participants' accuracy failed to reach significance (group: F = 0.848, df = 1, 56, p = 0.361, η^2 = 0.015; gender: F = 0.053, df = 1, 56, p = 0.819, η^2 = 0.001). And the group × gender interaction did not reach significance level (F = 0.205, df = 1, 56, p = 0.652, η^2 = 0.004).

For reaction time (RT), the main effect of group (MDD group and control group) on reaction time reached significance ($F_{(1, 56)}$ = 11.243, p = 0.001, η^2 = 0.167), and the reaction time was longer in MDD group than control group (MDD group: 495.3 ± 9.12 ms; control group: 452 ± 10.0 ms). The main effect of gender failed to reach significance ($F_{(1, 56)}$ = 0.827, p = 0.367, η^2 = 0.015). The group × gender interaction did not reach significance level ($F_{(1, 56)}$ = 0.306, p = 0.583, η^2 = 0.005).

ERP Analysis

As shown in **Figures 2A, B**, N1 and P2 components elicited at the posterior scalp by the deviant and standard stimuli regardless of block conditions in both healthy and MDD participants. As illustrated in **Figure 3**, the vMMN was observed on occipital areas at the time range between 150 and 300 ms.

Increment vMMN

Repeated measures ANOVA showed the main effect of group on increment vMMN amplitudes in occipital areas was significant ($F_{(1, 56)}$ = 6.130, p = 0.016, η^2 = 0.099), indicating that the vMMN mean amplitude decreased in MDD group. The main effect of gender was marginal significant ($F_{(1, 56)}$ = 4.980, p = 0.051, η^2 = 0.034). Moreover, the interaction of group × gender reached significance ($F_{(1, 56)}$ = 6.386, p = 0.014, η^2 = 0.102).

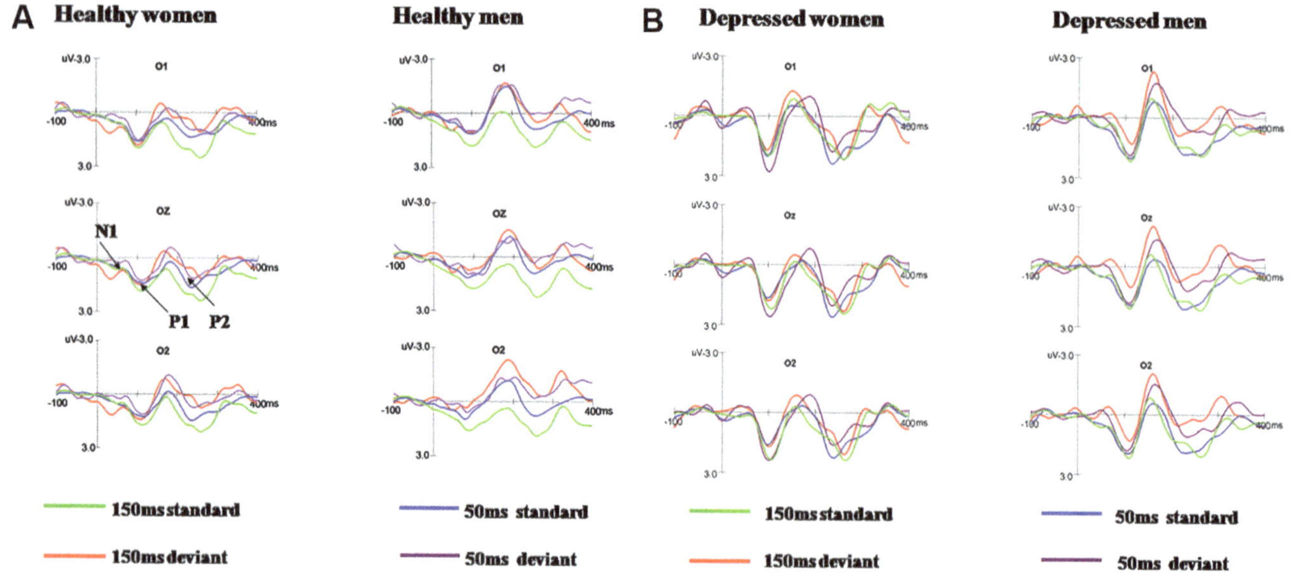

FIGURE 2 | Grand average ERPs in response to 50 ms and 150 ms deviant/standard visual stimuli in healthy participants **(A)** and MDD patients **(B)**.

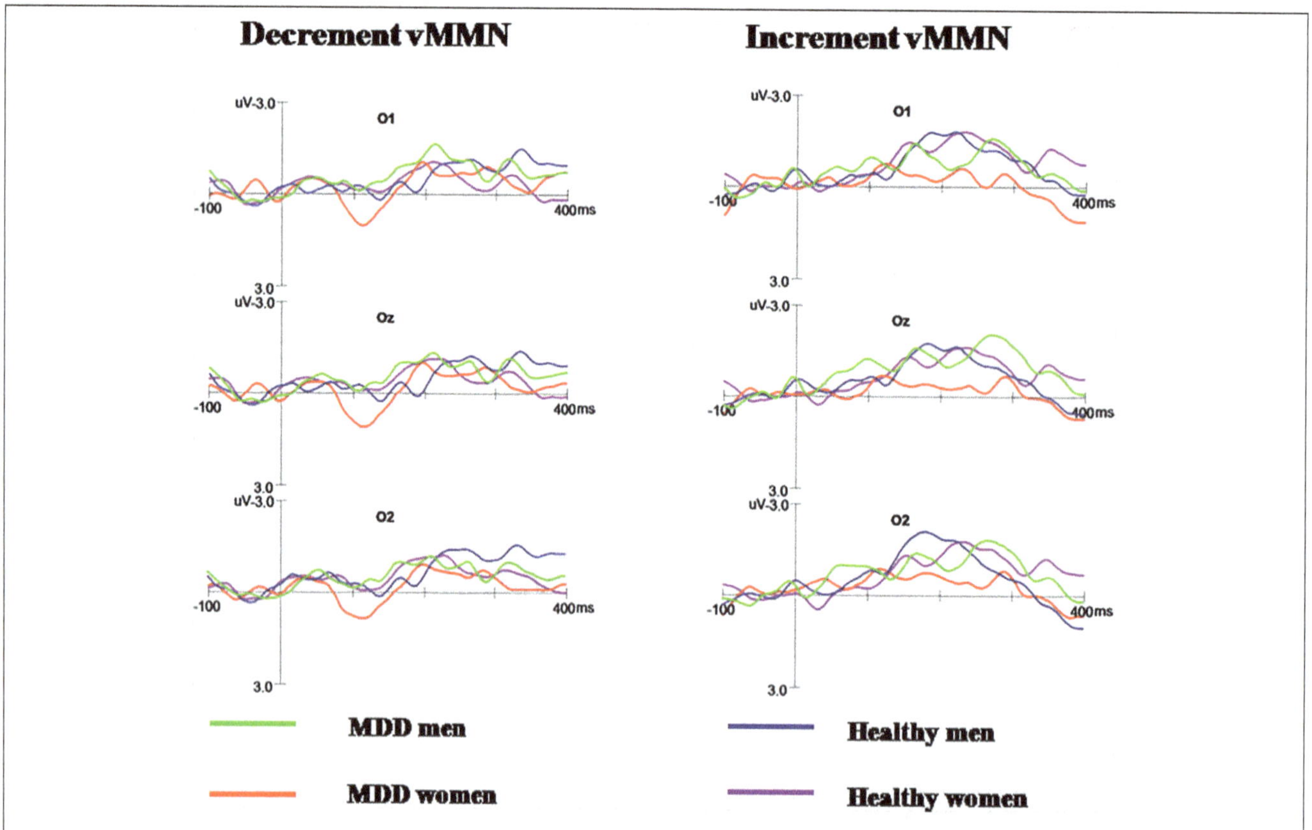

FIGURE 3 | The decrement and increment vMMN in MDD men, MDD women, healthy men, and healthy women. MDD women showed significantly reduced increment vMMN compared to MDD men and healthy women. Increment vMMN was smaller in healthy women than in healthy men.

Further post-hoc analysis revealed the amplitudes of increment duration vMMN in MDD women were significantly smaller compared to MDD men (−0.369 μV and −1.603 μV for MDD women and MDD men, respectively; $F_{(1, 56)} = 6.696$, $p = 0.008$). In addition, the increment vMMN in healthy men was higher than in healthy women ($F_{(1, 56)} = 6.219$, $p = 0.016$; healthy men: −1.916 μV, healthy women: −1.316 μV). The amplitude of increment vMMN was smaller in MDD women than in healthy women (−0.369 μV and −1.316 μV for MDD women and healthy women, respectively; $F_{(1,\ 56)} = 4.603$, $p = 0.036$) (**Figure 4**). No difference was found for increment vMMN between MDD men and healthy men ($F_{(1,\ 56)} = 2.074$, $p = 0.155$).

The main effect of hem and the interaction of hem × group × gender did not reach significance (hem: $F_{(2,\ 112)} = 0.868$, $p = 0.387$, $\eta^2 = 0.015$; hem × group × gender: $F_{(2,\ 112)} = 0.977$, $p = 0.353$, $\eta^2 = 0.017$).

Decrement vMMN

Repeated measures ANOVA showed no significant effect of group on decrement vMMN ($F_{(1,\ 56)} = 0.240$, $p = 0.626$, $\eta^2 = 0.004$). The main effect of gender was not significant ($F_{(1,\ 56)} = 0.557$, $p = 0.459$, $\eta^2 = 0.010$). Furthermore, there was no significant interaction for group × gender, indicating that the decrement vMMN amplitude was similar between different group for men and women. The main effect of hem was not significant ($F_{(2,\ 112)} = 0.707$, $p = 0.495$, $\eta^2 = 0.012$). And the interaction of hem × group × gender did not reach significance ($F_{(2,\ 112)} = 2.012$, $p = 0.153$, $\eta^2 = 0.035$).

Relationship Between the Amplitudes of Increment vMMN and Depressive Symptom (Scores of HRSD) in MDD Patients

Pearson correlation analysis was used to examine the relationship between the amplitudes of increment vMMN and the severity of depression (scores of HRSD). At the occipital electrode sites, neither the correlation between vMMN amplitude and depression symptoms in the MDD patients (e.g., O1: $r = 0.109$, $p = 0.678$, Oz: $r = 0.167$, $p = 0.302$, and O2: $r = 0.186$, $p = 0.396$) nor the correlation in all participants was significant (e.g., O1: $r = 0.126$, $p = 0.679$, Oz: $r = 0.149$, $p = 0.463$, and O2: $r = 0.201$, $p = 0.383$). In addition, the amplitudes of the increment vMMN did not relate to the symptom level in MDD women (e.g., Oz, $r = 0.185$, $p = 0.391$, O1, $r = 0.112$, $p = 0.634$, and O2, $r = 0.198$, $p = 0.367$).

DISCUSSION

In this study, we examined gender differences in pre-attentive information processing using vMMN in MDD patients.

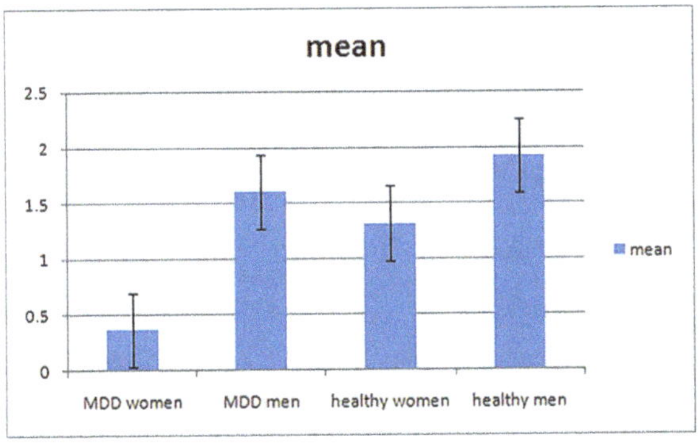

FIGURE 4 | The mean amplitudes of increment vMMN in four groups.

Consistent with our hypothesis, we found that detection of change in vMMN was impaired in MDD women compared to MDD men. The results can be summarized as following: 1) In healthy controls, increment vMMN was enhanced in men relative to women. 2) In depressed patients, the amplitude of the increment vMMN was smaller in MDD women than healthy women. In contrast, MDD men showed no differences in increment vMMN amplitudes as compared to healthy men. 3) The amplitude of the decrement vMMN in MDD women was equivalent to healthy women, as was the case for MDD men and healthy men. 4) MDD women showed smaller amplitude of the increment vMMN compared to MDD men, indicating a greater severity of impairment in pre-attentive information processing in MDD women. In contrast, MDD women showed no differences in decrement vMMN amplitudes compared to MDD men. 5) The amplitude of increment vMMN did not associate with depressive symptoms in women with MDD, indicating the impairment of pre-attentive change detection in patients is independent of depressive symptoms.

In line with our previous study, the amplitude of vMMN in healthy males is higher than that in healthy females, which indicates that there are inherent gender differences in visual information processing (24).

To explain the gender difference in the increment vMMN, we must consider the neurogenerator of vMMN: the right occipital visual extrastriate area (30). It is reported that the visual region was sexually dimorphic by quantitative analysis of the cellular structure of human primary visual cortex. The primary visual cortex (V 1/Brodmann region 17) and the volume of the motion sensitive region (hOc5) in men were larger than that of women (31), indicating that men have greater ability to process visual information. The enhanced VMMN observed in men in this study can indirectly demonstrate the gender differences in visual extrastriate areas. However, fMRI studies are needed to determine the gender differences in occipital visual extrastriate areas due to ERPs cannot directly reflect brain tissue structure.

Consistent with previous studies, MDD patients showed reduced vMMN compared to healthy controls, suggesting patients with MDD show impairment of pre-attentive processing. Our further analysis indicated that only MDD women exhibit smaller increment vMMN. The decreased vMMN indicates that impaired change detection function processing was evident in MDD women but not in MDD men. Although the neurobiological differences which may explain the gender-specific effect have not been elucidated, our results showed that male MDD patients differ from female patients in pre-attention information processing, which must be considered when comparing cognitive processing between MDD patients and healthy controls.

Although the amplitude of increment vMMN decreased in healthy women compared to healthy men and the same result in MDD women and MDD man, the amplitude decreased in MDD women compared to healthy women, while the amplitude in healthy man was similar to MDD men. Then we conclude that the pre-attentive change detection was impaired only in MDD women. And the results were mostly concordant with our hypothesis that there would be smaller vMMN amplitudes in MDD women than MDD men. Extensive studies have proved the role of personality factors in gender differences in depression and proposed the development of depression has been attributed to high levels of neuroticism (32, 33). Moreover, previous studies have found that levels of neuroticism were higher in MDD women compared with MDD men (34). In particular, MMN amplitude was positively correlated with neuroticism (35), and therefore it has been speculated that higher neuroticism may contribute to the difference of MMN between MDD women and MDD male.

It has been shown that MDD women make more errors during emotional processing tasks than healthy women and also MDD men (36). The differences in emotional processing between women and men during depressed states may result from different cognitive strategies regarding attention processing. In addition, studies have found that impairment of pre-attentive information processing may lead to more complex cognitive operations in patients with schizophrenia (14). Our findings that vMMN amplitude was smaller in MDD women compared to MDD men, as well as healthy women, suggests that gender differences in cognitive function during depressed states are related to the pre-attentive stage of information processing. Therefore, our results may partly explain disparities in the prevalence of MDD between women and men as well as the more severe impairments in cognitive function found in female patients. It is worth noting that given the link between depression and a narrow focus of attention, MDD women may have been impaired in detecting changes because their attention was more narrowly focused to the central task.

No significant effect for decrement vMMN was found between the MDD and healthy group, as well as between healthy men and women, while a significant effect was found for increment vMMN, which could be explained by different processing of increment and decrement vMMN. According to previous studies, stimulus parameters exert a differential influence on the vMMN for a duration decrement and increment of an equal magnitude. The increase in stimulus is detected by both a transient and a memory-comparison-based change detector system, while the decrease in stimulus is only activated by the change detector system (37, 38). The results of this study suggest that the impacts of stimulus parameters should be taken into account when comparing different studies in clinical settings.

Our previous studies indicated no association between the amplitudes of duration vMMN (17) or aMMN (28) and the severity of depressive symptoms in MDD patients. Furthermore, a few studies have reported that cognitive impairment remained evident regardless of the remission of depressive symptoms or the reduction of the HDRS score (39, 40). In the present study, the correlation between the severity of depressive symptoms and increment vMMN was not significant in MDD patients and MDD women, indicating that the pre-attentive change detection may be associated with depressive symptoms in patients with MDD. Taken together, our findings indicate the changes of vMMN are likely to be trait-dependent, but not state-dependent in MDD patients.

However, it should be noted that the cross-section design constrains conclusive evidence as to whether MDD affects pre-attentive processing or whether the impairment in pre-attentive processing is a risk factor for subsequently developing MDD in women. In addition, about 67% depressed patients have anxiety symptoms; our results could not exclude the effect of anxiety on our results. Moreover, Withall et al. found that compared with patients without melancholic symptoms, cognitive function of depressed patients with melancholy was severely impaired (41). Whether the subtypes of MDD affect the gender effect in pre-attentive processing needs further investigation. The evidence that symptom severity is not associated with vMMN suggests that the dysfunction of pre-attentive processing may be a significant trait of MDD but unrelated to the symptoms, and longitudinal data is required to verify whether vMMN abnormalities still exist if the depressive symptoms disappear. Last but not the least, the sample of our study is relatively small.

In conclusion, we found that the increment duration vMMN was reduced in MDD women but not in MDD men, indicating that MDD women have visual information processing dysfunction at the pre-attentive stage. Our study supports previous findings that cognitive impairment in MDD women was more severe than in MDD men. Therefore, we should take gender differences into account when exploring pre-attentive information processing in MDD patients. Moreover, the association between symptom severity and duration vMMN was not significant, reflecting that the dysfunction of pre-attentive processing was unrelated to the symptoms of MDD, it could be a distinguishing trait of MDD.

ETHICS STATEMENT

This study was carried out in accordance with the recommendations of the Ethics Committee of Harbin Medical University with written informed consent from all subjects. All subjects gave written informed consent in accordance with the Declaration of Helsinki. The protocol was approved by the Ethics Committee of Harbin Medical University.

AUTHOR CONTRIBUTIONS

YY and XY designed the experiment. XY and QW wrote the manuscript. ZQ, XQ, DH, CZ, and QW selected the participants and completed the experiment. XZ and ZQ analyzed the data.

FUNDING

This research was supported by the National Natural Science Foundation of China (Grant Nos. 81773536, 31271093, and 81302484) and National Science Foundation of Heilongjiang Province (Grant No: LH2019H032).

REFERENCES

1. Whiteford HA, Degenhardt L, Rehm J, Baxter AJ, Ferrari AJ, Erskine HE, et al. Global burden of disease attributable to mental and substance use disorders: findings from the Global Burden of Disease Study 2010. *Lancet* (2013) 382(9904):1575–86. doi: 10.1016/S0140-6736(13)61611-6
2. Kessler RC. Epidemiology of women and depression. *J Affect Disord* (2003) 74 (1):5–13. doi: S0165032702004263
3. Kuehner C. Gender differences in unipolar depression: an update of epidemiological findings and possible explanations. *Acta Psychiatr Scand* (2003) 108(3):163–74.
4. Lai CH. Major depressive disorder: gender differences in symptoms, life quality, and sexual function. *J Clin Psychopharmacol* (2011) 31(1):39–44. doi: 10.1097/JCP.0b013e318205a670 00004714-201102000-00008
5. Alexandrino-Silva C, Wang YP, Viana MC, Bulhões RS, Martins SS, Andrade LH. Gender differences in symptomatic profiles of depression: results from the São Paulo Megacity Mental Health Survey. *J Affect Disord* (2013) 147(1–3):355–64. doi: 10.1016/j.jad.2012.11.041
6. Shagass C, Roemer RA. Evoked potential topography in major depression. I. comparisons with nonpatients and schizophrenics. *Int J Psychophysiol* (1992) 13(3):241–54.
7. Fernandes LO, Keller J, Giese-Davis JE, Hicks BD, Klein DN, Miller GA. Converging evidence for a cognitive anomaly in early psychopathology. *Psychophysiology* (1999) 36(4):511–21.
8. Anderer P, Saletu B, Semlitsch HV, Pascual-Marqui RD. Structural and energetic processes related to P300: LORETA findings in depression and effects of antidepressant drugs. *Methods Find Exp Clin Pharmacol* (2002) 24 Suppl D:85–91.
9. Sarosi A, Gonda X, Balogh G, Szekely A, Sasvari M, Faludi G. [Gender differences in the neurocognitive components of depression]. *Neuropsychopharmacol Hung* (2008) 10(4):191–9.
10. Seri S, Pisani F, Thai JN, Cerquiglini A. Pre-attentive auditory sensory processing in autistic spectrum disorder. Are electromagnetic measurements telling us a coherent story? *Int J Psychophysiol* (2007) 63(2):159–63. doi: 10.1016/j.ijpsycho.2006.03.013 S0167-8760(06)00101-2
11. Light GA, Swerdlow NR, Braff DL. Preattentive sensory processing as indexed by the MMN and P3a brain responses is associated with cognitive and psychosocial functioning in healthy adults. *J Cogn Neurosci* (2007) 19(10):1624–32. doi: 10.1162/jocn
12. Fisher DJ, Labelle A, Knott VJ. The right profile: mismatch negativity in schizophrenia with and without auditory hallucinations as measured by a multi-feature paradigm. *Clin Neurophysiol* (2008) 119(4):909–21. doi: 10.1016/j.clinph.2007.12.005 S1388-2457(07)00900-5
13. Mathalon DH, Ford JM. Corollary discharge dysfunction in schizophrenia: evidence for an elemental deficit. *Clin EEG Neurosci* (2008) 39(2):82–6. doi: 10.1177/155005940803900212
14. Rissling AJ, Braff DL, Swerdlow NR, Hellemann G, Rassovsky Y, Sprock J, et al. Disentangling early sensory information processing deficits in schizophrenia. *Clin Neurophysiol* (2012) 123(10):1942–9. doi: 10.1016/j.clinph.2012.02.079 S1388-2457(12)00215-5
15. Takahashi H, Rissling AJ, Pascual-Marqui R, Kirihara K, Pela M, Sprock J, et al. Neural substrates of normal and impaired preattentive sensory discrimination in large cohorts of nonpsychiatric subjects and schizophrenia patients as indexed by MMN and P3a change detection responses. *Neuroimage* (2012) 66C:594–603. doi: 10.1016/j.neuroimage.2012.09.074 S1053-8119(12) 01001-4
16. Naatanen R, Pakarinen S, Rinne T, Takegata R. The mismatch negativity (MMN): towards the optimal paradigm. *Clin Neurophysiol* (2004) 115(1):140–4. doi: S1388245703003687
17. Qiu X, Yang X, Qiao Z, Wang L, Ning N, Shi J, et al. Impairment in processing visual information at the pre-attentive stage in patients with a major depressive disorder: a visual mismatch negativity study. *Neurosci Lett* (2011) 491(1):53–7. doi: 10.1016/j.neulet.2011.01.006 S0304-3940(11) 00008-5
18. Czigler I, Balazs L, Pato LG. Visual change detection: event-related potentials are dependent on stimulus location in humans. *Neurosci Lett* (2004) 364 (3):149–53. doi: 10.1016/j.neulet.2004.04.048 S0304394004004999
19. Pazo-Alvarez P, Amenedo E, Cadaveira F. Automatic detection of motion direction changes in the human brain. *Eur J Neurosci* (2004) 19(7):1978–86. doi: 10.1111/j.1460-9568.2004.03273.x EJN3273
20. Chang Y, Xu J, Shi N, Pang X, Zhang B, Cai Z. Dysfunction of preattentive visual information processing among patients with major depressive disorder. *Biol Psychiatry* (2011) 69(8):742–7. doi: 10.1016/j.biopsych.2010.12. 024S0006-3223(10)01316-8
21. Tales A, Haworth J, Wilcock G, Newton P, Butler S. Visual mismatch negativity highlights abnormal pre-attentive visual processing in mild cognitive impairment and Alzheimer's disease. *Neuropsychologia* (2008) 46 (5):1224–32. doi: 10.1016/j.neuropsychologia.2007.11.017 S0028-3932(07) 00406-X
22. Umbricht D, Koller R, Schmid L, Skrabo A, Grübel C, Huber T, et al. How specific are deficits in mismatch negativity generation to schizophrenia? *Biol Psychiatry* (2003) 53(12):1120–31. doi: 10.1016/j.biopsych
23. Langrova J, Kremlacek J, Kuba M, Kubova Z, Szanyi J. Gender impact on electrophysiological activity of the brain. *Physiol Res* (2012) 61 Suppl 2:S119–127. doi: 932421
24. Yang X, Yu Y, Lu C, Sun H, Qiao Z, Qiu X, et al. Gender differences in pre-attentive change detection for visual but not auditory stimuli. *Clin Neurophysiology Off J Int Fed Clin Neurophysiology* (2015) 127(1):431–41. doi: 10.1097/WNR.0b013e32836169b9
25. Schroger E, Wolff C. Mismatch response of the human brain to changes in sound location. *Neuroreport* (1996) 7(18):3005–8. doi: 10.1097/00001756-199611250-00041
26. Jacobsen T, Schroger E. Measuring duration mismatch negativity. *Clin Neurophysiol* (2003) 114(6):1133–43. doi: S1388245703000439
27. Evstigneeva MD, Aleksandrov AA. Mismatch negativity: the contribution of differences in the refractoriness of stimulus-specific neuron populations. *Neurosci Behav Physiol* (2009) 39(9):833–40. doi: 10.1007/s11055-009-9211-x
28. Qiao Z, Yu Y, Wang L, Yang X, Qiu X, Zhang C, et al. Impaired pre-attentive change detection in major depressive disorder patients revealed by auditory mismatch negativity. *Psychiatry Res* (2013) 211(1):78–84. doi: 10.1016/j.pscychresns.2012.07.006 S0925-4927(12)00177-1
29. Gratton G. Dealing with artifacts: The EOG contamination of the event-related brain potential. *Behav Res Methods Instrum Comput* (1998) 30(1):44–53.
30. Kimura M. Visual mismatch negativity and unintentional temporal-context-based prediction in vision. *Int J Psychophysiol* (2012) 83(2):144–55. doi: 10.1016/j.ijpsycho.2011.11.010 S0167-8760(11)00357-6
31. Amunts K, Armstrong E, Malikovic A, Homke L, Mohlberg H, Schleicher A, et al. Gender-specific left-right asymmetries in human visual cortex. *J Neurosci* (2007) 27(6):1356–4. doi: 10.1523/JNEUROSCI.4753-06.2007
32. Nolen-Hoeksema S, Larson J, Grayson C. Explaining the gender difference in depressive symptoms. *J Pers Soc Psychol* (1999) 77(5):1061–42. doi: 10.1037// 0022-3514.77.5.1061
33. Ormel J, Oldehinkel AJ, Brilman EI. The interplay and etiological continuity of neuroticism, difficulties, and life events in the etiology of major and subsyndromal, first and recurrent depressive episodes in later life. *Am J Psychiatry* (2001) 158(6):885–91. doi: 10.1176/appi.ajp.158.6.885
34. Goodwin RD, Gotlib IH. Gender differences in depression: the role of personality factors. *Psychiatry Res* (2004) 126(2):135–42. doi: 10.1016/j.psychres.2003.12.024 S0165178104000393
35. Hansenne M, Pinto E, Scantamburlo G, Renard B, Reggers J, Fuchs S, et al. Harm avoidance is related to mismatch negativity (MMN) amplitude in healthy subjects. *Pers Individ Dif* (2003) 34(6):1039–48.
36. Wright SL, Langenecker SA, Deldin PJ, Rapport LJ, Nielson KA, Kade AM, et al. Gender-specific disruptions in emotion processing in younger adults with depression. *Depress Anxiety* (2009) 26(2):182–9. doi: 10.1002/da.20502
37. Takegata R, Tervaniemi M, Alku P, Ylinen S, Naatanen R. Parameter-specific modulation of the mismatch negativity to duration decrement and increment: evidence for asymmetric processes. *Clin Neurophysiol* (2008) 119(7):1515–23. doi: 10.1016/j.clinph.2008.03.025
38. Macdonald M, Campbell K. Effects of a violation of an expected increase or decrease in intensity on detection of change within an auditory pattern. *Brain Cognit* (2011) 77(3):438–45. doi: 10.1016/j.bandc.2011.08.014

39. Hammar A. Automatic and effortful information processing in unipolar major depression. *Scand J Psychol* (2003) 44(5):409–13. doi: 10.1046/j.1467-9450.2003.00361.x
40. Preiss M, Kucerova H, Lukavsky J, Stepankova H, Sos P, Kawaciukova R. Cognitive deficits in the euthymic phase of unipolar depression. *Psychiatry Res* (2009) 169(3):235–9. doi: 10.1016/j.psychres.2008.06.042
41. Withall A, Harris LM, Cumming SR. A longitudinal study of cognitive function in melancholic and non-melancholic subtypes of major depressive disorder. *J Affect Disord* (2010) 123(1-3):150–7. doi: 10.1016/j.jad.2009.07.012 S0165-0327(09)00339-5

17

Dihydromyricetin Alleviates Diabetic Neuropathic Pain and Depression Comorbidity Symptoms by Inhibiting $P2X_7$ Receptor

*Shu Guan[1], Yulin Shen[1,2], Huixiang Ge[1], Wei Xiong[3], Lingkun He[3], Lijuan Liu[3], Cancan Yin[3], Xingyu Wei[4] and Yun Gao[1,5]**

[1] Department of Physiology, Basic Medical College, Nanchang University, Nanchang, China, [2] Sport Biological Centre, China Institute of Sport Science, Beijing, China, [3] Department of Preventive Dentistry, Affiliated Stomatological Hospital of Nanchang University, Nanchang, China, [4] Basic Medical College of Grade 2017, Nanchang University, Nanchang, China, [5] Jiangxi Provincial Key Laboratory of Autonomic Nervous Function and Disease, Nanchang University, Nanchang, China

***Correspondence:**
Yun Gao
gaoyun@ncu.edu.cn

Diabetic neuropathic pain (DNP) and major depressive disorder (MDD) are common complications of diabetes mellitus and mutually affect each other. As a member of the ATP-gated ion channel family, $P2X_7$ receptor is associated with the transduction of pain signal and the onset of depression. The aim of this study was to investigate the effects of dihydromyricetin (DHM) on rats with comorbid DNP and MDD. After the comorbid model was established, rat behavior changes were monitored by measuring the mechanical withdrawal threshold, thermal withdrawal latency, sugar water preference, immobility time in the forced-swim test, and open-field test parameters. The expressions of $P2X_7$ receptor in the dorsal root ganglia (DRGs), spinal cord, and hippocampus were assessed by quantitative real-time PCR, Western blotting, and double immunofluorescence. We found that hyperalgesia, allodynia, and depressive behaviors of rats with comorbid DNP and MDD were relieved by treatment with DHM or application of a short-hairpin RNA for $P2X_7$ receptor. The expression levels of $P2X_7$, phosphorylated extracellular signal–regulated kinase 1/2, tumor necrosis factor α, and interleukin 1β were increased in the DRGs, spinal cord, and hippocampus of rats in the model group but restored after DHM or $P2X_7$ short-hairpin RNA treatment. In conclusion, $P2X_7$ receptor in the DRGs, spinal cord, and hippocampus participates in the transduction of DNP and MDD signals. DHM seems to relieve comorbid DNP and MDD by reducing the expression of $P2X_7$ receptor in the DRGs, spinal cord, and hippocampus and may be an effective new drug for the treatment of patients with both DNP and MDD.

Keywords: dihydromyricetin, $P2X_7$ receptor, diabetic neuropathic pain, major depressive disorder, dorsal root ganglion, spinal cord, hippocampus

INTRODUCTION

Given the high prevalence of diabetes mellitus worldwide, diabetic neuropathic pain (DNP) has become a relatively common condition (1, 2). DNP often involves primary injury or dysfunction of the peripheral or central nervous system (3, 4). Although DNP is one of the main symptoms of diabetic neuropathy, its pathophysiological mechanisms are not yet fully understood (5).

Depression, also known as major depressive disorder (MDD), is a serious medical condition affecting public health. Mild and severe depression is closely associated with increased mortality rates in patients with diabetes mellitus (6). Painful diabetic polyneuropathy is a greater determinant of depression than other diabetes-related complications and comorbidities (7), and depression severity depends on the intensity of pain (8). Comorbid DNP and MDD seriously affect the quality of life and are more difficult to treat than either DNP or MDD in isolation. At present, the relevant mechanisms have not been thoroughly elucidated and require further research.

After nerve injury and inflammation, nerve endings release large amounts of adenosine triphosphate, an important neurotransmitter that activates several purinergic receptors and is necessary for many biological and pathological functions (9, 10). $P2X_7$ receptor is a ligand-gated nonselective cation channel receptor (11–13) that is closely associated with neuropathic pain and depression (14, 15). Many studies have confirmed that $P2X_7$ receptor activation is involved in depression progression (16–18). Our previous experiments confirmed that hippocampal $P2X_7$ receptor expression was noticeably higher in rats with comorbid DNP and MDD than in control rats (19). We speculate that $P2X_7$ receptor might be a common target for the two comorbid diseases. However, the effects of comorbid DNP and MDD on $P2X_7$ receptor expression in the dorsal root ganglia (DRGs) and spinal cord have not been reported.

The flavonoid dihydromyricetin (DHM) is the most abundant organic chemical in vine tea, which is made from *Ampelopsis grossedentata*, and provides myriad health benefits, including anti-inflammatory, antitumor, and rapid antidepressant-like effects (20, 21). Homology modeling and molecular docking analysis, which predicts ligand binding at a protein's active sites (22), suggested that DHM is capable of high-affinity binding to $P2X_7$ receptor (**Table 1** and **Figure 1**). Thus, we hypothesized that DHM could be used to treat the comorbid symptoms by acting on $P2X_7$ receptor. The aim of this study was to investigate whether DHM treatment can alleviate comorbid DNP and MDD by inhibiting $P2X_7$ receptor expression in the DRGs, spinal cord, and hippocampus.

TABLE 1 | MOE (Molecular Operating Environment, a docking software) score of $P2X_7$ receptor docking and dihydromyricetin (kcal/mol).

Mode	Affinity	Dist from best mode	
	(kcal/mol)	RMSD lb	RMSD ub
1	−7.4	0	0
2	−7.2	1.600	2.344
3	−7.1	16.017	18.330
4	−7.1	4.546	6.709
5	−7.0	16.775	19.643
6	−7.0	16.089	18.520
7	−6.9	62.551	65.298
8	−6.9	18.809	22.016
9	−6.8	21.204	23.029

*The predicted binding affinity is in kcal/mol (energy). *rmsd: RMSD values are calculated relative to the best mode and use only movable heavy atoms. Two variants of RMSD metrics are provided, rmsd/lb (RMSD lower bound: matches each atom in one conformation with itself in the other conformation, ignoring any symmetry) and rmsd/ub (RMSD upper bound: rmsd/lb[c1, c2] = max[rmsd'{c1, c2}, rmsd'{c2, c1}], and rmsd' matches each atom in one conformation with the closest atom of the same element type in the other conformation), differing in how the atoms are matched in the distance calculation. There is a strong reaction between ligand and protein when the binding affinity is bigger than −6.0 kcal/mol. The rmsd/lb and rmsd/ub of modes 1 to 5, as well as of modes 6 to 8 are much similar, which indicates that those modes are located in one docking pocket. In summary, molecular docking of dihydromyricetin on a mode-h protein $P2X_7$ is stable.*

MATERIALS AND METHODS

Animals and Treatments

Male Sprague–Dawley rats (180–220 g) were provided by the Centre of Laboratory Animal Science of Nanchang University. The procedures of this study were approved by the Animal Care and Use Committee of Nanchang University Medical School and were performed according to IASP(International Association for the Study Pain)'s ethical guidelines for pain research in animals. Rats were housed under controlled conditions at 25°C temperature and 60% humidity, with freely available food and water. Five rats were housed in each cage. The timeline of this study is shown in **Figure 2C**.

Generation of DNP and MDD Rat Model

During the week before the start of the experiment, rats were fed a normal diet. After that, they were fed high-glucose, high-fat diet for 4 weeks. After the end of the 4 weeks, rats were starved for more than 12 h and were then given an intraperitoneal (i.p.) injection of streptozotocin (STZ; 35 mg/kg). Blood glucose was measured after food consumption. Rats whose blood glucose levels were higher than 16.7 mmol/l were chosen as having type 2 diabetes mellitus. For the next 5 weeks after injecting STZ, chronic unpredictable stress (CUS) stimuli were given randomly. Meanwhile, we measured responses in several behavioral tests once a week to verify that rats had both DNP and MDD, as follows: thermal withdrawal and mechanical withdrawal tests, sucrose preference (SP) test, forced-swimming test (FST), and open-field test (OFT). The CUS stimuli included food deprivation (24 h), cold swimming (4°C, 5 min), water deprivation (24 h), heat stress (45°C, 5 min), reverse light/dark cycle, no stressor, and clip of the tail (1 min) (13). Rats were exposed to one of the seven daily stressors randomly for 5 weeks.

Treatments

Seventy-two male rats were randomly divided into six groups: (1) control, (2) control + DHM, (3) comorbid DNP and MDD model (model), (4) DHM treatment group (model + DHM), (5) $P2X_7$ receptor short-hairpin RNA (shRNA) treatment group (model + $P2X_7$ shRNA), and (6) scramble shRNA treatment group (model + scramble shRNA). Rats in the control + DHM and model + DHM groups were treated with DHM *via* i.p. injection once a day, at a dose of 30 mg/kg, for 14 consecutive days.

The transfection complex consisting of shRNA ($P2X_7$ or scramble shRNA) and transfection reagent at a ratio of 1:2 (μg/μl) was prepared using the Entranster™ *in vivo* transfection reagent (Engreen Biosystem Company of Beijing), according to the manufacturer's instructions. The complex was intrathecally injected into rats of the model + $P2X_7$ and model + scramble

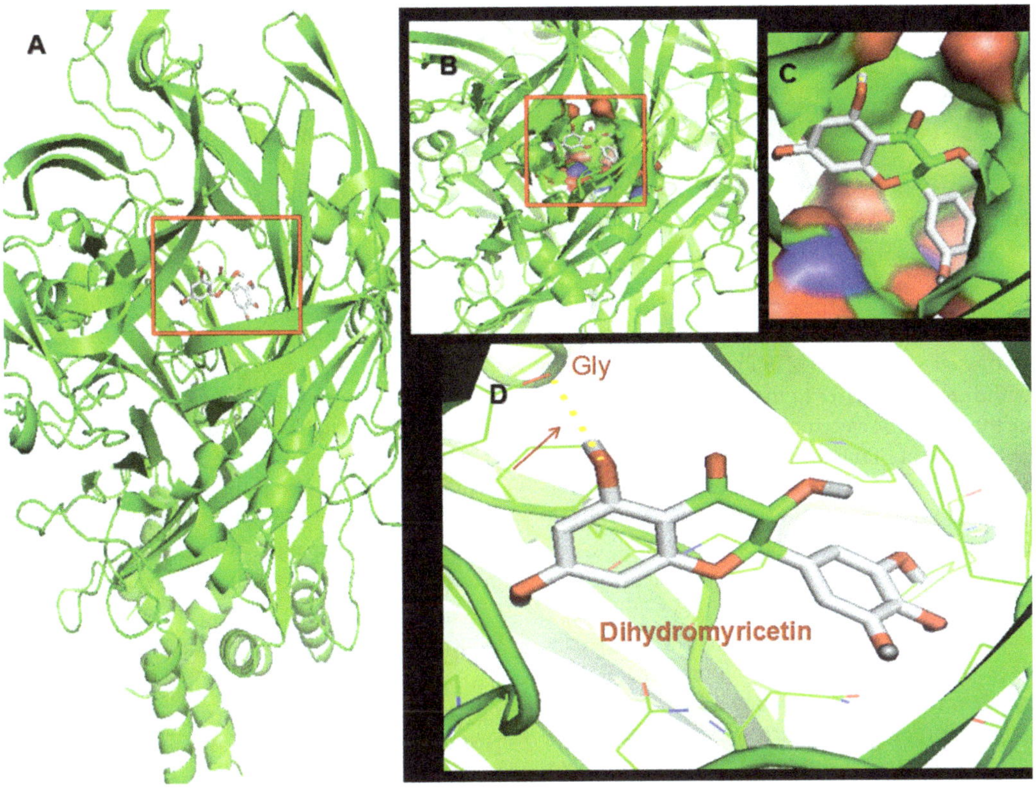

FIGURE 1 | Molecular docking of dihydromyricetin (DHM) on $P2X_7$ receptor. **(A)** Simulation modeling of DHM docking on $P2X_7$ receptor was performed by a computer. Molecular docking prediction of DHM on $P2X_7$ receptor was performed by AutoDock 4.2. **(B–D)** Enlarged view indicating the perfect match enabling DHM to interact with $P2X_7$ receptor.

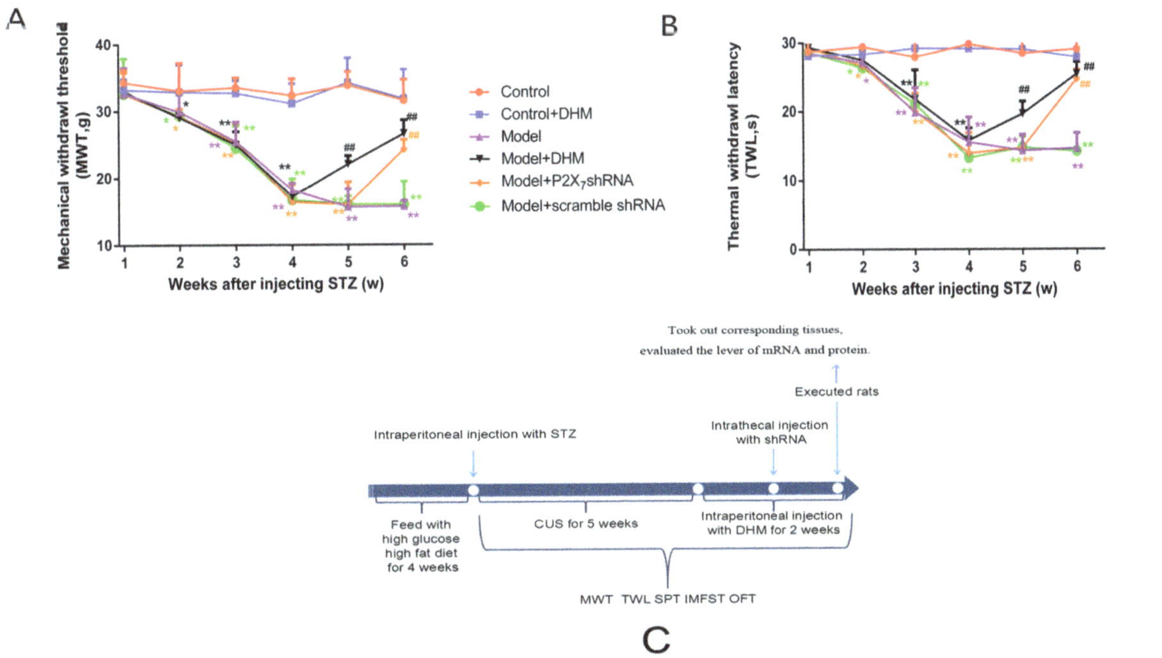

FIGURE 2 | Effects of dihydromyricetin (DHM) on mechanical withdrawal threshold (MWT; **A**) and thermal withdrawal latency (TWL; **B**) values in rats with diabetic neuropathic pain and major depressive disorder (model). **(C)** The timeline of treatments used in this study. Data are displayed as means ± standard errors of the means. $^{*}p<0.05$, $^{**}p<0.01$ vs. control group; $^{\#\#}p<0.01$ vs. model group.

shRNA groups. The behavior of rats in the two groups was assessed once a day after the intrathecal injection. The sequences of $P2X_7$ shRNA were as follows: ′-CACCGTGCAGTGAAT GAGTACTACGAATAGTACTCATTCACTGCAC-3′ and 3′-CACGTCACTTACTCATGATGCTTATCATGAGT AAGTGACGTGAAAA-5′.

DHM was purchased from Zelang, Nanjing, China. $P2X_7$ shRNA and scramble shRNA were synthesized by Novobio, Shanghai, China.

Mechanical Withdrawal Test

Mechanical withdrawal threshold (MWT) was evaluated by observing the withdrawal responses to mechanical stimulation, induced by using the BME-404 electronic mechanical stimulator (provided by the Institute of Biomedical Engineering of Chinese Academy of Medical Sciences). The end-face diameter of the test needle, the pressure measurement range, and pressure measurement resolution of the stimulator were 0.6 mm, 0.1 to 50 g, and 0.05 g, respectively. Before evaluation, each rat was placed in a clean glass box positioned on the sieve of a metal frame for an adaptive period of at least 30 min. The test needle touched the place between the third and fourth metatarsus of the left hind paws, until the rat attempted to withdraw its paw. The computer recorded the pressure values automatically. The stimulus alternated between the left and right hind paws at 5-min intervals. The MWT was calculated as the mean of three consecutive stable values, expressed in grams, and was determined by one observer.

Thermal Withdrawal Test

Thermal withdrawal latency (TWL) was evaluated by measuring the latency to hind paw withdrawal from a thermal stimulus, administered using the BME-410C Thermal Paw Stimulation System (provided by the Institute of Biomedical Engineering of Chinese Academy of Medical Sciences). Before evaluation, each rat was placed on a glass plate in a transparent, square, bottomless acrylic box, for an adaptive period of at least 30 min. A beam of radiant heat was oriented at the plantar surface of the rat's paws. The activation of the beam simultaneously activated a timer. The cutoff time for heat stimulation was 30 s. The light beam was switched off when the animal lifted its paw, and the timing was over. The time on the screen of the apparatus was designated as the TWL and was expressed in seconds. The hind paw withdrawal was tested in triplicate, and hind paws were alternated at 5-min intervals.

Sucrose Preference Test

Before the test, rats were fasted for 24 h and then placed individually in separate cages. Two identical water bottles, one containing 100 ml of 1% sucrose in water and another containing 100 ml of pure water, were placed in every cage at the same time. SP was evaluated by measuring the levels of sugar–water and pure-water consumption in 1 hour. The SP rate was calculated as the ratio of sugar water/total liquid consumption × 100%. This test reflects a lack of pleasure.

Forced Swimming Test

Rats were placed in an 80-cm-high glass cylinder with a 40-cm inner diameter. Water temperature was approximately 20, and water depth was 30 cm. The immobility time (IT) of rats in the water, i.e., when rats stopped struggling and floated in a fixed shape, and the swimming time of each rat were recorded for 5 min and expressed in seconds.

Open-Field Test

Before the test, rats were placed in the dark for 30 min to adapt to the environment. Then, they were placed in a black box that measured 40 × 60 × 50 cm. Each rat was placed gently in the middle of the box, and the distance navigated by the animal was recorded using a Canon Powershot A610 camera (Canon Co. local distributer, Tehran, Iran) during a 5-min session. The recorded videos were analyzed and processed using MATLAB (MathWorks Co., Natick, MA, USA) to determine the total distance traveled, expressed in centimeters. The apparatus was cleaned with a 10% ethanol solution before the next animal was introduced into the box.

Quantitative Real-Time PCR

Rats were anesthetized by i.p. injection of 10% chloral hydrate (batch no. 050101; Shanghai Xingya Medical Company, China). DRGs, the spinal cord at the level of L4–L5 vertebrae, and hippocampus were isolated immediately after sacrifice from rats in different groups, flushed with ice-cold phosphate-buffered saline (PBS), and stored in RNA Store solution at −20°C until further use. All instruments were treated with DEPC before use.

Total RNA was separately isolated from DRGs, spinal cord, and hippocampus using the TRIzol Total RNA Reagent (Beijing TransGen Biotech Co.). Complementary DNA synthesis was performed with 2 μg total RNA using the RevertAid™ HMinus First Strand cDNA Synthesis Kit. The primers were designed using Primer Express 3.0 Software (Applied Biosystems), and sequences were as follows: β-actin forward 5′-TAAAGACCTCTATGCCAACA -3′ and reverse 3′-CACGATGGAGGGGCCGGACTCATC-5′; $P2X_7$ forward 5′-GATGGATGGACCCACAAAGT-3′ and reverse 3′-GCTTCTTTCCCTTCCTCAGC-5′.

Quantitative real-time PCR was performed using the SYBR® Green Master Mix in the ABI PRISM® 7500 Sequence Detection System (Applied Biosystems Inc., Foster City, CA). The expression of each gene was quantified using the ΔΔCT method, with CT as the threshold cycle. The relative levels of target genes normalized to the sample with the lowest CT are presented as $2^{-\Delta\Delta CT}$.

Western Blotting

After rats were anesthetized, DRGs, spinal cord at L4–L5, and hippocampus were separated and flushed with ice-cold PBS. Tissues were positioned in the spherical part of a 2-ml homogenizer and homogenized in RIPA lysis buffer (50 mM Tris-Cl, pH 8.0, 150 mM NaCl, 0.1% sodium dodecyl sulfate, 1% Nonidet P-40, 0.02% sodium deoxycholate, 100 mg/ml phenylmethylsulfonyl fluoride, and 1 mg/ml aprotinin) containing protease inhibitors. Tissues were ground for 30 min on ice and centrifuged at 4°C at 12,000 rpm for 10 min. The supernatants were collected, diluted with 6× loading buffer, and heated to 95 for 10 min. The protein concentration was calculated with the BCA Protein Assay Kit, and samples were kept at −20°C until use. Proteins in samples from each group (20 µg) were separated by 12% sodium dodecyl sulfate–polyacrylamide gel electrophoresis, using Bio-Rad electrophoresis device, and transferred onto polyvinylidene fluoride membranes. Polyvinylidene fluoride membranes were blocked with 5% nonfat dry milk in 1× TBST (Tris-Buffered Saline and Tween 20) for 2 h at room temperature, followed by incubation with antibodies against $P2X_7$ (1:500; Alomone Labs, Jerusalem, Israel), β-actin (1:1,000; Beijing Zhongshan Biotech Co., China), extracellular signal–regulated kinases 1/2 (ERK1/2; 1:1,000; Cell Signaling Technology Inc, Boston, MA, USA), and phosphorylated (p)-ERK1/2 (1:1,000; Cell Signaling) at 4°C overnight. Membranes were washed three times with 1× TBST, 10 min each, incubated for 2 h at room temperature with horseradish peroxidase–conjugated secondary goat anti-rabbit immunoglobulin G and goat anti-mouse immunoglobulin G antibodies (1:2000; Beijing Zhongshan Biotech Co., China) in blocking buffer, and washed again three times with 1× TBST, 10 min each. Labeled proteins were then visualized with enhanced chemiluminescence on a Bio-Rad system. Band intensities were quantified using Image-Pro Plus software, and the intensities of target proteins were normalized against the respective β-actin internal control.

Double-Immunofluorescence Labeling

Rats were anesthetized with 10% chloral hydrate and were transcardially perfused with 4% paraformaldehyde (PFA). The DRGs, spinal cord at L4–L5, and hippocampus were removed and fixed in 4% PFA at 4°C for 2 h at room temperature. The tissues were immersed in 30% sucrose solution (in 4% PFA) for 24 h, at 4°C, for dehydration; solutions were changed every 8 h. Tissues were cut into 12- or 8-µm-thick slices in a cryostat (Leica). The sections were placed at 37°C for 2 h and then stored at −20°C until use.

Before staining, sections were balanced at room temperature, rinsed with 0.01 M PBS for 5 min × three times, incubated with 0.3% Triton X-100, and washed again with PBS for 5 min × three times. Then, slices were incubated in 10% goat serum for 1 h at 37°C, followed by incubation with the diluted antibodies (rabbit anti-$P2X_7$, 1:200, Alomone Labs; and mouse anti–glial fibrillary acidic protein [GFAP], 1:200, Millipore) overnight at 4°C. The next day, sections were placed at room temperature for 30 min and washed with PBS (three × 5 min); secondary antibodies (goat anti-mouse 1:800 and goat anti-rabbit 1:800; Abcam, USA) were added on sections at 37°C for 1 h. Sections were washed for 5 min × three times with PBS, sealed with antifade solution, and imaged using a fluorescence microscope (Olympus, Tokyo, Japan). Image-Pro Plus6.0 software was used to analyze the immunofluorescence intensity ratio of $P2X_7$ and GFAP coexpression normalized to control values.

Enzyme-Linked Immunosorbent Assay

For assessing the levels of tumor necrosis factor α (TNF-α) and interleukin 1β (IL-1β), we performed enzyme-linked immunosorbent assay (ELISA) using Rat PicoKine™ ELISA Kit (Boster Biological Technology), according to the manufacturer's instructions. Experimental samples (diluted to 100 µl) or control were loaded in triplicates, and 100 µl of antibody solution (1× biotinylated anti-rat TNF-α or IL-1β antibody) was added to each well and incubated for 60 min at 37°C. After washing three times with 1× wash buffer, 100 µl of 1× avidin–biotin–peroxidase complex was added to each well and incubated for 30 min at 37°C. Wells were washed five times with 1× wash buffer, and 90 µl of color developing reagent was added to each well and incubated in the dark for 25 min at 37°C. The reaction was stopped by adding 100 µl of stop solution to each well. The absorbance at 450 nm was read using a microplate reader.

Statistical Analysis

Statistical analyses were performed using SPSS 21.0 software. Data were analyzed by one-way analysis of variance. The experimental results are expressed as mean ± standard error of the mean and were considered significant at $p < 0.05$.

RESULTS

Effect of DHM on MWT and TWL in Rats With Comorbid DNP and MDD

We generated a comorbid symptom rat model by injecting rats with STZ and subjecting them to CUS stimulation for 5 weeks. After 5 weeks, both MWT and TWL were significantly lower in the model group than in the control group ($p < 0.05$), thus confirming the efficiency of our model. Two weeks after injection of DHM or 1 week after injection of $P2X_7$ shRNA, the MWT and TWL were significantly lower in the model + $P2X_7$ shRNA and model + DHM groups than in the model group ($p < 0.05$), indicating that both $P2X_7$ shRNA and DHM treatment relieve neuropathic pain-related behavior in rats with DNP and MDD (**Figures 2A, B**).

Effect of DHM on SP, Distance in the OFT, and IT in Rats With Comorbid DNP and MDD

Our analysis of SP in the respective test and of the distance traveled in the OFT showed that both values were markedly lower in the model than in the control group; in contrast, the IT in the FST was obviously higher in the model than in the control group, further confirming the successful generation of the DNP/MDD rat model ($p < 0.05$). Two weeks after injection with DHM or 1 week after injection with $P2X_7$ receptor shRNA, the values for SP and OFT distance were significantly lower in the model + $P2X_7$ shRNA and model + DHM groups than in the model group ($p < 0.05$). In addition, the IT in the FST was shorter in the model + $P2X_7$ shRNA and model + DHM groups than in the model group ($p < 0.05$). The above results indicate that treatment with DHM or $P2X_7$ shRNA relieves depression-like behaviors in model rats. Simultaneously, anhedonia improved, as evidenced by the higher values in the SPT and OFT and by the reduced IT in the FST in rats with DNP and MDD, indicating that DHM or $P2X_7$ shRNA may moderate depressive symptoms (**Figure 3**).

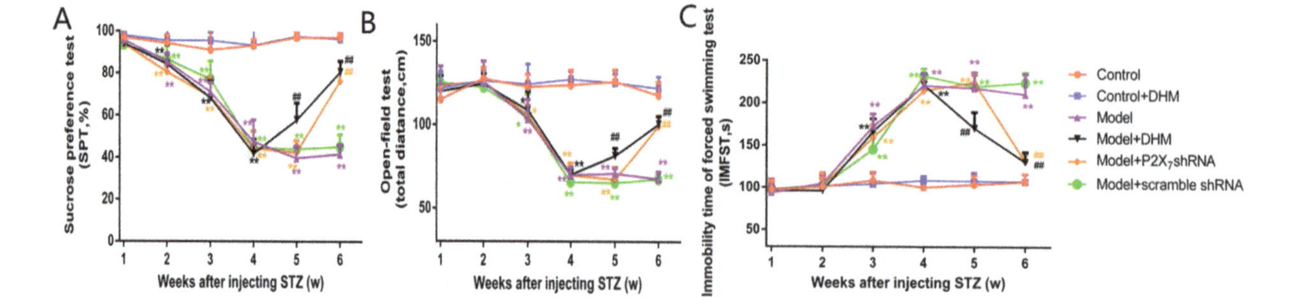

FIGURE 3 | Effects of dihydromyricetin (DHM) on sucrose preference (SP; **A**), distance traveled in the open-field test (OFT; **B**), and immobility time (IT) in the forced-swimming test **(C)** in rats with diabetic neuropathic pain (DNP) and major depressive disorder (MDD) (model). Data are displayed as the means ± standard error of the mean. $^{*}p<0.05$, $^{**}p<0.01$ vs. control group; $^{\#\#}p<0.01$ vs. model group.

Effects of DHM on the Expression Levels of $P2X_7$ Receptor in DRGs, Spinal Cord, and Hippocampus of Rats With Comorbid DNP and MDD

The expression levels of $P2X_7$ mRNA and protein were examined in the DRGs, spinal cord, and hippocampus in rats from each group by quantitative real-time PCR and Western blotting (**Figure 4**), respectively. In all tissues, the levels of $P2X_7$ mRNA and protein were higher in rats in the model than in the control group. However, treatment with DHM or $P2X_7$ shRNA significantly decreased the expression of $P2X_7$ mRNA and protein ($p<0.05$).

At the same time, the immunoreactivity of $P2X_7$ in the DRGs, spinal cord, and hippocampus was detected using double-immunofluorescence labeling for GFAP and $P2X_7$. GFAP marks satellite glial cells (SGCs). We found that $P2X_7$ and GFAP coexpression in these regions were higher in model than in control rats ($p<0.05$). However, the treatment with DHM or $P2X_7$ shRNA reversed these changes (**Figures 5–7**). The up-regulation of GFAP in the DRGs, spinal cord, and hippocampus of rats in the model group suggested the activation of SGCs after a nervous-injury stimulus. Moreover, we found that $P2X_7$ receptor was expressed by SGCs in all three regions. Therefore, DHM might decrease the expression of $P2X_7$ receptor in these regions in rats with comorbid DNP and MDD.

Effects of DHM on TNF-α and IL-1β Serum Levels in Rats With Comorbid DNP and MDD

ELISA was used to detect the levels of TNF-α and IL-1β in the serum of rats with comorbid DNP and MDD. In both cases, the levels were higher in the model than in the control group ($p<0.05$), while treatment with DHM or $P2X_7$ receptor shRNA significantly reduced them (**Figure 8**).

Effects of DHM on ERK1/2 Phosphorylation in DRGs, Spinal Cord, and Hippocampus of Rats With Comorbid DNP and MDD

The detection of p-ERK was performed by Western blotting. The levels of p-ERK in the DRGs, spinal cord, and hippocampus were higher in the model than in the control group ($p<0.05$). However, treatment with DHM or $P2X_7$ receptor shRNA reversed this increase (**Figure 9**).

Discussion

Diabetes mellitus leads to a series of complications, including DNP and MDD, both of which are risk factors for the development of diabetes mellitus and mutually affect each other (23–27). The comorbid presence of DNP and MDD is difficult to clinically manage and reduces the patients' quality of life to a greater extent than the individual presence of either DNP or MDD does (26, 28). In this study, we established a comorbid DNP and MDD rat model by administering a high-glucose and high-fat diet, STZ, and CUS (19). The successful generation of this model was confirmed by significantly reduced TWL values, MWT values, SP values, and OFT distances, as well as significantly increased ITs in the FST.

$P2X_7$ receptor is a member of the purinergic receptor family (11, 29) and plays a specific role in nociceptive signaling during chronic pain states (15). Studies have also shown that $P2X_7$ receptor is associated with anxiety and/or depressive symptoms, and $P2X_7$ receptor antagonists may exert an antidepressant effect (18, 30). Our previous work showed that $P2X_7$ receptors in the DRGs are involved in pain transmission in DNP and that down-regulation of $P2X_7$ receptor expression relieves DNP (31). Moreover, we found that $P2X_7$ receptor expression in the hippocampus was significantly higher in rats with comorbid DNP and MDD than in control rats (19). In the present study, we confirmed that comorbid DNP and MDD are associated with increased expression of $P2X_7$ receptor and the corresponding mRNA in the hippocampus, DRGs, and spinal cord.

DHM is a natural flavone extracted from *A. grossedentata* and has many pharmacological effects, including antioxidative, anti-inflammatory, and neuroprotective effects (32, 33). Homology modeling and molecular docking analysis can predict ligand binding to a protein's active sites. Molecular docking computations with AutoDock Vina (34) showed that DHM is capable of high-affinity binding to $P2X_7$ receptor. In this study, we found that treatment with DHM or $P2X_7$ receptor shRNA

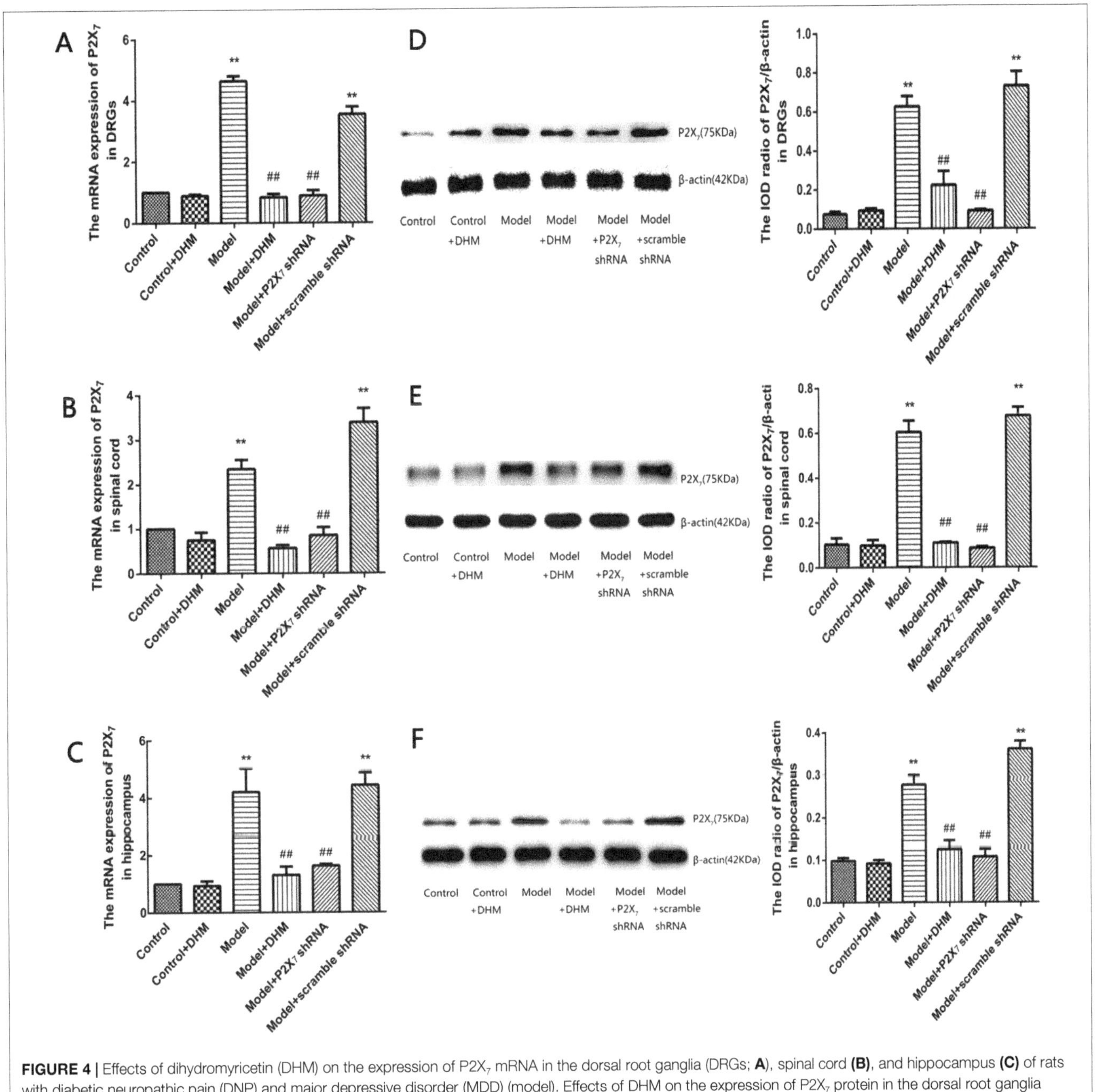

FIGURE 4 | Effects of dihydromyricetin (DHM) on the expression of $P2X_7$ mRNA in the dorsal root ganglia (DRGs; **A**), spinal cord **(B)**, and hippocampus **(C)** of rats with diabetic neuropathic pain (DNP) and major depressive disorder (MDD) (model). Effects of DHM on the expression of $P2X_7$ protein in the dorsal root ganglia (DRGs; **D**), spinal cord **(E)**, and hippocampus **(F)** of rats with model. Data are displayed as the means ± standard error of the mean. $^{**}p<0.01$ vs. control group; $^{\#\#}p<0.01$ vs. model group.

relieves neuropathic pain and depressive behaviors in rats with comorbid DNP and MDD and counteracts their elevated $P2X_7$ receptor expression levels. The antidepressant-like effect of DHM in our study is consistent with the findings of Ren et al. (21). In addition, DHM treatment also relieved DNP symptoms in our study. Therefore, DHM might be an effective medication for the comorbid disease, and $P2X_7$ receptor might be a key target for treatment.

Based on our findings, we hypothesize that patients with comorbid DNP and MDD have elevated $P2X_7$ receptor expression in the DRGs, spinal cord, and hippocampus, and treatment with DHM or $P2X_7$ receptor shRNA to inhibit $P2X_7$ receptor expression can alleviate the symptoms of comorbid DNP and MDD.

In the nervous system, $P2X_7$ receptor is expressed by glial cells, including satellite glia, astrocytes, and microglia (35–37). In this study, double-immunofluorescence labeling showed the coexpression of $P2X_7$ receptor and GFAP (a marker of satellite glia or astrocytes) (38) in the DRGs, spinal cord, and hippocampus; this was more enhanced in

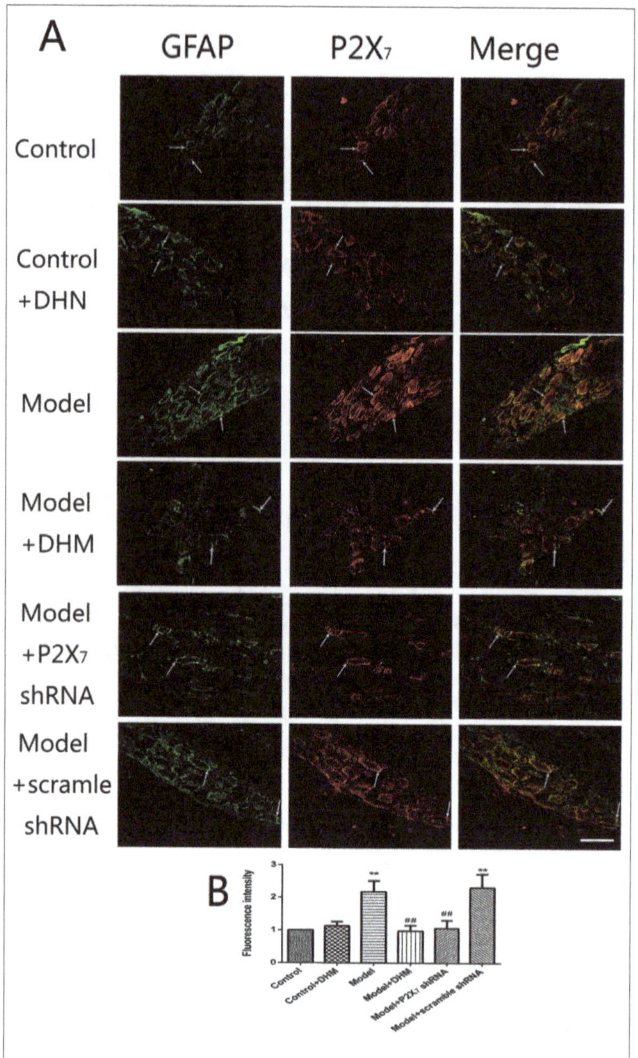

FIGURE 5 | Effects of dihydromyricetin (DHM) on the coexpression of $P2X_7$ and glial fibrillary acidic protein (GFAP) in the dorsal root ganglia (DRGs) of rats with diabetic neuropathic pain (DNP) and major depressive disorder (MDD) (model). Data are displayed as the means ± standard error of the mean. $^{**}p<0.01$ vs. control group; $^{\#\#}p<0.01$ vs. model group. Scale bars, 100 μm.

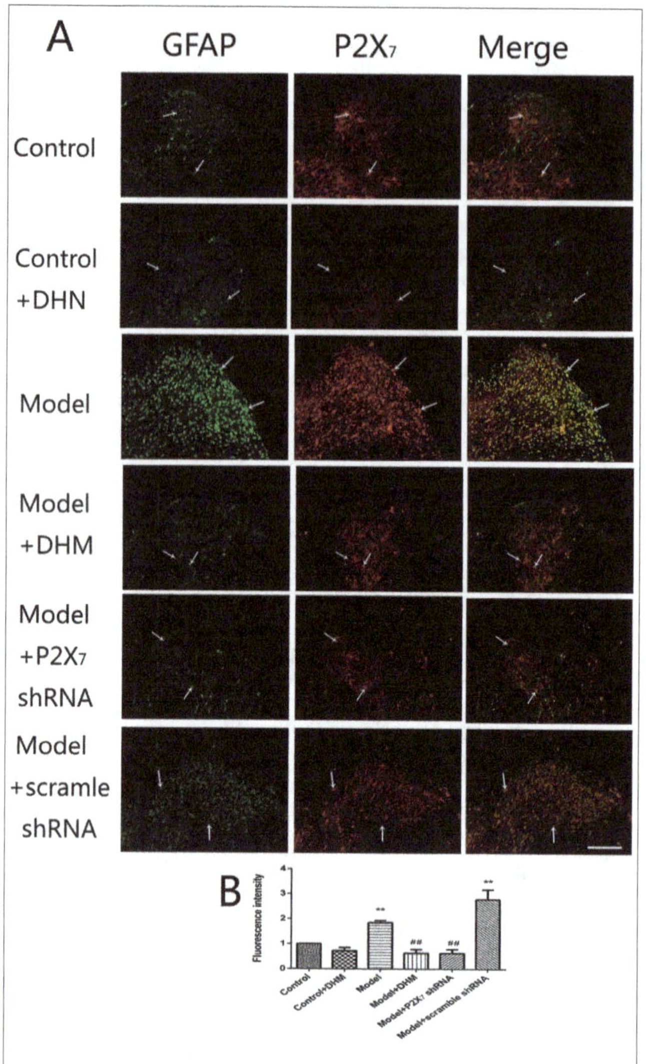

FIGURE 6 | Effects of dihydromyricetin (DHM) on the coexpression of $P2X_7$ and glial fibrillary acidic protein (GFAP) in the spinal cord of rats with diabetic neuropathic pain (DNP) and major depressive disorder (MDD) (model). Data are displayed as the means ± standard error of the mean. $^{**}p<0.01$ vs. control group; $^{\#\#}p<0.01$ vs. model group. Scale bars, 100 μm.

the model than in the control group, while DHM or $P2X_7$ receptor shRNA treatment reversed these changes. These results indicate that SGCs in the aforementioned regions are activated during DNP and MDD comorbidity, consistently with the observed increase in $P2X_7$ receptor expression. Glial cells participate in the immune response by activating $P2X_7$ receptor, thus enabling the release of a large number of proinflammatory cytokines (39). A significant feature of $P2X_7$ receptor activation is the release of proinflammatory cytokines, which in turn affects cell activity (13, 39). $P2X_7$ receptor plays an important role in the neuroinflammatory pathway, and its antagonists have been proposed as feasible drugs for the treatment of neuroinflammatory diseases (40, 41). Moreover, diabetes mellitus leads to increased expression of proinflammatory cytokines, such as TNF-α and IL-1β (42, 43), and increased inflammation is also considered to be involved in the pathogenesis of depressive symptoms in type 2 diabetes mellitus (44). Our team previously found that TNF-α and IL-1β serum levels were significantly higher in rats with DNP than in control rats (45, 46). In this study, we used ELISA and showed that the serum levels of IL-1β and TNF-α were significantly higher in model than in control rats but significantly decreased after DHM or $P2X_7$ receptor shRNA treatment. We hypothesize that $P2X_7$ receptor is activated in glial cells in the DRGs, spinal cord, and hippocampus during DNP and MDD comorbidity, thus stimulating the production and release of TNF-α and IL-1β to promote the pathogenesis of the two conditions.

Mitogen-activated protein kinase is involved in MDD and peripheral nerve injury-induced neuropathic pain, which

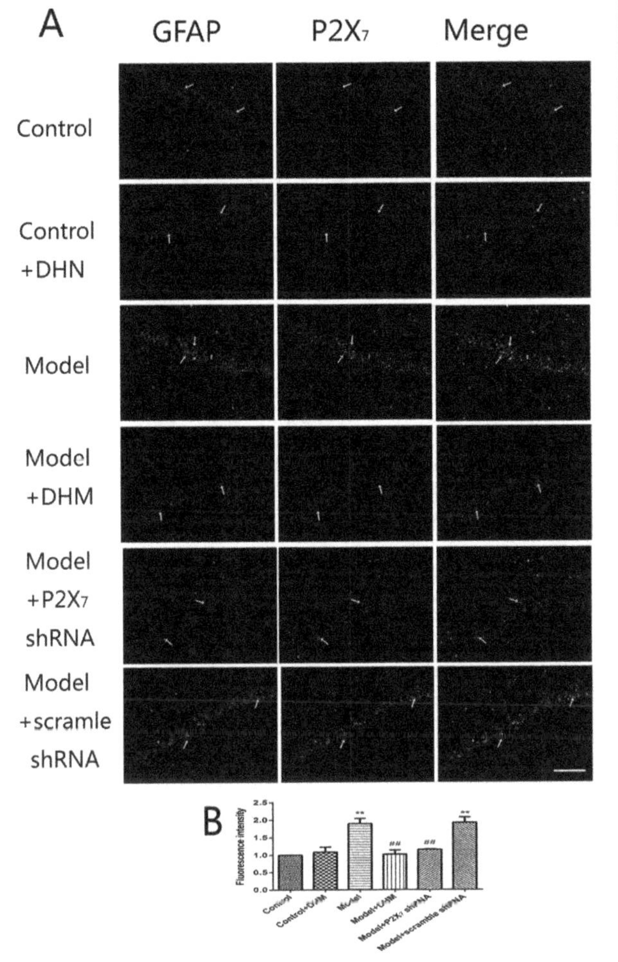

FIGURE 7 | Effects of dihydromyricetin (DHM) on the coexpression of $P2X_7$ and glial fibrillary acidic protein (GFAP) in the hippocampus of rats with diabetic neuropathic pain (DNP) and major depressive disorder (MDD) (model). Data are displayed as the means ± standard error of the mean. $^{**}p<0.01$ vs. control group; $^{\#\#}p<0.01$ vs. model group. Scale bars, 200 μm.

mainly includes three pathways: ERK, p38 kinase, and c-Jun N-terminal kinase (47, 48). Many studies have confirmed that ERK pathway is closely associated with DNP and MDD (49, 50) and that its activation is involved in P2X-mediated pain and depressive symptoms (10, 51). Our previous experiments also revealed that the phosphorylation of ERK1/2 in the hippocampus is noticeably higher in rats with DNP and MDD than in control rats (19). In this study, we did not detect any significant changes among groups in the total ERK1/2 levels, but the levels of ERK1/2 phosphorylation in the DRGs, spinal cord, and hippocampus were significantly higher in the model than in the control group, indicating that the activation of this pathway might mediate pain and depression signal transduction in the case of DNP and MDD comorbidity. The fact that DHM or $P2X_7$ receptor shRNA reduced the levels of p-ERK1/2 in the model group indicates that $P2X_7$ receptor is associated with ERK pathway activation, involved in DNP and MDD. We found that DHM and $P2X_7$ receptor shRNA treatments had similar effects. Therefore, DHM may inhibit the activation of ERK1/2 pathway by decreasing the expression of $P2X_7$ receptor, reducing the secretion of inflammatory cytokines in peripheral glial cells, restraining pain and depression transduction, and thereby alleviating the symptoms of pain and depression.

One limitation of our study is that we used a rat model. Due to the complexity of DNP and MDD, rat models cannot completely mimic the human symptoms. Moreover, multiple pathways and receptors are involved in the progression of these disorders, and there are drugs other than DHM that may also effectively treat these disorders, such as palmatine (19). Further mechanistic research into the interaction between DHM and the $P2X_7$ receptor, including research with human subjects, is therefore required.

In conclusion, we showed that $P2X_7$ receptors in the DRGs, spinal cord, and hippocampus participate in the transduction of DNP- and MDD-related signals. DHM decreases $P2X_7$ receptor expression in rats with comordid DNP and MDD, down-regulates ERK1/2 pathway activation, and reduces the release of the inflammatory

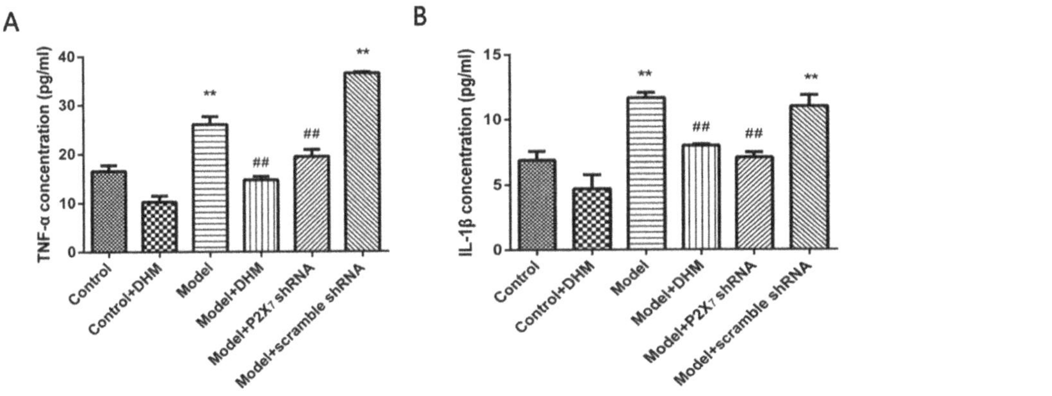

FIGURE 8 | Effects of dihydromyricetin (DHM) on the expression of tumor necrosis factor α (TNF-α) **(A)** and interleukin 1β (IL-1β) **(B)** in the serum of rats with diabetic neuropathic pain (DNP) and major depressive disorder (MDD) (model). Data are displayed as the means ± standard error of the mean. $^{**}p<0.01$ vs. control group; $^{\#\#}p<0.01$ vs. model group.

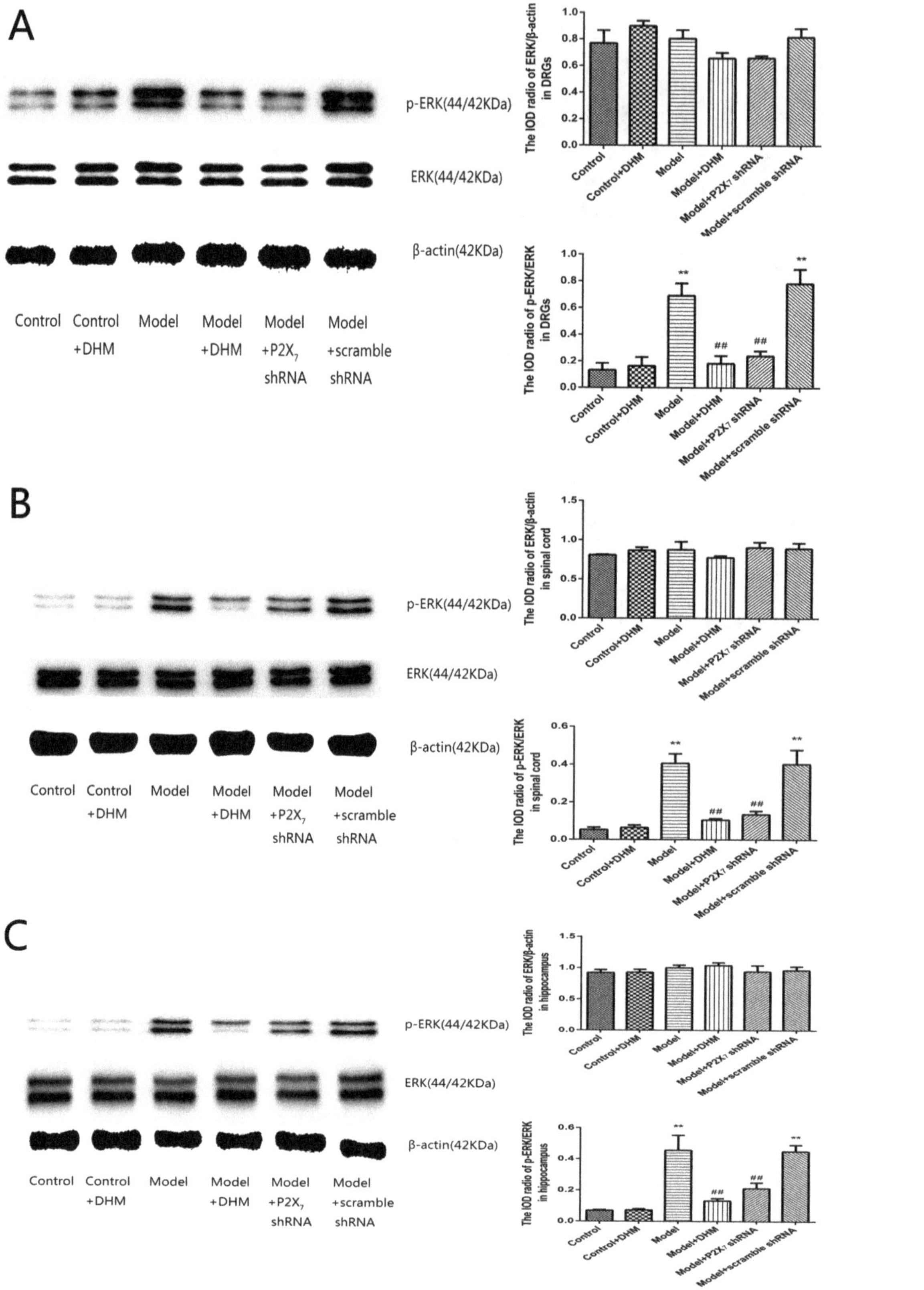

FIGURE 9 | Effects of dihydromyricetin (DHM) on the levels of phosphorylated extracellular signal–regulated kinase 1/2 (ERK1/2) in the dorsal root ganglia (DRGs; **A**), spinal cord **(B)**, and hippocampus **(C)** of rats with diabetic neuropathic pain (DNP) and major depressive disorder (MDD) (model). Data are displayed as the means ± standard error of the mean. $^{**}p<0.01$ vs. control group; $^{\#\#}p<0.01$ vs. model group.

factors TNF-α and IL-1β. These effects ultimately alleviate DNP and depressive behaviors. We propose that DHM may be an effective new drug for treating patients with comorbid DNP and MDD.

AUTHOR CONTRIBUTIONS

SG conducted the experiments with assistance from YS, HG, LL, CY, XW, LH, and WX. SG, WX, and YG contributed to the experimental design, data analysis and interpretation, and writing.

FUNDING

This study was supported by grants from the National Natural Science Foundation of China (nos. 81760152, 81460106, 81360136), Major Disciplines of Academic and Technical Leaders Project of Jiangxi Province (no. 20142BCB22001).

ACKNOWLEDGMENTS

We thank Prof. Shangdong Liang and Prof Guodong Li for assisting us in the experimental design.

REFERENCES

1. Zhao, JY, Yang, L, Bai, HH, Liu, JP, Suo, ZW, Yang, X, et al. Inhibition of protein tyrosine phosphatase 1B in spinal cord dorsal horn of rats attenuated diabetic neuropathic pain. *Eur J Pharmacol* (2018) 827:189–97. doi: 10.1016/j.ejphar.2018.03.012
2. Smith, HS, and Argoff, CE. Pharmacological treatment of diabetic neuropathic pain. *Drugs* (2011) 71:557–89. doi: 10.2165/11588940-000000000-00000
3. Erasso, D, Tender, GC, Li, Q, Yan, J, Culicchia, F, Abdi, S, et al. The effects of agrin isoforms on diabetic neuropathic pain in a rat streptozotocin model. *Anesth Analg* (2018) 127:1051–7. doi: 10.1213/ANE.0000000000002773
4. Mousa, SA, Shaqura, M, Khalefa, BI, Zollner, C, Schaad, L, Schneider, J, et al. Rab7 silencing prevents mu-opioid receptor lysosomal targeting and rescues opioid responsiveness to strengthen diabetic neuropathic pain therapy. *Diabetes* (2013) 62:1308–19. doi: 10.2337/db12-0590
5. Schreiber, AK, Nones, CF, Reis, RC, Chichorro, JG, and Cunha, JM. Diabetic neuropathic pain: physiopathology and treatment. *World J Diabetes* (2015) 6:432–44. doi: 10.4239/wjd.v6.i3.432
6. Katon, WJ, Rutter, C, Simon, G, Lin, EH, Ludman, E, Ciechanowski, P, et al. T. *Diabetes Care* (2005) 28:2668–72. doi: 10.2337/diacare.28.11.2668
7. Boulanger, L, Zhao, Y, Foster, TS, Fraser, K, Bledsoe, SL, and Russell, MW. Impact of comorbid depression or anxiety on patterns of treatment and economic outcomes among patients with diabetic peripheral neuropathic pain. *Curr Med Res Opin* (2009) 25:1763–73. doi: 10.1185/03007990902997309
8. D'Amato, C, Morganti, R, Greco, C, Di Gennaro, F, Cacciotti, L, Longo, S, et al. Diabetic peripheral neuropathic pain is a stronger predictor of depression than other diabetic complications and comorbidities. *Diab Vasc Dis Res* (2016) 13:418–28. doi: 10.1177/1479164116653240
9. Burnstock, G. Historical review: ATP as a neurotransmitter. *Trends Pharmacol Sci* (2006) 27:166–76. doi: 10.1016/j.tips.2006.01.005
10. Burnstock, G, Krugel, U, Abbracchio, MP, and Illes, P. Purinergic signalling: from normal behaviour to pathological brain function. *Prog Neurobiol* (2011) 95:229–74. doi: 10.1016/j.pneurobio.2011.08.006
11. Sluyter, R. The P2X7 Receptor. *Adv Exp Med Biol* (2017) 1051:17–53. doi: 10.1007/5584_2017_59
12. Burnstock, G, and Knight, GE. The potential of P2X7 receptors as a therapeutic target, including inflammation and tumour progression. *Purinergic Signal* (2018) 14:1–18. doi: 10.1007/s11302-017-9593-0
13. Volonte, C, Apolloni, S, Skaper, SD, and Burnstock, G. P2X7 receptors: channels, pores and more. *CNS Neurol Disord Drug Targets* (2012) 11:705–21. doi: 10.2174/187152712803581137
14. Chen, Y, Zhang, X, Wang, C, Li, G, Gu, Y, and Huang, LY. Activation of P2X7 receptors in glial satellite cells reduces pain through downregulation of P2X3 receptors in nociceptive neurons. *Proc Natl Acad Sci U S A* (2008) 105:16773–8. doi: 10.1073/pnas.0801793105
15. Donnelly-Roberts, DL, and Jarvis, MF. Discovery of P2X7 receptor-selective antagonists offers new insights into P2X7 receptor function and indicates a role in chronic pain states. *Br J Pharmacol* (2007) 151:571–9. doi: 10.1038/sj.bjp.0707265
16. Farooq, RK, Tanti, A, Ainouche, S, Roger, S, Belzung, C, and Camus, V. A P2X7 receptor antagonist reverses behavioural alterations, microglial activation and neuroendocrine dysregulation in an unpredictable chronic mild stress (UCMS) model of depression in mice. *Psychoneuroendocrinology* (2018) 97:120–30. doi: 10.1016/j.psyneuen.2018.07.016
17. Deussing, JM, and Arzt, E. P2X7 Receptor: a potential therapeutic target for depression? *Trends Mol Med* (2018) 24:736–47. doi: 10.1016/j.molmed.2018.07.005
18. Zhang, K, Liu, J, You, X, Kong, P, Song, Y, Cao, L, et al. P2X7 as a new target for chrysophanol to treat lipopolysaccharide-induced depression in mice. *Neurosci Lett* (2016) 613:60–5. doi: 10.1016/j.neulet.2015.12.043
19. Shen, Y, Guan, S, Ge, H, Xiong, W, He, L, Liu, L, et al. Effects of palmatine on rats with comorbidity of diabetic neuropathic pain and depression. *Brain Res Bull* (2018) 139:56–66. doi: 10.1016/j.brainresbull.2018.02.005
20. Hou, X, Tong, Q, Wang, W, Xiong, W, Shi, C, and Fang, J. Dihydromyricetin protects endothelial cells from hydrogen peroxide-induced oxidative stress damage by regulating mitochondrial pathways. *Life Sci* (2015) 130:38–46. doi: 10.1016/j.lfs.2015.03.007
21. Ren, Z, Yan, P, Zhu, L, Yang, H, Zhao, Y, Kirby, BP, et al. Dihydromyricetin exerts a rapid antidepressant-like effect in association with enhancement of BDNF expression and inhibition of neuroinflammation. *Psychopharmacology* (2018) 235:233–44. doi: 10.1007/s00213-017-4761-z
22. Yi, Y, Shen, Y, Wu, Q, Rao, J, Guan, S, Rao, S, et al. Protective effects of oxymatrine on vascular endothelial cells from high-glucose-induced cytotoxicity by inhibiting the expression of A2B receptor. *Cell Physiol Biochem* (2018) 45:558–71. doi: 10.1159/000487033
23. Bruce, DG, Davis, WA, Hunter, ML, Peters, KE, Davis, TM, and Starkstein, SE. Lifetime depression history and depression risk in type 2 diabetes: A case-control study. *J Diabetes Complications* (2016) 30:38–42. doi: 10.1016/j.jdiacomp.2015.10.010
24. Katon, W, Pedersen, HS, Ribe, AR, Fenger-Gron, M, Davydow, D, Waldorff, FB, et al. Effect of depression and diabetes mellitus on the risk for dementia: a national population-based cohort study. *JAMA Psychiatry* (2015) 72:612–9. doi: 10.1001/jamapsychiatry.2015.0082
25. Ho, N, Sommers, MS, and Lucki, I. Effects of diabetes on hippocampal neurogenesis: links to cognition and depression. *Neurosci Biobehav Rev* (2013) 37:1346–62. doi: 10.1016/j.neubiorev.2013.03.010
26. Sacco, WP, Bykowski, CA, and Mayhew, LL. Pain and functional impairment as mediators of the link between medical symptoms and depression in type 2 diabetes. *Int J Behav Med* (2013) 20:22–9. doi: 10.1007/s12529-011-9210-5
27. Gore, M, Brandenburg, NA, Dukes, E, Hoffman, DL, Tai, KS, and Stacey, B. Pain severity in diabetic peripheral neuropathy is associated with patient functioning, symptom levels of anxiety and depression, and sleep. *J Pain Symptom Manage* (2005) 30:374–85. doi: 10.1016/j.jpainsymman.2005.04.009
28. Bair, MJ, Brizendine, EJ, Ackermann, RT, Shen, C, Kroenke, K, and Marrero, DG. Prevalence of pain and association with quality of life, depression and glycaemic control in patients with diabetes. *Diabet Med* (2010) 27:578–84. doi: 10.1111/j.1464-5491.2010.02971.x
29. King, BF. Novel P2X7 receptor antagonists ease the pain. *Br J Pharmacol* (2007) 151:565–7. doi: 10.1038/sj.bjp.0707266
30. Basso, AM, Bratcher, NA, Harris, RR, Jarvis, MF, Decker, MW, and Rueter, LE. Behavioral profile of P2X7 receptor knockout mice in animal models of depression and anxiety: relevance for neuropsychiatric disorders. *Behav Brain Res* (2009) 198:83–90. doi: 10.1016/j.bbr.2008.10.018

31. Liu, S, Zou, L, Xie, J, Xie, W, Wen, S, Xie, Q, et al. LncRNA NONRATT021972 siRNA regulates neuropathic pain behaviors in type 2 diabetic rats through the P2X7 receptor in dorsal root ganglia. *Mol Brain* (2016) 9:44. doi: 10.1186/s13041-016-0226-2
32. Ling, H, Zhu, Z, Yang, J, He, J, Yang, S, Wu, D, et al. Dihydromyricetin improves type 2 diabetes-induced cognitive impairment via suppressing oxidative stress and enhancing brain-derived neurotrophic factor-mediated neuroprotection in mice. *Acta Biochim Biophys Sin (Shanghai)* (2018) 50:298–306. doi: 10.1093/abbs/gmy003
33. Hou, XL, Tong, Q, Wang, WQ, Shi, CY, Xiong, W, Chen, J, et al. Suppression of inflammatory responses by dihydromyricetin, a flavonoid from ampelopsis grossedentata, via inhibiting the activation of NF-kappaB and MAPK signaling pathways. *J Nat Prod* (2015) 78:1689–96. doi: 10.1021/acs.jnatprod.5b00275
34. Hill, AD, and Reilly, PJ. Scoring functions for AutoDock. *Methods Mol Biol* (2015) 1273:467–74. doi: 10.1007/978-1-4939-2343-4_27
35. Wu, B, Ma, Y, Yi, Z, Liu, S, Rao, S, Zou, L, et al. Resveratrol-decreased hyperalgesia mediated by the P2X7 receptor in gp120-treated rats. *Mol Pain* (2017) 13:1744806917707667. doi: 10.1177/1744806917707667
36. Chen, ML, Cao, H, Chu, YX, Cheng, LZ, Liang, LL, Zhang, YQ, et al. Role of P2X7 receptor-mediated IL-18/IL-18R signaling in morphine tolerance: multiple glial-neuronal dialogues in the rat spinal cord. *J Pain* (2012) 13:945–58. doi: 10.1016/j.jpain.2012.06.007
37. Gao, P, Ding, X, Khan, TM, Rong, W, Franke, H, and Illes, P. P2X7 receptor-sensitivity of astrocytes and neurons in the substantia gelatinosa of organotypic spinal cord slices of the mouse depends on the length of the culture period. *Neuroscience* (2017) 349:195–207. doi: 10.1016/j.neuroscience.2017.02.030
38. Nadeau, JR, Wilson-Gerwing, TD, and Verge, VM. Induction of a reactive state in perineuronal satellite glial cells akin to that produced by nerve injury is linked to the level of p75NTR expression in adult sensory neurons. *Glia* (2014) 62:763–77. doi: 10.1002/glia.22640
39. Chessell, IP, Hatcher, JP, Bountra, C, Michel, AD, Hughes, JP, Green, P, et al. Disruption of the P2X7 purinoceptor gene abolishes chronic inflammatory and neuropathic pain. *Pain* (2005) 114:386–96. doi: 10.1016/j.pain.2005.01.002
40. Chrovian, CC, Rech, JC, Bhattacharya, A, and Letavic, MA. P2X7 antagonists as potential therapeutic agents for the treatment of CNS disorders. *Prog Med Chem* (2014) 53:65–100. doi: 10.1016/B978-0-444-63380-4.00002-0
41. Gao, XF, Wang, W, Yu, Q, Burnstock, G, Xiang, ZH, and He, C. Astroglial P2X7 receptor current density increased following long-term exposure to rotenone. *Purinergic Signal* (2011) 7:65–72. doi: 10.1007/s11302-011-9218-y
42. Ratter, JM, Rooijackers, HM, Tack, CJ, Hijmans, AG, Netea, MG, de Galan, BE, et al. Proinflammatory effects of hypoglycemia in humans with or without diabetes. *Diabetes* (2017) 66:1052–61. doi: 10.2337/db16-1091
43. Ding, Y, Kantarci, A, Badwey, JA, Hasturk, H, Malabanan, A, and Van Dyke, TE. Phosphorylation of pleckstrin increases proinflammatory cytokine secretion by mononuclear phagocytes in diabetes mellitus. *J Immunol* (2007) 179:647–54. doi: 10.4049/jimmunol.179.1.647
44. Laake, JP, Stahl, D, Amiel, SA, Petrak, F, Sherwood, RA, Pickup, JC, et al. The association between depressive symptoms and systemic inflammation in people with type 2 diabetes: findings from the South London Diabetes Study. *Diabetes Care* (2014) 37:2186–92. doi: 10.2337/dc13-2522
45. Peng, H, Zou, L, Xie, J, Wu, H, Wu, B, Zhu, G, et al. lncRNA NONRATT021972 siRNA decreases diabetic neuropathic pain mediated by the P2X3 receptor in dorsal root ganglia. *Mol Neurobiol* (2016) 54:511–23. doi: 10.1007/s12035-015-9632-1
46. Jia, T, Rao, J, Zou, L, Zhao, S, Yi, Z, Wu, B, et al. Nanoparticle-encapsulated curcumin inhibits diabetic neuropathic pain involving the P2Y12 receptor in the dorsal root ganglia. *Front Neurosci* (2017) 11:755. doi: 10.3389/fnins.2017.00755
47. Gosselin, RD, Suter, MR, Ji, RR, and Decosterd, I. Glial cells and chronic pain. *Neuroscientist* (2010) 16:519–31. doi: 10.1177/1073858409360822
48. Liu, MG, Wang, RR, Chen, XF, Zhang, FK, Cui, XY, and Chen, J. Differential roles of ERK, JNK and p38 MAPK in pain-related spatial and temporal enhancement of synaptic responses in the hippocampal formation of rats: multi-electrode array recordings. *Brain Res* (2011) 1382:57–69. doi: 10.1016/j.brainres.2011.01.076
49. Ito-Ishida, A, Kakegawa, W, and Yuzaki, M. ERK1/2 but not p38 MAP kinase is essential for the long-term depression in mouse cerebellar slices. *Eur J Neurosci* (2006) 24:1617–22. doi: 10.1111/j.1460-9568.2006.05055.x
50. Wang, S, Xu, H, Zou, L, Xie, J, Wu, H, Wu, B, et al. LncRNA uc.48+ is involved in diabetic neuropathic pain mediated by the P2X receptor in the dorsal root ganglia. *Purinergic Signal* (2015) 12:139–48. doi: 10.1007/s11302-015-9488-x
51. Dutheil, S, Ota, KT, Wohleb, ES, Rasmussen, K, and Duman, RS. High-fat diet induced anxiety and anhedonia: impact on brain homeostasis and inflammation. *Neuropsychopharmacology* (2016) 41:1874–87. doi: 10.1038/npp.2015.357

18

Epistatic Interaction Between 5-HT1A and Vascular Endothelial Growth Factor Gene Polymorphisms in the Northern Chinese Han Population With Major Depressive Disorder

Dong Han[†]*, Zhengxue Qiao*[†]*, Dong Qi, Jiarun Yang, Xiuxian Yang, Jingsong Ma, Lin Wang, Xuejia Song, Erying Zhao, Jian Zhang, Yanjie Yang** *and Xiaohui Qiu**

Medical Psychology Department of Public Health Institute of Harbin Medical University, Harbin, China

***Correspondence:**
Yanjie Yang
yanjie1965@163.com
Xiaohui Qiu
qiuxiaohui1218@qq.com

[†]These authors have contributed equally to this work.

Aims: Serotonin 1A receptor (5-HT1A) and vascular endothelial growth factor (VEGF) are widely expressed in the neurons of the hippocampus and have significant roles in the pathophysiological processes of major depressive disorders (MDDs). The present study was designed to examine 5-HT1A and VEGF gene polymorphisms and whether the gene–gene interaction of 5-HT1A and VEGF gene variants was associated with MDD.

Methods: A total of 264 MDD patients and 264 healthy controls were included in the present genetic study. The rs6295, rs1364043, and rs878567 single-nucleotide polymorphisms (SNPs) in the 5-HT1A gene and the rs699947, rs833061, and rs2010963 SNPs in the VEGF gene were selected for genotypic analyses. The generalized multifactor dimensionality reduction method was employed to assess their interactions.

Results: The genotype distributions of the two genes' respective SNPs were significantly different between patients and controls for 5-HT1A rs6295 (p = 0.041) and VEGF rs2010963 (p = 0.035); however, no significant allelic variation in 5-HT1A (rs6295, rs1364043, and rs878567) and VEGF (rs699947, rs833061, and rs2010963) was found. The interactions between 5-HT1A (rs6295, rs1364043, and rs878567) and VEGF (rs699947, rs833061, and rs2010963) had a cross-validation (CV) consistency of 10/10 and a p value of 0.0107, which was considered as the best generalized multifactor dimensionality reduction (GMDR) model.

Conclusions: The interactions between 5-HT1A and VEGF gene polymorphisms may play a key role in the development of MDD in the Northern Chinese Han population.

Keywords: major depressive disorder, genetic association, 5-HT1A, vascular endothelial growth factor, gene–gene interaction

INTRODUCTION

Major depressive disorder (MDD) is one of the most common complex mental disorders, with symptoms that include loss of interest, periodic depression, and thoughts of suicide. Epidemiologic studies have shown that MDD afflicted an estimated 7%–11% of the general population (1, 2); yet, the underlying mechanism of MDD remains unclear. Genetic factors are likely to play a critical role in its etiology with the total contribution of heritability estimated at approximately 40% (3). Results from family, twin, and adoption studies provided further strong evidence for a genetic component to MDD (4); however, there are studies suggesting that single genetic loci offer weak predictive power for the identification of MDD (5). A large body of evidence found that gene–gene interactions are intricately involved in the phenotypic effect of variation in complex psychiatric diseases, particularly when a specific individual genetic variant is present (6, 7). There are numerous studies that suggest that overlaps exist between biological mechanisms underlying MDD (8). Thus, identifying the genetic mechanisms of MDD susceptibility may contribute to a better understanding of the etiological features of MDD (9).

Previous studies of neuroimaging and postmortem MDD patients found that the average volume of the hippocampus declined 9% and that atrophy of existing neurons and neurogenesis may lead to the pathophysiology of MDD (10–12). There is evidence to show that neurogenesis could decrease the levels of MDD and that chronic treatment with antidepressants may facilitate this decrease and also prevent reductions in hippocampal volume (13, 14). The above findings form the basis of the hypothesis that stress and antidepressants can affect hippocampal neurogenesis and are therefore likely have a role in MDD (15–17).

Increasing results of studies demonstrate that dysregulation of neurotrophic factors are associated with MDD (18, 19). Vascular endothelial growth factor (VEGF) and serotonin 1A receptor (5-HT1A) are widely expressed in neurons and have an important role in the pathophysiological processes of MDD (20, 21). Indeed, a previous study demonstrated that activation of the 5-HT1A gene is enough to induce VEGF expression in the neonatal hippocampus (22). The 5-HT1A gene is located on chromosome 5q11.2-q13 and encodes for one of the most abundant serotonin receptors in the brain. Several studies found that the 5-HT1A gene was in both presynaptic and postsynaptic neurons of the hippocampus (23). In addition, an increasing body of literature confirmed that impaired 5-HT1A expression or function was associated with MDD (24, 25). Subsequent studies showed that the rs6295(C-1019G) 5-HT1A promoter polymorphism was associated with MDD and the response to antidepressant therapy (26–28). The VEGF gene is located on chromosome 6p21.3 (29), which has been shown to play a role in hippocampal neurogenesis (30, 31) and in the response to stress. In addition, increasing numbers of studies have identified a role for VEGF in the pathophysiology of MDD and for the neurogenic and behavioral actions of antidepressants (32). So far, whether the 5-HT1A gene variants are able to stimulate VEGF expression is still unclear.

To date, no studies have been initiated to determine if an association between 5-HT1A/VEGF genetic polymorphisms and MDD exists using multilocus analyses in the Northern Chinese Han population. Hence, the aims of this study were to investigate the possible association of 5-HT1A and VEGF gene variants with MDD and to determine the potential susceptibility of gene–gene interactions in this disease.

MATERIALS AND METHODS

Sample

Blood samples were collected from 528 Chinese Han patients with MDD, who were outpatients and inpatients from the Psychiatry Department of the First Affiliated Hospital of Harbin Medical University. All patients underwent the Structured Clinical Interview for the Diagnostic and Statistical Manual of Mental Disorders (SCID, DSM-IV) to confirm the diagnosis of MDD. All the patients were in their first episode. We used the Hamilton Depression Scale Test to assess the severity of patients who had not received antidepression treatment for 2 weeks prior to participation. Patients with other major mental diseases, brain organic mental disorders, and comorbidity for other psychiatric disturbances were excluded. At the same time, 264 age-, education-, career-, and ethnically matched healthy controls were selected from the same hospital for a physical examination. This study was approved by the Ethics Committee of Harbin Medical University. All participants provided written informed consent.

Genotyping

Genomic DNA was isolated from blood samples using a MagNA Pure DNA Isolator (Roche, Indianapolis, IN, USA). After DNA extraction, PCRs were used to amplify specific regions of the VEGF and 5-HT1A genes, respectively. Single-nucleotide polymorphism (SNP) analyses were performed using the Taqman allelic discrimination assay on a 7900 systems (Applied Biosystem Inc) according to the manufacturer's instructions.

Statistical Analysis

SPSS 19.0 software was used for all analyses. The χ^2 test was used to analyze the between-group differences in gender and distributions of genotypes and alleles between the patient group and the control group. The Student's t test was used to compare continuous variables. The Hardy–Weinberg equilibrium was evaluated for the genotypic distribution of each SNP by using a Pearson goodness-of-fit test in both patients and controls. Haplotype frequencies in MDD patients and controls were estimated by Haploview 4.2 software. Those haplotypes with p value need to do permutation tests 1,000 times. A p value of less than 0.05 was considered statistically significant.

Generalized multifactor dimensionality reduction (GMDR) analysis was used to assess gene–gene interactions (33) and is an extension of the multifactor dimensionality reduction method. Briefly, we performed 10-fold cross-validation and tested two six-marker interaction models with 1,000 permutations. The best value of maximized cross-validation (CV), balanced accuracy, and the most significant gene–gene interaction model were provided by GMDR analysis. We used interaction graphs to interpret the SNP interactions of the best model (34).

RESULTS

A total of 528 participants were included in the present genetic study. **Table 1** shows the demographic and characteristics of study participants. No significant difference was found in mean age and sex ratio between patients and controls.

Haplotype frequencies in patients and controls were estimated by Haploview 4.2 software. The results of haplotype-based analysis are presented in **Table 2**. Strong LD was observed between rs878567 and rs6295 of the 5-HT1A gene ($D' = 1.0$, $r^2 = 0.72$), but haplotype-based analysis found that the 5-HT1A gene rs878567-rs6295 haplotype was not associated with MDD ($p = 0.040$, permuted $p = 0.242$).

Genotype distributions for 5-HT1A and VEGF gene polymorphisms were analyzed using the Hardy–Weinberg equilibrium. **Table 3** shows the distributions of genotypes and alleles for the six SNPs in patients and controls. The genotype distributions of two SNPs were significantly different between patients and controls for 5-HT1A rs6295 ($p = 0.041$) and VEGF rs2010963 ($p = 0.035$). However, no significant difference in allele distributions of 5-HT1A (rs6295, rs1364043, and rs878567) and VEGF (rs699947, rs833061, and rs2010963) between patients and controls were found.

In addition, gene–gene interactions were analyzed using GMDR software to assess the impact of combinations of the six SNPs in MDD. p values were calculated by permuting the cases and controls 1,000 times. The results of GMDR analysis for each 2-locus to 6-locus multilocus–genotype combination are shown in **Table 4**. The interactions between 5-HT1A (rs6295, rs1364043, and rs878567) and VEGF (rs699947, rs833061, and rs2010963) had a CV consistency of 10/10 and a p value of 0.0107, which was considered as the best GMDR model. The results indicated that there were potential gene–gene interactions between 5-HT1A and VEGF in MDD susceptibility.

After identifying the impacts of combinations of the six SNPs using GMDR, we used the entropy estimates to produce an interaction graph to interpret the relationship between these six SNPs. As shown in **Figure 1**, a negative interaction effect of rs6295 and rs878567 was found in the 5-HT1A gene with an interaction entropy of −0.77%, while a positive interaction effect of rs878567 was found in the 5-HT1A gene and of rs2010963 in the VEGF gene with an interaction entropy of 0.52. The most independent effect and the least effect were rs2010963 (0.92%) and rs699947 (0.14%), respectively.

TABLE 1 | Characteristics of study participants.

Variable	Case (n = 264)	Control (n = 264)	χ^2/t	p value
Age (mean ± SD)	43.30 ± 13.87	41.82 ± 12.41	1.29	0.20
Gender (males/females)	78/186	72/192	0.00	1.00
HAMD score	31.62 ± 4.84	–	–	–

TABLE 2 | Haplotype-based association analysis results.

Gene	Haplotype	MDD (%)	Control (%)	χ^2	P/permuted P
5-HT1A	GCC	0.612	0.600	0.18	0.671/1.000
	TTG	0.197	0.215	0.583	0.445/0.993
	TCC	0.119	0.141	1.268	0.260/0.865
	TCG	0.072	0.044	4.207	**0.040**/0.242

MDD, major depressive disorder.
The boldfaced value indicate $p < 0.05$.

DISCUSSION

In the present study, we explored the impact of the 5-HT1A and VEGF genes and gene–gene interactions on the risk of MDD in the Northern Chinese Han population. Our study investigated not only the main effects but also the joint effects of the 5-HT1A and VEGF genes. The results found that the VEGF gene had a few main effects on MDD, but when combined with the 5-HT1A gene, the interaction effect was definitively associated with MDD.

To date, we have found that the 5-HT1A and VEGF genes are widely expressed in the brain and have varied functions; both were reported to be involved in the antidepressant response. Previous studies also indicated that a decrease in expression of the 5-HT1A or in its function was associated with MDD. Although these studies highlighted the important role of genetic variants in the mechanism of MDD, the identification of the risk gene for MDD needs further investigation. The genotype frequencies of the 5-HT1A rs6295 polymorphism were a risk factor for MDD; however, our analyses show that there was no significant allelic association ($p = 0.486$) between the 5-HT1A rs6295 polymorphism and MDD.

Genetic association studies of 5-HT1A in MDD have produced contradicting results. Wu et al. found that rs6295 (C-1019G) was associated with MDD in the Chinese population (35, 36), while Albert and Lemonde reported that the 5-HT1A rs6295 (C-1019G) polymorphism had an effect on suicide, depression, anxiety, and antidepressant responses (37, 38). Moreover, Illi et al. demonstrated that no association was found between the 5-HT1A gene and MDD or antidepressant responses (39). Yet, Kato et al. reported that the 5-HT1A rs10042486 and rs1364043 polymorphisms were associated with MDD and antidepressant responses (26). A possible explanation for the above findings could be the small sample size employed in these respective studies. Compared with the study by Illi et al. for example, with 106 outpatient MDD patients of Finnish origin, we recruited 264 Chinese MDD samples. This larger sample size likely had a greater power effect than those studies with smaller sample sizes.

Previous studies have shown that a genetic association exists between the VEGF gene and MDD; however, similar to the 5-HT1A, the results have been inconsistent and at times contradictory. Two recent meta-analyses found that VEGF was

TABLE 3 | Distributions of genotypes and alleles for study participants.

Gene	SNP ID	Sample	Genotypes			P	Allele		P	OR (95% CI)
VEGF	rs699947		AA	AC	CC		A	C		
		Case	11	94	159	0.610	116	412	0.607	1.709 (0.808–1.439)
		Control	16	91	157		123	405		
	rs833061		CC	CT	TT		C	T		
		Case	11	95	158	0.389	117	411	0.558	1.090 (0.818–1.452)
		Control	18	89	157		125	403		
	rs2010963		CC	CG	GG		C	G		
		Case	56	143	65	**0.035**	255	273	0.423	1.104 (0.867–1.406)
		Control	64	114	86		242	286		
5-HT1A	rs6295		CC	CG	GG		C	G		
		Case	130	123	11	**0.041**	383	145	0.486	1.102 (0.838–1.449)
		Control	148	97	19		393	135		
	rs1364043		GG	GT	TT		G	T		
		Case	89	138	37	0.569	316	212	0.900	0.984 (0.769–1.259)
		Control	96	126	42		318	210		
	rs878567		CC	CT	TT		C	T		
		Case	165	92	7	0.093	422	106	0.760	0.955 (0.708–1.287)
		Control	170	78	16		418	110		

SNP, single-nucleotide polymorphism; VEGF, vascular endothelial growth factor; 5-HT1A, serotonin 1A receptor.
The boldfaced values indicate p < 0.05.

TABLE 4 | Gene–gene interaction analysis by generalized multifactor dimensionality reduction (GMDR).

Locus number	Best combination	Prediction error (%)	Cross-validation	*p* value
2	VEGF (rs2010963), 5-HTR1A (rs6295)	0.4743	6/10	0.6230
3	VEGF (rs2010963), 5-HTR1A (rs6295,rs1364043)	0.403	4/10	0.1719
4	VEGF (rs699947,rs2010963), 5-HTR1A (rs6295,rs1364043)	0.3685	9/10	0.0547
5	VEGF (rs699947,rs2010963), 5-HTR1A (rs6295,rs1364043,rs878567)	0.3493	9/10	**0.0107**
6	VEGF (rs699947,rs833061,rs2010963), 5-HTR1A (rs6295,rs1364043,rs878567)	0.3474	10/10	**0.0107**

The boldfaced values indicate p < 0.05.

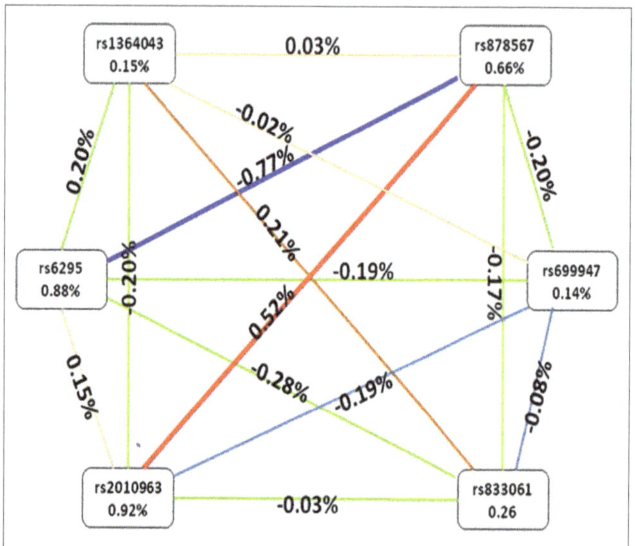

FIGURE 1 | Interaction graphs showed that the percentage at the bottom of each SNPs represented entropy of it, and there are a percentage on line represented the interaction percentage of entropy between two SNPs. The red line represented synergy redundancy interaction and the blue line represented redundancy interaction.

associated with MDD and response to antidepressants (40, 41). As for the analysis of single loci, Galecki et al.'s study reported that the frequency of the VEGF variant rs2010963(405G/C) increased in MDD patients compared with healthy controls (C-allele and genotype CC are the risk factors for MDD) (42). Several factors may help to explain the contradictory results in the above studies. Although the association between VEGF polymorphisms and MDD was found, ethnic differences might lead to inconsistent results in analyses of allele and genotype frequencies. In addition, MDD is a complex disease that is usually associated with single-gene or gene–gene interactions, and VEGF polymorphisms alone may not predispose MDD; therefore, it is significant to investigate gene–gene interactions among several genes to explain the complex pathogenic mechanisms of MDD.

We used the GMDR method to analyze the combined effects of the 5-HT1A and VEGF genes in MDD. We found that the 5-locus and 6-locus gene–gene interaction models conferred an increased risk of MDD. The interactions between 5-HT1A (rs6295, rs1364043, and rs878567) and VEGF (rs699947, rs833061, and rs2010963) had a CV consistency of 10/10 and a *p* value of 0.0107, which was considered as the best gene–gene interaction model. Of note, stress can exacerbate depressive episodes and down-regulate both VEGF and its major receptors in the brain, including fetal liver kinase-1 (Flk-1). We found that VEGF–Flk-1 signaling played a major role in the clinical effects of antidepressants. A possible mechanism was that the interaction effect that was activated by the 5-HT1A gene in neuronal and endothelial cell generated antidepressant effects (43). Some studies have also found that cAMP-response element binding protein (CREB) and VEGF can be activated by 5-HT1A gene stimulating pathways (extracellular-regulated kinase and protein kinase B) (44, 45). Several limitations of this study still need to be addressed. First, we collected our samples in the Northern Chinese Han population, and it is noteworthy that the positive associations may be due to chance or to a stratification effect. Second, the sample size of this study was relatively small; further studies with a large sample are needed to test our results. Future research should include other population and ethnicities with large sample sizes to explore interaction between these two genes in MDD.

CONCLUSIONS

In conclusion, the current study used single-locus and multilocus analyses to study genetic polymorphisms and gene-gene interactions between the 5-HT1A and VEGF genes in MDD. Our findings suggest that the interaction between the VEGF gene and the 5-HT1A gene may play a key role in the development of MDD.

ETHICS STATEMENT

This study was carried out in accordance with the recommendations of the Ethics Committee of Harbin Medical University with written informed consent from all subjects. All subjects gave written informed consent in accordance with the Declaration of Helsinki. The protocol was approved by the Ethics Committee of Harbin Medical University.

AUTHOR CONTRIBUTIONS

YY and XQ designed and conceived the study. DH, ZQ, DQ, JY, JM, and JZ wrote the manuscript and carried out all of the data analyses. XY, LW, XS, and EZ carried out edited manuscript drafts. All authors read and approved the final version of the manuscript.

FUNDING

This study was supported by the National Natural Science Foundation of China (81773536 to YY).

REFERENCES

1. Kessler RC, Merikangas KR, Wang PS. Prevalence, comorbidity, and service utilization for mood disorders in the United States at the beginning of the twenty-first century. *Annu Rev Clin Psychol* (2007) 3:137–58. doi: 10.1146/annurev.clinpsy.3.022806.091444
2. Klengel T, Binder EB. Gene-environment interactions in major depressive disorder. *Can J Psychiatry* (2013) 58(2):76–83. doi: 10.1177/070674371305800203
3. Sullivan PF, Neale MC, Kendler KS. Genetic epidemiology of major depression: review and meta-analysis. *Am J Psychiatry* (2000) 157(10):1552–62. doi: 10.1176/appi.ajp.157.10.1552
4. Duffy A, Grof P, Robertson C, Alda M. The implications of genetics studies of major mood disorders for clinical practice. *J Clin Psychiatry* (2000) 61(9):630–7. doi: 10.4088/JCP.v61n0906
5. Roetker NS, Yonker JA, Lee C, Chang V, Basson JJ, Roan CL, et al. Multigene interactions and the prediction of depression in the Wisconsin Longitudinal Study. *BMJ Open* (2012) 2(4):e000944. doi: 10.1136/bmjopen-2012-000944
6. Burmeister M, McInnis MG, Zollner S. Psychiatric genetics: progress amid controversy. *Nat Rev Genet* (2008) 9(7):527–40. doi: 10.1038/nrg2381
7. Murk W, DeWan AT. Exhaustive genome-wide search for SNP-SNP interactions across 10 human diseases. *G3 (Bethesda)* (2016) 6(7):2043–50. doi: 10.1534/g3.116.028563
8. Schulze TG, Akula N, Breuer R, Steele J, Nalls MA, Singleton AB, et al. Molecular genetic overlap in bipolar disorder, schizophrenia, and major depressive disorder. *World J Biol Psychiatry* (2014) 15(3):200–8. doi: 10.3109/15622975.2012.662282
9. Levinson DF. The genetics of depression: a review. *Biol Psychiatry* (2006) 60(2):84–92. doi: 10.1016/j.biopsych.2005.08.024
10. Sheline YI, Gado MH, Kraemer HC. Untreated depression and hippocampal volume loss. *Am J Psychiatry* (2003) 160(8):1516–8. doi: 10.1176/appi.ajp.160.8.1516
11. Neumeister A, Wood S, Bonne O, Nugent AC, Luckenbaugh DA, Young T, et al. Reduced hippocampal volume in unmedicated, remitted patients with major depression versus control subjects. *Biol Psychiatry* (2005) 57(8):935–7. doi: 10.1016/j.biopsych.2005.01.016
12. Janssen J, Hulshoff Pol HE, de Leeuw FE, Schnack HG, Lampe IK, Kok RM, et al. Hippocampal volume and subcortical white matter lesions in late life depression: comparison of early and late onset depression. *J Neurol Neurosurg Psychiatry* (2007) 78(6):638–40. doi: 10.1136/jnnp.2006.098087
13. Warner-Schmidt JL, Duman RS. Hippocampal neurogenesis: opposing effects of stress and antidepressant treatment. *Hippocampus* (2006) 16(3):239–49. doi: 10.1002/hipo.20156
14. Hviid LB, Ravnkilde B, Ahdidan J, Rosenberg R, Stodkilde-Jorgensen H, Videbech P. Hippocampal visuospatial function and volume in remitted depressed patients: an 8-year follow-up study. *J Affect Disord* (2010) 125(1–3):177–83. doi: 10.1016/j.jad.2010.01.002
15. Jacobs BL, van Praag H, Gage FH. Adult brain neurogenesis and psychiatry: a novel theory of depression. *Mol Psychiatry* (2000) 5(3):262–9. doi: 10.1038/sj.mp.4000712
16. Kempermann G, Kronenberg G. Depressed new neurons—adult hippocampal neurogenesis and a cellular plasticity hypothesis of major depression. *Biol Psychiatry* (2003) 54(5):499–503. doi: 10.1016/S0006-3223(03)00319-6
17. Dranovsky A, Hen R. Hippocampal neurogenesis: regulation by stress and antidepressants. *Biol Psychiatry* (2006) 59(12):1136–43. doi: 10.1016/j.biopsych.2006.03.082
18. Martinotti G, Pettorruso M, De Berardis D, Varasano PA, Pressanti LG, Remigis DV, et al. Agomelatine Increases BDNF serum levels in depressed patients in correlation with the improvement of depressive symptoms. *Int J Neuropsychopharmacol* (2016) 19(5):pyw003. doi: 10.1093/ijnp/pyw003
19. Fornaro M, Rocchi G, Escelsior A, Contini P, Ghio M, Colicchio S, et al. VEGF plasma level variations in duloxetine-treated patients with major depression. *J Affect Disord* (2013) 151(2):590–5. doi: 10.1016/j.jad.2013.06.055
20. Fournier NM, Duman RS. Role of vascular endothelial growth factor in adult hippocampal neurogenesis: implications for the pathophysiology and treatment of depression. *Behav Brain Res* (2012) 227(2):440–9. doi: 10.1016/j.bbr.2011.04.022
21. Miller JM, Hesselgrave N, Ogden RT, Zanderigo F, Oquendo MA, Mann JJ, et al. Brain serotonin 1A receptor binding as a predictor of treatment

outcome in major depressive disorder. *Biol Psychiatry* (2013) 74(10):760–7. doi: 10.1016/j.biopsych.2013.03.021
22. Samaddar S, Ranasinghe B, Tantry SJ, Debata PR, Banerjee P. Involvement of vascular endothelial growth factor in serotonin 1A receptor-mediated neuroproliferation in neonatal mouse hippocampus. *Adv Exp Med Biol* (2015) 842:375–88. doi: 10.1007/978-3-319-11280-0_23
23. Bermack JE, Debonnel G. Effects of OPC-14523, a combined sigma and 5-HT1a ligand, on pre- and post-synaptic 5-HT1a receptors. *J Psychopharmacol* (2007) 21(1):85–92. doi: 10.1177/0269881106063996
24. Miller JM, Brennan KG, Ogden TR, Oquendo MA, Sullivan GM, Mann JJ, et al. Elevated serotonin 1A binding in remitted major depressive disorder: evidence for a trait biological abnormality. *Neuropsychopharmacology* (2009) 34(10):2275–84. doi: 10.1038/npp.2009.54
25. Hesselgrave N, Parsey RV. Imaging the serotonin 1A receptor using [11C] WAY100635 in healthy controls and major depression. *Philos Trans R Soc Lond B Biol Sci* (2013) 368(1615):20120004. doi: 10.1098/rstb.2012.0004
26. Kato M, Fukuda T, Wakeno M, Okugawa G, Takekita Y, Watanabe S, et al. Effect of 5-HT1A gene polymorphisms on antidepressant response in major depressive disorder. *Am J Med Genet B Neuropsychiatr Genet* (2009) 150B(1):115–23. doi: 10.1002/ajmg.b.30783
27. Lemonde S, Du L, Bakish D, Hrdina P, Albert PR. Association of the C(-1019)G 5-HT1A functional promoter polymorphism with antidepressant response. *Int J Neuropsychopharmacol* (2004) 7(4):501–6. doi: 10.1017/S1461145704004699
28. Lemonde S, Turecki G, Bakish D, Du L, Hrdina PD, Bown CD, et al. Impaired repression at a 5-hydroxytryptamine 1A receptor gene polymorphism associated with major depression and suicide. *J Neuroscience* (2003) 23(25):8788–99. doi: 10.1523/JNEUROSCI.23-25-08788.2003
29. Lutty GA, McLeod DS, Merges C, Diggs A, Plouet J. Localization of vascular endothelial growth factor in human retina and choroid. *Arch Ophthalmol* (1996) 114(8):971–7. doi: 10.1001/archopht.1996.01100140179011
30. Jin K, Zhu Y, Sun Y, Mao XO, Xie L, Greenberg DA. Vascular endothelial growth factor (VEGF) stimulates neurogenesis in vitro and in vivo. *Proc Natl Acad Sci U S A* (2002) 99(18):11946–50. doi: 10.1073/pnas.182296499
31. Sun Y, Jin K, Xie L, Childs J, Mao XO, Logvinova A, et al. VEGF-induced neuroprotection, neurogenesis, and angiogenesis after focal cerebral ischemia. *J Clin Invest* (2003) 111(12):1843–51. doi: 10.1172/JCI17977
32. Greene J, Banasr M, Lee B, Warner-Schmidt J, Duman RS. Vascular endothelial growth factor signaling is required for the behavioral actions of antidepressant treatment: pharmacological and cellular characterization. *Neuropsychopharmacology* (2009) 34(11):2459–8. doi: 10.1038/npp.2009.68
33. Chen GB, Xu Y, Xu HM, Li MD, Zhu J, Lou XY. Practical and theoretical considerations in study design for detecting gene-gene interactions using MDR and GMDR approaches. *PLoS One* (2011) 6(2):e16981. doi: 10.1371/journal.pone.0016981
34. Moore JH, Gilbert JC, Tsai CT, Chiang FT, Holden T, Barney N, et al. A flexible computational framework for detecting, characterizing, and interpreting statistical patterns of epistasis in genetic studies of human disease susceptibility. *J Theor Biol* (2006) 241(2):252–61. doi: 10.1016/j.jtbi.2005.11.036
35. Wu Y, Xu Y, Sun Y, Wang YF, Li X, Lang XE, et al. Association between the serotonin 1A receptor C(-1019)G polymorphism and major depressive disorder in the northern Han ethnic group in China. *Chin Med J (Engl)* (2008) 121(10):874–6. doi: 10.1097/00029330-200805020-00002
36. Zhang K, Xu Q, Xu Y, Yang H, Luo J, Sun Y, et al. The combined effects of the 5-HTTLPR and 5-HTR1A genes modulates the relationship between negative life events and major depressive disorder in a Chinese population. *J Affect Disord* (2009) 114(1–3):224–31. doi: 10.1016/j.jad.2008.07.012
37. Albert PR, Lemonde S. 5-HT1A receptors, gene repression, and depression: guilt by association. *Neuroscientist* (2004) 10(6):575–93. doi: 10.1177/1073858404267382
38. Sawiniec J, Borkowski K, Ginalska G, Lewandowska-Stanek H. Association between 5-hydroxytryptamine 1A receptor gene polymorphism and suicidal behavior. *Przegl Lek* (2007) 64(4–5):208–11.
39. Illi A, Setala-Soikkeli E, Viikki M, Poutanen O, Huhtala H, Mononen N, et al. 5-HTR1A, 5-HTR2A, 5-HTR6, TPH1 and TPH2 polymorphisms and major depression. *Neuroreport* (2009) 20(12):1125–8. doi: 10.1097/WNR.0b013e32832eb708
40. Carvalho AF, Kohler CA, McIntyre RS, Knochel C, Brunoni AR, Thase ME, et al. Peripheral vascular endothelial growth factor as a novel depression biomarker: a meta-analysis. *Psychoneuroendocrinology* (2015) 62:18–26. doi: 10.1016/j.psyneuen.2015.07.002
41. Tseng PT, Cheng YS, Chen YW, Wu CK, Lin PY. Increased levels of vascular endothelial growth factor in patients with major depressive disorder: a meta-analysis. *Eur Neuropsychopharmacol* (2015) 25(10):1622–30. doi: 10.1016/j.euroneuro.2015.06.001
42. Galecki P, Galecka E, Maes M, Orzechowska A, Berent D, Talarowska M, et al. Vascular endothelial growth factor gene (VEGFA) polymorphisms may serve as prognostic factors for recurrent depressive disorder development. *Prog Neuropsychopharmacol Biol Psychiatry* (2013) 45:117–24. doi: 10.1016/j.pnpbp.2013.04.011
43. Greene J, Banasr M, Lee B, Warner-Schmidt J, Duman RS. Vascular endothelial growth factor signaling is required for the behavioral actions of antidepressant treatment: pharmacological and cellular characterization. *Neuropsychopharmacology* (2009) 34(11):2459–68. doi: 10.1038/npp.2009.68
44. Mendez J, Kadia TM, Somayazula RK, El-Badawi KI, Cowen DS. Differential coupling of serotonin 5-HT1A and 5-HT1B receptors to activation of ERK2 and inhibition of adenylyl cyclase in transfected CHO cells. *J Neurochem* (1999) 73(1):162–8. doi: 10.1046/j.1471-4159.1999.0730162.x
45. Cowen DS. Serotonin and neuronal growth factors—a convergence of signaling pathways. *J Neurochem* (2007) 101(5):1161–71. doi: 10.1111/j.1471-4159.2006.04420.x

19

Understanding the Relation Between Early-Life Adversity and Depression Symptoms: The Moderating Role of Sex and an Interleukin-1β Gene Variant

Robyn J. McQuaid[1*], *Robert L. Gabrys*[2], *Opal A. McInnis*[2], *Hymie Anisman*[1,2] *and* *Kimberly Matheson*[1,2]

[1] *The Royal's Institute of Mental Health Research, University of Ottawa, Ottawa, Canada,* [2] *Department of Neuroscience, Carleton University, Ottawa, ON, Canada*

Correspondence:
Robyn J. McQuaid
robyn.mcquaid@theroyal.ca

Pro-inflammatory cytokines, such as interleukin (IL)-6 and tumor necrosis factor-α (TNF-α), are thought to play a fundamental role in the pathogenesis of depression within a subset of individuals. However, the involvement of IL-1β has not been as consistently linked to depression, possibly owing to difficulties in detecting this cytokine in blood samples or that changes in circulating levels might only be apparent in a subgroup of patients who have experienced early-life adversity. From this perspective, the association between early-life adversity and depressive illness might depend on genetic variants regulating IL-1β activity. Considering the inflammatory-depression link, and that women are twice as likely to experience depression compared to men, the current study (N = 475 university students) examined the moderating role of three independent cytokine single nucleotide polymorphisms (SNPs; IL-1β rs16944, IL-6 rs1800795 SNP, TNF-α rs1800629) in the relationship between early-life adversity and depressive symptoms, and whether these relations differed between males and females. The relation between childhood adversity and depressive symptoms was moderated by the IL-1β SNP, and further varied according to sex. Specifically, among females, higher childhood maltreatment was accompanied by elevated depressive symptoms irrespective of the IL-1β SNP, but among males, this relationship was particularly pronounced for those carrying the GG genotype of the IL-1β SNP. These findings suggest that, in the context of early life adversity, genetic variations of IL-1β functioning are related to depressive symptomatology and this may vary among males and females. The present study also, more broadly, highlights the importance of considering the confluence of experiential factors (e.g., early life adversity) and personal characteristics (e.g., sex and genetics) in understanding depressive disorders, an approach increasingly recognized in developing personalized treatment approaches to this illness.

Keywords: cytokines, depression, inflammation, interleukin-1β, polymorphism, stress

INTRODUCTION

The role of inflammation in the pathogenesis of depression is well-established (1, 2). Depressed individuals display elevated circulating pro-inflammatory cytokine levels (3) and administering pro-inflammatory cytokines to adults (e.g., during the course of treatment for hepatitis C and for some types of cancer) induces symptoms of depression, an effect that could be reversed by antidepressants (4). A meta-analysis comprising 58 studies indicated that interleukin (IL)-6 and the acute phase reactant C-reactive protein (CRP) were elevated in major depressive disorder, and to a lesser extent, tumor necrosis factor (TNF)-α (5). Treatment with antidepressants, as expected, was accompanied by reduced peripheral IL-6, TNF-α, and the anti-inflammatory IL-10 (6).

When considering the link between IL-1β and depression, the results have been mixed. Some meta-analyses do not find an overall association between IL-1β and major depression (3, 5, 7), although it was suggested that this could be due to measurement issues as concentrations of IL-1β are very low in blood (5). Moreover, no differences were found in basal IL-1β levels in a recent paper with MDD patients, but proteins upstream IL-1β production were elevated (8). However, others have reported elevated IL-1β levels in major depression (9), and a separate meta-analysis found elevated IL-1β in patients affected with major depressive disorder, although, this was only when the studies included were rated as having high quality methodologies (10). It was suggested that IL-1β changes may be apparent in a subgroup of patients, including individuals with a history of childhood trauma (10). Consistent with this perspective, early-life adversity might be centrally involved in the relationship between depression and inflammation by promoting changes to inflammatory signaling (11). In this regard, females who reported sexual abuse in adolescence displayed higher plasma levels of the pro-inflammatory cytokine IL-6 (12). Scores on an early trauma inventory scale were positively associated with serum IL-6, TNF-α and IL-1β levels (13), and depressed individuals with experiences of childhood trauma displayed higher peripheral cytokine levels compared to individuals with major depressive disorder who did not experience childhood trauma (14).

Beyond plasma cytokine levels, genetic variants of pro-inflammatory cytokines that can alter gene transcription and thereby affect inflammatory proteins, including IL-1β, have been associated with a wide range of physical and psychological disturbances, such as major depression (15, 16). Secretion of IL-1β protein can be influenced by a single nucleotide polymorphism (SNP), rs16944 located in the promoter region of the gene (17). However, currently there are inconsistent reports about whether the GG genotype (18) or the A/A genotype (19) is associated with elevated IL-1β levels. Moreover, other reports have suggested that the functional role of this SNP might depend on promoter region haplotypes (17, 20). Despite the poor understanding of the functionality of this SNP, it has been tied to a number of psychological outcomes. Specifically, individuals carrying two copies of the G allele, were found to have an early age of onset of depression (21), higher depressive symptoms and poorer response to antidepressant treatment (22–24), elevated cortisol levels following dexamethasone (25), and greater depressive symptoms following chronic interpersonal stressor encounters (26). However, there have also been some conflicting findings, such that an elevated risk of depression among the minor allele A carriers for individuals with schizophrenia spectrum disorders (27), Alzheimer's disease (28), and following childhood adversity (29).

Altered IL-6 expression has been linked to the IL-6 rs1800795 SNP, which is also located in the promoter region of the gene (30, 31). However, this SNP has been inconsistently linked to depression, in that individuals homozygous for the G allele exhibited an increase in depressive symptoms (32), whereas no association was found between this SNP and depression in other reports (33–35). It was found, however, that following interpersonal stress (26), and recent negative events (36), the G-carriers of this IL-6 SNP expressed fewer depressive symptoms relative to CC homozygotes. The TNF-α rs1800629 SNP located in the promoter region has also been inconsistently linked to depression and a recent meta-analysis found no significant association to depression (37). Only one previous investigation examined the TNF-α SNP in association to interpersonal stress and depression, and found no moderating role of the TNF-α SNP (26).

As women are approximately twice as likely to be diagnosed with depression (38), and report greater severity and increased symptoms compared to men (39), the pathophysiology of depression might also differ by sex. In fact, a large-scale gene expression study revealed multiple transcription changes in opposite directions between men and women with major depressive disorder (40).

Considering the discrepant findings regarding the IL-1β SNP, the primary aim of the current study was to examine the moderating role of the IL-1β SNP and that of IL-6, and TNF-α in the relation between early life adversity and depressive symptoms, and to determine whether any such effects would be moderated by sex. In the present investigation we chose to assess these factors in a sample of university students, as it has long been known that ∼15–20% of students entering post-secondary educational institutions may have undiagnosed or subsyndromal symptoms of depression and anxiety (41). Moreover, early-life adverse experiences, such as childhood abuse and neglect, have been increasingly reported by college students and are thought to be contributing to large increases in the number of students presenting at university counseling services (42, 43). Given the considerable role for early life negative experiences in the evolution of adult depression, it was hypothesized that the GG carriers for the IL-1β SNP would display elevated depression scores following childhood maltreatment, although it was uncertain whether women or men might be more affected in this regard. Moreover, it was expected that the G-carriers of the IL-6 SNP would be linked to fewer depressive symptoms following childhood maltreatment compared to individuals with the CC genotype, but similarly, a sex effect was uncertain. The currently available data do not justify a hypothesis that early-life adversity and the TNF-α SNP would be associated with adult depression, but this

SNP was included in the present analysis to replicate previous null findings.

METHODS

Procedure

Students were recruited through the university's online computerized research system. Participants provided informed written consent, following which they completed measures of current depressive symptoms, experiences of early-life maltreatment, and a series of demographic questions (e.g., age, sex, and ethnicity). After completing the questionnaires, saliva samples were collected for later genotyping. Participants were debriefed and compensated with course credit. This study was approved by the Carleton University Ethics Committee for Psychological Research.

Genotyping

Norgen collection kits (Norgen Biotek Corp., Thorold, Ontario Canada) were used for the collection of saliva samples for genotyping. Genomic DNA was extracted from the sample collection kit according to the manufacturer's instructions and diluted to approximately equal concentration (10 ng/μL). Genotyping was performed at the McGill University and Génome Québec Innovation Center (Montreal, Canada). Polymerase chain reaction (PCR) was used to amplify the DNA, and QIAXcel determined amplification status. To remove all unincorporated dNTPs, shrimp alkaline phosphatase was used. One probe per marker was used to do a single base extension and the product was desalted using 6 mg of resin. Products were spotted on a Sequenom 384-well chip using a Samsung Nanodispenser and then read by a Mass Spectrometer. A manual analysis was done for each marker. Primer sequences were: IL-1β forward: ACGTTGGATGCTGTCTGTATTGAGGGTGTG, IL-1β reverse: ACGTTGGATGATTTTCTCCTCAGAGGCTCC, IL-1β probe: GTGCTGTTCTCTGCCTC, TNF-α forward: ACGTTGGATGTTCTGGGCCACTGACTGATT, TNF-α reverse: ACGTTGGATGAAGGAAACAGACCACAGACC, TNF-α probe: AGGCTGAACCCCGTCC, IL-6 forward: ACGTTGGATGGATTGTGCAATGTGACGTCC, IL-6 reverse: ACGTTGGATGAGTGGTTCTGCTTCTTAGCG, and IL-6 probe: TGTGACGTCCTTTAGCAT.

Measures

Depressive Symptoms

The 21-item Beck Depression inventory (BDI) (44) was used to assess depressive symptoms. For each item, participants selected one of four response options, which ranged from mild to severe indicators of depressive symptomatology. Total scores were calculated by summing across all items ($\alpha = 0.90$).

General Health

Participants completed a one-item question asking, "*In your opinion, how do you describe your health*," which ranged from one (poor) to five (excellent). This question was assessed to examine how BDI scores map onto other aspects of life/functionality. As expected, it was found that poorer health related to higher depressive symptoms, $r = -0.476, p < 0.001$.

Childhood Maltreatment

The 31-item Childhood Maltreatment Questionnaire (short form) (45) assessed levels of early life adversity, including psychological ($\alpha = 0.95$), physical ($\alpha = 0.90$), and sexual abuse ($\alpha = 0.97$) as well as neglect ($\alpha = 0.85$). Each item is rated from 1 (never) to 5 (very often) indicating the frequency of experiences. Total scores were calculated by obtaining the mean across all items ($\alpha = 0.95$).

Statistical Analyses

Statistical analyses were performed using SPSS for Windows 24.0 (SPSS Science, Chicago, Illinois, USA). Analyses assessing genotype differences on childhood maltreatment and depression scores were performed using a one-way analysis of variance (ANOVA), followed by Bonferroni corrected *t*-tests for any significant outcomes. Sex differences were examined using independent samples *t*-tests. Correlational analysis was performed using Pearson product moment correlations. To examine the moderating role of genotype and sex on the relationship between childhood maltreatment and depression scores, and any possible 3-way interactions, PROCESS (model 3) was used (46), in which moderations are tested in a single model. To be sure findings were not influenced by medications, such as anti-depressants, medications were included as a covariate in PROCESS and effects remained unchanged. Although it is ideal to keep all three genotypes separate whenever possible, as we have previously discussed in relation to OXTR genes [see (47) for a discussion on this topic], moderation analyses require a dichotomous moderator. For moderation analyses genotypes were collapsed into two groups to perform dominant tests because of power issues. A power calculation conducted using on online A-Prior sample size calculator for a Hierarchical Multiple Regression using three predictors in set A (Gender, Il-1B, and Childhood Maltreatment), one predictor in set B (3-way interaction term), a desired power level of 0.8, a *p*-value of 0.05 and the anticipated small effect size of 0.02. The power calculator provided a desired sample size of $N = 388$ (48). For the three main models conducted (one for each of the 3 SNPs), corrections for multiple testing were made such that models were considered significant if they were less than $p = 0.0167$, and effects remained significant.

RESULTS

Participants and Descriptive Information

The original sample comprised 925 Carleton University first year students of various ethnic backgrounds. Population stratification effects were found, in which the IL-1β rs16944, TNF-α rs1800629, and IL-6 rs1800795 genotype distributions significantly differed according to ethnic groups, $\chi^2_{(16)} = 77.0, p < 0.001$, $\chi^2_{(16)} = 39.1$, $p = 0.001$, and $\chi^2_{(16)} = 209.5$, $p < 0.001$, respectively. As an example of these differences, 97.3% of the Asian participants (Chinese, Japanese, Korean) displayed the GG genotype for the IL-6 SNP, whereas, only 36.3% of participants who reported

European white ethnicity had this genotype. Moreover, 89.9% of participants who identified as black (African, Haitian, Jamaican, and Somali) displayed the GG genotype for IL-6 SNP, which was more in-line with Asian participants, whereas individuals who reported South Asian ethnicity (East Indian, Pakistani, Punjabi, and Sri Lankan) had 59.4% GG carriers. This example highlights the large discrepancies of genotype distributions across ethnic groups and the importance of conducting gene x environment analyses within a single homogeneous ethnic group. Accordingly, the current study only examined the largest homogeneous ethnic group, which comprised 475 individuals of European white ethnicity. Of these individuals, there were 343 females and 132 males with a mean age of 19.45 years (SE = 0.11, range = 17–35 years).

Among participants five individuals were taking anti-inflammatory medications (1.1%), 20 individuals were taking anti-depressant medication (4.2%), six individuals were taking anti-anxiety medications (1.3%), and 34.9% reported other medications, which largely included birth control, asthma and allergy medications.

Genotype Distributions and Differences

Six individuals could not be genotyped for the IL-1β rs16944 SNP and the TNF- α rs1800629 SNP, whereas four individuals could not be genotyped for the IL-6 SNP, rs1800795. Genotype distributions and Hardy-Weinberg Equilibrium expectations are represented in **Table 1**.

TABLE 1 | Genotype frequencies, distributions, and Hardy-Weinberg equilibrium expectations.

Genotype distributions	GG	GA	AA	Hardy Weinberg equilibrium
IL-1β (total)	197 (42%)	225 (48%)	47 (10%)	$\chi^2_{(1)} = 2.22$, $p > 0.05$
Males	54 (41.2%)	61 (46.6%)	16 (12.2%)	$\chi^2_{(1)} = 0.04$, $p > 0.05$
Females	143 (42.3%)	164 (48.5%)	31 (9.2%)	$\chi^2_{(1)} = 2.74$, $p > 0.05$
	GG	**GA**	**AA**	
TNF-α (total)	324 (69.1%)	133 (28.4%)	12 (2.6%)	$\chi^2_{(1)} = 0.1$, $p > 0.05$
Males	93 (71.0%)	34 (26.0%)	4 (3.1%)	$\chi^2_{(1)} = 0.17$, $p > 0.05$
Females	231 (68.1%)	99 (29.3%)	8 (2.4%)	$\chi^2_{(1)} = 0.47$, $p > 0.05$
	GG	**GC**	**CC**	
IL-6 (total)	171 (36.3%)	225 (47.8%)	75 (15.9%)	$\chi^2_{(1)} = 0$, $p > 0.05$
Males	39 (38.7%)	67 (46.3%)	24 (15.0%)	$\chi^2_{(1)} = 0.26$, $p > 0.05$
Females	132 (30.0%)	158 (51.5%)	51 (18.5%)	$\chi^2_{(1)} = 0.11$, $p > 0.05$

There were no differences in childhood maltreatment total scores across genotypes for the IL-1β, $F_{(2,466)} = 0.69$, $p = 0.50$, TNF-α, $F_{(2,466)} = 0.14$, $p = 0.87$, or IL-6 SNPs, $F_{(2,468)} = 0.41$, $p = 0.67$. Depression scores, however, varied with the IL-1β genotype, $F_{(2,466)} = 4.00$, $p = 0.02$, $\eta^2 = 0.02$, with GG carriers reporting more severe depressive symptoms ($M = 10.23$, $SE = 0.57$), compared to GA carriers ($M = 8.11$, $SE = 0.54$), $p = 0.02$, whereas AA carriers did not significantly differ compared to the other groups. Depression scores, in contrast, did not vary based on the TNF-α genotypes, $F_{(2,466)} = 0.28$, $p = 0.76$, or the IL-6 SNP, $F_{(2,468)} = 0.84$, $p = 0.43$. **Table 2** shows means for genotype groups collapsed according to the dominant model.

Correlations

As expected, females report more severe depressive symptoms than males, $t_{(1,\,473)} = 3.19$, $p = 0.002$ (females $M = 9.92$, SE 0.44; males $M = 7.32$, SE 0.65), and also reported higher levels of childhood maltreatment, $t_{(1,\,332.0)} = 2.52$, $p = 0.012$ (females: $M = 1.53$, SE 0.03; males: $M = 1.41$, SE 0.04). As shown in **Table 3**, the relations between the childhood maltreatment total scores and depressive symptoms were significant, as were the relations between the different forms of maltreatment and depressive scores (reports of sexual abuse were very infrequent and as such, this subscale was not assessed as an independent measure).

Moderation Analyses

To examine whether sex and cytokine SNPs moderated the relationship between childhood maltreatment and depression scores, moderation analyses were conducted separately for each cytokine SNP. For IL-1β, the overall model was significant, $R^2 = 0.26$, $F_{(7,461)} = 23.11$, $p < 0.001$, revealing interactions between Childhood Maltreatment × IL-1β, $p = 0.03$, Childhood Maltreatment × Sex, $p = 0.005$, and IL-1β × Sex, $p = 0.003$, as well as a significant 3-way interaction between Childhood

TABLE 2 | Mean and standard deviation of childhood maltreatment and depressive symptoms collapsed across genotype groups.

Genotype groups	Childhood maltreatment ($M \pm SD$)	Depressive symptoms ($M \pm SD$)
IL-1β		
Males (GG)	1.32 (±0.34)	6.78 (±7.66)
Males (GA/AA)	1.48 (±0.46)	7.74 (±7.37)
Females (GG)	1.59 (±0.63)	11.53 (±8.96)
Females (GA/AA)	1.49 (±0.56)	8.74 (±7.37)
TNF-α		
Males (GG)	1.46 (±0.46)	8.04 (±8.00)
Males (GA/AA)	1.30 (±0.27)	5.63 (±5.75)
Females (GG)	1.51 (±0.59)	9.50 (±8.14)
Females (GA/AA)	1.57 (±0.60)	10.78 (±8.30)
IL-6		
Males (GG)	1.42 (±0.33)	7.59 (±6.94)
Males (GC/CC)	1.40 (±0.45)	7.00 (±7.42)
Females (GG)	1.50 (±0.05)	10.32 (±0.74)
Females (GC/CC)	1.55 (±0.58)	9.65 (±8.00)

TABLE 3 | Pearson correlations among childhood maltreatment total and subscales and depressive symptoms.

	1	2	3	4	5
1. Depressive symptoms	——				
2. Childhood maltreatment (total score)	0.47**	——			
3. Childhood physical abuse	0.31**	0.78**	——		
4. Childhood psychological abuse	0.48**	0.96**	0.63**	——	
5. Childhood neglect	0.41**	0.87**	0.65**	0.77**	——

**$p < 0.001$.

maltreatment × IL-1β × Sex, $R^2_{change} = 0.01$, $F_{(1, 461)} = 7.86$, $p = 0.005$. The findings of the 3-way interaction are shown in **Figure 1**, wherein a positive relationship between childhood maltreatment and depressive symptoms for females was significant for both GG and A carriers of the IL-1β SNP, $B = 6.78$, $t = 7.27$, $p < 0.001$, 95% CI [4.95, 8.61] and $B = 6.16$, $t = 6.84$, $p < 0.001$, 95% CI [4.39, 7.93], respectively. For males, the relationship between childhood maltreatment and depression was also significant for both genotype carriers, however, it was a much stronger effect for GG carriers, $B = 15.17$, $t = 5.36$, $p < 0.001$, 95% CI [9.61, 20.73], compared to A carriers $B = 4.55$, $t = 2.60$, $p = 0.01$, 95% CI [1.11, 7.98]. In fact, among males with low levels of childhood maltreatment, depression scores were low irrespective of the genotype. However, as levels of maltreatment increased, depression scores were appreciably higher, and more so among those with the GG alleles than among A carriers.

Due to the significant IL-1β SNP model when examining total child maltreatment scores, we conducted follow-up analyses for the different forms of abuse. Once more, 3-way interactions between IL-1β x Sex and each of the subscales of childhood maltreatment were evident: psychological maltreatment, $R^2_{change} = 0.01$, $F_{(1, 461)} = 5.43$, $p = 0.02$, neglect, $R^2_{change} = 0.01$, $F_{(1, 461)} = 5.57$, $p = 0.02$, and physical abuse, $R^2_{change} = 0.01$, $F_{(1, 461)} = 4.34$, $p = 0.04$. However, after correcting for multiple testing, these effects were no longer considered significant at $p < 0.0167$.

Analysis of the moderating relationships involving the TNF-α and IL-6 SNPs indicated that none of these interactions were significant.

DISCUSSION

The current study revealed that, although the effect size was small, depressive symptoms were higher among individuals with the GG genotype of the IL-1β rs16944 SNP, an outcome that was most pronounced among those who experienced childhood adversity. These findings align with earlier reports that the GG carriers show an earlier age of onset of depression (21), enhanced severity of depressive symptoms (24) and poorer responses to antidepressants (22–24). Moreover, individuals with the GG genotype also displayed greater depressive symptoms following chronic interpersonal stressor experiences (26). Thus, the current findings replicate this earlier report showing that the relation between childhood maltreatment and depressive symptoms was also stronger among individual homozygous for the GG genotype. However, it has also been reported that individuals with the GG genotype displayed lower depression scores following childhood adversity (29). Why these differences exist are uncertain, however, in Kovacs et al. report the relations to depression were only apparent among individuals who encountered the most marked childhood adversity. Maltreatment scores in the current study were modest and thus, comparisons or generalizations beyond this population would be inappropriate.

As commonly observed, depressive symptoms were higher in women than in men. Sex also interacted with the IL-1β SNP and childhood maltreatment in predicting depressive scores. Specifically, following maltreatment, males who carried the GG genotype of the IL-1β SNP showed particularly marked depressive symptoms. This finding appears to be in line with research examining systemic inflammation and sex, wherein a higher production of pro-inflammatory cytokines were associated with increasing depressive symptoms for males, however females exhibited reduced pro-inflammatory cytokines as depressive symptoms increased (49). It appears that there are gender differences in the relation between depressive symptoms and inflammatory patterns. Additionally, there have been several reports indicating that the sex differences in depression varied with SNPs on genes other than those coding for cytokines. For instance, the glucocorticoid receptor gene (NR3C1) SNP rs6195 was related to depression among females, but not males (50). Moreover, there was a sex-dependent moderation of a functional mineralocorticoid receptor (MA) haplotype in the relationship between childhood maltreatment and depression, revealing that males in the clinical sample were at increased risk of depression (51). As well, among boys and girls that carried the short allele of the serotonin transporter gene, 5-HTTLPR, displayed opposite responses to environmental stressors (52). In line with these reports, a meta-analysis suggested that pronounced gene expression differences exist between men and women with major depression, and even more relevant to the current findings is the suggestion that treatments aimed at suppressing immune function might be more appropriate for men with depression compared to women (40).

These findings highlight the importance of considering individual characteristics, such as sex, when examining the link between genetic variants and depression, and the treatment of this disorder. Personalized treatment approaches extend beyond this to also recognize the importance of contextual and environmental factors, such as early-life stressful experiences (53). Early-life stressors and/or trauma have been strongly linked to the later development of depression and may interact with individual genetic variants to contribute to depression (54). By example, it was reported that interactions between early-life adversity and the oxytocin receptor gene (OXTR) SNP rs5657 (55), and brain derived neurotrophic factor (BDNF) SNP (56, 57) were linked to depressed mood. Interactions have also been reported between early-life maltreatment and a polymorphism in the promoter region of the serotonin transporter gene (5-HTTLPR) (58). To be sure, considerable controversy exists concerning the reliability of such reports

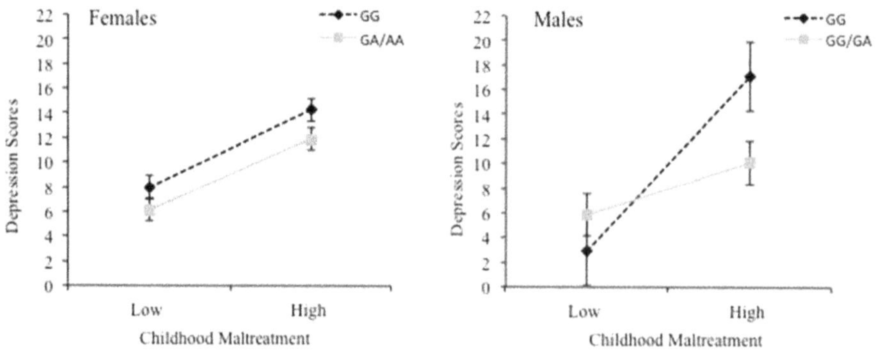

FIGURE 1 | The 3-way interaction between childhood maltreatment, the IL-1β rs16944 SNP (GG vs. GA/AA) and sex in relation to depression scores. Females are shown in the left graph and males are shown in the right graph.

(59), but it should be considered that there are differences in sample characteristics and contexts, such as the timing and type of stress experienced across studies, which highlight the importance of accurate characterization of the environmental exposures underlying the gene × environment effects (54, 60).

In the current study general depressive symptoms were examined, but it would be of particular interest to focus on specific symptoms or subtypes of depression, such as atypical depression, which might be differentially related to sex and/or the cytokine SNPs. As well, specific cytokine SNPs that were not tied to depression might be more strongly linked to suicide behaviors. In this regard, the GG genotype of the TNF-α SNP, rs1800629, was associated with increased risk for suicide attempts among patients with major depressive disorder (61), even though this TNF-α SNP was not linked to general depression and depressive symptomatology (26, 37). The current findings similarly did not show an association between this TNF-α SNP and depressive scores.

Although there have been several reports indicating that inflammatory factors, notably circulating IL-6 and TNF-α, were associated with major depressive illness (5, 62), as previously observed (33–35), the IL-6 rs1800795 SNP was not directly related to depression scores in the present study. Moreover, the IL-6 SNP did not interact with childhood maltreatment or sex to predict depression symptoms. This differs from earlier reports showing interactions between this SNP with interpersonal stress (26), and recent negative events (36), in relation to depression. Of course, early-life maltreatment ought to be distinguished from recent and/or acute stressors, which could explain the non-significant effects in the current study. Recently, this IL-6 SNP has been found to influence antidepressant treatment outcomes in major depressive patients, which might suggest a role for IL-6 in treatment resistant depression (63). As described earlier, support for IL-6 involvement in depression has also come from the many reports showing elevated levels of peripheral IL-6 in depressed patients (5). However, plasma cytokine levels do not necessary reflect levels of this cytokine within the brain. There is, indeed, reason to believe that inflammatory factors released from microglia (64, 65) may contribute to psychiatric disorders, including depression (66). However, it is unlikely that these cytokine variations can be detected in plasma, or that circulating cytokine levels would parallel brain cytokine variations [e.g., (67)].

There are several limitations associated with the current study. Specifically, early-life maltreatment was based on retrospective self-reports, and although this is common when examining childhood adversity, reports might be biased by the individuals' current affective state, and individuals could be unaware of events that took place years earlier. The current study also examined depressive symptoms among university students and thus the findings cannot be generalized to a clinically depressed population. Moreover, it should be noted that the mean scores for both childhood maltreatment and depressive symptoms were fairly low and the findings could differ within the context of higher maltreatment and depressive scores. An additional limitation concerned the relatively small sample size, even though it was determined that the sample size for the current study ($N = 495$ individuals of a homogeneous ethnicity) provided sufficient power to detect small effects, and significant effects survived correction for multiple testing. Due to population stratification effects, we had to limit our analyses to the largest homogenous ethnic group, which comprised individuals who identified as European/white. A larger sample ideally might have allowed for assessment of gene x environment variations among other ethnic groups. This is particularly of interest when we consider the importance of culture in personalized medicine (68, 69). Moreover, there is a possibility that the different cytokine SNPs assessed independently might be additively or interactively linked to depressive symptoms. For instance it has been reported that BDNF and 5-HTTLPR interactions were additive in predicting lifetime depression diagnosis (70), however, in the current sample we had limited power to add additional factors to our model. It is also problematic that the functionality of the IL-1β SNP is not well-understood (25). It would have been ideal to measure the relation between the rs16944 SNP frequency and gene expression levels (i.e., the expression quantitative trait loci [eQTLs; (71, 72)]. This approach could potentially facilitate a better understanding of the functional role of the IL-1β SNP. However, human eQTL studies typically involve analyses in blood-derived cells, as opposed to the saliva samples that were used in the present study, and it also appears that gene expression might vary with different cell types (71). Despite the potential benefits of eQTL analyses, the present data do not lend themselves to this approach. Finally, the current study precludes any causal effects to be inferred.

Together with earlier findings, the present report indicates that the IL-1β rs16944 SNP was associated with depressive symptoms. The current report shows that this relationship might be dependent on environmental contexts, including early-life maltreatment and individual characteristics, such as sex. In fact, sex differences appear to be especially critical in the relation between SNPs and depression, as new reports highlight gene-expression changes in opposite directions for men and women with major depression. These findings, together with other reports, highlight the importance of the social determinants of health when examining depression, an approach increasingly recognized in personalized approaches to medicine.

AUTHOR CONTRIBUTIONS

RM, OM, and HA contributed to the conception and design of the current experiment. Testing and data collection were performed by RM and OM. Data analysis and the writing of the manuscript were performed by RM, RG, HA, and KM. All authors approved the final version of the paper for submission.

FUNDING

This research was funded by the Canadian Institutes of Health Research (CIHR) (grant #86477). The funding source had no further role in the study or in the writing of this article.

ACKNOWLEDGMENTS

We thank Genome Quebec Innovation Center for performing the genotyping.

REFERENCES

1. Maes M. Major depression and activation of the inflammatory response system. In: Dantzer R, Wollman EE, Yirmiya R, editors. *Cytokines, Stress, and Depression*. Boston, MA: Springer (1999). p. 25–46.
2. Miller AH, Raison CL. The role of inflammation in depression: from evolutionary imperative to modern treatment target. *Nat Rev Immunol.* (2016) 16:22. doi: 10.1038/nri.2015.5
3. Dowlati Y, Herrmann N, Swardfager W, Liu H, Sham L, Reim EK, et al. A meta-analysis of cytokines in major depression. *Biol Psychiatry.* (2010) 67:446–57. doi: 10.1016/j.biopsych.2009.09.033
4. Dantzer R, O'Connor JC, Freund GG, Johnson RW, Kelley KW. From inflammation to sickness and depression: when the immune system subjugates the brain. *Nat Rev Neurosci.* (2008) 9:46. doi: 10.1038/nrn2297
5. Haapakoski R, Mathieu J, Ebmeier KP, Alenius H, Kivimäki M. Cumulative meta-analysis of interleukins 6 and 1β, tumour necrosis factor α and C-reactive protein in patients with major depressive disorder. *Brain Behav Immun.* (2015) 49:206–15. doi: 10.1016/j.bbi.2015.06.001
6. Köhler CA, Freitas TH, Stubbs B, Maes M, Solmi M, Veronese N, et al. Peripheral alterations in cytokine and chemokine levels after antidepressant drug treatment for major depressive disorder: systematic review and meta-analysis. *Mol Neurobiol.* (2017) 55:4195–206. doi: 10.1007/s12035-017-0632-1
7. Köhler CA, Freitas TH, Maes MD, De Andrade NQ, Liu CS, Fernandes BS, et al. Peripheral cytokine and chemokine alterations in depression: a meta-analysis of 82 studies. *Acta Psychiatr Scand.* (2017) 135:373–87. doi: 10.1111/acps.12698
8. Syed SA, Beurel E, Loewenstein DA, Lowell JA, Craighead WE, Dunlop BW, et al. Defective inflammatory pathways in never-treated depressed patients are associated with poor treatment response. *Neuron.* (2018) 99:914–24. doi: 10.1016/j.neuron.2018.08.001
9. Mota R, Gazal M, Acosta BA, de Leon PB, Jansen K, Pinheiro RT, et al. Interleukin-1β is associated with depressive episode in major depression but not in bipolar disorder. *J Psychiatr Res.* (2013) 47:2011–4. doi: 10.1016/j.jpsychires.2013.08.020
10. Ellul P, Boyer L, Groc L, Leboyer M, Fond G. Interleukin-1 β-targeted treatment strategies in inflammatory depression: toward personalized care. *Acta Psychiatr Scand.* (2016) 134:469–84. doi: 10.1111/acps.12656
11. Miller GE, Cole SW. Clustering of depression and inflammation in adolescents previously exposed to childhood adversity. *Biol Psychiatry.* (2012) 72:34–40. doi: 10.1016/j.biopsych.2012.02.034
12. Bertone-Johnson ER, Whitcomb BW, Missmer SA, Karlson EW, Rich-Edwards JW. Inflammation and early-life abuse in women. *Am J Prevent Med.* (2012) 43:611–20. doi: 10.1016/j.amepre.2012.08.014
13. Hartwell KJ, Moran-Santa Maria MM, Twal WO, Shaftman S, DeSantis SM, McRae-Clark AL, et al. Association of elevated cytokines with childhood adversity in a sample of healthy adults. *J Psychiatr Res.* (2013) 47:604–10. doi: 10.1016/j.jpsychires.2013.01.008
14. Lu S, Peng H, Wang L, Vasish S, Zhang Y, Gao W, et al. Elevated specific peripheral cytokines found in major depressive disorder patients with childhood trauma exposure: a cytokine antibody array analysis. *Comprehensive Psychiatry.* (2013) 54:953–61. doi: 10.1016/j.comppsych.2013.03.026
15. Bufalino C, Hepgul N, Aguglia E, Pariante CM. The role of immune genes in the association between depression and inflammation: a review of recent clinical studies. *Brain Behav Immun.* (2013) 31:31–47. doi: 10.1016/j.bbi.2012.04.009
16. Khazim K, Azulay EE, Kristal B, Cohen I. Interleukin 1 gene polymorphism and susceptibility to disease. *Immunol Rev.* (2018) 281:40–56. doi: 10.1111/imr.12620
17. Hall SK, Perregaux DG, Gabel CA, Woodworth T, Durham LK, Huizinga TWF, et al. Correlation of polymorphic variation in the promoter region of the interleukin-1β gene with secretion of interleukin-1β protein. *Arthritis Rheumatol.* (2004) 50:1976–83. doi: 10.1002/art.20310
18. Iacoviello L, Di Castelnuovo A, Gattone M, Pezzini A, Assanelli D, Lorenzet R, et al. Polymorphisms of the interleukin-1β gene affect the risk of myocardial infarction and ischemic stroke at young age and the response of mononuclear cells to stimulation *in vitro*. *Arteriosclerosis Thrombosis Vasc Biol.* (2005) 25:222–7. doi: 10.1161/01.ATV.0000150039.60906.02
19. Hwang IR, Kodama T, Kikuchi S, Sakai K, Peterson LE, Graham DY, et al. Effect of interleukin 1 polymorphisms on gastric mucosal interleukin 1β production in Helicobacter pylori infection. *Gastroenterology.* (2002) 123:1793–803. doi: 10.1053/gast.2002.37043
20. Chen H, Wilkins LM, Aziz N, Cannings C, Wyllie DH, Bingle C, et al. Single nucleotide polymorphisms in the human interleukin-1B gene affect transcription according to haplotype context. *Hum Mol Genet.* (2006) 15:519–29. doi: 10.1093/hmg/ddi469
21. Hwang JP, Tsai SJ, Hong CJ, Yang CH, Hsu CD, Liou UJ. Interleukin-1 beta−511C/T genetic polymorphism is associated with age of onset of geriatric depression. *Neuromol Med.* (2009) 11:322–7. doi: 10.1007/s12017-009-8078-x
22. Baune BT, Dannlowski U, Domschke K, Janssen DG, Jordan MA, Ohrmann P, et al. The interleukin 1 beta (IL1B) gene is associated with failure to

achieve remission and impaired emotion processing in major depression. *Biol Psychiatry*. (2010) 67:543–9. doi: 10.1016/j.biopsych.2009.11.004
23. Tadić A, Rujescu D, Müller MJ, Kohnen R, Stassen HH, Szegedi A, et al. Association analysis between variants of the interleukin-1β and the interleukin-1 receptor antagonist gene and antidepressant treatment response in major depression. *Neuropsychiatr Dis Treatment*. (2008) 4:269. doi: 10.2147/NDT.S2262
24. Yu WY, Chen TJ, Hong CJ, Chen HM, Tsai SJ. Association study of the interleukin-1beta (C-511T) genetic polymorphism with major depressive disorder, associated symptomatology, and antidepressant response. *Neuropsychopharmacology*. (2003) 28:1182. doi: 10.1038/sj.npp.1300172
25. Sasayama D, Hori H, Iijima Y, Teraishi T, Hattori K, Ota M, et al. Modulation of cortisol responses to the DEX/CRH test by polymorphisms of the interleukin-1beta gene in healthy adults. *Behav Brain Funct*. (2011) 7:23. doi: 10.1186/1744-9081-7-23
26. Tartter M, Hammen C, Bower JE, Brennan PA, Cole S. Effects of chronic interpersonal stress exposure on depressive symptoms are moderated by genetic variation at IL6 and IL1β in youth. *Brain Behav Immun*. (2015) 46:104–11. doi: 10.1016/j.bbi.2015.01.003
27. Rosa A, Peralta V, Papiol S, Cuesta MJ, Serrano F, Martínez-Larrea A, et al. Interleukin-1beta (IL-1beta) gene and increased risk for the depressive symptom-dimension in schizophrenia spectrum disorders. *Am J Med Genet B Neuropsychiatr Genet*. (2004) 124B:10–4. doi: 10.1002/ajmg.b.20074
28. McCulley MC, Day IN, Holmes C. Association between interleukin 1-β promoter (−511) polymorphism and depressive symptoms in Alzheimer's disease. *Am J Med Genet Part B Neuropsychiatr Genet*. (2004) 124:50–3. doi: 10.1002/ajmg.b.20086
29. Kovacs D, Eszlari N, Petschner P, Pap D, Vas S, Kovacs P, et al. Effects of IL1B single nucleotide polymorphisms on depressive and anxiety symptoms are determined by severity and type of life stress. *Brain Behav Immun*. (2016a) 56:96–104. doi: 10.1016/j.bbi.2016.02.012
30. Cole SW, Arevalo JM, Takahashi R, Sloan EK, Lutgendorf SK, Sood AK, et al. Computational identification of gene-social environment interaction at the human IL6 locus. *Proc Natl Acad Sci USA*. (2010) 107:5681–6. doi: 10.1073/pnas.0911515107
31. Schultze-Florey CR, Martínez-Maza O, Magpantay L, Breen EC, Irwin MR, Gündel H, et al. When grief makes you sick: bereavement induced systemic inflammation is a question of genotype. *Brain Behav Immun*. (2012) 26:1066–71. doi: 10.1016/j.bbi.2012.06.009
32. Bull SJ, Huezo-Diaz P, Binder EB, Cubells JF, Ranjith G, Maddock C, et al. Functional polymorphisms in the interleukin-6 and serotonin transporter genes, and depression and fatigue induced by interferon-α and ribavirin treatment. *Mol Psychiatry*. (2009) 14:1095. doi: 10.1038/mp.2008.48
33. Clerici M, Arosio B, Mundo E, Cattaneo E, Pozzoli S, Dell'Osso B, et al. Cytokine polymorphisms in the pathophysiology of mood disorders. *CNS Spectrums*. (2009) 14:419–25. doi: 10.1017/S1092852900020393
34. Mihailova S, Ivanova-Genova E, Lukanov T, Stoyanova V, Milanova V, Naumova E. A study of TNF-α, TGF-β, IL-10, IL-6, and IFN-γ gene polymorphisms in patients with depression. *J Neuroimmunol*. (2016) 293:123–8. doi: 10.1016/j.jneuroim.2016.03.005
35. Misener VL, Gomez L, Wigg KG, Luca P, King N, Kiss E, et al. Cytokine Genes TNF, IL1A, IL1B, IL6, IL1RN and IL10, and childhood-onset mood disorders. *Neuropsychobiology*. (2008) 58:71–80. doi: 10.1159/000159775
36. Kovacs D, Eszlari N, Petschner P, Pap D, Vas S, Kovacs P, et al. Interleukin-6 promoter polymorphism interacts with pain and life stress influencing depression phenotypes. *J Neural Transmission*. (2016b) 123:541–8. doi: 10.1007/s00702-016-1506-9
37. Shin KH, Jeong HC, Choi DH, Kim SN, Kim TE. Association of TNF-alpha g-308a gene polymorphism with depression: a meta-analysis. *Neuropsychiatr Dis Treatment*. (2017) 13:2661. doi: 10.2147/NDT.S143434
38. Nolen-Hoeksema S. Gender differences in depression. *Curr Directions Psychol Sci*. (2001) 10:173–6. doi: 10.1111/1467-8721.00142
39. Kornstein SG, Schatzberg AF, Thase ME, Yonkers KA, McCullough JP, Keitner GI, et al. Gender differences in chronic major and double depression. *J Affect Disorders*. (2000) 60:1–11. doi: 10.1016/S0165-0327(99)00158-5
40. Seney ML, Huo Z, Cahill K, French L, Puralewski R, Zhang J, et al. Opposite molecular signatures of depression in men and women. *Biol Psychiatry*. (2018) 84:18–27. doi: 10.1016/j.biopsych.2018.01.017
41. Offer D, Spiro RP. The disturbed adolescent goes to college. *J Am Coll Health*. (1987) 35:209–14. doi: 10.1080/07448481.1987.9940443
42. American College Health Association. American college health association national college health assessment (ACHA-NCHA) spring 2005 reference group data report (abridged). *J Am Coll Health*. (2006) 55:5. doi: 10.3200/JACH.55.1.5-16
43. Benton SA, Robertson JM, Tseng WC, Newton FB, Benton SL. Changes in counseling center client problems across 13 years. *Professional Psychol Res Pract*. (2003) 34:66. doi: 10.1037/0735-7028.34.1.66
44. Beck AT, Ward CH, Mendelson M, Mock J, Erbaugh J. An inventory of measuring depression. *Arch Gen Psychiatry*. (1961) 4:561–71.
45. Demare, D. *The Childhood Maltreatment Questionnaire: Examining Long-Term Correlates of Childhood Maltreatment*. Toronto, ON: Paper presented at APA (1996).
46. Hayes AF. *PROCESS: A Versatile Computational Tool for Observed Variable Mediation, Moderation, and Conditional Process Modeling*. (2012). Available online at: http://www.afhayes.com/public/process2012.pdf
47. McQuaid RJ, McInnis OA, Matheson K, Anisman H. Distress of ostracism: oxytocin receptor gene polymorphism confers sensitivity to social exclusion. *Soc Cogn Affect Neurosci*. (2015) 10:1153–9. doi: 10.1093/scan/nsu166
48. Soper DS. *The Free Statistics Calculators Website: A-priori Sample Size Calculator for Hierarchical Multiple Regression (Version 2.0)*. (2010). Available online at: https://www.analyticscalculators.com/calculator.aspx?id=16
49. Majd M, Graham-Engeland JE, Smyth JM, Sliwinski MJ, Lipton RB, Katz MJ, et al. Distinct inflammatory response patterns are evident among men and women with higher depressive symptoms. *Physiol Behav*. (2018) 184:108–15. doi: 10.1016/j.physbeh.2017.11.009
50. Sarubin N, Hilbert S, Naumann F, Zill P, Wimmer AM, Nothdurfter C, et al. The sex-dependent role of the glucocorticoid receptor in depression: variations in the NR3C1 gene are associated with major depressive disorder in women but not in men. *Eur Arch Psychiatry Clin Neurosci*. (2017) 267:123–33. doi: 10.1007/s00406-016-0722-5
51. Vinkers CH, Joëls M, Milaneschi Y, Gerritsen L, Kahn RS, Penninx BW, et al. Mineralocorticoid receptor haplotypes sex-dependently moderate depression susceptibility following childhood maltreatment. *Psychoneuroendocrinology*. (2015) 54:90–102. doi: 10.1016/j.psyneuen.2015.01.018
52. Sjöberg RL, Nilsson KW, Nordquist N, Öhrvik J, Leppert J, Lindström L, et al. Development of depression: sex and the interaction between environment and a promoter polymorphism of the serotonin transporter gene. *Int J Neuropsychopharmacol*. (2006) 9:443–9. doi: 10.1017/S1461145705005936
53. Khoury MJ, Iademarco MF, Riley WT. Precision public health for the era of precision medicine. *Am J Prevent Med*. (2016) 50:398–401. doi: 10.1016/j.amepre.2015.08.031
54. Heim C, Binder EB. Current research trends in early life stress and depression: review of human studies on sensitive periods, gene-environment interactions, and epigenetics. *Exp Neurol*. (2012) 233:102–11. doi: 10.1016/j.expneurol.2011.10.032
55. McQuaid RJ, McInnis OA, Stead JD, Matheson K, Anisman H. A paradoxical association of an oxytocin receptor gene polymorphism: early-life adversity and vulnerability to depression. *Front Neurosci*. (2013) 7:128. doi: 10.3389/fnins.2013.00128
56. Caldwell W, McInnis OA, McQuaid RJ, Liu G, Stead JD, Anisman H, et al. The role of the Val66Met polymorphism of the brain derived neurotrophic factor gene in coping strategies relevant to depressive symptoms. *PLoS ONE*. (2013) 8:e65547. doi: 10.1371/journal.pone.0065547
57. Hosang GM, Shiles C, Tansey KE, McGuffin P, Uher R. Interaction between stress and the BDNF Val66Met polymorphism in depression: a systematic review and meta-analysis. *BMC Med*. (2014) 12:7. doi: 10.1186/1741-7015-12-7
58. Caspi A, Hariri AR, Holmes A, Uher R, Moffitt TE. Genetic sensitivity to the environment: the case of the serotonin transporter gene and its implications for studying complex diseases and traits. *Focus*. (2010) 8:398–416. doi: 10.1176/foc.8.3.foc398
59. Culverhouse RC, Saccone NL, Horton AC, Ma Y, Anstey KJ, Banaschewski T, et al. Collaborative meta-analysis finds no evidence of a strong interaction between stress and 5-HTTLPR genotype contributing to the development of depression. *Mol Psychiatry*. (2018) 23:133–42. doi: 10.1038/mp.2017.44

60. Karg K, Burmeister M, Shedden K, Sen S. The serotonin transporter promoter variant (5-HTTLPR), stress, and depression meta-analysis revisited: evidence of genetic moderation. *Arch General Psychiatry.* (2011) 68:444–54. doi: 10.1001/archgenpsychiatry.2010.189
61. Kim YK, Hong JP, Hwang JA, Lee HJ, Yoon HK, Lee BH, et al. TNF-alpha- 308G> A polymorphism is associated with suicide attempts in major depressive disorder. *J Affect Disorders.* (2013) 150:668–72. doi: 10.1016/j.jad.2013.03.019
62. Ma K, Zhang H, Baloch Z. Pathogenetic and therapeutic applications of tumor necrosis factor-α (TNF-α) in major depressive disorder: a systematic review. *Int J Mol Sci.* (2016) 17:733. doi: 10.3390/ijms17050733
63. Carvalho S, Santos M, Lima L, Mota-Pereira J, Pimentel P, Maia D, et al. IL6-174G> C genetic polymorphism influences antidepressant treatment outcome. *Nordic J Psychiatry.* (2017) 71:158–62. doi: 10.1080/08039488.2016.1242650
64. Allen NJ, Barres BA. Neuroscience: glia—more than just brain glue. *Nature.* (2009) 457:675–7. doi: 10.1038/457675a
65. Donegan JJ, Girotti M, Weinberg MS, Morilak DA. A novel role for brain interleukin-6: facilitation of cognitive flexibility in rat orbitofrontal cortex. *J Neurosci.* (2014) 34:953–62. doi: 10.1523/JNEUROSCI.3968-13.2014
66. Mondelli V, Vernon AC, Turkheimer F, Dazzan P, Pariante CM. Brain microglia in psychiatric disorders. *Lancet Psychiatry.* (2017) 4:563–72. doi: 10.1016/S2215-0366(17)30101-3
67. Gibb J, Hayley S, Poulter MO, Anisman H. Effects of stressors and immune activating agents on peripheral and central cytokines in mouse strains that differ in stressor responsivity. *Brain Behav Immun.* (2011) 25:468–82. doi: 10.1016/j.bbi.2010.11.008
68. Kirmayer LJ, Crafa D. What kind of science for psychiatry? *Front Hum Neurosci.* (2014) 8:435. doi: 10.3389/fnhum.2014.00435
69. Matheson K, Bombay A, Anisman H. Culture as an ingredient of personalized medicine. *J Psychiatry Neurosci.* (2018) 43:3. doi: 10.1503/jpn.170234
70. Carver CS, Johnson SL, Joormann J, LeMoult J, Cuccaro ML. Childhood adversity interacts separately with 5-HTTLPR and BDNF to predict lifetime depression diagnosis. *J Affect Disorders.* (2011) 132:89–93. doi: 10.1016/j.jad.2011.02.001
71. Nica AC, Dermitzakis ET. Expression quantitative trait loci: present and future. *Philos Trans Roy Soc B Biol Sci.* (2013) 368:20120362. doi: 10.1098/rstb.2012.0362
72. Battle A, Montgomery SB. Determining causality and consequence of expression quantitative trait loci. *Hum Genet.* (2014) 133:727–35. doi: 10.1007/s00439-014-1446-0

20

Cognitive Impairment and Endoplasmic Reticulum Stress Induced by Repeated Short-Term Sevoflurane Exposure in Early Life of Rats

Fu-Yi Shen [1†], *Ying-Cai Song* [1†], *Fei Guo* [2†], *Zhen-Dong Xu* [1], *Qian Li* [1], *Bing Zhang* [1,2,3], *Yu-Qin Ma* [2,3], *Yue-Qi Zhang* [1], *Rong Lin* [1], *Yang Li* [2*] and *Zhi-Qiang Liu* [1*]

[1] Department of Anesthesiology, Shanghai First Maternity and Infant Hospital, Tongji University School of Medicine, Shanghai, China, [2] Key Laboratory of Receptor Research, Shanghai Institute of Materia Medica, Chinese Academy of Sciences, Shanghai, China, [3] University of Chinese Academy of Sciences, Beijing, China

***Correspondence:**
Yang Li
liyang@simm.ac.cn
Zhi-Qiang Liu
drliuzhiqiang@163.com

† These authors have contributed equally to this work and are co-first authors.

Sevoflurane is one of the most commonly used volatile anaesthetics for children, but the safety of prolonged or repeated clinical use of sevoflurane in infants or children is controversial. Here, we investigated the effects of sevoflurane on rats in early life and the time scale of those effects. Our behavioral results indicated that repeated short-term exposure of new-born rats to sevoflurane caused learning and memory impairment, while a single exposure of rats to sevoflurane was relatively safe. Further mechanistic investigation revealed that repeated sevoflurane exposure impaired long-term potentiation (LTP), downregulated the expression of certain synaptogenesis-related proteins (GluR1, PSD95) and upregulated proteins related to endoplasmic reticulum (ER) stress in the hippocampus. An ER stress inhibitor, tauroursodeoxycholic acid (TUDCA), reversed the changes in the levels of synaptic plasticity proteins. Our results provide new evidence for the clinical concerns regarding repeated sevoflurane anesthesia.

Keywords: sevoflurane, repeated exposure, cognitive dysfunction, synaptic plasticity, endoplasmic reticulum stress

INTRODUCTION

Sevoflurane, a volatile anesthetic, is commonly used in pediatric anesthesia, owing to its rapid onset, short recovery time, sweet smell and nonflammability. Sevoflurane has been used clinically for decades, and most studies have supported its safety for adults. However, studies have shown that sevoflurane causes stress and neurotoxicity in the developing brains of rodents and non-human primates (NHPs) (1, 2). In addition, a large number of clinical observations have demonstrated that childhood exposure to anesthesia can cause long-term cognitive impairment (3, 4). Since the developing brain is susceptible to anesthetics (5, 6), the US Food & Drug Administration (FDA) has also raised concerns regarding the effects of repeated or prolonged anesthetic exposure in children (7).

As the developing brain is highly sensitive to different environmental factors such as sensory stimuli, drugs and stress, children's brains can be at high risk of being remodeled by severe anesthetic exposure. Since sevoflurane is one of the most commonly used volatile anesthetics for children, its safety deserves further investigation. Many reports have confirmed that a single exposure to sevoflurane has no effects on the infants or children (8). However, some research has reported long-term cognitive impairment caused by repeated sevoflurane exposure (2, 9–11). Unfortunately, some major surgeries in clinical practice require repeated sevoflurane exposure for infants or children; therefore, it is urgent to clarify the effects of repeated sevoflurane anesthesia and its long-term effects later in life.

In the present study, we investigated the time scope of sevoflurane exposure in neonatal rats by comparing single and repeated exposure to sevoflurane. Our results indicate that repeated exposure of young rats to sevoflurane results in severe deterioration of memory and cognition later in life, while a single sevoflurane exposure is relatively safe. Furthermore, the mechanism underlying the adverse effects of repeated sevoflurane exposure may involve dysfunction of synaptic plasticity and endoplasmic reticulum (ER) stress.

MATERIALS AND METHODS

Animals

The present study was approved by the Animal Care Committees of Shanghai Institute of Materia Medica, Chinese Academy of Science, and the experiments were carried out in accordance with EU Directive 2010/63/EU on the protection of animals used for scientific purposes. Four-day-old male Sprague Dawley (SD) rats obtained from Shanghai Sippr-BK Laboratory Animal Co were housed with their dams under controlled illumination (12-h/12-h light/dark cycle, light from 07:00 to 19:00) at 24 ± 1°C. The rats were given free access to food and water. On postnatal day (P) 7, all neonatal rats were randomly divided into 2 groups: a control group and a sevoflurane (sevo) group. The neonatal rats in the sevo group were exposed to 3% sevoflurane for 2 h per exposure on P7, P10, and P13, whereas those in the control group were subjected to the same conditions without receiving sevoflurane. Changes in synaptic plasticity and ER-stress-associated protein levels were then analyzed by western blotting ($n = 4$ for each group). On P21, all the young rats were weaned and housed in groups of 2 per cage in standard conditions. Behavioral tests were later conducted: the open field test for locomotor activity was performed on P42, and the Morris water maze test for learning and memory ability was performed from P43 to P48 (control group: $n = 10$, sevo group: $n = 9$). Subsequently, rats that had undergone behavioral tests were subjected to field excitatory postsynaptic potential (fEPSP) experiments to detect whether synaptic transmission was affected (**Figure 1**, $n = 6$ for each group).

Anesthesia

The neonatal rats in the sevo group received 3% sevoflurane in 50% O_2/N_2 for 2 h on P7, 10, and 13 in a sealed box at a set temperature of 37 ± 1°C. The rats in the control group received 50% O_2/N_2 at the same flow rate in a similar box on the same days. The neonatal rats breathed spontaneously. The concentrations of sevoflurane and oxygen were measured continuously (Vamos, Drager, Germany). Following sevoflurane exposure, the neonatal rats were returned to their dams after recovering their righting reflex.

Drug Treatment

Tauroursodeoxycholic acid (TUDCA, sodium salt; Sigma-Aldrich) was dissolved in 0.9% saline at a concentration of 50 mg/ml and was intraperitoneally injected 1 h before each sevoflurane exposure at a dosage of 50 mg/kg body weight. The rats were randomly divided into four groups: the saline-treated control group (control), the TUDCA-treated control group (TUDCA), the saline-treated sevo group (sevo) and the TUDCA-treated sevo group (sevo+TUDCA).

Western-Blotting Analysis

Rats were deeply anesthetized with an injection of chloral hydrate (400 mg/kg, intraperitoneally). Immediately after decapitation, the hippocampus was dissected and homogenized by sonic disruption. The homogenate was centrifuged at 14,000 rpm for 10 min at 4°C. Total protein concentrations were measured using a BCA assay (Pierce, Rockford, IL). The proteins were separated on SDS-PAGE gels and transferred to nitrocellulose membranes. The membranes were blocked and then incubated overnight at 4? with primary antibodies (anti-GRP 78, 1:1,000, Sigma-Aldrich; anti-PERK, 1:1,000, Sigma-Aldrich; anti-eIF-2α, 1:1,000, Sigma-Aldrich; GluR1 subunit (pSer845), 1:1,000, Sigma-Aldrich; anti-PSD95, 1:1,000, Sigma-Aldrich; anti-CREB, 1:1,000, Sigma-Aldrich; anti-GAPDH, 1:1,000, Sigma-Aldrich). Band intensities were measured using Image Processing and Analysis in Java (ImageJ) software.

Open Field Test

The open field test is the standard way to obtain an overview of locomotor activity. We performed this test on P42 according to a previously described protocol (12, 13). First, the SD rats were allowed to habituate to the testing room. Subsequently, they were placed in the middle of a square box (100 × 100 × 45 cm) made of black acrylic plastic. The rats were permitted to explore in the box for 10 min, and their movements were video tracked. The total distance moved was calculated offline with an analysis-management system (Viewer 2 Tracking Software, Ji Liang Instruments, China).

Morris Water Maze

The Morris water maze test was conducted 24 h after the open field test. The Morris water maze test consisted of 5 days of place navigation training and a probe trial on day 6. The maze was composed of a circular black metal tank (180 cm in diameter, 60 cm in height) filled with water (24 ± 2°C); a video camera set in the ceiling and was connected to a computer equipped with an analysis-management system (Viewer 2 Tracking Software, Ji Liang Instruments, China). The maze was divided into 4 equal quadrants, one of which contained a hidden escape platform (10 cm diameter) in the middle, 0.5 cm below the

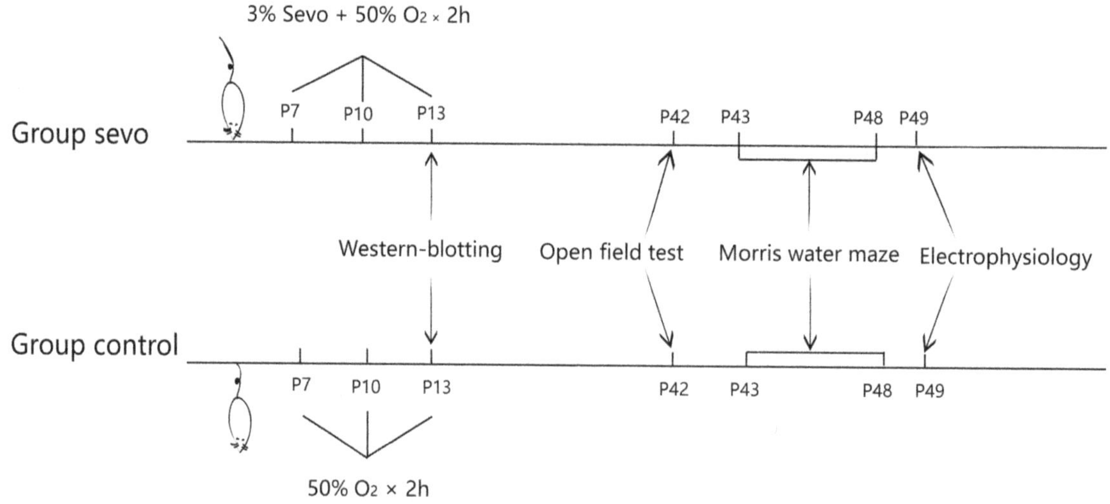

FIGURE 1 | Schematic timeline of the experimental procedure.

surface of the water. White marks were located equidistantly around the edge of the maze in all start positions. On P43, each rat was allowed to swim freely in the pool for 60 s for habituation. From P44 to P47, a hidden escape platform (10 cm in diameter) was submerged 0.5 cm below the surface of the water in the middle of the target quadrant. During navigation training, four trials separated by 30 s were conducted daily for each rat. Each day, rats were placed into four different starting quadrants, and entry from the north, south, east, or west point was varied in a quasi-random order. Each rat was allowed a maximum of 60 s to locate the platform. If the rat did not find the platform within 60 s, it was guided to the location. The time that the rat took to reach the submerged platform (escape latency) was recorded to assess spatial learning ability. On P48, a probe test consisting of a 60 s trial with the platform removed was conducted to assess memory. The amount of time spent in the target quadrant was recorded. The target quadrant was defined as the quadrant that previously contained the platform, whose radius was limited to 16 cm in this assessment.

Slice Preparation

SD rats at P49-P55 were deeply anesthetized with an injection of chloral hydrate (400 mg/kg, intraperitoneally) and euthanized by decapitation. The brain tissue was obtained immediately. The hippocampus was cut into 400-μm-thick sections using a vibratome (Leica VT1000 S, USA) in ice-cold, oxygenated modified artificial cerebrospinal fluid (mACSF, in mM: 25.0 $NaHCO_3$, 1.25 NaH_2PO_4, 2.5 KCl, 0.5 $CaCl_2$, 7.0 $MgCl_2$, 25.0 glucose, 11.0 choline chloride, 11.6 ascorbic acid and 3.1 pyruvic acid, gassed with 5% CO_2 and 95% O_2). The cut slices were quickly placed into a chamber and incubated in normal oxygenated ACSF (118 NaCl, 2.5 KCl, 26 $NaHCO_3$, 1 NaH_2PO_4, 10 glucose, 1.3 $MgCl_2$ and 2.5 $CaCl_2$ in mM, gassed with 5% CO_2 and 95% O_2) at 32°C for 1 h. Finally, the slice was transferred to the recording chamber at room temperature.

Electrophysiology

We recorded fEPSPs by using a Multiclamp 700B amplifier (Molecular Devices, USA) under a microscope (Olympus, Japan). For fEPSP recording, both bipolar stimulating and recording electrodes were placed at CA3/Schaffer collateral-CA1 synapses in the stratum radiatum of the CA1 area. The data were filtered at 2 kHz, sampled at 10 kHz using a Digidata 1440A (Molecular Devices, USA) and analyzed with Clampfit 10.2 software (Molecular Devices, USA). The stimuli consisted of 100-μs pulses delivered at 0.03 Hz using an electronic stimulator (Nihon Kohden Corporation, Japan), and the stimulus intensity was adjusted to 65% of the maximal response. The evoked response was monitored for 10 min at this intensity to ensure stable recording prior to the drug treatment. After 10-min stable recording at baseline, the long-term potentiation (LTP) was induced by application of the high frequency intensity (HFS) protocol consisting of 1 s trains of 100 Hz stimulation repeated two times 20 s apart. All recordings were continued for 60–80 min.

Statistical Analysis

The data are expressed as the means ± SEM. The software Statistical Package for the Social Sciences (SPSS, Version 19.0; SPSS Inc., Chicago, IL, USA) was used for statistical analysis. The results of the open field test, and western blots in SD rats were analyzed using unpaired *t*-tests. The results of Morris water maze test were analyzed using a repeated ANOVA in which treatment was used as the between factor and time (weeks) was used as the within factor, and a *post-hoc* LSD test was performed. p-values < 0.05 were considered statistically significant.

RESULTS

Early-Life Repeated Sevoflurane Exposure Led to Long-Term Cognitive Impairment

We first performed the open field test to detect differences in locomotor activity between groups. The results showed

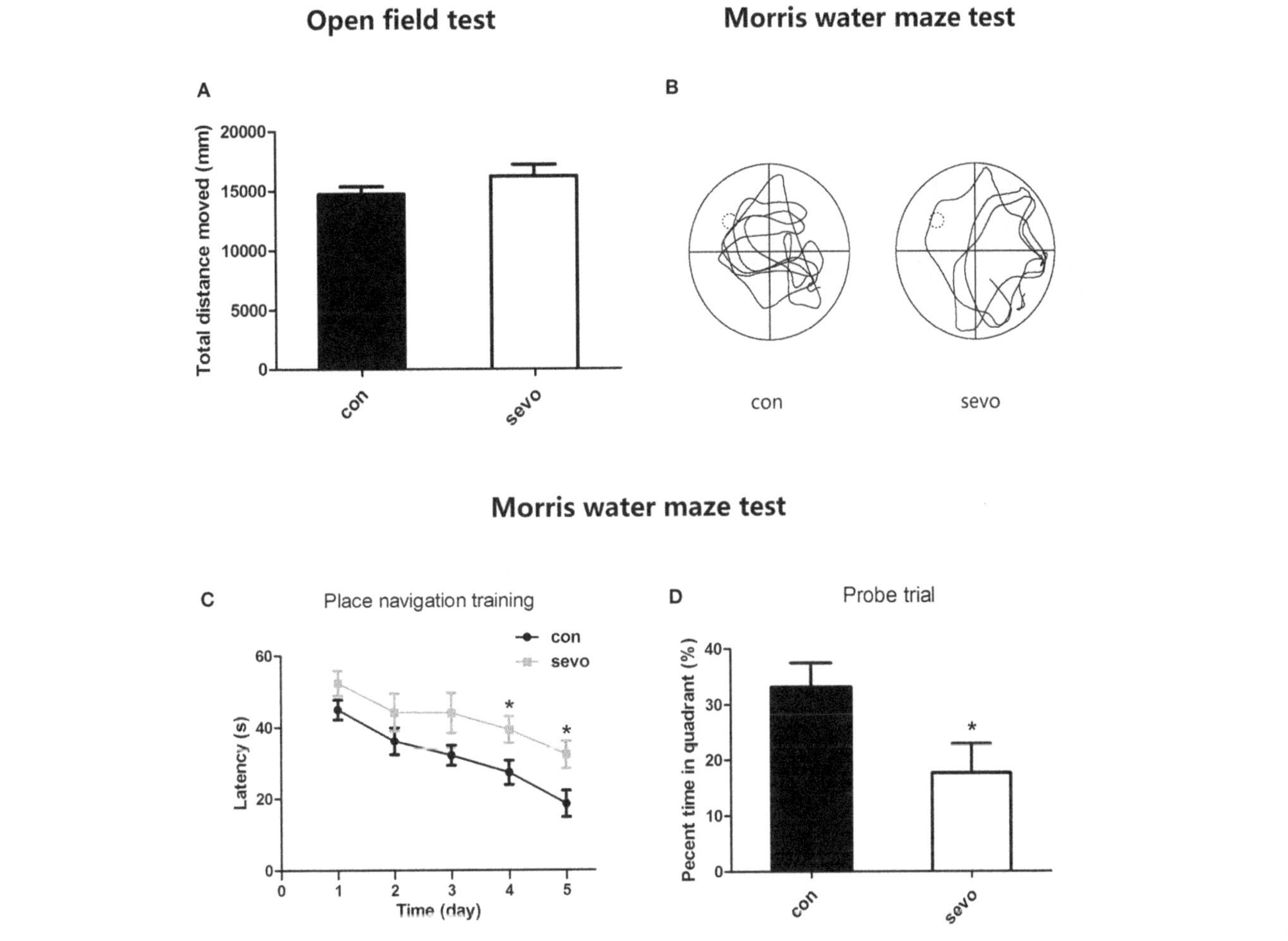

FIGURE 2 | Effects of repeated early-life sevoflurane exposure on behavior. **(A)** In the open field test, no significant difference was observed between the control group and the sevoflurane group in total distance moved. **(B)** A typical path during the probe trial for each group. **(C)** The latency to find the platform during the place navigation training phase of the Morris water maze test. **(D)** The percentage of time spent in the target quadrant during the probe trial of the Morris water maze test. $N = 10$ rats for each group. Repeated ANOVA with a *post hoc* least significant difference (LSD) test and unpaired *t*-tests were performed for **(A,C,D)**, respectively; $^{*}p < 0.05$. Data are presented as the mean ± SEM.

that there was no significant difference in total distance moved between the control group and the sevoflurane group, indicating that repeated early-life sevoflurane exposure did not affect the psychomotor ability of animals (**Figure 2A**).

To examine the long-term effects of early sevoflurane exposure on cognitive function, we administered the Morris water maze test from P43 to P48, consisting 5 days of place navigation training to evaluate learning ability and 1 day (P48) containing a probe trial to assess memory ability. The results suggested that the latency to locate the hidden platform was significantly longer in the sevoflurane group than in the control group on days 4-5 (P46-47) of navigation training, indicating much lower learning ability in sevoflurane-treated animals (**Figure 2C**). Moreover, the probe trial results showed that the percentage of time spent in the target quadrant was higher for the control group than for the sevoflurane group (**Figure 2D**). Taken together, all those results imply that repeated early-life sevoflurane exposure caused long-term dysfunction of learning and memory.

Repeated Short-Term Sevoflurane Exposure Caused Dysfunction of Synaptic Plasticity in the Hippocampus

Sevoflurane exposure may cause an impairment of hippocampal synaptic plasticity, as a severe deficiency of learning and memory ability was observed in the above results (as shown in **Figure 2**). We then examined the LTP at CA3/Schaffer collateral-CA1 synapses of behaviorally tested rats. Our results showed that the slopes of fEPSPs were significantly decreased in the CA1 area of the hippocampus in the sevoflurane group compared to the control group (**Figure 3**). This result suggests that early-life repeated sevoflurane exposure abolished LTP, indicating a dysfunction of synaptic plasticity in the hippocampus.

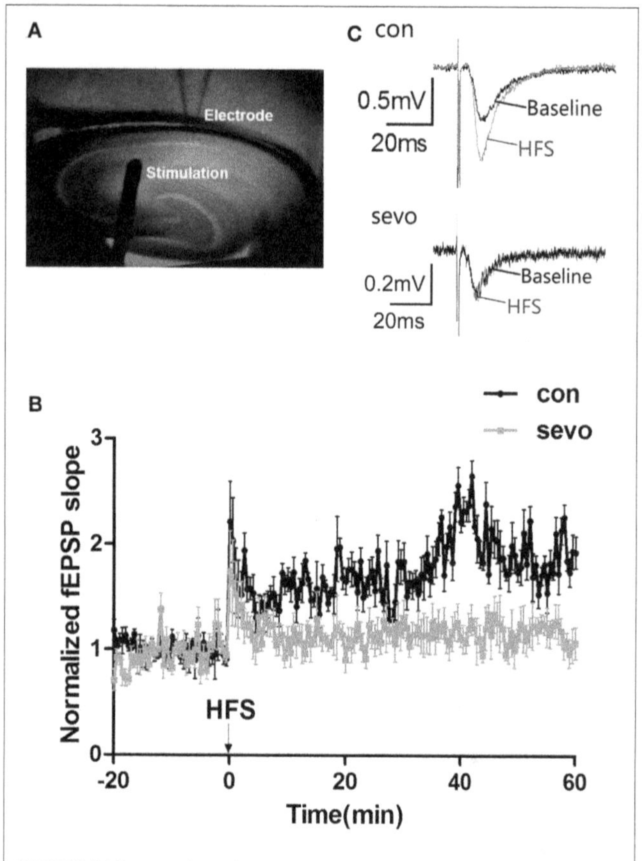

FIGURE 3 | Repeated sevoflurane exposure abolished LTP in the hippocampus. **(A)** Schematic representation of bipolar stimulating and recording electrode placement. **(B)** Tetanic stimulation (one bout of stimulation at 100 Hz) induced LTP in the Schaffer collateral-CA1 pathway of rat hippocampal slices. **(C)** Representative traces of the fEPSP waves were recorded at baseline (the black line) and after repeated sevoflurane exposure (the gray line); early-life sevoflurane exposure impaired LTP in the rat hippocampus. $N = 9$ slices, 4 rats for the control group; $n = 8$ slices, 4 rats for the sevo group.

Expression of Proteins Associated With Synaptic Plasticity Decreased in the Sevoflurane-Exposed Hippocampus

To explore possible mechanisms relating to cognitive dysfunction caused by early-life repeated sevoflurane exposure, we further determined the expression levels of synaptic-plasticity-associated proteins under repeated sevoflurane exposure. We examined the expression levels of GluR1, postsynaptic density protein 95 (PSD95) and cAMP response element-binding protein (CREB) in the hippocampus. The results showed that the expression levels of GluR1, PSD95, and CREB were significantly decreased by repeated sevoflurane exposure (**Figures 4A,B**). Interestingly, the expression levels of the abovementioned proteins did not change with a single sevoflurane exposure (Supplemental Figures S1A,B). These results suggest that repeated sevoflurane exposure but not single exposure decreased hippocampal synaptic plasticity.

Levels of ER-Stress-Related Proteins in the Hippocampus Were Elevated by Repeated Sevoflurane Exposure

ER stress commonly occurs under severe conditions, such as prolonged anesthetic exposure. It is possible that ER stress might play a critical role in deficits of synaptic plasticity (14). To determine whether sevoflurane exposure was associated with ER stress in the hippocampus, we analyzed the levels of ER-stress-associated proteins in the hippocampus. The results showed that the expression level of glucose-regulated protein 78 (GRP 78), a crucial biomarker of ER stress (15), was significantly elevated by sevoflurane exposure (**Figures 5A,B**). PKR-like ER kinase (PERK) is a critical transmembrane ER signaling protein that mediates an important signaling pathway when dissociated from GRP 78, and eukaryotic initiation factor 2α (eIF-2α) is a critical protein in the PERK pathway (16, 17). The levels of PERK and eIF-2α were also significantly elevated in the sevoflurane group compared with the control group (**Figures 5A,B**). As expected, we did not observe any significant change in GRP 78, eIF-2α or PERK in the group that underwent single sevoflurane exposure (Supplemental Figures S1C,D). These results suggest that the activation of PERK pathway may promote ER stress as a consequence of repeated but not single sevoflurane exposure.

TUDCA Reversed the Decrease in the Expression of Synaptic-Plasticity-Associated Proteins in the Sevoflurane-Exposed Hippocampus

To clarify the correlation between ER stress and synaptic plasticity, we injected the rats with TUDCA (an ER stress inhibitor) intraperitoneally before each sevoflurane exposure, and then we analyzed the levels of ER-stress-associated proteins and synaptic-plasticity-related proteins in the hippocampus. The results showed that the expression levels of GRP 78, PERK and eIF-2α were significantly increased in the sevo group and that the increases were reversed by application of TUDCA (**Figures 6A,B**). The expression levels of GluR1, PSD95, and CREB were significantly decreased in the sevo group, but the decrease in expression was prevented by treatment with TUDCA (**Figures 6C,D**). These results suggested that the ER stress inhibitor TUDCA, could reverse the changes in synaptic plasticity protein levels that were induced by repeated sevoflurane exposure in early life.

DISCUSSION

Our results showed that repeated short-term exposure to sevoflurane resulted in impairment of learning and memory. Furthermore, we found that proteins related to ER stress were unusually abundant and synaptogenesis-related proteins markedly decreased after repeated sevoflurane exposure, indicating that ER stress and dysfunction in hippocampal synaptic plasticity may be associated with deficits in spatial learning and memory induced by repeated sevoflurane exposure.

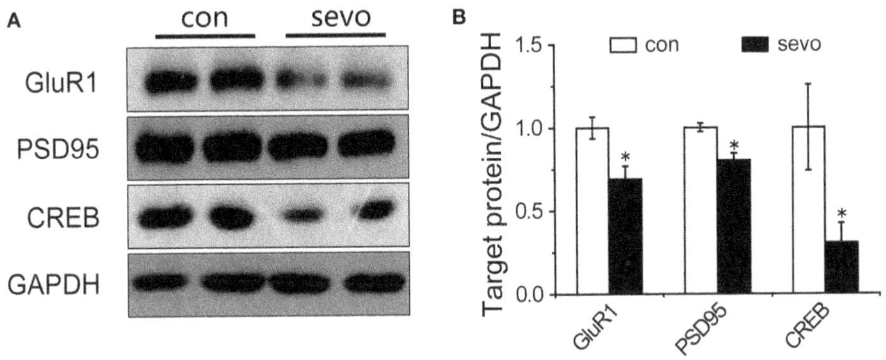

FIGURE 4 | Repeated sevoflurane exposure decreased the expression of GluR1, PSD95, and CREB. **(A)** Representative samples showing the hippocampal expression levels of GluR1, PSD95, and CREB in the control group and the sevoflurane group. **(B)** Densitometric analysis of GluR1, PSD95, and CREB. $N = 4–6$ times for each protein. Unpaired *t*-tests; $^{*}p < 0.05$ vs. control. Data are presented as the means ± SEM

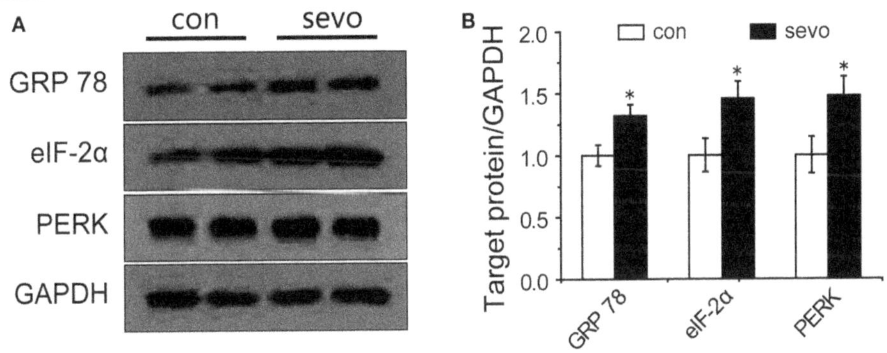

FIGURE 5 | Repeated sevoflurane exposure increased the expression of GRP 78, PERK, and eIF-2α. **(A)** Representative samples showing the expression levels of GRP 78, PERK, and eIF-2α in the hippocampi of the control group and the sevoflurane group; **(B)** Densitometric analysis of GRP 78, PERK, and eIF-2α. $N = 4–6$ times for each protein. Unpaired *t*-tests; $^{*}p < 0.05$ vs. control. Data are presented as the means ± SEM.

Most studies on the effects of sevoflurane have focused on a single prolonged exposure, whereas only a few studies have examined repeated short-term exposure. Extremely long exposure to sevoflurane is rare for infants in the clinic, whereas repeated short-term exposure to sevoflurane, although more common and well worth exploring, receives less attention.

In clinical studies, Flick et al. have found that repeated exposure to anesthesia before the age of 2 is a significant independent risk factor for the later development of learning disabilities (6); similarly, Wilder et al. have found that multiple exposure to anesthesia, but not single exposure, is a significant risk factor for the later development of learning disabilities in children (18). Our results indicated that both learning and memory were impaired by repeated exposure to sevoflurane, in accordance with those clinical studies.

Synaptic plasticity is closely related to the structural modification of synapses and to synaptic transmission (19). The impairment of synaptic plasticity can lead to deficits in cognitive function (8). LTP is widely considered the neuronal basis for learning and memory. A change in LTP function can be reflected in the strength of postsynaptic neurotransmission. Our current results showed that repeated sevoflurane exposure markedly impaired LTP at CA3/Schaffer collateral-CA1 synapses of the hippocampus, in agreement with findings from previous studies (20). Furthermore, the inhibition of LTP caused weakness in postsynaptic transmission and changes in the morphological and structural development of synapses.

The reduction of LTP may be related to the expression of synaptic proteins. We found that the expression levels of GluR1, PSD95 and CREB in the hippocampus were all markedly decreased in rats that received repeated sevoflurane exposure. GluR1 is a glutamate receptor and cation channel that is integral to plasticity and synaptic transmission at many postsynaptic membranes. The underlying physiological correlate of increases in EPSP size is postsynaptic upregulation of GluR1 at the membrane (21). The upregulation of GluR1 at the membrane results in a long-lasting increase in EPSP size, which underlies LTP. In the current study, repeated sevoflurane exposure downregulated the expression of GluR1 and led to reduced LTP. The transcription of GluR1 in

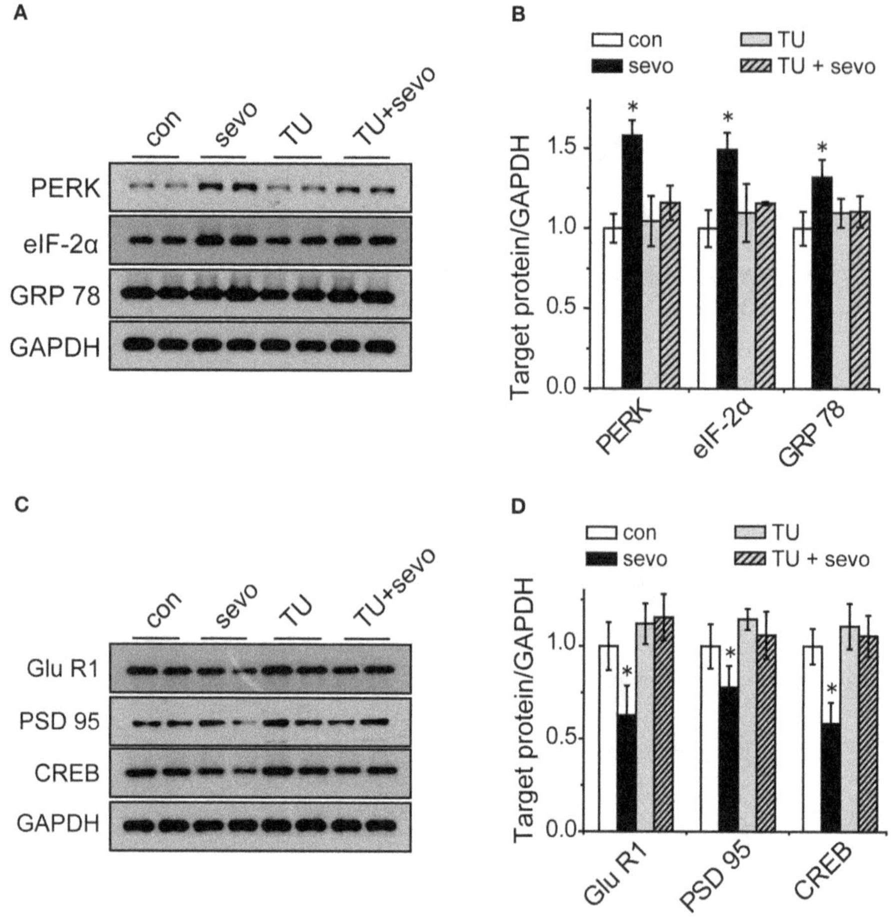

FIGURE 6 | Increased expression of GRP 78, PERK, and eIF-2α and decreased expression of GluR1, PSD95, and CREB were reversed by the ER stress inhibitor TUDCA. **(A)** Representative samples showing the expression levels of GRP 78, PERK and eIF-2α in the hippocampi of the control group, the sevoflurane group, the TUDCA group and the TUDCA+sevoflurane group; **(B)** Densitometric analysis of GRP 78, PERK, and eIF-2α. $N = 3$–6 times for each protein. One-way ANOVA; $^{*}p < 0.05$ vs. control. Data are presented as the means ± SEM. **(C)** Representative samples showing the expression levels of GluR1, PSD95, and CREB in the hippocampi of the control group, the sevoflurane group, the TUDCA group and the TUDCA+sevoflurane group; **(D)** Densitometric analysis of GluR1, PSD95, and CREB. One-way ANOVA; $^{*}p < 0.05$ vs. control. Data are presented as the means ± SEM.

long-term memory is controlled through CREB. CREB is a cellular transcription factor that has been extensively linked to learning, memory (22) and LTP (23). Gene transcription of the transcription factor CREB is closely related to hippocampus-mediated memory consolidation (24). In agreement with results from previous studies (25–27), our western blotting results revealed that repeated sevoflurane exposure was associated with downregulated expression of CREB, which led to a decrease in neurogenesis (28). PSD95 is a postsynaptic marker (29). Downregulated expression of PSD95 results in disrupted synaptic structure (30, 31). The decrease in synaptogenesis-related proteins in the hippocampus indicated deficits in synaptic plasticity, which might lead to dysfunction of spatial learning and memory.

Previous studies have revealed that sevoflurane induces Ca^{2+} release from the ER to the cytosol via the inositol 1,4,5-trisphosphate receptor (IP3R) and ryanodine receptor (RyR), which suggests an influence of sevoflurane on calcium homeostasis in neurons (32–34). However, whether repeated short-term sevoflurane exposure can induce ER stress that impairs synaptic plasticity and long-term memory is still unknown. In our study, repeated sevoflurane exposure increased the expression of GRP 78, PERK and eIF-2α. GRP 78 is a crucial biomarker of ER stress (15). When misfolded proteins accumulate, GRP 78 is released, thereby permitting aggregation of transmembrane signaling proteins and triggering the ER stress response (15). PERK is a critical transmembrane signaling protein (35), and eIF-2α is a key protein in the PERK pathway (36). TUDCA is a neuroprotective drug via inhibiting ER stress (37). We found that TUDCA reversed the decline in the expression of GluR1, PSD95, and CREB. These results revealed that ER stress might play a critical role in deficits of synaptic plasticity, which may correspond to the recent finding that impaired LTP could be rescued by the ER stress inhibitor TUDCA in a chronic intermittent hypoxia model (14).

CONCLUSIONS

Our results showed that repeated short-term exposure to sevoflurane resulted in impairment of learning and memory abilities, and the underlying mechanism included hippocampal synaptic dysfunction and ER stress. ER stress and decreased expression of synaptic proteins may be involved in this impairment of synaptic function, which can be reversed by the ER stress inhibitor TUDCA.

AUTHOR CONTRIBUTIONS

YL and Z-QL designed and supervised the project. F-YS, Y-CS, FG, and Z-DX performed behavioral test and western-blotting experiments. FG, BZ, and Y-QM performed electrophysiological experiments. F-YS, Y-QZ, RL, and BZ performed ER stress experiments. F-YS, BZ, Z-DX, YL, and Z-QL wrote the manuscript. All authors discussed the data and read the manuscript.

FUNDING

This work was supported by the China National Natural Science Foundation [31200771, 31171011, 31371066, 31671049, 81771188], Science and Technology Commission of Shanghai Municipality [14411966700, 16411967400], the Shanghai Municipal Health and Family Planning Commission [grant numbers 20144Y0209, 20134y129], Shanghai municipal medical and health discipline construction projects [2017ZZ02015] and the "Xinchen Cup" Young Anaesthesiologists Incubation Fund of Shanghai Medical Association Anaesthesiology Branch.

REFERENCES

1. Raper J, Alvarado MC, MurphyKL, Baxter MG. Multiple anesthetic exposure in infant monkeys alters emotional reactivity to an acute stressor. *Anesthesiology* (2015) 123:1084–92. doi: 10.1097/ALN.0000000000000851
2. Jevtovic-Todorovic V, Hartman RE, Izumi Y, Benshoff ND, Dikranian K, Zorumski CF, et al. Early exposure to common anesthetic agents causes widespread neurodegeneration in the developing rat brain and persistent learning deficits. *J Neurosci.* (2003) 23:876–82. doi: 10.1523/JNEUROSCI.23-03-00876.2003
3. DiMaggio C, Sun LS, Li G. Early childhood exposure to anesthesia and risk of developmental and behavioral disorders in a sibling birth cohort. *Anesth Analg.* (2011) 113:1143–51. doi: 10.1213/ANE.0b013e3182147f42
4. Ing C, DiMaggio C, Whitehouse A, Hegarty MK, Brady J, von Ungern-Sternberg BS et al. Long-term differences in language and cognitive function after childhood exposure to anesthesia. *Pediatrics* (2012) 130:e476–85. doi: 10.1542/peds.2011-3822
5. Qiu L, Zhu C, Bodogan T, Gómez-Galán M, Zhang Y, Zhou K, et al. Acute and long-term effects of brief sevoflurane anesthesia during the early postnatal period in rats. *Toxicol Sci.* (2016) 149:121–33. doi: 10.1093/toxsci/kfv219
6. Flick RP, Katusic SK, Colligan, RC, Wilder RT, Voigt RG, Olson MD, et al. Cognitive and behavioral outcomes after early exposure to anesthesia and surgery. *Pediatrics* (2011) 128:e1053–61. doi: 10.1542/peds.2011-0351
7. Andropoulos DB, Greene MF. Anesthesia and developing brains - implications of the FDA warning. *N Engl J Med.* (2017) 376:905–7. doi: 10.1056/NEJMp1700196
8. Xiao H, Liu B, Chen, Y, Zhang, J. Learning, memory and synaptic plasticity in hippocampus in rats exposed to sevoflurane. *Int J Dev Neurosci.* (2016) 48:38–49. doi: 10.1016/j.ijdevneu.2015.11.001
9. Kodama M, Satoh Y, Otsubo Y, Araki Y, Yonamine R, Masui K, et al. Neonatal desflurane exposure induces more robust neuroapoptosis than do isoflurane and sevoflurane and impairs working memory. *Anesthesiology* (2011) 115:979–91. doi: 10.1097/ALN.0b013e318234228b
10. Wei H, Kang B, Wei W, Liang G, Meng QC, Li Y, et al. Isoflurane and sevoflurane affect cell survival and BCL-2/BAX ratio differently. *Brain Res.* (2005) 1037:139–47. doi: 10.1016/j.brainres.2005.01.009
11. Shen X, Liu Y, Xu S, Zhao Q, Guo X, Shen R, et al. Early life exposure to sevoflurane impairs adulthood spatial memory in the rat. *Neurotoxicology* (2013) 39:45–56. doi: 10.1016/j.neuro.2013.08.007
12. Stanford SC. The open field test: reinventing the wheel. *J Psychopharmacol.* (2007) 21:134–5. doi: 10.1177/0269881107073199
13. Garza JC, Guo M, Zhang W, Lu XY. Leptin restores adult hippocampal neurogenesis in a chronic unpredictable stress model of depression and reverses glucocorticoid-induced inhibition of GSK-3beta/beta-catenin signaling. *Mol Psychiatry.* (2012) 17:790–808. doi: 10.1038/mp.2011.161
14. Xu LH, Xie H, Shi ZH, Du LD, Wing YK, Li AM, et al. Critical role of endoplasmic reticulum stress in chronic intermittent hypoxia-induced deficits in synaptic plasticity and long-term memory. *Antioxid Redox Signal.* (2015) 23:695–710. doi: 10.1089/ars.2014.6122
15. Xu C, Bailly-Maitre B, Reed JC. Endoplasmic reticulum stress: cell life and death decisions. *J Clin Invest.* (2005) 115:2656–64. doi: 10.1172/JCI26373
16. Harding HP, Zhang Y, Bertolotti A, Zeng H, Ron D. Perk is essential for translational regulation and cell survival during the unfolded protein response. *Mol Cell* (2000) 5:897–904. doi: 10.1016/S1097 2765(00)80330-5
17. Scheuner D, Song B, McEwen E, Liu C, Laybutt R, Gillespie P, et al. Translational control is required for the unfolded protein response and *in vivo* glucose homeostasis. *Mol Cell* (2001) 7:1165–76. doi: 10.1016/S1097-2765(01)00265-9
18. Wilder RT, Flick RP, Sprung J, Katusic SK, Barbaresi WJ, Mickelson C, et al. Early exposure to anesthesia and learning disabilities in a population-based birth cohort. *Anesthesiology* (2009) 110:796–804. doi: 10.1097/01.anes.0000344728.34332.5d
19. Gomez-Palacio-Schjetnan A, Escobar ML. *In vivo* BDNF modulation of adult functional and morphological synaptic plasticity at hippocampal mossy fibers. *Neurosci Lett.* (2008) 445:62–7. doi: 10.1016/j.neulet.2008.08.069
20. Ishizeki J, Nishikawa K, Kubo K, Saito S, Goto, F. Amnestic concentrations of sevoflurane inhibit synaptic plasticity of hippocampal CA1 neurons through gamma-aminobutyric acid-mediated mechanisms. *Anesthesiology* (2008) 108:447–56. doi: 10.1097/ALN.0b013e318164cfba
21. Maren S, Tocco G, Standley S, Baudry M. Thompson RF. Postsynaptic factors in the expression of long-term potentiation (LTP): increased glutamate receptor binding following LTP induction *in vivo*. *Proc Natl Acad Sci USA* (1993) 90:9654–8. doi: 10.1073/pnas.90.20.9654
22. Bourtchuladze, R, Frenguelli B, Blendy J, Cioffi D, Schutz G, Silva AJ, et al. Deficient long-term memory in mice with a targeted mutation of the cAMP-responsive element-binding protein. *Cell* (1994) 79:59–68. doi: 10.1016/0092-8674(94)90400-6
23. Impey S, Mark M, Villacres EC, Poser S, Chavkin C, Storm DR, et al. Induction of CRE-mediated gene expression by stimuli that generate long-lasting LTP in area CA1 of the hippocampus. *Neuron* (1996) 16:973–82. doi: 10.1016/S0896-6273(00)80120-8

24. Carlezon WA Jr, DumanRS, Nestler EJ. The many faces of CREB. *Trends Neurosci.* (2005) 28:436–45. doi: 10.1016/j.tins.2005.06.005
25. Xiong WX, Zhou GX, Wang B, Xue ZG, Wang L, Sun HC, et al. Impaired spatial learning and memory after sevoflurane-nitrous oxide anesthesia in aged rats is associated with down-regulated cAMP/CREB signaling. *PLoS ONE* (2013) 8:e79408. doi: 10.1371/journal.pone.0079408
26. Xie H, She GM, Wang C, Zhang LY, Liu CF. The gender difference in effect of sevoflurane exposure on cognitive function and hippocampus neuronal apoptosis in rats. *Eur Rev Med Pharmacol Sci.* (2015) 19:647–57.
27. Jia M, Liu WX, Yang JJ, Xu N, Xie ZM, Ju LS, et al. Role of histone acetylation in long-term neurobehavioral effects of neonatal Exposure to sevoflurane in rats. *Neurobiol Dis.* (2016) 91:209–20. doi: 10.1016/j.nbd.2016.03.017
28. Nakagawa S, Kim JE, Lee R, Malberg JE, Chen J, Steffen C, et al. Regulation of neurogenesis in adult mouse hippocampus by cAMP and the cAMP response element-binding protein. *J Neurosci.* (2002) 22:3673–82. doi: 10.1523/JNEUROSCI.22-09-03673.2002
29. Takeuchi, M, Hata Y, Hirao K, Toyoda A, Irie M, Takai Y. SAPAPs. A family of PSD-95/SAP90-associated proteins localized at postsynaptic density. *J Biol Chem.* (1997) 272:11943–51. doi: 10.1074/jbc.272.18.11943
30. Li G, Xue Q, Luo Y, Hu X, Yu B. S6 inhibition contributes to isoflurane neurotoxicity in the developing brain. *Toxicol Lett.* (2015) 233:102–13. doi: 10.1016/j.toxlet.2014.11.026
31. Rubino T, Realini N, Braida D, Guidi S, Capurro V, Viganò D, et al. Changes in hippocampal morphology and neuroplasticity induced by adolescent THC treatment are associated with cognitive impairment in adulthood. *Hippocampus* (2009) 19:763–72. doi: 10.1002/hipo.20554
32. Schroder M, Kaufman RJ. The mammalian unfolded protein response. *Annu Rev Biochem.* (2005) 74:739–89. doi: 10.1146/annurev.biochem.73.011303.074134
33. Yang H, Liang G, Hawkins BJ, Madesh M, Pierwola A, Wei H. Inhalational anesthetics induce cell damage by disruption of intracellular calcium homeostasis with different potencies. *Anesthesiology* (2008) 109:243–50. doi: 10.1097/ALN.0b013e31817f5c47
34. Liu X, Song X, Yuan T, He J, Wang X, Wang Q. Effects of calpain on sevoflurane-induced aged rats hippocampal neuronal apoptosis. *Aging Clin Exp Res.* (2016) 28:633–9. doi: 10.1007/s40520-015-0466-5
35. Harding HP, Zhang Y. Ron D. Protein translation and folding are coupled by an endoplasmic-reticulum-resident kinase. *Nature* (1999) 397:271–4. doi: 10.1038/16729
36. Shi Y, Vattem KM, Sood R, An J, Liang J, Stramm L, et al. Identification and characterization of pancreatic eukaryotic initiation factor 2 alpha-subunit kinase, PEK, involved in translational control. *Mol Cell Biol.* (1998) 18:7499–509. doi: 10.1128/MCB.18.12.7499
37. Cheng F, Ma C, Sun L, Zhang X, Zhai C, Li C, et al. Synergistic neuroprotective effects of Geniposide and ursodeoxycholic acid in hypoxia-reoxygenation injury in SH-SY5Y cells. *Exp Ther Med.* (2018) 15:320–6. doi: 10.3892/etm.2017.5395

21

Evidence Based Dyadic Therapies for 0- to 5-Year-Old Children With Emotional and Behavioral Difficulties

*Reem M. A. Shafi, Ewa D. Bieber, Julia Shekunov, Paul E. Croarkin and Magdalena Romanowicz**

Department of Psychiatry and Psychology, Mayo Clinic, Rochester, MN, United States

Correspondence:
Magdalena Romanowicz
romanowicz.magdalena@mayo.edu

As many as one in four preschool-aged children are estimated to struggle with psychosocial stress and social-emotional issues; yet, interventions are often postponed until older ages when change is actually more difficult. Reasons for this include limited interventions, paucity of FDA approved medications for young children, as well as the dearth of clinicians adequately trained in psychotherapeutic approaches for young children. This commentary outlines indications of the four most commonly used evidence-based dyadic psychotherapies for young children: Child-Parent Psychotherapy (CPP) and Trauma-Focused Cognitive Behavioral Therapy (TF-CBT), used primarily for young children with trauma, and Parent-Child Interaction Therapy (PCIT) and Child Parent Relationship Therapy (CPRT), used mostly for children with behavioral issues. Rooted in attachment theory and further supported by the premise that the quality of the child–caregiver dyad is paramount to psychological wellbeing, these therapies focus on strengthening this relationship. Literature indicates that insecure or disorganized early attachments adversely affect an individual's lifelong trajectory. These therapies have demonstrated efficacy leading to positive behavioral changes and improved parent–child interactions. The major challenges of clinical practice focused on young children and their families include proper diagnosis and determining the best therapeutic strategy, especially for families who have not benefited from prior interventions. At this time, it is still unclear which therapy is best indicated for which type of patients and it mostly has been driven by convenience and provider preference or training. Further research is required to tailor treatments more successfully to the child's needs.

Keywords: young child, Psychotherapy, emotional regulation, behavioral issues, mental health

INTRODUCTION

It is estimated that as many as one in four preschool-aged children struggle with psychosocial stress and social-emotional issues, both of which may be precursors to later disease (1). The period of 0–3 years is the most formative in human brain development (due to the critical period of synaptogenesis, pruning, and myelination) and carries the potential for lifelong consequences, both positive and negative (2, 3). However, despite the acknowledgement of increasing pediatric mental health concerns and interventions aimed at reducing the raising suicide rates, the quality of training, implementation, and dissemination of interventions focused on the 0- to 5-year-old patient population remains inadequate.

While many psychiatric disorders emerge in adolescence (2), their underpinnings can be seen much earlier. For example, oppositional defiant disorder (ODD) is a highly prevalent condition in young children (6–15%) (3). Yet, the ones who develop serious externalizing behaviors early in life have a two- to three-fold higher risk of developing conduct disorder (CD), which is more difficult to manage and has a worse prognosis (4–6). According to a longitudinal follow-up study by Luby et al. (2009), internalizing disorders such as major depressive disorder (MDD) in preschool children also show stability over time. Here, preschoolers diagnosed with depression at baseline had a higher risk of developing depression at 12 and/or 24 months later in comparison to the control group (7). In another study by Luby et al. (2014), preschool-onset depression was shown to be a predictor of MDD in later childhood. In addition to non-supportive parenting, the Adverse Childhood Experiences (ACE) score could also affect depression severity and oppositional behaviors (8–10).

Importantly, early interventions aimed at emotional and behavioral disturbances are more effective when done at preschool age rather than school age (11). Since early childhood onset of externalizing disorders (such as ODD or CD) and internalizing disorders (such as MDD or anxiety disorder) can have a lasting, detrimental impact on later life, it is imperative that early identification by trained providers occurs with implementation of safe, effective psychotherapeutic treatment modalities (11).

PSYCHOTHERAPY WITH YOUNG CHILDREN—GENERAL OVERVIEW

Infant and Early Childhood Mental Health has been recognized by the field of psychiatry for over 75 years. There are a number of clinical interventions driven by various theories; however, it is safe to say that a great majority of them are founded on dyadic psychotherapy. Young children do not function without their caregivers, and as such, dyadic therapies aim to effectively address the parent, the child, and their relationship. The latter is particularly important as young children function and grow only within the context of their relationship with caregivers.

Most dyadic therapies try to address at least three different "parties" involved. It is a difficult task and attrition rate is usually high. Zeanah and Boris (12) describe several challenges of dyadic treatment. First, young children develop and change rapidly between 0 and 5 years old. This rapid development necessitates an urgency to address any issues so that ongoing development continues and acquisition of milestones is reached appropriately. Children have a limited repertoire of self-expression for some time and often irritability or anger can be a sign of a number of diagnostic categories which further complicates assessment. Clinicians have to rely predominantly on parental or other caregiver descriptions of the child's behaviors, which may be inaccurate. Lastly, while the debate as to whether nature or nurture contributes to human behavior has largely subsided with acknowledgment of the contribution of both, including the interactions with the caregiver, it remains challenging in a clinical setting to precisely identify which of the factors plays the most pivotal role for a particular patient.

There are also a number of external factors that limit access to care for young children and their families for early symptoms. Unfortunately, even with optimal identification of children who could benefit from psychiatric or psychotherapeutic treatment, there is a critical shortage of qualified providers, particularly in infant mental health. Unfortunately, despite numerous studies, there remains a misconception among some providers that young children will grow out of their difficulties or simply forget traumatic experiences (13). Clinicians working with these children need to be attuned to this and be familiar with both child and adult psychopathology, which requires specialized training.

This commentary outlines indications of the most commonly used evidence-based dyadic psychotherapies for young children: Child-Parent Psychotherapy (CPP), Trauma-Focused Cognitive Behavioral Therapy (TF-CBT), Parent-Child Interaction Therapy (PCIT), and Child Parent Relationship Therapy (CPRT). CPP, TF-CBT and CPRT are used primarily for young children with trauma, and (PCIT) is used mostly for children with behavioral issues.

All four therapies are well-known. The basic theory describing their background and detailed evidence of efficacy is beyond the scope of this article. Here, we will summarize the primary characteristics of each treatment's methods, paying special attention to the indications, goals, and specific interventions.

CHILD-PARENT PSYCHOTHERAPY (CPP)

CPP was initially studied as a treatment for traumatized children and their parents and continues to be the main indication. However, it has since been found to be useful for early childhood disorders such as anxiety, bonding difficulties, behavioral issues, and others. The main premise of CPP, recommended for children ages 0–6, is to attempt to help the child's mental health issues while supporting and strengthening primary attachment relationships (14). The attachment system between the child and caregiver is the leading organizing system that helps the child with his or her responses to dangerous situations. A trusting relationship within this paradigm is the most important protective factor for a young child (14, 15).

A manual of CPP, "Don't Hit My Mommy" (16), is available, but master level clinicians are required to complete formal training and supervision in order to be considered qualified providers. CPP takes approximately 1 year to complete and consists of the therapist meeting with the child and parent on a weekly basis. The initial assessments are typically scheduled with the primary caregiver to create the treatment plan; they are then followed by joint child–parent play sessions. The therapist selects developmentally appropriate toys before each session for the child to use. If there is a history of trauma, toys usually are used to elicit trauma material. During the course of the treatment, the therapist may schedule individual sessions with the primary caregiver as clinically indicated to review progress.

CPP is a psychodynamic oriented treatment, and interpretation during play is one of the main techniques. In order to address both the parent and the child, the therapist delivers their interpretation in a two-prong way. The main goal of the interpretation is to show compassion for the parent (many of whom have experienced past abuse or traumatic events) and help them realize, in the presence with their child, that their previous experiences affect their relationship. The idea behind such an approach is that the better parents remember their past, the less likely it is for them to repeat it with their children. It is also easier for parents to be more protective and have compassion modeled by the therapist for their child. The danger of burying traumatic events and not being able to talk about them is despite best intentions there is the potential of parental reenactment of maladaptive events with their own children. Parents may also use defense mechanisms such as denial or avoidance to fend off uncomfortable feelings, impacting their ability to enjoy the relationship with their child (17).

In CPP therapy, the therapist is required to be fairly flexible and creative when working with patients. The length of sessions often depends on the level of engagement of the child and parent. Depending on age, this may vary from 30 to 45 min. Infants always accompany their parents during sessions, but with toddlers and preschoolers, the session may be divided. This may involve spending a portion of the session with the child and in the remainder the therapist engages in "grown up talk." Alternatively, the therapist may meet separately with the parent and then the child (especially in situations when parental mental health is in peril and needs to be addressed immediately).

The main goals of CPP may be divided into two categories: global goals and trauma-related goals. Global goals of CPP revolve around supporting normal development and helping the child and parent develop a strong and loving relationship. Part of this includes teaching the parent how to help the child manage their emotions and control their behaviors. Trauma related goals are directed to help both the child and parent resolve trauma related symptomatology, re-build trust, and normalize their responses. Through play and the therapist's interpretations, the child and parent are encouraged to create a trauma narrative that is meaningful to them both and developmentally appropriate to the child (18).

CPP was empirically validated in a randomized controlled study conducted by Lieberman et al. on a sample of 75 preschoolers who experienced domestic violence (19). Since then, CPP has been well studied in at least nine randomized controlled trials with sample sizes ranging from 50 to 198 dyads across a number of different populations, including but not limited to Latino toddlers and their mothers with a history of trauma (20), depressed mothers and their toddlers (21), and children from the welfare system with a history of abuse (19). The effect size in the seminal paper by Lieberman et al. was around 0.4 both for the child and the parent (22).

TRAUMA FOCUSED COGNITIVE BEHAVIORAL THERAPY (TF-CBT)

One of the most common evidence-based treatments for trauma in children is TF-CBT (23, 24), a treatment model delivered to young children that is a components-based treatment, requiring full involvement of the child's non-offending caregivers. Although initially tested on children with a history of sexual abuse, it has since been successfully applied to children, ages 3–18, with diverse and sometimes complex trauma: physical, sexual, and emotional or neglect. TF-CBT also addresses parental secondary trauma and helps parents with addressing difficult behaviors in their children that resulted of trauma. Typical treatment involves 8–20 sessions divided between individual sessions for the child and the caregiver, followed by conjoint sessions. Due to children's short attention spans, especially for exploring difficult trauma, sessions should not exceed 30 min in length. The remainder of the session can be devoted to the caregiver, or brief activities such as learning relaxation skills, coloring, or other positive activities that allow the child to take a short break.

TF-CBT is structured so that the child and caregiver both gradually engage in exposure exercises. This begins at the assessment session. First, the therapist must ensure that the child has memory of the trauma and sufficient verbal skills to acknowledge it took place. Then slowly, the child and caregiver participate in the process of learning coping skills, such as relaxation skills and deep breathing, to help manage reminders of the trauma. They are also encouraged to narrate the trauma story and make meaning of their experience.

Engaging primary caregivers from the very beginning is crucial for a number of reasons, starting with compliance. Caregivers who understand the indications and goals of therapy are more likely to complete treatment (25, 26). Additionally, the primary focus is on positive parenting skills, largely praising, and rewarding good behaviors. Parents are taught that negative consequences may be used but that relying on them without praise is not sufficient to change behaviors. Negative consequences are intended to be benign and brief (for example a short time-out). Psychoeducation is provided to both the child and their caregivers. child and their caregivers. Caregivers are counseled on the differentiation between problematic behaviors that are in the context of trauma and normal behaviors that are to be expected as a normal course of development. This should help the caregivers avoid misinterpreting new behaviors as pathological in the aftermath of trauma and to respond effectively (23, 27).

Psychoeducation to children should be delivered in a developmentally appropriate way and the therapist is encouraged to assess the child's understanding of the material as the treatment progresses. The relaxation and affect expression training are very similar to other CBT treatment protocols in that even very young children are capable of discussing simple emotions such as sad, mad, and happy. Likewise, young children can be taught cognitive coping skills, for example, with the help of age-appropriate books (28).

Additionally, one of the most important elements of treatment is trauma narrative, which can be accomplished by a creation of a book with drawings and stories of trauma. If the child is very young and prefers to play, then dolls, puppets, and other play materials may be used. Narration of trauma provides an opportunity to plan for *in vivo* mastery. Often planning for gradual exposures with caregivers is necessary, as avoidance behaviors frequently occur outside of therapy sessions. It is very helpful to share the trauma narrative in conjoint sessions towards the end of the treatment. Conjoint sessions are also beneficial in practicing communication between the caregiver and the child, and to identify behavioral interventions that are best for the dyad.

TF-CBT is manualized and certification typically consists of formal in-person training as well as consultation calls (29, 23). The most commonly cited study supporting the use of TF-CBT in young children by Cohen et al. (30) found TF-CBT to be superior to nondirective supportive therapy in addressing sexual trauma. Specifically, there was a significant decrease in PTSD symptomatology and sexualized behaviors in TF-CBT subjects even at 1 year follow up in comparison to the control group. Since then, further studies have found TF-CBT to be beneficial in addressing symptoms resulting from emotional and physical abuse, natural disasters, and complicated grief (24, 25, 31). There are at least 10 randomized control studies with sample sizes ranging from 36 to 229 dyads and 6 review studies of TF-CBT. Studies showed medium to large effects that were defined as standardized mean differences of Cohen's d ≥.40 (medium effects), and large effects were defined as d ≥.75 (32).

PARENT CHILD INTERACTION THERAPY (PCIT)

PCIT is an evidence-based behavioral treatment for 2–7 year olds with behavioral disturbances arising from internalizing and externalizing disorders (33). The aim of treatment is to improve symptoms by improving the child–caregiver relationship. The distinguishing feature of PCIT is the use of a "bug in the ear system" that allows the therapist to coach the caregiver in real time. This discrete method allows for in the moment training and feedback as the caregiver interacts with their child while the therapist watches and teaches behind a one-way mirror.

PCIT is implemented in two stages: Child Directed Interaction (CDI) and Parent Directed Interaction (PDI). CDI involves teaching PRIDE (Praise, Reflection, Imitation, Description, and Enthusiasm) "do" skills that the caregiver is taught to utilize during interactions and play with the child (**Table 1**). At the same time, the caregiver is taught to avoid "don't" skills during CDI (**Table 2**). Once mastery of the PRIDE skills is attained, the therapy transitions onto PDI. Here, the caregiver learns appropriate disciplinary techniques, such as effective time-outs, and the phrasing of clear directions or commands (direct commands) (34, 35). Sessions are usually 45 min long, although in the second part of treatment- PDI, they may be extended to 60–90 min depending on the child's response. For example, if the child does not comply with a direct command given to them by their parent, they have to sit in a time out chair for 3 min followed by 5 seconds of silence

TABLE 1 | (19, 34, 35) CDI "do" skills.

CDI "do" skills	Explanation	Example
Praise	Caregiver is encouraged to praise all good behaviors in order to positively reinforce them and increase their frequency. Of the two types (Labeled and Unlabeled Praise), labeled praise is preferred as it clearly specifies the behavior for which the child receives praise.	Labelled Praise: "I love how you are sitting quietly", "Thank you for using your walking feet" Unlabeled Praise: "Great Job!", "Nice work!"
Reflection	Caregiver repeats or summarizes what child says, showing them they are attentive to them. Additionally, this helps to increase the child's vocabulary.	Child: "I like apples" Caregiver: "You like apples" Child: "I don't know how to fix this truck" Caregiver: You are wondering how to fix the truck"
Imitation	Caregiver allows the child to lead play and imitates positive behaviors.	Child: Begins to draw a sun Caregiver: Also starts drawing a sun
Behavioral Description	Caregiver acts as a "sports commentator" describing what the child is doing, creating an opportunity to teach without asking questions.	Child: Playing with a cube Caregiver: "You are picking up the yellow cube and putting it on top of the box"
Enjoyment	Caregiver expresses enthusiasm during the play and learns to enjoy the time with the child encouraging engagement.	Therapist: "(Child) loves spending time with you", "When you smile it really causes (Child) to brighten up!"

TABLE 2 | (19, 34, 35) CDI "don't skills".

CDI "don't skills"	Explanation	Examples
Questions	These can push the adult's agenda and inhibit child-lead play.	"What color is this?" "Where do you want to put this block?"
Commands	Indirect Command: often phrased as a question and offers a choice. Direct Command: clear and explicit in what parent expects of child.	Indirect: "Can you put your coat on?" Direct: "Put your coat on please"
Criticism	Caregivers are taught to avoid criticism of any kind.	"No, silly" "That is not a clever way to fix it!"

(the latter is important for the child to learn that only calm behavior will get them out of the chair). Likewise, if the child gets off the chair prematurely, they have to go to the time out room, or if the room is unavailable, parents practice a "swoop and go" strategy, where they collect all the toys that are in the room and tell the child that they will be standing right outside the door until the child is ready to sit in the chair. The recommendation is that parents should wait at least a minute that is followed by 5 s of silence before approaching the child to put them in the time out chair. PDI also includes a public outing session where parents have the opportunity to practice their newly acquired skills in a park or a store. There is also a sibling session where parents practice their skills with all their children. This is particularly helpful for children who have difficult relationships with their siblings.

PCIT has a wide body of evidence supporting its use, including randomized controlled trials indicating long term improvement in parenting strategies and diminished behavioral issues, as compared with treatment-as-usual groups (36). PCIT has traditionally been used for developmentally normal children between the ages of 2–7 years. However, there is evidence that PCIT can be modified to benefit children with behavioral problems as a result of autism, severe developmental delay, and intellectual disability (37–39). In addition to externalizing conditions such as ODD, adaptations to PCIT have increasingly targeted and been found to be efficacious for internalizing conditions such as depression and anxiety.

Luby et al. (2018) developed PCIT with an Emotion Development (ED) component as an addition to the therapy. This is now referred to as PCIT-ED and lengthens the series from an average of 12 to 18 sessions. After completion of standard PCIT, the caregiver is taught specifically how to coach the child to identify and understand emotions in themselves and others with a stronger emphasis on the caregiver acting as an external regulator of the child's emotions (2, 40). PCIT based treatments such as the Coaching Approach behavior and Leading by Modeling (CALM) Program have been effectively used to treat a spectrum of anxiety disorders by focusing on parent led exposures and behavioral modeling (41).

In summary, PCIT has applicability outside its traditional indications of normally developed children with externalizing disorders. Standard PCIT technique and adaptations described above offer safe and effective alternatives to psychotropic medications for a range of externalizing and internalizing disorders such as oppositional defiant behaviors, ADHD, anxiety, depression, and trauma in young children (2).

Based on comparative studies, PCIT demonstrated large effect sizes for helping with negative parent and child behaviors as well as increasing positive parenting skills and improving child behaviors (42). There are at least 12 meta-analyses and reviews of PCIT research (43, 44). Based on one analysis, PCIT has a large effect size of d = 1.65 (decrease in externalizing symptoms in children) (45). PCIT has also been studied in various settings such as in school therapy (TCIT- Teacher Child Interactive Therapy) (46), in-home settings (47), mothers who are incarcerated, as well as Primary Care Practice (group format) (48, 49).

CHILD–PARENT RELATIONSHIP THERAPY (CPRT)

CPRT is an evidence-based humanistic, child-centered, and play-based treatment program. It was initially developed for children ages 3–8 years old with more recent adaptations available for 1- to 3-year-old children as well as pre-teens. Other components of the treatment are 30 min, weekly, non-directive play sessions for the parent and the child (50, 51). Parents use skills learned in group therapy in their play interactions with children. Parents practice in a supervised environment how to better address their child's emotional and behavioral needs and children learn that they can always depend on their parents. CPRT utilizes concepts of Child Centered Play Therapy (CCPT). Therapy is designed for a wide range of issues that include attachment disorders or difficulties bonding, for adoptive families and for those with a history of abuse in families with resulting emotional and behavioral problems in children. For the latter group, the aims of the treatment include decreasing parental stress and their secondary trauma symptoms, and helping with their child's behavioral issues (52–55). Behavioral issues are addressed by parents serving as role models for their children and their ability to interact with them in a non-judgmental way with empathy and respect.

Group sessions in CPRT are structured and address various components that include education on CCPT skills (delivered mostly in sessions 1–3), as well as supervision and discussion of the video recordings of the in-home play sessions in a small group format (delivered mostly in weeks 4–10). Parents have the opportunity to process their concerns and ask appropriate questions as well as receive support (56).

Bratton et al. formalized the CPRT created treatment manual available for the therapists (56). The certification process contains a number of steps for mental health providers to undertake, including educational training, which allows therapists to conduct group therapy but not home visitations (parents may get certified as well). In addition, therapists must receive training in CCPT, complete CPRT certification exam, and have sufficient supervision of their clinical experience.

CPRT is considered an evidence-based treatment model based on at least 20 outcome studies that included 15 Randomized Control Trials (57). Based on a meta-analysis (Bratton et al., 2005) that assessed 93 studies, the effect size for CPRT is in the moderate range (d = 0.80). CPRT also has been implemented in various settings (e.g., school based) and across diverse populations (57, 58).

CONCLUSIONS

Significant psychiatric conditions such as depression, anxiety, post-traumatic stress disorder, and ODD occur in very young children and early identification and treatment is of paramount importance. The long term effects of psychotropic medication remain uncertain, though its use has become increasingly common (2). The treatment modalities of CPP, TF-CBT, PCIT, and CRPT

TABLE 3 | Summary of three main evidence-based psychotherapeutic interventions in young children.

Type of therapy	Age (years)	Indications	Goals of therapy	Length of treatment/frequency and duration of sessions
CPP	0–6	PTSD and other trauma related disorders, anxiety, behavioral issues, attachment difficulties	Global Goals: Improve child–caregiver attachment Trauma Goals: Reduce trauma related symptoms	1 year/1–2 times a week/30–60 min
TF-CBT	3–18	PTSD and other trauma and stressor related disorders Grief	Gradual exposure to trauma narrative and learning of coping skills as a way to reduce symptoms	8–20 sessions/weekly/30 min
PCIT	2.5–7	Disruptive behavior in context of ODD, CD, autism, attention deficit hyperactivity disorder (ADHD), anxiety, selective mutism, depression	Increase positive interactions between caregiver and child, improve communication and teach appropriate disciplinary techniques to strengthen the caregiver–child relationship	8–12 sessions/weekly/45–90 min
CPRT	3–8	Attachment difficulties, children of adoption, families with history of abuse	CPRT utilizes concepts of Child Centered Play Therapy (CCPT). The main aim is to strengthen or create secure attachment between parent and a child. Behavioral issues are addressed by parents serving as role models for their children and their ability to interact with them in non-judgmental way with empathy and respect.	10 sessions of weekly group therapy (for parents only)/120 min plus 30 min weekly in home, video recorded play therapy (parent and child)

are evidence-based, valuable options for young children with a history of trauma, internalizing and externalizing disorders, and their caregivers. See **Table 3** for a summary of individual goals, indications, and length of treatment for each therapy. By focusing on the powerful influence of a positive caregiver–child relationship during a sensitive period of neurodevelopment these therapies may positively impact a child's trajectory.

Although many providers are familiar with one of the discussed treatment modalities, it is very rare to find a clinician trained in multiple therapies. One of the major challenges in clinical practice with young children and their families is proper diagnosis but also being able to determine the best therapeutic strategy, especially for families who have had a weak or null response with previous treatment.

In TF-CBT, the non-offending caregiver is required to participate in the sessions that are different from CPP or CPRT where an abusive parent, as long as they are motivated for change, would be a viable candidate for treatment. This is an important aspect of various treatments that needs to be taken into consideration. Similar to PCIT and CPRT, parents who, for example, have lost custody due to abuse and who are now interested in reconciliation may use the treatment to reconnect with their children. Another important factor is the age of the patient. All four therapies are designed for very young children; however, only CPP takes on infants 0–12 months. TF-CBT also does not accept patients with dangerous acting-out or suicidal behaviors. While suicidal behaviors would be extremely rare in children 3–6 years old, dangerous acting-out is not uncommon, especially in patients with a history of significant abuse. It is often a difficult clinical decision whether to first address the behaviors with treatment such as PCIT or focus on the traumatic response with a referral to TF-CBT, CPP, or CPRT. Rarely is it a good idea to conduct both therapies at the same time due to "dilution" of the effectiveness of each therapy and high dropout rate. Although dual therapy is typically avoided, there remains a lack of guidance and no studies on the type of therapy that is best suited for a particular patient, and until recently, this was mostly driven by therapist's availability and training as well as the patients' preference.

In the absence of evidence and based on clinical practice alone, children who do present with such difficult behaviors are referred to PCIT for stabilization before undergoing TF-CBT, CPP, or CPRT to learn how to better cope with their trauma history. That being said, all four therapies address difficult behaviors in some capacity. CPRT is the only therapy that offers group sessions for parents, and if that is their preference, such therapy should be considered as a first line treatment. Further research is required to tailor the type of treatment quickly, more successfully, and according to the child's and caregiver's needs.

AUTHOR CONTRIBUTIONS

RS and MR drafted the manuscript. EB, JS, and PC made revisions to the manuscript. All authors read and approved the final manuscript.

REFERENCES

1. Brown CM, Copeland KA, Sucharew H, Kahn RS. Social-emotional problems in preschool-aged children: opportunities for prevention and early intervention. *Arch Pediatr Adolesc Med* (2012) 166(10):926–32. doi: 10.1001/archpediatrics.2012.793
2. Luby JL, Barch DM, Whalen D, Tillman R, Freedland KE. A randomized controlled trial of parent-child psychotherapy targeting emotion development for early childhood depression. *Am J Psychiatry* (2018) 175(11):1102–10. doi: 10.1176/appi.ajp.2018.18030321
3. Rice D, Barone S, Jr. Critical periods of vulnerability for the developing nervous system: evidence from humans and animal models. *Environ Health Perspect* (2000) 108 Suppl 3:511–33. doi: 10.1289/ehp.00108s3511
4. Loeber R, Farrington DP. Young children who commit crime: epidemiology, developmental origins, risk factors, early interventions, and policy implications. *Dev Psychopathol* (2000) 12(4):737–62. doi: 10.1017/S0954579400004107

5. Loeber R, Keenan K, Lahey BB, Green SM, Thomas C. Evidence for developmentally based diagnoses of oppositional defiant disorder and conduct disorder. *J Abnorm Child Psychol* (1993) 21(4):377–410. doi: 10.1007/BF01261600
6. Podolski CL, Nigg JT. Parent stress and coping in relation to child ADHD severity and associated child disruptive behavior problems. *J Clin Child Psychol* (2001) 30(4):503–13. doi: 10.1207/S15374424JCCP3004_07
7. Luby JL, Si X, Belden AC, Tandon M, Spitznagel E. Preschool depression: homotypic continuity and course over 24 months. *Arch Gen Psychiatry* (2009) 66(8):897–905. doi: 10.1001/archgenpsychiatry.2009.97
8. Luby JL, Gaffrey MS, Tillman R, April LM, Belden AC. Trajectories of preschool disorders to full DSM depression at school age and early adolescence: continuity of preschool depression. *Am J Psychiatry* (2014) 171(7):768–76. doi: 10.1176/appi.ajp.2014.13091198
9. Hunt TKA, Slack KS, Berger LM. Adverse childhood experiences and behavioral problems in middle childhood. *Child Abus Negl* (2017) 67:391–402. doi: 10.1016/j.chiabu.2016.11.005
10. Heim C, Nemeroff CB. The role of childhood trauma in the neurobiology of mood and anxiety disorders: preclinical and clinical studies. *Biol Psychiatry* (2001) 49(12):1023–39. doi: 10.1016/S0006-3223(01)01157-X
11. Eyberg SM, Boggs SR, Algina J. Parent-child interaction therapy: a psychosocial model for the treatment of young children with conduct problem behavior and their families. *Psychopharmacol Bull* (1995) 31(1):83–91.
12. Zeanah CH, Boris NW. Disturbances and disorders of attachment in early childhood. In: *Handbook of infant mental health*, 2nd edition Guilford Press (2000).
13. Osofsky JD, Lieberman AF. A call for integrating a mental health perspective into systems of care for abused and neglected infants and young children. *Am Psychol* (2011) 66(2):120–8. doi: 10.1037/a0021630
14. Lieberman AF SR, Pawl JH. Infant-parent psychotherapy: core concepts and current approaches. In: *Handbook of infantmental health*, 2nd ed Guildford Press (2000).
15. Bowlby J. *Attachment and loss*. New York: Basic Books (1969).
16. Lieberman AF VHP. *Don't hit my mommy: a manual for child-parent psychotherapy with young witnesses of family violence*. Washington, DC: zero to three press (2005).
17. Lieberman AE, Van Horn P. Psychotherapy with Infants and Young Children: Repairing the Effects of Stress and Trauma on Early Attachment. New York, The Guilford Press: (2008)
18. Willheim E. Dyadic psychotherapy with infants and young children: child-parent psychotherapy. *Child Adolesc Psychiatr Clin North Am* (2013) 22(2):215–39. doi: 10.1016/j.chc.2013.01.003
19. Lieberman AF, Van Horn P, Ippen CG. Toward evidence-based treatment: child-parent psychotherapy with preschoolers exposed to marital violence. *J Am Acad Child Adolesc Psychiatry* (2005) 44(12):1241–8. doi: 10.1097/01.chi.0000181047.59702.58
20. Lieberman AF, Weston DR, Pawl JH. Preventive intervention and outcome with anxiously attached dyads. *Child Dev* (1991) 62(1):199–209. doi: 10.1111/j.1467-8624.1991.tb01525.x
21. Cicchetti D, Rogosch FA, Toth SL. The efficacy of toddler-parent psychotherapy for fostering cognitive development in offspring of depressed mothers. *J Abnorm Child Psychol* (2000) 28(2):135–48.
22. Lieberman AF, Ghosh Ippen C, Van Horn P. Child-parent psychotherapy: 6-month follow-up of a randomized controlled trial. *J Am Acad Child Adolesc Psychiatry* (2006) 45(8):913–8. doi: 10.1097/01.chi.0000222784.03735.92
23. Deblinger E, Mannarino AP, Cohen J, Runyon MK, Heflin AH. *Child sexual abuse: a primer for treating children, adolescnets and their non-offending parents*. 2nd ed. New York, NY: Oxford University Press (2015). doi: 10.1093/med:psych/9780199358748.001.0001
24. Cohen JA, Deblinger E, Mannarino AP, Steer R. A multi-site, randomized controlled trial for children with abuse-related PTSD symptoms. *J Am Acad Child Adolesc Psychiatry* (2004) 43(4):393–402. doi: 10.1097/00004583-200404000-00005
25. Dorsey S, Conover KL, Revillion Cox J. Improving foster parent engagement: using qualitative methods to guide tailoring of evidence-based engagement strategies. *J Clin Child Adolesc Psychol* (2014) 43(6):877–89. doi: 10.1080/15374416.2013.876643
26. McKay MM, Bannon WM, Jr. Engaging families in child mental health services. *Child Adolesc Psychiatr Clin North Am* (2004) 13(4):905–21. doi: 10.1016/j.chc.2004.04.001
27. Allen B, Hoskowitz NA. Structured trauma-focused CBT and unstructured play/experiential techniques in the treatment of sexually abused children: a field study with practicing clinicians. *Child Maltreat* (2017) 22(2):112–20. doi: 10.1177/1077559516681866
28. W. P. *The little engine that could*. New York: Grosset and Dunlap (2012).
29. Cohen JA, Mannarino AP, Deblinger E. *Treating trauma and traumatic grief in children and adolescents*. 2nd ed. New York, NY: Guilford (2017).
30. Cohen JA, Mannarino AP. Factors that mediate treatment outcome of sexually abused preschool children: six- and 12-month follow-up. *J Am Acad Child Adolesc Psychiatry* (1998) 37(1):44–51. doi: 10.1097/00004583-199801000-00016
31. O'Callaghan P, McMullen J, Shannon C, Rafferty H, Black A. A randomized controlled trial of trauma-focused cognitive behavioral therapy for sexually exploited, war-affected Congolese girls. *J Am Acad Child Adolesc Psychiatry* (2013) 52(4):359–69. doi: 10.1016/j.jaac.2013.01.013
32. de Arellano MA, Lyman DR, Jobe-Shields L, George P, Dougherty RH, Daniels AS, et al. Trauma-focused cognitive-behavioral therapy for children and adolescents: assessing the evidence. *Psychiatr Serv (Washington, DC)* (2014) 65(5):591–602. doi: 10.1176/appi.ps.201300255
33. Lieneman CC, Brabson LA, Highlander A, Wallace NM, McNeil CB. Parent–child interaction therapy: current perspectives. *Psychol Res Behav Manage* (2017) 10:239–56. doi: 10.2147/PRBM.S91200
34. Eyberg SM, Nelson MM, Duke M, Boggs SR. Manual for the dyadic parent-child interaction coding system. 3rd ed. Thousand Oaks, CA: Sage Publications (2004)
35. Foote RC, Schuhmann EM, Jones ML, Eyberg SM. Parent-child interaction therapy: a guide for clinicians. *Clin Child Psychol Psychiatry* (1998) 3(3):361–73. doi: 10.1177/1359104598033003
36. Bjorseth A, Wichstrom L. Effectiveness of parent-child interaction therapy (PCIT) in the treatment of young children's behavior problems. A Randomized Controlled Study. *PloS One* (2016) 11(9):e0159845. doi: 10.1371/journal.pone.0159845
37. Solomon M, Ono M, Timmer S, Goodlin-Jones B. The effectiveness of parent-child interaction therapy for families of children on the autism spectrum. *J Autism Dev Disord* (2008) 38(9):1767–76. doi: 10.1007/s10803-008-0567-5
38. Bagner DM, Eyberg SM. Parent-child interaction therapy for disruptive behavior in children with mental retardation: a randomized controlled trial. *J Clin Child Adolesc Psychol* (2007) 36(3):418–29. doi: 10.1080/15374410701448448
39. Shafi RMA, Vande Voort JL, Croarkin PE, Romanowicz M. Parent-child interaction therapy in a case of global developmental delay and leukoencephalopathy. *Front Psychiatry* (2018) 9(427). doi: 10.3389/fpsyt.2018.00427
40. Luby J, Lenze S, Tillman R. A novel early intervention for preschool depression: findings from a pilot randomized controlled trial. *J Child Psychol Psychiatry* (2012) 53(3):313–22. doi: 10.1111/j.1469-7610.2011.02483.x
41. Carpenter AL, Puliafico AC, Kurtz SM, Pincus DB, Comer JS. Extending parent-child interaction therapy for early childhood internalizing problems: new advances for an overlooked population. *Clin Child Fam Psychol Rev.* (2014) 17(4):340–56. doi: 10.1007/s10567-014-0172-4
42. Eyberg SM, Nelson MM, Boggs SR. Evidence-based psychosocial treatments for children and adolescents with disruptive behavior. *J Clin Child Adolesc Psychol* (2008) 37(1):215–37. doi: 10.1080/15374410701820117
43. Funderburk BW ES. *History of psychotherapy: continuity and change*. 2nd ed. American Psychological Association, Washington DC, USA (2011)
44. Drewes, A. A., Bratton, S. C., & Schaefer, C. E. (Eds.). (2011). Integrative play therapy. New York, NY: Wiley. doi: 10.1002/9781118094792
45. Ward MA, Theule J, Cheung K. Parent–child interaction therapy for child disruptive behaviour disorders: a meta-analysis. *Child Youth Care Forum* (2016) 45(5):675–90. doi: 10.1007/s10566-016-9350-5
46. Lyon AR, Gershenson RA, Farahmand FK, Thaxter PJ, Behling S, Budd KS. Effectiveness of Teacher-Child Interaction Training (TCIT) in a preschool setting. *Behav Modif* (2009) 33(6):855–84. doi: 10.1177/0145445509344215

47. Self-Brown S, Valente JR, Wild RC, Whitaker DJ, Galanter R, Dorsey S, et al. Utilizing benchmarking to study the effectiveness of parent–child interaction therapy implemented in a community setting. *J Child Family Stud* (2012) 21(6):1041–9. doi: 10.1007/s10826-012-9566-4
48. Scudder AT, McNeil CB, Chengappa K, Costello AH. Evaluation of an existing parenting class within a women's state correctional facility and a parenting class modeled from Parent–Child Interaction Therapy. *Child Youth Serv Rev* (2014) 46:238–47. doi: 10.1016/j.childyouth.2014.08.015
49. Berkovits MD, O'Brien KA, Carter CG, Eyberg SM. Early identification and intervention for behavior problems in primary care: a comparison of two abbreviated versions of parent-child interaction therapy. *Behav Ther* (2010) 41(3):375–87. doi: 10.1016/j.beth.2009.11.002
50. Landreth, GL (1991). *Play therapy: the art of the relationship*. Accelerated Development, Muncie, Ind.
51. Landreth GL, Bratton SC. Child parent relationship therapy (CPRT): a 10-session filial model. New York: Brunner-Routledge (2005) 1–258. doi: 10.4324/9780203956342
52. Cornett N, Bratton SC. A golden intervention: 50 years of research on filial therapy. *Int J Play Ther* 24(3):119–133.
53. Costas M, Landreth G. Filial therapy with nonoffending parents of children who have been sexually abused. *Int J Play Ther* (1999) 8(1):43–66. doi: 10.1037/h0089427
54. Landreth GL. Therapeutic limit setting in the play therapy relationship. *Prof Psychol Res Pract* (2002) 33(6):529–35. doi: 10.1037//0735-7028.33.6.529
55. Rennie R, Landreth G. Effects of filial therapy on parent and child behaviors. *Int J Play Ther* (2000) 9(2):19–37. doi: 10.1037/h0089434
56. Bratton SC, Landreth GL, Kellam T, Blackard SR. *Child parent relationship therapy (CPRT) treatment manual: a 10-session filial therapy model for training parents*. New York, NY, US: Routledge/Taylor & Francis Group (2006) p. 258–x. doi: 10.4324/9780203956793
57. Bratton S, Ray D, Rhine T, Jones L. The efficacy of play therapy with children: a meta-analytic review of treatment outcomes. *Prof Psychol Res: and Pract* (2005) 36:376–390. doi: 10.1037/0735-7028.36.4.376
58. Baggerly JN, Ray DC, Bratton SC. Eds. Child-centered play therapy research: the evidence base for effective practice. Hoboken, NJ, US:John Wiley & Sons Inc. (2010) doi: 10.1002/9781118269626

22

Effects of Xiaoyaosan on the Hippocampal Gene Expression Profile in Rats Subjected to Chronic Immobilization Stress

Xiao-Hong Li[1,2†], *Xue-Ming Zhou*[1,3†], *Xiao-Juan Li*[1,4], *Yue-Yun Liu*[1], *Qun Liu*[1], *Xiao-Ling Guo*[1], *Li-Qiang Yang*[2] *and Jia-Xu Chen*[1,4*]

[1] *School of Traditional Chinese Medicine, Beijing University of Chinese Medicine, Beijing, China,* [2] *School of Basic Medical Sciences, Guangxi University of Chinese Medicine, Nanning, China,* [3] *School of Basic Medical Sciences, Heilongjiang University of Chinese Medicine, Harbin, China,* [4] *Formula-pattern Research Center, School of Traditional Chinese Medicine, Jinan University, Guangzhou, China*

Correspondence:
Jia-Xu Chen
chenjiaxu@hotmail.com

† *These authors have contributed equally to this work*

Objective: This study examined the effect of Xiaoyaosan and its anti-stress mechanism in rats subjected to chronic immobilization stress at the whole genome level.

Methods: Rat whole genome expression chips (Illumina) were used to detect differences in hippocampal gene expression in rats from the control group (CN group), model group (M group) and Xiaoyaosan group (XYS group) that were subjected to chronic immobilization stress. The Gene Ontology terms and signaling pathways that were altered in the hippocampus gene expression profile were analyzed. The network regulating the transcription of the differentially expressed genes was also established. To verify the results from the gene chips, real-time quantitative polymerase chain reaction was used to determine the expression of the GABRA1, FADD, CRHR2, and CDK6 genes in hippocampal tissues. *In situ* hybridization (ISH) and immunohistochemistry were used to determine the expression of the GABRA1 and CRHR2 genes and proteins, respectively.

Results: Compared with the CN group, 566 differentially expressed genes were identified in the M group. Compared with the M group, 544 differentially expressed genes were identified in the XYS group. In the M and XYS groups, multiple significantly upregulated or downregulated genes functioned in various biological processes. The cytokine receptor interaction pathway was significantly inhibited in the hippocampus of the model group. The actin cytoskeleton regulation pathway was significantly increased in the hippocampus of the XYS group. The inhibition of hippocampal cell growth was the core molecular event of network regulating the transcription of the differentially expressed genes in the model group. Promotion of the regeneration of hippocampal neurons was the core molecular event of the transcriptional regulatory network in the XYS group. The levels of the GABRA1, FADD, CRHR2 and CDK6 mRNAs, and proteins were basically consistent with the results obtained from the gene chip.

Conclusion: XYS may have the ability of resistance to stress, enhancement immunity and promotion nerve cell regeneration by regulating the expression of multiple genes in numerous pathways and repaired the stress-induced impairments in hippocampal structure and function by inducing cytoskeletal reorganization. These results may provide the possible target spots in the treatment of stress in rats with XYS.

Keywords: Xiaoyaosan, chronic immobilization stress, the hippocampus, gene expression profile, signal pathways, network regulating gene transcription

INTRODUCTION

Xiaoyaosan (XYS) which was first recorded in the *Prescriptions of the Bureau of Taiping People's Welfare Pharmacy* contains Radix Bupleuri, Rhizoma Atractylodis Macrocephalae, Radix Paeoniae Alba, Poria, Radix Angelicae Sinensis, Herba Menthae, Rhizoma Zingiberis Recens, and Radix Glycyrrhizae. The long-term studies of our research group have confirmed that XYS has reliable effectiveness in preventing and curing chronic stress. XYS increases the appetite and weight of stressed rats (1) and improves the learning and memory of stressed rats (2). XYS exerts an obvious anti-depressant effect (3). At early stage, the research group studied multiple brain regions including the central hippocampus, the hypothalamus (1), the amygdala (4), the cortex and the pituitary (5), etc., in stressed rats; in particular, the hippocampus was studies using multiple research methods. XYS increases the levels of the post-synaptic density protein 95 (PSD−95) and synaptophysin (SYP) proteins in the hippocampus (2). XYS also increases the hippocampal expression of the proopiomelanocortin (POMC) (6), corticotropin releasing factor-2 (CRF-2) (5), neurotrophic protein 3 (NT3) (7), brain derived neurotrophic factor (BDNF) (8), glutamate receptor-2 (GluR2) (9), N-methyl-D-aspartic acid (NMDA) receptors subunits NR2A and NR2B (10) mRNAs and proteins, reverses the decrease in glucocorticoid receptor levels (11) in the hippocampus and decreases the hippocampal expression of the enkephalin, prodynorphin (11), glutamate receptor-1 (GluR1) (9), and tyrosine kinase B (TrkB) mRNAs and proteins (8), among other effects.

XYS exerts a bi-directional effect on the central nervous system, participates in the integrated function of the neuro-endocrine-immune network and exerts an anti-stress effect. To date, the mechanism by which XYS inhibits stress and injury in the hippocampus has not been clearly determined. Therefore, this study used an Illumina ratref-12 full-genome expression spectrum chip containing 22,226 genes to determine the profile of differentially expressed genes in the hippocampal tissues from rats subjected to chronic immobilization stress. We systematically discuss the mechanism by which XYS induces resistance to chronic stress injury in the hippocampus from the perspective of the whole genome.

MATERIALS AND METHODS

Animals and Grouping

Sixty-nine male Sprague-Dawley rats were purchased from the Beijing Vitalriver Laboratory Animal Research Center [animal license No. SCXK (Beijing) 2006-0009]. All rats were SPF-grade and weighed 225 ± 10 g. The rats were adaptively fed for 1 week, and then randomly divided into three groups of 23 rats each: a control group (CN group), model group (M group), and Xiaoyaosan group (XYS group). Five rats from each group were placed in one cage. The rats were raised in a common animal room with a temperature of 22 ± 2°C and a relative humidity of 50–60%. The rats in each group were provided conventional feed water *ad libitum*. In this study, all animal experiments were approved by the Institutional Animal Care and Use Committee of Beijing University of Chinese Medicine and conformed to the animal welfare guideline (BUCM-4-2014070401-3001). All efforts were made to minimize animal suffering and the number of animals needed to produce reliable data.

Drugs, Reagents, and Instruments

The Chinese herbal compound prescription used in the experiment was Xiaoyaosan which was recorded in the "Prescriptions of the Bureau of Taiping People's Welfare Pharmacy." Xiaoyaosan consists of the following eight herbs: Chinese thorowax root (30 g), Angelica sinensis (30 g), Radix Paeoniae Alba (30 g), Rhizoma Atractylodis (30 g), Wolfiporia extensa (30 g), Radix Glycyrrhizae (15 g), Ginger (15 g), and Mint (10 g). The preparation of herbal drugs was purchased from Beijing Tongrentang Group Co., Ltd., and dissolved in solution at a concentration of 1.67 g/ml. SYBR ExscriptTM RT-PCR kits and TRIzol, PrimeScript^{TM} RT Reagent kits were purchased from TaKaRa Company (Japan). The hybridization kit and chip tester

Abbreviations: AHSP, alpha-hemoglobin-stabilizing protein; ARHGEF7, Rho guanine nucleotide exchange factor 7; BDNF, brain-derived neurotrophic factor; C3, complement component 3; CIS, chronic immobilization stress; CRF-2, corticotropin releasing factor-2; Ct, cycle threshold; DA, dopamine; CXCL9, chemokine (C-X-C motif) ligand 9; DβH, dopamine beta hydroxylase; ECM, extracellular matrix; ECs, endothelial cells; ERAF, erythroid-associated factor; FGF, fibroblast growth factor; GC, glucocorticosteroid; GluR1, glutamate receptor-1; GluR2, glutamate receptor-2; GRs, glucocorticoid receptors; HF, hepatic fibrosis; HPA, hypothalamic-pituitary-adrenal; HSCs, haematopoietic stem cells; IFN, interferon; IOD, integrated optical density; IRF7, interferon regulatory factor 7; ISH, *in situ* hybridization; KLF5, Kruppel-like factor 5; LPS, lipopolysaccharide; MAPK, mitogen-activated protein kinase; MAF, macrophage activation factor; MALT1, mucosa-associated lymphoid tissue lymphoma transport protein 1; NE/NA, norepinephrine; Neg, negative; NF-κB, nuclear factor-κB; NMDA, N-methyl-D-aspartic acid; NT3, neurotrophic protein 3; OCM, oncomodulin; Pak4, p21-activated kinase 4; PCs, progenitor cells; POMC, proopiomelanocortin; Pos, positive; PSD-95, post-synaptic density protein 95; SYP, synaptophysin; TCR, T cell receptor; TF, transcription factor; TFBS, transcription factor binding site; TrkB, tyrosine kinase B; TSS, transcription start site; XYS, Xiaoyaosan.

including a hybridization oven, rat expression profile chip, a chip scanner, a chip washing system, and all other reagents were provided by Illumina Company (USA). *In situ* hybridization kits for GABRA1 and CRHR2 were provided by Boster (Wuhan). Mouse anti-GABRA1 and rabbit anti-CRHR2 antibodies were provided by Abcam.

Method Used to Establish the Model

The rat model of stress was produced by exposing the animals to chronic immobilization stress (CIS) (12). In the model and Xiaoyaosan group, rats were bound to a special binding rack for 3 h a day for 21 days. The rats in the control group were not exposed to stress. In the Xiaoyaosan group, rats were administered Xiaoyaosan via the intragastric route daily before they were subjected to the stress procedure, and the control group and model group were administered the same volume of normal saline (1/d). The emotional behavior of rats were evaluated by open field test (OFT) and Y maze experiment (YME), as shown in **Supplementary Figure 1**.

Sampling

On the morning of the second day after the 21-day stress protocol, 2% sodium pentobarbital was injected into the abdominal cavity of rats to induce deep anesthesia (40 mg/kg). The rats used for gene expression and spectroscopy analyses were decapitated rapidly, the brain was removed and the hippocampus was dissected on ice on a super-clean bench. The hippocampus was placed in liquid nitrogen, and then stored in a −80°C freeze until further use. The rats used for *in situ* hybridization and immunohistochemistry were perfusion-fixed via the left ventricular ascending aorta, and then decapitated. The brain tissues were placed in 4% paraformaldehyde at 4°C for 12 h and then embedded in paraffin for subsequent use.

Gene Chip Detection of the Differentially Genes in the Hippocampus

Total RNA was extracted from the hippocampus using TRIzol reagent. The purity and concentration of total RNA were measured with an ultraviolet spectrophotometer. Formaldehyde-denaturing agarose gel electrophoresis was performed to assess the RNA integrity. The mRNA samples extracted from hippocampal tissues from three rats per group were mixed for the chip experiment, and three biological replicates of the samples from each group were analyzed. The differentially expressed genes between the experimental and control groups were considered significant at $P < 0.05$. If the ratio of mean fluorescence intensity of the gene in the experimental group /mean fluorescence intensity of the gene in the control group was $\leqq 0.67$ or $\geqq 1.5$, the difference in expression between two specimens was considered significant (13).

Verification of Some of the Differentially Expressed Genes in the Hippocampus Using Real-Time qPCR

The upregulation of FADD and GABRA1 genes and the downregulation of the CDK6 and CRHR2 genes were verified using real-time qPCR. All the selected RNA specimens were same as those used in the chip experiment. The Invitrogen Company synthesized the PCR primers. A 10 μl reaction was established for each gene and included 1 μl of the cDNA templates, 1 μl upstream primer, 1 μl downstream primer, and 0.5 μl SYBR Green I. The reaction conditions were set as follows: denaturation for 2 min at 95°C and 30 cycles of 94°C for 10 s, 62°C for 10 s, and 72°C for 20 s. The plate was analyzed, and then a melting curve was performed by increasing the temperature from 55 to 95°C. The reaction was terminated, and the samples were cooled to 4°C.The $2^{-\Delta\Delta}$Ct method was used to calculate the relative expression of various genes (14). Data are presented as the means ±SD; $P < 0.05$ was considered as statistically significant.

Detection of the Hippocampal Expression of the GABRA1 and CRHR2 mRNAs and Proteins Using *in situ* Hybridization (ISH) and Immunohistochemistry, Respectively

In situ Hybridization

Sections were dewaxed with xylene and a gradient of ethanol solutions. Then, 3% H_2O_2 was used to inactivate the endogenous peroxidases. The mRNA nucleic acid fragments were generated by adding a freshly prepared 3% pepsase solution in citric acid to each section in a dropwise manner. Subsequently, each section was incubated with pre-hybridization liquid without probe in a 42°C incubator for 2 h. Afterwards, each section was incubated with hybridization liquid in a 42°C incubator overnight (PBS replaced the probe hybridization solution as a negative control). Next, the sections were incubated with SABC. Then, the sections were incubated with peroxidase-conjugated biotin. For detection, sections were stained with the DAB chromogen and counterstained with haematoxylin. Finally, the sections were dehydrated with ethanol, cleared with xylene, and eventually sealed with neutral gum.

Immunohistochemical Staining

Paraffin sections were dewaxed with xylene and a gradient of ethanol solutions. Then, sections were treated with 3% H_2O_2 to inactivate the endogenous peroxidases. Subsequently, sections were incubated at a high temperature and high pressure. Afterwards, sections were incubated with a blocking solution at 37°C in a humid chamber for 20 min. Sections were sequentially incubated with the primary antibody, secondary antibody, ABC and chromogen. Next, sections were counterstained. Finally, sections were dehydrated and mounted. TBS was used in place of the primary antibody as a negative control.

Image Processing

We chose the similar coronal sections from each group and captured images with an Olympus BX60 microscope equipped with a Nikon D700 digital camera. Using 20X objective, images of the CA_1, CA_3 and DG regions were captured. Image Pro Plus 6.0 image analysis software was used to analyse the images of 10 randomly selected sections from each group. Using a method described in the literature (15), the images of the hippocampal partition were processed. Before treatment, we corrected the space and optical density in microscale (the minimum scale of 0.01 mm) images and images of blank sections captured under the same conditions. The CA_1 region was selected in a $200 \times 100\ \mu m^2$ area along the pyramidal layer, CA_3 and DG regions were selected in $200 \times 200\ \mu m^2$ areas. The positive area and integrated optical density (IOD) of each slice was calculated, and calculate the MOD (MOD = IOD/area). The IOD represents the relative mRNA and protein levels. Data are presented as the means ± SD. $P < 0.05$ was considered to indicate statistically significant differences.

Bioinformatics Analysis of the Hippocampal Profile of Differentially Expressed Genes

(1) The biological processes, cellular components, and molecular functions of differentially expressed genes were classified using the Database for Annotation, Visualization and Integrated Discovery (DAVID) (16, 17) and Gene Ontology (GO) (18) database. Fisher's exact probability test was employed.

(2) The signaling pathways in which the differentially expressed genes were involved were classified and analyzed using Biocarta (www.biocarta.com) and Kyoto Encyclopedia of Genes and Genomes (KEGG, www.genome.jp/kegg/pathway.html) databases. The MSigDB database provided all of the pathway information. According to the hypergeometric distribution, the pathways in which significantly differentially expressed genes were involved were determined.

(3) Establishment of differentially expressed transcription regulation network.

According to the literature (19), the strategy of comparative genomics combined with promoter region sequence transcription factor binding site (TFBS) detection technology was used to establish the network regulating the transcription of the differentially expressed genes. First, the promoter sequences were collected. The data for rat promoter sequences were downloaded from the UCSC (http://genome.ucsc.edu/) genome database. Using the accession numbers of differentially expressed genes in the model and XYS groups, the promoter sequences of these differentially expressed genes were screened to predict the TFBS of potential target genes in the regulatory network. The first 20 optimal motifs were selected in each group (differentially expressed genes) of regulatory events. An analysis of the evolutionary conservation of the motifs in calculated and predicted promoter sequences was performed to identify additional potential TF regulatory regions. The analysis of the conservation of the promoter sequences in the whole genome of eight vertebrate animals was conducted using the most recent version of the UCSC database and the phast Cons software algorithm based on a Two-State Hidden Markov Model (20). For each promoter region and binding site identified using the motif probe algorithm, the corresponding conservation of the respective motif was obtained, as the PhastCons value. Then, the predicted motifs were used to perform a position weight matrix (PWM) analysis with the TFBS binding sites in the most recent transcription factor databases TRANSFAC and JASPAR using the Motif Compare algorithm (21, 22). The PWM similarity P-value obtained from the comparison should not exceed 10E-4 (or 10^{E-4}). Meanwhile, the corresponding TF binding sequences involved in regulating gene expression were located in the conserved sequences and mapped onto the considered motif position. The score for the corresponding conserved TF binding sequences was ≧0.8 (1 represents the most conserved sequence,

TABLE 1 | Classification of the upregulated and downregulated genes involved in the significant bioprocesses of the model group compared with the control group.

	Term	Genes	*P*-value
Up-regulated genes in model group	Biological regulation	EFNA1, DDR2, ASGR2, MAX, TTR, CDCA7, SLC2A3, SOSTDC1, TRPV4, KCNQ1, AKT3, TAAR3, FANCC, AR, BTNL8, PTGER3, OTX2, RAB4B, FADD, VAX2, VAX1, PPARGC1A, TRDN, CD38, OLR1701, MSX1, RASGRF2, ARRB2, F5, HIPK3, ARPC5L, RIN2, RIPK3, AKAP7, ZFP212, UNG, ENPP3, LOC295015, ASB13, GCGR, SNIP, ACE, SNRK, OLR1714, PRKAA2, COL8A1, NFATC3, FZD9, ERG, TRPC6, ESRRB, TBX2, CTLA4, ACACA, RPS9, TEAD2, USF2, SHOX2, RAB31, RGS1, PPP1R2, LRP6, CHRNB4, RHBDL2, CD79B, ATP6V0A4, CHRNG, CACNA1B	2.96E-02
Down -regulated genes in model group	Immune system process	RT1-CE7, CRP, STAT5B, C5, CDK6, CCL5, DBH, TERC, RT1-A3, CCL25, OAS1I, CD34, IRF7, ERAF, DEFB1	2.25E-05
	Developmental process	WNT5A, STAT5B, C5, STRN, CCL5, GJA5, TERC, HEMGN, FOXH1, ERAF, ODF4, CHM, PCDHA13, FANCA, TBPL1, KLF5, PLD2, MAFB, CCNF, CYP26A1, CDK6, DBH, PTPN12, PRM2, NFIC	3.70E-03
	Biological regulation	WNT5A, RAB3C, IL9R, PANX1, C5, STAT5B, CRP, PRND, STRN, CCL5, TERC, SCTR, HEMGN, ADPRHL1, FOXH1, STAT4, ERAF, CHM, FANCA, CEACAM1, TBPL1, KLF5, PLD2, MAFB, ZHX2, CYP26A1, OLR1504, CDK6, DBH, RT1-A3, CRHR2, NAALAD2, P2RX1, RPS6KA2, PLK1, IRF7, REM1, KCNH7, NFIC, ZFHX2, IL22RA2	5.97E-03
	Multicellular organismal process	OLR210, WNT5A, RAB3C, C5, STAT5B, STRN, GJA5, TERC, HEMGN, FOXH1, OLR482, STAT4, ERAF, CHM, ODF4, PCDHA13, FANCA, TBPL1, KLF5, PLD2, OLR693, MAFB, OLR220, CCNF, CYP26A1, OLR1504, CDK6, DBH, PTPN12, NAALAD2, P2RX1, IRF7, PRM2, NFIC	1.18E-02

TABLE 2 | Classification of the upregulated and downregulated genes involved in the significant bioprocesses of the XYS group compared with the model group.

	Term	Genes	*P*-value
Upregulated genes in XYS group	Developmental process	WNT5A, TACR3, EVX2, GRB2, C5, STRN, HEMGN, APOA5, ERAF, SOX18, GPNMB, PCDHA13, FRS2, FIGF, FANCA, RUNX3, ANAPC2, LYN, ARHGEF7, SMAD6, MYO1E, CDK6, MALT1, DBH, PRPH2, IRS1, GNAT2, ATP7A, ALOX15, UCP3, HDAC1, SPATA18, NAB1, USH1C, TGFB1I1, COL1A1, PRM2, TCF12	2.18E-04
	Multicellular organismal process	TACR3, EVX2, STRN, HEMGN, OLR1392, APOA5, ERAF, SOX18, FRS2, FANCA, ANAPC2, OLR790, LYN, ARHGEF7, LOC367539, CDK6, IRS1, SAG, MMP11, ALOX15, OLR450, SPATA18, NAB1, USH1C, OLR194, COL1A1, TGFB1I1, WNT5A, OLR1073, GRB2, C5, RPL10L, IL23A, GPNMB, PCDHA13, OLR112, FIGF, RUNX3, OLR1609, OLR220, MYO1E, SMAD6, MALT1, DBH, PRPH2, GNAT2, ATP7A, OLR1384, HDAC1, OLR1726, PRM2, TCF12	1.03E-03
	Immune system process	LYN, MYO1E, SMAD6, RT1-M1-2, C5, CXCL9, MALT1, CDK6, CXCL11, DBH, ATP7A, IL23A, ERAF	1.33E-02
	Response to stimulus	WNT5A, TACR3, OLR1073, PANX1, GRB2, C5, RT1-M1-2, CXCL9, STRN, CXCL11, IL23A, OLR1392, SLC2A1, APOA5, OLR112, OLR1609, OLR790, LYN, OLR220, SMAD6, NEIL1, TRIM25, MALT1, DBH, PRPH2, IRS1, SAG, CYP4B1, GNAT2, PCK1, ATP7A, OLR1384, HAO1, CRHR2, UCP3, HDAC1, OLR450, OLR1726, OLR194, TGFB1I1, COL1A1	4.47E-02
Down regulated genes in XYS group	Multicellular organismal process	IBSP, PCDHA6, OLR851, ERBB4, EFNA1, EFNA2, MUTED, PGAM2, DNASE1L2, EPHB3, CDH22, GPX2, OLR488, SOSTDC1, NOS3, COL8A1, TWIST1, OTOP1, FANCC, NES, PTGER3, ESRRB, SMAD5, ACACA, DLL3, ANG1, OLR247, DPYSL3, VAX1, SLCO1A5, TNNI2, MSX1, F5, ARRB2, KCNJ8, CLDN1, OLR1288, FABP1, SEMA4D, OLR855, CTNS	3.22E-03
	Developmental process	IBSP, PCDHA6, ERBB4, EFNA1, EFNA2, MUTED, DNASE1L2, EPHB3, CDH22, SOSTDC1, NOS3, COL8A1, TWIST1, OTOP1, FANCC, NES, ESRRB, SMAD5, DLL3, ANG1, DPYSL3, VAX1, SLCO1A5, MSX1, KCNJ8, CLDN1, SEMA4D, CTNS	4.58E-03
	Biological adhesion	CDH22, PCDHA6, IBSP, WISP2, F5, PCDHB3, CLDN1, LOC498972	2.8E-02

$P < 0.05$ was considered to be statistically significant, and arranged in the order of the significant difference. Genes: The differential genes which were screened in the bioprocess in this experiment.

whereas 0 represents the least conserved sequence). The first five optimal TFs of each group were exported after the comparison. The TFs that potentially regulated the differential expression of genes in the model and XYS groups were obtained. Finally, networks regulating the cis-transcription of the differentially expressed in the model and XYS groups were established. The core genes in the network structure were calculated using the PageRank algorithm (23). The regulatory network was visualized using Cytoscape (http://www.cytoscape.org/) (24).

RESULTS

Gene Chip Detection

A total of 566 differentially expressed genes were identified in the model group compared with the control group, of which 365 were upregulated and 201 were downregulated. The results are shown in **Supplementary Table 1**.

A total of 544 differentially expressed genes were identified in the XYS group compared with the model group, of which 265 were upregulated and 279 were downregulated. The results are shown in **Supplementary Table 2**.

Go Function Analysis

In the model and XYS groups, the significant biological processes of the differentially expressed genes in the hippocampus mainly included biological regulation, immune system process, development, reproduction, multicellular organism, response to stress, and adhesion, among others. **Tables 1**, **2** list the names and *P*-values for biological processes that were significantly activated or suppressed, as well as the number of differentially expressed genes.

Signaling Pathway in Which the Differentially Expressed Genes Were Involved

Compared with the control group, differentially expressed genes were involved in 4 significant signaling pathways in the model group. The function of the cytokine-cytokine receptor interaction pathway was significantly inhibited, with one upregulated gene and four downregulated genes. The upregulated gene was IL17RB. The downregulated genes were IL22RA2, IL9R, CCL5, and CCL25. The pathway diagram has been published in the Li et al. (19). Compared with the model group, differentially expressed genes in the XYS group were involved in 4 significant pathways. The actin cytoskeleton regulation pathway changed significantly, with upregulation of the ARHGEF7 gene and downregulation of the FGF14 and PAK4 genes. The pathway diagram is shown in **Figure 1**. **Tables 3**, **4** list all the significant signaling pathways in which the differentially expressed genes in the model and XYS groups were involved (the pathways

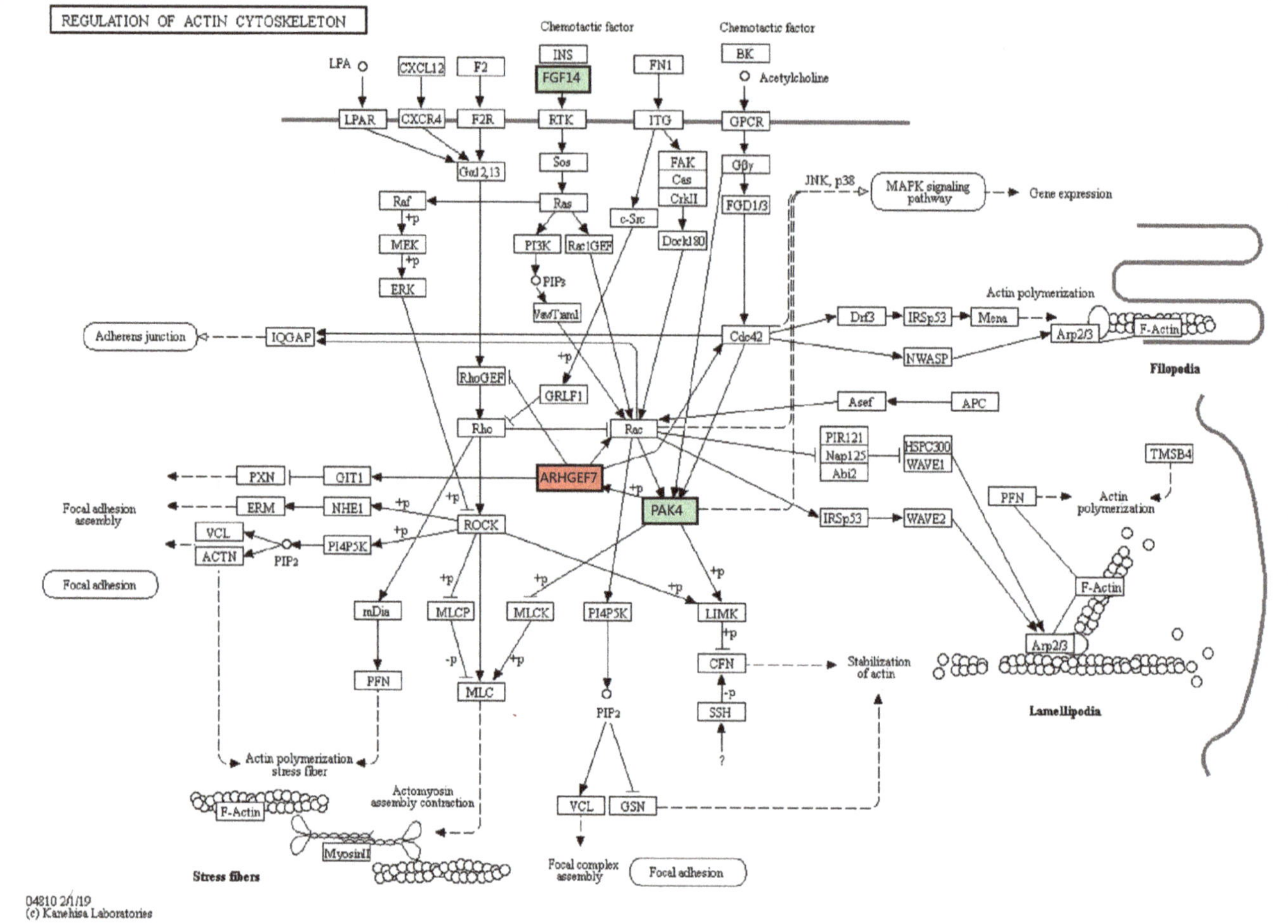

FIGURE 1 | Signaling pathways regulating the actin cytoskeleton. Diagram of the most significant signaling pathways in which the differentially expressed genes in the XYS group were involved compared with the model group. The green label represents the downregulated FGF14 and PAK4 genes; the red label represents the upregulated ARHGEF7 gene.

with the HAS prefix were obtained from the KEGG database, and the others without a unified prefix were obtained from the Biocarta database), the number of genes in each pathway in the database, the number of differentially expressed genes, the names of upregulated genes and downregulated genes and *P*-values are shown.

Establishment of Networks Regulating the Transcription of the Differentially Expressed Genes

(1) Compared with the control group, 39 genes were involved in the establishment of transcriptional regulatory networks for the 566 differentially expressed genes in the model group, of which 22 were upregulated and 17 were downregulated.

One hundred two transcription factors (TF) were predicted. One hundred forty-one nodes (including transcription factors and target genes) and 384 pairs of TF→ RTFT potential relationships were identified in the transcriptional regulatory network. (2) Compared with the model group, 40 genes were involved in the establishment of the transcriptional regulatory networks for the 544 differentially expressed genes in the XYS group, of which 15 were upregulated and 25 were downregulated. One hundred twelve transcription factors (TF) were predicted. One hundred fifty-two nodes (including transcription factors and target genes) and 478 pairs of TF→ RTFT potential relationships were identified in the transcriptional regulatory network. **Table 5** lists the PageRank values of the first 10 core genes in the network structure and their common TFs. **Figure 2** show the diagrams of the regulatory network structures. Red and green represent upregulated and downregulated genes, respectively, and gray represents TFs. The direction of regulation between the TF and TFT is presented as an arrow.

Real-Time Fluorescence Quantitative PCR

The $2^{-\Delta\Delta Ct}$ method was used to compute the relative expression of the verified gene. The ratio of the mean fluorescence intensities of the genes in the gene chip experimental group to the mean fluorescence intensities of the genes in the control

TABLE 3 | Analysis of the differential gene pathways of model group compared with the control group.

Pathways	Genes in geneset (K)	Genes in overlap (k)	Up-regulated Genes	Down-regulated Genes	*P*-value
HSA04060-CYTOKINE_CYTOKINE_RECEPTOR_INTERACTION	257	5	IL17RB	IL22RA2, IL9R, CCL5, CCL25	1.98E-02
HSA04810_REGULATION_OF_ACTIN_CYTOSKELETON	212	4	ITGB6, FGF14 ARPC5	ITGA10	2.95E-02
ACE_INHIBITOR	8	2	AGTR1, ACE		3.92E-02
SIG_PIP3_SIGNALING_IN_B_YMPHOCYTES	36	4	ITPR2, AKT3 DAPP1	RPS6KA2	4.82E-02

TABLE 4 | Analysis of the differential gene pathways of XYS group compared with the model group.

Pathways	Genes in geneset (K)	Genes in overlap (k)	Up-regulated Genes	Down-regulated Genes	*P*-value
HSA04810_REGULATION_OF_ACTIN_CYTOSKELETON	212	3	ARHGEF7	FGF14 PAK4	2.71E-02
TERTPATHWAY	8	2	HDAC1	MAX	3.10E-02
CALCIUM_REGULATION_IN_CARDIAC_CELLS	143	3	FXYD2	ARRB2, RGS1	4.34E-02
HSA04060_CYTOKINE_CYTOKINE_RECEPTOR_INTERACTION	257	6	IL22RA2, CNTFR, IL23A, CXCL11, CXCL9, LTBR		4.49E-02
GPCRDB_CLASS_A_RHODOPSIN_LIKE	185	3		PTGER1, CNR1, GPR30	5.14E-02
IL4PATHWAY	11	2	GRB2, IRS1		5.43E-02

$P < 0.05$ was considered to be statistically significant, and arranged in the order of the significant difference genes in geneset (K): the number of genes in this pathway in the database; genes in overlap (k): the number of differential genes screened in this experiment. Up-regulated Genes and Down-regulated Genes: The up-regulated and down-regulated genes of the differential genes on the pathway in the experiment.

group served as relative parameter to confirm the data. In the relative quantitative analysis of real-time PCR data, a relative expression ratio of the experimental group to the control group of ≦1.5 or ≧0.67 suggested that the trends for the upregulation or downregulation of gene expression, respectively, were consistent with the gene chip results. The difference in the relative expression of each gene between groups was statistically analyzed, and the results were basically consistent with the differentially expressed genes identified using the gene chip (**Figure 3**).

Effects of Xiaoyaosan on the Expression of the CRHR2 and GABRA1 Proteins and m RNAs in the Rat Hippocampus

In situ hybridization and immunohistochemistry were used to detect the expression of the CRHR2 and GABRA1 mRNAs and proteins, respectively. The expression of the CRHR2 and GABRA1 mRNA in the hippocampal CA_1, CA_3 and DG regions is shown in **Figure 4A**. CIS reduce the area in which the CRHR2 mRNA was expressed in the hippocampal CA_1 region ($P < 0.01$), which was reversed by the XYS treatment ($P < 0.05$) (**Figure 4B**a). The integrated optical density of CRHR2 mRNA expression in the hippocampal CA_1, CA_3 and DG regions in model group ($P < 0.01$ or 0.05) was reduced, and this change was reversed by the XYS treatment ($P < 0.05$) (**Figure 4B**b). CIS increased the area and integrated optical density of the GABRA1 mRNA in the hippocampal DG region ($P < 0.01$ or 0.05), which was reversed by the XYS treatment ($P < 0.05$; **Figures 4B**c,d). Significant differences in the area and integrated optical density of GABRA1 mRNA expression in the CA_1 and CA_3 regions were not observed (**Figures 4B**c,d). The expression of the CRHR2 and GABRA1 proteins in the hippocampal CA_1, CA_3 and DG regions is shown in **Figure 5A**.

CIS reduce the area in which the CRHR2 protein was expressed in the hippocampal CA_1 region ($P < 0.01$), which was reversed by the XYS treatment ($P < 0.01$) (**Figure 5B**a). The CRHR2-positive area showed a decreasing trend in the CA3 and DG regions, but the differences between groups were not significant ($P > 0.05$; **Figure 5B**a). The integrated optical density of the CRHR2 protein was reduced in the hippocampal CA_1, CA_3 and DG regions ($P < 0.01$ or 0.05) of the model group, and these changes were reversed by the XYS treatment ($P < 0.05$) (**Figure 5B**b). CIS increased the area and integrated optical density of GABRA1 expression in the hippocampal DG region ($P < 0.01$ or 0.05), changes that were reversed by the XYS treatment ($P < 0.05$; **Figures 5B**c,d). Significant differences in the area and integrated optical density of GABRA1 expression were not observed in the CA_1 and CA_3 regions (**Figures 5B**,c,d).

TABLE 5 | PageRank values of the first 10 core genes in the network structure diagram and their common TFs.

Gene	Transcription factor	PageRank
M-N		
Klf5	AP-2,v-Maf,LMAF,SRY,odd,Myf,AP-2alphaA,HAP5, COMP1,HEN1,NFE2L2,AZF1,NHP10,CAC-binding,MAC1, bZIP910,Dde,Nrf-2,Adf-1	0.052951
Lfng	SWI5,E2A,Adf-1,myogenin,AP-2alphaA,LMAF,GAMYB, SMAD3,Myf,Spz1, AP-2, ARF, LBP-1,MET32,hth,achi, REST,odd,HEB,HEN1,AP-4,Kr, MyoD, MyoD,CAC-binding, NHP10	0.049318
Cryba2	Dfd,bZIP910,NRSF,INO2,AtMYB-15,c-Ets-1,INO4, Osf2	0.043825
Pter	Achi,Dde,Lmo2,ZEB1,sna,TBX5,E2A,Brachyury, MyoD,T,LMAF,SMAD3,CACD,MAC1,LF-A1	0.0403
Ppargc1a	TAL1,SP1,MAZ, AP-4,RAP1,Tra-1,TFII-I,SPIB,ISGF-3 CUP2,Retroviral,PEND,myogenin,PU.1,AZF1, EWSR1-FLI1,UF1H3BETA, Klf4,LBP-1,NHLH1,Elf-1,Dfd,E47,sna,SFL1, CAC-binding,Myf, Dde	0.039645
Krt1-19	Achi,TFII-I,EWSR1-FLI1,SP1,E2A,ARF,Skn-1,HTF, SMAD3,Oct-1, Opaque-2, MATALPHA2	0.036807
Tacstd2	Kr,Dde,E2A,MAC1,LMAF,HSF,TBF1,MEF-2,ESR1, SZF1-1,RAP1,Cdx,LUN-1,LF-A1	0.033357
Nxf	ARF,MEF-2,KR,PEND,E2A, Retroviral,Ttk,SPIB,SFL1, TBF1,SZF1-1,LUN-1,CUP2,Elf-1,HSF,PU.1,AZF1	0.031067
Tgm1	NHLH1,Sp1,AP-4,E47,myogenin,GC,AZF1, PEND,Klf4,sna,KROX,TAL1,SUT1, Myf,DAL81,LBP-1,Elf-1	0.025603
Cyp26a1	LMAF,bZIP910,bZIP911,c-Myc,sna,MAC1,TAL1,E47, LF-A1,NF-muE1,E12,Dde,HAP5	0.025388
XYS-M		
Ocm	MEF-2, Caup, STB5, GATA-1, MATALPHA2, GATA-2, GLN3, GATA-4, Kr, Spz1, MEIS1A-HOXA9, SZF1-1, CG11617, Opaque-2, YY1, ARF, ESR1, AR, Optix, TBF1	0.061146
Vof16	AZ, PEND, Elf-1, AZF1, HSF, MSN4, Lentiviral, ARF, SPIB, ttx-3_c, PU.1, Lyf-1, NFATC2 _D, ZNF219, c-Rel, MAZR, Nkx6-1, Foxd3, UF1H3BETA, SFL1, HNF3alpha, STE11, MSN2, MZF1, TFII-I, SP1, Dl, FOXP1, TFIIA, dl_1, br_Z1, MZF1_5-13, RGM1, dl_2	0.05971
Kcna1	Alfin1, Ets, Pax4, MZF1_5-13, MZF1, PU.1, SPIB, Optix, ETF, MAZ, BLIMP1, Egr, MCM1+SFF, LMAF, NFATC2, SP1, EDS1, SPI1, KAISO, Dl, Elf-1, So, PEND, AZF1, id1, STAT5A, UF1H3BETA, Helios, CG11617, dl_1, FEV, ZNF219, FZF1, E47, Cdc5, GLN3, HEB, MAC1	0.05841
Aqp1	PU.1, Sp1, AZF1, MAZ, Elf-1, FXR-RXR-alpha, Tra-1, ZEB1, PEND, ZNF219, GBF, ROM, UF1H3BETA, E47, SREBP-1, E12, SFL1, MSN4, RGM1, Myogenin, MSN2, Pax4, HMG-I_Y, Klf4, SPIB, Sna, SPI1, Alfin1	0.04028
Cnr1	CDC5, LMAF, Dde, MAC1	0.033435
Tnni2	PEND, Klf4, LMAF, Ets, MAC1, SPIB, AP-4, Myf, PU.1, TFIIA, AZF1, Myogenin, Ttk, E47, TAL1, GATA-4, KAISO, HEB, SFL1, Elf-1, SPI1, STAT1, CDC5, Sna, Dde, NHLH1, HSF	0.03207
Msx1	FEV, dl_1, Sp1, RGM1, ZNF219, NFATC2, MZF1, PU.1, STRE, MSN4, Dl, Helios, STAT5A, MSN2, E2A, id1, Klf4, EDS1, MAZ, Egr, BLIMP1, UF1H3BETA, GATA-1, MZF1_5-13, MCM1+SFF, MAZR, Tal1_Gata1	0.030168
Gja9	ZEB1, Sn, E47, AREB6, EmBP-1, T, MyoD, sna	0.030136
Efna1	FOXP1, STE11, HSF, Foxd3, Nkx6-1, ttx-3_c, Ttk, AZF1, br_Z1, HNF3alpha_D	0.027062
Ltbr	Kr, SZF1-1, SPI1, ESR1, STB5, MEF-2, SPIB, sna, E47, PU.1, Spz1, ROM, E12, myogenin, PEND, TBF1, Elf-1, SFL1, Tra-1, AZF1, ZEB1	0.02606

The names of the first 10 core genes in the model group and XYS group in the network structure in descending order according to the PageRank value. Transcription factor column lists the predicted transcription factor of regulating and controlling each core gene.

DISCUSSION

In this study, we applied gene expression chip and bioinformatics technology to determine the central hippocampal profile of differentially expressed genes in rats exposed to CIS after the administration of the XYS intervention, and relevant research results are described above. The gene chip results for the GABRA1, FADD, CRHR2, and CDK6 genes were verified using real-time fluorescent quantitative PCR in hippocampal tissues from the rats in each group. The ISH results for the GABRA1 and CRHR2 genes, and the immunohistochemical staining for the GABRA1 and CRHR2 proteins were similar to the gene chip results. The gene chip data were verified to be reliable at the tissue and cell levels.

The most important characteristic of stress reactions is the activation of the hypothalamic-pituitary-adrenal (HPA) axis and the subsequent increase in glucocorticosteroid (GC) secretion. Activation of the HPA axis is the most important adaptative and protective response to stress, but during chronic stress, the HPA axis tends to be in a continuously highly reactive state, leading to the secretion of large amounts of GCs and the dysfunction of the nervous, endocrine, and immune systems, among others. The hippocampus is one of the most important brain regions that mediates the stress response. The hippocampus plays crucial roles in learning and memory. Because the hippocampus expresses glucocorticoid receptors (GR) at the highest levels in the central nervous system, high levels of GCs induced by stress will selectively act on the hippocampus, impairing hippocampal neuronal plasticity, disrupting the balance between apoptosis and regeneration, leading to atrophy and the loss of neurons, and eventually local damage to the hippocampal structure and function (25, 26).

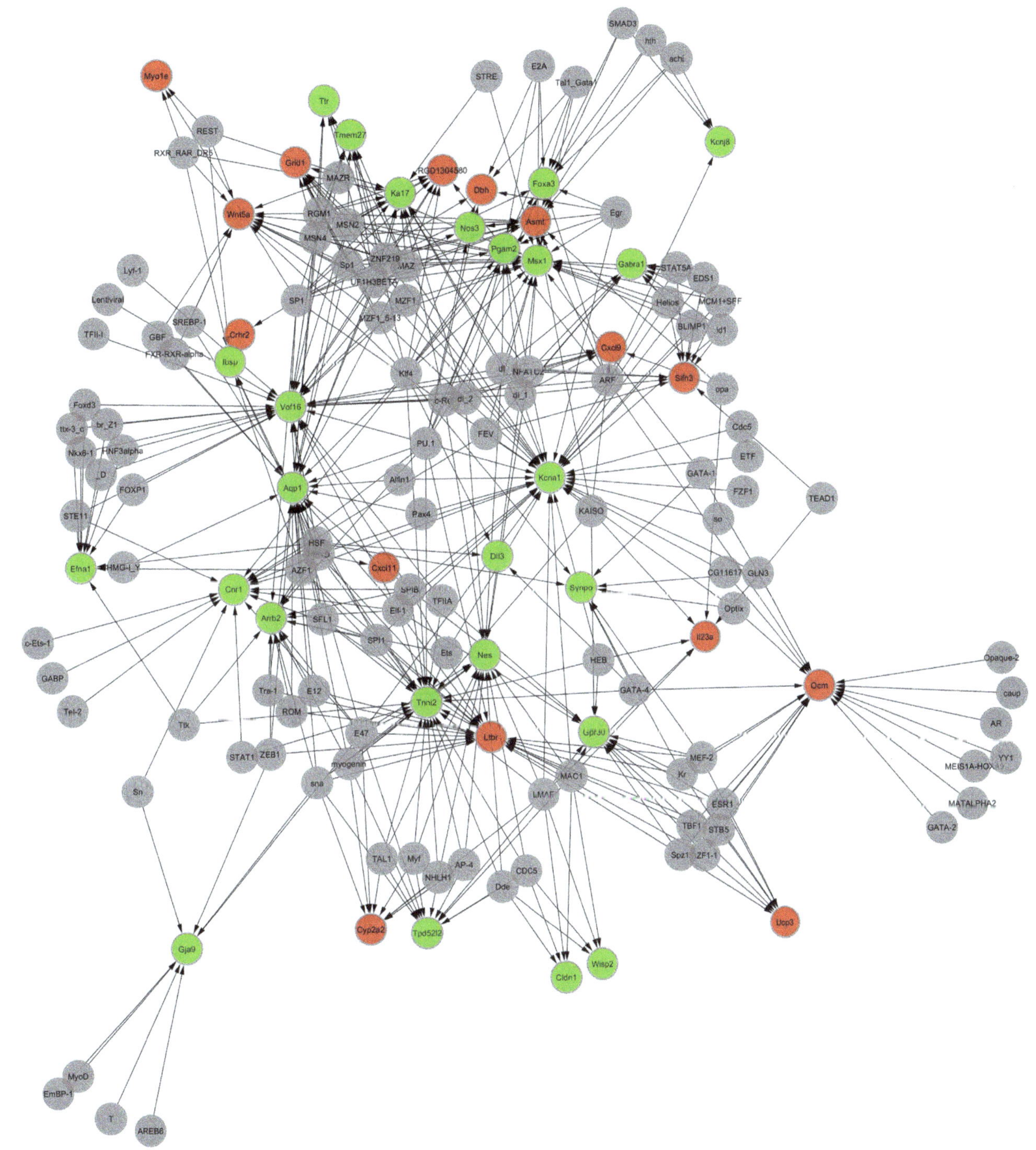

FIGURE 2 | Diagram of the networks regulating the transcription of the differentially expressed genes in the model group compared with the XYS group. Red and green represent upregulated and downregulated genes, respectively, and gray represents TFs. The arrow indicates the direction in which the TF target (TFT) genes are regulated by transcription factors (TFs).

We genetically confirmed the reliability of previous findings. Based on the dynamic analysis of the central hippocampal profiles of differentially expressed genes in rats exposed to 21 days of chronic immobilization stress, (1) the HPA axis of the stressed rats is hyperactivated. The function of the hippocampal immune system was significantly inhibited, and the number and function of T lymphocytes were abnormal. (2) An imbalance in the synthesis and degradation of extracellular matrix (ECM)

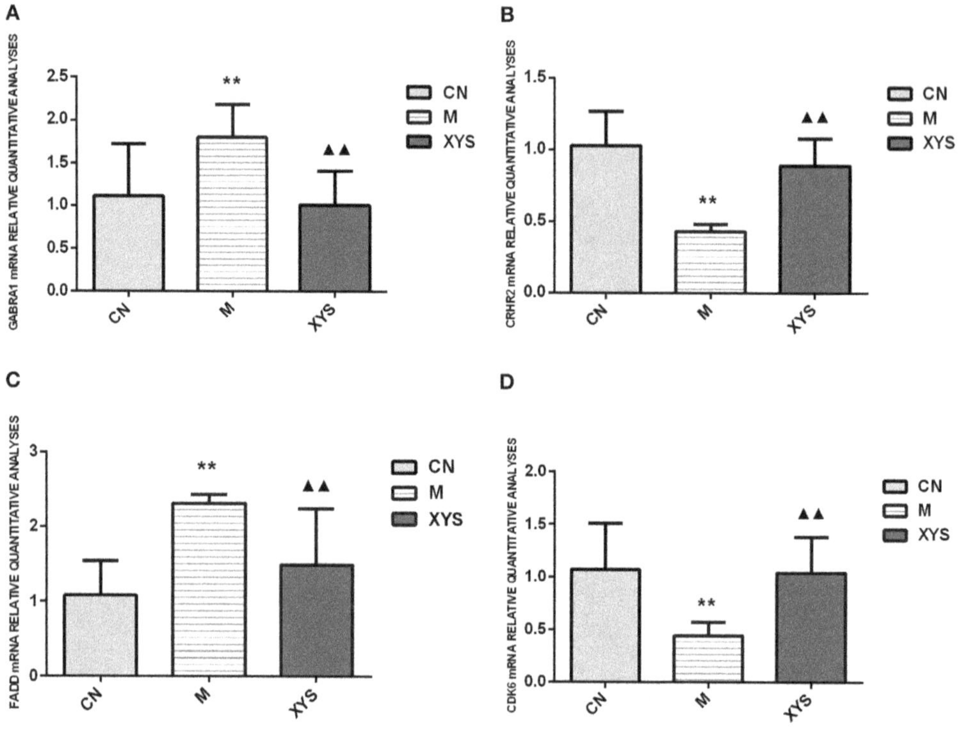

FIGURE 3 | Relative quantitative analyses of the expression of the GABRA1, CRHR2, FADD, and CDK6 mRNAs in the rat hippocampal tissues from each group. **(A)** Relative quantitative analyses of GABRA1 mRNA expression in each group. **(B)** Relative quantitative analyses of CRHR2 mRNA expression in each group. **(C)** Relative quantitative analyses of FADD mRNA expression in each group. **(D)** Relative quantitative analyses of CDK6 mRNA expression in each group. $^{**}P < 0.01$ compared with the control group. ▲▲$P < 0.01$ compared with the model group.

of hippocampus tissues was observed. The synthesis of ECM increased, and the degradation was reduced. Collagen synthesis was increased. The overdeposition of ECM and collagen resulted in a certain degree of hardening of the hippocampus, and the inflammatory response in the hippocampal tissue is a key factor promoting the overdeposition of ECM and collagen. (3) The balance between the growth and apoptosis of hippocampal neurons was disrupted. The growth of hippocampal neurons was inhibited, but apoptosis was accelerated. A detailed explanation of these conclusions has been published in the Li et al.

XYS is widely used as modern clinical treatment for diseases. It has been used to cure more than 165 different diseases by physicians in the fields of psychiatry, neurology, cardiology, gastroenterology, gynecology, surgery, etc., (27). It is most commonly used for psychiatric diseases and neurological diseases (28) and the most common symptoms treated are depression, followed by anxiety, cardiac symptoms, neuroses, sleep disorders, etc., (29). The regulatory effect of XYS on chronic stress has also been studied extensively. The stress-induced abnormalities in the function of the central nervous system are significantly improved or eliminated by XYS and its components, including learning and memory deficits, depression, and sleep disorders caused by psychological stress. XYS and its components also display calming, analgesic, anti-convulsant, anti-anxiety, and anti-chronic depression properties. Its effect on chronic depression is similar to imipramine (30). Research on the pharmacology of modern Chinese medicine also shows that XYS exerts a strong central pharmacological action. Among the 8 components (Radix Bupleuri, Rhizoma Atractylodis Macrocephalae, Radix Paeoniae Alba, Poria, Radix Angelicae Sinensis, Herba Menthae, Rhizoma Zingiberis Recens, and Radix Glycyrrhizae), Radix Bupleuri exhibits sedative and anti-convulsant activities, and improves central nervous excitability (31); *Angelica Sinensis* has sedative, analgesic, anti-convulsant, nerve repair, memory enhancing, anti-inflammatory, and immune boosting properties and obviously promotes the haematopoietic function of the circulatory system (32); Paeoniae has anti-inflammatory, immunomodulatory, analgesic, sedative, anti-depressant, anti-fibrotic, anti-apoptotic, and neuroprotective properties and enhances learning, and memory (33); Rhizoma Atractylodis Macrocephalae regulates the nervous and immune systems, functions as a sedative and stimulates Th1 lymphocyte growth (34); Poria exerts anti-inflammatory and sedative effects, and particularly adjusts the ratio of T cell subgroups and enhances immunity (35) Radix Glycyrrhizae enhances immune function and protects nerves (36); Rhizoma Zingiberis Recens has a dual regulatory effect on the excitation and inhibition of the central nervous system (37) Herba Menthae excites the central nervous system (38). Thus, the components of XYS regulate the function of the central nervous system.

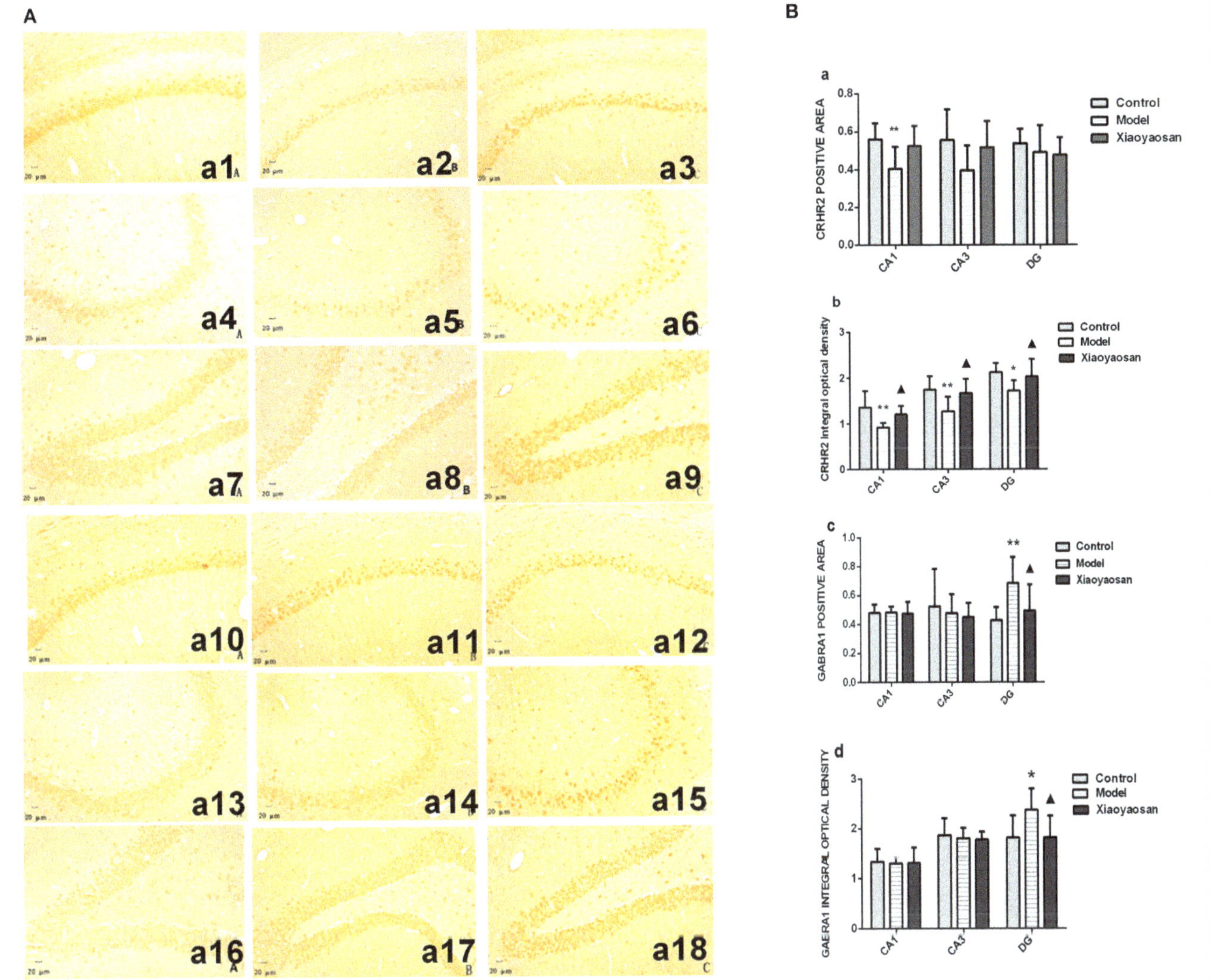

FIGURE 4 | Effects of Xiaoyaosan on the expression of the CRHR2 and GABRA1 mRNAs in the rat hippocampus. **(A)** The expression of the CRHR2 and GABRA1 mRNAs in the hippocampal CA_1, CA_3 and DG regions. The expression of the CRHR2 mRNA in the hippocampal CA_1 **(a1–a3)**, CA3 **(a4–a6)**, DG **(a7–a9)** regions of the control, model, and Xiaoyaosan groups is shown. The expression of the GABRA1 mRNA in the hippocampal CA_1 **(a10–a12)**, CA3 **(a13–a15)**, DG **(a16–a18)** regions of the control, model, Xiaoyaosan groups is shown. **(B)** Changes in the expression of the CRHR2 and GABRA1 mRNAs in the rat hippocampus. **(a)** CRHR2-positive area in ISH. **(b)** Integrated optical density of the ISH for CRHR2. **(c)** GABRA1-positive area in ISH. **(d)** Integrated optical density of the GABRA1 ISH. Values are presented as the means ± SD from 10 rats per group. $^{*}P < 0.05$ and $^{**}P < 0.01$ compared with the control group. $^{▲}P < 0.05$ compared with the model group.

We were encouraged to note that XYS reversed the stress-induced hippocampal damage. XYS is a multi-target, multi-pathway, and multi-channel agent with a dual regulatory function.

First, the GO analysis of the hippocampal gene expression profile in the XYS group showed that XYS restored the functions of multiple downregulated biological pathways in the stressed rats. As shown in **Table 2**, XYS not only regulated the downregulated developmental process and multicellular biological processes in stressed rats to ensure a new dynamic balance but also significantly inhibited the effects of and increased the function of the immune system in the stressed rats. The mechanism by which XYS regulated the immune system of the stressed rats might be related to the increased expression of the C5, DβH, ERAF, CDK6, RT1-M1-2, MALT1, SMAD6, CXCL9, CXCL11, IL23A, LYN, MYO1E, and ATP7A genes. In these upregulated genes, the expression of C5, DβH, ERAF, and CDK6 was downregulated in the model group. XYS play a direct reversal effect.

The increased expression of C5 showed that XYS reversed the complement-activated cascade reaction that was inhibited by 21 days of stress and restored the decreased humoural immune function of the stressed rats. The expression of the RT1 and M1-2 MHC class III genes was upregulated. MHC class III is mainly involved in regulating the innate immune response. Therefore, XYS not only restores the decreased

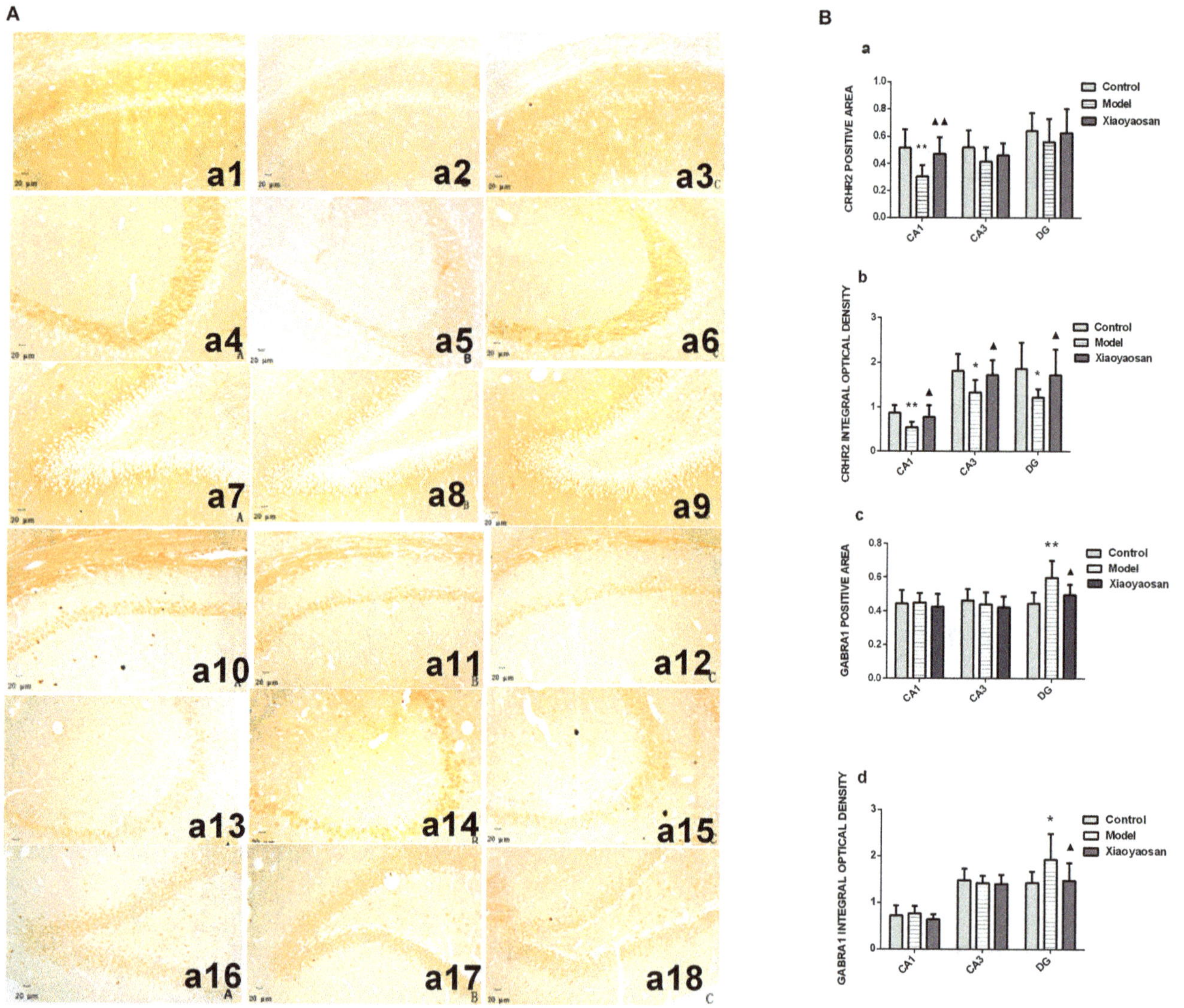

FIGURE 5 | Effects of Xiaoyaosan on the levels of the CRHR2 and GABRA1 proteins in the rat hippocampus. **(A)** Levels of the CRHR2 and GABRA1 proteins in the hippocampal CA_1, CA_3, and DG regions. Levels of the CRHR2 protein in hippocampal CA_1 **(a1–a3)**, CA_3 **(a4–a6)**, DG **(a7–a9)** regions of the control, model, and Xiaoyaosan groups. Levels of the GABRA1 protein in the hippocampal CA_1 **(a10–a12)**, CA_3 **(a13–a15)**, DG **(a16–a18)** regions of the control, model, and Xiaoyaosan groups. **(B)** Changes in the levels of the CRHR2 and GABRA1 proteins in the rat hippocampus. **(a)** CRHR2-positive area. **(b)** Integrated optical density of the CRHR2 protein. **(c)** GABRA1-positive area. **(d)** Integrated optical density of the GABRA1 protein. Values are presented as the means±SD from 10 rats per group. $^{*}P < 0.05$ and $^{**}P < 0.01$ compared with the control group. $^{\blacktriangle}P < 0.05$ and $^{\blacktriangle\blacktriangle}P < 0.01$ compared with the model group.

humoural immunity but also improves the innate immune response of stressed rats. An increase in innate immunity is an important aspect of improving the overall immunity of the body.

Dopamine beta hydroxylase (DβH) is the key enzyme that catalzses the transformation of dopamine (DA) to norepinephrine (NE/NA). In response to stress, increased NA synthesis and the subsequent increase the capacity to adapt to the external environment mediate the adaptable regulation of the body (39, 40). XYS reversed the downregulation of DβH expression in the stressed rats and increased NA levels in the hippocampus of the stressed rats; thus, the mechanism regulating the resistance of the hippocampus to stress were enhanced.

Erythroid-associated factor (ERAF), which is also called alpha-hemoglobin-stabilizing protein (AHSP), is a protein that is expressed at high levels in erythrocytes and is closely related to the functions of these cells (41, 42). The downregulated expression of AHSP in the model group of rats revealed that 21-day CIS altered the haemopoietic system of rats. In combination with the downregulated expression of CD34 in immune system of the model group, the haemopoietic system was undoubtedly altered. The CD34 antigen is selectively expressed on the surface of haematopoietic stem cells (HSCs), progenitor cells (PCs), and endothelial cells (ECs), and promotes the formation of haematopoietic progenitor cells. XYS reversed the changes in ERAF expression during the production of erythroid cells in stressed rats, restored cell homeostasis, and maintained the function of red blood cells.

The main biological function of CDK6 is to regulate the transition between different phases of the cell cycle (43). The decreased expression of CDK6 revealed an abnormality in the cell cycle of hippocampal neurons in the stressed rats, and neuronal growth was inhibited, leading to the aging and death of neurons. XYS reversed the abnormal cell cycle of hippocampal neurons in stressed rats by up-regulating the expression of CDK6.

Here, we will focus on the expression of the SMAD6, MALT1, CXCL9, CXCL11, IL23A, LYN, MYO1E, and ATP7A genes to clarify the mechanism by which XYS restored the function of suppressed immune system. These genes were not differentially expressed in the model group, but their expression was upregulated in the XYS group.

SMAD6 is an important downstream molecule in the TGF -β/Smad signaling pathway, and it is an inhibitory Smad protein (I-Smad). The TGF-β/Smad signaling pathway has been studied extensively in a hepatic fibrosis (HF) model.ds signaling pathway has been studied extensively in hepatic fibrosis (HF) model (44). Increased Smad6 expression negatively regulates the TGFβ/Smad signaling pathway, exerts an anti-fibrotic effect (45), In addition, Smad6 blocks the SMAD signal mediated by TGF β by blocking receptor-induced SMAD phosphorylation, thus inhibiting apoptosis (46). We observed substantial collagen deposition in the hippocampus of rats subjected to 21 days of chronic stress. The expression of some collagen proteins, such as Col8a1 (ratio: 3.17, the numbers in parentheses following each protein are all ratios), Col1a1 (1.52), Col1a1 (1.89), Col1a2 (1.53), Col3a1 (2.0), Col4a2 (1.7), and Col8a2 (1.93), was increased. Collagen inhibits cell proliferation (47, 48). The induction of collagen synthesis may promote the sclerosis of the hippocampus to some extent, resulting in the loss of some neurons. In combination with the analysis of signaling pathways, XYS not only increased the expression of the inhibitory Smad, Smad6 but also decreased the expression of the regulatory protein SMAD5 and negatively regulated the TGF-β signaling pathway (TGF_BETA_SIGNALING_PATHWAY, although the difference was not significant, $P = 0.196$). Thus, the balance between the synthesis and degradation of extracellular matrix in hippocampal neurons was restored, thus preventing hippocampal sclerosis, repairing the hippocampal damage, inhibiting the apoptosis of hippocampal neurons, increasing the number of hippocampal neurons, and restoring the suppressed immune function of hippocampus.

In addition, XYS also restored the immune function of the hippocampus by up-regulating the expression of MALT1. MALT1 is involved in the activation and function of T lymphocytes. A MALT1 deficiency reduces T cell proliferation (49), inhibits T cell activation by antigens (50). In our study, we have analyzed the number and impaired function of T lymphocytes, which is the main reason for the decrease in the immune function of stressed rats. XYS promoted the activation and proliferation of T lymphocytes by increasing the expression of MALT1.

Chemokine (C-X-C motif) ligand 9 (CXCL9) and CXCL11 are type I chemotactic factors or type Th1 chemotactic factors (51). These chemokines exert substantial effects on Th1 cell recruitment (52), and promote the production of Th1 type cytokines by decreasing the levels of Th2 cytokines. Th1 cytokines can promote the repair of normal tissues and play an important role in controlling infection and tissue damage (53, 54). In our study, the Th1/Th2 balance in the hippocampus of rats subjected to 21 days of chronic stress was disrupted, and the Th1 cells were suppressed. By increasing the expression of CXCL9 and CXCL11 (CXCL11 exhibited a significant increase, ratio: 95.67), XYS induced the accumulation of Th1 cells in the hippocampus, increased the proportion of Th1 cells in the hippocampus, and restored the Th1/Th2 cell balance. XYS not only reduced the hippocampal damage induced by Th2 cells but also promoted the repair of the hippocampal structure by increasing the number of Th1 cells. At the same time, the increased expression of CXCL9 and CXCL11 induced the accumulation of macrophages in the hippocampus by chemotaxis. As inflammatory cells, macrophages engulf and destroy the damaged tissue and help initiate the recovery process.

In addition, interleukin 23 (IL-23) and alpha subunit p19 (IL23a) increased the proportion of hippocampal Th1 cells. IL-23 is a new member of the IL-12 family that mainly functions as a proinflammatory cytokine. It promotes the proliferation of activated T cells and memory T cells and induces and activates T cells and DC to generate type Th1 cytokines, such as IFN-γ and IL-12. IL-23 causes a more persistent Th1 immune response than IL-12 (55).

In many autoimmune diseases, CXCL9 and CXCL11 are involved in the immune dysfunction in the target organs and excess amplification of the local inflammatory response in patients with various diseases (56, 57). The increased expression of CXCL9 and CXCL11 may also excessively activate the hippocampal type Th1 immune and inflammatory response and trigger autoimmune diseases, but the upregulated expression of LYN (ratio: 2.06) eliminated our concerns.

LYN is mainly expressed in inflammatory cells such as mononuclear macrophages (58). Lyn is a kinase with anti-inflammatory properties (59–61). LYN also has a very important role in maintaining the normal immune state of the body. A LYN deficiency can cause autoimmune diseases (62–64). In our study, the chronic inflammatory response in the hippocampus of the stressed rats was responsible for the decrease in the hippocampal function, and the inflammatory response was mainly a Th2 type response. Inflammation damaged the organized structure of the hippocampus, and increased the incidence of a spontaneous immune disease. An inflammatory response was also observed in the hippocampus after the administration of XYS, but it was mainly a type Th1 inflammatory response. As mentioned above, the XYS treatment activated and induced the accumulation of macrophages in the hippocampal tissue, and CXCL9 and CXCL11 induced the chemotaxis of Th1 cells to the hippocampus. The upregulated expression of LYN further may promote the activation of macrophages, enhance the inherent immune function of the hippocampus, induce the production of cytokines, and help hippocampus initiate the repair and remodeling processes. At the same time, the upregulated expression of Lyn restricted the excessive amplification of the inflammatory response. While repairing the damaged structure of the hippocampus, the Th1/Th2 cells achieved a new dynamic balance, thus avoiding the occurrence of autoimmune diseases. XYS exerted a dual regulatory effect.

MYO1E is type I myosin. MYO1E participates in numerous cell activities associated with actin fibers, such as endocytosis, signal transduction, maintenance of the cell membrane structure and tension, etc. (65), and this protein is closely related to the actin cytoskeleton. MYO1E is an indispensable component that maintains normal cellular morphology and functions (66–68). The 21-day CIS protocol increased the levels of pro-apoptosis proteins in hippocampal neurons (for example, the expression of Fadd increased) and affected the ability of hippocampal neurons to maintain a normal cytoskeleton. One of the mechanisms by which XYS restores the function of the immune system may be to increase the expression of MYO1E to repair the damaged cytoskeleton in hippocampal neurons and the damage to the structure and function of hippocampal neurons.

In addition, ATP7A is also associated with the cytoskeleton in and apoptosis of hippocampal neurons (69, 70). Increased expression of ATP7A promotes the repair of the cytoskeleton and decreases hippocampal neuron apoptosis, and it restores the structure and function of the hippocampus.

XYS reversed the core molecular events that significantly affected the structure and function of the hippocampus in stressed rats. The Th1 type inflammatory response plays an important role in the repair of the pathological damage to the hippocampal tissue in the stressed rats. The analysis of the gene regulation network and signaling pathways further confirmed the repair of the hippocampal structure and function in stressed rats.

The analysis of the gene regulation network showed that XYS reversed the pathological process of accelerated apoptosis and inhibited growth of hippocampal neurons in the stressed rats, and the regeneration of hippocampal neurons was the core molecular event in the regulatory network. The core of the network was no longer the KLF5 gene that inhibited cell growth, but the oncomodulin (OCM, Ratio was 2.03) gene that promoted cell growth. Previous studies have confirmed that confirmed that OCM was a new kind of neuronal growth factor in the central and peripheral nervous systems (71). It is an effective growth factor in the innate immune system and neurons (72). The key step in central nervous system regeneration is the growth of axons, and OCM promotes axon regeneration in the central nervous system and peripheral nervous system *in vivo* and *in vitro*. Cultured cells and the experimental mice showed that OCM obviously promotes the growth of the optic nerve, enhances the axonal regeneration capacity of the dorsal root ganglion (71, 72), and influences the direction of growth of the regenerating optic nerve axons in mice (73). Combined with the previous analysis, in our study, the increased OCM expression promoted the growth of hippocampal neurons, and OCM may also be mainly derived from activated macrophages. CXCL11 expression was significantly increased, and CXCL11 induced macrophage accumulation in the hippocampus by chemotaxis. Of course, OCM may also be derived from neutrophils, and CXCL11 can also induce granulocytes accumulation in the hippocampus by chemotaxis.

Based on the analysis of signaling pathways in hippocampal tissues from the 21-day stress group, the cytokine and cytokine receptor signaling pathway exhibited the most significant changes. We had already analyzed the upregulated IL17RB gene and downregulated IL22RA2, IL9R, CCL5, and CCL25 genes in the pathway, and the changes in the expression of these cytokines and cytokine receptors indicated that the Th2 inflammatory response predominated in the hippocampal tissues of the stressed rats. As the exposure to stress increased, the inhibitory effect on Th1 cells was more remarkable, and a lesion occurred in the hippocampal tissue (19). However, the most significant change in the XYS group occurred in the pathway regulating the actin cytoskeleton. Changes in the cytoskeleton are closely related to neuronal injury, and the extension of the axon and dendrites of neurons are related to the cytoskeleton. Significant increases in the expression of the Rho guanine nucleotide exchange factor 7 (ARHGEF7) gene, (ratio: 14.4), and significant decreases in the expression of the FGF14 (ratio: 0.43) and PAK4 (ratio: 0.56) genes in this pathway were observed.

Previous studies examining the function of RhoGEFs have frequently studied the effect on the actin cytoskeleton. ARHGEF7 regulates the actin cytoskeleton through CDC42 and PAKs (74, 75). ARHGEF7 modulates the function of PAKs that are important for regulating downstream proteins that maintain F-actin stability, such as LIM-kinases and ADF/cofilins (74, 76). ARHGEF7 affects the hyperplasia of neurites by regulating actin polymerization, and increase ARHGEF7 expression increases neurite growth (77, 78). ARHGEF7 has recently been shown to guide the actin cytoskeleton in the growth cone. The downregulation of ARHGEF7 significantly reduces neurite hyperplasia, while ARHGEF7 overexpression increases the number of neuronal growth cones (79). The increased expression of ARHGEF7 suggests that XYS induced the formation of neurites in hippocampal neurites of stressed rats and enhanced the regeneration of hippocampal neurons. By restructuring of cytoskeleton, XYS repaired the structure and function of the damaged hippocampal tissue.

P21-activated kinase 4 (PAK4) is a class II molecule in the PAKs family. PAK has many biological functions, such as regulating the cytoskeleton, cell survival and apoptosis, and the transduction and transformation of cell growth signals (80–82). Combined with the previous analysis of ARHGEF7 expression, we propose that the downregulation of PAK4 restricts the significant upregulation of ARHGEF7 expression, and the mutual interaction between the two repairs the structure and function of the hippocampal tissue.

FGF14 was downregulated in this pathway (ratio: 0.43). Previous studies on fibroblast growth factor (FGF) have focused on the central nervous system and liver fibrosis. The biological function of FGF14 is unclear. FGF14 is widely expressed in the developing and mature central nervous system, including the hippocampus, cerebral cortex (temporal lobe), putamen and cerebellum and is related to nerve signal conduction, axon transport and synaptic transmission (83). It plays important roles in spatial learning and synaptic plasticity (84, 85). We speculated that FGF14 is related to the synthesis and degradation of collagen and ECM in the hippocampus, based on the functions of FGF in the liver fibrosis model.

As mentioned above, the liver tissue of the liver fibrosis model presents obviously aberrant increase in the expression and excessive deposition of collagen fibers and extracellular matrix. FGF contributes to hepatic fibrosis. The mice that lack FGF1 and FGF2, liver fibrosis was decreased (86). Improving the expression of FGF9 in hepatic cells will lead to hepatic cell proliferation and collagen deposition (87). In patients with liver cancer, FGFs (FGF2, FGF4, FGF5, FGF9, and FGF22) are overexpressed (88). We did not identify direct reports of the role of FGF14 in hepatic fibrosis, but the FGF11-14 subfamily members interact with mitogen-activated protein kinase (MAPK) (89). The MAPK signaling pathway is closely related to the occurrence and development of fibrosis in various organs (90–92). For instance, the MAPK signaling pathway mediate the formation of liver fibrosis by regulating the activation, proliferation and apoptosis of hepatic stellate cells. Although the function of the MAPK signaling pathway was not significantly altered in response to 21 days of stress, changes in its activation or inhibition were observed. Compared with control group, the MAPK signaling pathway was activated in the 21-day stressed rats. Among the genes in the pathway, FGF14 gene (2.25), was upregulated. Compared with model group, the MAPK signaling pathway was inhibited in the 21-day XYS group. Among the genes in the pathway FGF14 (0.43), was downregulated. In this case, we hypothesized that FGF14 may be involved in the deposition and degradation of collagen and ECM in hippocampal tissue, and the downregulation of FGF14 would facilitate the degradation of collagen and the ECM in the hippocampal tissue, enabling ARHGEF to promote the growth of the hippocampal neurons and increase the number of growth cones. Of course, further studies using multiple techniques are needed to determine whether FGF14 promotes the degradation of collagen and the ECM in the hippocampal tissue under physiological and pathological conditions in the future.

In summary, the interaction of ARHGEF, Pak4, and FGF14 regulates the actin cytoskeleton in hippocampal neurons through an intricate regulatory network. ARHGEF7 positively regulates hippocampal neurons and the growth of their axons. The downregulated expression of FGF14 and Pak4 appears to inhibit the growth of hippocampal neurons, but this negative regulation balances the growth and apoptosis of hippocampal neurons. The intercoordination of positive and negative regulatory pathways enables the network of hippocampal nerve cells to be in a new equilibrium state.

In summary, we have obtained a understanding of the mechanism by which XYS enhances the resistance of the rat hippocampus to stress by bi-directionally regulating multiple genes, targets and pathways. XYS may enhance the immunocompetence and neuronal regeneration in the hippocampus of the stressed rats, and repaire the stress-induced damage to the structure and function of the hippocampus by reorganizing the cytoskeleton. The Th1 inflammatory response and CXCL11, LYN, OCM, and ARHGEF7 genes play a crucial role in the repair of the pathological damage to the hippocampus of stressed rats. XYS may exert therapeutic effects on autoimmune diseases and thalassaemia, among others. In the future, we will perform an in-depth analysis to verify the gene expression profile and provide reliable experimental evidence for the clinical application of XYS.

ETHICS STATEMENT

In this study, all animals were carried out in accordance with the guidelines of the P. R. China legislations on the ethical use and care of laboratory animals. All efforts were made to minimize animal suffering and the number of animals needed to produce reliable data.

AUTHOR CONTRIBUTIONS

X-HL and X-MZ contributed equally to this work. J-XC was responsible for the conception and design of the study and the supervision of experiments and contributed to revising the manuscript. X-HL, X-MZ, X-JL, Y-YL, QL, X-LG, and L-QY performed the experiments. X-HL, X-MZ, and X-JL analyzed the data. X-MZ and X-HL contributed to the drafting of the manuscript. All authors have read and agreed with the submission of manuscript.

FUNDING

This research was supported by grants from National Funds for Distinguished Young Scientists of China (No. 30825046), National Natural Science Foundation of China (No. 81630104, 81360526, 81560750), as well as the 111 project of MOE (B07007).

REFERENCES

1. Wang SX, Chen JX, Yue GX, Bai MH, Kou MJ, Jin ZY. Xiaoyaosan decoction regulates changes in neuropeptide y and leptin receptor in the rat arcuate nucleus after chronic immobilization stress. *Evid Based Complement Alternat Med.* (2012) 2012:381278. doi: 10.1155/2012/381278
2. Meng ZZ, Chen JX, Jiang YM, Zhang HT. Effect of Xiaoyaosan decoction on learning and memory deficit in rats induced by chronic immobilization stress. *Evid Based Complement Alternat Med.* (2013) 2013:297154. doi: 10.1155/2013/297154
3. Liang Y, Guo XL, Chen JX, Yue GX. Effects of the chinese traditional prescription Xiaoyaosan decoction on chronic immobilization stress-induced changes in behavior and ultrastructure in rat hippocampus. *Evid Based Complement Alternat Med.* (2013) 2013:984797. doi: 10.1155/2013/984797
4. Jiang YM, Zhang HT, Chen JX. Effect of Xiaoyao powder on the expression of Bax and Bcl-2 in amygdala of ratsinduced

by chronic restrain stress. *China J TCM Pharm.* (2012) 27:882–5.

5. Chen JX, Tang YT. Effect of Xiaoyao powder on changes of relative brain zone CRF gene expression in chronic restrained stress rats. *Zhongguo Ying Yong Sheng Li Xue Za Zhi.* (2004) 20:71–4.
6. Chen JX, Tang YT. Change of relative brain zone POMC gene expression and effect of Chinese medicine on chronic restrained stress modelrats. *Chinese Remedies andClinics.* (2003) 3:223–6.
7. Chen JX, Li W, Zhao X. Effects of three TCM formulas on the behavior and NT3 in the cortex and hippocampus in the rats irritated by the chronic stressor of restraint. *J Beijing Univ TCM.* (2004) 27:19–23.
8. Chen JX, Li W, Zhao X. Effects of three Chinese formulas on BDNF,TrkB in rat contex and hippocampus with chronic immobilization stress. *Zhong guo Bing Li Sheng Li Za Zhi.* (2007) 23:1296–300.
9. Ding J, Chen JX, Rao HM, Yue GX, Liang Y, Zhang QL. Influence of Xiaoyao powder on expressions of GluRl and GluR2 of central nervous system in rat model of liver-stagnation and spleen deficiency syndrome. *Beijing Zhong Yi Yao Da Xue Xue Bao.* (2009) 32:389–93.
10. Wang ZF, Wang BJ, Yue GX. Influence of Xiaoyao powder on expression of NR2A and NR2B in brain NMDA receptor by chronic restraint stress. *Beijing J Tradit Chin Med.* (2013) 32:300–4.
11. Chen JX, Yang JX, Zhao X, Wang ZF, Yue GX. Effects of Chinese herbs on glucocorticoid receptor in rat brain regions with chronic immobilization stress. *Zhongguo Ying Yong Sheng Li Xue Za Zhi.* (2005) 21:402–6.
12. Chen JX, Li W, Zhao X, Yang JX. Effects of the Chinese traditional prescription Xiaoyaosan decoction on chronic immobilization stress-induced changes in behavior and brain BDNF, TrkB, and NT-3 in rats. *Cell Mol Neurobiol.* (2008) 28:745–55. doi: 10.1007/s10571-007-9169-6
13. Toshinai K, Mondal MS, Nakazato M, Date Y, Murakami N, Kojima M. Upregulation of Ghrelin expression in the stomach upon fasting, insulin-induced hypoglycemia, and leptin administration. *Biochem Biophys Res Commun.* (2001) 281:1220–5. doi: 10.1006/bbrc.2001.4518
14. Bustin SA, Benes V, Nolan T, Pfaffl MW. Quantitative real-time RT-PCR–a perspective. *J Mol Endocrinol.* (2005) 34:597–601. doi: 10.1677/jme.1.01755
15. Martens U, Capito B, Wree A. Septotemporal distribution of [3H]MK-801, [3H]AMPA and [3H]Kainate binding sites in the rat hippocampus. *Anat Embryol.* (1998) 198:195–204. doi: 10.1007/s004290050177
16. Huang DW, Sherman BT, Lempicki RA. Systematic and integrative analysis of large gene lists using DAVID bioinformatics resources. *Nature Protoc.* (2009) 4:44–57. doi: 10.1038/nprot.2008.211
17. Huang DW, Sherman BT, Lempicki RA. Bioinformatics enrichment tools: paths toward the comprehensive functional analysis of large gene lists. *Nucleic Acids Res.* (2009) 37:1–13. doi: 10.1093/nar/gkn923
18. Osborne JD, Zhu LJ, Lin SM, Kibbe WA. Interpreting microarray results with gene ontology and MeSH. *Methods Mol Biol.* (2007) 377:223–42. doi: 10.1007/978-1-59745-390-5_14
19. Li XH, Chen JX, Yue GX, Liu YY, Zhao X, Guo XL. Gene expression profile of the hippocampus of rats subjected to chronic immobilization stress. *PLoS ONE.* (2013) 8:e57621. doi: 10.1371/journal.pone.0057621
20. Siepel A, Bejerano G, Pedersen JS, Hinrichs AS, Hou M, Rosenbloom K. Evolutionarily conserved elements in vertebrate, insect, worm, and yeast genomes. *Genome Res.* (2005) 15:1034–50. doi: 10.1101/gr.3715005
21. Mahony S, Auron PE, Benos PV. DNA familial binding profiles made easy: comparison of various motif alignment and clustering strategies. *PLoS Comput Biol.* (2007) 3:e61. doi: 10.1371/journal.pcbi.0030061
22. Mahony S, Benos PV. STAMP: a web tool for exploring DNA-binding motif similarities. *Nucleic Acids Res.* (2007) 35:W253–W258. doi: 10.1093/nar/gkm272
23. Brin S, Page L. The anatomy of a large-scale hypertextual Web search engine. In: *International Conference on World Wide Web.* Brisbane, QLD.
24. Shannon P, Markiel A, Ozier O, Baliga NS, Wang JT, Ramage D. Cytoscape: a software environment for integrated models of biomolecular interaction networks. *Genome Res.* (2003) 13:2498–504. doi: 10.1101/gr.1239303
25. Chao HM, Ma LY, McEwen BS, Sakai RR. Regulation of glucocorticoid receptor and mineralocorticoid receptor messenger ribonucleic acids by selective agonists in the rat hippocampus. *Endocrinology.* (1998) 139:1810–4. doi: 10.1210/endo.139.4.5896
26. Kempermann G, Kronenberg G. Depressed new neurons–adult hippocampal neurogenesis and a cellular plasticity hypothesis of major depression. *Biol Psychiatry.* (2003) 54:499–503. doi: 10.1016/S0006-3223(03)00319-6
27. Zhang HJ, Zhang J, Guo XZ. The establishment of self rating scale of depression in elderly patients with depression. *Liaoning J Tradit Chin Med.* (2009) 36:1691–2.
28. Ji B, Chen JX, Lu ZL. Thoughts on the clinical applica.tion of Xiaoyao Powder. *J Beijing Univ TCM.* (2001) 24:4–7.
29. Chen XT, Shi XD. Application of Xiaoyao powder in the disease of mental and nervous system. *Jiangsu J Tradit Chin Med.* (2007) 39:66–7.
30. Sun Q, Ao HQ, Guo W. Research progress of Xiaoyao powder on counteracting chronic stress. *J New Chin Med.* (2011) 43:105–7.
31. Lv XH, Sun ZX, Su RQ. Pharmacological actions of Radix bupleuri and its active components research advances. *Chin J Inf Tradit Chin Med.* (2012) 19:105–7.
32. Liu YH, Yang SY, Ma WL. Research progress on pharmacological effects of Angelica sinensis. *China Mod Med.* (2014) 21:192–4.
33. Li Y. Progress of pharmacological research on radix paeoniae alba and its chemical constituents. *Occup Health.* (2015) 31:2153–5.
34. Yang E, Zhong YM, Feng YF. Advance on the chemical constituents and pharmacological effects of *Atractylodes macrocephala* Koidz. *J Guangdong Pharm Univ.* (2012) 28:218–21.
35. Niu S, Hao LM, Zhao SX, Chen Q. Research Progress in Polysaccharides from Poria cocos. *Food Sci.* (2012) 33:348–53.
36. Li QY, Jin YJ, Huang XX, Wang XN, Liu Y, Wu XJ. Overview of the role of licorice and its extract on bodily systems. *J Jilin Med Coll.* (2014) 35:139–44.
37. Lim WC, Seo JM, Lee CI, Pyo HB, Lee BC. Stimulative and sedative effects of essential oils upon inhalation in mice. *Arch Pharm Res.* (2005) 28:770–4. doi: 10.1007/BF02977341
38. Shen MF, Li XM, Shan QY. Research progress of chemical compositions and pharmacological actions of *Mentha canadensis. Chin Arch Tradit Chin Med.* (2012) 30:1484–7.
39. Zhou QY, Quaife CJ, Palmiter RD. Targeted disruption of the tyrosine hydroxylase gene reveals that catecholamines are required for mouse fetal development. *Nature.* (1995) 374:640–3. doi: 10.1038/374640a0
40. Thomas SA, Palmiter RD. Thermoregulatory and metabolic phenotypes of mice lacking noradrenaline and adrenaline. *Nature.* (1997) 387:94–7. doi: 10.1038/387094a0
41. Feng L, Gell DA, Zhou S, Gu L, Kong Y, Li J. Molecular mechanism of AHSP-mediated stabilization of alpha-hemoglobin. *Cell.* (2004) 119:629–40. doi: 10.1016/j.cell.2004.11.025
42. Mi L, Menzel S, Jiang J. Abstracts of the 14th conference on hemoglobin switching Orcas Island,Washington. *Blood Cells Mol Dis.* (2005) 34:71–134.
43. Ohtani N, Yamakoshi K, Takahashi A, Hara E. The p16INK4a-RB pathway: molecular link between cellular senescence and tumor suppression. *J Med Invest.* (2004) 51:146–53. doi: 10.2152/jmi.51.146
44. Schuppan D, Kim YO. Evolving therapies for liver fibrosis. *J Clin Invest.* (2013) 123:1887–901. doi: 10.1172/JCI66028
45. Zhang CH, Li C, Li HJ, Guo LY, Jia YJ. Effects of Tanshinone IIA on expression of transforming growth factor-β/Smads signaling pathway related factors in the liver tissue of rats with hepatic fibrosis. *Chin J Tissue Eng Res.* (2015) 19:4345–50. doi: 10.3969/j.issn.2095-4344.2015.27.015
46. Patil S, Wildey GM, Brown TL, Choy L, Derynck R, Howe PH. Smad7 is induced by CD40 and protects WEHI 231 B-lymphocytes from transforming growth factor-beta -induced growth inhibition and apoptosis. *J Biol Chem.* (2000) 275:38363–70. doi: 10.1074/jbc.M004861200
47. Henriet P, Zhong ZD, Brooks PC, Weinberg KI, DeClerck YA. Contact with fibrillar collagen inhibits melanoma cell proliferation by up-regulating p27KIP1. *Proc Natl Acad Sci USA.* (2000) 97:10026–31. doi: 10.1073/pnas.170290997
48. Lemons ML, Condic ML. Combined integrin activation and intracellular cAMP cause Rho GTPase dependent growth cone collapse on laminin-1. *Exp Neurol.* (2006) 202:324–35. doi: 10.1016/j.expneurol.2006.06.008
49. Ruland J, Duncan GS, Wakeham A, Mak TW. Differential requirement for Malt1 in T and B cell antigen receptor signaling. *Immunity.* (2003) 19:749–58. doi: 10.1016/S1074-7613(03)00293-0

50. Du MQ. MALT lymphoma: many roads lead to nuclear factor-kappab activation. *Histopathology.* (2011) 58:26–38. doi: 10.1111/j.1365-2559.2010.03699.x
51. Groom JR, Luster AD. CXCR3 in T cell function. *Exp Cell Res.* (2011) 317:620–31. doi: 10.1016/j.yexcr.2010.12.017
52. Romagnani P, Crescioli C. CXCL10: a candidate biomarker in transplantation. *Clin Chim Acta.* (2012) 413:1364–73. doi: 10.1016/j.cca.2012.02.009
53. Zeremski M, Petrovic LM, Chiriboga L, Brown QB, Yee HT, Kinkhabwala M. Intrahepatic levels of CXCR3-associated chemokines correlate with liver inflammation and fibrosis in chronic hepatitis C. *Hepatology.* (2008) 48:1440–50. doi: 10.1002/hep.22500
54. Butcher EC, Picker LJ. Lymphocyte homing and homeostasis. *Science.* (1996) 272:60–6. doi: 10.1126/science.272.5258.60
55. Ha SJ, Kim DJ, Baek KH, Yun YD, Sung YC. IL-23 induces stronger sustained CTL and Th1 immune responses than IL-12 in hepatitis C virus envelope protein 2 DNA immunization. *J Immunol.* (2004) 172:525–31. doi: 10.4049/jimmunol.172.1.525
56. Lacotte S, Brun S, Muller S, Dumortier H. CXCR3, inflammation, and autoimmune diseases. *Ann N Y Acad Sci.* (2009) 1173:310–7. doi: 10.1111/j.1749-6632.2009.04813.x
57. Antonelli A, Ferrari SM, Giuggioli D, Ferrannini E, Ferri C, Fallahi P. Chemokine (C-X-C motif) ligand (CXCL)10 in autoimmune diseases. *Autoimmun Rev.* (2014) 13:272–80. doi: 10.1016/j.autrev.2013.10.010
58. Okutani D, Lodyga M, Han B, Liu M. Src protein tyrosine kinase family and acute inflammatory responses. *Am J Physiol Lung Cell Mol Physiol.* (2006) 291:L129–41. doi: 10.1152/ajplung.00261.2005
59. Abram CL, Lowell CA. The diverse functions of Src family kinases in macrophages. *Front Biosci.* (2008) 13:4426–50. doi: 10.2741/3015
60. Cheung R, Ravyn V, Wang L, Ptasznik A, Collman RG. Signaling mechanism of HIV-1 gp120 and virion-induced IL-1beta release in primary human macrophages. *J Immunol.* (2008) 180:6675–84. doi: 10.4049/jimmunol.180.10.6675
61. Yew KH, Carsten B, Harrison C. Scavenger receptor A1 is required for sensing HCMV by endosomal TLR-3/-9 in monocytic THP-1 cells. *Mol Immunol.* (2010) 47:883–93. doi: 10.1016/j.molimm.2009.10.009
62. Flores-Borja F, Kabouridis PS, Jury EC, Isenberg DA, Mageed RA. Decreased Lyn expression and translocation to lipid raft signaling domains in B lymphocytes from patients with systemic lupus erythematosus. *Arthritis Rheum.* (2005) 52:3955–65. doi: 10.1002/art.21416
63. Gutierrez T, Halcomb KE, Coughran AJ, Li QZ, Satterthwaite AB. Separate checkpoints regulate splenic plasma cell accumulation and IgG autoantibody production in Lyn-deficient mice. *Eur J Immunol.* (2010) 40:1897–905. doi: 10.1002/eji.200940043
64. Beavitt SJ, Harder KW, Kemp JM, Jones J, Quilici C, Casagranda F. Lyn-deficient mice develop severe, persistent asthma: Lyn is a critical negative regulator of Th2 immunity. *J Immunol.* (2005) 175:1867–75. doi: 10.4049/jimmunol.175.3.1867
65. Bi J, Chase SE, Pellenz CD, Kurihara H, Fanning AS, Krendel M. Myosin 1e is a component of the glomerular slit diaphragm complex that regulates actin reorganization during cell-cell contact formation in podocytes. *Am J Physiol Renal Physiol.* (2013) 305:F532–44. doi: 10.1152/ajprenal.00223.2013
66. Michaud JL, Hosseini-Abardeh M, Farah K, Kennedy CR. Modulating alpha-actinin-4 dynamics in podocytes. *Cell Motil Cytoskeleton.* (2009) 66:166–78. doi: 10.1002/cm.20339
67. Krendel M, Osterweil EK, Mooseker MS. Myosin 1E interacts with synaptojanin-1 and dynamin and is involved in endocytosis. *FEBS Lett.* (2007) 581:644–50. doi: 10.1016/j.febslet.2007.01.021
68. Chase SE, Encina CV, Stolzenburg LR, Tatum AH, Holzman LB, Krendel M. Podocyte-specific knockout of myosin 1e disrupts glomerular filtration. *Am J Physiol Renal Physiol.* (2012) 303:F1099–106. doi: 10.1152/ajprenal.00251.2012
69. Tanzi RE, Petrukhin K, Chernov I, Pellequer JL, Wasco W, Ross B, et al. The Wilson disease gene is a copper transporting ATPase with homology to the Menkes disease gene. *Nat Genet.* (1993) 5:344–50. doi: 10.1038/ng1293-344
70. Hu J, Jiao XT, Liu XQ, Yu XG, He ZJ, Zhang YJ. Cell apoptosis and expression of ATP7A in brain of Atp7btx-J mice. *J Shanghai Jiaotong Univ.* (2013) 33:916–9. doi: 10.3969/j.issn.1674-8115.2013.07.004
71. Yin Y, Henzl MT, Lorber B, Nakazawa T, Thomas TT, Jiang F. Oncomodulin is a macrophage-derived signal for axon regeneration in retinal ganglion cells. *Nat Neurosci.* (2006) 9:843–52. doi: 10.1038/nn1701
72. Yin Y, Cui Q, Gilbert HY, Yang Y, Yang Z, Berlinicke C. Oncomodulin links inflammation to optic nerve regeneration. *Proc Natl Acad Sci USA.* (2009) 106:19587–92. doi: 10.1073/pnas.0907085106
73. Charalambous P, Hurst LA, Thanos S. Engrafted chicken neural tube-derived stem cells support the innate propensity for axonal regeneration within the rat optic nerve. *Invest Ophthalmol Vis Sci.* (2008) 49:3513–24. doi: 10.1167/iovs.07-1473
74. Bagrodia S, Taylor SJ, Jordon KA, Van Aelst L, Cerione RA. A novel regulator of p21-activated kinases. *J Biol Chem.* (1998) 273:23633–6. doi: 10.1074/jbc.273.37.23633
75. Manser E, Loo TH, Koh CG, Zhao ZS, Chen XQ, Tan L. PAK kinases are directly coupled to the PIX family of nucleotide exchange factors. *Mol Cell.* (1998) 1:183–92. doi: 10.1016/S1097-2765(00)80019-2
76. Bernard O. Lim kinases, regulators of actin dynamics. *Int J Biochem Cell Biol.* (2007) 39:1071–6. doi: 10.1016/j.biocel.2006.11.011
77. Shin EY, Woo KN, Lee CS, Koo SH, Kim YG, Kim WJ. Basic fibroblast growth factor stimulates activation of Rac1 through a p85 betaPIX phosphorylation-dependent pathway. *J Biol Chem.* (2004) 279:1994–2004. doi: 10.1074/jbc.M307330200
78. Shin EY, Lee CS, Cho TG, Kim YG, Song S, Juhnn YS. betaPak-interacting exchange factor-mediated Rac1 activation requires smgGDS guanine nucleotide exchange factor in basic fibroblast growth factor-induced neurite outgrowth. *J Biol Chem.* (2006) 281:35954–64. doi: 10.1074/jbc.M602399200
79. Habig K, Gellhaar S, Heim B, Djuric V, Giesert F, Wurst W. LRRK2 guides the actin cytoskeleton at growth cones together with ARHGEF7 and Tropomyosin 4. *Biochim Biophys Acta.* (2013) 1832:2352–67. doi: 10.1016/j.bbadis.2013.09.009
80. Gnesutta N, Minden A. Death receptor-induced activation of initiator caspase 8 is antagonized by serine/threonine kinase PAK4. *Mol Cell Biol.* (2003) 23:7838–48. doi: 10.1128/MCB.23.21.7838-7848.2003
81. Gnesutta N, Qu J, Minden A. The serine/threonine kinase PAK4 prevents caspase activation and protects cells from apoptosis. *J Biol Chem.* (2001) 276:14414–9. doi: 10.1074/jbc.M011046200
82. Siu MK, Chan HY, Kong DS, Wong ES, Wong OG, Ngan HY. p21-activated kinase 4 regulates ovarian cancer cell proliferation, migration, and invasion and contributes to poor prognosis in patients. *Proc Natl Acad Sci USA.* (2010) 107:18622–7. doi: 10.1073/pnas.0907481107
83. Wang Q, Bardgett ME, Wong M, Wozniak DF, Lou J, McNeil BD. Ataxia and paroxysmal dyskinesia in mice lacking axonally transported FGF14. *Neuron.* (2002) 35:25–38. doi: 10.1016/S0896-6273(02)00744-4
84. Wozniak DF, Xiao M, Xu L, Yamada KA, Ornitz DM. Impaired spatial learning and defective theta burst induced LTP in mice lacking fibroblast growth factor 14. *Neurobiol Dis.* (2007) 26:14–26. doi: 10.1016/j.nbd.2006.11.014
85. Xiao M, Xu L, Laezza F, Yamada K, Feng S, Ornitz DM. Impaired hippocampal synaptic transmission and plasticity in mice lacking fibroblast growth factor 14. *Mol Cell Neurosci.* (2007) 34:366–77. doi: 10.1016/j.mcn.2006.11.020
86. Yu C, Wang F, Jin C, Huang X, Miller DL, Basilico C. Role of fibroblast growth factor type 1 and 2 in carbon tetrachloride-induced hepatic injury and fibrogenesis. *Am J Pathol.* (2003) 163:1653–62. doi: 10.1016/S0002-9440(10)63522-5
87. Antoine M, Wirz W, Tag CG, Gressner AM, Marvituna M, Wycislo M. Expression and function of fibroblast growth factor (FGF) 9 in hepatic stellate cells and its role in toxic liver injury. *Biochem Biophys Res Commun.* (2007) 361:335–41. doi: 10.1016/j.bbrc.2007.06.189
88. Mas VR, Maluf DG, Archer KJ, Yanek KC, Fisher RA. Angiogenesis soluble factors as hepatocellular carcinoma noninvasive markers for monitoring hepatitis C virus cirrhotic patients awaiting liver transplantation. *Transplantation.* (2007) 84:1262–71. doi: 10.1097/01.tp.0000287596.91520.1a
89. Schoorlemmer J, Goldfarb M. Fibroblast growth factor homologous factors are intracellular signaling proteins. *Curr Biol.* (2001) 11:793–7. doi: 10.1016/S0960-9822(01)00232-9

90. Qiang H, Lin Y, Zhang X, Zeng X, Shi J, Chen YX. Differential expression genes analyzed by cDNA array in the regulation of rat hepatic fibrogenesis. *Liver Int.* (2006) 26:1126–37. doi: 10.1111/j.1478-3231.2006.01353.x
91. Chopra P, Kanoje V, Semwal A, Ray A. Therapeutic potential of inhaled p38 mitogen-activated protein kinase inhibitors for inflammatory pulmonary diseases. *Expert Opin Investig Drugs.* (2008) 17:1411–25. doi: 10.1517/13543784.17.10.1411
92. Schwer CI, Guerrero AM, Humar M, Roesslein M, Goebel U, Stoll P. Heme oxygenase-1 inhibits the proliferation of pancreatic stellate cells by repression of the extracellular signal-regulated kinase1/2 pathway. *J Pharmacol Exp Ther.* (2008) 327:863–71. doi: 10.1124/jpet.108.136549

Permissions

All chapters in this book were first published by Frontiers; hereby published with permission under the Creative Commons Attribution License or equivalent. Every chapter published in this book has been scrutinized by our experts. Their significance has been extensively debated. The topics covered herein carry significant findings which will fuel the growth of the discipline. They may even be implemented as practical applications or may be referred to as a beginning point for another development.

The contributors of this book come from diverse backgrounds, making this book a truly international effort. This book will bring forth new frontiers with its revolutionizing research information and detailed analysis of the nascent developments around the world.

We would like to thank all the contributing authors for lending their expertise to make the book truly unique. They have played a crucial role in the development of this book. Without their invaluable contributions this book wouldn't have been possible. They have made vital efforts to compile up to date information on the varied aspects of this subject to make this book a valuable addition to the collection of many professionals and students.

This book was conceptualized with the vision of imparting up-to-date information and advanced data in this field. To ensure the same, a matchless editorial board was set up. Every individual on the board went through rigorous rounds of assessment to prove their worth. After which they invested a large part of their time researching and compiling the most relevant data for our readers.

The editorial board has been involved in producing this book since its inception. They have spent rigorous hours researching and exploring the diverse topics which have resulted in the successful publishing of this book. They have passed on their knowledge of decades through this book. To expedite this challenging task, the publisher supported the team at every step. A small team of assistant editors was also appointed to further simplify the editing procedure and attain best results for the readers.

Apart from the editorial board, the designing team has also invested a significant amount of their time in understanding the subject and creating the most relevant covers. They scrutinized every image to scout for the most suitable representation of the subject and create an appropriate cover for the book.

The publishing team has been an ardent support to the editorial, designing and production team. Their endless efforts to recruit the best for this project, has resulted in the accomplishment of this book. They are a veteran in the field of academics and their pool of knowledge is as vast as their experience in printing. Their expertise and guidance has proved useful at every step. Their uncompromising quality standards have made this book an exceptional effort. Their encouragement from time to time has been an inspiration for everyone.

The publisher and the editorial board hope that this book will prove to be a valuable piece of knowledge for researchers, students, practitioners and scholars across the globe.

List of Contributors

Rui Wang, Wei Wang, Jingjing Xu, Dexiang Liu, Hong Jiang and Fang Pan
Department of Medical Psychology and Medical Ethics, Cheeloo College of Medicine, Shandong University, Jinan, China
Department of Medical Psychology and Ethics, School of Basic Medical Sciences, Shandong University, Jinan, China

Xiaqing Qin and Arslan Khalid
Department of Medical Psychology and Ethics, School of Basic Medical Sciences, Shandong University, Jinan, China

Hui Li and Yan Wu
Department of Anatomy, Capital Medical University, Beijing, China

Tong Wang, Yutao Yang, Xiaoxiao Li and Zhi-Qing David Xu
Beijing Key Laboratory of Neural Regeneration and Repair, Beijing Laboratory of Brain Disorders (Ministry of Science and Technology), Department of Neurobiology, Beijing Institute of Brain Disorders, Capital Medical University, Beijing, China

Cuige Shi
Department of Cell Biology, National Research Institute of Family Planning, Beijing, China

Qing Tian
Institute of Neuroscience, Medical College, University of South China, Hengyang, China

Lei Chen, Wei Zou and Ping Zhang
Institute of Neuroscience, Medical College, University of South China, Hengyang, China
Institute of Clinical Research, Affiliated Nanhua Hospital, University of South China, Hengyang, China

Bang Luo, Yong You and Xiao-Qing Tang
Institute of Neuroscience, Medical College, University of South China, Hengyang, China
Institute of Clinical Research, the First Affiliated Hospital, University of South China, Hengyang, China

Huiling Tian, Xiaoli Li, Qisheng Tang, Wen Zhang, Qingmeng Li, Xinyue Sun, Ruizhen Zhao, Haipeng Liu and Fei Han
Department of Encephalopathy, The Third Affiliated Hospital, Beijing University of Chinese Medicine, Beijing, China

Ai-Ping Wang
Institute of Clinical Research, Affiliated Nanhua Hospital, University of South China, Hengyang, China

Yushan Gao and Chongyang Ma
Research Institute, Beijing University of Chinese Medicine, Beijing, China

Yixue Lou
College of Psychology and Sociology, Shenzhen University, Shenzhen, China
Faculty of Education and Psychology, University of Jyväskylä, Jyväskylä, Finland
Center for Neurogenetics, Shenzhen Institute of Neuroscience, Shenzhen, China

Yi Lei, Ying Mei and Hong Li
College of Psychology and Sociology, Shenzhen University, Shenzhen, China
Center for Neurogenetics, Shenzhen Institute of Neuroscience, Shenzhen, China

Paavo H. T. Leppänen
Faculty of Education and Psychology, University of Jyväskylä, Jyväskylä, Finland

Jessica L. Hamilton
Department of Psychiatry, University of Pittsburgh, Pittsburgh, PA, United States

Ryan C. Brindle
Department of Psychology and Neuroscience Program, Washington and Lee University, Lexington, VA, United States

Lauren B. Alloy
Department of Psychology, Temple University, Philadelphia, PA, United States

Richard T. Liu
Department of Psychiatry and Human Behavior, Alpert Medical School of Brown University, Providence, RI, United States

Man Li
Department of Psychology, Tianjin Normal University, Tianjin, China
Academy of Psychology and Behavior, Tianjin Normal University, Tianjin, China
Center of Collaborative Innovation for Assessment and Promotion of Mental Health, Tianjin, China
CAS Key Laboratory of Mental Health, Institute of Psychology, Beijing, China

Hang Xu and Weiwen Wang
CAS Key Laboratory of Mental Health, Institute of Psychology, Beijing, China
Department of Psychology, University of Chinese Academy of Sciences, Beijing, China

Xiaoming Zhong, Guanze Li and Zhen Huang
Department of Chinese Medical Resources, College of Pharmacy, Zhejiang Chinese Medical University, Hangzhou, China

Fengmei Qiu
Pharmacy Teaching Experiment Centre, College of Pharmacy, Zhejiang Chinese Medical University, Hangzhou, China

Cyrus S. H. Ho and Roger C. M. Ho
Department of Psychological Medicine, Yong Loo Lin School of Medicine, National University of Singapore, Singapore, Singapore

Jianguo Li
Laboratory for Microbiome Sciences, Institute of Biomedical Sciences, Shanxi University, Taiyuan, China
Key Laboratory of Chemical Biology and Molecular Engineering of Ministry of Education, Shanxi University, Taiyuan, China

Luwen Hou, Cui Wang and Xueyang Jia
Modern Research Center for Traditional Chinese Medicine, Shanxi University, Taiyuan, China

Xuemei Qin
Key Laboratory of Chemical Biology and Molecular Engineering of Ministry of Education, Shanxi University, Taiyuan, China
Modern Research Center for Traditional Chinese Medicine, Shanxi University, Taiyuan, China

Changxin Wu
Laboratory for Microbiome Sciences, Institute of Biomedical Sciences, Shanxi University, Taiyuan, China

Jiarun Yang, Xueyan Zhao, Jingsong Ma, Zhengxue Qiao, Xiuxian Yang, Erying Zhao, Yanjie Yang, Xiaohui Qiu, Qihe Wang, Dong Han, Dong Qi, Lin Wang, Xuejia Song and Jian Zhang
Department of Medical Psychology, Institute of Public Health, Harbin Medical University, Harbin, China

Bo Ban
Department of Endocrinology, Affiliated Hospital of Jining Medical University, Jining, China

Depin Cao
Department of Medical Education Management, Harbin Medical University, Harbin, China

Rucui Yang, Haoran Sun and Yani Wu
Department of Clinical Medicine, Weifang Medical University, Weifang, China

Guohua Lu, Yanyu Wang, Hongwei Sun and Lin Sun
Department of Psychology, Weifang Medical University, Weifang, China

Qi Li
Department of Psychiatry and Centre for Reproduction Growth and Development, University of Hong Kong, Hong Kong, Hong Kong

Jin Zhou
College of Pharmacy, Weifang Medical University, Weifang, China

Yi Zhang, Lei Wang, Xin Wang, Chuting Li and Xiongzhao Zhu
Medical Psychological Center, The Second Xiangya Hospital, Central South University, Changsha, China

Yuting Wang
Medical Psychological Center, The Second Xiangya Hospital, Central South University, Changsha, China
Department of Clinical Psychology, Maternal and Child Health Hospital of Hunan Province, Changsha, China

Kerun Cao, Chongkun Shen and Yafei Shi
School of Fundamental Medical Science, Guangzhou University of Chinese Medicine, Guangzhou, China

Yumei Yuan
Shenzhen Baoan Hospital of Chinese Medicine, Shenzhen, China

Shasha Bai, Lei Yang and Rong Zhang
Institute of Clinical Pharmacology, Guangzhou University of Chinese Medicine, Guangzhou, China

Lili Guo
Third Affiliated Hospital of Henan University of Chinese Medicine, Henan University of Chinese Medicine, Zhengzhou, China

Zhexue Xu and Miao Qu
Department of Neurology, Xuan Wu Hospital Capital Medical University, Beijing, China
Department of Neurology, Third Affiliated Hospital, Beijing University of Chinese Medicine, Beijing, China

Jing Zhang
Department of Neurology, Xuan Wu Hospital Capital Medical University, Beijing, China

Di Wang
Department of Clinical Psychology, Beijing Anding Hospital, Beijing, China

Ting Wang
Nanjing Municipal Hospital of Traditional Chinese Medicine, Nanjing, China

Shu Zhang
Department of Neurology, Fengtai Integrated Chinese and Western Medicine Hospital of Beijing, Beijing, China

Xi Ren
Department of Neurology, Third Affiliated Hospital, Beijing University of Chinese Medicine, Beijing, China

Xiaolei Zhu and Atsushi Kamiya
Department of Psychiatry and Behavioral Sciences, Johns Hopkins University School of Medicine, Baltimore, MD, United States

Jiliang Fang
Department of Radiology, Guang'anmen Hospital China Academy of Chinese Medical Sciences, Beijing, China

Congpei Zhang
The First Special Hospital of Harbin, Harbin, China

Shu Guan and Huixiang Ge
Department of Physiology, Basic Medical College, Nanchang University, Nanchang, China

Yulin Shen
Department of Physiology, Basic Medical College, Nanchang University, Nanchang, China
Sport Biological Centre, China Institute of Sport Science, Beijing, China

Wei Xiong, Lingkun He, Lijuan Liu and Cancan Yin
Department of Preventive Dentistry, Affiliated Stomatological Hospital of Nanchang University, Nanchang, China

Xingyu Wei
Basic Medical College of Grade 2017, Nanchang University, Nanchang, China

Yun Gao
Department of Physiology, Basic Medical College, Nanchang University, Nanchang, China
Jiangxi Provincial Key Laboratory of Autonomic Nervous Function and Disease, Nanchang University, Nanchang, China

Robyn J. McQuaid
The Royal's Institute of Mental Health Research, University of Ottawa, Ottawa, Canada

Robert L. Gabrys and Opal A. McInnis
Department of Neuroscience, Carleton University, Ottawa, ON, Canada

Hymie Anisman and Kimberly Matheson
The Royal's Institute of Mental Health Research, University of Ottawa, Ottawa, Canada
Department of Neuroscience, Carleton University, Ottawa, ON, Canada

Fu-Yi Shen, Ying-Cai Song, Zhen-Dong Xu, Qian Li, Yue-Qi Zhang, Rong Lin and Zhi-Qiang Liu
Department of Anesthesiology, Shanghai First Maternity and Infant Hospital, Tongji University School of Medicine, Shanghai, China

Fei Guo and Yang Li
Key Laboratory of Receptor Research, Shanghai Institute of Materia Medica, Chinese Academy of Sciences, Shanghai, China

Bing Zhang
Department of Anesthesiology, Shanghai First Maternity and Infant Hospital, Tongji University School of Medicine, Shanghai, China
Key Laboratory of Receptor Research, Shanghai Institute of Materia Medica, Chinese Academy of Sciences, Shanghai, China
University of Chinese Academy of Sciences, Beijing, China

Yu-Qin Ma
Key Laboratory of Receptor Research, Shanghai Institute of Materia Medica, Chinese Academy of Sciences, Shanghai, China
University of Chinese Academy of Sciences, Beijing, China

Reem M. A. Shafi, Ewa D. Bieber, Julia Shekunov, Paul E. Croarkin and Magdalena Romanowicz
Department of Psychiatry and Psychology, Mayo Clinic, Rochester, MN, United States

Xiao-Hong Li
School of Traditional Chinese Medicine, Beijing University of Chinese Medicine, Beijing, China
School of Basic Medical Sciences, Guangxi University of Chinese Medicine, Nanning, China

Xue-Ming Zhou
School of Traditional Chinese Medicine, Beijing University of Chinese Medicine, Beijing, China
School of Basic Medical Sciences, Heilongjiang University of Chinese Medicine, Harbin, China

Xiao-Juan Li and Jia-Xu Chen
School of Traditional Chinese Medicine, Beijing University of Chinese Medicine, Beijing, China
Formula-pattern Research Center, School of Traditional Chinese Medicine, Jinan University, Guangzhou, China

Yue-Yun Liu, Qun Liu and Xiao-Ling Guo
School of Traditional Chinese Medicine, Beijing University of Chinese Medicine, Beijing, China

Li-Qiang Yang
School of Basic Medical Sciences, Guangxi University of Chinese Medicine, Nanning, China

Index